THE NEW OXFORD HISTORY OF ENGLAND

General Editor · J. M. ROBERTS

Plantagenet England

1225–1360

MICHAEL PRESTWICH

CLARENDON PRESS · OXFORD

OXFORD

UNIVERSITY PRESS

Great Clarendon Street, Oxford OX2 6DP

Oxford University Press is a department of the University of Oxford.
It furthers the University's objective of excellence in research, scholarship,
and education by publishing worldwide in

Oxford New York

Auckland Bangkok Buenos Aires Cape Town Chennai
Dar es Salaam Delhi Hong Kong Istanbul Karachi Kolkata
Kuala Lumpur Madrid Melbourne Mexico City Mumbai Nairobi
São Paulo Shanghai Taipei Tokyo Toronto

With offices in

Argentina Austria Brazil Chile Czech Republic France Greece
Guatemala Hungary Italy Japan South Korea Poland Portugal
Singapore Switzerland Thailand Turkey Ukraine Vietnam

Published in the United States
by Oxford University Press Inc., New York

© Michael Prestwich 2005

The moral rights of the author have been asserted
Database right Oxford University Press (maker)

First published 2005

British Library Cataloguing in Publication Data

Data available

Library of Congress Cataloging in Publication Data

Data available

Typeset by SPI Publisher Services, Pondicherry, India
Printed in Great Britain
on acid-free paper by
Biddles Ltd,
King's Lynn, Norfolk

ISBN 0-19-822844-9

1 3 5 7 9 10 8 6 4 2

For J.O.P.
In memoriam

General Editor's Preface

The first volume of Sir George Clark's *Oxford History of England* was published in 1934. Undertaking the General Editorship of a *New Oxford History of England* forty-five years later it was hard not to feel overshadowed by its powerful influence and well-deserved status. Some of Clark's volumes (his own among them) were brilliant individual achievements, hard to rival and impossible to match. Of course, he and his readers shared a broad sense of the purpose and direction of such books. His successor can no longer be sure of doing that. The building-blocks of the story, its reasonable and meaningful demarcations and divisions, the continuities and discontinuities, the priorities of different varieties of history, the place of narrative—all these things are now much harder to agree upon. We now know much more about many things, and think about what we know in different ways. It is not surprising that historians now sometimes seem unsure about the audience to which their scholarship and writing are addressed.

In the end, authors should be left to write their own books. None the less, the *New Oxford History of England* is intended to be more than a collection of discrete or idiosyncratic histories in chronological order. Its aim is to give an account of the development of our country in time. It is hard to treat that development as just the history which unfolds within the precise boundaries of England, and a mistake to suggest that this implies a neglect of the histories of the Scots, Irish, and Welsh. Yet the institutional core of the story which runs from Anglo-Saxon times to our own is the story of a state-structure built round the English monarchy and its effective successor, the Crown in Parliament, and that provides the only continuous articulation of the history of peoples we today call British. It follows that there must be uneven and sometimes discontinuous treatment of much of the history of those peoples. The state story remains, nevertheless, an intelligible thread and to me appears still to justify both the title of this series and that of its predecessor.

If the attention given to the other kingdoms and the principality of Wales must reflect in this series their changing relationship to that central theme, this is not only way in which the emphasis of individual volumes will be different. Each author has been asked to bring forward what he or she sees as the most important topics explaining the history under study, taking account of the present state of historical knowledge, drawing attention to areas of dispute and to matters on which final judgement is at present difficult (or, perhaps, impossible) and not merely recapitulating what has recently been the fashionable centre of professional debate. But each volume, allowing for its special approach and proportions, must also provide a comprehensive account, in which politics is always likely to be prominent. Volumes have to be demarcated chronologically but continuities must not be obscured; vestigially or not, copyhold survived into the 1920s and the Anglo-Saxon shires until the 1970s (some of which were to be resurrected in the 1990s, too). Any single volume should be an entry-point to the understanding of processes only slowly unfolding, sometimes across centuries. My hope is that in the end we shall have, as the outcome, a set of standard and authoritative histories, embodying the scholarship of a generation, and not mere compendia in which the determinants are lost to sight among the detail.

J. M. ROBERTS

Preface

The period covered by this book ranged over two volumes of the previous *Oxford History of England*. A hundred and thirty-five years, from 1225 to 1360, for this book, is significantly more than my predecessors had to deal with. I have an understandable jealousy of those authors of later volumes in this series who have to cover a mere forty years or so. The logic to the particular dates selected is that by not picking the obvious beginnings and endings of reigns different themes may emerge. The year 1225 marks the beginning, in a sense, of Henry III's personal rule, while 1360 saw the end of a major phase of the Hundred Years War. Any dates have advantages and disadvantages; the main problem with the concluding date is that it is not possible to provide a full account of the consequences of the Black Death of 1348, for that involves looking far beyond 1360, and therefore to the next volume in this series.

The plan of this book needs some explanation. While the past is seamless, I do not find it possible to write about it without cutting it up into segments, and in this case some of the pieces are chronological and others thematic. It may be helpful for readers to note that Chapters 3 to 11 provide a narrative framework, while the others address distinct themes. Just as the book as a whole does not use reigns as starting or ending points, so too the chapters adopt a slightly different chronology from that conventionally employed; it makes sense, for example, to see the period from 1290 to 1311 as a whole in political terms, rather than to break at the death of Edward I in 1307. I have not tried to cover all aspects of the history of thirteenth- and fourteenth-century England in equal depth; to have done so would have made a long book even longer. Nor is it possible for one person to write a fully comprehensive study. Intellectual and artistic life is no more than very briefly sketched, while the history of the Church has not been made into a separate theme. There is, as a result, no extended treatment of topics such as the advent of the friars to England, or the development of Benedictine monasticism; I have aimed rather to include discussion of the Church, where relevant, in chapters that are centred on other subjects. It would also have been possible to treat parliament as a separate topic, as I have done in previous publications, but instead, material on parliament has been integrated into various parts of this book.

It has, for very good reasons, become fashionable in recent years to write British, rather than English, history. Among other things, this has the advantage of providing a comparative dimension. I have not, however, taken this course; the title of the series is *The New Oxford History of England*, and I have taken this in a literal sense. I was taught, many years ago, by A. J. P. Taylor, who adopted this view with considerable force in his volume of the original *Oxford History of England*. There are good reasons why it makes sense to write the history of a single country, which in the period covered by this book had a clear, distinct, and developing identity. In this volume Wales and Scotland each receive a chapter, but the emphasis is very much on the role of the English in those countries. Ireland and Gascony were important parts of the dominions of the kings of England, but as this is a history of England, not of the lands ruled by English kings, they do not receive separate treatment.

The amount that has been published since the previous Oxford Histories appeared is immense; in many areas the subject has been transformed. In this book I have taken a deliberate decision not to refer to modern historians in the text, and I hope that the many upon whose work I have relied do not take this amiss. My hope is that the footnote references, together with the bibliographical section, will make sufficiently clear my immense debt to all those who have worked on this period.

I owe many thanks. This is the second book that John Roberts suggested that I should write, and it is very sad that he did not live to see this one completed. I would like to thank Oxford University Press, and in particular Ruth Parr, Anne Gelling, Louisa Lapworth, Kay Rogers, and Laurien Berkeley for the help they provided, from the earliest stages to the final production of the book. I am grateful to the University of Durham for awarding me a Sir Derman Christopherson fellowship, which allowed me a year free of teaching duties. The University Library and the Cathedral Library have both provided splendid support. Anthony Musson kindly read two of the chapters concerned with the law, and other chapters have been read by my long-suffering colleagues Ben Dodds and Christian Liddy. I must thank other colleagues at Durham, particularly Robin Frame and Richard Britnell, for much help over many years. Robert Bartlett and John Maddicott have read the entire book in draft; I am deeply grateful for their suggestions, even for those I was unable to take up. Research associates are a relatively new feature of academic life for historians, and although they have not worked on this particular project, I owe thanks for ideas and inspiration to Andy King, Matthew Holford, and Alastair Dunn. I have learned much from my research students, and, though they may be surprised to learn this, from my undergraduate students as well. The role of my wife, Maggie, has, as ever, been invaluable; she has had to put up with many conversations about this book, and the form that it should take, and has done an immense amount to improve and correct its contents. I owe a lifetime debt to another medieval historian, my father, John Prestwich. It was he who first motivated me to work on the medieval period, and his rigorous scholarship provided a constant inspiration. This book is dedicated to his memory.

November 2004   M.C.P.

Contents

PART II   POLITICS AND WARS

PART III   SOCIETY AND PEOPLE

Plates

Tables

Maps

Abbreviations and Conventions

All manuscript references, unless otherwise indicated, are to to documents in The National Archives (formerly the Public Record Office).

Agrarian History	*The Agrarian History of England and Wales*, ii: *The Middle Ages*, ed. H. E. Hallam (Cambridge, 1988)
Ann. Dunstable	'The Dunstable Annals', in *Annales Monastici*, ed. H. R. Luard, 5 vols. (RS, 1864–9), vol. iii
Ann. Lond.	'Annales Londonienses', in *Chronicles of the Reigns of Edward I and Edward II*, ed. W. Stubbs, 2 vols. (RS, 1882–3), vol. i
Ann. Mon.	*Annales Monastici*, ed. H. R. Luard, 5 vols. (RS, 1864–9)
Anon. Chron.	*The Anonimalle Chronicle 1333–1381*, ed. V. H. Galbraith (Manchester, 1927)
Anonimalle	*The Anonimalle Chronicle 1307 to 1334*, ed. W. R. Childs and J. Taylor (Yorkshire Archaeological Society, 1991)
Avesbury	*Robertus de Avesbury De Gestis Mirabilibus Regis Edwardi Tertii*, ed. E. M. Thompson (RS, 1889)
Baker	*Chronicon Galfridi le Baker de Swynebroke*, ed. E. M. Thompson (Oxford, 1889)
BIHR	*Bulletin of the Institute of Historical Research*
BL	British Library
Cal. Anc. Corr. Wales	*Calendar of Ancient Correspondence concerning Wales*, ed. J. G. Edwards (Cardiff, 1935)
Cal. Ch. Rolls	*Calendar of Charter Rolls*
Cal. Fine Rolls	*Calendar of Fine Rolls*
Cal. Lib. Rolls	*Calendar of Liberate Rolls*
Cal. Plea and Mem. Rolls	*Calendar of Plea and Memoranda Rolls of the City of London, 1323–1364*, ed. A. H. Thomas (Cambridge, 1926)

CCR	*Calendar of Close Rolls* (London, 1892–)
CDS	*Calendar of Documents relating to Scotland*, i–iv, ed. J. Bain (Edinburgh, 1881–8); v, ed. G. G. Simpson and J. D. Galbraith (Edinburgh, 1986)
CIM	*Calendar of Inquisitions Miscellaneous*
CIPM	*Calendar of Inquisitions Post Mortem*
Complete Peerage	G. E. C[ockayne], *The Complete Peerage of England, Scotland, Ireland, Great Britain and the United Kingdom*, ed. V. Gibbs *et al.*, 13 vols. in 14 (London, 1910–59)
Cotton	*Bartholomaei de Cotton, Historia Anglicana*, ed. H. R. Luard (RS, 1859)
CPR	*Calendar of Patent Rolls* (London, 1891–)
CR	*Close Rolls of the Reign of Henry III* (London, 1902–38)
DBM	*Documents of the Baronial Movement of Reform and Rebellion 1258–1267*, ed. R. F. Treharne and I. J. Sanders (Oxford, 1973)
EcHR	*Economic History Review*
EHR	*English Historical Review*
Flores	*Flores Historiarum*, ed. H. R. Luard, 3 vols. (RS, 1890)
Foedera	T. Rymer (ed.), *Foedera, Conventiones, Litterae et Acta Publica*, ed. A. Clarke and F. Holbrooke, 4 vols. (London, 1816–69)
Froissart	*Chroniques de Jean Froissart*, ed. S. Luce, G. Raynaud, L. Mirot, and A. Mirot, 15 vols. (Société de l'histoire de France, 1869–1975)
Gesta Edwardi	'Gesta Edwardi de Carnarvan auctore canonico Bridlingtonensi', in *Chronicles of the Reigns of Edward I and Edward II*, ed. W. Stubbs, 2 vols. (RS, 1882–3), vol. i
Guisborough	*The Chronicle of Walter of Guisborough*, ed. H. Rothwell, Camden 3rd ser., 89 (1957)
Knighton	*The Chronicle of Henry Knighton*, ed. G. H. Martin (Oxford, 1995)
KW	R. A. Brown, H. M. Colvin, and A. J. Taylor (eds.), *The History of the King's Works*, i and ii: *The Middle Ages* (London, 1963)

Lanercost	*Chronicon de Lanercost*, ed. J. Stevenson (Maitland Club, Edinburgh, 1839)
Le Bel	*Chronique de Jean le Bel*, ed. J. Viard and E. Déprez (Paris, 1904)
Liber Quotidianus	*Liber Quotidianus Contrarotulatoris Garderobae anno regni Regis Edwardi Primi vicesimo octavo*, ed. J. Topham (London, 1787)
Melsa	*Chronica Monasterii de Melsa*, ed. E. A. Bond, 3 vols. (RS, 1866–9)
Murimuth	*Adae Murimuth, Continuatio Chronicarum*, ed. E. M. Thompson (RS, 1889)
Paris, *Chron. Maj.*	*Matthaei Parisiensis, Monachi Sancti Albani, Chronica Majora*, ed. H. R. Luard, 7 vols. (RS, 1872–83)
Parl. Writs	*Parliamentary Writs*
Pauline Annals	'Annales Paulini', in *Chronicles of the Reigns of Edward I and Edward II*, ed. W. Stubbs, 2 vols. (RS, 1882–3), vol. i
Pierre de Langtoft	*Édition critique et commentée de Pierre de Langtoft: Le Règne d'Édouard Ier*, ed. J. C. Thiolier (Créteil, 1989)
Political Songs	*The Political Songs of England from the Reign of John to that of Edward II*, ed. T. Wright (Camden Society, 1839)
Rishanger	*Willelmi Rishanger, Chronica et Annales*, ed. H. T. Riley (RS, 1865)
Rot. Parl.	*Rotuli Parliamentorum*, 6 vols. (London, 1783)
RS	Rolls Series
Scalacronica	*Scalacronica by Sir Thomas Gray*, ed. J. Stevenson (Maitland Club, Edinburgh, 1836)
SR	*Statutes of the Realm*, 11 vols. (London, 1810–28)
TCE	*Thirteenth Century England*, i–v, ed. P. Coss and S. Lloyd; vi–x, ed. M. C. Prestwich, R. H. Britnell, and R. F. Frame (Woodbridge, 1986–2004)
Tout, *Chapters*	T. F. Tout, *Chapters in the Administrative History of Mediaeval England*, 6 vols. (Manchester, 1920–33)
TRHS	*Transactions of the Royal Historical Society*

Trokelowe

Johannis de Trokelowe et Henrici de Blaneford... Chronica et Annales, ed. H. T. Riley (RS, 1866)

VCH

Victoria County History

Vita Edwardi

Vita Edwardi Secundi, ed. N. Denholm-Young (London, 1957)

Wendover

The Flowers of History by Roger of Wendover, ed. H. G. Hewlett, 3 vols. (RS, 1886–9)

Worcester Annals

'Annales Prioratus de Wigornia', in *Annales Monastici*, ed. H. R. Luard (RS, 1864–9), vol. iv

Wykes

'Chronicon vulgo dictum Chronicon Thomae Wykes, 1066–1289', *Annales Monastici*, ed. H. R. Luard (RS, 1864–9), vol. iv

Note on Money

During most of the period covered by this book, the silver penny was the only coin in circulation. Halfpennies and farthings were first minted under Edward I, but their numbers were never large. In 1344 Edward III introduced the first English gold coinage. This, the English florin, was not produced in large quantities, but the gold noble, first minted in 1351, proved a great success. For accounting purposes, money was normally counted in pence, shillings (each worth 12 pence), and pounds (each worth 20 shillings, or 240 pence). An alternative system used marks. A mark was worth two-thirds of a pound, and was therefore equal to 13 shillings and 4 pence. In the text, sums are given in the form £10 10s. 10d., for 10 pounds, 10 shillings, and 10 pence.

PART I

Introductory

CHAPTER I

The Environment

Life was hard in the thirteenth and fourteenth centuries. Most men and women lived in cold, damp, uncomfortable, and unhygienic dwellings. They were at the mercy of the weather, and were exposed to a range of unpleasant and sometimes fatal diseases. Even good harvests were poor by the standards of more recent periods. Both the achievements of the period and the disasters need to be set against this physical backcloth.

In 1289 there was a great storm, which caused widespread flooding and battered down the standing corn, ruining the harvest. That, for the St Albans chronicler William Rishanger, marked the end of good weather. For the next forty years grain harvests were poor.[1] This, of course, was an exaggeration, but Rishanger was expressing a view echoed by many historians, who view the early fourteenth century as a period that witnessed a marked deterioration in the English climate. Should the history of this period be seen against a background of good times in the thirteenth century, of golden summers and rich harvests, which were abruptly succeeded by years of frosts, torrential rain, coastal erosion, and consequent misery?

THE CLIMATE

Climate mattered in the middle ages. People remembered the weather. Witnesses to a church court, testifying to having seen their neighbours engaging in sexual activity, recalled that they had seen what they were doing because it had been a moonlit night, with snow lying. On another occasion it was noted that the land where a couple were engaged in amorous activity had not been sown, and that it was a fine day with the sun shining.[2] One cleric, William Merle, was so aware of the weather that he kept a detailed record, month by month, for the years 1337 to 1344. He provided descriptions of frost, cloud cover, strength

---

[1] Rishanger, 119.

[2] *Select Cases from the Ecclesiastical Courts of the Province of Canterbury c.1200–1301*, ed. N. Adams and C. Donahue, Jr. (Selden Society, 1981), 96, 101.

and direction of winds, as well as other details.[3] The weather was more than simply a matter of interest; it had a very direct effect on people's lives. There was little capacity to store food supplies beyond a single year, and bad harvests could therefore be disastrous. Storms and floods could have a severe impact. Thirteenth- and fourteenth-century England appears to have been prone to very variable and sometimes extreme weather conditions, and chroniclers recorded unusual weather. In the 1250s, as noted by the St Albans chronicler Matthew Paris, each year brought some problem. A violent thunderstorm in May 1251 brought down thirty-five oaks in Windsor Forest. A gale in the following January caused much damage. From April until July 1252 there was a severe drought, and the next year saw drought in spring and summer, followed by autumn rains and floods. A severe frost began on 1 January 1254 and did not end until 12 March. In the summer there were strong winds for three months. In 1255 there was drought in April, and in the next year a severe storm in June did much damage. The year 1257 began with floods, and from February until May the weather was very bad. The severe cold from early February to the end of March 1258 was highly noteworthy. Matthew's last year-end summary was very gloomy: there had been much rain, and the harvest had been seriously damaged. Grain and fodder were in short supply: people were forced to sell their flocks and to leave their land uncultivated. Famine caused many deaths, and corpses were so numerous that they had to be thrown into common pits.[4] Hard winters were especially memorable. One chronicler noted that in 1280 there was hard frost, with lying snow, for seven weeks up to 12 March. No one could remember such weather.[5] Storms could have disastrous consequences. In 1283 wind and rain for two nights and one day in Lincolnshire caused many animal deaths, and led to breaches in the sea defences and extensive flooding.

The years that Rishanger saw as the worst were those from the 1290s, and there is clear evidence of poor weather from other chronicles, particularly in the early fourteenth century, to support his view. One London chronicle noted the fact that the Thames froze over in the winter of 1309–10; it was even possible to build a bonfire in the middle of the river.[6] The appalling weather of 1315 and 1316, years of incessant rain, was widely recorded in chronicles and elsewhere.

---

[3] *Merle's MS: Consideraciones Temperiei pro 7 Annis... The Earliest Known Journal of the Weather, 1337–1344*, ed. G. J. Symons (London, 1891).

[4] Paris, *Chron. Maj.* v. 263–4, 272, 317, 395, 427, 495, 561, 630, 674, 728.

[5] BL, Cotton MS Vesp. B. xi, fo. 28^{r-v}. Ann. Dunstable, 285, refers to frost lasting for fifty days.

[6] Ann. Lond. 158.

Ruls is our rye, and rotted in the straw,
For wicked weather by brook and by brink[7]

was how one poet put it. These were two exceptional years, with disastrous harvests, consequent high prices, and, for many, famine.

The evidence of the chronicles, with their incidental references to the weather, cannot do much more than identify individual poor years. Despite Rishanger's statement, chroniclers were not in a good position to determine long-term climatic changes in this period. A fuller story is provided by the estate accounts. From these it is possible to calculate the yield of grain, which was of course heavily dependent on the weather. In addition, the clerks often added explanatory notes, which often refer to weather conditions such as drought, flood, or abnormal temperatures. Grain yields fluctuated considerably from year to year, but the overall pattern is one of relative stability. This evidence is largely derived from the Winchester estates in the south of England, but there is no reason to suppose that this region was atypical. Of course, yields can change for reasons other than the weather. Different farming practices could affect them, and might indeed compensate for deterioration in the climate. A contraction in the amount of land under cultivation might improve yields if the more marginal, poorly performing lands were abandoned first. The overall pattern suggests that average yields were at their best in the first half of the thirteenth century (the period for which the data are thinnest), that there was then a decline in the second half of the century, and that levels then remained fairly static in the first half of the fourteenth century.[8] This evidence does not provide support for the view that there was an overall long-term deterioration in the climate, with a marked turning point around 1300. The overall decline that took place in the course of the thirteenth century might, however, fit into a very long-term pattern of a shift from a warm early middle ages to a cold early modern period.

Long-term changes to the climate may not have presented great problems. Certain crops, notably vines, might be abandoned, and other adjustments made. Any shifts, however, were not so fundamental as to affect the essential basis of the English arable and pastoral economy. It was short-term changes that could bring disaster. In an analysis of yields and weather based on the Winchester accounts, the harvests of 1283, 1290, 1310, 1315, 1316, 1339, 1343, 1346, 1349, and 1350 were identified as particularly poor. Analysis of the accounts of Norwich cathedral priory produced slightly different results, where the years 1294, 1295, 1315, 1316, 1317, 1319, and 1321 rated as very

---

[7] *Political Songs*, 152. Although Wright placed this poem in Edward I's reign, it clearly dates from 1315–16.

[8] D. L. Farmer, 'Prices and Wages', in *Agrarian History*, 721–3.

bad. These bad harvests might result from a wet autumn followed by a wet winter and summer, or from a wet autumn followed by a dry summer. A hard winter was not an important factor, and might indeed be followed by a good harvest. This evidence of bad harvests might appear to support the view that there was a clear downturn in the climate in the fourteenth century, but account also needs to be taken of the years, ten in all, in the first half of the century when, by the same calculations, there were outstandingly good harvests.[9] What the evidence of grain yields strongly suggests is that the weather became more variable and more unpredictable in the early fourteenth century. This unpredictability was difficult to cope with, but what caused the most problems was the fact that the successive years 1315 and 1316, and in some regions 1317 as well, saw extremely poor weather with incessant rain. The years around 1350 also saw disastrous harvests, but it is likely that the poor yield figures are more a reflection of the disruption to the labour market that followed the Black Death of 1348 than of appalling weather. In broad terms, it was the first quarter of the fourteenth century that saw the climate at its worst.

The weather of 1315 and 1316 was by far the most serious episode in its effects. The scale of the rains was quite unprecedented. It was not just that low-lying land was flooded; fields everywhere were turned to mud, and topsoil was washed away. If crops grew at all, they would be beaten down before they ripened. Moulds and fungal infections spread in the damp, causing further problems. Yields of wheat on the Winchester and Westminster estates fell to 64 per cent of the average in 1315, and to 56 per cent in the following year. In some cases grain yielded less seed than had been sown.[10] Some of the effects of the rain are not so immediately obvious. Salt, for example, was in short supply, for the salt pans near the coasts could not evaporate in the normal way. The fact that this dreadful weather persisted for so long created quite exceptional difficulties. People did not have sufficient supplies to see them through for two years and more of disastrous harvests. Famine was the result, and hunger went hand in hand with disease. Such an event did not necessarily imply that there was a long-term downturn in the weather, but it might not be easy for the economy to recover swiftly.

The weather could have severe local effects. In 1296 the earl of Lincoln's north Lancashire estates were hard-hit; on one manor the yield per acre was half that of a good year, while on another the course of Calder Water had to be

[9] J. Z. Titow, 'Evidence of Weather in the Account Rolls of the Bishopric of Winchester 1209–1350', *EcHR*, 2nd ser., 12 (1959–60), 363; H. E. Hallam, 'The Climate of Eastern England 1250–1350', *Agricultural History Review*, 32 (1984), 124–32.
[10] W. C. Jordan, *The Great Famine: Northern Europe in the Early Fourteenth Century* (Princeton, 1996), 32, 52–3.

diverted to save the park paling.[11] Yet this was not a year that other statistics suggest was particularly poor. On a much larger scale the east coast of England suffered from localized problems, with storms and high tides having a devastating impact on the low-lying areas. The years 1250 and 1287–8 were especially serious, causing among other things the abandonment of the original port of Winchelsea. There were, however, many other floods. In 1289, 2,857 acres in Kent were 'in the peril of the sea', and over the half-century prior to an inquiry made in 1341, 2,120 acres of arable land in a dozen Sussex villages were said to have been lost. At West Walton in Norfolk eighty-five houses were lost to the sea between 1307 and 1347. Ravenserodd, on the Humber estuary, lost 145 houses and much land in the 1330s and 1340s. At Dunwich about a quarter of the town was lost between 1278 and 1326. Around the Severn estuary, however, there were fewer problems, though Goldcliff priory on the Gwent levels saw much land flooded, resulting in reduced valuations by 1324.[12] It would, however, be wrong to generalize from these local disasters and conclude that the whole of England was suffering.

The weather had a very obvious immediate impact on the economy. It also had wider effects on politics and war. The harvest was below average in 1257, following heavy rains, and in 1258 there was again much rain, with grain prices rising to over twice the average level for the period.[13] This was a significant element in the political crisis of 1258, a crisis that saw widespread popular resentment directed at the government. Poor harvests from 1294 to 1297 coincided with the immense efforts put into war on three fronts and a consequent political crisis. In the disastrous years of 1315 and 1316 the government was dominated by Thomas, earl of Lancaster, who had many failings as a politician, but his task was undeniably made much more difficult by the weather of those awful years. Again, there is a coincidence between a bad harvest in 1339, heavy expenditure on war, and a political crisis in the next year. The weather could also affect war. In 1356 the Black Prince aimed to join forces with the duke of Lancaster on the Loire, but the bridges had been broken, and the river, with its multiple channels, was running too fast and high, following rains, for a crossing to be possible. The great storm of 13 April 1360, on what became known as Black Monday, devastated Edward III's army to an extent that the French were not capable of, as vast hailstones terrified the

---

[11] M. A. Atkin, 'Land Use and Management in the Upland Demesne of the De Lacy Estate of Blackburnshire c.1300', *Agricultural History Review*, 42 (1994), 16.

[12] M. Bailey, '*Per Impetuum Maris*: Natural Disaster and Economic Decline in Eastern England, 1275–1350', in B. M. S. Campbell (ed.), *Before the Black Death: Studies in the 'Crisis' of the Early Fourteenth Century* (Manchester, 1991), 192–4; S. Rippon, *The Severn Estuary* (London, 1997), 242.

[13] Titow, 'Evidence of Weather', 372.

horses, even killing many. On occasion the English were able to take advantage
of the weather. At the naval battle of Sluys in 1340, for example, one of the
reasons for Edward III's triumph was that the wind and tide were with his
ships when they attacked the tightly packed formations of the French navy.
One of the explanations for the English victory at Crécy was that a shower of
rain just before the engagement had soaked the cords on the crossbows used by
the Genoese mercenaries, rendering the weapons useless.[14]

Why the climate altered is difficult to tell. Changes have been the object of
much scientific study. A battery of evidence is available, such as tree-ring
analysis, studies of ice cores to reveal variations in oxygen isotopes, examination of the extent of glaciers, and astronomical data about sunspot cycles.
Many interpretations of the data support conclusions of the kind suggested by
the documentary and literary evidence. It is widely accepted that it was around
the end of the thirteenth century that the climate began to shift markedly, from
the medieval warm period into the little ice age of early modern times. The
scientific evidence, however, is hard to interpret, and, drawn as much of it is
from worldwide sources, does not provide conclusive proof of the nature of the
English climate. The data are not entirely consistent, and often cannot provide
chronological precision. Further, the historical evidence adduced in support of
the scientific conclusions has sometimes been used in a somewhat cavalier
fashion.[15] Tree-ring evidence taken from oak, however, is especially interesting, for it strongly suggests that, after a stable period in the thirteenth century,
there was a dramatic slowdown in growth rates from about 1320, which can be
associated with colder temperatures.[16]

More important than an overall cooling was the fact that these were years in
which the climate became less reliable and more unpredictable. Why this was
is, for the most part, mysterious. One event that can be explained is the bad
weather and cold in 1258–9. Study of an ice core taken in Greenland provides
unambiguous evidence for volcanic eruptions. Signs of volcanic acids can be
easily detected, and for these specific years there is a massive trace. However,
which volcano had erupted is unknown. It almost certainly lay in the tropics,
and left a much stronger marker behind than even the great eruption of
Tamboro in Indonesia in 1815. It will have created a veil of cloud, leading to

[14] Murimuth, 106; *The Chronicle of Jean de Venette*, ed. R. A. Newhall (New York, 1953), 43.
[15] M. K. Hughes and H. F. Diaz (ed.), *The Medieval Warm Period* (Dordrecht, 1994). See
H. H. Lamb, *Climate, History and the Modern World*, 2nd edn. (London, 1995), 195–9. Lamb's
attempt to reconstruct the weather pattern of the summer of 1315 is a remarkable exercise in
imagination, of limited scientific validity.
[16] M. G. L. Baillie, 'Dendrochronology Provides an Independent Background for Studies of
the Human Past', in S. Cavaciocchi (ed.), *L'uomo et la foresta: Secc. XIII–XVIII* (Prato, 1996),
109–10.

cold in winter and spring, and perhaps to summer storms by 1260. The same explanation cannot fit other years of bad weather. Although volcanic activity was higher in the later thirteenth century than in the earlier years, it was not such as to cause a significant long-term shift in the climate. There is no evidence of eruptions taking place on a sufficient scale to explain the appalling weather of 1315 and 1316.[17]

THE PEOPLE AND THEIR HEALTH

The population grew rapidly in the thirteenth century, and reached its peak by about 1300. What that peak was is a matter of some controversy, but it was probably around 5 million. The level stayed relatively static in the first half of the fourteenth century, though the severe weather of 1315–16 brought famine and disease and a consequent short-term fall in the population. Demographic catastrophe came with the advent of the Black Death in 1348. The scale of this is barely imaginable, for between a third and a half of the population died.[18]

The people who lived in thirteenth- and fourteenth-century England were, it is commonly assumed, very much shorter than in modern times. The difference was in fact less than in the Victorian period, when average heights fell to their minimum. Measurements of medieval skeletons show a range of between 165 cm (5′ 5″) and 178 cm (5′ 10″) for men.[19] One calculation of an overall average is 171 cm (5′ 7¼ ″) for males and 159 cm (5′ 2½ ″) for females. For London, the figures are 172 cm for males, and 160 cm for females. A York cemetery shows a slightly shorter medieval population, with the average male at 1.69 cm, and the average female at 157 cm. These figures compare with 177 cm for modern males and 163 for modern females. Analysis of skeletons reveals other interesting features. The York evidence shows that the most common skull type was brachycephalic, or wide. This contrasts intriguingly with narrower skulls from the early medieval period. Faces tended to be broad, with a third of the foreheads being low. Noses tended to be wide.

Archaeology provides some indications of the diseases and conditions that affected people. There is a little evidence for rickets in childhood, perhaps the result of swaddling babies and wearing clothing that prevented any sunlight from reaching the skin. The condition of cribra orbitalia, a pitting of the skull, is indicative of a deficiency of iron in the diet, leading to severe anaemia;

[17] C. U. Hammer, H. B. Clausen, and W. Dansgaard, 'Greenland Ice Sheet Evidence of Post-Glacial Volcanism and its Climatic Impact', *Nature*, 288 (1980), 230–5; R. B. Stothers, 'Climatic and Demographic Consequences of the Massive Volcanic Eruption of 1258', *Climatic Change*, 45 (2000), 361–74.

[18] For further discussion of population levels, see below, 531–8.

[19] J. Schofield and A. Vince, *Medieval Towns* (Leicester, 1994), 197.

hospital sites have yielded a high proportion of cases. Excavations in York and at the deserted village of Wharram Percy show that over half the population in these places suffered from sinusitis, though this condition was not so common elsewhere. Periostitis, a non-specific condition indicative of infections such as leprosy and tuberculosis, has been shown to have affected 14 per cent of skeletal remains from the eleventh to the sixteenth centuries. Some skeletons of monks show signs of diffuse idiopathic skeletal hyperostosis, suggestive of diabetes or (more probably in these cases) obesity resulting from over-eating. There is of course evidence of diseases such as osteoarthritis, but little indication that the pattern was significantly different from that in the modern population. Vitamin C deficiency might be expected from the nature of the medieval diet, but skeletal remains do not show significant indications of scurvy.[20] Analysis of mid-fourteenth-century remains found in London cemeteries shows that almost 90 per cent of the populace died before reaching 45. The indications from a wider range of excavations are that, on average, men might expect to live to just over 30, women to just under that age.[21] However, a young adult of 20 might expect to live another twenty or thirty years, and if people survived to 50, it was quite probable that they would live on to old age.

The environment of thirteenth- and fourteenth-century England was unhealthy, with appalling sanitation and hygiene presenting a particularly acute problem in the crowded towns. The micro-organisms, bacteria, viruses, and parasites, in the medieval environment presented a major threat to man and his animals. Fleas and lice were constant companions. The sources, unfortunately, rarely specify diseases, and where they are named, it is not always possible to identify them with modern ailments. It is not known, for example, what 'le felon' was, but it killed Gunnilda, daughter of Agnes Marsh, in Wiltshire in 1249. Nor is it clear why large numbers suffered an illness in the summer of 1340 that caused them to make a noise like dogs barking. The widespread cases of dementia observed by one chronicler in 1355 are unexplained, though ergotism is a possibility.[22] However, a plausible argument suggests that a

---

[20] C. Roberts and M. Cox, *Health and Disease in Britain* (Stroud, 2003), 233–5, 248; C. Daniell, *Death and Burial in Medieval England* (London, 1997), 134–42; A. Werner, *London Bodies* (London, 1998), 60–7, 108; J. R. Dawes and J. R. Magilton, *The Cemetery of St Helen-on-the-Walls, Aldwark* (York, 1980), 27–9, 40, 82–3. Figures for the modern population are based on analysis of a cohort born in 1958: see C. Power, O. Manor, and L. Li, 'Are Inequalities in Height Underestimated by Adult Social Position? Effects of Changing Social Structure and Height Selection in a Cohort Study', *British Medical Journal*, 325 (2002), 131–4. This shows that those in the upper classes today are about 1.6 cm taller than those in the lowest; unfortunately it is not possible to produce similar class-based calculations for the medieval period.

[21] Daniell, *Death and Burial in Medieval England*, 133–4.

[22] *Crown Pleas of the Wiltshire Eyre, 1249*, ed. C. A. F. Meekings (Wiltshire Archaeological and Natural History Society, 1961), 244; Knighton, 36–7; *Melsa*, ii. 111.

sudden increase in 1333–4 in deaths in Thornbury, Gloucestershire, may well have been due to malaria.[23] Leprosy was probably on the decline by this period, but was still a danger, which could only be dealt with by isolation of the unfortunate victims. The famine years of 1315 and 1316 saw considerable mortality; probably 10 to 15 per cent of the people died. Hunger alone is unlikely to have been the cause; a weakened population was inevitably a prey to disease. Just as it was beginning to recover from the losses caused by famine, the population was hit by a catastrophe of unprecedented proportions. The Black Death reached England in 1348. The population had not been exposed to this disease previously, and so lacked any form of immunity. The effect was devastating. What the Black Death was is discussed in Chapter 13; it probably killed off up to half the population.

The environment was not only unhealthy, but also unsafe, presenting many risks to its inhabitants. In Wiltshire in 1249, for example, John de Puntrefeud was crushed in a marl pit. Robert de la Forde was accidentally struck on the leg with a scythe; the wound became infected, and he died. Felicity of Wrockshall was crushed to death by part of a grindstone in an accident. William, son of Roger of Alinton, fell on a pair of shears and died ten days later. Nicholas Spyrun was drowned in a ditch. Thomas le Norreys was found crushed to death in a quarry. William de la Pyrie was crushed by a heavily laden cart. Eve Scolace was scalded to death. Mabel, wife of Crum, who was epileptic, had a fit while holding a small boy; she dropped him into a fire, and he died. Three-year-old Christiana was trampled to death by a horse. This was a world in which a dog might run through a village street carrying a dead baby in its jaws.[24] Even sport might prove dangerous. One man died after a collision while playing with a ball; his opponent had a knife hanging from his belt, and even though it was sheathed, the force was such that it penetrated.[25] A wrestling match near Stafford in 1289 ended with more violence than was intended when the maidservant of one of the participants was accidentally killed.[26]

THE LANDSCAPE

The landscape the people inhabited was stable, and long settled, and while it evolved in many ways under the pressure of population growth, it underwent no dramatic changes during this period. The landscape was very varied; England was a country of regions very different in character. This was not

[23] P. Franklin, 'Malaria in Medieval Gloucestershire: An Essay in Epidemiology', *Transactions of the Bristol and Gloucestershire Archaeological Society*, 101 (1983), 111–22.
[24] *Crown Pleas of the Wiltshire Eyre*, 187–90, 203, 308.
[25] *CIM* i, no. 2242.
[26] *CIM* i, no. 2310.

due solely to the geographical contrasts between lowland and highland zones, but was also the result of long tradition and contrasting histories. There were many different economies, with great differences between the densely populated eastern counties, notably Norfolk, the long-settled midlands, with their great sweeping open fields, and the uplands in the west and north. There has been much scholarly debate about field systems and their origins, but by the thirteenth century they were well established. The classic open fields, divided into long strips, normally featured the very distinctive ridge and furrow pattern, which is usually thought to have been created by careful ploughing. It was intended, at least on heavy soils, to make drainage easier. The extent of this practice, extending to high and marginal lands such as the Wiltshire downs, shows the extraordinary extent of arable cultivation by the late thirteenth century. Ridge and furrow, however, was not universal. It was not to be found, for example, in the great grain-producing region of East Anglia, where the open fields were subdivided to a much greater extent than elsewhere. In the midland system the proportion of arable land was extraordinarily high. A calculation for Leicestershire covering the period 1254 to 1350 suggests that 87.9 per cent of the land was arable, with meadow 8.7 per cent and pasture a mere 3.4 per cent. This did not mean that there was virtually no pasture; fallow fields were available to provide grazing for the sheep and cattle. In east Devon, in contrast to the midlands, arable was 68.6 per cent, meadow 8.8 per cent, and pasture 22.6 per cent.[27] Different systems of crop rotation operated, but the two main methods were the two-field and the three-field system. In the former, one field was left fallow; in the latter, one field would be autumn-sown, one spring, with the third fallow. The main cereal crops were wheat, oats, and barley; in some districts rye was also grown on a substantial scale. Beans and peas also featured, while relatively small quantities of fruit and vegetables were grown in gardens.[28] The cereal crops were very different in appearance from those of the present day; the plants were very tall, yielding excellent straw but little seed. In many manors, in a good year, a fivefold return on seed was all that might be expected. In the highland regions of the north and the west, patterns of agriculture were very different, with smaller hamlets and isolated farmsteads rather than the nucleated villages of the midlands. There was much more pasture land, but far fewer rich meadows. Here rye and oats were the main grains harvested, rather than wheat.

The landscape, contrary to widespread popular impression, was not heavily or uniformly wooded. Much of the midlands and Yorkshire had no woods at

[27] H. S. A. Fox, 'Some Ecological Dimensions of Medieval Field Systems', in K. Biddick (ed.), *Archaeological Approaches to Medieval Europe* (Kalamazoo, Mich., 1984), 121, 124.

[28] For a detailed analysis of various cropping systems, see B. M. S. Campbell, *English Seigniorial Agriculture, 1250–1450* (Cambridge, 2000), 249–305.

MAP 1.1. The counties of England

all, and woods were scarce in East Anglia. The Weald and the Chilterns, however, had extensive tracts of woodland. Conifer forests were largely unknown; the woods of this period were mostly of lime, oak, ash, elm, and hazel. Woods were a vital resource, and were carefully managed, with extensive coppicing. Of the trees in English woods, oak was particularly prized, and was a significant element in royal patronage, with grants of oaks from royal forests being made on a regular basis. Timber was needed on a huge scale for building; it has been calculated that it took 333 trees to construct a substantial timber-framed farmhouse. On a much larger scale, when Edward III was building at Windsor in the mid-fourteenth century, a whole wood at Cagham was bought to provide 3,004 oaks.[29] Large oaks would be needed for roof timbers in large buildings and for the great crucks that were the main frames of a peasant house; coppiced wood cut into laths, hazel rods, and the like served for wattle-and-daub.[30] Ideally, new timber was cut in the winter months so that it would have time to dry out in the summer.[31] Wood was also needed for fuel on a very extensive scale. Trees were highly valued. One valuation set oak trees at 5s. each, apple trees at 2s., and ash trees at 1s. 6d.[32] The oaks growing in the marketplace at Causton in Norfolk protected buyers and sellers from 'all blasts and changes in the weather', and their loss was much regretted when they were cut down by an asset-stripping landlord.[33] Financial gain was not the only reason for destroying woodland. There were occasions when it had to be cleared for military reasons. Orders were issued in 1224 for all woods around the new castle at Montgomery to be chopped down and the land cleared: it was obviously essential to have good lines of sight from the castle walls.[34] Edward I used axemen to create ways through the forests of north Wales to provide easier routes for his armies and the multiplicity of supplies that they needed.

As well as timber, woodland provided pasture for deer and pigs. Much woodland was included in parks.[35] These might be royal, but many were in private hands, the proud possessions of the more important landowners. They

[29] L. F. Salzman, *Building in England down to 1540* (Oxford, 1952), 237.

[30] O. Rackham, 'The Forest: Woodland and Wood-Pasture in Medieval England', in Biddick (ed.), *Archaeological Approaches to Medieval Europe*, 78.

[31] Salzman, *Building*, 239.

[32] 'Plea Rolls of the Reign of Edward III', ed. G. Wrottesley, in *Collections for a History of Staffordshire*, 12 (William Salt Archaeological Society, 1891), 31.

[33] *CDS* iii, no. 532.

[34] J. K. Knight, 'Excavations at Montgomery Castle, Part I', *Archaeologia Cambrensis*, 141 (1992), 107.

[35] Forests, parks, and chases are discussed in L. Cantor, *The English Medieval Landscape* (London, 1982), 56–85. For a detailed local analysis, see J. Hunt, *Lordship and the Landscape: A Documentary and Archaeological Study of the Honor of Dudley c.1066–1322*, British Archaeological Reports, British Series, 264 (1997), 110–19.

were substantial areas, usually enclosed by a ditch and bank, serving as reserves where deer were hunted for sport and for food. Calculations vary, but there may have been almost 2,000 parks in England by 1300, most between 100 and 200 acres. The thirteenth and early fourteenth centuries witnessed a huge increase in the number of these parks. Deer were not strictly speaking farmed, but food might be put out for them in winter. Much work was done to ensure that parks were properly stocked, and the maintenance of fences was often a major expense. In 1332–3 the bishop of Winchester spent about £100 on his deer parks in Hampshire, of which about £70 went on maintenance and the rest on hunting. The Black Prince even went to the lengths of having the lawns in two of his Cornish parks dug up so as to get rid of the moss and to improve the grazing for the deer. The numbers of animals in these parks were considerable. At the royal park of Havering, over 1,000 acres in size, there were about 500 deer in the fourteenth century.[36]

Forests were not the same as woodland and parks. The status of the forest was a legal one. In the forest the common law was supplemented by special forest law. The crown had special rights in the forest, which were intended to preserve hunting, notably of 'the beasts of the forest': red deer, roe deer, fallow deer, and wild boar. There were, as a result, prohibitions on the carrying of bows and arrows. Dogs had to have their claws removed. The woods in which the deer lived were also protected. Clearing (or assarting) land within the bounds of the forest, the construction of hedges and ditches, and much of the business of agriculture were strictly controlled. A typical entry in a New Forest record reads: 'Richard Pinnock holds one acre enclosed with a hedge without warrant and for which enclose he was fined at the last forest eyre [judicial visitation]. Let the hedge be thrown down.'[37] The landscape within the bounds of the forest was significantly affected by these legal constraints. There was a widespread belief that the crown had been improperly extending the bounds of the forest, and around 1300 this became a major political issue. It was not a simple matter to remove land from forest jurisdiction; when the bishop of Bath and Wells proposed to enclose some forest land in Edward II's reign, a commission reported in very adverse terms.[38] The private equivalent of the royal forest was the chase. Cannock Chase, for example, had been royal forest until it was granted to the bishop of Chester in 1290. The lowest level at which hunting rights were granted was that of free warren. Such a grant gave the recipient the right to hunt rabbits, hares, foxes, and wildcats over their

---

[36] J. Birrell, 'Deer and Deer Farming in Medieval England', *Agricultural History Review*, 40 (1992), 112–26.

[37] *A Calendar of New Forest Documents 1244–1334*, ed. D. J. Stagg, Hampshire Record Series, 3 (1979), 75.

[38] SC 1/19, no. 19.

lands. In the early fourteenth century it was possible to buy a charter of free warren for £7 11s. 8d.[39]

Pressure from a rising population in the thirteenth century made men seek ways of increasing the area under cultivation; extension of agriculture was a much easier solution than intensification. Cutting back woodland was one solution, but that was often difficult, given the conflicting needs of lords to maintain and improve their hunting. Even so, it has been estimated that the overall area of forest decreased by about a third between 1250 and 1325, and with that process woodlands were encroached upon by fields; the sound of the axe was very familiar.[40] With the removal of the legal constraints on those who lived within the bounds of the forest, expansion of arable and pasture became much easier.

Reclamation of marsh and fen was another answer, with the two most notable examples being the Fens of East Anglia and the Somerset levels. This was a long-established process involving the building of elaborate sluices, dykes, and banks, often on a massive scale. Many settlements were created as new land came under the plough. In the Lincolnshire hundred of Elloe some 18 square miles were added when the last of five great medieval banks was completed in the mid-thirteenth century.[41] In the Somerset levels there was little new land won from the sea in the thirteenth and early fourteenth centuries, but extensive work was done to create major artificial channels and to improve drainage and flood defences.[42] Drainage schemes, however, were not invariably successful. The Pevensey levels were severely damaged by flooding in 1287, and subsequent measures to drain the land themselves caused further floods. In 1317 Edward II optimistically made a grant to one of his household knights and his wife 'that they may enclose as much as they can of the marsh of Pevensey, which is submerged by the flow of the sea'.[43] A dam built in Norfolk by Walter Langton, bishop of Coventry and Lichfield, enabled him to drain lands in one of his Cambridgeshire manors nearby. However, the dam both prevented river-borne trade on the Nene and, it was later claimed, caused extensive flooding to 110,000 acres of fenland. After twenty-eight years a case was brought in the courts, and the dam was duly destroyed in a great public ceremony.[44]

[39] D. Crook, 'A Dying Queen and a Declining Knight', in C. Richmond and I. Harvey (eds.), *Recognitions: Essays Presented to Edmund Fryde* (Aberystwyth, 1996), 106.

[40] C. R. Young, *The Royal Forests of Medieval England* (Leicester, 1979), 116–24.

[41] *Agrarian History*, ii. 142–74.

[42] Rippon, *Severn Estuary*, 206–19.

[43] E. Searle, *Lordship and Community: Battle Abbey and its Banlieu 1066–1538* (Toronto, 1974), 254 n.; *Calendar of Chancery Warrants, 1244–1327*, 474.

[44] *The Eyre of Northamptonshire, iii–iv: Edward III*, ed. D. W. Sutherland (Selden Society, 97, 1981), pp. i, xxxviii–xxxix, 227–9.

High ground, too, was brought under cultivation, with farms being created out of rough moorland in areas such as the south-west and the fringes of the North Yorkshire Moors. Cistercian monasteries in the north were very active in this process, but much work was also done by ordinary villagers in an unplanned fashion. It is impossible to calculate the total acreage that was brought into cultivation in this way between the early thirteenth century and the mid-fourteenth, but the extent to which the countryside was transformed through the efforts of villagers and lords, by the extension of the area of cultivation, should not be underestimated.

ANIMALS

The wild and domestic animals of medieval England included some that are no longer found in the British Isles. Wolves were a threat to farmers in some remote regions: on the earl of Lincoln's Lancashire estates, in 1303–4, eleven cattle were lost to wolves, though disease took a much larger toll, with 123 dying.[45] Others were relative newcomers, and some had not spread to the extent they have today. Fallow deer were a recent and highly successful introduction. Rabbits were carefully looked after in warrens, and were not a widespread pest. In 1235 Henry III made a gift of ten live rabbits from a warren at Guildford—the first documentary evidence of them in mainland England.[46] The extent to which rats and mice were common is an important question, given the significance of rats as a vector in spreading bubonic plague. There is startlingly little evidence, either documentary or archaeological, to suggest that there was a large rat population in the country. References such as that in the accounts for the Durham manor of Bearpark, where rats and mice destroyed all the stock of beans and peas in 1333–4, are rare.[47] Yet the way in which grain and other produce were stored in barns left them wide open to infestation. It may be that losses were so common that they were simply not recorded, but normally those presenting accounts were anxious to provide every possible explanation for low yields and poor performance.

The main domesticated animals were, of course, horses, cattle, sheep, and pigs. Breeding techniques have transformed farm animals almost out of recognition from their medieval ancestors, which were much smaller, and far less productive of milk, wool, and meat. England was above all a country of sheep. Accurate overall figures for the sheep population cannot be worked out, in the absence of details of the size of peasant flocks, but there are very impressive

---

[45] Atkin, 'Land Use and Management in the Upland Demesne of the De Lacy Estate of Blackburnshire c.1300', 8.

[46] Cantor, *English Medieval Landscape*, 83.

[47] Durham cathedral muniments, manorial accounts 3, 1334–5.

figures for great estates. In the first half of the fourteenth century Durham cathedral priory had flocks of some 4,000, Furness abbey perhaps twice that number; Crowland abbey had just over 5,000. In 1349 the earl of Arundel had 5,345 sheep on his estates in the Welsh marches.[48] Dogs were kept largely for hunting. Pets included cats. John de Engayne was accused of catching a domestic cat belonging to Millicent de Mohaut when out hunting wolves, foxes, and wildcats. More exotically, one bishop of Durham, 'in the manner of modern prelates', kept two monkeys so as to relieve him of stress.[49]

Animals suffered from different plagues from humans. The period of greatest difficulty, when animals died in their thousands, was the second decade of the fourteenth century, the same period that saw the worst weather and the most disastrous harvests. Cattle were probably afflicted by rinderpest, a highly contagious viral infection quite as devastating to cattle as plague was to humans. In the aftermath of the famine of 1315–16 figures show losses of 50 per cent to have been common. At Ramsey abbey records show herds declining from forty-eight to six, and from forty-five to two.[50] Sheep suffered from what contemporaries called murrain, a general term for animal plagues. There were severe epidemics in the 1280s, and again in the aftermath of the famine years in the early fourteenth century. Which of the various diseases that affected sheep were the most serious cannot be determined, but whether it was liver fluke or some other ailment, there was no cure available. It is conceivable that anthrax, which would affect both cattle and sheep, was one of the agents involved.

BUILDINGS

The built environment was very varied, ranging as it did from grand castles and churches to simple wooden shacks for the poorest of the peasantry. In physical terms, aristocratic lordship was defined by castles. There was much castle-building in the thirteenth and fourteenth centuries. For the most part this was a matter of rebuilding and adding to existing structures. There were not many major new castles such as the early thirteenth-century Bolingbroke in Lincolnshire, or the great early fourteenth-century unfinished castle at Dunstanburgh in Northumberland, and a good many small castles fell into disuse. A reasonable estimate is that there were some 400 to 500 castles in the country in this period, though any such figure depends on difficult issues of definition. Even the practice of licensing is of less help than might be expected. From the early thirteenth century it was necessary to obtain a royal licence to crenellate in order to build a castle; but such licences might also be given for buildings

---

[48] *Agrarian History*, ii. 310, 409, 486.   [49] JUST 1/620, m. 25ᵛ; *Lanercost*, 114.
[50] Jordan, *Great Famine*, 38.

that cannot be categorized as castles, such as the cathedral close at Lichfield. Stokesay, in Shropshire, was licensed, but is often conventionally regarded as a fortified manor house rather than a castle.

It was not only the higher aristocracy whose lordship was symbolized in part by buildings. For the gentry, manor houses and moated sites provided a means of displaying wealth and demonstrating a position in society. Types of manorial building varied considerably and might be in either stone or wood. The usual elements were a hall and a chamber block, with which a kitchen and other service elements were usually combined. Early timber buildings usually had an aisled hall, but by the end of the thirteenth century the fashion was for halls constructed without aisle posts, using arches or hammer-beams to support the roof.[51] There appears to have been a huge expansion in the number of moated sites in the thirteenth and fourteenth centuries, with over 5,000 identified. One estimate is that about 70 per cent of these came into being between 1200 and 1325, making a major contribution to the transformation of the landscape, particularly in eastern England and the west midlands.[52]

Alongside the castles, manor houses, and moated sites, abbeys and churches dominated the landscape. Here there was a less dramatic transformation in the thirteenth and fourteenth centuries, for there were no new major monastic foundations. Newly established friaries and chantries did not have such an impact on the landscape of England as did the great Cistercian foundations of the twelfth century. Much of the building of these great houses, however, took place in the thirteenth century, while at Vale Royal in Cheshire, Edward I began, but did not complete, what would have been the largest Cistercian church in England. Much of England was a country of towns and villages rather than of isolated farms. Villages took many different forms, and generalization is impossible. Some were carefully planned, with standard-sized holdings ranged along a straight road, with back lanes formed parallel to it. Others were centred on a green, which might be irregular in shape. Churches or manor houses might provide an alternative focus for the settlement. In the north and the west settlement might be much more dispersed than in the nucleated villages of much of the country.

Relatively little is known about peasant housing, for wooden buildings have not left much trace on sites that have undergone frequent rebuilding. There was undoubtedly much regional variation. Longhouses, which combined human habitation with animal, were not unknown, but the house was frequently separate from a barn or byre. The most common form of building was

---

[51] J. Munby, 'Manorial Building in Timber in Central and Southern England, 1200–1550', in G. Meirion-Jones and M. Jones (eds.), *Manorial Domestic Buildings in England and Northern France* (London, 1993), 49–64.
[52] Cantor, *English Medieval Landscape*, 140.

to use crucks, massive frames set some 15 feet apart. Houses could be of one or more bays, depending on how many crucks were erected. It was normal for there to be at least two rooms, one a substantial hall and the other a much smaller chamber which provided a degree of privacy. A central hearth provided heat, as well as smoke and soot. The foundations for these buildings might be no more than post-holes in the ground, but increasingly they consisted of stone walls or pad stones on which the timbers rested. The walls would usually have been of timber, with a wattle-and-daub construction. Little is known of the costs of peasant housing, but isolated cases suggest that a cottage could be built for as little as 10s. The evidence seems to show that housing standards improved in the thirteenth century, but much more excavation is needed to prove the point. Despite improvements in building methods, some dwellings were flimsy and inadequate. In 1249 it was reported that Agnes of Lavinton had been crushed when an old house in Devizes collapsed. The value of the timber in the ruin was set at no more than 18d.[53]

Just as the pressure of a growing population saw the area under cultivation increase, so it also saw the towns both expand and proliferate. Many towns were clearly marked out from the surrounding countryside by their walls, though the development of suburbs extending beyond the gates blurred the distinction. The great towns of England in this period were not, with the sole exception of London, very large. London may have had a population of 70,000 or more by 1300, putting it on a similar level to great European cities such as Paris and Florence. No other town is likely to have exceeded 20,000, and most would have been far below that figure. Shrewsbury, which was the eighth most important town in terms of tax raised, probably had a population in the region of 5,000.[54] The most striking development in the thirteenth century is the extraordinary number of new towns founded, most with well-organized regular ground plans. About fifty were created in the hundred years from 1220, with the greatest number (fifteen) in the decade 1221–30.[55] Stratford upon Avon is a classic example of a new town of this period, founded by the bishop of Worcester, with quarter-acre plots of land carefully set out. There was a legal distinction between a borough and a village, for the inhabitants of the former had clearly established freedoms and rights. Not all boroughs, however, performed the economic function of a town, and not all towns possessed the

[53] C. Dyer, *Everyday Life in the Middle Ages* (London, 1994), 160–9; *Agrarian History*, ii. 898–915; *Crown Pleas of the Wiltshire Eyre*, no. 231.
[54] B. M. S. Campbell, J. A. Galloway, D. Keene, and M. Murphy, *A Medieval Capital and its Grain Supply: Agrarian Production and Distribution in the London Region c.1300* (London, 1993), 10–11; *The Wealth of Shrewsbury in the Early Fourteenth Century*, ed. D. and R. Cromarty (Shropshire Archaeological and Historical Society, 1993), 29.
[55] M. W. Beresford, *New Towns of the Middle Ages* (London, 1967), 330.

0 100 miles

0 80 160 km

Berwick

Dunstanburgh

Newcastle

Carlisle

Durham Hartlepool

Scarborough

Boroughbridge

Lancaster York

Pontefract Hull

Wakefield Ravenserodd

Grimsby

Lincoln

Conwy Chester Boston

Caernarfon Vale Royal

Harlech Shrewsbury Stafford King's Yarmouth

Lichfield Lynn Norwich

Leicester

Coventry Ely Dunwich

Kenilworth Northampton Cambridge

Worcester Stratford Bury St

Hereford Edmunds

Evesham St Albans

Oxford

Gloucester London

Bristol

Devizes Windsor Gillingham

Bath Canterbury

Dover

Salisbury

Glastonbury Winchester

Southampton Lewes Winchelsea

Pevensey

Exeter Portsmouth

MAP 1.2. Major towns, with other places mentioned in the text

legal status of a borough. Nor is the distinction between small towns and villages always easy to make in an economic or a physical sense. Tax returns might include under the heading of a borough some nearby villages, while significant urban suburbs might be returned under some nearby vill. Attempts to calculate the proportion of the population that lived in towns are beset by difficulties of definition, and vary between 5 and 20 per cent. Using a broad definition of 'town', the latter is probably nearer to the truth.[56]

Most of the buildings in towns were wooden, and many roofs were thatched. Streets were narrow, and fire was a constant danger. Carlisle suffered a serious fire in 1292, and in 1296 much of the city was again burned as a result of a Scottish attack. In 1303 yet another fire destroyed half the city, but recovery and rebuilding was swift, largely because so much of what was built was flimsy.[57] The urban environment was crowded and unhygienic, with pigs and other animals wandering the streets, and water supplies polluted. Sanitation was primitive; latrines opened onto cesspits, or into open drains. Butchers were careless about what they did with the offal from carcases. The smell must have been extremely unpleasant. Most people had to put up with this, but Edward I's mother, Queen Eleanor, wrote to him on one occasion saying that she had left Gillingham sooner than expected because of the poor quality of the air, which was especially smoke-filled in the evenings. Edward himself used the foul air of London as an excuse for leaving the city when he wanted to avoid political embarrassment. People had low standards of personal hygiene. At Carlisle the air was 'so corrupted and tainted by dung and manure heaps and much other filth put in the streets and lanes that the men dwelling there and coming to the city for its defence are stricken with a dreadful horror'. Henry, duke of Lancaster, felt some guilt at his very understandable reaction to the smell of the sick and the poor.[58]

TECHNOLOGY AND TRANSPORT

The thirteenth and fourteenth centuries were not notably inventive in terms of technology. There were very highly skilled craftsmen, but this was not an age of startling breakthroughs. In the thirteenth century, with an expanding population, labour was cheap, and there was little incentive to find new or more efficient ways of doing things. This is not to say that there were no

[56] Dyer, *Everyday Life in Medieval England*, 285, 302.

[57] H. Summerson, *Medieval Carlisle: The City and the Borders from the Late Eleventh to the Mid-Sixteenth Century* (Cumberland and Westmorland Antiquarian and Archaeological Society, extra ser., 25, 1993), 190–2.

[58] SC 1/16/157; M. C. Prestwich, *Edward I* (London, 1988), 520; *CPR 1343–45*, 507–8; K. Fowler, *The King's Lieutenant: Henry of Grosmont, First Duke of Lancaster* (London, 1969), 195.

changes. Metalworking saw a significant advance around the year 1300, with the development of more efficient furnaces capable of producing larger single blooms of iron than in the past. Those produced in the mid-fourteenth century at Tudeley in Kent weighed about 30 lbs, double what had been possible in classical times; larger blooms would make it easier to produce items such as plate armour. Water power was used from the early fourteenth century to shape the blooms.[59] Gunpowder was introduced, and employed by Edward I in his Scottish wars as an explosive, and primitive guns were soon produced, though they had little effect.

An interesting technological advance in the measurement of time began in this period. Patterns of work followed the pattern of daylight, not the passing of hours and minutes. Time was normally measured by the monastic day, with its frequent services such as prime, nones, and vespers. Its passing might be noted by the ringing of bells. The first signs of a transformation came in the mid-fourteenth century. In the early 1350s a clock driven by weights and striking the time was installed in the keep at Windsor. The first such instrument known in England, it was brought to the castle from London, probably having been constructed by Italians.[60]

Power was chiefly available from wind, water, and animals. Windmills first appeared in England in the twelfth century, but they were still sufficiently striking in the later thirteenth century for the artist of the so-called Windmill Psalter to depict one at the head of a magnificent capital E. As for the medieval post mill, the whole structure pivoted on a huge central post: a long tail-pole provided the miller with a means of swinging the mill so that it faced the wind. A simple gearing system translated the horizontal rotation of the main shaft into a vertical rotation which turned the millstones.[61] Watermills were not new in this period, but the development of the 'overshot' type greatly increased the power they made available. This involved diverting the stream, digging mill-ponds, and fitting sluice-gates, all of which could involve a very considerable investment. Such mills, an innovation in the early fourteenth century, were not common. Mills were, of course, mostly used for grinding grain. Although fulling mills, which used a cam mechanism to power one of the finishing processes of cloth manufacture, were known, it would be wrong to see their introduction as an early stage in the industrialization of cloth production, for the fulling mill did not spur the similar mechanization of any other elements in the production cycle.

[59] J. Blair and N. Ramsay (eds.), *English Medieval Industries: Craftsmen, Techniques, Products* (London, 1991), 169–73.
[60] *KW* ii. 875–6.
[61] E. J. Kealey, *Harvesting the Air: Windmill Pioneers in Twelfth-Century England* (Woodbridge, 1987), 147 and *passim*.

Animal power was essential for transport and for agriculture. The great improvements in harnessing horses had taken place earlier, with the introduction of the stiff, solid horse collar which enabled the horse to pull far more effectively than with a softer harness, which had a throttling effect. Minor improvements in harnessing continued, however, and better carriages and carts made land transport somewhat easier. There was a steady increase in the use of horses rather than oxen.

Ships and boats provided the cheapest form of bulk transport. Little is known about the many boats and barges that were used on England's inland waterways, but seagoing ships were of various types, ranging from open vessels of Viking type to far more sophisticated decked ships. Methods of construction defined the distinction between hulks, which did not have stem and stern posts and which might be built using a 'reverse clinker' method, and the more advanced cogs, high-sided and flat-bottomed, with conventional clinker build. All had a simple square sail on a single mast. There were many other types, many of which cannot be identified. One of the more important developments of the period was the shift from the Viking-type steering oar to the central rudder mounted on a stern post, which took place very gradually during the thirteenth and early fourteenth centuries. One of the galleys built for Edward I in 1295 had both steering oar and stern rudder, whereas the *Philippe* of 1337 had just a stern rudder. 'Castles' might be added to stem and stern, and even masthead, to convert vessels for use in war.[62]

Transport by land was slow. Most people did not travel much, with the nearest market as far as many would go. This was perhaps fortunate, for the transport system of medieval England was inadequate. The great Roman roads remained as major thoroughfares, but little work was done to create new routes, with the exception of causeways in the fenland and similar areas. In many cases it was simply the passage of men, carts, and animals that served to keep tracks open. Bridges were vital if communications were to be maintained, and these were the main medieval contribution to land transport. In one case, that of Rochester Bridge on the Medway, elaborate accounts by the bridge wardens have survived, to show how the crossing was maintained. Rivers were much used, offering as they did a much easier way of transporting goods in bulk than muddy roads. When Edward I went to Lincolnshire in 1300, Reginald the Janitor was sent on in advance to repair bridges and to hire boats for transport of the royal household from Peterborough to Ely.[63]

Many accounts survive of the speed of travel in this period. In 1300 Pierre Aimery went to Rome and back on Edward I's behalf; the journey took him four months each way. It took three days for thirty carters to take some of the

---

[62] I. Friel, *The Good Ship* (London, 1995), 35–8, 79–81.   [63] *Liber Quotidianus*, 89.

royal tents from Newcastle to Carlisle in 1300, a distance of about 60 miles. Six days were needed to take 1,000 marks from York to Lochmaben, just over twice as far. A round trip from London to Caerlaverock in the same year took twenty-five days; the distance involved was about 650 miles. The earl of Ross took eighteen days to travel from London to Berwick, some 300 miles. That was somewhat leisurely: at the end of Edward II's reign it took royal servants six days to go from York to London, just over 200 miles. A royal envoy in the late 1330s, John de Thrandeston, took seven days to go from Sandwich to York, about 280 miles. To travel from Oxford to Ponteland, just outside Newcastle, a journey of some 260 miles, took fellows of Merton College seven or eight days.[64]

CONCLUSION

This account may suggest, with some cause, that the thirteenth- and four-teenth-century environment was grim and that life was hard. The climate deteriorated, with the second decade of the fourteenth century witnessing particularly severe conditions. Disease, both in people and in animals, pre-sented problems that could not be dealt with. Technological advances were limited. Life was not, however, without its distractions. Even a small place such as Sherburn-in-Elmet, in Yorkshire, had its pleasures, for in the early fourteenth century the local vicar lived life to the full, frequenting taverns and other such places by day and night, feasting and drinking, taking part in theatrical performances, fighting and scolding, not to mention fornicating.[65] People were proud of England. Robert of Gloucester, who wrote his chronicle in English in about 1300, began by stating that 'England is a well good land.' The country was full of fruit, trees, woods, and parks. Animals were abundant, both wild and tame, and there was ample fish, saltwater and fresh. There was a wealth of minerals, and the corn was good. There were great wonders, notably the hot waters of Bath and the great stones of Stonehenge. The inhabitants were the fairest people in the world.[66] Nor was it just a matter of literary expression. The abbot of Battle used to go to Barnhorn on the edge of the Pevensey levels in the summer, to enjoy the sport which the marshland could provide. For a modern commentator, this is 'a grey, bleak world of sea, sky and

---

[64] Ibid. 64–5, 86, 92; *CDS* ii, no. 1403; Society of Antiquaries of London, MS 122, p. 84; *Œuvres de Froissart*, ed. Kervyn de Lettenhove (Brussels, 1867–77), xviii. 154–5, 157, 159; *The History of the University of Oxford*, i: *The Early Oxford Schools*, ed. J. I. Catto (Oxford, 1984), 338–9.

[65] *The Register of William Greenfield, Lord Archbishop of York 1306–15*, ed. W. Brown (Surtees Society, 1931), i. 117–18.

[66] *The Metrical Chronicle of Robert of Gloucester*, ed. W. A. Wright (RS, 1887), i. 1–2, 11, 13.

birds . . . overlooking tumbledown marsh pastures'.[67] It may not be to modern tastes, but the monks of the thirteenth and fourteenth centuries would not have visited it if they had not enjoyed it. The priory and manor of Bearpark, just outside Durham, provided similar rest and recreation for the cathedral monks. Set on a bend of the river Wear, overlooked by cliffs and surrounded by dense woodland, it is still a beauty spot, and it is impossible to imagine that the monks did not appreciate their surroundings when they went there. The countryside could be idealized. One poet wrote:

> Therefore I will stay in the wood, in the lovely shade
> Where there is no falseness, nor any bad laws.
> In the wood of Belregard, where the jay flies
> And the nightingale sings without delay every day.[68]

[67] Searle, *Lordship and Community*, 254.
[68] *Political Songs*, 232 (my translation).

CHAPTER 2

The Crown and Kingship

The kings of England had grand titles. When Henry III came to the throne, he was king of England, lord of Ireland, duke of Normandy and Aquitaine, and count of Anjou. The claim to Normandy and the counties of Anjou, Maine, Touraine, and Poitou was abandoned in 1259, but Edward III added no less than the kingdom of all France to his title in 1340.[1] The elements of the title emphasize the cosmopolitan character of the English monarchy; this was an Anglo-French dynasty. Henry III was an Angevin, descended from Geoffrey, count of Anjou, and the Norman Matilda, daughter of Henry I. He married Eleanor, daughter of the count of Provence, two of whose sisters married into the French royal house. His son Edward I was married first to Eleanor of Castile, and second to Margaret, daughter of Philip III of France. Edward II married Isabella, daughter of Philip IV of France, and their son Edward III married Philippa, daughter of the count of Hainault. The international connections were further increased by the marriages of other members of the royal family. Edward I's brother Edmund of Lancaster, for example, married Blanche, dowager countess of Champagne. This was a dynasty deeply embedded in the complex structures of the ruling families of Europe.

The marriages of the kings of this period were important in establishing international connections; they were also important in their primary purpose of continuing the dynasty. All of the queens proved to be good at what can be seen as their primary duty, that of bearing children. Eleanor of Castile produced an impressive fifteen or sixteen, and Philippa of Hainault a dozen. Eleanor of Provence probably had nine. Isabella, queen to Edward II, had four children, while Edward I's second queen, Margaret, had three. Not all children survived; only one of Eleanor of Castile's male children, the future Edward II, lived to be an adult.

---

[1] For a brief period at the end of Edward II's reign, Aquitaine was omitted from the royal title, following the grant of the duchy to the king's son, the future Edward III, in 1325. See P. Chaplais, *Medieval English Diplomatic Practice*, pt. 1 (London, 1982), i. 68–70, and ibid., i. 154–5 for Edward III's royal style.

Royal blood was important, and the English dynasty possessed an exceptionally long lineage. This ran back to the royal house of Wessex, through
Henry I's marriage to Matilda, who was descended from Æthelred the Unready. From the kings of Wessex it was an easy task for any medieval genealogist to trace descent from Woden; for Henry III, it was more important to be
able to recite the names of the saintly kings of the Anglo-Saxon past.[2] Edward I
did not share his father's enthusiasm for the devout Confessor after whom he
was named. He looked back rather to a different past, that of legend, and made
a very interesting attempt to link his kingship with that of the mythical King
Arthur. Where Henry III had the remains of the Confessor translated in 1269,
Edward I conducted a successful archaeological excavation at Glastonbury in
1278, in which the bodies of Arthur and Guinevere were discovered and then
reburied. Edward's conquest of Wales and his ambitions in Scotland were
viewed by some as Arthurian. When a letter was sent in Edward's name to the
pope in 1301, it was argued that when King Arthur held a feast at Caerleon, the
king of Scotland, Angusel, had performed the service of carrying his sword,
which demonstrated his subjection to the British king. The chronicler Peter
Langtoft, however, made a very different Arthurian comparison when he
pointed out that, among other things, Arthur got up earlier in the morning
than Edward.[3] Edward III also made something of the Arthurian precedent; his
unsuccessful attempt to create a round table of 300 knights in 1344 looked back
to the legendary British king.[4]

THE CORONATION AND SACRED KINGSHIP

The greatest ceremony that celebrated the position and role of the monarchy
was, of course, the coronation. Before being crowned, the king was anointed, an
act seen as endowing him with spiritual authority. He was then invested with
spurs and a sword, symbolic of secular power. Unusually, Henry III was
crowned twice. The first was at Gloucester in 1216, by the papal legate
Guala in the difficult days immediately after John's death. Since this was
held in the wrong place, with the wrong person conducting the ceremony,
the second was held in Westminster, with the archbishop of Canterbury
presiding. Speed had been necessary in 1216, but when Edward I came to
the throne in 1272 he was absent from the country on crusade, and the
coronation did not take place until 1274. There was no questioning of the

    [2] Paris, *Chron. Maj.* v. 617.
    [3] E. L. G. Stones (ed.), *Anglo-Scottish Relations, 1174–1328* (London, 1965), 98; Pierre de
Langtoft, 401.
    [4] *Melsa*, iii. 52.

king's authority because he had not been crowned. Edward II was not crowned until February 1308, over seven months after his accession. In Edward III's case, however, there was a need to proceed fast, following the deposition of his father: Edward II was deposed on 20 January 1327, and his son was crowned on 1 February. The ceremony did not always go smoothly. There would be arguments in advance over who had the right to perform certain ceremonial roles, such as bearing the swords and sceptres. It seems likely that Edmund, earl of Lancaster's claim to carry the sword *Curtana* was rejected in 1274, and that as a result he refused to attend the ceremony. When Edward II was crowned in Westminster abbey, so great was the throng of people present that a wall collapsed and a knight was killed.[5] At the coronation the new king swore an oath. Its precise form before 1308 is not known, but it is probable that in additional to swearing to uphold the laws of Edward the Confessor, to work for the peace of the Church and people, and to prevent rapacity and oppression, both Henry III and Edward promised to preserve and recover the rights of the crown.[6] When Edward II was crowned in 1308, he promised to maintain the laws and customs of his predecessors, particularly the Confessor, and to maintain peace and do justice. A new clause was added, in which he agreed 'to maintain and preserve the laws and rightful customs which the community of your realm shall have chosen', a promise which has created far more interest among historians than it did among those who heard it.[7]

The coronation was a religious ceremony, and there was a strong sacral element to the monarchy. There were also other religious ceremonies in which the king took part that helped to reinforce this aspect of his role. In 1234, when Henry III freed himself from the regime dominated by Peter des Roches, he made a solemn pilgrimage to Bromholm, where he placed a silver statuette of himself on the altar as a form of votive offering.[8] Henry III developed the cult of Edward the Confessor, naming his eldest son, Edward, in honour of the last legitimate Anglo-Saxon king, and rebuilding Westminster abbey, the centre of the Confessor's cult. The Confessor was a slightly odd choice in that he had not been successful in war, nor had he managed to perpetuate his dynasty. For Henry, however, his sanctity doubtless made up for any failings, and in addition the link to the Confessor emphasized both the Englishness and the legitimacy of the monarchy. In 1247 the king made a gift of some of what was thought to be Christ's blood to his great abbey at Westminster, on the

---

[5] D. A. Carpenter, *The Minority of Henry III* (London, 1990), 13, 187–8; Prestwich, *Edward I*, 90; *Chronicles of the Reigns of Edward I and Edward II*, ed. W. Stubbs (RS, 1882–3), i. 153, 261.

[6] Carpenter, *Minority of Henry III*, 189; Prestwich, *Edward I*, 90–1.

[7] *Foedera*, ii/1. 36. For discussion of this new clause, see below, p. 179.

[8] N. Vincent, 'Pilgrimages of the Angevin Kings of England', in C. Morris and P. Roberts (eds.), *Pilgrimage: The English Experience from Becket to Bunyan* (Cambridge, 2002), 27.

Confessor's feast day. He walked barefoot as a pilgrim, but did so under a pall carried on four spears, like that borne over the king in his coronation procession.[9] In 1265 the king's recovery of power was emphasized by his celebration of the feast of the translation of the Confessor. The culmination came in 1269, when the remains of the Confessor were formally translated and reburied, on the same Sunday in October—the 13th—as the first translation in 1163. The ceremony coincided, quite deliberately, with the opening of a parliament; it was at one and the same time a religious and a political statement.[10] Such measures were not always, it should be noted, as effective as the king wished. Henry's donation to Westminster abbey of the holy blood did not result in the development of a popular cult. There were other, better-attested examples of divine blood in existence, and it was that which Edmund of Cornwall brought from Germany, which he divided between Hailes abbey and his college at Ashridge, which proved far more successful in drawing pilgrims.[11]

Henry III was a man whose strong personal piety was closely connected to his sense of kingship. His authority was, he undoubtedly considered, God-given. His son Edward I was a man of conventional religious belief, and this was an important element in his kingship. In 1278 the new cathedral at Norwich was consecrated, and a new bishop enthroned. The bishops of London, Hereford, and Waterford were there, and each dedicated an altar. This was a Church occasion, but the presence of the king and queen, along with a number of earls of barons, made it also a royal one.[12] The religious element of Edward's kingship was demonstrated in building works, though not spectacularly as had been the case under Henry III with Westminster abbey. Edward founded Vale Royal abbey in Cheshire, but this was an act of personal piety, in fulfilment of a vow made when shipwreck threatened, rather than an expression of the sacrality of the crown. In what seems to have been a capricious decision, he abandoned his interest in the project in 1290. The building of St Stephen's chapel at Westminster was probably intended to provide the English monarchy with an equivalent to Louis IX's Sainte-Chapelle in Paris. Work began in 1292, but financial stringency brought it to a close in 1297, and it was not resumed until the 1320s.[13] Edward gave full backing to the demands for the canonization of Thomas Cantilupe, the bishop of Hereford, who died in 1282, for he was eager 'to have as a sympathetic

[9] N. Vincent, *The Holy Blood: King Henry III and the Westminster Blood Relic* (Cambridge, 2001), 3.

[10] D. Carpenter, 'Westminster Abbey in Politics, 1258–1269', in *TCE* viii. 49–58; B. Weiler, 'Symbolism and Politics in the Reign of Henry III', in *TCE* ix. 23.

[11] Vincent, *The Holy Blood*, 137–53.

[12] Cotton, 157.

[13] *KW* i. 248–52, 510–14.

patron in heaven him who we had in our household on earth'.[14] One of Edward's most prized acquisitions in the Welsh war was the Croes Naid, which was said to contain part of the wood of the Cross itself. No doubt he felt that this was an important addition to his power. It is striking that in his wars against the Scots he made sure that among the banners carried forward were those of St Cuthbert of Durham and St John of Beverley. Edward III was a man whose personal religious convictions were as conventional as those of his grandfather. Again, during his Scottish wars he associated his monarchy with the saints of the north, adding to Cuthbert and John the figures of Oswin of Tynemouth and Wilfrid of Ripon. Apart from a devotion to the Virgin Mary, he displayed throughout his reign a patriotic concern for English cults, notably those of Thomas Becket, Edmund of Bury, Thomas Cantilupe, and Edward the Confessor.[15] Consciously or unconsciously, he was bolstering not only the crown, but also a sense of English identity.

A regular cycle of religious ceremonies took place in the royal court, or more specifically in the royal chapel. Alms were allocated on a standard basis. Henry III claimed that it was his custom to feed 500 paupers each week; by the end of the thirteenth century the number stood at 666. In addition, on major feast days special provision was made for large numbers of poor men. In the week that began on Christmas Day 1300 no fewer than 4,000 received alms. The birthday of the heir to the throne was the occasion for substantial almsgiving, with 1,700 being favoured. On some occasions the paupers received cash, and on others food or clothing. In addition, there were ceremonies for those who claimed to suffer from the king's evil. Possibly Henry III, and certainly Edward I and his successors, were believed to have the ability to heal the sick, specifically those suffering from scrofula. It may be that the practice was begun in France, by Louis IX, after his return from crusade in 1254, and soon copied by Henry in England. The earliest alms account shows that in 1276–7 at least 627 men were blessed, or touched, by Edward I; in 1305–6 the number was a staggering 2,002, a figure that does not appear to have been matched by subsequent monarchs. Full figures for Edward II and Edward III are lacking, but there is nothing to suggest that they touched for the king's evil on this scale. Between 1314 and 1317 Edward II blessed just 108 people, but in 1319–20 the number was 315, though it fell to 79 in the following year. Clearly, Edward II lacked his father's charisma, but under Edward III the numbers of sick who came forward did not rise as might have been expected. Between

---

[14] Quoted by R. Bartlett, *The Hanged Man: A Story of Miracle, Memory, and Colonialism in the Middle Ages* (Princeton, 2004), 120.

[15] M. W. Ormrod, 'The Personal Religion of Edward III', *Speculum*, 64 (1989), 858–9; BL, Add. MS 9951, fo. 3ᵛ; Add. MS 17362, fos. 4, 5.

November 1341 and April 1343 Edward III touched 396 individuals.[16] Another ceremony took place on Good Friday, when it was customary for the king to offer money before the cross, which was then made into curative rings said to be effective against muscular cramps and epilepsy.[17]

Emphasis on the sacral quality of kingship provided a way of strengthening the monarchy when it was threatened. Edward II, who needed to find ways of bolstering his authority more than any of the other kings in this period, claimed in 1319 that he had been brought a phial of oil, which had been presented by the Virgin Mary to Thomas Becket. This would have given the English monarchy an equivalent to the oil that had been presented to the Capetian dynasty by the Holy Ghost. Edward asked the pope if he could go through a process of reanointment, but the request for a public ceremony was rejected.[18]

SECULAR KINGSHIP AND THE CROWN

Kingship was also a form of secular lordship. The king was the feudal overlord, and his tenants in chief owed him homage and fealty. Various specific obligations resulted from this, of which the most important were the king's right to wardship should the heir to a lordship be under age, and the right to arrange or sell the marriages of under-age heiresses and widows. Military service was another obligation, as was the obligation to pay an aid on the occasion of the marriage of the king's eldest daughter, and the knighting of his eldest son. When Edward I requested such an aid in 1306, this was said to be 'by right of his royal crown'.[19] Perhaps more significant than such specific rights was the general obligation of men to the ultimate lord. When, in 1297, Edward I was faced with war with France and domestic discontent, his propaganda emphasized his lordship. He stressed that he was doing all he could for his people, and claimed to be acting for the common profit of the realm, which was in danger of destruction and perdition. He was the liege lord, the ultimate overlord.[20]

And it seems to our lord the king that he could not do more for them than put his body and his life at risk for them, as for those whom he loves loyally and wishes to guard and maintain them in honour with all his power, as if it was for his own body. So they will naturally wish to have regard and to do their duty towards their lord with good will, as

---

[16] Ormrod, 'Personal Religion of Edward III', 862.

[17] M. C. Prestwich, 'The Piety of Edward I', in W. M. Ormrod (ed.), *England in the Thirteenth Century* (Grantham, 1985), 120–6.

[18] J. R. S. Phillips, 'Edward II and the Prophets', in W. M. Ormrod (ed.), *England in the Fourteenth Century* (Woodbridge, 1986), 196–201.

[19] G. O. Sayles, *The Functions of the Medieval Parliament* (London, 1988), 275.

[20] *Documents Illustrating the Crisis of 1297–8 in England*, ed. M. C. Prestwich, Camden 4th ser., 24 (1980), 128, 134.

good and loyal people should, and are bound to do towards their liege lord in so great and mighty a business. And with this, pray for him that God gives him by his grace to do and work so well in this expedition that this will be to the honour of God and of him and of all his realm.[21]

When Edward II addressed parliament in 1324, trying to ensure that he had as full support as possible for war with France over his duchy of Gascony, he appealed to the fealty and allegiance that he was owed:

And I have requested on this your counsels, aid and power, that you do, owe and demonstrate at your peril, as you wish to avow now and in the future, and that each of you severally and individually give me his counsel and his advice as to what I should do. That said, I wish that it should be entered for perpetual memory in the parliament roll, that I am asking you again on your fealty and allegiance that you say it again to me, each of you severally and individually.[22]

There were, in addition to the feudal concepts of kingship, ideas of royal authority that derived from Roman law. The concept of necessity is particularly relevant. If the king could show that there was an urgent necessity, his subjects were under a clear obligation to provide him with the assistance he needed. Taxes still had to be granted if there was a necessity, but there was no right of refusal. In the words of Thomas Aquinas, 'a prince who fights for the interests of his country may make use of the resources of the community and lay a charge on the community either through the normal forms of taxation or, if such are insufficient, through individual contributions'.[23] In 1294 Edward I justified his seizure of wool in terms of the 'certain and urgent necessity' that existed.[24] In 1297 the arguments he put to the clergy made appeal to the doctrine of necessity; he was tailoring his case to his audience, and the clergy would have been well aware of the position of the ruler as defined in Roman and canon law.[25] Under Edward III requests for taxation were made in terms of the need to provide for the defence of the realm, using the language of necessity. Roman law concepts of the rights of the prince underlay this.

Concepts of kingship did not go unchallenged. A celebrated mid-thirteenth-century interpolation in Bracton's treatise argued that the king was under the law, and that if he was not, he should be bridled by his associates, the earls and barons, unless they were also unbridled.[26] Arguments about the theoretical

---

[21] Ibid. 122.

[22] *The War of Saint-Sardos (1323–1325)*, ed. P. Chaplais, Camden 3rd ser., 87 (1954), 95.

[23] Cited by G. L. Harriss, *King, Parliament and Public Finance in Medieval England to 1369* (Oxford, 1975), 22. Harris emphasizes the importance of Roman law concepts of necessity.

[24] Cotton, 245.

[25] *Documents Illustrating the Crisis of 1297–8*, ed. Prestwich, 28.

[26] *Bracton on the Laws and Customs of England*, ed. G. E. Woodbine, trans. and rev. S. E. Thorne (Cambridge, Mass., 1968), ii. 110.

powers of kings were set out with great clarity in a remarkable poem written after the defeat of the royalist forces in the battle of Lewes of 1264. One case was set out in absolutist terms: the king should have the right to decide whom he should appoint to earldoms, to the custody of castles, and to ministerial positions. The command of the king should have the force of law, and his decisions should be binding on his subjects. Every earl was his own master, able to make appointments as he chose; surely the king should be in the same position. The alternative case, which the author of the poem supported, was set out much more fully. Kings owed their position to God, and their duty was to rule in obedience to divine authority. It was the duty of a king not to oppress his subjects, but to win the favour of his people by conferring benefits on them in accordance with divine law. A king who ruled rightly, in accordance with the law, was truly free. An unwise king should be advised by the community of the kingdom, and should not rely on foreigners, for those who are ruled by the laws know them best. 'The law rules over the king's dignity, for we believe that the law is the light, and without it the ruler will wander from the right path.'[27]

In the early thirteenth century little distinction was drawn between the king and the crown, but the theoretical concept of the crown changed and developed over the next century and a half. It is striking that in the many political arguments that took place in the hectic years following the Oxford parliament of 1258, there was a great deal of debate about the powers and authority of the king, but the idea of the crown as a permanent institution, distinct from an individual rule, was not stressed. Debate was about kingship, not the crown. One indication from this period, however, that the crown might be regarded as distinct from the person who wore it came when the king's son Edward received a massive grant of lands in England, Wales, Gascony, and Ireland in 1254, for it was laid down that these should not be alienated from the crown. In 1261 Henry III argued, in a set of complaints against the baronial-controlled council, that it had allowed his son Edward to squander the possessions that had been given to him to strengthen the crown. Elham in Kent had been granted to Edward on the specific condition that it should not be separated from the crown.[28]

Under Edward I there was much greater stress placed on the concept, or institution, of the crown. The distinction between it and the king began to emerge more clearly. In 1293 a case was brought against the archbishop of York, who had excommunicated Anthony Bek, royal councillor and bishop of Durham. It was argued that he had acted 'in contempt of the king, the injury of his royal dignity, and contrary to the reverence due to the king', but also 'in

---

[27] *Political Songs*, 72–121.   [28] *CPR 1247–58*, 382; *CR, 1261–4*, 117; *DBM* 216–17.

contempt of the king, and contrary to his crown and royal dignity'. He had 'endeavoured, so far as lay in his power, to occupy and usurp the royal crown and dignity'.[29] The oath that was sworn by the king's councillors also used language that separated the crown from the king himself. The councillors were to do all they could to maintain the rights of the king and of the crown. If they knew of any rights of the crown or the king that were concealed, they should make them known to Edward, and they should loyally do what they could to increase the crown's authority.[30]

The concept of the crown was particularly important in a legal context. In Bracton's treatise, written earlier in the thirteenth century, the idea was put forward that all judicial franchises were held from the crown, and could be revoked by the king. Early in Edward I's reign it was a strongly held belief in royal circles that magnates and others had usurped many royal rights, and in the series of *quo warranto* inquiries attempts were made, with limited success, to reassert the rights of the crown.[31] In the context of the recovery of royal rights which Edward had granted out before he came to the throne, Gilbert de Thornton, a lawyer acting for the king, claimed that he 'was of another condition to what he was previously, as if he was another person'.[32] In 1290 a notable case was heard between the earls of Gloucester and Hereford, in the course of which it was argued that the king, 'for reasons of common utility, was in many cases through his prerogative above the laws and customs used in the realm'.[33] The qualification of common utility was important; this was not a claim to absolute power.

Arguments based on the crown could be turned against the king. Soon after Edward II's coronation the earl of Lincoln presented a protest. This began dramatically with the statement that homage and the oath of allegiance were due more to the office of the crown than to the person of the king. The document laid stress of the power and dignity of the crown, and argued that the crown was enfeebled by the activities of the king's favourite Piers Gaveston.[34] This was startling indeed. The opposition to Edward II, as it developed, did not make further use of this clear distinction between crown and king. The Ordinances of 1311, however, referred to the crown on several occasions. The document was concerned to preserve 'the estate of the king and

[29] *CCR 1288–96*, 332–3, 334.
[30] E 159/68, m. 64. This is the 1294 version of the oath, which is better known from the almost identical 1307 version.
[31] Prestwich, *Edward I*, 259–64.
[32] Cited by F. Pollock and F. W. Maitland, *The History of English Law*, 2nd edn. (Cambridge, 1898), i. 524.
[33] *Rot. Parl.* i. 71.
[34] H. G. Richardson and G. O. Sayles, *The Governance of Medieval England* (Edinburgh, 1963), 467–8.

of his crown', and it was argued that the crown had been seriously damaged by gifts of royal lands that Edward II had made. One specific example was given, that of Bamburgh castle, which was said to belong to the crown. At the same time the Ordinances demanded that various matters previously regarded as being for the king to decide should be subject to baronial consent in parliament. Chief among these was the king's right to leave the realm and make war. Another was control of the coinage.[35]

The concepts of the crown and the person of the king in the early fourteenth century were not monopolized by the critics of Edward II's government. When it came to undoing the Ordinances in the Statute of York of 1322, reference was made to 'the royal power of our lord the king or his heirs', to 'the estate of our lord the king or his heirs', to 'the estate of the crown', and to 'the estate of the realm and people'. What the subtle distinction between these categories was intended remains mysterious. It is striking that, while matters concerning the estate of the king and the estate of the realm and people could be discussed in parliament as in the past, questions relating to royal power and the estate of the crown were excluded.[36] Ideas about the crown were becoming commonplace in political discussion. In his address of 1324 to parliament, Edward II laid stress on it:

My lords, I have shown you certain matters which belong to the crown which are under discussion, as he who is your chief and who maintains sovereignty, and is ready to maintain the crown in all its rights by your counsel and aid, and to defend it as a man can with the power of all your force. I have always asked for your counsels about this, and have not done anything in this matter without counsel, by which I mean that I have done what is mine to do.[37]

Defending the rights of the crown was exactly what Edward II was thought not to have done, when it came to his deposition early in 1327. The deposition, however, did not involve any attack on the institution of the crown. The core of the complaints was that Edward had failed to preserve the lands that he had inherited, and had listened to evil counsel. He was a *rex inutilis*, a worthless king, and the charges against him followed a line that went back to the accusations made by Pope Gregory VII against the emperor Henry IV.[38]

It might be expected that deposition of Edward II would have been a disaster for the crown. Ironically, it served rather to demonstrate the strength of the institution. There was no question of replacing Edward with anyone save his

---

[35] The Ordinances are given in *SR* i. 157 ff.   [36] *SR* i. 189–90.
[37] *The War of Saint-Sardos*, ed. Chaplais, 95.
[38] W. Stubbs, *The Constitutional History of England*, 4th edn. (Oxford, 1906), ii. 383. See also E. Peters, *The Shadow King: Rex Inutilis in Medieval Law and Literature, 751–1327* (New Haven, 1970), 237–42.

son, and there was no attempt to reduce royal authority. There was a difficult balance that Edward III needed to strike, between condemning or justifying the actions of each of his parents and maintaining the dignity of the crown, but the problem was one that was skilfully managed. Edward II's death following his removal from the throne may even have had the effect of enhancing the monarchy in the eyes of some by providing it with a new martyr.

There were many aspects to the authority of the crown. There was, for example, a special jurisdiction around the king's person. Twelve miles around the royal person was the verge, an area where the ordinary local courts did not have jurisdiction, where justice was done through the courts of the household. It was even claimed that this jurisdiction was still valid when the king was abroad. Most of the cases that came up were not particularly serious, and the income derived from them not substantial, but the existence of the verge was yet another way in which the king's authority was marked out as special and different. This was not always welcome; in some instances local communities would pay a lump sum to be free of the attentions of the household courts of the hall and the market.[39] Anyone in the vicinity of the king was under his protection. In 1292 four clerics, one of them a notary, attempted to summon Anthony Bek, bishop of Durham, to answer charges before a church court. The king argued that 'secretaries and others of his household staying by his side ought not without the king being consulted to be cited by any ordinaries or other ecclesiastical persons'. To do so was in contempt of the king, to the impressive tune of £10,000.[40]

The way that the king was addressed provides an indication of how royal authority was regarded. In some cases, the style adopted was surprisingly informal. Taking some examples from Edward I's reign, laymen might write 'to our lord the king of England', or send a petition 'to our lord the king and his council'. The language was simple, a straightforward reference to the lordship exercised by the king. Churchmen, in contrast, tended to use more solemn language, for example writing to their 'most excellent prince and lord, Edward king of England', to 'the most high prince and honourable lord sir Edward', and to 'the most honourable prince and their dear lord Edward'. Foreign rulers would also use elaborate formulas, referring to the king as prince. 'To the most wise, noble and excellent prince, his dear lord and father' was how John, count of Holland, Edward I's son-in-law, addressed the king.[41]

Modes of address suggest that alongside the formal rights and authority of the crown, there was a more intangible aura of royal power. To some extent

---

[39] Prestwich, *Edward I*, 167.   [40] *CIM* i, no. 1588.
[41] *Documents Illustrating the Crisis of 1297–8*, ed. Prestwich, 90, 119, 131, 160, 177, 186; N. Saul, 'Richard II and the Vocabulary of Kingship', *EHR* 110 (1995), 859.

this depended on the individual king: Edward I and Edward III were far more formidable individuals than Henry III or Edward II. The tall figure of Edward I was imposing enough, but it was surely because he was king that he frightened both a dean of St Paul's and an archbishop of York to death.[42] Yet Henry III too was very well aware of the dignity of his position, and was capable of putting men down with a pointed riposte, or worse. In the case of a justice against whom various accusations were brought in 1251, he declared, 'If anyone kills Henry of Bath, he shall be quit of his death, and I will declare him quit.'[43] Even after his defeat at the battle of Lewes in 1265, Henry was treated with respect; he was the anointed king. Edward II, for all his evident failings, could also find himself treated with the awe appropriate to a king. At Burton upon Trent early in 1322 he was pursuing Thomas, earl of Lancaster, with his army. The younger Hugh Despenser, Edward's favourite, prostrated himself before Edward in the snow with his arms outstretched, and begged him not to unfurl his banner. To do so would be a sign of war.[44] Edward II, however, was the one king in this period who quite evidently lacked the personal qualities required to rule. In 1318 a lunatic came to the court at Oxford, and claimed that he was the real king. He claimed that he had been exchanged for Edward as a baby. There was, of course, no conceivable truth in this bizarre story, and the man's parents were summoned, to declare that he was indeed their true son. Yet the affair attracted wide attention, and was included in the majority of contemporary chronicles, for it drew notice neatly to Edward's unkingly ways. A man who was fond of digging ditches, who liked the company of the low-born, and who enjoyed water sports such as rowing and swimming, was hardly appropriate to occupy the throne of England.[45]

By Edward III's reign, the legal and constitutional concept of the crown was well developed. There was a crown estate, lands that belonged by tradition to the crown, which should not be granted out. The crown had overriding rights of jurisdiction. Private jurisdictions existed, but these were regarded as being delegated by the crown. It was not possible to sue the crown in the king's own courts. 'Our lord the king can not be summoned or receive a command from any one' was the statement made in a judgement as early as 1234.[46] The crown had the right to coin money, and although there were a very few mints under private (particularly episcopal) control, they were closely controlled in that

[42] Prestwich, *Edward I*, 405, 547.

[43] Paris, *Chron. Maj.* v. 223.

[44] 'Gesta Edwardi Secundi', in *Chronicles of the Reigns of Edward I and II*, ed. Stubbs, ii. 75.

[45] W. R. Childs, ' "Welcome my Brother": Edward II, John of Powderham and the Chronicles, 1318', in I. N. Wood and G. A. Loud (eds.), *Church and Chronicle: Essays Presented to John Taylor* (London, 1991), 149–63; H. Johnstone, 'The Eccentricities of Edward II', *EHR* 48 (1933), 264–7.

[46] Cited by Pollock and Maitland, *History of English Law*, i. 516.

they could use only dies supplied by the crown. The king also had the right to make war, though it was an unwise ruler who did not choose to obtain some form of parliamentary consent for his decisions. Rather curiously, the crown was regarded as being always under age, and therefore subject to all the protections that were applied to land while the holder was a minor.[47]

Queenship made a significant contribution to the crown. Intercession by the queen, seeking pardon for those who had approached her, was a traditional role. This might be more than simply a matter of seeking the exercise of mercy; intercession might have a valuable political role. Eleanor of Provence was certainly well aware of this, and Philippa of Hainault's celebrated intercession on behalf of the burghers of Calais was a well-calculated move that enabled the king to display generosity without weakness.[48] In broader terms, the formal institutions of the monarchy did not provide for a substantial role for queens, but expectations that they would play a role as peacemakers were significant. The contribution of queens to kingship varied greatly, for much depended on the personal relationships involved. Eleanor of Provence was a powerful personality, whose influence not only over her husband, Henry III, but also over her son Edward I should not be underestimated. Edward I was himself remarkably close to his first queen, Eleanor of Castile. Her role in advising him cannot be discerned from the documents that survive, but the fact that she did not play a markedly independent role certainly does not mean that she was unimportant. In contrast, the independent role that Queen Isabella played, and above all her part in the fall of Edward II, shows the potential scale of a queen's political influence.

SYMBOLS AND CEREMONIES

In discussing the crown, historians have largely concentrated on the written evidence, which survives in profusion. Many of the king's subjects were no doubt familiar with the writs and charters that were churned out by the royal chancery, and with the formulas they contained. The power of the monarchy however, was, also expressed in visual terms, and these were important.[49]

---

[47] Ibid. i. 525.

[48] Intercession is discussed by J. C. Parsons, 'The Intercessionary Patronage of Queens Margaret and Isabella of France', in *TCE* vi. 146–56. For a useful discussion of queenship in more general terms, see M. Howell, 'Royal Women of England and France in the Mid-Thirteenth Century: A Gendered Perspective', in B. K. U. Weiler (ed.), *England and Europe in the Reign of Henry III (1216–1272)* (Aldershot, 2002), 163–81.

[49] J. Watts, 'Looking for the State in Later Medieval England', in P. Coss and M. Keen (eds.), *Heraldry, Pageantry and Social Display in Medieval England* (Woodbridge, 2002), 267, argues that 'the visual representation of those elements of later medieval government which approach the sense of a "state" was distinctly thin'.

Firstly, there was the crown itself. There was not one single royal crown, but many. The most important was that known as St Edward's Crown, which had the status of a relic, and which was used at coronations. There were many others. Henry III had a new crown made in 1229, and it seems to have been usual for there to be several in the royal treasury. These were of open type, richly encrusted with precious stones. In 1253 the king bought a crown for 500 marks from an overseas merchant. An inventory made in 1300 describes one great gold crown, with emeralds, oriental sapphires, rubies, and huge pearls, which the king customarily wore when he left the church after his coronation, and at the dinner which followed the ceremony. This was valued at 2,800 *livres tournois*, or £700. According to a later inventory, Edward III had one described as the great crown, another was the minor or second crown, and there were no less than seven others. There were also a dozen gold circlets. The queen also had crowns. Near the end of his life Edward I gave his second queen, Margaret, jewels and a crown worth £130 as a New Year's present. An impression of the grandeur of these emblems of monarchy is given by the description of one of these, pawned by Edward III in 1339 in exchange for 3,472 florins. It had nine roses, each formed of nine pearls with a ruby at the centre.[50] When Henry III led an expedition to Brittany in 1230, he took with him a set of royal regalia, including crown and sceptre, clearly with the intention of using them on some ceremonial occasion.[51] The kings of the thirteenth and fourteenth centuries did not, however, wear their crowns very often, for there were no regular ceremonies at which they would do this. In 1269 it seems that the king initially intended to wear the crown at the ceremony to celebrate the translation of Edward the Confessor, but arguments over who would perform what services led to his abandoning the plan.[52]

It is not clear how often the king sat on his throne, but this was another important symbol. Henry III was much concerned with the visual splendour of monarchy, and wrote in 1245: 'Because we recall that you have said that it will be much grander to make the two leopards, which will be on either side of our new chair at Westminster, of bronze rather than of marble or carved, we command you that they should be made of metal as you have suggested.' At Windsor, Henry had a 'royal seat' decorated with a picture of a king holding a sceptre, and no doubt there were further thrones in other major royal residences.[53] Edward I

[50] *Cal. Lib. Rolls, 1251–60*, 105; *Liber Quotidianus*, 353; *The Wardrobe Book of William de Norwell 12 July 1338 to 27 May 1340*, ed. M. Lyon, B. Lyon, and H. S. Lucas (Brussels, 1983), 414, 447; E 101/369/11, fo. 170.

[51] F. M. Powicke, *King Henry III and the Lord Edward* (Oxford, 1947), i. 181.

[52] Weiler, 'Symbolism and Politics in the Reign of Henry III', 35–6; *De Antiquis Legibus Liber*, ed. T. Stapleton (Camden Society, 1846), 116–17.

[53] *CCR 1242–7*, 293; *KW* i. 868.

had a splendid concept for a new throne. He ordered one to be made of bronze, which would encase the Scottish Stone of Destiny, which he had brought to Westminster as part of the spoils of war in 1296. The cost, however, was too great, and instead a cheap wooden version was constructed, which survives, somewhat battered, to this day. From any distance, it would have looked magnificent enough, decorated and gilded as it was by Walter of Durham, the king's painter.

Not many subjects would have seen the king seated, crowned, on his throne. Images of the king, however, were common. That which was most familiar to English people was the representation of the king on the silver pennies that were the sole form of currency until 1344. This was hardly a realistic portrait; but the contrast with other countries was striking, for nowhere else in Europe was there only one legal currency which bore the king's head. Even private mints, held by bishops, had to produce their coins with the same image as those turned out by the royal mints. From 1344 the prestige of the monarchy was further enhanced by the production of gold coins, called nobles, which showed the majestic and over-large figure of the king aboard a warship such as had recently achieved notable success in the battle of Sluys.

Royal documents carried the royal seal to authenticate them. The king was better represented on his great seal than on his coins. It carried an equestrian image on one side, with the king seated on a splendid throne supported by two lions on the other. The symbolism was important. In 1259 Henry III ceased to be shown holding a sword, but in its place grasped a sceptre. The coincidence of the king's abandoning his claims to Normandy, Maine, Anjou, and Touraine, and his giving up the sword, was duly noted.[54] Two castles on Edward II's seal were in deference to his mother, Eleanor of Castile. Edward III's seals after 1340 show the English royal arms of three leopards quartered with the French fleur-de-lis, since he claimed both kingdoms. Coins and seal impressions were an important reminder of royal authority.

Ceremonial provided opportunities to display the power of the crown. Religious ceremonies have already been discussed, but there were also important secular occasions. There were feasts of considerable grandeur, often coinciding with the holding of parliament, or the celebration of a royal marriage. Edward I held the Feast of the Swans in 1306, on the occasion of the knighting of his eldest son, when some 300 other young men were accorded the same status. A series of oaths were sworn, intended to ensure that the struggle against the Scots would be continued. An extraordinary array of minstrels provided a musical commentary on the proceedings. At the start of Edward

---

[54] Cotton, 138.

III's struggle with the French, literary evidence suggests that the king held the Feast of the Heron, at which, like the Feast of the Swans, those present swore oaths for the prosecution of the war, though the lack of documentary proof casts some doubt on this ceremony.[55] Tournaments were patronized by Edward III and used as a form of propaganda. The fall of Roger Mortimer in 1330 was celebrated with tournaments staged in London, and similar events marked the successful conclusion of campaigns in Scotland and in France. The king himself was an eager, and skilful, participant.[56] Grand shows were put on in London to celebrate major royal events. After the birth of Edward II in 1312 the fishmongers organized a procession featuring a ship in full sail, which was borne through the city. With much singing the queen was escorted to Eltham.[57] In 1356 the Black Prince was met outside the city by the mayor and the citizens organized in their guilds. The city was thronged with people anxious to see the prince; the fountain in Cheap was splendidly decorated in his honour with figures of two girls, their long hair flowing free.[58] A record of payment to forty men carrying torches when the king and queen processed from Clerkenwell to Westminster on the occasion of the marriage of their daughter Joan of Acre in 1290 gives another glimpse of how royalty was put on show in public.[59]

The splendour of the monarchy was expressed in many ways, as it displayed its wealth. Gold, silver, along with rich fabrics, offered ways in which kings could emphasize their position, power, and wealth, and put across an ideological message. Kings possessed significant quantities of gold and silver plate, and old, outdated pieces were regularly sent to goldsmiths to be remade in the most up-to-date style. Goldsmiths such as Roger Frowyk, who sold plate to the crown under Edward II up to a value of £450 a year, were surely artist–craftsmen of great ability. The so-called King John Cup (Plate 10) dates from about 1340, and is a silver-gilt goblet with foot and cover. It is decorated with twenty enamel panels showing scenes of hunting and hawking. Its dividing ribs are botanical in inspiration, like many architectural features of the period. The workmanship is of the highest quality, and while this piece cannot be proven to be of royal origin, accounts show that the crown possessed work of this type. The cost in Edward II's reign of one silver-gilt enamelled cup, with foot and handle, similar in weight to the King John Cup at about 6 pounds, was £18.[60] There were other

[55] M. Vale, *The Princely Court: Medieval Courts and Culture in North-West Europe* (Oxford, 2001), 213–14, 218–20.

[56] J. R. V. Barker, *The Tournament in England 1100–1400* (Woodbridge, 1986), 68–9.

[57] Ann. Lond. 221; C. M. Barron, *London in the Later Middle Ages: Government and People 1200–1500* (Oxford, 2004), 18–20.

[58] *Anon. Chron.* 41.

[59] C 47/4/5, fo. 14ᵛ.

[60] J. Alexander and P. Binski (eds.), *Age of Chivalry: Art in Plantagenet England 1200–1400* (London, 1987), 435–6; Society of Antiquaries of London, MS 120, fo. 69ᵛ.

precious objects in the inventories. A king could not play chess with ordinary pieces, and Edward I had a set made of jasper and crystal.[61]

Clothes were important as an indication of wealth and status. Edward III was one of the best-dressed of all English monarchs, sporting such magnificent garments as a jupon made of blue taffeta and white silk, decorated with a pound of gold and a multitude of silver buckles. In 1360 the king and queen, with the princes and princesses of the royal family, were all dressed in clothes of 'marbryn', variegated cloth. Edward III's own suit was made up of four garments, including a long cloak, and two hoods. The trimmings were of narrow gold ribbons, and the lining was of miniver and ermine. Queen Philippa's dress was enhanced with reddish cloth, which must have contrasted tastefully with the 'marbryn'. While the whole royal group wore similar clothes, those of the king and queen were a little more luxurious, with rather more fur and gold ribbon.[62] However, it was not always a matter of dressing grandly; in 1247 when Henry bore the relic of the Holy Blood, he wore a plain cloak without a hood, the garb of a poor penitent.[63] In doing so, he emphasized his own piety, and with it, the sacrality of the monarchy.

By long tradition, members of the king's household were entitled to receive liveries of robes twice a year, and there is evidence to suggest that from Henry III's time these might be cut from cloth of a standard type and colour. In 1240 the king handed out fifty tunics to members of his entourage, each embroidered with a red R, for Rex. Green was the normal colour for the knights, and blue for the clerks. Squires and valets had striped robes. John Droxford, keeper of Edward I's wardrobe, was resplendent in red.[64] It is likely, however, that it became increasingly common to make a money payment in lieu of providing actual robes. At Christmas 1304 robes were handed out, but this was only after a specific instruction from the king.[65] Under Edward III there were occasions when the king and his knights wore similar clothes to make a grand show. In 1336, for example, black and red cloth was bought for this purpose.[66] At the Dunstable tournament of 1342 the king and his knights

---

[61] *Liber Quotidianus*, 351.

[62] N. H. Nicolas, 'Observations on the Institution of the Most Noble Order of the Garter', *Archaeologia*, 31 (1846), 33–4; S. M. Newton, *Fashion in the Age of the Black Prince* (Woodbridge, 1980), 65–6.

[63] Paris, *Chron. Maj.* iv. 641.

[64] M. C. Hill, *The King's Messengers 1199–1377* (London, 1961), 28; Vale, *Princely Court*, 110–12; *CR, 1242–7*, 493, implies that there were standard robes for household knights and officials.

[65] F. Lachaud, 'Liveries of Robes in England, *c*.1200–*c*.1330', *EHR* 111 (1996), 294.

[66] BL, MS Nero C. VIII, fo. 214ᵛ.

appeared in green suits embroidered with Catherine wheels and the motto
'It is as it is'.[67]

BUILDINGS

Another way in which the crown could express its authority was through
architecture. Henry III created a new central focus for the English monarchy,
with his rebuilding of Westminster abbey.[68] This was a huge project, started in
1245. The building, and its meaning, is very complex. It has strong affinities
with the cathedral at Reims. No doubt this is in part because the chief mason,
Henry of Reyms, though quite probably an Englishman, had worked on the
great French cathedral. The links between Reims and the French Capetian
monarchy must also have been highly relevant: Henry III will have wanted his
royal abbey to be as magnificent as the church in which the French kings were
crowned. The widespread use of Purbeck marble in Henry III's scheme gave
Westminster a rare, and surely deliberate, regal quality. The same marble was
used in his chapel at Windsor. Not all of the design of Westminster, however,
should be seen as a form of royal propaganda. Contrasting with the mature
Gothic style of the abbey as a whole are the remarkable Cosmati pavements, the
work of Roman craftsmen in the 1260s. Their symbolism was cosmological
rather than regal.[69] Westminster was a truly exceptional church, which Henry,
and many of his subjects, must have considered a marvellous celebration of
monarchy. Strikingly, it also honoured the king's most important subjects,
incorporating their coats of arms and emphasizing their cooperation with the
crown in what must have seemed a rather ironical way, given the opposition of
so many to Henry's policies. There was no doubt, however, of the superiority
of the crown. In 1245 Henry ordered a splendid banner, yellow and black with
a red–gold dragon on it, with flashing eyes of red crystal, to be hung in
Westminster abbey. This was to be larger than any of the other banners
there, emphasizing the power and might of the monarchy.[70]

Edward I further developed the focus on Westminster. Whereas the An-
gevins had used the abbey of Fontevraud as their mausoleum, and King John
was buried at Worcester, Westminster now became the English royal burial
place. Henry III and Eleanor of Castile have magnificent gilt bronze effigies.
Henry's half-brother William de Valence's memorial is a remarkable Limoges

---

[67] Newton, *Fashion in the Age of the Black Prince*, 42.

[68] P. Binski, *Westminster Abbey and the Plantagenets* (London, 1995), for a full discussion.

[69] Binski, ibid. 100, argues that the Cosmati work was not completed until 1280, but see
D. Carpenter, 'King Henry III and the Cosmati Work at Westminster Abbey', in his *The Reign of
Henry III* (London, 1996), 409–25.

[70] *CR, 1242–7*, 331.

enamel effigy. Edward I's brother Edmund of Lancaster has an exceptionally grand canopied tomb. However, Edward's own tomb is astonishingly plain; it is a stark Purbeck marble sarcophagus with no effigy or image of the king. This may have been in deliberate imitation of the tomb of Louis IX, while another possibility is that it was intended to resemble the stone coffin in which the bones of Arthur and Guinevere had been placed in 1278. The tradition of burial at Westminster was not maintained for the deposed Edward II, whose tomb is at Gloucester. The magnificence of his tomb there, however, made a statement about the importance of the crown and the royal dynasty which was highly significant in view of the personal failings of the king. Subsequently Westminster regained its key role as the royal resting place, though Edward II's queen, Isabella, was buried in the Franciscan church at Newgate, along with a casket containing her husband's heart.[71]

The funerary style of the monarchy was also extended by Edward I with a most remarkable series of monumental crosses built to commemorate the resting places of the cortège that bore the body of his queen, Eleanor, back to London (see Plate 7). There was a French precedent in the crosses used to mark the progress of the bones of St Louis from Paris to Saint-Denis, but the Eleanor crosses were built on a magnificent scale, reflecting simultaneously the king's devotion to his queen, and the power of the English monarchy.

St Stephen's chapel, in the palace of Westminster, was begun by Edward I in 1292. It was, in its original intention, more a place of private worship than a public royal statement, though Edward surely also intended it as a way of keeping up with the French monarchy and its splendid Sainte-Chapelle. Work stopped in 1297, when the king decided that money was better spent on the prosecution of war than the pursuance of prayer. Building began again in 1319, but it was not until Edward III's reign that the chapel was completed. It was decorated in the most lavish way imaginable, with every possible surface coloured or gilded. Leopards and fleurs-de-lis echoed Edward's claim to be king of both England and France, and the inclusion of arms of the English baronage emphasized the political unity of the realm. In 1348 Edward III created a college for the chapel, with a dean, a dozen canons, and thirteen vicars, so as to provide properly for the religious needs of the royal family.[72]

Secular as well as religious buildings were used to project the power of the monarchy, and the palace of Westminster was one of the most splendid outside Byzantium. The so-called Painted Chamber was constructed under Henry III within the existing twelfth-century fabric. It was paved with glazed tiles, and

[71] M. Duffy, *Royal Tombs of Medieval England* (Stroud, 2003), 74–99, 118–32; N. Coldstream, *The Decorated Style: Architecture and Ornament 1240–1360* (London, 1994), 127.
[72] *KW* i. 510–27.

had a magnificent patterned and painted roof. Its main glory lay in the great series of paintings that decorated the walls. They were seriously damaged by fire in 1263, but were restored; a further series of paintings depicting Judas Maccabeus were probably added under Edward I. In the chamber was the king's state bed, with green posts round it decorated with gold stars (Henry III's favourite style of interior decoration). It probably had an elaborate canopy as well as curtains. How the bed was used in ceremonial terms is not clear, but it is possible that the king used it for formal audiences. The Painted Chamber, and other parts of the palace of Westminster, became increasingly a public, not a private, space. In the 1320s two Irish friars visited London. The main sights were London Bridge, the Tower, St Paul's, Westminster abbey, and the palace of Westminster. The latter was particularly notable to these fourteenth-century tourists, where they were especially impressed by the Painted Chamber.[73]

The crown possessed fifty-eight castles when Henry III came of age, and though this number had fallen to forty-seven by Edward I's accession, this was still an impressive total. Many royal castles, however, were poorly maintained and did little to enhance the prestige of the crown. A handful, on the other hand, clearly demonstrated royal power and wealth. The Tower dominated the city of London, physically if not politically. A great deal of work was done to extend and modernize the fortifications under Henry III, with the construction of an up-to-date towered curtain wall. Progress was not straightforward, for in 1240 a new gatehouse collapsed, as did a section of wall. Henry's Tower contained one very unusual building, an elephant house for the beast that was sent to the king as a present by Louis IX. Edward I had a taste for the large-scale, and his works at the Tower greatly extended an already splendid castle. A ten-year programme saw the Tower developed into a fully concentric fortress, with an elaborate entry route through barbican and gatehouses well calculated to impress any visitor. In addition, Edward built a magnificent new watergate, St Thomas's Tower, on the Thames. This was more residence than castle, and bore an interesting resemblance to the barbican at the Louvre in Paris. The Tower was a most imposing reminder of the power of the crown, dominating as it did the largest city in the realm.

Edward I's fame as a castle-builder rests primarily on the great Welsh castles with which he cemented his conquest. That at Caernarfon in particular was designed to make an intriguing statement. With its multi-angular towers and with dark bands of stonework enlivening the walls, it was in concept partly derived from the Theodosian walls of Constantinople. Caernarfon was claimed in Welsh legend as the birthplace of the emperor Constantine, and Edward's

[73] P. Binski, *The Painted Chamber at Westminster* (London, 1986), 1.

castle can be seen as an arrogant claim to imperial status expressed in stone, though one that was not echoed on the parchment of official documents. The symbolism of the castle was complex: eagles on the turrets could be seen as a reference to the Roman imperial past, but also to the Savoyard background of Otto de Grandson, Edward's constable of Caernarfon (See Plate 5).[74]

Henry III spent lavishly on Windsor castle, making it a fine residence more than a fortress. It was, however, Edward III who converted Windsor into a palatial castle of quite extraordinary splendour. The works began in 1350, and the king 'caused many excellent buildings in the castle of Windsor to be thrown down, and others more beautiful and sumptuous to be set up'.[75] There is nothing specifically royal in the form of the buildings, but the scale of the works, which cost over £50,000 between 1350 and the end of the reign, was such that only the crown could have undertaken them. So many masons were employed, almost 600 in 1360, that a real shortage of labour was created elsewhere in the country. No one who saw Windsor could have doubted that Edward III was a powerful king: the castle was a magnificent physical embodiment of his rule and his success.

COURT AND HOUSEHOLD

The king lived in his court, or household; the queen had her own separate household. Historians would like contemporaries to have used terms with precision, but they rarely did so, and court and household are hard to separate. A letter written by a royal clerk, Thomas of Swansea, in 1300 included the line 'When I was at the king's court last Easter', and the household accounts specify his return to 'court' that year. Reginald, the king's janitor, was sent 'out of court' to catch fish and send them back to the 'court'. The sheriff of Essex and Hertfordshire packed two tuns full of salted whalemeat, and sent them to the 'court' at Stamford. It was, however, for the king and his 'household' (*familia*) that billeting arrangements were made at Berwick, while a clerk came from York to Caerlaverock with £1,000 for the expenses of the king's 'household' (*hospicium*).[76] The author of the *Vita* of Edward II described the way in which the Ordainers banned Piers Gaveston's followers from the 'court' after their master was sent into exile. The official text of that expulsion, however, detailed a number of household knights who were to be 'ousted from office and position and out of the service of the king so that they no longer come near him'. Robert Darcy, Edmund Bacon, and others were to be removed from the king's

[74] *KW* i. 371. [75] Higden's *Polychronicon*, cited in *KW*, i. 877.
[76] *Receuil de lettres anglo-française 1265–1399*, ed. F. J. Tanquerey (Paris, 1916), 75; *Liber Quotidianus*, 55, 74, 76, 89.

'household' (*oustill*). The only people who were to be ousted specifically from
the 'court' were, curiously, the carters.[77] 'Court' was perhaps a looser term that
could be applied to all those around the king, whether or not they were retained
in his service, while the 'household' was a more clearly established institution.[78]

The royal household was a very large body, which could number 500
or more. In part it was purely domestic in character. The provision and
preparation of food was a large-scale business and required many separate
departments, such as those of the hall, kitchen, buttery, saucery, spicery,
pantry, bakery, and scullery. The stable, for the king's horses, was a substantial
organization in itself. The king's hunting with falcons, hawks, and dogs
required a large establishment. These various sections came under the overall
control of the main household department, the wardrobe; there was, in addition, the more private section of the chamber, which came into particular
prominence in Edward II's final years.

The transport of the household from place to place was no small affair,
needing many carts and horses. According to a household ordinance of 1279,
ten carts, six of them long ones, were needed for transport. By 1318 the number
had risen to twenty long carts.[79] Water transport was often the simplest means
of moving the royal household, though the operation was still a major enterprise. When the king and queen went from Westminster in 1290, each had a
barge with twenty-three crew, while their son Edward travelled in a boat
manned by fifteen. Three additional boats were needed; the total crew for all
the vessels was ninety-six.[80]

In addition to its private role, the household had what might be termed
public functions. It was the central department of government, from where
royal orders were issued under the privy seal. At times, as during Edward I's
wars, it was the main government spending department, organizing and
financing the royal campaigns. The main clerical officers of the household,
the keeper of the wardrobe and his colleagues, were among the king's most
important ministers. The king also retained a body of household bannerets and
knights. They, along with the squires and sergeants-at-arms, had an obvious
role in warfare. They provided the king with a force that could be deployed
quickly, as in Edward I's Welsh wars, and were a core element in royal armies.
Their role was far from solely military, for they served the king in many other
ways, as agents and administrators. They might act as diplomats, perform

---

[77] *Vita Edwardi*, 21; Ann. Lond. 199–200.

[78] The issues around this question are discussed by N. Saul, *Richard II* (London, 1997),
327–33.

[79] Tout, *Chapters*, ii. 163; T. F. Tout, *The Place of the Reign of Edward II in English History*
(Manchester, 1914), 301.

[80] C 47/4/5, fo. 4^v.

peacekeeping duties at home, or act as royal commissioners in other ways. The number of bannerets and knights might vary considerably. Under Henry III it was between thirty and seventy; in the 1280s Edward I had over a hundred, but at the end of the reign fewer than fifty. In 1314–15 Edward II retained over 120, but that was exceptional. Even at a time of active campaigning, with the siege of Calais, Edward III had no more than seventy bannerets and knights of the royal household.[81]

A list from the 1330s gives the composition of Edward III's household:

7 bannerets
24 knights
26 sergeants-at-arms
22 sergeants of offices (these were the departments such as the hall, kitchen, pantry, buttery, and scullery)
4 clerks
79 squires
14 huntsmen and falconers
20 minstrels
9 sub-clerks
4 watchmen
2 washerwomen
8 chamber valets
48 valets of offices
9 messengers
22 huntsmen's valets
2 falconers' valets
20 carters
14 purveyors (dealing with food supply)
54 sumptermen (for the sumpter horses, used for carriage)
108 palferers (for the palfreys, used for riding).[82]

The total came to 496 people. Another list from the same period yields a total of 529 individuals. It enumerates more valets of the household offices, sixty-four in all, and a more substantial military contingent, with twenty-two bannerets and thirty-nine knights.[83] Numbers were not static; a list from 1353–4 shows nine bannerets and ten knights, with sixty-seven esquires, sixty-eight valets of the offices, and in all a total of just below 300.[84] The

[81] For a convenient tabulation, see C. Given-Wilson, *The Royal Household and the King's Affinity 1360–1413* (London, 1986), 205.
[82] BL, Cotton MS Nero C. viii, fos. 225 ff.
[83] E 101/398/14.
[84] E 101/392/12.

costs of running so large an establishment were considerable. Figures are very incomplete for Henry III's reign, but in 1236–7 expenditure on the domestic household stood at about £4,000. Under Edward I the figure ranged from just below £7,000 a year to just over £14,000, and remained in a similar range under his son, save for the final years of his reign, when the level fell dramatically, to about £4,500 in 1324–5. There were considerable fluctuations under Edward III. In the early years expenses were around £10,000–£12,000 a year, but they began to rise in the 1340s to around £20,000 a year. This was still the level in 1358–9.[85] In quantitative terms, the royal household was on a completely different scale from those of even the greatest magnates, who were unlikely to have had households numbering more than two to three hundred. There was one exception. Thomas of Lancaster, in Edward II's reign, had a household that matched that of the king in size, if not quite in total cost.[86]

Orders to collect food for grand occasions testify to the splendour of the court. In 1245 the sheriff of Cambridgeshire and Huntingdonshire was asked to supply ten boars, with their heads whole and well pickled, half-a-dozen peacocks, a dozen cranes, two dozen swans, fifty bitterns, and 10,000 eels, all for Christmas. Similar orders went out to ten other royal officials, with hares, rabbits, and partridges featuring on the lists. A further slaughter of rare birds took place for the following Whitsunday feast.[87] Diet accounts of the royal household show how certain days were the occasion for grand feasts. In 1292 kitchen expenses were especially high at Christmas at £116, as against a normal level of little more than £10. On Easter Day in the following year the cost was £60, and at Whitsun £83. When the king's daughter Eleanor married the count of Bar there must have been a sumptuous banquet, for the kitchen cost was £184. All Saints' Day was also an occasion for celebrations, with the bill coming to £119.[88] The grandeur of the occasions is suggested by the purchase in Edward II's reign of a tapestry depicting the king and the earls, which was to be used to decorate the hall on the occasion of major feasts.[89]

There was much entertainment in the court, as payments to minstrels testify. Edward I and his court were entertained by no fewer than 125 minstrels at Saint-Macaire in Gascony at Christmas 1287.[90] A somewhat bizarre scene when Edward II was at Pontoise in France in 1313 was the appearance before

---

[85] These figures are conveniently tabulated by Tout, *Chapters*, vi. 74–91; see also Given-Wilson, *The Royal Household and the King's Affinity*, 14.

[86] C. M. Woolgar, *The Great Household in Late Medieval England* (London, 1999), 12, estimates the size of Lancaster's household in 1318–19 at 708.

[87] *Cal. Lib. Rolls, 1245–51*, 12–13, 51.

[88] E 101/352/10.

[89] Society of Antiquaries of London, MS 121, fo. 13.

[90] E 36/201, fo. 52.

him of no less than fifty-five naked dancers, led by Bernard the Fool.[91] A pleasant scene is evoked by the entry in an account book recording payment of the impressive sum of 20 marks to Lulielino le Piper, the earl of Northampton's minstrel, for playing before the king and queen at the request of the king's young son Lionel, in the early 1340s.[92]

There is surprisingly little evidence about the more private ceremonies and protocols of the court. There was a ceremony of New Year gifts, with the presentation of rings. At Christmas 1305 the king's children by his first queen received rings valued at 10 marks each; his two young sons by Margaret received ones worth £3, as did Aymer de Valence and the king's granddaughter Eleanor de Clare.[93] Edward II was more generous. In 1317 the queen received an enamelled silver-gilt bowl, with foot and cover, worth £17, as her New Year's present. Rings worth up to £10 each went to the king's niece Elizabeth de Burgh, his sons Edward and John, and Margaret, the widow of Piers Gaveston. The latter's daughter Joan got a gold ring with two emeralds and three pearls, worth 32s.[94]

On Easter Mondays, at the end of the period of Lenten abstinence, there was a jovial ritual. In Edward I's reign some of the queen's ladies would demand a ransom from the king before they would allow him to go from his bed to that of their mistress. Early in Edward II's reign, in contrast, it was three chamber knights who had the task of dragging the king from his bed on Easter Monday morning, for which they received a reward of £20.[95]

There is surprisingly little evidence of courtly behaviour, though the absence of guides to ceremonial and etiquette does not mean that people behaved in a coarse and uncivilized manner. The household ordinance of 1318 provides some hints on how the king himself was treated. It is clear that, as in more modern times, servants surrounded the king himself, and did virtually everything for him. There were two sergeants to cook personally for him, with five valets under them. There was an esquire to supervise the meats given to the king to eat, another to carve for him, and a third actually to serve him. A pair of large knives for the king's personal service had grand enamelled silver handles, and cost 33s. 4d. There was an 'esquire fruiterer', who was to take figs, raisins, and spiced confections from the clerk of the spicery, for the king's own use; he was also to buy apples, pears, cherries, and other fruit. Two grooms of the chamber were to make the royal bed, and fetch and carry torches.[96]

---

[91] E 101/375/8, fo. 32.   [92] E 36/204, fo. 82.   [93] E 101/368/6, fo. 20.
[94] Society of Antiquaries of London, MS 120, pp. 132–5.
[95] J. Parsons, *Eleanor of Castile: Queen and Society in Thirteenth-Century England* (New York, 1995), 50; C 47/4/1, m. 27ᵛ; BL, Cotton MS Nero C. viii, fo. 85ᵛ.
[96] Tout, *Place of Edward II*, 276, 280–1, 291–2; BL, Stowe MS 553, fo. 26.

In addition to the evidence of the formalities, the household accounts provide some very human touches, even in the case of so formidable a king as Edward I. Pets are rarely referred to, but in 1278 a boy was sent to Winchester to find two kittens belonging to the king. References to Edward I's losses playing dice, and to the game called *tabula*, reveal how some of the king's leisure hours might be spent.[97] In his later years Edward I may have suffered some digestive problems: four goats were bought in March 1301 by John Hayward for the king's use, so he could have milk in the summer. Hayward was still keeping the royal goats in 1306.[98]

The court provided an opportunity for the display of wealth and style. Under Edward III in particular, the world of the court was a glamorous one in which public show and ostentation was important. Soon after the coup that put the king in power in 1330, splendid jackets of velvet and silk embroidered with gold and silver thread were given to those who had taken part in the conspiracy. The king's own jacket was especially splendid, with red velvet, green cindon, taffeta, silk, and even pieces of coloured glass.[99] Under Edward's leadership, tournaments were great occasions for display and ceremony, as well as for feats of arms. There was an element of the masque at times, with a great deal of dressing up, with knights disguised as Tatars, or wearing fantastic masks. One year Edward wore a splendid jousting doublet made of white linen, with a design of golden clouds and twisted vines carrying the words 'It is as it is'. Another of his somewhat mysterious mottoes was 'Sure as the woodbine'; the motto on the Garter, 'Honi soit qui mal y pense', was but one of many that were used at court.[100]

The extent to which the culture of the court provided a model is difficult to assess; indeed, court culture itself is hard to define. Royal patronage was of course of great importance, and Henry III in particular, with his keen interest in architectural detail, was well aware of the most up-to-date trends in building. The question of whether there was a true 'court style' is controversial. It has been a popular concept among art historians, but it is not so evident that there was such conceptual unity as to warrant its use. 'Court eclectic' might be a better term.[101] Under Edward I the use of Savoyard masons made the great

---

[97] C 47/4/1, fo. 18ᵛ.

[98] BL, Add. MS 7966a, fo. 31ᵛ; E 101/369/11, fo. 51.

[99] C. Shenton, 'Edward III and the Coup of 1330', in J. S. Bothwell (ed.), *The Age of Edward III* (Woodbridge, 2001), 24.

[100] J. Vale, *Edward III and Chivalry: Chivalric Society and its Context 1270–1350* (Woodbridge, 1982), 62–75; Newton, *Fashion in the Age of the Black Prince*, 42, 57.

[101] For example, J. Bony, *The English Decorated Style: Gothic Architecture Transformed 1250–1350* (Ithaca, NY, 1979), 10–13, presents an analysis in terms of a 'court style'; for a different view, Binski, *Westminster Abbey*, 44–51, and Coldstream, *The Decorated Style*, 186–92.

castles he built in Wales distinctive in architectural detail. The great gateway at Caernarfon was copied by the earl of Lincoln at Denbigh, and some Savoyard detail can be discerned in the country house built by the chancellor Robert Burnell at Acton Burnell, and in Chester cathedral. The works at the Tower of London, however, did not feature Savoyard elements; the new watergate there was almost certainly built following the example of the Louvre in Paris, and was unique in England. Edward III's great works at Windsor were typical of mid-fourteenth-century architecture, rather than being in the forefront of development.

Painting is still more difficult to assess than architecture. Kings were responsible for commissioning some remarkable works, of which the most notable was probably the Painted Chamber at Westminster. This is now lost, but is known from eighteenth- and nineteenth-century drawings. Certain painters were favoured by Henry III and Edward I, but there was no permanent royal workshop, and a distinctive court style cannot be identified. It is more likely that the paintings produced for the court reflected current London fashions. No doubt, because of the resources available, the works of art produced for the crown were among the finest to be found, but as has been wisely remarked, 'the court circle had as many styles as it had members'.[102] Similarly, although there are very fine surviving manuscripts commissioned by members of the king's family and entourage, there is no school of manuscript illustration that can be clearly identified with the court, and that can be shown to have had widespread influence.[103]

In one cultural area there can be no doubt that the court's influence was negligible. No major literary works are associated with the monarchy. To those accustomed to the monarchy of the twentieth and twenty-first centuries this may come as no surprise, but in the twelfth century the courts of Henry I and Henry II had been centres of learning and literary activity. Matthew Paris, the greatest chronicler of the age, met Henry III, but there is no question of his work being in any sense court chronicles. It is curious that no thought appears to have been given to the production of any 'official' history; Edward I and his advisers might well have considered this prudent after having had a search made of monastic works in the hope of finding solid evidence to justify the king's claims to the superior lordship of Scotland. There are scraps to suggest that Edward may have had a taste for Arthurian literature. When he was in Sicily on his way to the east on crusade, he lent a book or books to Rustichello of Pisa, which served as the basis for a work by the Italian. However, the only work that the king is known to have quoted, or rather misquoted, was a satire of

[102] Binski, *The Painted Chamber*, 108–9.
[103] This argument is set out fully by Coldstream, *The Decorated Style*, 117–32.

almost unimaginable obscenity.[104] His son Edward II has the distinction of being one of the few English monarchs to have been credited with authorship of a poem, but in practice he is most unlikely to have written it.[105] There was, however, a substantial collection of books recorded in the accounts of the privy wardrobe for the later years of Edward II's reign and the early part of his son's reign, including fifty-nine termed romances. The account suggests, however, that Edward III had only to see a book to lend it or give it away; there is little indication that he was an active patron of literature.[106]

The crown provided England's rulers with the theoretical authority that they needed. Kingship had many roots: lineage and lordship of a feudal character combined with concepts of public authority derived from Roman law. There was also a sacral element to kingship, very evident in the coronation ceremony, but also displayed in the personal piety of individual rulers. Symbols, buildings, and ceremonies emphasized the position of the king in a variety of ways. All this, however, did not enable the kings of England to govern their realm, nor could this be done solely through the mechanisms provided by the royal household, elaborate as it was. The household may have been at the heart of government, but an elaborate bureaucracy, at both the central and local levels, was required in addition.

[104] Prestwich, *Edward I*, 118.
[105] C. Valente, 'The "Lament of Edward II": Religious Lyric, Political Propaganda', *Speculum*, 77 (2002), 422–39.
[106] Ormrod, 'Personal Religion of Edward III', 857; Vale, *Edward III and Chivalry*, 49–50.

CHAPTER 3

Government

There are very different opinions of government in England in the thirteenth and fourteenth centuries. One view is that the country enjoyed a remarkably sophisticated bureaucratic system; another is that it suffered from a surfeit of government, with quite unnecessarily complex administrative procedures that achieved little. No other country in western Europe approached it in terms of the complexity of both central and local government. There was what at times appears to have been an obsession with supervision, control, and above all record-keeping. The quantity of documents produced increased rapidly in the course of the thirteenth century. One indicator is that the chancery used 3 to 4 pounds of wax a week for sealing the documents it produced in the 1220s and 1230s, whereas by the late 1260s over 30 pounds was needed. It is questionable whether the impressive industry of the clerks yielded comparable results in terms of the efficiency with which the country was run. The total quantity of outgoing correspondence produced by central government may well have approached 50,000 writs a year by the mid-fourteenth century. A single sheriff in the 1330s might have expected to receive some 1,500 writs in the course of a year.[1]

The chancery and other departments kept copies on rolls of the documents they issued. Patent rolls, close rolls, charter rolls, and many others provide tangible evidence of the immense labours of the clerks. The exchequer not only produced the great annual pipe rolls, recording the sheriffs' accounts, but also memoranda, receipt, and issue rolls. Tally sticks were cut to act as receipts and to record payments. The royal household kept accounts, both at the level of individual departments and in a consolidated form. The law courts all kept prolific records of the cases that came before them.[2] The survival of so many of

---

[1] M. T. Clanchy, *From Memory to Written Record: England 1066–1307* (London, 1979), 43; D. A. Carpenter, 'The English Chancery in the XIIIth Century', in K. Fianu and D. J. Guth (eds.), *Écrit et pouvoir dans les chancelleries médiévales: Espace français, espace anglais* (Louvain-La-Neuve, 1997), 26, 34; W. M. Ormrod, 'Accountability and Collegiality: The English Royal Secretariat in the Mid-Fourteenth Century', ibid. 61.

[2] M. C. Prestwich, 'English Government Records', in R. H. Britnell (ed.), *Pragmatic Literacy East and West, 1200–1330* (Woodbridge, 1997).

these records is astonishing. In part, it bears witness to how little they were used; the pristine condition of many rolls today demonstrates how few people had any need to read them. Many, of course, could not understand them, for the main language of government was Latin, 'un language formal de mettre en briefs' ('a formal language to put in writs'), as one chief justice described it.[3] This meant that the country was administered in a tongue that the great majority of the population could not follow, much as was the case in British India in the nineteenth century. Most charters and writs were in Latin; this was also the language of accountancy, not just in the rolls produced by the exchequer, but also in the myriad of manorial accounts kept by landlords, great and small. French was also used. Much of the more private royal correspondence was in French, and by the early fourteenth century this was the language used for the accounts of the royal chamber. In the royal law courts the records were kept in Latin, while pleading took place in French. It was only among the lower levels of the hierarchy of courts that English may have been employed.

In many cases administrative procedures appear needlessly complex. By the fourteenth century it was possible for a single royal order to be issued first of all under the king's secret seal, and sent to the privy seal office. The privy seal office would instruct the chancery, which would prepare the final writ. Three documents were used where one would have sufficed. This might lead to long delays. The letters and writs produced by government departments were all dated. These dates, however, might bear very little relationship to the reality of when they were actually issued and received. It was usual practice for the chancery to date letters using the date given on the initial instruction it had received in a privy seal document. Once the letters were written, there might be a considerable wait before they were entrusted to a messenger for delivery. The evidence suggests that where matters were urgent, the government machinery acted expeditiously. If they were not, it might take up to six months for a writ to be delivered. Study of the writs sent to the bishop of Worcester in the years 1302–7 shows that three writs were received within ten days of the date on the document, while three took over twenty weeks to arrive.[4]

The complexity of record-keeping was particularly remarkable where financial matters were concerned. One payment might appear on a document issued by the keeper of the wardrobe, in the wardrobe account book, on the exchequer issue and receipt rolls (in triplicate), on the chancery's *liberate* rolls, and possibly even on the pipe roll, as well as being recorded in notches made on

---

[3] B. H. Putnam, *The Place in Legal History of Sir William Shareshull* (Cambridge, 1950), 112.
[4] J. F. Willard, 'The Dating and Delivery of Letters Patent and Writs in the Fourteenth Century', *BIHR* 10 (1932), 1–11.

a tally stick.[5] While such matters as the appointment of tax-collectors was done efficiently and promptly, since the money was normally urgently needed, other business might take a very long time. The auditing of accounts was carried through methodically and carefully, with the result that in some cases it might be very many years before an issue was finally settled. Some of the wardrobe accounts of Edward I's later years were never finally agreed and audited; others had to wait until the 1320s.

THE STRUCTURE OF GOVERNMENT

The essential structures of government were well established by the early thirteenth century. The king and his council were at the apex. The term 'council' could have various meanings, from great councils to which large numbers of magnates might be summoned, to the working council at the core of government. This usually contained some magnates, lay and ecclesiastical, and officials with administrative knowledge and experience, notably the chancellor and treasurer, as well as judges. In 1236 a council of twelve was named, and its members swore to give the king faithful counsel.[6] A new oath was established in 1257, and a more elaborate version was used from 1294.[7] The composition of the council was a political issue in Henry III's reign: the political revolution of 1258 saw a council of fifteen set up. Under Edward II part of the political settlement achieved in 1318 involved setting up a council of seventeen. Such councils imposed on the king were significant, but the way in which the council evolved as a working body, in which the official element normally dominated, was more important. The council has left few records, but surviving memoranda and agenda notes show that the business was wide-ranging. Under Edward I it can be shown to have dealt with diplomatic and financial issues. It was also much concerned with legal questions, particularly where it was necessary to create a new remedy to deal with a particular matter. By Edward III's reign the council had acquired a permanent home, in what would become the Star Chamber in the palace of Westminster. It was acquiring increasing judicial importance, hearing cases involving the great, and those that could not easily be resolved under common law procedures.[8] The fundamental importance of the council lay not in any executive authority, but in the expert

[5] Carpenter, 'English Chancery in the xiiith Century', 25–53.
[6] Ann. Dunstable, 145–6.
[7] Prestwich, *Edward I*, 437. The medieval oaths are a considerable contrast to the modern privy councillor's oath, for, as is appropriate in a country where no more than lip-service is paid to principles of open government, the modern oath lays much stress on the need for secrecy: *The Times*, 2 Mar. 2004.
[8] W. M. Ormrod, *The Reign of Edward III* (London, 1990), 74–7.

advice and assistance that it gave to the king. Membership of the council, almost of an honorific type, though with an annual fee, might be granted to foreigners. Berto de Frescobaldi early in Edward II's reign provides one example; early in the next reign Antonio Pessagno and Niccolo de' Fieschi of Genoa, Reymund Corneli of Aragon, and Cardinal Annibald were all retained in this way.[9]

The king's household provided for much more than the domestic needs of the court, and was in many ways the hub of government. Within the household, the wardrobe was the department of greatest importance; despite its name, it was the main financial section of the household. At some periods, such as the 1290s, virtually all central government expenditure was channelled through it, for it was through this office that royal military campaigns were financed. This continued to be the case under Edward II and Edward III. The clerks of the household were the men at the heart of the organization of war, supervising recruitment, victualling, and pay. Importantly, the household provided the king with a personal writing office, which was used for writs sent out under a personal seal. Orders to the chancery and to the exchequer, for example, were issued under the privy seal. This was kept in the wardrobe until Edward II's reign, when it began to acquire independence as a separate office, with four clerks writing writs. In the same reign the secret seal came into use; in 1322 it was used to instruct the keeper of the privy seal to issue letters to the sheriff of Oxfordshire and Buckinghamshire. It was used for matters particularly close to the king, as when he stated in a letter to the exchequer 'so that you know that we have this business at heart, we are writing to you under our secret seal'. Under Edward III one of the secret seals was so private to the king that it took the form of a signet ring he might wear. The complexity of the household seals was increased by the addition in 1335 of the griffin seal, used for almost twenty years alongside the privy and secret seals. It was used for business relating to the lands whose revenues were assigned to the chamber.[10]

The central departments of state were the exchequer and the chancery. The exchequer was divided into two sections, the lower, which dealt with money paid in and the issue of receipts in the form of wooden tallies, and the upper, which was the court where accounts were rendered and heard. The sheriffs were to appear, at least in theory, twice a year at the upper exchequer, once for a 'view' of their account, and once at Michaelmas for the full accounting process. In this, the chequered cloth from which the office derived its name was used as a form of abacus, with counters set out on the columns to represent

---

[9] J. F. Willard and W. A. Morris (eds.), *The English Government at Work, 1327–1336*, i (Cambridge, Mass., 1940), 142–3.
[10] Tout, *Chapters*, v. 167–8, 181 ff.

the sums that were due. The exchequer systems were long-established, but of course required occasional revision and overhaul. In 1234 Alexander Swereford was appointed chief baron of the exchequer, and he undertook the major task of sorting and organizing the complex records that were kept. The *Red Book of the Exchequer* represents the fruits of his labours. Another period when massive labours took place was the 1320s. In Walter Stapledon, Edward brought in as treasurer a man who had ample experience of running his diocese of Exeter but no experience of royal government. A fresh eye brought swift improvements to the way in which things were done. Record-keeping was overhauled; much material, such as that relating to old debts, was stripped from the great annual accounts, the pipe rolls, and put in separate rolls. The pipe rolls were for the accounts presented by the sheriffs; so-called 'foreign accounts', which included those of the wardrobe, were to be dealt with separately. Accounts for castle garrisons and victualling, like those of the royal stud farms, were to be presented directly to the exchequer, and not to the wardrobe. The exchequer ordinances of 1323, 1324, and 1326 reformed existing practice, and set out the blueprint for the way the department would operate for the rest of the medieval period.[11]

The extent to which the exchequer really controlled the royal finances varied. It was the ultimate court of audit, but if the accounts of the keeper of the wardrobe were not presented on a regular annual basis (as was the case at the end of Edward I's reign), then the supervision it could exercise was necessarily limited. If most of the money that the sheriffs and other officials received was paid out straight away by them to the wardrobe, or to others on the instructions of household officials, then little would be received in cash at Michaelmas. In Edward I's later years the exchequer had virtually no control over the wardrobe and the scale of debt that it incurred. No wardrobe accounts were enrolled at the exchequer. Wardrobe expenditure was authorized by means of writs of *liberate*, and in theory these provided a means of controlling spending, but at this period these writs were made out in huge sums, up to £20,000 in a single tranche, and they were often made out long after payments had been made. The ideal practice was set out in the Ordinances of 1311, which provided that all royal revenue should be paid into the exchequer. The treasurer and chamberlains should then pay out funds as appropriate, to pay for the expenses of the royal household.[12] This may have been correct in theory, but was difficult to put into effect, such was the pressure on government. However, exchequer control was increasingly reasserted, if not directly because of the Ordinances, at least because of the ideas expressed in them.

---

[11] Ibid. ii. 258–68. [12] *SR* i. 157–67, Ordinances 4 and 8.

Under Edward III there was a full recognition of the supremacy of the exchequer in financial administration, but both in the early campaigns of the late 1330s of the French war, and with the king's last campaign, that of 1359–60, nearly all the expenditure was channelled through the wardrobe, just as it had been under Edward I.[13] The wardrobe, however, was not able to run up debts in the way it had in the late thirteenth and early fourteenth centuries; it was instead the exchequer that assigned revenue before it had been collected.

Without the chancery, and the multiplicity of writs that emanated from it, government could not have operated. Early in Henry III's reign the chancery was closely linked to the household. The clerks and sergeants of the chancery even had a role in the royal chapel. The chancery was still close to the king in the first half of Edward I's reign. In the late 1280s, when the king went to Gascony, he took his chancellor, Robert Burnell, with him. The chancery was then divided, with the majority of the clerks remaining in England, based at Westminster. After the king's return to England in 1289, the chancery became increasingly separate from the household. During the Welsh war of 1294–5 the chancellor and his clerks moved to Chester, rather than accompanying the king on campaign, and during Edward I's Scottish wars the chancery similarly did not stay by the king's side, but remained at York. The fact that letters issued by the chancery gave the king's whereabouts as the place of issue makes it difficult to determine where the office actually was, but by Edward III's reign it had a permanent presence at Westminster. When the king went to Flanders in 1338, there was no division of the chancery; it remained in England, using not the normal great seal, but a seal of absence. The way in which the chancery moved 'out of court' was a significant element in the evolution of the central machinery of government. By the fourteenth century it employed about a hundred clerks; in 1324 they produced about 29,000 writs, at an average rate of eighty a day. The department was headed by twelve 'masters', senior clerks of great importance, often termed 'of the first form', because they occupied the front bench. Below them were the clerks 'of the second form', also numbering twelve. Below them again were twenty-four cursitors, the men who wrote the standardized 'writs of course'. There were in addition large numbers of assistant clerks and servants.[14]

The law courts were another important part of the machinery of government. There were two main central courts, King's Bench and Common Pleas; the exchequer also had a judicial function. King's Bench, created in the early 1230s, in theory followed the king on his travels (though by the fourteenth century this was no more than theory), while Common Pleas was fixed at

[13] Tout, *Chapters*, iii. 178.
[14] Ibid. ii. 63–4, 79–81; iii, 57 n. 2, 211; Carpenter, 'English Chancery in the XIIIth Century', 34.

Westminster, apart from fairly brief periods when the whole government machinery was moved to York. King's Bench heard cases that came to it by way of appeal from lower courts, and increasingly became concerned with criminal matters, while the court of Common Pleas concentrated more on property cases, and in the fourteenth century a wide range of matters that came under the general heading of trespass.[15] It was hard work being a judge. In the late 1220s one justice wrote to Hubert de Burgh asking to be relieved of the task of serving any more alongside Martin of Patishall. The work began at sunrise, and ended at night. Patishall, the writer said, was a strong man, but he and his colleague William Raleigh could not keep up with the pace.[16]

A powerful historical interpretation of the development of royal administration saw rivalry and competition between departments as very important. Above all, government based on the royal household on the one hand, and on the great offices of state—chancery and exchequer—on the other, were seen as alternatives. Edward II's reign provided the best example of this pattern, with the king and his favourites reliant upon the household, and his opponents seeking to deprive the household department of the wardrobe of independent sources of finance.[17] This concept provided a convenient and effective tool for historians, which made sense of complex issues. It is less clear, however, that this is how contemporaries regarded the administrative structures of medieval government, and it makes more sense to think in terms of the cooperation of the various departments under the overall control of the crown. The later years of Edward I's reign saw the wardrobe in an apparently dominant position, for the exchequer had little effective control over the expenditure it was incurring. There was, however, no rivalry between the treasurer, Walter Langton, who headed the exchequer, and the keeper of the wardrobe, John Droxford. When Langton had to leave the country to go to Rome, Droxford stepped up as his deputy, and the administrative arrangements that were made demonstrate that both men fully accepted the ultimate primacy of the exchequer. It was the pressures of war and other business that had led to the situation in which the wardrobe achieved virtual day-to-day independence of the exchequer, rather than a policy of developing the household as an alternative structure of government.[18]

---

[15] A convenient account of these courts is in A. Musson and W. M. Ormrod, *The Evolution of English Justice: Law, Politics and Society in the Fourteenth Century* (London, 1999), 12–20.

[16] *Royal and Other Historical Letters Illustrative of the Reign of Henry III*, ed. W. W. Shirley, 2 vols. (RS, 1862–6), i. 342.

[17] This, summarized very briefly, was an underlying theme of Tout's great work *Chapters in the Administrative History of Medieval England*. See also his *Place of Edward II*, where, on pp. 62–3, he wrote that 'The king's wardrobe was, speaking roughly, the financial and secretarial department of the king's household, the domestic and semi-private exchequer of the king, hopelessly overlapping the national exchequer and chancery in all its functions.'

[18] Prestwich, *Edward I*, 535–6.

CAREERS IN ROYAL ADMINISTRATION

An alternative approach to an analysis based on the changing role of different departments is to examine the careers of individual administrators. Much is known about the careers of the officials who ran the central departments as they moved up from post to post, with the really able (or perhaps ambitious and unscrupulous) ending up on the episcopal bench. Their personalities, however, very rarely appear through the reams of parchment that they produced. For contemporaries, the most noteworthy feature of Silvester de Everdon's life was the way he left it in 1254, thrown by a lively horse. He had prospered as a result of serving Ralph Neville, bishop of Chichester and chancellor to 1238, and remained in the chancery until 1246. Clearly an effective administrator, he received his rewards in the form of a number of lucrative church livings, which included a couple of cathedral canonries and the post of archdeacon of Chester. Remarkably, when he was first offered the see of Carlisle, he rejected it. He may have been modest, and felt himself to be inadequate, or, more probably, he may have had doubts about the custom of promoting civil servants to bishoprics. His qualms of conscience, however, did not last long, and at the second time of asking he accepted the position, which he filled with some distinction.[19]

Networks were important to those developing careers in royal administration. This is very clear from the study of one very remarkable group who came to dominance in the early fourteenth century. These were men who came from the region around the Humber, south Yorkshire, and north Lincolnshire. William Hamilton (or Hambledon, from his birthplace near Selby) was probably the first to enter royal service in the 1260s; he was a shrewd lender, and a highly successful accumulator of ecclesiastical benefices. Robert Barlby and Adam Osgodeby followed in his wake, as did his kinsman John Markingfield. William Airmyn was a notable figure in Edward II's chancery; he came from close to Goole. John Sandal was an important administrator in Edward I's later years, and a major figure in the exchequer under his son. William Melton entered the royal household as a clerk in 1294, left the administration when he became archbishop of York in 1315, and returned as treasurer in 1325–6, and again in 1330. He was responsible for introducing a host of his relations and neighbours to royal service: William, John, and Richard Ferriby, Nicholas Huggate, William Cliffe, and John Swanland were among them. The most notable of those who owed their careers to Melton's patronage was John Thoresby, his clerk in 1325–6. Thoresby rose to be chancellor in 1349, and

---

[19] H. Summerson, 'The King's Clericulus: The Life and Career of Silvester de Everdon, Bishop of Carlisle, 1247–1254', *Northern History*, 28 (1992), 71–6, 88.

then in 1352, like his master, Melton, was promoted to the archbishopric of York. No doubt the intermittent presence of the exchequer and other departments in York because of the Scottish wars helped to encourage these Yorkshire clerks to seek careers in the king's service, but more important surely were personal connections and links, with perhaps a sense of loyalty to their home region. These men served in a range of different departments, both within the household and in chancery and exchequer, but no doubt retained some sense of collective regional identity.[20]

Adam Limber provides a good example of a member of this group, and of the second rank of civil servants. He came from north Lincolnshire, and began his career as the personal clerk of the keeper of the wardrobe, the unpopular Ingelard Warley, in 1309. By the next year he was a king's clerk, and then in 1311 he moved to the exchequer, where he held the office of king's remembrancer until 1322. The next two years he spent in Gascony, as constable of Bordeaux, returning to England to raise troops for the defence of the duchy against the French. He was in a good position when it came to the *coup d'état* of 1327, for he had been keeper of the young Edward III's wardrobe for a time. His loyalty to the new regime was rewarded with the office of keeper of the privy seal. In 1331 he became chancellor of Ireland, but came back to England as a baron of the exchequer in 1334, an office he held until 1339, when his service to the crown came to an end.[21] His career admirably demonstrates the flexibility of a good civil servant, and the range of duties that might be expected. His abilities must have been considerable, for he served in two overseas dominions, and acted in both the exchequer and the household.

Men could rise meteorically in royal service. Thomas Hatfield was another clerk who came from south Yorkshire, near the Humber. He became a clerk of the king's chapel in October 1337; previously he had been in royal service organizing building works in Scotland at Stirling and Bothwell. A year later he became receiver of the chamber, and in 1345 he moved out of royal service when he became bishop of Durham.[22] He must have had obvious skills and political awareness, though the records that survive do not demonstrate anything that marks Hatfield out from his contemporaries. Unfortunately for historians, after the king had approved Hatfield's chamber accounts, the records were burned so as to ensure that no one in future could dredge up charges with which to vex him.[23]

---

[20] J. L. Grassi, 'Royal Clerks from the Archdiocese of York in the Fourteenth Century', *Northern History*, 5 (1970), 12–33.
[21] Tout, *Chapters*, iv. 74; v. 4–5.
[22] BL, Cotton MS Nero C. VIII, fo. 215; Tout, *Chapters*, vi. 55.
[23] *CPR 1343–5*, 371.

The career of William Edington shows how a really successful fourteenth-century civil servant developed his career. Like Hatfield, his rise to prominence was very rapid. A Wiltshire man, he was an associate of Adam Orleton, bishop first of Worcester and then of Winchester. He entered royal service as a clerk in 1335. In 1340–1 he was a collector of the tax of a ninth, and was then suddenly promoted to be keeper of the wardrobe. In 1345 he was moved to the exchequer, as treasurer, and in 1356 he moved again to the chancery, as chancellor. He therefore had experience in the household, and in both of the great departments of state; his career demonstrates the fundamental unity of royal government. Like so many high royal ministers, his main reward for his service was a bishopric; he succeeded Adam Orleton at Winchester in 1346.[24]

For the most part, the officials of central government were trained in post. Some, however, considered that it was important to provide universities with patronage. In the thirteenth century Merton College at Oxford was founded by the notable royal clerk Walter de Merton. Family advancement was high on Walter's agenda. His intention was to provide for clerks studying at Oxford, and in particular for eight of his nephews.[25] No doubt he hoped that some at least would follow his example and serve the crown. Adam de Brome, founder in 1326 of Oriel College, Oxford, was a royal clerk who served in the chancery and as royal almoner. He envisaged that the first ten of the scholars in the college would study theology. Half a dozen more would study canon law, and might be allowed to study civil law, good qualifications for careers in Church or State service.[26] John Winwick also had ambitions to found an Oxford college, where the scholars would study canon and civil law. Although the scheme was approved by both king and pope, it failed since Winwick's heirs would not give it their support.[27] The crown itself took a limited interest in university education: in 1317 Edward II authorized the maintenance of a clerk and twelve children from the royal chapel at Cambridge, and in 1337 his son provided an endowment which transformed the foundation into the King's Hall. The explicit intention was to train young men for service in Church and State.[28]

Nearly all the king's servants in the household, chancery, and exchequer were clerics. Yet some at least rode to war with entourages as splendid as those of true military men. John Droxford, keeper of the wardrobe and future bishop of Bath and Wells, had a retinue of six knights and twenty-two squires on the Scottish

---

[24] Tout, *Chapters*, iii. 203.
[25] G. H. Martin and J. R. L. Highfield, *A History of Merton College* (Oxford, 1997), 11.
[26] *The History of the University of Oxford*, i.: *The Early Oxford Schools*, ed. Catto, 237.
[27] Tout, *Chapters*, v. 37.
[28] A. B. Cobban, *The King's Hall Within the University of Cambridge in the Later Middle Ages* (Cambridge, 1969), 9–14.

campaign of 1300.[29] His colleague John Benstead, who achieved high rank in Edward I's wardrobe as controller, had less of a clerical vocation than Droxford, and early in Edward II's reign abandoned his clerical orders, married, and became a knight.[30] Ralph Manton, another of Edward I's wardrobe officials, before his death at the battle of Roslin in 1303 was berated by the Scot Simon Fraser for wearing an iron hauberk rather than a habit suitable for a churchman.[31]

After the political crisis of 1340–1 there was an exceptional period when the king appointed laymen to high administrative office. This was a reaction to the way in which Archbishop Stratford, former chancellor, had played a leading role in opposing the king. Robert Bourchier became chancellor for ten months, and was succeeded by Robert Parving. On his death in 1343 another layman, Robert Sadington, took over. In 1345, however, his successor was John Offord, a cleric. There is nothing to suggest that the lay chancellors had not been efficient and effective. Indeed, the evidence is to the contrary, showing that they took a more active interest in the day-to-day running of the chancery than their clerical predecessors. Under Sadington, a significant change took place with the creation of two new seals, one for King's Bench, and one for Common Pleas. There were, however, difficulties with lay officials, above all that they could not be rewarded in the same way as clerics, with fat church livings. The normal allowance of £500 a year had to be doubled.[32] The fact that in this brief period the chancery had laymen at its head did not mean that there was any broader process of the laicization of government.

One area in which laymen increasingly dominated was the law. Laymen had commonly been employed as judges, but it was only from Edward I's reign that lay professional lawyers came to be appointed. Gilbert of Thornton had been a serjeant in the courts since the start of Edward I's reign, and was in royal service in the 1280s. In 1290, on the disgrace of Ralph Hengham, he became chief justice of King's Bench. Other lay justices had backgrounds in royal and baronial administration.[33] By Edward III's reign the ranks of the justices were almost exclusively lay, and were dominated by men best described as professional lawyers. One of the most notable was Geoffrey le Scrope, who became a king's serjeant in 1315. He was one of those professional men whose skills were such that he sailed through the political disturbances of the 1320s, remaining in favour with each successive regime. He became a justice of Common Bench in 1323, and was then promoted in the following year to the King's Bench. He was chief justice from 1324 until 1338, when he accompanied the king to Flanders, and where he died in 1340. He had a central role in determining legal policy for

---

[29] *Liber Quotidianus*, 202–3.   [30] Tout, *Chapters*, ii. 193.
[31] Pierre de Langtoft, 410–11.   [32] Tout, *Chapters*, iii. 151–7.
[33] P. Brand, *The Making of the Common Law* (London, 1992), 135–68.

many years, particularly where matters of law and order were concerned. Fifteen statutes were issued while he was chief justice, and while his specific contribution to them cannot be isolated, it was undoubtedly considerable. Nor was his role a purely legal one, for he served with distinction as a diplomat.[34]

GOVERNMENT IN THE LOCALITIES

It would be wrong to make too clear a distinction between local and central government; there is no indication that contemporaries thought in such terms, but they are convenient labels for historians to use. Government at a local level was structured in accordance with the long-established county structure, though in some cases, such as Nottinghamshire and Derbyshire, or Shropshire and Staffordshire, counties were paired under a single sheriff. The sheriff was the chief royal officer; he was primarily accountable to the exchequer. The question of how he should be chosen, and what sort of man he should be, could be a political issue. There was a shift under Henry III, from 1236, away from the appointment of powerful men of the court (who would exercise the office through deputies) towards the use of local knights. The early 1270s saw more *curiales* in office, but the long-term trend against the use of such men was not reversed. Demands for local election of sheriffs surfaced in the heady years of reform in the late 1250s, and again near the end of Edward I's reign, but feelings over this probably never ran very high. When Edward I conceded the right to local election in 1300, there was little enthusiasm to take up the offer. In an exceptional case in 1303 in Shropshire and Staffordshire (which shared a sheriff) the election was overturned, as some of the magnates and knights of the counties registered their opposition, and the exchequer officials simply nominated a local knight in place of the original man elected.[35]

The sheriff had an under-sheriff and a number of clerks, one of whom was in charge of the finances of the shire, and another who had custody of the writs. There were in addition bailiffs and sub-bailiffs. The duties of the sheriffs and their officials were wide-ranging. There were financial responsibilities. The sheriff was responsible for the annual county farm, and from this and other resources there were outlays on royal castles and other buildings, and a range of other matters. Legal matters were a major preoccupation. The sheriff presided over the county court, and made his regular tourn, appearing twice a year in the

---

[34] E. L. G. Stones, 'Sir Geoffrey le Scrope *c*.1280 to 1340, Chief Justice of the King's Bench', *EHR* 69 (1954), 1–17.

[35] D. A. Carpenter, 'The Decline of the Curial Sheriff in England', in his *The Reign of Henry III* (London, 1996), 151–82; W. A. Morris, *The Medieval English Sheriff to 1300* (Manchester, 1927), 184–5. For sheriffs in the 14th century, see R. Gorski, *The Fourteenth-Century Sheriff* (Woodbridge, 2003).

hundred courts of the county. He was the main instrument used by the crown for communication with the localities, and would be charged with making various proclamations. It was in the county court that elections took place of those to represent the county in parliament. It is striking that even when (as was often the case) there was a rapid turnover of sheriffs, there was no evident disruption to the operation of the administrative machinery. Local government, like central, was bureaucratic, and full attention was paid to enrolling copies of the large number of writs that came in and recording the action that was taken.[36]

The sheriff and his small staff could not undertake all the multiplicity of tasks that needed to be done. There were other officials as well. There were normally two escheators in England, one north of the Trent and one to the south. Their task of enforcing royal rights of wardship, holding inquisitions on the death of tenants-in-chief, and looking after lands that escheated to the crown, was done at county level by sub-escheators, appointed by the escheators. Coroners were also important, within their own area of a county. Their main duties were judicial, involving the holding of inquests, dealing with those who abjured the realm, and similar tasks. Unlike sheriffs, they might hold office for life. When taxes were granted, it was normal for special appointments of assessors and collectors to be made. By Edward I's reign there were many special commissions appointed, for tasks ranging from the recruitment of troops to the hearing of cases, and for these the crown had to rely on the willingness of members of the local gentry to serve. The scale of their involvement in local government was very impressive. It has been estimated that of those men listed by the sheriff of Warwickshire as knights in 1324, three-quarters had undertaken some major task in the county. It becomes difficult to find knights who were not involved in some way in serving on a commission or holding some local office.[37]

In addition to the county structure, the royal forests formed a further, distinct strand of local government with a different hierarchy of officials, from the chief justices of the forest (in the early thirteenth century) down to the verderers and agisters, who received no formal reward for their duties. The sheer extent of royal forest gave these positions considerable importance and their holders considerable unpopularity.

Royal justice in the localities was the responsibility of a number of different agencies. Justices were sent round the country on circuits. In the thirteenth century the general eyre was a massive inquiry at county level into a wide range of issues. In theory, each county was visited once every seven years. With the

---

[36] H. Jenkinson and M. H. Mills, 'Rolls from a Sheriff's Office of the Fourteenth Century', *EHR* 43 (1928), 21–32.
[37] P. Coss, *The Origins of the English Gentry* (Cambridge, 2003), 174, 179.

outbreak of war with France in 1294, the eyre was abandoned, a move that was intended to be temporary, but that was never fully reversed. Other types of court took its place. Assize circuits heard property cases such as those under the assize of novel disseisin; from the late thirteenth century these were increasingly combined with sessions of gaol delivery, when the cases of those held in prison, or on bail, were heard. Trailbaston inquiries were first set up by Edward I, and looked specifically into questions of crime and public order; again, justices were sent out on circuit to hear these. Keepers of the peace were commissioned from the mid-thirteenth century. They had authority to pursue and arrest criminals, and to receive indictments, but only rarely before a statute of 1361 did they have the power to determine cases.[38]

Much of the country was not under the direct control of central government. The medieval state was in some ways more federal than unitary, and a great many rights of jurisdiction and other powers were in the hands of magnates and others. The range of liberties in the hands of the king's subjects was immense. At the top, within England, were the great palatinates, where the royal writ did not run. The palatinate of Durham was in many ways virtually independent. It was an exaggeration, and unwise, for a knight in Anthony Bek's entourage to declare that the bishop was king between Tyne and Tees, but it was not far from the truth.[39] An alternative view came from the crown, arguing that 'the bishop, since he holds the said liberty, is so far the king's minister for upholding and carrying out in the king's name and in due manner what belongs to the royal authority within the same liberty'. Edward II, however, 'for the great devotion which the king has for the glorious confessor, St Cuthbert', was careful not to take action 'by which the franchise of the bishop might be blemished'.[40] Durham was particularly distinctive. It did not pay the same taxes as the rest of the country, and did not even send representatives to parliament. Cheshire also enjoyed palatine status; within the county, writs were issued by the earl of Chester's chancery. Pleas could not be removed from the county court of Chester to central royal courts. Like Durham, Chester had no parliamentary representation. Lancaster gained palatine status in 1351, when the earl was raised to ducal rank. There were some differences from Chester. The king retained the right to pardon life and limb, and could reverse erroneous judgments made in the duke's courts. In contrast to the other two palatinates, Lancaster continued to send representatives to parliament.[41]

---

[38] Musson and Ormrod, *The Evolution of English Justice*, 42–53.
[39] C. M. Fraser, *A History of Anthony Bek* (Oxford, 1957), 196–7.
[40] H. M. Cam, *Liberties and Communities in Medieval England* (Cambridge, 1944), 184; *Calendar of Chancery Warrants, 1244–1327*, 336.
[41] Fowler, *King's Lieutenant*, 173–4.

The liberties of the Welsh march were even greater than those of the great English palatinates. The king's writ did not run here, and the marchers were not liable to pay English taxes. In the great lordships such as Glamorgan or Brecon, the courts had full competence, and were not subject to any supervision from royal officials. Nor was there any right to appeal to English royal courts. The list of rights was long, and included the capacity to create new boroughs, markets, and fairs, power over life and limb, and the ability to exercise rights jealously guarded by the crown in England, such as those over treasure trove, wreck, and such royal fish as whales and porpoises. The marchers also claimed the right to determine disputes among their number by, if it came to it, private war.[42] It was only in the most exceptional circumstances that the king could intervene in the affairs of the lordships of the march. When franchisal rights were tested by Edward I in the *quo warranto* inquiries, he did not extend the investigations to the marches.

There were many other great liberties. Some were held by ecclesiastics. That of Bury St Edmunds in eastern England was notable, and in the same region there were those of Peterborough, Ely, and Ramsey. At Bury the abbot could exercise all the authority that a sheriff would normally possess over eight and a half hundreds in west Suffolk. Within this area lay the liberty itself. There no royal official could act; all power lay with the abbot. Bury was also an ecclesiastical liberty, dependent directly on the pope and free from any episcopal interference. The liberty of St Etheldreda, belonging to the see of Ely, was such that all royal officials were excluded. The bishop's justices heard all pleas, including pleas of the crown. Cases were successfully removed by the bishop from the jurisdiction of King's Bench and of Common Pleas.[43] The liberty held by the archbishop of Canterbury demonstrates the way that there might be a hierarchy of franchises, for it had the liberties of the prior of Canterbury, of Tonbridge (held by the earls of Gloucester), and of the see of Rochester below it.[44]

Many lords held lesser liberties, such as the right to hold the view of frankpledge, and there were very many hundreds held in private hands. Here lords or their men, rather than royal officials, exercised the jurisdiction of the hundred courts. The potential result of this was cases such as that of the sheriff of Shropshire, who complained in 1341 that he could not collect a debt of 4s. owed by Hugh Mortimer as it was inside the hundred of Cleobury. This was held by the earl of Northampton, and 'he neither could enter that hundred nor dared to do so'.[45] It has been estimated that in 1272 of the 628 hundreds in

---

[42] R. R. Davies, *Lordship and Society in the March of Wales 1282–1400* (Oxford, 1978), 217–19.
[43] A. Gransden, 'John de Northwold, Abbot of Bury St Edmunds', in *TCE* iii. 92; E. Miller, *The Abbey and Bishopric of Ely* (Cambridge, 1951), 323–5.
[44] D. Crook, 'The Later Eyres', *EHR* 97 (1982), 257.
[45] E. B. Fryde, 'Magnate Debts to Edward I and Edward III: A Study of Common Problems and Contrasting Royal Reactions to Them', *National Library of Wales Journal*, 27 (1992), 252.

England, 270 were royal and 358 in private hands. The geographical spread
was not even. In Buckinghamshire and Warwickshire there were no private
hundreds, but in Sussex all were in private possession. In Devon only two out
of the thirty-five hundreds were held by the crown. The fact that a hundred
was in private hands meant that the profits were paid to the lord, rather than to
the crown. He would normally pay an annual farm to the sheriff or to the
exchequer for it. The extent to which these private hundreds were independent
from royal government varied considerably. If the lord had the franchise of
return of writ, then the sheriff would not be able to enter the hundred, and
royal instructions would have to be handed over to the lord or his officials. In
other cases, although the lord would appoint the bailiff of the hundred, it
would differ very little from a hundred in royal hands. Its officials would act
just like royal ones, and would be answerable to the sheriff. It would be a part of
the complex structure of royal government.[46]

THE CHURCH

The Church was in theory separate from the State, with its own systems of
government. In practice, there were overlaps, and areas of cooperation as well
as of dispute, and although the Church was not a part of government, it assisted
greatly in the governing of England. The structure of the Church was not
coincident with that of secular government; the boundaries of dioceses did not
equate with those of counties. The evidence for the way in which the Church
was ruled is very different from that which royal government has left behind,
but the substantial numbers of bishops' registers that survive demonstrate, for
the most part, the professionalism and competence of another highly bureaucratic institution. As already shown, many bishops attained their office after
long service to the crown. Robert Burnell, Edward I's great chancellor, became
bishop of Bath and Wells, although the king failed to secure either Canterbury
or Winchester for him. Walter Langton, treasurer in Edward's later years and a
man not noted for his piety, was bishop of Coventry and Lichfield, a post he
filled with some distinction. In part bishoprics went to such men because the
king was in a position to influence their appointment, and the appointment was
an excellent way of rewarding good service. At the same time, cathedral
chapters may well have welcomed the elevation of men of proven administrative ability, even when, as was the case with Burnell and Langton, their
personal morality might be called into question.

There were, of course, bishops who gained office through other routes, of
which the most notable was that of academic achievement. In the thirteenth

[46] H. M. Cam, *The Hundred and the Hundred Rolls* (London, 1930), 137–45.

century it is striking that in Edmund of Abingdon, John Pecham, and Robert Winchelsey the see of Canterbury had three very notable archbishops whose careers rested on their scholarship and who had no experience in royal government. Robert Grosseteste, bishop of Lincoln, was one of the most eminent academic minds of the thirteenth century. Edward II's reign provides in Walter Stapledon an exceptional example of a university *magister*, Oxford trained, who had no background in royal government when elected bishop of Exeter in 1307, but who was suddenly pitchforked into the high office of treasurer in 1320.[47]

The government of the Church offers both parallels and contrasts to secular rule. The structure of archbishoprics and dioceses was quite distinct and different from that of the shires. Bishoprics varied greatly in size and consequently wealth, from small ones such as Rochester, to that of Lincoln, which extended from the Humber to the Thames and included eight archdeaconries and about 1,600 parishes. A bishop had various men to rely on, who formed a significant bureaucracy. There was the chancellor of the diocese, and the bishop's official, who presided over the consistory court. The register, in which a whole range of different documents were recorded, was kept by the registrar. Archdeacons had an important part to play, as did the dean and chapter of the cathedral. There was much routine business to be conducted, notably the many ordinations of new priests. Visitation was an important part of the duties of the bishop, but there were variations in how extensively this was done. Bishop Grosseteste took his duties very seriously, and, in addition to inspecting religious houses, would assemble the local populace in every deanery 'to hear the word of God'.[48] Bishop Stapledon of Exeter made six visitations of two of the archdeaconries in his diocese and four of another. Religious houses would be inspected in the course of visitations; the records of these can often suggest that the strict rules of religious orders were honoured in the breach. Stapledon's instructions for nunneries suggest that these were institutions where the inhabitants had their own private maids, no longer dined in common, failed to keep the feast of Corpus Christi, and did not maintain silence.[49]

While much of the concern of episcopal administration was with spiritual matters in a very broad sense, the Church, like the secular State, had to collect money. Collections were taken, legacies received, fines accumulated, and gifts sought in order to pay for building operations. There were also taxes imposed by the papacy, or negotiated by the crown. Rather than provide a new assessment for each tax, the Church relied on fixed assessments of income.

[47] For Stapledon's career, see M. Buck, *Politics, Finance and the Church in the Reign of Edward II: Walter Stapledon, Treasurer of England* (Cambridge, 1983).
[48] R. W. Southern, *Robert Grosseteste: The Growth of an English Mind in Medieval Europe* (Oxford, 1986), 258.
[49] Buck, *Politics, Finance and the Church*, 61–2.

One was made in 1217, and another, known as the valuation of Norwich, in 1254. This calculated the value of clerical income at about £102,000, a considerable under-assessment. Further valuations took place at regular intervals. That made in the early 1290s was particularly important, for it continued to be used thereafter as the basis for taxes levied by the papacy, with revisions made for the north of England in the early fourteenth century as a result of the damage caused by the Scots. Collectors and deputy collectors had a large and difficult task. In 1292 the deputy collectors were ordered to keep a full record of all payments, to take no money not of full weight, to keep the receipts safe, and to record acquittances properly.[50]

Ecclesiastical officials were no more popular than their secular counterparts. The men of Devon complained early in the fourteenth century about the way in which the officials of the bishop of Exeter and the archdeacons maltreated innocent laymen, by threats and actions of excommunication. All sorts of secular rights were being trampled. The 'poor commons' of Devon and Cornwall complained that more was levied in fines and in other ways by church courts than by secular ones.[51]

CORRUPTION

Inevitably, government offered opportunities for corruption. At the highest level, there were some major drives against crooked officials, notably after periods of royal absence abroad. In 1289 Edward I returned to England from three years in Gascony; in November 1340 Edward III suddenly took ship from the Low Countries and arrived totally unexpectedly at the Tower of London. In both cases, the kings clearly considered that things had gone badly wrong while they were out of the country.

Edward I's main target in 1289 was the royal justices. Thomas Weyland, chief justice of Common Pleas, had protected two of his men after they had committed a murder. His lands were confiscated, and he was driven into exile. It may be that this case alerted the king to the possibility that there was corruption on a much wider scale. A commission was set up to hear complaints against royal officials; in all some 1,000 defendants were named in about 670 different actions. Ralph Hengham, chief justice of King's Bench, was fined 8,000 marks; the sum seems hardly commensurate with his main offence of misdating a writ. William de Brompton was fined 6,000 marks for taking bribes, forcing a jury to change its mind, adjourning cases incorrectly, and

---

[50] For a detailed discussion of clerical taxation, see W. A. Lunt, *Financial Relations of the Papacy with England to 1327* (Cambridge, Mass., 1939), 355 and *passim*.
[51] Buck, *Politics, Finance and the Church*, 65–6.

other offences. William de Saham, one of Hengham's judicial colleagues, was fined 2,500 marks. The records of the trials strongly suggest that the scale of corruption was not as serious as the level of fines, and the comments of the chroniclers, implied. On the other hand Adam Stratton, the chamberlain of the exchequer, probably was guilty of much misdoing. One of the counts on which he was convicted involved the forgery of a deed relating to Bermondsey priory, a house from which he had acquired five manors. When he was arrested, about £13,000 in cash was discovered in his house, a huge hoard which such a man was hardly likely to have built up by legal means. Henry de Bray, the escheator for southern England, committed suicide; his post had put him in a good position to acquire estates illicitly.[52]

In 1341 Richard Willoughby was accused of selling laws 'as if they had been oxen or cattle', and in 1346 an ordinance of the king's council attempted to deal with corruption among the judges. They were not to take fees or robes from anyone save the king himself, and could only accept gifts of food and drink of little value. Their fees were increased to compensate them for lost income as a result of this. In 1350, however, William Thorpe, chief justice of King's Bench, was put on trial for accepting bribes. He confessed his guilt, and was imprisoned for a time, only to be pardoned and restored to favour in 1352. The ordinance had been well intentioned, but it did not work. Thorpe himself had the effrontery to continue to receive fees from Ramsey abbey, and almost certainly from other sources as well, even after 1352.[53]

Opportunities for self-enrichment abounded at the local level, and are well documented, thanks to the efforts that were made to investigate abuses. In 1258 the eyre headed by Hugh Bigod conducted extensive investigations. The great Hundred Rolls inquiry of 1275 was on a massive scale. In 1298, in the aftermath of political crisis, Edward I launched judicial inquiries into the way in which officials had acted during the preceding years of high taxation and heavy demands for foodstuffs and wool in support of the war effort. Edward III responded in similar fashion in 1341 to the widespread complaints about the activities of local officials. The legal proceedings revealed extensive extortion in the localities, of money, foodstuffs, wool, and other goods. In Lincolnshire alone there were 784 accusations of trespasses by officials. Gilbert Ledred, recently sheriff, was charged with a wide range of offences. His demands for money from the countess of Lincoln before he would hold an inquest into her second husband's lands led to his imprisonment. A typical

[52] Prestwich, *Edward I*, 339–41.
[53] Musson and Ormrod, *The Evolution of English Justice*, 38–9; J. R. Maddicott, *Law and Lordship: Royal Justices as Retainers in Thirteenth- and Fourteenth-Century England, Past and Present*, suppl. 4 (1978), 40–1, 48–51, 56–7.

incident was the claim that the abbot of Ramsey in Huntingdonshire had paid one royal official £7 13s. 6d. to leave the abbey's lands alone.[54]

All of these investigations revealed that there were many ways in which those acting on behalf of the crown could, quite improperly, better themselves. Sheriffs were accused of a wide range of offences. They were often adept at manipulating the processes of law, and ensuring that some of funds passing through their hands stuck to their fingers. In 1355 a range of charges was brought against the sheriff of Devon. He had levied fines at will, rigged juries, imprisoned people without cause, and was 'a common fabricator of false indictments'.[55] The most remarkable story was that of the sheriff of Essex in 1267. There was a real possibility that royal forces would put London under siege, and the sheriff took a wide range of supplies, which he did not pay for, and which he appropriated for his own use. A true confidence trickster, he even persuaded some gullible villagers to hand over forty cocks, which he claimed would be used to burn down London. Tow would be tied to their feet, set alight, and the birds released to fly into the city.[56]

Purveyance was one of the most unpopular activities of royal officials at the local level. It was easy to take grain or other foodstuffs, using the royal right of prise, and not to pass on all that was collected. In 1359 Hugh de Stoke took bribes from people in Yorkshire in lieu of foodstuffs, while he took food from others without giving them proper receipts or tallies. The deputy sheriff of the same county was accused of corruption in taking hay and corn. He purveyed 500 quarters of corn in the North Riding for the king's horses, using a raised, or heaped, measure, but when he delivered the grain, it was by a razed measure. A wide range of other abuses were reported at the same time. Nor were abuses confined to Yorkshire; similar problems were recorded by commissioners in Norfolk.[57]

Bribes might be accepted from men anxious to avoid service in the king's armies. In 1294 the under-sheriff of Lincolnshire took 4s. from Ingoldmells, and in return promised not to recruit anyone from the place for service in Wales.[58] Tax assessors might take bribes in cash or kind from people wanting to see their assessment set at a low level. In 1323, for example, the tax-collectors for Staffordshire were found guilty of taking much money for their own use. One was fined £40, the other 50 marks. All of the sub-taxers were also found

---

[54] *The 1341 Royal Inquest in Lincolnshire*, ed. B. W. McLane (Lincoln Record Society, 1988), pp. xxv, 116–17; E 101/21/38.

[55] *Proceedings Before the Justices of the Peace in the Fourteenth and Fifteenth Centuries*, ed. B. H. Putnam (London, 1938), 73–8.

[56] Cam, *The Hundred and the Hundred Rolls*, 101–2.

[57] *CIM* iii, nos. 352, 411.

[58] *A Lincolnshire Assize Roll for 1298*, ed. W. S. Thomson (Lincoln Record Society, 1944), 59.

guilty, and fined varying amounts. Further enquiries revealed that there had been similar corruption in the three preceding taxes, so all the sub-taxers who could be found were fined 340 marks. Their dubious explanation was that they had not done the assessment according to the true value of people's goods, but that they had put their trust in 'the common interest of the whole community of the county'.[59] The Leicester urban accounts for 1300 reveal payment of £1 to the sheriff, to have his favour with regard to the royal prohibition on purchasing wool, hides, and tin with anything other than sterling coin. His clerks were paid 13s. 4d. The under-sheriff was paid £1, for unspecified reasons, as were his two clerks.[60] Such sums were the essential oil that lubricated local government; men needed to be rewarded, and the crown did not pay its officials the fees and wages that would have been needed to prevent them taking money from those prepared to offer it.

Corruption led naturally to unpopularity. When the king's bailiffs were about to summon the men of the hundred of Westerham in Kent to appear before royal justices, Nicholas French told them that they 'deserved to be hanged for they never did good when they could do ill'.[61] Not surprisingly, popular poetry contains complaints about the heavy hand of government.

> Justices, sheriffs, mayors, bailiffs, if I read it right
> They can make the fair day into the dark night.
>
> . . . .
>
> And bailiffs and bedels under the sheriff
> Each one finds how best men to grieve.
> The poor men are all summoned to the assize
> And the rich sit at home, and to shine their silver they rise.

Another poet complained that 'they hunt us as a hound does a hare on a hill'.[62] When, early in Edward II's reign, Bartholomew Burchull, the king's bailiff of Northampton, tried to arrest some wrongdoers in the town for attacking his carters, the cry went up 'At him! At him! He is the king's man.'[63] William March acted as tax-collector and purveyor under Edward II, and was commissioned by the younger Despenser to guard the Norfolk coast. Plainly much disliked; he accused a number of men of threatening to murder him, following

---

[59] 'Extracts from the Plea Rolls of the Reign of Edward II', ed. Wrottesley, in *Collections for a History of Staffordshire*, 9 (1888), 94–5.

[60] *Records of the Borough of Leicester*, ed. M. Bateson (London, 1899), 234.

[61] *CIM* i, no. 760.

[62] *Political Songs*, 152, 336, 338.

[63] R. W. Kaeuper, 'Law and Order in Fourteenth-Century England: The Evidence of Special Commissions of Oyer and Terminer', *Speculum*, 54 (1979), 747–8.

a case he had brought against them. His fear was justified, for in 1331 he was beheaded, and his body burned.[64]

Related to the issue of corruption is a more specific question about the extent to which officials were in practice under the control not of the king, but of great landowners. The practice of retaining men by means of grants of fees and robes, often termed 'bastard feudalism', might lead to such a situation. Accusations on these lines were certainly made. In about 1330 John Berkeley of Dursley complained that he could not obtain justice in Gloucestershire, because Thomas Berkeley retained the sheriff and bailiffs with fees and robes, as members of his household. It was said of Thomas de Lisle, bishop of Ely, that 'all the people of value from the county of Cambridge are the tenants of the bishop or otherwise [are beholden] to his fees and robes', though this was denied by the king's council, which claimed that there were 1,000 people in the county not in this position.[65] The networks in local society were complex, and no doubt royal officials had a range of connections. There were complications as men moved from private to royal administration. Yet, for all that there were fears that local government was falling into the hands of the magnates through the influence they could exercise, the evidence does not suggest that the problem was as extensive or as serious as some of the complaints imply.

The scale of corruption should not be exaggerated. The fundamental structures of government were sound. Offices were not routinely bought and sold, as had been the case under Henry I, and as would be the case in the sixteenth and seventeenth centuries. Enormous fortunes were not to be made out of the illicit profits of office; a case such as that of Adam Stratton was highly exceptional. There is, of course, no way of knowing what proportion of corrupt officials was caught by the various judicial inquiries that were held, but it is unlikely that it was just the unlucky ones who were caught.

CONCLUSION

This chapter began by asking whether government in this period was sophisticated and effective, or whether it was excessively bureaucratic, bogged down in its own complex procedures. There is no easy answer, but while there can be little doubt that administration could have been carried out in a more streamlined fashion, the governments of this period largely met the challenges that

---

[64] A. Musson, *Public Order and Law Enforcement: The Local Administration of Criminal Justice, 1294–1350* (Woodbridge, 1996), 272–4.

[65] N. Saul, *Knights and Esquires: The Gloucestershire Gentry in the Fourteenth Century* (Oxford, 1981), 266; J. Aberth, *Criminal Churchmen in the Age of Edward III: The Case of Bishop Thomas de Lisle* (University Park, Pa., 1996), 106, 108.

faced them. The greatest test that was faced was that of organizing war. This involved raising the necessary funds, recruiting up to 30,000 men, and ensuring that the armies were sufficiently well provided with foodstuffs and other necessary provisions. The record is not uniform, but as will be apparent in later chapters, the challenge was one that was met with considerable success. For all that the procedures of exchequer and chancery were bound by tradition, the administrative structures were able to adjust to the massive demands imposed by war.

Direct taxation was levied on a valuation of people's movable goods, and until 1334 a new assessment was carried out each time a tax was levied. This seems over-elaborate, and the evidence shows that the assessments were far from accurate. Yet this method of taxation meant that it was possible to raise large sums with considerable speed. This required flexibility on the part of the government, with a capacity to recruit new assessors and collectors to meet immediate needs. Similar flexibility was shown in conducting purveyance, the compulsory purchase of foodstuffs for the armies. Central government worked out what was needed, and at a local level the sheriffs were able both to use their existing staff, and to recruit additional officials, to put the orders into effect. The quantities actually provided did not equate to the initial requests as closely as tax receipts matched the assessments, but nevertheless the achievements were impressive.

One significant limitation of the government's capability was that overall budgeting and forecasting of income and expenditure were rarely attempted. The accounting systems used in the exchequer and the wardrobe were primarily intended to ensure that officials and others accounted properly for the money in their charge, not to provide information for decision-making. Budgets of a sort were produced in 1284 and 1324, but there was no regular attempt to ensure that income matched expenditure, much less overall commitments. This meant that periods of continuous warfare could create major financial problems, as expenditure spiralled out of control. The mid-1290s and the late 1330s provide notable examples, demonstrating the limitations of the administrative methods available to Edward I and his grandson.

Familiarity with the innumerable records produced by the government during this period may lead to the conclusion that this was an unnecessarily bureaucratic age, and that there could have been easier and quicker ways of doing things. The overriding impression, however, is of men who were doing their best and working very hard.

PART II

Politics and Wars

CHAPTER 4

Politics Under Henry III

In the evening of 4 August 1265 the mutilated body of Simon de Montfort, earl of Leicester, lay on the battlefield of the Green Hill outside Evesham. This gruesome scene dominates the story of the politics of Henry III's reign; it was the culminating point of a ferocious civil war. Yet, for all that there was at times much bitter faction fighting, for the thirty years from the early 1230s England had been at peace. The civil war of John's final months on the throne, and of the early years of Henry III's minority, lay in the past. If it were not for the bloody events of the civil war of 1264–5, Henry's reign might be seen as one in which brutal conflict was replaced by political manoeuvring, in which groups of foreigners were integrated into English society with increasing success, and as one in which major advances were made in government and law.

The bloodstains on that Green Hill in 1265, however, tell a different story, one in which the clash between different political interests and ideals could in the end be settled only by force. Henry's reign was an age of conflict within the circles of the court, with rival groups jockeying for power with little sense of principle. Foreign influence was extensive, with the Savoyard relations of the queen and their followers striving against the Poitevins, of whom the king's half-brothers were the most notable in terms of birth if not ability. It was also an age when political principles were important, as crisis succeeded crisis. Simon de Montfort, earl of Leicester and brother-in-law to the king, was one of those remarkable people of real charisma who, at rare intervals, dominate political life. His opposition to the king was partly bred from personal quarrels and financial disputes, but it was also characterized by a deep resentment at the way in which government was conducted.

One chronicler of these years, Matthew Paris (Plate I), stands above all others; this gossipy, prejudiced, and at the same time brilliant writer provided a very personal interpretation, which distorts as well as illuminates complex events. His work, most notably the *Chronica Majora*, provides an astonishingly vivid depiction of the years up to his death in 1260, characterized by an intense inquisitiveness. His talents extended to illustrating his works; he was an artist of real ability.

HENRY III

In an age when politics were intensely personal, the character of the king himself was a crucial element. Personality can be difficult to extract from medieval records, but in Henry's case, the character of the man is more transparent than is the case with most monarchs. He was in many ways an attractive person. He was a man of great aesthetic sensibility, and had nothing of the cruel streak that was one of his father's many flaws. When news reached him of the death of Richard Marshal in 1234, there was no rejoicing at the fate of a rebel; Henry burst into tears and ordered masses to be said for Richard's soul.[1] A sense of humour is suggested by a writ of 1237, authorizing William Peretot to cut the long hair of his household clerks, and comb out their curls.[2]

One view of Henry is that he had a very exalted view of his position as king, and that he espoused what amounted to absolutist ideas. According to Matthew Paris he declared in 1248 that 'inferiors should be directed at the will of the lord', and in 1252 he claimed to be able to set aside previously granted charters at will. He anticipated the policies of his son Edward I in ordering his sheriffs to maintain the rights of the crown, and not to allow the magnates to exercise various judicial rights without proper warrant. He also made statements that stressed the sanctity of his kingship. 'The All Highest has constituted us defender of the church, which, His grace allowing, we will and must defend.' He had hymns in praise of the monarchy, the Laudes Regiae, sung with great frequency.[3] It has, however, been argued that there was a substantial gap between Henry's statements and his actions. In practice he did not challenge the judicial liberties exercised by the magnates in any really significant manner. Rather, liberties were extended with no opposition from the king. Henry's style of kingship was never aggressive in the manner of his father, John, or his son Edward.[4]

There is no doubting Henry's ambition. He was a man whose vision extended across Europe. His family connections encouraged him in this. His queen, Eleanor of Provence, was one of four granddaughters of the count of Savoy. One of her sisters married Louis IX of France; the others married younger brothers of the kings of England and France. Henry's sister Isabella married the emperor Frederick II in 1235. Henry's younger brother Richard, earl of Cornwall, was elected to the German throne in 1257, and the king had plans in the 1250s to make his second son, Edmund, king of Sicily. Henry also

---

[1] Wendover, iii. 88.   [2] *CPR 1232–47*, 202.

[3] M. T. Clanchy, 'Did Henry III Have a Policy?', *History*, 53 (1968), 203–16.

[4] Carpenter, 'King, Magnates and Society: The Personal Rule of King Henry III, 1234–1258', in his *Reign of Henry III*, 75–106.

hoped to lead a crusade, and took the cross in 1250. His aspirations, however, far exceeded the reality of what he achieved; he was never the major player on the European stage that he imagined himself to be.

Henry took a deep interest in the detailed workings of government in England. In 1256, for example, he appeared at the exchequer, and made a speech setting out the fines that were to be paid by sheriffs and others if they were late appearing at Michaelmas and Easter. It was unusual for a king to intervene directly in such a matter; that he did so strongly suggests that it was on his own initiative. It was also typical of him that the heavy penalties he demanded were not put into effect; he was a man all too ready to back away.[5] The king's political methods were demonstrated in 1242, when he sought a subsidy. Faced with a general refusal, he summoned men one by one, as if, said Matthew Paris, he were a priest asking people to confess. Each was told how much others had promised, and was shown a roll recording the amounts, but his trickery failed to persuade many, so determined were they to stick to the line that they had agreed in common.[6]

For all his grand ideas about what it meant to be a king, Henry was a nervous man. When a madman tried to murder him by climbing through a window at Woodstock in 1238, his response was to have iron bars fitted across every possible entry point to his chambers, even including the outflow of the royal latrine at Westminster.[7] In 1258 he was terrified by the thunder and lightning of a storm that erupted when he was travelling by boat along the Thames. When, in the same year, the barons appeared armed at the Westminster parliament, the king said, 'What is it, my lords? Wretch that I am, are you taking me captive?' This was hardly the reaction of a confident king.[8]

The king was a great enthusiast for building, and something of a perfectionist when it came to detail. When he had the Tower of London whitewashed in 1240, he ordered drainpipes to be fitted right down to ground level, so that the walls would not be stained by rainwater. The interior of Winchester castle demonstrated the king's taste. The hall had a tiled floor and glazed windows. A *mappa mundi* decorated one wall; stained glass added a further touch of luxury. In the king's chamber Bible stories were painted within circles on the green walls, which were further decorated with gold stars. The queen's chamber had a marble fireplace, and was fully panelled in wood. The king's main passion was for the rebuilding of Westminster abbey. He gave England a

---

[5] Carpenter, 'Matthew Paris and Henry III's Speech at the Exchequer', in his *Reign of Henry III*, 137–50.
[6] Paris, *Chron. Maj.* iv. 182.
[7] *KW* i. 122.
[8] 'Annals of Tewkesbury', in *Ann. Mon.* i. 164.

magnificent church that could match the great cathedrals of France. Whether Henry of Reyms, one of its builders, was a native of Reims, or an Englishman who had worked there for some time, is of little import; what is plain is the connection that existed between the great English church and one of the triumphs of French thirteenth-century architecture. The church at Westminster had an eclectic character, for it included the remarkable Cosmati pavement, the work of Italian craftsmen, quite distinctive in style and manner. The concept of the building as a whole, however, as well as much of its detailing, was strongly French.[9] The Londoners who gazed in admiration at the great new church must also have been impressed by the extensive works that the king ordered at the Tower of London, where it has been estimated that he spent almost £10,000.[10] Henry never visited Ireland, but he contemplating doing so in the late 1240s and in preparation had a hall built at Dublin, which was to be decorated with portraits of himself and his queen surrounded by the Irish magnates.[11]

There is no doubting Henry's personal piety; the rebuilding of Westminster abbey was just one reflection of this. He had laudable ambitions in alms-giving, and in 1263 ordered his officials to provide for no less than 100,000 poor at the feast of St Edward, a quite impractical number.[12] Unlike his son Edward I, Henry was not superstitious; he had no truck with the story of the Anglo-Saxon St Frideswide and her curse on royalty who entered the city of Oxford.

THE EARLY YEARS

The legacy of Henry III's minority, which finally ended in 1227, was mixed.[13] When King John died in 1216, England was in the throes of civil war. The throne had been offered to Louis, eldest son of Philip II of France, who had established himself in the south-east and had control of London. The position of the young Henry III, aged 9, was precarious in the extreme. Yet the leadership provided by William Marshal, earl of Pembroke, acting with the assistance of the papal legate Guala, proved decisive. Dover castle held out against the French. In 1217 the Marshal was victorious at the battle of Lincoln, and Hubert de Burgh achieved naval success against the French off Sandwich. Reissues of Magna Carta, in revised form, in 1216 and 1217, were an important

[9] Binski, *Westminster Abbey*, 10–51.
[10] *KW* i. 714; ii. 710, 861. For Westminster abbey, see above, 44.
[11] *Calendar of Documents relating to Ireland*, ed. H. S. Sweetman and G. F. Handcock (London, 1875–86), vol. i, no. 2793.
[12] *CPR 1358–66*, 202–3.
[13] For this period, see Carpenter, *The Minority of Henry III*, and R. Stacey, *Politics, Policy and Finance Under Henry III, 1216–1245* (Oxford, 1987).

element in political reconciliation. The finances of the kingdom slowly began to recover. The achievements of the minority government in rebuilding the country were remarkable; the task had been immense. However, there were problems. The Marshal died in 1219, and Pandulf, who succeeded Guala as papal legate, left England in 1221. Political unity was rent by conflict between Hubert de Burgh, the justiciar, and Peter des Roches, bishop of Winchester and guardian of the king. In 1223 civil war seemed close, but Hubert de Burgh, with Stephen Langton, archbishop of Canterbury, gained control. A major redistribution of control of royal castles was an important step. In the following year Falkes de Bréauté, one of John's former mercenary captains, was humbled when his castle of Bedford fell to royal forces. Magna Carta was reissued once more, in 1225, and a tax granted that helped to transform the financial situation. In 1227 the king declared that, with the agreement of the magnates, he would from now on issue charters under his own seal. Although this was not a full declaration of his majority, it marked the end of the minority and the start of Henry's personal rule. The minority had seen Plantagenet authority restored, but factional divisions remained.

The declaration of 1227 was not a revolutionary step in any way; Hubert de Burgh remained the dominant figure in government, but he faced increasing difficulties. The king was enthusiastic about the prospect of a campaign in Poitou, and he was understandably angry at the failure of the plans to mount an expedition in 1229. He considered rightly that de Burgh had been less than wholehearted about the operation. When the campaign did take place in the following year, the results were not what he expected.[14] Nor were expeditions into Wales in 1228 and 1231 any more successful. De Burgh also faced difficulties over demands for a reduction in the extent of the royal forest. In 1232 he failed to persuade the magnates to make a grant of taxation. At the same time, he was very successful in terms of his own personal aggrandisement. He was created earl of Kent, and he was firmly established in the Welsh marches and Wales. He held the powerful lordship of the Three Castles, and received hereditary grants of Montgomery, Cardigan, and Carmarthen, among many others. He was even quit of the jurisdiction of shire and hundred courts, and given the right on his estates to hold all pleas that sheriffs would normally have been responsible for.[15] Resentment was inevitable.

In 1232 de Burgh lost power.[16] His fall was engineered by Peter des Roches when he returned from five years abroad, in which he had increased his reputation by going on crusade. With him came the return to power of men

---

[14] See below, 294–5.   [15] *Cal. Ch. Rolls*, i. 12–13, 54, 81, 83, 100.

[16] Hubert's fall is analysed by Carpenter, 'The Fall of Hubert de Burgh', in his *Reign of Henry III*, 45–60; and see also N. Vincent, *Peter des Roches: An Alien in English Politics 1205–1238* (Cambridge, 1996), 303–20.

who had lost in a bitter struggle in 1223–4. Some were English, such as the earl of Chester and Brian de Lisle, but des Roches, whose own origins lay in Touraine, inevitably relied on his fellow countrymen from the dominions in France that had been lost by John. Engelard de Cigogné was one unpopular figure, but the most important was Peter de Rivallis, very probably a nephew of des Roches.[17] Hubert failed to provide the king with the revenues he needed, especially for war with the Welsh. 'We have at present no money with us and are in the greatest need,' claimed Henry. The justiciar did his best to maintain his position, but accusations that he was involved in riots directed against Italian clerics appointed by the pope to benefices in England brought him down. He was driven from the court, and hauled in fetters from a chapel in which he had sought sanctuary. He was sent to the Tower, put on trial, and sent to Devizes castle as an abject prisoner for an indefinite period. He had to surrender the lands he held from the crown.

The regime headed by des Roches and de Rivallis was, it used to be argued, characterized by innovation and a new sense of efficiency in financial management. De Rivallis was appointed sheriff to over twenty-one counties, and this was seen as the first step in a radical review of royal finances at a local level. Improvements in exchequer record-keeping were accompanied by determined efforts to collect debts owed to the crown. In practice, it seems more likely that the reason why so many counties were put in des Rivallis's hands was in order to facilitate their eventual redistribution to new sheriffs. In some cases, when new sheriffs were appointed, the charges they were expected to pay were increased; in others, however, the level was lowered. The intention of the new regime was to put as much power as possible into the hands of its supporters, and there are few signs of de Roches, de Rivallis, and their associates carrying out significant financial reforms. Instead, it seems that the excessive concentration of power into the hands of one man led to muddle and mismanagement. In particular, the way in which the administration of all escheats and wardships was entrusted to him alone created confusion and inadequate accounting. Financial solvency came as a result of the grant of a tax of a fortieth in 1232, not as a result of greater administrative efficiency.[18]

The ways in which de Rivallis overreached himself were many, and they soon brought him down. His acquisition of de Burgh's interests in south Wales, such as the lordship of the Three Castles of Grosmont, White Castle,

---

[17] I have adopted the spelling 'de Rivallis', following Vincent's arguments. Peter is also known as des Rivaux, and as des Rievaux. Roger of Wendover regarded him as des Roches's son, but a more distant relationship seems more probable: Vincent, *Peter des Roches*, 27, 293.
[18] The older view was the work of M. H. Mills, 'The Reforms at the Exchequer (1232–1242)', *TRHS*, 4th ser., 10 (1927), 111–34; for criticism of it, see Vincent, *Peter des Roches*, 343–57, and Carpenter, *Reign of Henry III*, 163–6.

and Skenfrith, aroused the hostility of the lords of the marches. Grants to him of lands in Ireland following de Burgh's fall were resented by the young Richard Marshal, and his associates. In England one of Richard's close associates, Gilbert Basset, came under attack from the regime headed by the bishop of Winchester, Peter des Roches. He had been granted the manor of Upavon in Wiltshire by Henry III in 1229, but in 1233 the manor was given to Peter de Maulay, an adherent of Peter. This was followed by the loss of the manor of Sutton in Surrey, which Basset had held since John's reign. The situation was further complicated by the desertion of some Marshal adherents to the faction headed by des Roches and de Rivallis.[19] Richard had many reasons for disliking the regime headed by des Roches, but the root of his problems lay in the threat to his power and the injustice done to his followers. The outcome was civil war in the Welsh marches. Early in 1234 the Marshal left Wales, and went to Ireland, where his lands were under severe pressure. Roger of Wendover claimed that de Rivallis sent letters under the king's seal, but of which the king was kept in ignorance, that told Maurice FitzGerald, Walter and Hugh de Lacy, Richard de Burgh, and others in Ireland that the Marshal had been found guilty of treason and had been exiled from England.[20] This tale was probably the flight of fancy of a conspiracy theorist, but the outcome of the Marshal's Irish adventure was his severe wounding in battle, and subsequent death in April 1234.[21]

The king had already faced a major crisis at a council in February, when Edmund of Abingdon, archbishop elect of Canterbury, spoke out against Peter des Roches and Peter de Rivallis in forthright terms. They were responsible for everything that had gone wrong since the loss of Normandy in 1204. Native-born Englishmen were driven from the king's counsels. The law of the land was overturned, and it was most unlikely that proper accounts would be presented for the wardships and escheats that they held. In April the king bowed to the pressure on him, notably in the form of threats of excommunication, and dismissed des Roches. Henry declared, according to Roger of Wendover, that had de Rivallis not been a priest, he would have torn out both his eyes. The Poitevin supporters of the pair were also ordered back to their homeland. Reconciliation with the Marshal was ordered.[22] This was too late; the Marshal had already died. The remaining rebels were restored to favour, as was Hubert de Burgh, at least in nominal terms.

The regime that emerged out of this crisis was a moderate one, dominated by the archbishop of Canterbury, the earls of Cornwall and Lincoln, and men

---

[19] Vincent, *Peter des Roches*, 334–6, 377–8.   [20] Wendover, iii. 72–3.
[21] Vincent, *Peter des Roches*, 372–4, 377; B. Smith, 'Irish Politics, 1220–1245', in *TCE* viii. 13–21.
[22] Wendover, iii. 75–9.

such as Geoffrey of Crowcombe and Ralph FitzNicholas, the stewards of the household. The treasurer and chancellor, who were bishops of Carlisle and Chichester respectively, also had major parts to play. It is likely that there was considerable jockeying for power, but none of the obvious contenders emerged in a dominant position. Instead, the situation was transformed with the king's marriage in 1236 to Eleanor of Provence. With her came her uncle William of Savoy, bishop-elect of Valence. He rapidly established himself in power, with astonishing skill. He obtained the ear of the pliable king, and soon drove the household stewards from office. William was appointed as chief councillor, and swiftly began a programme of financial and administrative reform. Inquiries were set up into the value of the demesne lands held by the crown, and into the knights' fees which owed service to the crown.[23] The new regime did not succeed in all it wanted. According to Matthew Paris, the chancellor, Ralph Neville, was asked to give up his office, but he said that there was no way he could do this: he had been appointed by common counsel of the realm, and it was only by common assent that he could be removed.[24] In other respects, the regime moved fast and acted thoroughly. In 1237 there was a shake-up of the shrievalties, with new appointments made to seventeen counties. The new men appointed were not creatures of the court, but local men, selected not through political influence, but by the exchequer officials who were looking for men who would accept, and carry through, new policies. They were appointed on much less favourable terms than their predecessors, and no longer had charge of the royal demesnes. They swore oaths not to accept bribes and to be moderate in their demands. Royal revenues rose as a result of these changes.[25] Much work was done to audit accounts, and to collect all debts due from taxes levied since 1225. William of Savoy was not the only man driving change in this period. William Raleigh, chief justice of the King's Bench, was probably responsible for the Provisions of Merton, issued early in 1236, and for changes in the way that the law was administered. For example, an order went out in April 1236 that all cases involving a questionable point of law should be transferred to the King's Bench.[26] It is very possible that Raleigh was the main author of the great legal treatise known as Bracton, one of the corner-stones of English law in this period. Much of the treatise was written in the 1220s or 1230s, with revisions made in the 1250s. The two judges most cited in

[23] Stacey, *Politics, Policy and Finance*, 40, 93–5, 96–8.
[24] Carpenter, 'Chancellor Ralph de Neville and Plans of Political Reform', in his *Reign of Henry III*, 62, accepts this story, but Stacey, *Politics, Policy and Finance*, 100, dismisses it as the result of confusion between the events of 1236 and 1238.
[25] Carpenter, 'Decline of the Curial Sheriff', 167–71.
[26] Stacey, *Politics, Policy and Finance*, 105.

it were Raleigh and Martin of Patishall, whose clerk Raleigh had been. Henry of Bracton was, in turn, Raleigh's clerk.[27]

It was William Raleigh who sparked off a new crisis in 1237. In January a parliament met to hear the chief justice put the case for the grant of a new tax of a thirtieth. The argument was expressed in terms of the failure of past officials to account properly for the royal receipts, and Raleigh promised that the income from the tax would be spent on the needs of the realm, according to the advice of elected magnates. The request was not well received. King Henry had to promise to confirm Magna Carta. Earl Warenne, William de Ferrers, and John FitzGeoffrey were added to the membership of the royal council. The latter replaced Geoffrey of Crowcombe as royal steward.[28]

In January 1238 opposition came from what must have been a totally unexpected quarter. The king's brother Richard, earl of Cornwall, took violent exception to the secret marriage of his sister Eleanor to Simon de Montfort, earl of Leicester. Eleanor was the widow of William Marshal, earl of Pembroke, elder brother of Richard Marshal; Simon, at this stage of his career, was little more than a foreign adventurer seeking his way in Henry's court. There were also objections to the marriage of the daughter of John de Lacy, earl of Lincoln, to the son of the earl of Gloucester. More general arguments also appear to have been put, over the question of the composition of the royal council. Richard of Cornwall took to arms, along with Gilbert Marshal, earl of Pembroke (the brother of William and Richard Marshal), the earl of Winchester, and others. The issue never came to a fight. Henry agreed to accept the terms demanded of him; Simon de Montfort and the earl of Lincoln made their peace with Richard of Cornwall. This amounted to a betrayal of the baronial cause; for Matthew Paris, Richard's reputation was gravely blackened. The chronicler would have thought it blacker still had he been aware of the 6,000 mark bribe that Richard accepted. The problem for historians about what was no more than a small-scale rising is to determine whether, and to what extent, wider and more fundamental issues were raised than that of the king's sister's marriage. Matthew Paris is the main source for these events. He stated that the king agreed to accept certain conditions, which were duly written down, sealed, and made public. What these were, however, is not clear, but they probably related to the tax of a thirtieth, and how it was to be spent. It may well be, though the connection cannot be proved, that it was as a result of the rebellion and the

---

[27] *Bracton De Legibus et Consuetudines Angliae*, ed. and trans. S. E. Thorne, 4 vols. (Cambridge, Mass., 1968–77). P. Brand, 'The Age of Bracton', in J. Hudson (ed.), *The History of English Law: Centenary Essays on 'Pollock and Maitland'* (Oxford, 1996), 65–89, summarizes the debate on the date and authorship of Bracton.
[28] Paris, *Chron. Maj.* iii. 3804; Stacey, *Politics, Policy and Finance*, 112–15.

demands made during it that William of Savoy left England, not to return. He died in Italy in 1239.[29]

In 1238 the chancellor, Ralph Neville, lost control of his office. He had been in charge of the chancery since 1218, and had held the title of chancellor since 1226. He quarrelled with the king over the issue of the bishopric of Winchester, vacant as result of the death of Peter des Roches, which he sought for himself, and to which the chapter elected him. Henry wanted the see for William of Savoy, bishop-elect of Valence, and persuaded the pope to quash the choice of Neville. As a result, the seal was taken from Neville, though he was allowed to retain the title of chancellor until his death in 1244.[30] Neville had not been the chapter's first choice. That had been the justice William Raleigh. The king's retort when he heard this showed a flash of the anger he had inherited from his Angevin forebears: 'You refused the bishop-elect of Valence, saying he was a man of blood, and you elect William Raleigh, who has killed more men with his tongue than the other has with his sword.' Raleigh, not surprisingly, withdrew from government after this. The continuing dispute over Winchester illustrated the king's determination and, at the same time, his readiness to support a cause that proved increasingly insupportable. An appeal to Rome by the chapter, seeking the right of free election so that, as Matthew Paris had it, they would not have to accept a foreigner imposed on them, made the king furious.[31] Raleigh, meanwhile, was elected to the see of Norwich. The Winchester chapter received papal permission to proceed. The consequent election was divided, with a majority still wanting Raleigh and the minority, Boniface of Savoy. The king displayed his fury in 1243, refusing to greet Raleigh with the customary kiss of peace. Henry ordered the gates of Winchester to be shut against the new bishop. Raleigh went barefoot to the gates of the city, and finding them closed against him, imposed an interdict on the place. Eventually, in 1244, Henry accepted the papal verdict in the case, and abandoned his attempts to prevent Raleigh's installation.[32]

There was a striking failure in these years to establish a solid, lasting regime. The dominant figure from 1239 until his death in 1241 was Stephen Segrave, who had been justiciar from 1232–4. He was a man of obscure origins, a cleric who abandoned his orders to become a knight. Matthew Paris caustically remarked of him that he 'managed almost all the affairs of the kingdom at his

---

[29] Paris, *Chron. Maj.* iii. 475–9; N. Denholm-Young, *Richard of Cornwall* (Oxford, 1947), 35–9; Stacey, *Politics, Policy and Finance*, 119–22.

[30] Carpenter, 'Chancellor Ralph Neville and Plans of Political Reform', in his *Reign of Henry III*, 62–3; Paris, *Chron. Maj.* iii. 491, 525.

[31] Paris, *Chron. Maj.* iii. 494, 630.

[32] Powicke, *King Henry III and the Lord Edward*, i. 271–3; Paris, *Chron. Maj.* iv. 263–6.

will, but always more in his own interests than in the commonwealth's'.[33] The government in the early 1240s contained few men of high rank and influence. Paul Piper, steward of the household and a man of humble origins, became the king's chief councillor along with the clerk John Mansel in 1244. These two were described as 'prudent and circumspect', but for all their ability, they lacked status. The tensions of the time were clear in 1241, when Peter of Savoy determined to hold a tournament, in which he and the foreigners of the court challenged the nobility of England. Various Englishmen, however, were bribed to join the alien cause, which resulted in much understandable bad feeling. The situation was only resolved when the king gave orders cancelling the event. Tournaments at this time were not the courtly events of later period, and were capable of developing into small-scale battles. It was from injuries received in a tournament that Gilbert Marshal, along with one of his knights, died later in the same year.[34]

In 1244 there were renewed political difficulties as a result of the king's demand for taxation. Henry put the request for a grant personally in parliament, explaining that it was needed to pay off the debts incurred in the recent Gascon campaign. The magnates, lay and ecclesiastical, agreed that they should establish common cause, and set up a committee of twelve to take matters forward. There were complaints that the terms of Magna Carta were being ignored and previous grants of taxation had not been spent to the profit of the king or the kingdom. Writs had been issued that were contrary to justice, and the demand was made for the appointment of a chancellor and justiciar who would run the affairs of state properly. The king refused to act under compulsion, but agreed to consider the issues that had been raised. A date was set for a new meeting of parliament. Negotiations were lengthy, as the king tried to divide his opponents. A papal letter encouraging the prelates to make a grant was produced. The earl of Leicester and others set out the king's position to the clergy, and explained the need for a tax so that the government could deal with the dangers of war in Gascony and rebellion in Wales. In the event, the opposition to the king came to nothing, for Henry abandoned his request for taxation, so depriving his critics of their one effective weapon, the power to impose conditions on a grant. In the following year the king obtained agreement for the collection of an aid on the occasion of the marriage of his eldest daughter, a tax he was fully entitled to collect.[35] This crisis has attracted much attention, for in his account of it Matthew Paris included a statement of the terms that the committee of twelve agreed, a document that has become known as the 'paper constitution'.

[33] Paris, *Chron. Maj.* iv. 169, trans. Stacey, *Politics, Policy and Finance*, 134–5.
[34] Paris, *Chron. Maj.* iv. 88, 135–6, 294.   [35] Ibid. iv. 362–74.

The most striking provision of the paper constitution was for the appoint-ment of four magnates who would be members of the royal council. Two of them should be present at all times at court, to hear complaints and remedy grievances. These councillors should supervise the expenditure of the money raised in taxes granted by all, and they should act as conservators of liberties. The document also provided for the election of the justiciar and the chancellor. Measures included the revocation of writs that had been issued contrary to custom.[36] The document was not put into effect, and one suggestion is that Matthew Paris inserted it at the wrong point in his chronicle, that it belonged in 1238. It certainly sits somewhat uneasily in the chronicler's narrative for 1244, but provided that it is read as no more than a draft, never put into effect, there are no compelling arguments for redating it.[37] What is significant about the document is not its date, but the fact that so radical a solution to the political problems of this period was suggested. The four were envisaged as possessing remarkably comprehensive authority, but perhaps more striking still was the ultimate authority which it was envisaged lay with the political community of the realm.

At this juncture the level of the king's financial demands was a central issue, while it was also considered that the money raised had not been spent as it should have been. Matthew Paris inserted in his chronicle a list of all the taxes that had been levied since 1224. There had been a tax on ploughlands, a fifteenth on movable goods, a scutage, a fortieth, a thirtieth, and a feudal aid assessed on ploughlands. These were not the only ways in which money had been raised; the list also included the sums that the king had demanded as gifts on the occasion of the birth of his eldest son.[38] The overall burden of taxation was not in fact particularly high, when seen in comparison with the levels that had been witnessed under Richard I, or those that would be seen in the 1290s or late 1330s, but the principles were strongly felt. Resistance to taxation meant that Henry III was not able to negotiate a tax in 1244, or indeed any further direct taxes after that of 1237. There were arbitrary, but less satisfactory, alternatives. In 1253 a feudal aid was collected, ostensibly to pay for the knighting of the king's eldest son, and in the same year a tallage of 5,000 marks was imposed on the Jews. The request in the following year for a grant of taxation to meet the king's expenses in Gascony met with an understandable refusal.

---

[36] Paris, *Chron. Maj.* iv. 366–8.

[37] N. Denholm-Young, 'The "Paper Constitution" Attributed to 1244', in his *Collected Papers on Medieval Subjects* (Oxford, 1946), 130–53; C. R. Cheney, 'The "Paper Constitution" Pre-served by Matthew Paris', *EHR* 65 (1950), 213–21.

[38] Paris, *Chron. Maj.* iv. 373–4.

The difficulties in obtaining grants of taxation meant that the crown had to find other means of raising money. In 1241 the system that had been in place since 1236 whereby sheriffs received allowances for their expenses and accounted for their profits at the exchequer was changed. Sheriffs were in future charged increments in addition to the traditional amount due from their counties. In 1241–2 the increments totalled £1,540. Ten years later they amounted to about £2,320, and by 1256–7 the sum was almost £2,500. This inevitably meant that greater pressures were loaded onto the counties, with higher sums charged on the local hundreds, and every effort made to increase revenue.[39] This naturally added to the powerful undercurrents of hostility to Henry's government that existed in the shires. Levies on the Jews were imposed at levels that were unsustainable in the long term.

FOREIGNERS

Although finance remained a significant issue, other matters came to the fore in the 1240s. One was the role of foreigners in Henry III's court and administration.[40] Matthew Paris made much of this, but the extent to which the writing of one somewhat xenophobic individual mirrored more general attitudes is a difficult question. Matthew was enraged by the two main groups of aliens, as he termed them, the Savoyards and the Poitevins. The Savoyards obtained their introduction to England through Henry III's marriage to Eleanor of Provence, whose mother was Beatrice of Savoy. Rarely can a queen have been able to use her position as Eleanor was, to advance her compatriots. Henry III was only too receptive to her persuasive charms and the influence of her relations. The queen's uncle Peter of Savoy came to England in 1240, and at once received the full force of Henry III's generosity. In 1241 he was granted the honour of Richmond, and then that of Pevensey, along with the wardship of John de Warenne. In 1241 another uncle, Boniface of Savoy, was elected to the see of Canterbury. His compatriot Peter of Aigueblanche had become bishop of Hereford in 1240. The link between England and Savoy was cemented by treaty in 1246, when the count of Savoy agreed to become Henry III's vassal for four of his castles, which controlled major Alpine passes. For young and ambitious Savoyards, both laymen and clerics, England must have seemed like the Promised Land. Offices, good marriages, lands, and influence were there almost for the asking. No fewer than 170 members of the Savoyard connection have been identified in England, two-thirds of them clerics. Thirty-nine received lands from the king, and about forty had revenues

[39] Carpenter, *Reign of Henry III*, 171–2.
[40] For a valuable discussion of the Savoyards and Poitevins from which much of the detail that follows is taken, see H. Ridgeway, 'King Henry III and the "Aliens", 1236–1272', in *TCE* iii. 81–92.

of at least 100 marks. Eble des Montibus married Joan de Somery, the wealthy widow of the royal steward Godfrey de Crowcombe. Peter of Geneva married Maud de Lacy; after his death she married Geoffrey de Geneville, who came from Champagne, and who was closely related to the Savoyard dynasty.[41] There was some inevitable hostility to the marriages of English heiresses to foreigners in this way. Joan Piper took exception to Stephen de Salines as her proposed husband. To the king's fury, she married John de Grey.[42] The petition of the barons at the Oxford parliament of 1258 demanded that the practice of marrying heiresses to foreigners should cease.[43]

The second group of foreigners was the Poitevins. They were a smaller group than the Savoyards. It has been estimated that they probably numbered about a hundred, of whom some two-thirds were laymen. Only twenty-eight obtained significant revenues from Henry III. The decline of English influence in Poitou, with the failure of Henry III's campaigns, led to some Poitevins abandoning their homeland and seeking fresh pastures in England. Peter Chaceporc was one of the first. His brother was married to a relation of Henry III's through his mother, Isabella of Angoulême. He became keeper of the wardrobe in 1241, succeeding Peter of Aigueblanche and retaining the post until his death in 1254.[44] There was little problem in employing such a man, an efficient administrator. The Poitevins who aroused resentment were Henry III's half-brothers, Isabella's children by Hugh de Lusignan, count of La Marche. In 1247 the king invited his four half-brothers William de Valence, and Aymer, Geoffrey, and Guy de Lusignan to England, along with their sister Alice. The flow of patronage was swiftly diverted in their direction. In the absence of more permanent rewards, the two younger brothers, Geoffrey and Guy, received substantial incomes from the exchequer, even though they did not settle permanently in England. William did exceptionally well, with his marriage to Joan de Mountchesney, the Pembroke heiress. Aymer was a cleric, and duly received the bishopric of Winchester. Alice married the young John, Earl Warenne. It has been pointed out that in many cases such marriages worked well and helped to integrate the foreigners; John de Warenne was heartbroken when his wife died in 1256. In contrast, the marriage of Gilbert de Clare to Henry III's niece Alice de Lusignan in 1253 appears to have been a disaster in personal terms. This may help to explain the xenophobia that marked Gilbert's political career in the 1260s.[45]

---

[41] M. Howell, *Eleanor of Provence: Queenship in Thirteenth-Century England* (Oxford, 1998), 30–1, 47, 49–53.
[42] Ann. Dunstable, 182–3.
[43] *DBM* 80.
[44] Tout, *Chapters*, i. 263–4.
[45] Ridgeway, 'King Henry III and the "Aliens"', 88; M. Altschul, *A Baronial Family in Medieval England: The Clares, 1217–1314* (Baltimore, 1965), 103.

It is hardly surprising that newcomers such as the Savoyards and Poitevins were resented. Some of them received very considerable grants, or acquired substantial lands through marriage. In the southern Welsh marches William de Valence, through marriage, possessed much of the great Marshal inheritance. Ludlow and much of the Lacy inheritance went likewise to Peter of Geneva. The power of the bishop of Hereford added to the Savoyard influence in this region. Peter of Savoy held the great lordship of Richmond in the north. Maud de Lacy's marriages to Peter of Geneva and Geoffrey de Geneville were one of the ways in which the Savoyards obtained a substantial foothold in Ireland. The extent to which Henry's patronage was directed towards the foreigners is demonstrated by the fact that in the years from 1247 to 1258 twenty-four wardships were granted to Poitevins, whereas earls and barons outside the court circle received only seven. The rewards Henry gave to one Poitevin, William de St Ermino, demonstrate his generosity. His first grant, in 1253, was of an annual fee of £20 a year. This was soon raised to 40 marks. By 1258 he had received the marriages of two widows, £40 of land from one wardship, and £20 from another. He received a wardship and marriage, which he sold on, and was given the royal manor of Havering at farm. It is hardly surprising that the opposition would demand William's expulsion from England in 1258.[46] England did not provide an inexhaustible supply of land for royal patronage; one solution was to turn to Ireland, where from 1248 the king made a considerable number of grants of land that was at best no more than half-conquered. Close links were created between the court and Ireland, though a plan to grant Geoffrey de Lusignan £500 in Thomond was unsuccessful.[47]

Tournaments continued to provide a focus for the rivalry between the aliens and the English nobility. In 1247 the king prohibited one that was to be between Richard, earl of Gloucester, and his followers, and Guy de Lusignan. In 1249 many English knights were defeated in a tournament at Brackley by the court aliens, who had been joined on this occasion by their former opponent, the earl of Gloucester. The year 1251 saw a further conflict, this time at Rochester, which the English won, forcing their opponents to flee to the town for safety. This, according to Matthew Paris, did much to aggravate the hatred between the English and the foreigners.[48]

At a local level there was hostility towards the way in which the aliens profited from the grants they had received. Their officials were frequently high-handed and oppressive. Although Peter of Savoy employed compatriots

---

[46] S. L. Waugh, *The Lordship of England: Royal Wardships and Marriages in English Society and Politics 1217–1327* (Princeton, 1988), 242–4.

[47] R. F. Frame, 'King Henry III and Ireland: The Shaping of a Peripheral Lordship', in his *Ireland and Britain 1170–1450* (London, 1998), 46–51.

[48] Paris, *Chron. Maj.* iv. 633; v. 83, 265.

as his stewards, it has been pointed out that the stewards and bailiffs employed by the Lusignans were nearly all Englishmen, such as William de Bussay, who served both William de Valence and Geoffrey de Lusignan. Analysis of William de Valence's following shows that only one of the Poitevin knights who accompanied him to England in 1247 remained in his service. His retinue was largely English.[49] The dislike of the Poitevins cannot, therefore, be analysed in simple chauvinist terms. Dislike of them was more because of the patronage they received, and the way in which they behaved, than because of their origins in Poitou.

English resentment at the extent of royal favour to the aliens undoubtedly embittered politics from the late 1240s. The situation was made worse by the rivalry between the Savoyards and Poitevins. In 1252 there was a dispute between Boniface of Savoy and Aymer de Valence, bishop elect of Winchester, which required royal intervention before the two were reconciled.[50] There was competition between the two groups for control of the heir to the throne, Edward. He was very much under the influence of the Savoyards, and particularly of his uncle Peter of Savoy, until 1257. Then, he made common cause with the Poitevins. William de Valence lent him funds in return for the towns of Stamford and Grantham. Edward was planning to make Geoffrey de Lusignan his seneschal in Gascony, and Guy keeper of Oléron and the Channel Islands.[51] The Savoyards must have been very put out at this, and it is not surprising that Peter of Savoy was one of those seeking reform, and the expulsion of the Lusignans, in 1258.

One foreigner who was to prove more important than any other actor in the dramas of Henry's reign was not a member of either the Savoyard or Poitevin faction. Simon de Montfort's family came from the Île de France, and had a claim to the earldom of Leicester through marriage.[52] Simon arrived in England in 1230 to try to make this claim good. Negotiations with Ranulf, earl of Chester, custodian of the Leicester lands, were successful. Henry III gave his full backing to Simon, whose powers of persuasion were clearly considerable. By the late 1230s Simon was high in the king's immediate circle. In 1238 he married Henry's sister Eleanor, widow of William Marshal, a strong-minded and energetic woman. The marriage was clandestine; it was an extraordinary move for so important a lady, who had sworn vows of chastity, to marry a foreigner without any consultation taking place with the English magnates. Henry must have been delighted when Simon's first-born was christened

[49] H. Ridgeway, 'William de Valence and his *Familiares*, 1247–72', *Historical Research*, 65 (1992), 239–57.

[50] 'Annals of Tewkesbury', in *Ann. Mon.* i. 151; Paris, *Chron. Maj.* v. 348–54.

[51] Prestwich, *Edward I*, 21–2.

[52] For Simon de Montfort's career, see J. R. Maddicott, *Simon de Montfort* (Cambridge, 1994).

Henry after him. In 1239 Simon was given the title of earl of Leicester; his importance is demonstrated by the fact that in the first half of the year he witnessed more royal charters than anyone else. In August, however, Henry turned against his brother-in-law. Simon had used Henry's name as security for a loan without permission, and the king accused him of having seduced Eleanor prior to her marriage. Serious as this breach was, it did not drive a permanent wedge between the two men. In the 1240s, when he was in England, Earl Simon appears to have lent full support to his brother-in-law. In 1248 Henry appointed him as his lieutenant in Gascony for seven years. The methods Simon adopted there were tough. There was no indication of the future idealistic reformer in the way he seized castles, took hostages, and disregarded legal custom. His rule aroused protest, and in 1252 he was brought back to England and put on trial in Westminster Hall. Words between Simon and the king were bitter. 'Who can believe that you are a Christian? Have you ever confessed?' asked Simon, as he went for the jugular, accusing the king of bad faith in failing to adhere to the terms of the agreement between the two men.[53] Simon did not lose the case, and a settlement of sorts was achieved later in the year, when the king promised the earl £500 to cover his losses in Gascony and made elaborate arrangements for the payment of a substantial annual fee of 600 marks.

Earl Simon went to join Henry III in Gascony in 1253, and his presence was influential in persuading the king's opponents there to submit to him. It appeared that relations between the king and Montfort had been repaired. There were, however, many complex financial issues between the two men that were not resolved to Montfort's satisfaction. There was the long-standing issue of the payments for his wife's dower. She was entitled to this as the earl of Pembroke's widow, and felt cheated of her rights. Henry III had agreed to pay this himself, at a rate of £400 a year. The scheme was that he should then recover the money from the Pembroke heirs. The sum was inadequate, and payment was intermittent. There were also difficulties over the payment of the 600 mark fee due to the earl. By the end of 1257 the debt owed to Montfort stood at £1,199. Yet he continued to cooperate with the king, and Henry continued to employ him. It made sense to use him on diplomatic business, for he had extensive connections abroad. He went to Scotland in 1254, and in 1257 was employed as one of the English ambassadors to negotiate with the French. He was a member of the king's council in that year, and witnessed a significant number of royal charters.[54] There was little indication that he would emerge as the king's leading political opponent. Yet, according to Matthew Paris, in

---

[53] Ibid. 87. [54] Ibid. 135–6, 142–3.

1258, after the storm that so terrified the king, Henry met Montfort, who said, 'What are you afraid of? The storm has passed over.' The king replied, 'By God's head, I fear you more than all the thunder and lightning in the world.'[55]

PARLIAMENT

One institutional development in the 1240s and 1250s had a major impact on the way in which politics worked. Parliament was emerging as the key political forum. The term 'parliament' was first used in a legal context, in 1236, when a case was adjourned until parliament next met. It was, of course, nothing new for the king to summon the great men of the realm to discuss matters of state. What was new in this period was the way in which such gatherings were combined with judicial business. The exchequer, chancery, and courts of King's Bench and Common Pleas would all be present at time of parliament. The core of the assembly consisted of the king's council. There was now a proper occasion for the discussion of the great political issues of the day. The king could not obtain grants of taxation without consent, and parliament offered by far the most convenient way of obtaining such consent. As early as 1237 it was clear that the power to grant taxes gave those attending parliaments a weapon for controlling the king.

The composition of these early parliaments cannot be demonstrated from official lists of summons, as can be done from 1290. There are, however, some hints. When Magna Carta was confirmed in 1225, in return for a grant of a fifteenth, it was witnessed by the archbishop of Canterbury and eleven bishops, twenty abbots, the justiciar, nine earls, and twenty-three barons. An equivalent list for 1237 consisted of fourteen bishops, eight earls, and eighteen barons. In 1258 the Oxford parliament was also the occasion for a military summons to deal with Welsh affairs. Twenty-two abbots, five earls, and eighty-seven barons received individual summonses to attend. It is likely that, as under Edward I, the king and his officials decided which magnates were most appropriate to invite to parliamentary assemblies. Some assemblies saw, in addition, wider representation. There is some clear evidence for the summons of knights; indeed, there was precedent for doing this from John's reign. In 1226 four knights were asked to come to Lincoln from each county, to present complaints against the way in which the sheriffs were interpreting the clauses of Magna Carta. In 1254 two knights were summoned from each shire to agree a grant of taxation, which was not in fact forthcoming. For the first time returns survive, giving the names of those selected in Middlesex and Northumberland. In the former case, the first two who were nominated refused to serve and had to be

[55] Paris, *Chron. Maj.* v. 706.

replaced. Evidence for the attendance of knights at other gatherings is not so solid. However, Matthew Paris implies that at parliaments where taxation was discussed, the numbers present were normally large. The preamble to the 1237 grant of a thirtieth claimed, with exaggeration, that consent had been obtained from 'earls, barons, knights and free men for themselves and for their villeins'. This should not be taken literally in the sense of full representation, but interestingly the Tewkesbury annals suggest that urban representatives were present on this occasion, though no mention is made of knights. It is even possible therefore that urban representation preceded that of the counties, and may have been a model for the latter.[56]

THE CHURCH

Part of the general background to the enthusiasm for reform in the mid-thirteenth century was the position in the Church. Innocent III's Lateran Council of 1215 had legislated on a very wide range of issues, and provided a basis for action by the Church in England. Most important was the emphasis placed on pastoral care. Richard le Poore, bishop of Chichester, was present at the council. When he became bishop of Salisbury, he issued an important set of constitutions, which he reissued when he was moved a second time, to the see of Durham, which he held from 1228 to 1237. Similar constitutions were issued in other dioceses, though not, for example, in that of Ely. The matters that were covered included the conduct of the clergy, who were to be tonsured, unmarried, and should behave in a seemly fashion, not getting drunk in taverns. They were not to hold more than one benefice, and simony, the buying and selling of positions in the Church, was forbidden. Regular confession and communion were required of the laity. One verdict is that these constitutions 'fall very short of a determined campaign on the part of the bishops to exterminate the evils which corroded the church and to arouse a spirit of enthusiasm and reform'.[57] However, the fact is that there was, in most dioceses, a programme set out in legislative form intended to deal with abuses. If this could be done in the Church, it could also be done in the secular sphere.

Robert Grosseteste, bishop of Lincoln, was a remarkable man, surely a genius, if not without flaws. He was committed to reform in both Church

---

[56] J. R. Maddicott, 'The Earliest Known Knights of the Shire: New Light on the Parliament of April 1254', *Parliamentary History*, 18 (1999), 112–14; id., ' "An Infinite Multitude of Nobles": Quality, Quantity and Politics in the Pre-Reform Parliaments of Henry III', in *TCE* vii. 19–21, 34–7, 40; *Select Charters and Other Illustrations of English Constitutional History from the Earliest Times to the Reign of Edward the First*, ed. W. Stubbs, 9th edn. rev. H. W. C. Davis (Oxford, 1913), 353, 358, 366; 'Annals of Tewkesbury', in *Ann. Mon.* i. 102.

[57] M. Gibbs and J. Lang, *Bishops and Reform 1215–1272* (Oxford, 1934), 108–13, 122–30.

and State. A notable scholar, Grosseteste was no ivory tower academic, nor was he a man troubled by self-doubt. He tackled the issues of reform within his diocese with determination, undertaking visitations on a wholly novel scale, and taking on pastoral responsibilities in an unprecedented way. Drunken carousing, miracle plays, and Christmas festivities all came in for attack. Some of his reforming ideas were radical and unacceptable: Matthew Paris was not impressed by his method of testing the local nuns for chastity by feeling their breasts.[58] His relationship with Simon de Montfort meant that some of his ideas about the nature of the State and its relationship to the Church found a ready hearer. Near the end of his life, in 1250, he went to Lyons, where he addressed a no doubt incredulous pope on the failings of the Church. Innocent IV proved as unappreciative of Grosseteste's ideas of reform as all save their author must have expected. It may have made logical sense to see the papal curia as the root of all that was wrong in the Church, but it was not good politics to tell the pope this.

There were further strong pressures for reform in the Church, with the influence of the friars.[59] The Dominicans were the first to come to England, in 1221, while the first Franciscans, a little group of nine, arrived in England in 1224. The movement spread very rapidly; its spiritual conception and its ideals of austerity were very attractive. By about 1260 there were thirty-six Dominican houses in England, and a similar number of Franciscan ones. The friars were in the forefront of intellectual change in the thirteenth century. Oxford was one of their most important targets; Adam Marsh was a leading figure among them there. Cambridge also quickly became a significant centre. The friars were closely associated with reforming bishops. Alexander Stavensby of Coventry and Lichfield always had Dominicans in his company, and Robert Grosseteste, bishop of Lincoln, had strong links with the Franciscans, notably Adam Marsh. Grosseteste gave the Franciscans advice, which they gladly received, to study and devote their energies to divinity. The political sympathies of the Franciscans for the cause of reform are very clear. John of Wales, one of the leading Oxford members of the order, writing in the mid-1260s, set out to justify the subjection of rulers to the law, the duty of the prince to choose appropriate councillors, and the obligation on his officials to act equitably, all fundamental principles of the political reformers. Thomas Docking, another Oxford Franciscan, included in his biblical commentaries remarks that can have given his listeners no doubt about his political sympathies.[60]

---

[58] Southern, *Grosseteste*, 156–7, 160, 257–61; Paris, *Chron. Maj.* v. 227.

[59] For a general account, see M. D. Knowles, *The Religious Orders in England* (Cambridge, 1948), i. 127 ff.

[60] Maddicott, *Simon de Montfort*, 253–4.

The political attitudes of the Dominicans were less clear. John of Darlington was a Dominican and an intellectual with a reputation as a theologian and philosopher. He became a councillor and confessor to Henry III, was active as a royal adviser, and under Edward I became a collector of papal taxes in England.[61] The order was particularly favourably regarded by Henry III, and was not such a seedbed of revolutionary ideas as were the Franciscans. There is an argument that the Dominicans may have provided a precedent for the development of parliament, in that the principles of representation might have been copied from the methods used by the friars in their convocations.[62] There is no evidence, however, to demonstrate that there was any connection, and it may just have been that similar solutions sprang from a common ground of political ideas.

In addition to a general commitment to reform, there were specific issues that concerned the Church. There was much resentment at the financial demands of the papacy, aided by the crown. In 1251 Henry III asked the prelates to agree that a tax imposed by the pope, intended to pay for a crusade, should be collected. Agreement of a sort was not reached until 1253, and was made conditional upon the king reconfirming Magna Carta. The money was to be handed over only when the crusade expedition began. Further papal taxes imposed in 1256 created more hostility; since the money was intended to go to the crown, antagonism was directed at both papacy and crown. The monks of Durham wrote of the financial exactions as bringing 'the vilest servitude into the church of Christ'.[63]

POLITICS IN CRISIS, 1258–1264

In 1258 matters came to a head. Events began to unfold that would culminate in that gruesome scene of Simon de Montfort's corpse lying, obscenely mutilated, on the field of battle at Evesham in 1265. One important element in the crisis was hostility to foreigners. The behaviour of the king's half-brothers the Lusignans was a key element in the crisis of 1258. An immediate scandal, which focused attention on this issue, was the attack on 1 April, shortly before parliament began, on some servants of John FitzGeoffrey by a gang operating, so it was claimed, on the orders of Aymer, bishop-elect of Winchester. One of the victims of this assault died of his wounds.[64] On 12 April a powerful group of seven, headed by the earls of Leicester, Gloucester, and Norfolk, with Peter

[61] Knowles, *Religious Orders*, i. 167; W. E. Lunt, *Financial Relations of the Papacy with England to 1327* (Cambridge, Mass., 1939), 313.
[62] E. Barker, *The Dominican Order and Convocation* (Oxford, 1913), 72–4.
[63] Lunt, *Financial Relations*, 271.
[64] Carpenter, 'What Happened in 1258', in his *Reign of Henry III*, 192–3.

of Savoy, John FitzGeoffrey, Hugh Bigod (Norfolk's brother), and Peter de Montfort, made a sworn alliance that appears to have been directed against the Lusignans. At the end of April the earls, barons, and knights went armed to Westminster Hall, laid down their swords, and compelled the king to agree to accept measures of reform, to be determined by a committee of twenty-four. Roger Bigod, earl of Norfolk, took the lead in demanding the removal of the Lusignans: 'Let the wretched and intolerable Poitevins and all foreigners flee from your face.' In June the Oxford parliament took place; one of the demands made by the barons was that all royal castles should be put in charge of native-born Englishmen. After much manoeuvring, and a further parliament at Winchester, the Lusignans were driven out.[65] According to the early four-teenth-century chronicler Walter of Guisborough, in the Winchester parliament it was decided, among other measures, that all foreigners, of whatever status or nationality, should be expelled from the realm. Decisions were made dealing with the problems of minors who held land from both the king and other lords. Sales of wool abroad, or to foreigners, were forbidden, and only English-made cloth was to be worn in England. No other chronicles, nor any record, corroborates this, but the story very probably reflects the temper of the times.[66]

For the king, the most pressing business in 1258 was the Sicilian affair. In 1254 Henry had accepted the papal offer of the Sicilian throne for his second son, Edmund. Pope Innocent IV was anxious to find a candidate who would be an effective alternative to the Hohenstaufen rulers of Sicily and southern Italy. What the papacy wanted above all was financial backing; the terms agreed upon by Henry included not only the sending of a military force to Sicily, but the payment of the debts that had been run up by the papacy there, amounting to some 135,000 marks. In 1255 Rostand, papal nuncio and tax-collector, arrived in England. The young Edmund was ceremonially invested with the Sicilian kingdom. In April 1257 the king paraded his son in parliament, dressed in what passed for south Italian costume, and set out the financial obligations. These were hard to meet. The clergy offered a substantial but inadequate 52,000 marks.[67] The proceeds of loans and taxes on the Church imposed by the pope

[65] Paris, *Chron. Maj.* v. 695–8; 'Annals of Tewkesbury', in *Ann. Mon.* i. 163–5; *DBM* 80–1. Carpenter, 'What Happened in 1258', 183–97, argues strongly that the Tewkesbury account is the most reliable. The chronicle has its difficulties, however. It contains two accounts, not one, with minor differences between them. The author confused and conflated the parliaments at Westminster and Oxford, making it difficult to be clear what he thought happened at each. It is, however, clearer than Matthew Paris's account that it was a demonstration of force at Westminster that compelled the king to accept reform.

[66] Guisborough, 186. See R. F. Treharne, *The Baronial Plan of Reform 1258–63*, 2nd edn. (Manchester, 1971), 80.

[67] Paris, *Chron. Maj.* v. 623–4.

were also insufficient. By 1258 Henry was being threatened with excommunication and his kingdom with interdict as a result of his failure to meet the terms demanded by the papacy, which by now included his sending 8,500 men to fight in Sicily.

Historians have condemned Henry for the grandiose folly of his plans, and for contemporaries, notably Matthew Paris, there was a very clear contrast between the extravagant and unrealistic ambition of putting Edmund on the Sicilian throne and the election of Henry's brother Richard of Cornwall as king of Romans (in effect king of Germany) in 1256. It would, however, be wrong to assume that the Sicilian venture was fatally flawed in its whole conception; after all, in the next decade Charles of Anjou, Louis IX's brother, was to establish himself as ruler of the Sicilian kingdom. Richard I in his crusade had demonstrated that it was possible for an English force to fight to great effect in far distant lands, and the financial burden imposed by the papacy was comparable with the ransom that was paid on Richard's behalf to the emperor Henry VI. The diplomatic preparations that Henry made were skilful and appropriate, and it would have been possible to recruit an effective mercenary force to fight in Sicily.[68] There is no doubt, however, that the affair aroused great hostility, above all from within the English Church. Matthew Paris in his chronicle wrote sarcastically about it, and laid great stress on the financial burden it entailed.

The Sicilian affair helped to bring matters to a head in 1258, when Henry III took the question of the papal demands to parliament. The leading barons pointed out to the pope that the king had undertaken the business without consultation and consent.[69] It would, however, have been remarkable for a major crisis to erupt solely over an issue of foreign policy that did not even directly threaten the security of the realm. This was no more than one element in a complex situation, nor did its significance continue. The last that was heard of it was in 1261, when Henry III complained that the baronial council had not pursued the Sicilian business as they had promised, allegedly leaving him in debt to the tune of 200,000 marks. The council responded that it was not on their advice that the arrangement had been made.[70]

Problems in Wales were another important issue. The position of the marcher lords was threatened, and theirs was a powerful voice in English politics. Rebellion in the north in 1256 was followed by major successes for the Welsh under Llywelyn ap Gruffudd. A royal campaign in 1257 was as

---

[68] B. Weiler, 'Matthew Paris, Richard of Cornwall's Candidacy for the German Throne, and the Sicilian Business', *Journal of Medieval History*, 26 (2000), 71–92; id., 'Henry III and the Sicilian Business: A Reinterpretation', *Historical Research*, 74 (2001), 127–50.

[69] Ann. Dunstable, 170.

[70] *DBM* 230–3.

unsuccessful as were most of Henry III's military ventures. The dejected English forces had to withdraw from Degannwy, driven out of Wales by hunger and the triumphant Welsh. The problem of Wales was high on the royal agenda in 1258. According to Matthew Paris, there was much hostility to a summons of feudal service for a muster in June. The nobles were, it was claimed, being impoverished, and the whole country would be hard-hit by the accompanying levy of scutage.[71] It was inevitable that the Welsh should take advantage of the political troubles affecting England. In 1261 the king complained that he was virtually disinherited in Wales, for the baronial council had promised to deal with the question in 1258 but nothing had been done. As a result, Builth castle was lost, and much land.[72]

By 1258 the government in Henry III's hands was seen as being incompetent and inadequate. The most fundamental step taken in the Oxford parliament was the creation of a new council, which would have executive authority. This council of fifteen was elected by a complex mechanism. The process began with the election of twelve from the royalist side and twelve from the baronial. Each twelve then selected two from the opposing ranks, and the four thus chosen had the authority to choose the council. There were to be three annual parliaments, at which the council would negotiate with baronial representatives. The major ministers, justiciar, treasurer, and chancellor were to hold office for a year, and were accountable to the king and council.[73] This marked a stage forward from the plan worked out in 1244, and appeared to provide an effective means of limiting the king's freedom of action.

The new system worked well in the early, heady days of reform. The king had little alternative other than to accept the decisions of the council. It was not until July 1259 that he was able to take a significant decision without its approval, when he succeeded in having letters of safe conduct issued, permitting a papal envoy, Velascus, to enter the country, bearing a papal bull ordering the restoration of the king's half-brother Aymer to his see of Winchester.[74]

At the Oxford parliament in 1258 the widespread dissatisfaction over the way in which government and law operated at a local level was clear. Legislation was needed to deal with the relationships between lords and their tenants, the procedures of the royal courts, and issues relating to the criminal law. There had been no major act of legislation since Magna Carta; the Provisions of Merton of 1236 was a limited measure (only five clauses of its eleven clauses were actually enacted in 1236).[75] The Petition of the Barons set out the grievances of various groups. Twenty-nine clauses covered a wide range of

---

[71] Paris, *Chron. Maj.* v. 677.   [72] *DBM* 232–3.   [73] *DBM* 96–113.
[74] Treharne, *Baronial Plan of Reform*, 143–4.
[75] P. Brand, *Kings, Barons and Justices: The Making and Enforcement of Legislation in Thirteenth-Century England* (Cambridge, 2003), 409.

issues. Questions of inheritance and feudal custom were important: safeguards were requested to protect the rights of heirs against rapacious lords. Heiresses should not be married to foreigners. There were issues regarding the royal forests. It was thought that the crown had brought back within the forest boundaries lands that had been deforested. Lay landlords requested protection against their land falling into the hands of the Church, as a result of which they would lose valuable rights. Unfair practices of fining men for not appearing at royal courts were condemned. The way in which debts owed to Jewish moneylenders were bought up by great men, who then refused to hand back the lands of the debtor even when he was prepared to pay off the debt, was condemned. Abuse of prise, the king's right to compulsory purchase of food-stuffs, was another subject of complaint. Other matters were also covered. There is much that is striking about this document. It is remarkable that it was drafted in such a short space of time. It betrays no indication of a clerical input, but is purely secular in character. The fact that the grievances it sets out were not simply those of the higher baronage is particularly significant. Many clauses were, of course, in the interests of the great men, but others favoured sub-tenants and ordinary freemen. The document pulled together complaints from very different groups.[76]

There was no quick solution to the problems the Petition pinpointed. At Oxford arrangements were swiftly set up for commissions of four knights in each county to investigate local affairs. Highly detailed articles of inquiry were set out; every aspect of administration, both royal and private, was to be covered. Hugh Bigod, brother of the earl of Norfolk, newly appointed as justiciar, began hearing cases, brought before him by a process of informal complaint, or *querela*. Bigod had no legal training. This may have been an advantage, making it easier for him to cut through the potential complexities of his position. Analysis of the cases that came before him shows that he did a remarkable job. The range of those who brought complaints was most impressive. At one end of the scale were great men such as John FitzGeoffrey, and at the other an outlaw, Richard of Glaston, who was able to use the *querela* procedure against the sheriff of Northampton's men, who had assaulted him. Of course, Bigod could not visit the whole country, and the unfree had no access to his court, but his achievement was none the less remarkable.[77]

When a new parliament sat in October 1258, regret was expressed that matters had not proceeded faster. No legislation had been produced in response to the Petition of the Barons. Now, an ordinance was drafted, and

---

[76] *DBM* 76–91; Brand, *Kings, Barons and Justices*, 20–4.

[77] A. Hershey, 'Success or Failure? Hugh Bigod and Judicial Reform During the Baronial Movement, June 1258–February 1259', in *TCE* v. 65–87.

issued to all counties. The sheriffs were to swear an elaborate oath, in which they promised to do justice to all and to engage in no corrupt practices. New sheriffs were appointed on different terms to those of recent years. They were no longer to hold their counties 'at farm', that is, for a fixed sum. Instead, they were to account for all the money that they actually received. Eighteen new sheriffs (two-thirds of the total), all influential local men, were appointed.[78] There can have been little disagreement over this. In other respects, however, arguments were beginning to surface over the direction that reform was taking. A document known as the Provisions of the Barons of England was probably prepared for the next parliament, which met in February 1259. It dealt at length with the question of the obligation of tenants to attend courts. The document explained that those who were not accustomed to do this, but who had in recent years been compelled by great men and others to do suit of court, should not be put under such pressure in future. This shows how the reformers were moving on from abuses of royal government to discuss issues affecting the administrations of great landlords. The Provisions were part of the debate over what legislation was needed, and were intended as a draft of future measures. They were not put into effect.[79] At the end of March 1259, however, the Ordinances of the Magnates was published. In this document the king's councillors announced that they would observe towards their men the same laws and customs that the king had agreed to. The same terms and procedures that applied to sheriffs would be applied to the officials of baronial liberties and franchises.[80]

Parliament met again in October at Westminster. There was growing frustration at the slow pace of legislative reform. This showed itself in the remarkable protest made by a group calling itself the Community of the Bachelors of England, who protested to Edward, the earl of Gloucester, and members of the council sworn in at Oxford. They pointed out that the king had done all that had been asked of him while the barons had done nothing to improve matters. They threatened to implement the Oxford agreement by other means if the barons did not act. Various suggestions have been made about who formed this group; the most plausible guess is that it was made up of the knights attending the parliament.[81] It would be wrong to make too much of an incident recorded in just one chronicle, but it may well have helped to

---

[78] *DBM* 118–23; Treharne, *Baronial Plan*, 121; H. W. Ridgeway, 'Mid Thirteenth-Century Reformers and the Localities: The Sheriffs of the Baronial Regime, 1258–1261', in P. Fleming, A. Gross, and J. R. Lander (eds.), *Regionalism and Revision: The Crown and its Provinces in England 1200–1650* (London, 1998), 63–70.

[79] *DBM* 122–31; Brand, *Making of the Common Law*, 333–46, and for texts, ibid. 357–67.

[80] *DBM* 130–7; Treharne, *Baronial Plan of Reform*, 137–9.

[81] Burton Annals, in *Ann. Mon.* i. 471; Maddicott, *Simon de Montfort*, 185.

persuade Edward to ally himself with his uncle Simon de Montfort in mid-October. He issued formal letters announcing his commitment to the baronial enterprise.[82] The mysterious bachelors' protest may also have helped to hasten the publication of the Provisions of Westminster on 24 October.

A document in French survives from the Westminster parliament, which appears to be a set of memoranda for the council, rather than formal legislation. A new judicial eyre was ordered. The *querela* procedure was extended: men were to be appointed to hear complaints dating back up to seven years. The arguments over the investigation of baronial franchises were settled with a decisive clause: 'Let them also inquire about the bailiffs of the rich men in the land, and about the rich men themselves.' Four knights in each county were to review the wrongs committed by the sheriffs. Royal forests were to be investigated. The justices of the King's Bench and the barons of the exchequer were to be supervised by appropriate representatives of the community. Wise men were to be appointed to see to the reform of the exchequer, and of the exchequer of the Jews. The state of the royal forests was to be investigated. It is very clear that there was still much business to be done.[83] This parliament saw the publication of a major act of legislation, subsequently known as the Provisions of Westminster.[84] Some of the twenty-four clauses took forward issues such as suit of court and attendance at the sheriff's tourn, which had been brought up in the earlier baronial provisions. Grants of land to monastic houses were forbidden, save with the permission of the chief lord from whom the land involved was held. While some measures were not in the interests of great landholders, a clause dealing with bailiffs who absconded instead of presenting their accounts was something that they must have welcomed. Royal rights received some protection, which suggests a degree of compromise. No one, for example, was to force free tenants to answer for their freeholds without a royal writ. Pleas of false judgment were reserved to the crown. The document covered an extensive range of issues, and marked the culmination of the process that had begun at Oxford. Important as this legislation was in the reform movement, no further measures of this sort were taken until after the defeat of Simon de Montfort. In the Statute of Marlborough of 1267 many of the measures instituted at Westminster in 1259 were re-enacted.

In financial policy, the intention of the reformers had been clear: the king's freedom of action needed to be curtailed. The Provisions of Oxford had stated that all revenues should go to the exchequer and nowhere else; this was directed at the practice of paying funds directly into the household department

---

[82] Carpenter, 'The Lord Edward's Oath to Aid and Counsel Simon de Montfort, 15 October 1259', in his *Reign of Henry III*, 241–52.

[83] *DBM* 148–57; Brand, *Making of the Common Law*, 347 n. 108.

[84] Brand, *Kings, Barons and Justices*, 414–27.

of the wardrobe. In the years before the crisis well over three-quarters of the wardrobe's income had derived from sources other than the exchequer. The new principle had some effect; in the period from 1258 to 1261 about three-fifths of the total wardrobe receipt of about £12,000 a year came from the exchequer. The change was therefore marked, but it was far from complete, and receipts from ecclesiastical vacancies and even some counties continued to be paid directly into the wardrobe, rather than being properly accounted in, and controlled by, the exchequer.[85]

The formal schemes of reform and the legislation of this period do not fully reveal the very real and fundamental ideological differences that existed between the king and his opponents. This was, above all in the early stages, a crisis over matters of principle. Henry III's view of kingship was expressed in the grievances against the baronial council set out in 1261. His royal power and dignity should be maintained. He was of full age, and it was his right to appoint officials, including the most important ministers, the justiciar, chancellor, and treasurer. In cases of disagreement with the council, the king's will should prevail. He should preside over the hearing of legal cases, so that people could obtain redress from the king's court.[86] The case that was put for the king's side in the 'Song of Lewes' of 1264 was similar, in laying stress on the king's capacity to appoint whomsoever he chose to serve him as his ministers, though the 'Song' added a legal dimension, using the terminology of Roman law to suggest that the king claimed that his commands had the force of law.[87]

The alternative view of kingship was rooted not only in past opposition to Henry III's policies, but also in the intellectual world of the schools. In 1251 Robert Grosseteste, bishop of Lincoln, sent Simon de Montfort part of a speech he made at the papal curia, in which he expounded the differences between just rule and tyranny. This was perhaps intended to rebuke Simon for the character of his regime in Gascony, but the links that the king's chief opponent had with Grosseteste and the Franciscan Adam Marsh would have made him well aware of advanced ideas about the nature of kingship. Another Franciscan, John of Wales, wrote in about 1265 on the subjection of the prince to the law, the need for him to employ wise councillors, and the obligation of his officials to act equitably, refusing bribes and avoiding extortion. The 'Song of Lewes' was very probably also the work of a Franciscan. It explained that if a king was less wise than he should be, then he should be advised by the community of the kingdom.[88] This concept of community was important to

---

[85] *DBM* 106–7; Tout, *Chapters*, i. 301–2; J. A. Collingwood, 'Royal Finance in the Period of Baronial Reform and Rebellion, 1255–1270' (Ph.D. thesis, London University, 1995), 175.

[86] *DBM* 212–17.

[87] *Political Songs*, 97.

[88] Maddicott, *Simon de Montfort*, 94–5, 253; *Political Songs*, 110.

Henry's opponents. The crisis of 1258 had been initiated by seven magnates who acted together as a sworn band. The Provisions of Oxford set out the oath to be sworn by the community of England. There was a powerful belief in a cooperative, communal enterprise, which provided a moral force behind the baronial opposition to the king. Events, however, would prove the baronial unity of purpose to be superficial.

No further measures to control the king were introduced at the Westminster parliament in October 1259. An important aim for the reformers was to establish peace with France, and in mid-November Henry left England for Paris, taking with him at least six members of the council of fifteen, including both Gloucester and Montfort. It was far less easy to control the king in Paris than it was in England, and the initiative began to slip back in his direction. He wrote to Hugh Bigod on 26 January 1260, telling him that, in the light of the danger from the Welsh, he was to 'set up or permit no parliament to be held before our return to England'. On 19 February he made the same point in a further letter to members of the council of fifteen. 'It is not our will that any parliament is held in our realm in our absence, since this would not be fitting, and we do not believe that it would enhance our honour.'[89] The point was important. Postponing the assembly meant abandoning the scheme for three annual parliaments, while at the same time it was made clear that the assembly was a royal one.

Fatal fissures divided the baronial ranks. Simon de Montfort was a divisive figure who found collaboration difficult. He saw himself as the one person whose behaviour was fully consistent with the oath he had sworn to the Provisions of Oxford, and this may have made it difficult for him accept the compromises that were inevitably necessary. Others must have found his undoubted arrogance irksome. His relations with the earl of Gloucester were crucial. Richard de Clare, earl of Gloucester, was in many ways an unlikely reformer who became increasingly unhappy in 1258 over suggestions that baronial administrations should be subject to the same scrutiny as that of the crown. At the end of parliament early in 1259 Montfort rebuked him: 'I do not want to live or have dealings with men who are so changeable and deceitful.'[90] The two men made up that quarrel, but when they were both in Paris negotiating with the French in April of the same year, they quarrelled again. Montfort, pursuing his own claims against Henry III, was holding up the discussions: the issue was the refusal of his wife, no doubt at Simon's bidding, to renounce her claims to the former Angevin lands in France. For most of 1260 relations between the two earls were very bad, until reconciliation was achieved in the autumn. It looks as if Montfort agreed to change those elements

---

[89] DBM 168, 172.   [90] Paris, Chron. Maj. v. 744.

of the Provisions that Gloucester saw as a threat, while Gloucester agreed to block the king's efforts to pursue Montfort's trial.[91] Gloucester, however, did not support Montfort for long, and from 1261 until his death in the following year lent his backing to the king.

By 1261 the initiative lay firmly with the king. Henry showed considerable low cunning, claiming on the one hand that he intended to observe the Provisions, while at the same time seeking papal absolution from his promises. He agreed to try to settle Montfort's claims against him in their private quarrels, so as to neutralize a dangerous opponent. Articles setting out Henry's grievances against the baronial council were drawn up with a view to settling matters by arbitration supervised by the French king, Louis IX. He complained, among other things, that the financial situation had deteriorated. Justice was in a parlous condition. His wishes were being disregarded, and the council held meetings in his absence. The officials the councillors appointed were unsatisfactory; when he nominated good people for the major offices of state, the councillors appointed far less satisfactory men. The king's power and royal dignity had been taken away, and his commands were worth less than those of the most junior member of the council. The indictment was lengthy, and was rebutted at greater length by the councillors.[92]

Henry cannot have believed that arbitration would offer a solution, but the proposal provided a delay while he built up his position.[93] His real intentions became clear when William de Valence returned to England in April, and when in the next month the king dismissed Hugh Bigod as constable of Dover castle, replacing him with a royalist, Robert Walerand. In London, Hugh Despenser was replaced in command of the Tower. In May the royal clerk John Mansel returned from Rome, bearing a papal bull absolving the king from his oath to uphold the Provisions. The royalist Philip Basset was named as justiciar, and Walter de Merton, veteran royal clerk, became chancellor. The conciliar experiment of 1258 was over. In July royalist sheriffs replaced baronial ones in thirty-four counties. In November the baronial leaders came to terms in the treaty of Kingston. Three negotiators from each side were nominated, but if they failed to agree, the king's brother Richard of Cornwall was to arbitrate, a provision that effectively assured success for the royalist arguments. Simon de Montfort left England in disgust.

The king's success in the autumn of 1261 proved illusory. One move that proved disastrous early in the following year was the disgrace of his son

[91] Maddicott, *Simon de Montfort*, 201–3.

[92] *DBM* 218–39; H. Ridgeway, 'King Henry III's Grievances Against the Council in 1261: A New Version and a Letter Describing Political Events', *Historical Research*, 61 (1988), 227–42.

[93] For these events, see Maddicott, *Simon de Montfort*, 208–15; Treharne, *Baronial Plan of Reform*, 260–72.

Edward's companion and supporter Roger Leyburn. Charged with misappro-
priating funds, Leyburn and an influential group of young men who had also
been associated with Edward were driven into opposition. Henry, unwisely,
went to France in July. One of his aims was to settle any remaining arguments
with the French king over the peace that had been agreed between the two in
1259, but more important for Henry was the opportunity to settle his dispute
with Montfort by means of French arbitration. It is hardly surprising that a
settlement was not achieved. The earl of Gloucester died in the summer; while
Henry was within his rights in refusing to allow his 19-year-old heir immediate
possession of his father's lands, his action was politically foolish. The young
earl was a determined opponent of foreigners. He had been married in 1253, as
a boy, to Alice de Lusignan, Henry III's niece, but far from linking him to the
Lusignans, marriage to someone he heartily disliked had had precisely the
opposite effect.[94] In the autumn of 1262 a Welsh revolt began, achieving
considerable success. The situation was becoming critical, and Henry's decision in January to reissue the Provisions of Westminster did not resolve the
problems he faced, or win him the support he needed.

Finance was an increasing problem for the king. Revenues had declined
since the 1240s. Initially, in the period of reform both royal income and
expenditure had risen, and receipts were at a very reasonable level in 1261–2
at over £30,000. However, they fell sharply to around £15,000 in 1262–3. The
store of gold that the king had built up in the 1250s was largely exhausted, and
resources that could be used to resist his opponents were lacking.[95]

In April 1263 Simon de Montfort returned to England, probably in response
to an appeal from Roger Leyburn and Edward's other disaffected former
supporters. He was in determined mood, and declared, according to one
account, that he was on a crusade, as willing to die fighting wicked Christians
for the liberty of England and the Church as against the pagans.[96] In May
Henry III rejected demands that he should observe the Provisions of Oxford.
Disorder broke out in the marches, where the earl of Gloucester and other
lords turned on the Savoyard bishop of Hereford, Peter of Aigueblanche.
Thomas Turberville drove him out of his church, to custody at Eardisley.
'Par Christ,' said the bishop, 'Sir Thomas, tu est mauveis.'[97] The lands of
the see were ravaged, and the estates of other Savoyards treated similarly.
There were widespread attacks on aliens, particularly foreign clergy. As one

[94] Altschul, *Baronial Family*, 102–3.
[95] Collingwood, 'Royal Finance in the Period of Baronial Reform and Rebellion, 1255–1270',
195, 200–1.
[96] C. Tyerman, *England and the Crusades, 1095–1588* (Chicago, 1988), 146.
[97] *The Metrical Chronicle of Robert of Gloucester*, ed. Wright, ii. 738.

chronicler had it, 'Anyone who did not know how to speak English was despised and treated with contempt.' Edward's recruitment of foreign mercenaries that summer was notably unpopular. In July 1263 peace was agreed and a royal decree issued that required all foreigners to leave the land, with the exception of those found acceptable by all.[98]

Baronial backing for Montfort at this time was relatively limited. Of the earls, Gloucester, Norfolk, Derby, and Oxford provided support to a varied degree. Lists drawn up in December 1263 agreeing to French arbitration name twenty-four Montfortian supporters. Besides members of Montfort's family and immediate retainers, the barons named were mostly middling men, such as Baldwin Wake and Adam of Newmarket. Two important Northumberland lords, Robert de Ros and John de Vescy, were listed.[99] London was solidly Montfortian in its sympathies, and there was support in other towns. One dramatic demonstration of the views of the Londoners came in 1263 when a mob pelted stones and insults at the queen from London Bridge as she tried to go by water from the Tower to Windsor.[100] Episcopal backing for Montfort was striking, but not surprising given his earlier connections with Robert Grosseteste, bishop of Lincoln. Walter Cantilupe, of Worcester, Henry of Sandwich, of London, and Richard Gravesend, of Lincoln, were the most important of the bishops to support the earl of Leicester. Thomas Cantilupe, future bishop of Hereford and saint, was another important churchman to side very openly with him.[101] Support from the friars was another important element, for they could help to whip up popular support.

Edward was not ready to give in when his father did, in the summer of 1263, and in August he re-established his links with Roger Leyburn and his other former supporters. It may be that they were influenced by the growing accord between Montfort and Llywelyn ap Gruffudd, which threatened their interests in the marches.[102] The violence that had disfigured the earlier part of the year may have discredited the baronial cause in some eyes. The Dunstable annalist was highly critical of the attacks on anyone considered to be opposed to the Provisions of Oxford. 'This was contrary to law, and could not stand.'[103] Negotiations failed to produce an effective settlement in parliament in September. Later that month discussions were held at Boulogne with the French king, Louis IX, following representations from Henry III. Remarkably, the

[98] *Flores*, ii. 481; Carpenter, 'King Henry III's Statute Against Aliens', in his *Reign of Henry III*, 261–80.
[99] Maddicott, *Simon de Montfort*, 248–9; *DBM* 284–5.
[100] Ann. Dunstable, 223.
[101] Maddicott, *Simon de Montfort*, 251–5.
[102] J. Beverley Smith, *Llywelyn ap Gruffudd, Prince of Wales* (Cardiff, 1998), 161.
[103] Ann. Dunstable, 222.

outcome favoured Montfort, but although Louis appears to have approved the Provisions of Oxford, he also demanded the restitution of property to those who had suffered in the recent disturbances in England. This was one of the issues on which peace foundered, but most important was Edward's opposition. His seizure of Windsor castle, and the support he received from the marcher lords, demonstrated that the royalist position was still strong. Neither side, however, was prepared to see matters settled on the battlefield, and in December both parties agreed to submit the dispute to Louis IX. Louis's verdict, the Mise of Amiens, gave full support to Henry III. The French king had indicated approval of the Provisions in September; now, in January 1264, he condemned them outright. The influence of Queen Eleanor was important in achieving what seemed to be a striking volte-face on the part of the French king. Henry III should be able to appoint ministers as he chose. The statute of 1263 against aliens was quashed. All that the king's opponents got out of the arbitration was an instruction that they should be pardoned.[104] One chronicler summed up the decision by stating that 'the king of France wanted England to be ruled by foreigners as well as native-born men, at the free will of the king of England, as was done before the Provisions of Oxford'.[105] This was not a recipe for peace, and left Simon de Montfort with few options.

THE CIVIL WAR AND MONTFORT'S RULE

When it came to civil war in 1264, Montfort's backing was strongly centred on the midlands, where he had no effective rivals. Although he had obtained no more than half of the original earldom of Leicester, the other half was in the hands a largely absentee landlord, Roger de Quency, earl of Winchester, himself a baronial supporter. Roger died in April 1264, leaving no heir. It was not surprising that his tenants should look to Montfort for leadership. William Mauduit became earl of Warwick in 1263, but following his capture in April 1264 was in no position to provide political leadership in the midlands.[106] London continued to provide backing for Montfort: the city would suffer a fine of 20,000 marks for its involvement in the rebellion. Nor was urban support confined to London; there was widespread backing for Montfort in many towns. Outside England, Montfort could count on support from Llywelyn ap Gruffudd, though the Welsh prince was understandably reluctant to commit any troops to an English civil war.

[104] DBM 280–91.

[105] The Historical Works of Gervase of Canterbury, ed. W. Stubbs (RS, 1880), ii. 232.

[106] Maddicott, Simon de Montfort, 62–3; D. Williams, 'Simon de Montfort and his Adherents', in W. M. Ormrod (ed.), England in the Thirteenth Century (Harlaxton, 1985), 166–77.

The war began in February 1264, when Montfort sent his sons Simon and Henry to attack Roger Mortimer in the marches. The advantage in the civil war, however, soon lay with the royalists. In March Henry III summoned an army, using a traditional feudal summons. This was ostensibly recruited to attack Llywelyn ap Gruffudd, but the Montfortians were the real targets. At Northampton the royal army achieved a major triumph, capturing the younger Simon de Montfort and a host of leading baronial figures. Campaigning then switched to the south-east, where London provided the baronial cause with significant support. Simon de Montfort failed to capture Rochester castle, and the king set about re-establishing control of Kent and Sussex. Montfort marched out of London, hoping either to negotiate or to challenge the king. The royalists rejected the terms that were offered, which included the maintenance of the Provisions. The outcome was, therefore, battle.[107] Montfort's army went into the fight armed with a sense of religious mission. They were absolved of their sins on the night before the battle, and they wore crusader crosses, front and back.[108] God was recruited to their cause, and the sense of moral zeal that underlay the baronial movement was very evident.

The battle of Lewes should have been a royalist triumph, for there is little doubt that the king's army was superior both in absolute numbers and in the number of trained knights. Montfort, however, obtained a tactical advantage from high ground, and the success that Edward achieved in routing the Londoners who faced him was negated by the fact that, in chasing them for several miles, he left the rest of the royal army vulnerable to the rest of Montfort's forces. Henry III, his brother Richard of Cornwall, and the remainder of the royalists were roundly defeated. However, the victory was not total, for the king, Edward, the marcher lords, and many others took refuge in Lewes priory.[109] A settlement, the Mise of Lewes, was accordingly negotiated during the night that followed the battle. The terms have not survived, but it is clear that the Provisions were to be maintained, baronial supporters pardoned, and foreigners with other undesirables removed from the royal council. Complex procedures for arbitration, by English and French panels, were set up. The marcher lords were to go free, while Edward and his cousin Henry of Almain would be held as hostages.[110]

Montfort's rule after his triumph at Lewes was narrowly based; he had to rely to a great extent on giving broad authority to his sons. After the battle a new conciliar form of government was set up. There would be three electors,

<hr />

[107] For these events, see Maddicott, *Simon de Montfort*, 264–70.
[108] Tyerman, *England and the Crusades*, 147–8.
[109] D. A. Carpenter, *The Battles of Lewes and Evesham 1264/5* (Keele, 1987), 19–34.
[110] J. R. Maddicott, 'The Mise of Lewes, 1264', *EHR* 98 (1983), 588–63; D. A. Carpenter, 'Simon de Montfort and the Mise of Lewes', *BIHR* 58 (1985), 1–11.

who would choose nine councillors. Three of these would always be in attendance at court, to supervise the affairs of the realm. The electors were Simon de Montfort, Gilbert de Clare, earl of Gloucester, and Stephen Berksted, bishop of Chichester. The scheme was in broad accord with the fundamental principles of the Provisions of Oxford, but it lacked the checks and balances provided in that scheme, with its royal and baronial twelves. Montfort, as one of the electors, was in a dominant position. The other two electors were thoroughgoing supporters of his, and a clear majority of the nine were strong backers of his cause.[111] The scheme allowed the king no effective role in government at all.

The character of Montfort's rule did little credit to his image as a man determined to uphold his oath to the Provisions of Oxford, a reformer of powerful spiritual convictions.[112] He did well at first, seeing off a serious threat of invasion from France by recruiting a huge army. A threat from the marcher lords was swiftly dealt with. Montfort, however, appears to have been far more determined to pursue his private ambitions than he was to continue with the programme of reform. There were many opportunities to acquire the lands from the defeated, and substantial ransoms were available from those wishing to buy their way out of captivity. He maintained a huge household, bringing in knights from abroad to reinforce it. His acquisition of Chester and the lordship of the Peak in December 1264 was a blatant piece of self-aggrandizement and enrichment. In 1265 Montfort tried to increase his authority when he sought information on the rights that were attached to his hereditary position of steward of England. Montfort's sons profited immensely from their father's position of power. Their arrogance and greed paralleled that of the Lusignans earlier. Guy de Montfort received charge of Richard of Cornwall's lands in the south-west. The young Simon de Montfort dispossessed William de Braose of his lands in Sussex. Henry de Montfort was singled out to receive the lordships of Chester and the Peak.

The work that was done to further the cause of reform during the period of Montfort's rule in 1264-5 was limited. A positive step was taken in June 1264 when new sheriffs were appointed, on the same basis as in 1258-9. The government insisted on the maintenance of the Provisions; copies were made and sent out to the shires in December. There was no major new legislation such as had characterized the early days of the reform movement; it would be unreasonable, perhaps, to expect it in circumstances of increasing tension and difficulty. Montfort is, of course, celebrated in popular mythology for his parliaments, notably that held early in 1265. Knights of the shire were summoned, and also

[111] *DBM* 294-9.
[112] For full details of what follows, Maddicott, *Simon de Montfort*, 279-345.

representatives of the towns. This was a gathering of the faithful, not a fully comprehensive parliament. The fact that only five earls and eighteen other magnates were summoned shows how Montfort's support was dwindling among those of real political importance. The summons of an extraordinary number of abbots and priors, just over a hundred, may have given the assembly spiritual strength, but that was not what was needed at this juncture.

Support for Simon de Montfort was nevertheless extensive. Statistical analysis of those identified as rebels in the aftermath of these events suggests that there was wide support for the Montfortian cause throughout the social classes. It has been argued, by extrapolating from a sample, that over half the knights in the country were rebels. About half of the identifiable rebels were from the rural populace below knightly rank, with a significant measure of peasant support.[113] In some cases what jurors reported reads more like incidents of petty crime than political activity, but there can be no doubts about cases such as that of Richard de Spechesleye, a Worcestershire man who possessed 2 carucates of land and a windmill, and who died at Evesham. Many must have felt like the Kentishman Nicholas French, who said to the king's bailiffs that they 'deserved to be hanged for they never did good when they could do ill'. The jurors were clear that this made French an open enemy of the king, but the case was hardly a strong one.[114]

Popular support, however, was no substitute for the backing of the magnates. Simon lost a very important supporter in the spring of 1265 when the young earl of Gloucester defected from his cause. When the king's son Edward escaped from custody in May, the scene was set for the final act in Montfort's tragedy. Edward joined forces with Gloucester and other marcher lords, notably Roger Mortimer. Montfort's decision to enter into a formal alliance with Llywelyn ap Gruffudd won him no friends in England and little support from the Welsh. The first major success for Edward came at Kenilworth, where he surprised the younger Simon de Montfort. Montfort himself was then outmanoeuvred by Edward. He found himself cut off from the midland heartland of his support, on the wrong bank of the Severn. He was trapped at Evesham by royalist forces, which, it must have seemed to him, were advancing from every direction. Divine approval for his cause was not as evident as it had been at Lewes: the white crusader crosses worn by his men were matched by red crosses adopted by the royalists. There is a clear sense of martyrdom about the final battle on 4 August. As he saw his enemies approach, Montfort declared, 'How skilfully they are advancing. Our bodies are theirs, our souls are God's.' The outcome was inevitable. A special assassination squad was

---

[113] C. Valente, *The Theory and Practice of Revolt in Medieval England* (Aldershot, 2003), 94–7.
[114] *CIM* i. 231, 284.

nominated to deal with Montfort. The baronial forces could not resist the charges by the royalists; they were not helped by the fact that the earl of Hereford, in command of the infantry, had taken up position in the rear, rather than the van. Montfort was slain. 'Such torment has not been heard of anyone; they cut his privy parts clean off.'[115]

Montfort's hideous death on the field at Evesham was not quite the end of the story. Those who resisted can have had little hope of success, but for some, resistance was the only possible course of action against a government that seemed determined on revenge. When parliament met at Winchester in September 1265, it was decided to disinherit all those who had rebelled, with limited provision for the wives and widows of the king's opponents. The king and his son Edward were in a mood to make no concessions. The royalists were vengeful, and sought their rewards. The younger Simon de Montfort engaged in fruitless resistance in Lincolnshire, in the Isle of Axholm, surrendering at Christmas. In Kent the Cinque Ports abandoned resistance in May, after a campaign led by Roger Leyburn. John d'Eyville and others, however, continued to hold out in the Isle of Ely. The most difficult problem in military terms for the royalists was presented by the great fortress of Kenilworth castle, well defended by a series of artificial lakes as well as by stout walls. There Henry de Hastings held out with a band of increasingly desperate men. The siege, which began in the early summer of 1266, was an operation on a very large scale. Despite the use of the latest military engines, assault and battery proved to be in vain. It was increasingly clear that the rebellion could not be finally crushed by military force, and at the end of August a committee of twelve was set up to produce a scheme for peace. At the end of October the Dictum of Kenilworth was proclaimed. This set out a scheme whereby men were allowed to buy back their lands at a price that varied according to the level of their involvement in the rebellion.[116] The garrison at Kenilworth did not accept the terms, but conditions within the castle had become so unbearable as the end of the year approached that surrender was the only option left to them. In the following summer the last embers of resistance, which John d'Eyville had kept alight in the Isle of Ely, were finally extinguished.

ARMIES OF THE CIVIL WAR

An aspect of this period that has not received much attention is the question of how, and on what scale, the armies of the civil war were recruited. In March

[115] O. de Laborderie, J. R. Maddicott, and D. A. Carpenter, 'The Last Hours of Simon de Montfort: A New Account', *EHR* 115 (2000), 378–412. The translation of the final quotation is mine.
[116] *DBM* 317–37.

1264 Henry III issued summonses to some 115 lay magnates, and to bishops and abbots in addition, requesting that they should muster at Oxford. The reason given was the activity of the Welsh under Llywelyn ap Gruffudd, though clearly this was not the real explanation. The men were asked to come in response to the fealty and affection they owed the king, and to bring all the service that they owed. It was curious that no direct appeal was made to homage, as was normal in a summons requesting the *servitium debitum*, feudal service. When a replacement summons was sent to a group of northern magnates (the messengers taking the first ones having been robbed of them in Sherwood Forest), the customary reference to homage was included. Later in the month summonses to men from Oxfordshire and Berkshire made it clear that the coming civil war was the reason. In this case, appeal was simply made to the fealty that they owed. Then a further summons was sent to the sheriffs, reverting to the explanation that the king intended to campaign against the Welsh. Proclamations were to be made requiring all who owed military service to provide it. In addition, the sheriffs were to bring all the knights, sergeants, and squires they could, to serve at the king's wages.[117] The king was using every available means to recruit cavalry troops, though there is no evidence to show what was done to provide infantry.

The start of Montfort's rule saw recruitment planned on a huge scale, since there was real fear of invasion from France. Orders went out that four, six, or eight men from each place in the threatened counties should muster at London. They were to be provided with expenses for forty days by their local communities. The magnates received a much more traditional summons, asking for the provision of service in accordance with their homage and fealty to the crown. The force was assembled on Barham Down in Kent; no muster rolls survive to show how successful the recruitment was in reality, but contemporaries judged this to be a huge army.[118] The final writ recorded on the close roll before the battle of Evesham, issued on 1 July 1265, was a desperate plea to the sheriff of Hereford. The sheriff was ordered to summon sixty named men, and all other knights and squires in his county, to muster at Hereford, mounted and equipped for war. There was no appeal to fealty and homage, nor was there any offer of pay, but there was a threat that if the order was disobeyed, the result would be disinheritance in perpetuity.[119]

It is difficult to know, from the record of the summonses that were issued, what the armies of this period were really like. Accounts for the force commanded by Roger Leyburn after Montfort's defeat provide some clues. He went to attack Sandwich with 106 horses in his troop. When he besieged

---

[117] *CR, 1261–4*, 377–82.   [118] Ibid. 395, 400–1; Maddicott, *Simon de Montfort*, 290.
[119] *CR, 1264–8*, 127.

Hastings, 232 archers were hired for two days and 254 for one. In all, he had 577 archers at royal wages. A little later, he had thirty-two paid knights in his following, and 500 Welsh archers from the royal household, each paid 3d. a day.[120] The implication of this is that the armies of this period contained a very normal mix of cavalry and infantry, and that at least a substantial proportion was paid. The emphasis on archers is important, for it demonstrates that Edward I's use of bowmen in his Welsh and Scottish wars was not novel. The Weald was a particularly important recruiting ground for archers in this period; in 1266, for example, the sheriff of Surrey and Sussex was ordered to recruit 200 to serve under John, Earl Warenne.[121]

One of the themes of this book is the way in which government and society was affected and altered by war. This period of civil war, however, was too brief to have a significant impact on military organization or methods of fighting, though it would, of course, have given many a rare taste of the awful reality of battle. Much of the recruitment that took place must, in practice, have been a matter of magnates persuading, by whatever means possible, their dependants and tenants to join in their armed retinues. The formal institutions of military obligation are unlikely to have been of much relevance in the weeks leading up to Evesham.

CONCLUSION

England faced huge problems in the aftermath of the civil war. The period of actual warfare had been short, and the extent of physical destruction limited, but the struggle had been a bitter one, very largely as a result of the actions of one man. Simon de Montfort was an extraordinary figure who had dominated English politics by the charismatic force of his personality in a way that few have matched. There were many contradictions about him. He had a great military reputation, which seems to have been based more on his own self-evaluation rather than on notable successes in the field. He was a foreigner who headed a political movement that aimed to expel aliens from the land. A letter, probably originating in the earl of Gloucester's circle, warned against Montfort in 1263, pointing out that, although he was ready to send some foreigners into exile, he was ready to protect others.[122] It would be facile to condemn Montfort from the viewpoint of a modern-day political morality, for permitting his private interests to take precedence over his public concerns. Montfort would have had no respect from his contemporaries had he not pursued his

---

[120] A. Lewis, 'Roger Leyburn and the Pacification of England, 1265–7', EHR 54 (1939), 200–4.
[121] CR, 1264–8, 191.
[122] 'Annals of Tewkesbury', in Ann. Mon. i. 180.

private concerns. It is, in the end, difficult to argue that his approach was a purely cynical one, for all that a commitment to reform is hard to discern in his career prior to 1258. His decisions to fight in the interest of his cause, both at Lewes and at Evesham, were not those of a self-seeking man; he had surely come to believe that his cause was rightful and just, and indeed that he had divine approbation for the disastrous course he had undertaken. There was a powerful motivation behind the movement that he came to lead; this was no self-interested baronial rebellion.

The baronial movement may have suffered defeat and humiliation at Evesham and Kenilworth, but many of the concepts that had powered it did not die. There could be no further question of confining the king by imposing a council upon him, but equally much of the work of reform that had taken place since 1258 could not be written off. The challenge facing those responsible for restoring the country after the civil war was massive. It extended from the complexities of settling the inevitable territorial disputes and re-establishing public order, to the much deeper problems of creating a political consensus that took appropriate account of the ideas and achievements of the reformers.

CHAPTER 5

Reconstruction and Reform, 1266–1294

The disturbed and divisive years that had ended with the dejected garrison of Kenilworth trudging out in bitter surrender in 1266 were followed by a period of remarkable achievement lasting until the early 1290s. There was a great programme of legislation. Parliament developed, and became increasingly central to the running of the English State. Royal finances were placed on a new and more secure footing. The recovery from the disasters of the civil war was astonishing. This was an outstanding period of positive development.

THE SETTLEMENT OF ENGLAND

The prospects when the civil war ended were not good. At the parliament held at Winchester, shortly following the victory at Evesham, a policy of confiscation of rebel property was formalized. Inquisitions taken subsequently reveal an orgy of seizures of lands and goods, as royalists took their revenge. Edward and his followers, and the earl of Gloucester, all took advantage of the situation.[1] There were, however, voices of reason, notably that of the papal legate Ottobuono. The Dictum of Kenilworth of October 1266, with its scheme setting out fines for the repurchase of their land by former rebels, on a scale reflecting their involvement in the rising, was a major advance. It took the threat of renewed civil war from Gilbert, earl of Gloucester, before it was agreed that the disinherited could be allowed to recover their lands before, not after, the payment of the fines. Even so, there were substantial gains for the royal family. The king's second son, Edmund, received not only Simon de Montfort's earldom of Leicester, but also, in 1269, the Ferrers earldom of Derby. The promulgation of the Statute of Marlborough in 1267 was a very important positive move. This measure incorporated a great deal of the reforming legislation of 1259, and showed that the crown was not insensitive to sensible demands for change.

[1] *CIM* i. 187–288.

For King Henry, a great moment came on 13 October 1269, when the ceremony of the translation of the remains of Edward the Confessor took place in the splendid church at Westminster. Prelates and magnates were summoned, as well as leading townspeople. The saint's remains were carried by Henry himself, his brother, the king's sons Edward and Edmund, along with Earl Warenne and Philip Basset.[2] The realm was at peace; the great building project had been largely carried through. The ritual was a celebration of the monarchy as well as of the royal saint, and it was marred only by the refusal of the bishops of the Canterbury province to follow the archbishop of York as he processed behind the Confessor's body.[3]

Evesham had been Edward's triumph, but the extent of his influence on royal policies in the next few years should not be exaggerated. His concern was increasingly with his planned crusade, and the one legislative act for which he, with his cousin Henry of Almain, was undoubtedly responsible was the lifting of the prohibition of tournaments. Edward's relations with the earl of Gloucester deteriorated, to such an extent that the earl refused to attend parliament in 1269, fearing for his safety at the hands of the king's son. Arbitration by Richard of Cornwall in the following year resolved the problem, at least in the short term.[4] In 1270 Edward departed for the east, not to return to England until 1274.

There was no question of abandoning the use of parliament in the aftermath of the civil war, despite the way that the institution had been used to their advantage by Simon de Montfort and the king's opponents. In the late 1260s representatives attended more frequently than in the past. Edward's crusade had to be paid for, and in a series of parliaments between 1268 and 1270 negotiations took place for the grant and collection of a tax. The evidence for these gatherings is thin and somewhat ambiguous, but it seems likely that representatives were summoned to York in September 1268. Few appeared, and a new parliament was organized for October, at which knights were present. They were again present at parliaments in 1269 and 1270, when it was finally agreed that the tax should go ahead.[5]

The death of Henry III in 1272, and the absence of the new king on crusade, might appear at first sight to have been a recipe for crisis. In fact, although historians are not in full agreement about this period, it seems that the country was well ruled in these difficult years, despite financial problems and some

---

[2] Wykes, 226–7.

[3] D. A. Carpenter, 'Westminster Abbey in Politics, 1258–1269', in *TCE* vii. 49–58.

[4] Wykes, 228–9.

[5] J. R. Maddicott, 'The Crusade Taxation of 1268–1270 and the Development of Parliament', in *TCE* ii. 93–117. A key question is whether the term *maiores* used by the chroniclers was employed at this period to mean knights and perhaps also burgesses.

continuing disorder. One important step had been taken before Edward departed from England. In 1270 some twenty-five counties with their royal castles had been transferred into Edward's hands. New officials were appointed, with Edward's associates naturally prominent among them. The purpose of the changes was clearly to ensure that in the event of the king's death, men loyal to the new ruler would already be in positions of power in the localities.[6] When Edward left England, he appointed Richard of Cornwall as guardian of his children. The archbishop of York, with Roger Mortimer, Philip Basset, and Robert Walerand, was to look after his lands. A significant change to the arrangements took place when Robert Burnell, Edward's chancellor, stayed in England rather than accompanying Edward as had been intended, and replaced Walerand. Burnell became the leading figure in the government after Henry III's death. While there were significant problems, such as that presented by Llywelyn of Wales, and by a trade dispute with Flanders, which were not resolved until Edward returned to England, the government under Burnell's guidance achieved much. A representative parliament was held, and an important step was taken when an inquiry into lost or alienated royal rights was set up in a number of counties.[7] Burnell continued, of course, to play a central role in government as chancellor until his death in 1292.

THE NEW KING

The first task facing Edward on his return to England in 1274 was the coronation, a splendid affair. Building costs alone, for pulpits in Westminster abbey, new kitchens, lodgings, a stable, stone seats in Westminster Hall, and other items, came to over £1,000.[8] Once the ceremonies were over, the reshaping of the administration was tackled. The replacement of most of the sheriffs showed that a new broom was at work. A massive inquiry was then held. Commissioners put a series of questions to local juries between November 1274 and March 1275. The inquiry was wide-ranging. Edward was concerned that the crown had lost rights and liberties, but the jurors were also asked about the misdeeds of officials, both royal and private. Extensive returns, known as the Hundred Rolls, were produced, which suggested a need both for new legislation and for proceedings against a great many corrupt local officials. The Dunstable annalist's comment that 'nothing good came of it' was unduly

---

[6] H. A. Waite, 'The Household and Resources of the Lord Edward, 1239–1272' (D.Phil. thesis, Oxford University, 1988), 138–53.

[7] R. Huscroft, 'Robert Burnell and the Government of England', in *TCE* vii. 59–70. J. R. Maddicott, 'Edward I and the Lessons of Baronial Reform', in *TCE* i. 1–9, takes a pessimistic view of this period.

[8] E 372/118, m. 36^v.

cynical.[9] The way forward was to produce legislation so as to meet grievances and improve government. Edward explained his achievements in 1275 in a draft of a letter to the pope. This explained how in parliament 'we ordained many things there which with God's help will make for the bettering of the state of the English church and the reform of the kingdom and produce an increase in the general welfare of the people'.[10] The king had started on an astonishingly energetic and productive programme, which achieved much of what the reformers of 1258 had been looking for.

With the legislation of 1275 Edward was building on previous achievements. The Statute of Marlborough of 1267 had shown what might be done by means of statutory legislation, and set a precedent for the measures of Edward I's reign. In 1275 the first Statute of Westminster dealt with many issues that had been raised in the course of the inquiry set up in the previous year. Although it would not have been possible to process all of the returns by the time that the statute was drafted, very many of the measures it contained were a reflection of popular demand and grievance. It attempted to deal with problems of disorder and with such abuses by magnates as the misuse of distraint. Above all, it dealt with the conduct of local administration. The new measures of 1275 were publicized in a way that shows that they were intended to win popularity for the king and his officials. The parliament at which the statute was issued was by far the largest of the reign, with four knights requested from each county and up to six burgesses from each city. In addition, more towns were asked to send representatives than was normal. In part this was in order to gain as full consent as possible to the new customs duties on wool exports, but the massive attendance, combined with the provisions for the public proclamation of the new statute in the localities, ensured that the content of the legislation would be widely known.[11]

The process of inquiry followed by legislation was reminiscent of Bigod's eyre of 1259 and the subsequent Provisions of Westminster. Edward's reign was characterized by many inquiries, and his officials must at times have suffered from severe information overload. The inquiry of 1274–5 was followed by an extraordinarily wide-ranging one in 1279, which concentrated on investigating who held what land, and by what services, and which yielded very detailed responses. In 1285 what was known as Kirkby's Quest took place, which provided information about what knights' fees were held from the crown, and about jurisdictional liberties.[12] Inquiries also took place at Edward's

[9] Ann. Dunstable, 263. Many, though not all, of the returns are printed in Rotuli Hundre-dorum, 2 vols. (London, 1812–18).

[10] Sayles, The Functions of the Medieval Parliament, 141.

[11] Maddicott, 'Edward I and the Lessons of Baronial Reform', 15.

[12] Prestwich, Edward I, 235–7.

behest in Gascony and in Wales. While it was far from unknown for thirteenth-century rulers (especially in France) to carry out surveys and make wide-ranging investigations, the English regime was remarkable in its thirst for information.[13] The first Statute of Westminster was followed by much further legislation. The year 1285 saw the second Statute of Westminster, another measure that covered a wide range of issues, and that is sometimes known by its most notable clause, *de donis conditionalibus*. In 1290 the Statute of *Quia Emptores* made important changes to the land law, in response to magnate pressure. Inquiries were of course just one source for the new measures. In many cases, clauses were a direct response to problems that had emerged in the courts. For example, Osbert Giffard's abduction of two nuns lay behind the drafting of part of a clause in the second Statute of Westminster.[14]

Another element in the legislative programme of 1275 was the issue of a statute to deal with the Jews. This provided for the total abolition of interest payments, and made it more difficult for creditors to obtain repayment of loans. The implication was that Jews should turn to trade and manual labour, a view that Robert Grosseteste had expressed in harsh terms in the 1230s. They were restricted in where they were allowed to live, being confined to towns where they had customarily resided, and were defined as being the king's serfs. The separateness of the Jews was emphasized by the requirement, following the ecclesiastical legislation of the fourth Lateran Council, that they should wear a distinctive badge on their clothing.[15] Like much of the legislation, this had roots in the later years of Henry III's reign. The Petition of the Barons of 1258 had complained about the way in which Jewish debts were transferred to magnates and others, who used them to acquire the lands of the debtors.[16] In 1269 Walter de Merton, with Edward, drew up the Provisions of the Jewry, which dealt with the question of debts owed to the Jews. Two years later instructions to justices prevented Jews from holding land in any form of freehold.[17] Indebtedness to Jewish moneylenders had been a significant element in the discontent of some landholders in the mid-thirteenth century, and it made good political sense for Edward to take steps to deal with the issue.

While elements of the legislation drew on the work of the reformers of the late 1250s, not all Edward's motives were the same as theirs had been. He was determined to recover and maintain royal rights. The *quo warranto* inquiries made this very clear. It was initially intended to challenge private rights to

---

[13] S. Raban, 'Edward I's Other Inquiries', in *TCE* ix. 43–57.

[14] Prestwich, *Edward I*, 270.

[15] *SR* i. 220–1. For Grosseteste's views, see Southern, *Grosseteste*, 249.   [16] *DBM* 87.

[17] R. Mundill, *England's Jewish Solution: Experiment and Expulsion, 1262–1290* (Cambridge, 1998), 58–9.

exercise jurisdiction in parliament, but by 1278 it was clear that the weight of business was too great, and that a different solution was needed. At the Gloucester parliament that summer it was decided that anyone who held rights of jurisdiction should appear before justices in eyre to set out their claims. The crown could use writs of *quo warranto* to find out by what right, or warrant, they exercised their rights. The view was that all judicial authority derived from the king, and that many royal rights had been usurped. In the early stages of the proceedings the earl of Gloucester was singled out for particular attention. The process was undoubtedly resented by many magnates, but there were no concerted protests. Partly this was because the inquiries were not held simultaneously, and partly it was because the crown did not in practice recover many rights. In many cases there was no proper conclusion, since the crown had not laid down proper principles to determine what types of claim should be allowed, and what not. Confrontation eventually took place, at Easter 1290, after a new chief justice, Gilbert de Thornton, began to take an aggressively royalist line in his judgments. A statute was then produced that allowed anyone who claimed continuous tenure of a franchise by himself and his ancestors since 1189 to retain their rights.[18] Edward was not opposed to franchises as a matter of principle; in 1297 he wrote sympathetically to the countess of Pembroke, who had complained that royal bailiffs were taking an aggressive attitude towards her franchise of Castle Gaweyn.[19] Some of the lawyers and officials acting on his behalf may have gone further on occasion than the king intended, but there is no doubt that Edward was firm that royal rights had to be maintained, and that franchises should be properly run.

FINANCIAL REORGANIZATION

The financial basis of government was transformed during Edward's early years on the throne. What can be called a fiscal state was coming into being. Taxation provided the means to increase the resources available to the crown massively, while at the same time the need to obtain consent shifted the political balance. Representatives were needed in parliament to provide the fullest possible agreement to the financial levies. Taxation was not the only answer to the king's needs; a credit system was required so that funds would be available promptly.

The currency itself was in a poor condition. No recoinage had taken place since 1247–50. The chronicler Thomas Wykes claimed, with some

---

[18] D. W. Sutherland, *Quo Warranto Proceedings in the Reign of Edward I, 1278–1294* (Oxford, 1963); Prestwich, *Edward I*, 258–64, 346–7.
[19] *Cal. Anc. Corr. Wales*, 212–13.

exaggeration, that as a result of clipping, coins weighed only half what they should, and that, as a result, foreign merchants were no longer coming to England. Prices had consequently risen.[20] The Jews were widely blamed for coin-clipping, and justices were appointed to inquire into their activities. As a result, in a vicious campaign it is likely that almost 300 Jews were hanged, while many others forfeited their property.[21] In 1279 a full-scale recoinage began, master-minded by a moneyer from Marseilles, William de Turnemire. Use of the old coins was forbidden, and by the end of the process some £700,000 of the new ones had been minted. A new technique for producing coin was used. Instead of being cut from thin sheets of silver, silver droplets, standard in weight, were poured onto a flat surface.[22]

The traditional foundation of royal finance was the land that the king held, and it made sense to try to modernize the way in which these estates were run. This, however, was one area where an attempted reform failed. In 1275 three stewards were appointed to take charge of royal lands and escheats in three groups of counties. The escheators, one north of the Trent and one to the south, were abolished. The new arrangements suggest that the government realized that by adopting more up-to-date methods of direct management of estates, following the example of many great landlords, income could be maximized. The task was too much for the three new stewards. A letter from one of them, Richard de Holbrook, reveals the problems of the new system. He was overworked, his health was suffering, and the sheriffs were not providing him with the cooperation he needed. In 1282 the experiment was abandoned. It had, however, shown that the government was ready to think in radical ways.[23]

Taxation was a more profitable way forward than trying to squeeze more revenue out of royal estates. In 1275 Edward achieved a notable success when he negotiated a grant in parliament in perpetuity of a customs duty of 6s. 8d. on each sack of wool exported. There was a precedent for this, for in 1266 Edward had imposed a duty on foreign merchants in exchange for his protection. By 1274 the proceeds of this tax had been granted to an Italian firm of merchant bankers, the Ricciardi of Lucca, who had assisted Edward in his crusading venture and were anxious for a more permanent, secure form of repayment.[24] It was possible to gain consent for the grant by offering to abandon the embargo on wool exports that had been imposed in 1270 in the course of a dispute

[20] Wykes, 278.

[21] P. Brand, 'Jews and the Law in England, 1275–90', EHR 115 (2000), 1148.

[22] C. E. Challis (ed.), A New History of the Royal Mint (Cambridge, 1992), 121, 127.

[23] Maddicott, 'Edward I and the Lessons of Baronial Reform', 21–3; Prestwich, Edward I, 102–3; SC 1/10/157.

[24] Ricciardi is the correct Italian spelling for this firm, often spelt Riccardi in English sources.

with Flanders. The new duties yielded roughly £10,000 a year in the 1270s, and provided an effective means of repaying the Italian merchants for their loans.[25]

Direct taxation could not be developed on a permanent basis in the same way as the customs duties. Taxes had to be negotiated. There had been a long period when none had been granted, for Henry III had been unable to obtain agreement from his magnates and other subjects between the grant of a thirtieth in 1237, and that of a twentieth to pay for Edward's crusade. In the second parliament of 1275 the argument was made that the king had spent much of his and his father's wealth on the crusade, and that it was therefore necessary to ask for assistance.[26] A fifteenth was duly granted, which raised some £80,000. It was perhaps only in the optimistic circumstances of the start of a new reign that such a request for taxation could be agreed so easily, with no concessions apparently being demanded.

In addition to these lay taxes, Edward negotiated grants of taxation from the clergy. A fifteenth from the Canterbury archdiocese was agreed in 1279, with a tenth from York. In 1283 Canterbury agreed a twentieth, and three years later York a thirtieth. In 1290 a tenth was negotiated; appropriately a higher rate was paid when the Jews had been expelled from England. These ecclesiastical taxes were not levied on the same basis as the lay ones. They were based on a fixed assessment, made in 1254 with another in 1291, so that the papacy could levy crusading taxes.

It was not possible to manage the government's finances without making use of credit. As the financial position improved, so it became easier to borrow money from Italian merchants, and in particular from the company of the Ricciardi of Lucca. It was possible to raise large sums for the enterprise of the Welsh war, and then pay the Italians back over the succeeding years. The Ricciardi played a major role in the collection of the tax of a fifteenth of 1275, and acted as Edward's agents in raising money from other Italian merchants operating in England. The crown's aggregate debt to them from the start of the reign until 1294 came to about £392,000. The Ricciardi never received full repayment for the loans that they made. In 1294 they were owed almost £19,000. The balance sheet, therefore, favoured the crown. By borrowing massively from the Italians, Edward acquired not only useful funds, but also agents who could act on his behalf. The Italians were no doubt dissatisfied at not being repaid in full, but they did receive other benefits. With the weight of royal favour behind them, they found it easier to recover other debts that were owed to them. The main technique used by the crown for repayment was to

---

[25] Prestwich, *Edward I*, 98–100.
[26] *The Historical Works of Gervase of Canterbury*, ed. W. Stubbs (RS, 1880), ii. 281.

hand over the proceeds of the customs, and this provided the Italians with valuable capital in the main English export ports, money that could be used to finance their wool-trading operations.[27]

Major efforts were made to improve financial administration in the mid-1280s. The Statute of Rhuddlan of 1284 dealt with the matter of debts owed to the crown. Those that were regarded as unrecoverable were removed from the main exchequer accounts, the pipe rolls. The inquiry known as Kirkby's Quest looked into these debts with a view to getting them paid off. In 1284 a financial statement was drawn up. The regular county farms, the sums due from the sheriffs every Michaelmas, were put at £10,168 a year. The only other substantial regular item was the customs duties, estimated to be worth £8,000 a year. Profits of justice were valued at £1,100. Vacant bishoprics and abbeys were expected to yield £666, and wardships £333. The chancery would bring in £666, from the fees payable for writs and charters, and payment of debts owed to the crown that were allowed to be paid off in instalments was put at £1,414. In all (and there were various other miscellaneous sources of income) revenue was calculated to be £26,828 3s. 9d. a year.[28] The figure shows that, for all the work that had been done, the finances of the crown were still not on a regular and assured footing.

CHURCH AND STATE

These were not years in which the king's authority was questioned in the course of political crises. The secular nobility were in no mood to challenge so successful a king as Edward. There were, however, arguments with the Church. In 1279 John Pecham was appointed to the see of Canterbury by the pope. He at once began a programme of reform at a council held at Reading, and went so far as to have Magna Carta read out, with sentences of excommunication issued against anyone who interfered with the liberties of the Church. Moves against pluralism were seen as an attack on those royal clerks who had successfully accumulated a number of church livings. In parliament Pecham was forced to withdraw his sentences of excommunication on those who sought writs that would remove cases from the Church's jurisdiction, and to make various other concessions, including the removal of copies of Magna Carta

[27] R. W. Kaeuper, *Bankers to the Crown: The Riccardi of Lucca and Edward I* (Princeton, 1973), provides a full study. See also M. C. Prestwich, *War, Politics and Finance Under Edward I* (London, 1972), 206–8, and id., 'Italian Bankers in Late Thirteenth and Early Fourteenth Century England', in Centre for Medieval and Renaissance Studies (ed.), *The Dawn of Modern Banking* (New Haven, 1979), 77–104.
[28] M. H. Mills, 'Exchequer Agenda and Estimate of Revenue, Easter Term 1284', *EHR* 40 (1925), 229–34; Prestwich, *Edward I*, 242–4.

posted in churches. It was at this same parliament that the king issued the Statute of Mortmain, which prohibited the grant of land to the Church. This was not an act of retaliation, for Pecham submitted before the statute was published, but it was symptomatic of the atmosphere between lay and ecclesiastical powers at this time, and was a pointed demonstration of royal authority. Grievances drawn up in 1280 went so far as to include a complaint that royal writs of prohibition were being used to prevent tithes from being collected from newly constructed mills, which met with a royal denial.[29] Pecham held another council, this time at Lambeth, in 1281. Demands for concessions from the king were met with a blunt refusal, since they would not benefit him, the Church, or the estate of the realm. No further dispute took place, however, perhaps because the king realized that Pecham did not represent a major threat to his authority.[30] Vigorous debate took place in 1285, when the clergy put forward seventeen articles of grievance, mostly going back to the issues raised at Reading and Lambeth. The boundaries of lay and ecclesiastical jurisdiction were disputed, particularly in the light of the recent murders of Laurence Duket in London, and of the precentor of Exeter cathedral, which involved members of the clergy. An inquiry in Norfolk revealed over 150 cases in which the church courts had overstepped their bounds. The crisis was calmed, however, by the issue of a writ known as *Circumspecte Agatis*, instructing Richard of Boyland, the justice active in Norfolk, to act cautiously. It set out the cases that were appropriate for church courts to hear, and offered a convenient compromise. Edward I had left England for Paris and Gascony, and was not anxious to see a serious dispute taking place with the Church.[31]

There was much else to concern churchmen in this period. The purpose of Pecham's appointment had been so that he might implement the reforming decrees of the second Council of Lyons. Issues of pluralism and absenteeism were important. The archbishop's decree, *Ignorantia Sacerdotum*, provided parish priests with a guide to how they were to instruct their flocks. Decrees covered a wide range of issues, such as the giving of the sacrament, and the taking of confession. A comprehensive programme of visitations showed Pecham's concern with pastoral issues and his desire to restore the purity of religious life. At Romsey he had to deal with an abbess who kept hounds and a pet monkey, and allowed her nephew the run of the premises. Inappropriate and superstitious celebrations, such as those at Christmas, were prohibited. He also became involved in bitter controversy with the bishop of Hereford,

[29] *Councils and Synods*, ii: *A.D. 1205–1313*, ed. F. M. Powicke and C. R. Cheney (Oxford, 1964), 873–86.

[30] D. Douie, *Archbishop Pecham* (Oxford, 1952), 95–142.

[31] Prestwich, *Edward I*, 255–8.

Thomas Cantilupe, displaying both bad temper and an exalted view of his own position.[32]

The universities, particularly Oxford, presented problems. In 1277 Archbishop Kilwardby, who had studied in the intellectual hotbed of Paris, publicly condemned thirty propositions, many of them derived from Aristotle and the work of Aquinas, that were being taught in the arts faculty at Oxford. His intervention had little effect, though the changes he instituted at Merton College entitle him to a place of honour in the history of university administration.[33] Pecham also became involved in problems at Merton, where the warden and fellows were in dispute. The latter understandably resented the scale of emoluments received by the former. In 1284 Pecham reiterated his predecessor's condemnation of the thirty propositions. This was seen by the Dominicans as an attack on them by the Franciscans, Pecham's order, and a bitter controversy followed. The attempt to impose an old-fashioned orthodoxy failed; the ideas that Kilwardby and Pecham criticized themselves developed into a new orthodoxy.[34]

PARLIAMENT AND LEGISLATION

The development of parliament was a vital element in the changing political structure of this period. Parliaments were frequent, with two or even three held in most years. The king himself had a central role in the assembly. The great Easter parliament of 1275 was unable to complete its work because Edward was ill.[35] The composition of the magnate element of parliament probably remained similar to that of Henry III's reign. For the Shrewsbury parliament of 1283, the attendance of ten earls and a hundred barons was requested; the lists used for military summonses were used to identify those who should come to

---

[32] Douie, *Pecham*, 134–8, 156–8; R. C. Finucane, 'The Cantilupe–Pecham Controversy', in M. Jancey (ed.), *St Thomas Cantilupe Bishop of Hereford: Essays in his Honour* (Hereford, 1982), 103–23.

[33] He ordered the appointment of a sub-warden, bursars, and no less than three deans, and might thus be considered responsible for the beginning of the movement that has in much more recent times seen a considerable increase in the proportion of university administrators as compared to mere academics. Further, in common with modern university financial officers, he forbade the carrying-over of credit balances from one financial year to the next: Martin and Highfield, *History of Merton College*, 48. The situation in the medieval period was, however, very different from that in modern times. A. Cobban, *English University Life in the Middle Ages* (London, 1999), 235, notes, for example, that 'In no way were administrative staff permitted to share in policy-making. Their task was to serve, not to manage.'

[34] *The History of the University of Oxford*, i: *The Early Oxford Schools*, ed. Catto, 116–19; Douie, *Archbishop Pecham*, 288–93.

[35] Sayles, *Functions of the Medieval Parliament*, 141–2.

parliament.[36] There was no question yet of receipt of a summons to parliament being an established right, much less a hereditary right. It is likely that the numbers of barons summoned to parliament varied considerably from one assembly to another. Representatives of shire and borough were not an essential element in parliament. It is conceivable that they may have been present on more occasions than are recorded; with the exception, however, of the Shrewsbury parliament of 1283 their known attendance corresponds with grants of taxation, and this was surely no coincidence. The first parliament of 1275 saw exceptionally heavy representation, with more townsmen present than in any other medieval parliament; at Shrewsbury, in contrast, it was only London and twenty other towns that were represented.[37] When representatives were summoned to Northampton in 1283, they were asked to come 'having full powers for their communities', and in 1290 shire representatives were to come 'with full powers for themselves and the whole community of the shire'. This terminology was important, for it ensured that the communities fully accepted that their representatives were empowered to make grants of taxation on their behalf.[38]

In parliament in 1278 sixty-one petitions were presented to the crown. This appears to have been a novelty, and was probably the result of positive encouragement by the king. There is certainly no evidence of petitions being presented in this way under Henry III. The process provided a convenient route for the king's subjects to bring complaints against royal officials in the localities. In 1279 proclamations in the shires asked people to bring to parliament complaints against Adam Stratton, a notably corrupt exchequer official.[39] By 1280 so many petitions were being brought forward in parliament that arrangements were made to streamline the way in which they were handled, so as to free up the king and council for discussion of major affairs of state.[40] The process of petitioning in parliament was one way in which Edward's government appeared far more open and responsive than had that of his father.

Justice was a central concern of parliaments.[41] Not only were cases determined and petitions heard in parliament, but also legislation was promulgated

[36] *Parl. Writs*, i. 15–16, 245–6.

[37] M. McKisack, *The Parliamentary Representation of the English Boroughs During the Middle Ages* (Oxford, 1932), 5–6.

[38] J. G. Edwards, 'The *Plena Potestas* of English Parliamentary Representatives', in E. B. Fryde and E. Miller (eds.), *Historical Studies of the English Parliament* (Cambridge, 1970), i. 136–49.

[39] J. R. Maddicott, 'Parliament and the Constituencies, 1272–1377', in R. G. Davies and J. H. Denton (eds.), *The English Parliament in the Middle Ages* (Manchester, 1981), 63–4.

[40] Sayles, *Functions of the Medieval Parliament*, 172.

[41] For Richardson and Sayles, justice provided the essential, central and defining function of parliament, but such a view distorts understanding of the nature of the assembly. See Prestwich, *Edward I*, 441.

there. Just as 1275 had been a great year for legislation, so was 1285. The Welsh war had been concluded, and in parliament the substantial statute known as Westminster II was promulgated. Its first clause, *de donis conditionalibus*, dealing with the question of conditional land settlements, was to have a fundamental impact on the workings of the land market. The king's intention was that the wishes of donors should be observed.[42] A wide range of other issues were dealt with in the statute; use of the writ of novel disseisin, for example, was extended, and the use of bogus arguments ('false exceptions') was forbidden. New procedures were introduced to deal with unreliable bailiffs. One clause allowed the chancery to issue novel writs, when 'a writ is found in one case, but none is found in a similar case'. A new writ was made available so that men could recover damages awarded by a court more easily than in the past.[43] Another important legislative act in the same year, 1285, was the Statute of Winchester, Edward's major measure dealing with the criminal law; this will be discussed in a later chapter.

The Statute of Merchants, also issued in 1285, revised and took further existing legislation. One of the problems that faced merchants was that of how to enforce payment of debts that they were owed. This issue had been tackled by Edward I and his council in the Statute of Acton Burnell of 1283. In a petition presented to the king in the summer of that year, Raymond Trespas explained that he had sold goods in London, Salisbury, and Winchester, and that although he had been given tallies and written promises of payment, he could not obtain the money that he was owed. The new statute allowed merchants to register debts before the mayors of London, York, and Bristol. If repayment did not take place, the mayor was empowered to sell the debtors' goods, and if all else failed, the final threat was one of imprisonment. The statute of 1285 set up more towns as registries, and provided that if a debt was not paid off promptly, the debtor was to be imprisoned and given three months to find the money. If he failed to do so, then his creditor was entitled to receive all his lands and goods, and to hold them until the debt was fully paid out of the proceeds. The scheme, though intended to meet the grievances of merchants, was in practice used much more widely, notably by royal officials such as Walter Langton.[44]

POLITICS AND PATRONAGE, 1289–1294

Edward spent the years from 1286 to 1289 in Gascony. His actions on his return suggest that he did not believe that England had been ruled properly in his absence, and was convinced that his ministers had been responsible for major abuses. The chief justice, Thomas Weyland, and many of his colleagues

---

[42] See below, 422–3.   [43] Prestwich, *Edward I*, 273–8.   [44] Ibid. 277–8.

were put on trial. Cases were brought against a large number of royal officials. Edward must have expected that this would be a popular move, but in fact it did him little credit. Although the downfall of judges and officials was welcome, the fact that they were mostly fined rather than being more severely punished led to suspicions that financial motives were more important for the king than was justice.[45]

In 1290 Edward was in urgent need of funds. The government at home had faced the costs of a Welsh rebellion in 1287; Edward himself had incurred debts of some £110,000 to his Italian bankers, partly as a result of financial commitments entered into in order to secure the release of Charles of Salerno from Aragonese captivity. In parliament in April 1290 the king obtained agreement to collect a feudal aid, a tax to which he was entitled on the occasion of the marriage of his daughter. Consent for this was not required, but it was tactful to put the issue to parliament. Collection of the aid, however, was shelved: it was unlikely to raise the sort of sums required. Knights of the shire were summoned to Westminster for a meeting on 15 July, at which they gave their consent to a tax of a fifteenth, to which the magnates had already given their consent. The tax yielded about £116,000, and was the most successful of any in Edward's reign.

The quid pro quo was evident three days after the fifteenth was granted, when an edict was promulgated for the expulsion of the Jews from England.[46] This met with contemporary approval, though it has done little for Edward I's reputation in more recent times. The reasons for the expulsion were complex. The Statute of Jewry of 1275 had set a period of fifteen years during which the Jews could acquire lands for leases of up to ten years. The fifteen years were now up, and one argument is that the Jews had failed to meet the terms set in 1290 and had not abandoned their usurious practices. Many of the bonds entered into by Jews in their last years in England saw values expressed in cereals or wool, rather than in cash. The existence of such commodity bonds suggests that they were indeed involved in trade, not simply moneylending. One objection to this analysis is that the values of the goods to be repaid were regularly fixed above market prices, suggesting that there was an element of disguised interest. In some cases at least, the bonds do look to have been genuine, and demonstrate that there was a degree of Jewish involvement in trade in grain and wool.[47] This, however, was too little and too late.

[45] State Trials of the Reign of Edward I, ed. T. F. Tout and H. Johnstone, Camden 3rd ser., 9 (1906), passim; P. A. Brand, 'Edward I and the Judges: The "State Trials" of 1289–93', in TCE i. 31–40.

[46] R. Stacey, 'Parliamentary Negotiation and the Expulsion of the Jews from England', in TCE vi. 77–101.

[47] Mundill, England's Jewish Solution, 108–45, argues that the bonds were genuine. But see also N. Vincent's review in EcHR 52 (1999), 568–9, and Brand, 'Jews and the Law'.

For the crown, there was a simple financial equation. How much were the Jews worth, in terms of the money that could be extracted from them in taxation, as compared to the likely yield from a tax? The Jewish communities had been taxed so hard that there was little more to be obtained from them. Henry III had imposed a 20,000 mark tallage on the Jews in 1241–2 (which raised just over £9,000), and one of 60,000 marks in 1244–50. These massive levies gravely weakened English Jewry, crippling it financially. In contrast, when a tallage of 5,000 marks was ordered in 1272, it yielded £1,289. Further tallages were imposed, and one calculation is that the Jews paid at least £5,301 to the crown between 1272 and 1278. The Jews were spared further taxation for much of the 1280s, but a tallage of 1287–8 raised almost £4,000. In all, it has been calculated that Edward I raised £9,271 from the Jews in the course of his reign.[48] A tax granted by the laity in parliament was worth far more than that, and in the event the fifteenth of 1290, as has been seen, raised about £116,000. The crown, however, maintained its concern to extract money from the Jews to the very end; an account reveals that £23 6s. was extracted by royal officials as a customary charge on the carriage of 1,335 Jews from London to France at 4d. a head, and to make matters worse still, 2d. a head on 126 poor Jews.[49]

The expulsion could be seen as in part an element of Simon de Montfort's legacy. The earliest known document issued by Montfort in England was his grant to the townspeople of Leicester announcing that no Jews should live there.[50] Appalling anti-semitic riots in London had characterized the support that Montfort received from the city. The issue of anti-semitism, however, was much wider than this. The influence of Edward's mother, Eleanor of Provence, is another possibility, for in 1275 she had expelled the Jews from the towns she held in dower. She also showed some enthusiasm for the conversion of the Jews.[51] There were horror stories of ritual murder, such as that which came up before the king in parliament, about 'the death of a certain Christian boy, who was crucified by these Jews and blasphemously and wretchedly slain in insult to the name of Jesus Christ and in breach of the peace of the realm and who was cast ashore at Dowgate by the flood-water of the Thames'.[52] The attitude of the Church towards the Jews is demonstrated by ecclesiastical legislation of 1287, echoing earlier measures, which forbade Christians from working in Jewish households, prohibited the eating of meals with Jews, made Jews stay within

---

[48] Stacey, *Politics, Policy and Finance*, 154–5; Mundill, *England's Jewish Solution*, 76–7, 88–90.
[49] E 101/4/5.
[50] Maddicott, *Simon de Montfort*, 15.
[51] Howell, *Eleanor of Provence*, 299–300, casts doubt on Eleanor's influence, seeing the expulsion of 1290 solely in financial terms.
[52] Sayles, *Functions of the Medieval Parliament*, 146.

their houses on Good Friday with windows closed, ordered Christians not to take medicines from Jews, and limited the building of synagogues. The atmosphere was one that favoured expulsion, though there is no evidence that Edward I himself was notably anti-semitic in his attitudes. There was, in addition, a Continental context. In France increasing restrictions were being placed upon the Jews in this period. In 1287 Edward himself expelled the Jews from Gascony. This may have been connected with the king's decision to take the cross; certainly it was not prompted by similar financial considerations to those that applied to England. In 1289 Charles of Sicily expelled the Jews from Maine and Anjou.[53] The expulsion of the Jews from England in 1290 was part of a pattern, not a unique event.

The years from 1290 to the outbreak of war with France in 1294 were to a considerable extent taken up by Scottish affairs, with the hearing of the great case over the succession to the throne. There were, however, other important issues. In a major case concerning two important earls, Gloucester and Hereford, the king showed his determination. There was a territorial dispute between the two earls in the Welsh marches, which had been running for some years. Gloucester was building a castle at Morlais, which Hereford claimed was his territory. The traditional method of settling disputes in the marches was by private war, but Hereford chose to appeal to the king. Gloucester, no doubt thinking that he was safe in the king's favour following his marriage to Edward's daughter Joan in May 1290, raided Hereford's lands in June and again later in the year. In January the king appointed a commission to investigate. A jury of twenty-four was assembled, and further hearings were planned to be held before the king at Abergavenny in September 1291. Hereford's men had conducted a retaliatory raid on Gloucester's lands by the time they took place. Both men were therefore tried before the king and his council. Both men were imprisoned and promptly bailed. They came before the king in parliament in January 1292. The sentences were fierce. Gloucester's liberty of Glamorgan, and Hereford's of Brecon, were to be confiscated. Both earls were to be imprisoned. Release was prompt; Gloucester was fined 10,000 marks, and Hereford 1,000. It was not long, however, before the lands were restored. The fines were never paid. Lists of the magnates who acted as guarantors for the two earls suggest that they both had considerable support; Edward was almost certainly wise not to proceed with the punishments that had been ordered. Nevertheless, the incident demonstrated the very different way in which Edward was prepared to act in comparison to his father. Further interventions in the Welsh marches emphasized the point.[54]

---

[53] Mundill, *England's Jewish Solution*, 50, 279–83.   [54] Prestwich, *Edward I*, 348–51.

This period from the king's return from Gascony to the start of war with France also saw changes among those close to the king, which help to explain the shifting character of Edward's government. In 1290 the queen, Eleanor of Castile, died. Judgements on her character have been varied. Her acquisition of land, particularly her use of Jewish debts for this purpose, was unpopular, and led to protests from the archbishop of Canterbury, Pecham. She did not act as an intermediary in requesting pardons to the same extent as did her mother-in-law, or Edward's second queen, Margaret of France. She was, on the other hand, cultured, possessing a library of romances. Some Arthurian works were dedicated to her. Above all, the king was devoted her. She had accompanied him on crusade, and went with him whenever possible on his travels within the British Isles, even giving birth to the future Edward II at Caernarfon. She performed her wifely duty of presenting the king with children with considerable efficiency; the couple probably had fifteen in all.[55] Eleanor was no cipher, and was ready to argue with Edward. When news came to the king in 1287 that Newcastle Emlyn had been taken by the Welsh, Edward was furious, blaming the earl of Cornwall. Eleanor, however, took a different view, accepting the argument that the capture was the fault of the keepers of the castles, who had not been prepared to garrison them adequately.[56]

The death of the queen mother, Eleanor of Provence, in 1291, marked the end of an era, but was not of great political significance. She had certainly not been reluctant to interfere in affairs of state, advising and instructing her son on diplomatic matters where she had an interest. She frequently interceded with Edward in favour of those who had approached her for help. Eleanor had, however, retired to the convent at Amesbury in Wiltshire in 1286, and the death of this strong-minded, remarkable woman did little to change the character of Edward's government.[57]

In the early 1290s there were also significant changes in the personnel of government. In part these were the result of the trials of the justices and officials, but death also deprived Edward of valuable servants. John Kirkby, exchequer stalwart, died in 1290, and more importantly, the death took place in 1292 of Robert Burnell. The surviving documents do not make it easy to assess Burnell's role in government, but this was a man whose influence went back to the later years of Henry III's reign. He had been largely responsible for holding government and country together in the years up to Edward's return from Gascony in 1274. He had his faults. He was acquisitive, and his morals were not those expected of a bishop. Some of the letters to him suggest, however, that he was a man who was well liked. Gloucester addressed him as his 'dear

---

[55] Ibid. 123–4; Parsons, *Eleanor of Castile*, 149–56.   [56] *Cal. Anc. Corr. Wales*, 174–5.
[57] For Eleanor, see Howell, *Eleanor of Provence*.

friend', and Roger Mortimer went further, with a letter beginning 'To his very dear and special friend'.[58] As chancellor, he did not transform the office he controlled. Yet he must have been one of the driving influences behind the great programme of reform. With his death, along with the departure from office of Chief Justice Hengham, much of the impetus for change was gone. The next generation of officials would not have experienced the heady excitements of the reform movement that began in 1258, and would not have the same commitment to change. At the same time, the challenges that they faced would be very different.

The years from the final collapse of the Montfortian cause to the early 1290s witnessed remarkably little political argument in England. One of the reasons for the difficulties of Henry III's reign had been the way in which royal patronage operated, above all with the favours that went to the Poitevins and the Savoyards. Edward I's approach was very different from that of his father. In one famous phrase, he 'preferred masterfulness to the arts of political management'.[59] Yet some political management was needed. In part Edward's position was easier than that of his father, for he did not face the same sort of demands. He had no half-brothers greedy for land, and his queen, Eleanor of Castile, did not bring a host of avaricious followers to England with her. Edward did, however, need to reward those upon whom he relied most. The links he had established with the Savoyards as a young man were not forgotten. One of his closest associates was Otto de Grandson. Otto did not receive land on any scale in England. He was given charge of the Channel Islands, and estates in Ireland, but little in England. This was not sufficient for him to abandon his homeland for good, and on the death of Edward he returned to Savoy, preferring not to serve the incompetent Edward II. Members of his family, however, remained in England, one becoming bishop of Exeter. Geoffrey de Geneville had family links with Savoy, and prospered in Edward's service; again, his main territorial interests lay in Ireland, not in England. His success in royal service therefore was not so much of a threat to established interests. Other Savoyards in Edward's service included Jean de Bevillard, who played an important part in the conquest of Wales, and the chief masons, notably James of St George, whom the king employed on his great castle-building programme, were also from Savoy. The way in which these men were managed and rewarded, however, never led to hostility against them in the way that had happened with the previous generation.

Edward was much concerned to provide his own family with sufficient lands. He was able to do this by manipulating the processes of inheritance in ways that

[58] SC 1/22/60; SC 1/22/68.
[59] K. B. McFarlane, *The Nobility of Later Medieval England* (Oxford, 1973), 267.

did not appear to threaten the nobility as a whole. His brother Edmund benefited immeasurably from the defeat of Simon de Montfort and the treatment of Robert Ferrers, acquiring as he did both the Leicester and Derby estates. In 1278 the king acquired the estates of Aveline de Forz, a major heiress who died childless. What appears to have been a fraudulent claimant was supported by the king, who gained the lands of Holderness, Skipton, and Cockermouth as a result. Aveline's mother, Isabella de Forz, countess of Aumale, was on her deathbed in 1293 when she agreed to a deal that gave the crown the Isle of Wight and other lands, effectively disinheriting her rightful heir, Hugh de Courtenay. The deal struck when the king's daughter Joan of Acre married the earl of Gloucester in 1290 fits into the same pattern of land acquisition for family purposes. Earl Gilbert's children from his previous marriage were disinherited, and arrangements were made to ensure that the great Gloucester inheritance would pass to Joan's children. Future earls would be closely linked to the crown by blood.[60] There may have been individual resentment at what took place, but the king's actions did not arouse widespread hostility.

While Edward's patronage was in some respects limited, conquest provided opportunities for generosity, and early in the second Welsh war, in October 1282, Earl Warenne, the earl of Lincoln, and Reginald de Grey all received major grants of land in north Wales. The Mortimers were also well rewarded for their part in the war, as was John Giffard. Not all the magnates, however, were so well treated, and the earls of Gloucester and Hereford, along with William de Valence, might have felt aggrieved that their efforts on Edward's behalf in south Wales did not produce dividends of the same sort.

CONCLUSION

The achievements in this period at home were remarkable, but they also need to be set against a background of further success, with the conquest of Wales and the management of Gascony. Edward also did much in the 1280s to promote peace in Europe. He succeeded in avoiding service with the French against the kingdom of Aragon in 1285, and played a role as a mediator. The release of Edward's cousin Charles of Salerno, son of Louis IX's brother Charles of Anjou, from captivity in Aragon was achieved at considerable cost to the English. Edward's ultimate ambition, however, was not to be fulfilled. Negotiations for a crusade in which the English king would take a leading role were lengthy and complex; issues of how the expedition was to be financed

[60] Ibid. 254–8.

were difficult. In 1287 Edward took the cross. There were ambitious hopes of winning the support of the Mongols (thought, wrongly, to be Christian), and of launching a concerted attack to rescue the Holy Land. The fall of Acre in 1291 did not galvanize the West as it might have done. An English embassy to the Persian Il-Khan in 1292 achieved nothing. Though Edward remained determined on a crusade, the problems he faced in Scotland and, from 1294, France made it impossible.

How much of the credit for the achievements of these years should go to the king himself is a difficult question. Edward's character is not easy to analyse, for he had no chroniclers of the calibre of Matthew Paris to record his actions. There is little surviving correspondence of a personal character. At the time of his accession he was not obviously suited to the task that faced him. His career since 1258 had given him a reputation for unreliability. He had initially opposed the Provisions of Oxford, had then entered into an alliance with his uncle Simon de Montfort, only to be brought back into the royal fold. He had shown political ability in 1263, when he did much to maintain the royalist cause at a difficult juncture, but there was nothing to suggest that he was a man of principle. Of his generation, it was his cousin Henry of Almain who looked to be the statesman, rather than the opportunistic Edward; Henry, however, was murdered at Viterbo in 1271 by two of Simon de Montfort's sons. What Edward had in his favour was a depth of experience and an iron will. He was a conventional man in many ways. His tastes were those of the aristocratic class to which he belonged. He enjoyed the hunt, both with falcon and bow, and was a keen participant in tournaments. His almsgiving was generous, and while Henry III had the great church at Westminster built, Edward founded Vale Royal abbey in Cheshire. Had it been completed, this would have had the largest church of any Cistercian abbey. Mysteriously, however, he declared in 1290 that he would have nothing more to do with the abbey, perhaps because his attention was diverted to Westminster, which, with his queen's burial, was beginning to emerge as a royal mausoleum. Edward was no scholar, and it is likely that it was men such as Ralph Hengham and Robert Burnell who provided the intellectual drive behind the reforms of these constructive years. Nevertheless, the king had a quick grasp of the problems of the law, and a clear understanding of the opportunities it presented him with. He was strong-willed and difficult to divert from his purpose; what is not so clear is whether he was a man of great vision.

CHAPTER 6

Wales

In 1284 a group of Welshmen came to Edward I at Conwy and presented him with a reliquary cross, the Croes Naid, containing some of the wood of the Cross itself. The surrender of this to the English king was a symbolic, moving acknowledgement of conquest, for the cross had been the prized possession of Llywelyn ap Gruffudd, prince of Wales.[1] Edward spent most of 1284 on a tour of Wales, no doubt content in the knowledge that Llywelyn's head adorned a pike mounted on the Tower of London. Conquest may appear, with the benefit of hindsight, to be the logical end of a process that began in the eleventh century, if not earlier, but to men in the early thirteenth century it would not have seemed an obvious outcome. What would have seemed far more probable was that the political authority of the Welsh princes would become more and more attenuated as their lands were divided between heirs, and that they would be increasingly integrated into the society of the marcher lords. This was the pattern in mid- and west Wales; the policies adopted by the princes of Gwynedd meant that the story for the country as a whole, and for the north in particular, was very different.

WALES AND THE MARCHES

Wales was a complex country, with traditions of political fragmentation rather than of unity.[2] Welsh princes ruled much of the country; but the power of the lords of the marches was also very considerable, particularly in the south. In the lands ruled by the Welsh, concepts of feudal lordship sat uneasily alongside older notions of authority. The three main kingdoms of Gwynedd, Powys, and Deheubarth all suffered divisions in the twelfth century. In the early thirteenth century, however, Llywelyn ap Iorwerth (Llywelyn the Great) established himself as ruler of Gwynedd, and obtained wider acknowledgement, partly

---

[1] J. B. Smith, *Llywelyn ap Gruffudd, Prince of Wales* (Cardiff, 1998), 580–1.
[2] For what follows, the best recent account is that provided by R. R. Davies, *Conquest, Coexistence and Change: Wales 1063–1415* (Oxford, 1987), 216–51.

by formal agreement and partly by more personal links, of his leadership in all of Wales. As for his attitude towards the English, 'Our liberties are no less than those of the king of Scots,' he wrote in 1224.[3] The confusion of civil war in England between 1215 and 1217 provided him with opportunities he gladly exploited. Llywelyn died in 1240. His son Dafydd succeeded him, but outlived his father by a mere six years, leaving no son himself. The next in line were his nephews, four sons of Gruffudd, grandson of Llywelyn ap Iorwerth. There was no principle of primogeniture as in England, and Owain, Llywelyn, Rhodri, and Dafydd were in a position either to share the lands of Gwynedd between them, or to compete one with another. Agreement that Owain and Llywelyn should share authority foundered when in 1255 Llywelyn defeated Owain and Dafydd at Bryn Derwin. He imprisoned the former and came to terms with the latter. Rhodri, in contrast to the other three brothers, never attempted to gain power in Wales, and instead settled with Llywelyn in 1272, accepting 1,000 marks in return for abandoning his claims. Llywelyn was the most successful of the brothers, succeeding in rebuilding an effective principality in Gwynedd and taking every advantage of the difficulties faced by Henry III in the 1260s. Dafydd's was a more maverick career. He plotted against his brother and supported Edward I against him in 1277. In the final tragedy of the dynasty, however, Llywelyn and Dafydd were united against the English foe.

The line of Llywelyn ap Iorwerth was not the only Welsh princely dynasty, though it was by far the most successful in this period. Powys had been powerful in the late twelfth century, but suffered from frequent divisions between the sons of its rulers. Gruffudd ap Gwenwynwyn, who ruled southern Powys from 1241, was not strong enough to exercise independent rule. By the 1270s it was clear to him that there was more likely to be a secure future for his dynasty under the protection of the English crown than under the aggressive authority of the rulers of Gwynedd. As a result, his was indeed the one Welsh dynasty to survive the catastrophe of the Edwardian conquest.

Deheubarth in south Wales had been a highly successful principality in the late twelfth century under Rhys ap Gruffudd, but after his death in 1197 the problems of partible inheritance and the vicious family feuds this engendered became extreme. Bitter quarrels laid Deheubarth open to intervention by the rulers of other parts of Wales, and more seriously by the lords of the marches and the English crown. While princely authority was consolidated in Gwynedd, it was fragmented elsewhere in Wales. Although south Wales was economically more prosperous than the mountainous regions of the north, in

---

[3] *Royal Letters Illustrative of the Reign of Henry III*, ed. Shirley, i. 229.

the thirteenth century it was Gwynedd alone that offered the leadership and the ambition that provided a challenge to eventual English dominance.

The lands of the marchers were a further element making up the complex mosaic of thirteenth-century Wales. The marcher lords had a strong sense of their separate, distinct identity, and it was by no means a foregone conclusion that their sympathies would necessarily lie with the rulers of England. Although primogeniture gave the social structure of the marches greater stability than the lands of 'pure' Wales, there were major transformations as a result of dynastic collapses, notably the failure of the line of Marshal earls of Pembroke in 1245. The marches were not clearly defined in geographical terms; military success for the English meant an expansion of marcher rule, notably

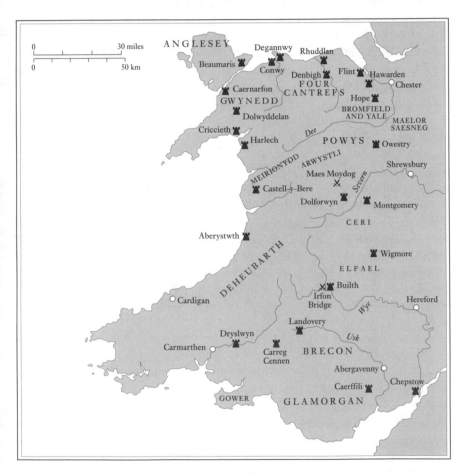

MAP 6.1. Wales

with the conquest of 1282–3. The earls of Gloucester had immense power in the south, where they held the lordship of Glamorgan, dominated from the late 1260s by the great castle of Caerffili. Brecon, held by the earls of Hereford, and Chepstow (or Striguil) held by the earls of Norfolk, were other powerful marcher lordships. The Braose lordship of Gower was another important bastion of marcher authority and independence in the south. Further north, in the middle marches, there were major lordships such as that held by the Mortimers of Wigmore. Other important marcher families included the FitzAlan earls of Arundel, the Cliffords, the Lestranges, and the Corbets. The Lacy lands in the march were divided after the death of Walter de Lacy in 1241 between his two daughters, one of whom married into the Verdun family and the other the Genevilles. In the north there was the earldom of Chester, which was held by the crown from 1237, when the last of the original line of earls, John the Scot, died. In 1254 it went to the king's eldest son, Edward. With the Edwardian conquest there came new families to rule great lordships in the northern marches, with the earl of Lincoln established at Denbigh and Earl Warenne in Bromfield and Yale. Reginald de Grey and John Giffard were also established as major marcher lords in the region.

The marcher lordships were characterized by a remarkable degree of juris-dictional authority.[4] This had complex origins; in part it was because of the way in which Norman lords had conquered these lands, taking over and adding to the rights of their Welsh predecessors. In part it was because the English shire system had not been extended into the marches. In 1247 Richard Siward complained that the earl of Gloucester 'was lord and virtually king and justiciar' in his court.[5] Royal writs were not valid in a great liberty such as that of Glamorgan, and there the pleas normally reserved to the crown were heard by the earls of Gloucester. The law that operated in the marches was marcher law, not the law of England. Significant elements of Welsh law survived in the marches, while the English law that operated there was not as up to date in some respects as the law in England. The thirteenth century saw a gradual closer delineation of the very considerable rights of these liberties, though even Edward I did not dare to investigate marcher authority by means of the *quo warranto* inquiries he used in England.

The interface between the marchers and the Welsh was not one of automatic hostility. Welsh lords were increasingly assimilated into marcher society, as the case of Gruffudd ap Madog of Bromfield illustrates. A Welshman whose land of Maelor Saesneg divided Cheshire from northern Shropshire, he had strong

---

[4] R. R. Davies, *Lordship and Society in the March of Wales 1282–1400* (Oxford, 1978), 149–75, discusses justice in the marches.

[5] M. Altschul, *A Baronial Family in Medieval England: The Clares* (Baltimore, 1965), 73.

marcher connections. In the early 1240s he married Emma Audley, and he employed a number of English servants, possibly even possessing two households, one English and one Welsh.[6] Even Llywelyn ap Iorwerth married his daughters into marcher families, while his wife had an affair with William de Braose. Roger Mortimer of Wigmore, who played such an important part in the Barons' Wars, was his grandson. Yet despite the long history of dealings at all levels between English and Welsh, cultural and linguistic problems remained. As a group of marchers pointed out in 1244 to the royal justiciar in south Wales, 'It is not easy in our region to reward or restrain the Welsh, unless this is done by someone of their own tongue.'[7]

The relationship between Welsh princes and marcher lords might be one of intermarriage, but it was also frequently one of conflict, of raid and counter-raid characterized by the destruction of settlements and even headhunting. In 1233 an English soldier, Richard de Muneton, and his companions received a bounty of 57s. for slaying that number of Welshmen who had been raiding Strattondale, near Montgomery, and bringing their heads as evidence. In 1249 a Welsh force raided the Montgomery district. Though the powerful castle of Montgomery did not fall, it was not capable of providing effective defence for the town, which the Welsh burned. A string of villages was destroyed. There was much destruction again in 1257. In 1263 the bailiff of Montgomery castle led a night-time raid into Welsh territory, only to be ambushed on his return.[8] Fortification was one answer to the problem presented by the tit-for-tat of border warfare, but strong walls were no use without men to provide active defence. As a result, marcher society was more highly militarized than that of the rest of England.

Wales, therefore, presented complex threefold problems involving the English crown, the marchers, and the native Welsh rulers. From the point of view of the English government, it was important to get full acknowledgement from the Welsh of English suzerainty. There was a pattern of brief royal campaigns in Wales, followed by a renegotiation of the relationship. For the marchers, it was important to retain the jurisdictional rights they claimed, and to expand the territory that they controlled. As for the Welsh, despite the many divisions that existed, there was a real and increasing sense of nationhood and a desire for independence.

---

[6] D. Stephenson, 'The Laws of Court: Past Reality or Present Ideal?', in T. M. Charles-Edwards, M. E. Owen, and P. Russell (eds.), *The Welsh King and his Court* (Cardiff, 2000), 404–5.
[7] *Royal Letters*, ed. Shirley, i. 426. For the correct date, see W. H. Waters, *The Edwardian Settlement of West Wales 1277–1343* (Salford, 2000), 92.
[8] F. Suppe, *Military Institutions on the Welsh Marches: Shropshire*, A.D. *1066–1300* (Woodbridge, 1994), 9, 12, 21, 23.

HENRY III AND WALES

Llywelyn ap Iorwerth was a difficult opponent. Conflict with the English was centred on the middle marches, where Hubert de Burgh's government provided limited support to the lords of the area in three campaigns against the Welsh prince in 1223, in Montgomery, in 1228 in Ceri, not far from Montgomery, and in 1231 in Elfael, a little further south.[9] These three campaigns achieved very little, and did much to discredit de Burgh's regime. In each case a reasonably substantial English army moved only a short distance into Welsh territory. There was a castle built, or planned, on each occasion; in 1223 a magnificent new castle overlooking Montgomery, in 1228 the castle known as Hubert's Folly was barely started before it was abandoned, and in 1231 Painscastle was reconstructed. One chronicler, however, unkindly noted that on this occasion Llywelyn had destroyed ten castles in the marches.[10] The resources that the English were able to deploy were quite substantial. One calculation is that, for the Ceri campaign, Hubert de Burgh had at his disposal a feudal host of about 425 knights, with a further 120 knights provided by the royal household, as well as infantry troops.[11] Yet the problems of the terrain, the difficulties of providing adequate supplies, and the skill of the Welsh meant that very little was achieved.

Llywelyn's death transformed the situation in Wales. A brief campaign in 1241, launched from Chester rather than the middle marches, led to his successor Dafydd's abject submission to the English king. Lands seized by the Welsh since 1216 were to be restored. Degannwy was handed over to the English. In the south, Carmarthen and Cardigan were surrendered, and other lands were taken over by the English. The English position was, however, far from secure. Welsh rebellion in 1244 looked serious. John Lestrange wrote in considerable alarm early in 1245 about the advances that the Welsh had made. They had even constructed siege engines to threaten English-held castles, and Lestrange feared that the king 'will not be able to do for ten thousand pounds what he could previously have done for a thousand'.[12] Henry's response to the problem must have cost a good deal more than £10,000, for he launched a large-scale campaign in north Wales.

Henry III's army in 1245 mustered in response to a feudal summons. A part record of the muster survives. It shows that the level of service provided was very much lower than the traditional twelfth-century quotas; this had become normal in the thirteenth century. The FitzWalter barony of Little Dunmow in

---

[9] R. F. Walker, 'Hubert de Burgh and Wales, 1218–1232', *EHR* 87 (1972), 465–94.
[10] Ann. Dunstable, 422.
[11] Walker, 'Hubert de Burgh and Wales', 480, 489.   [12] *Cal. Anc. Corr. Wales*, 22.

Essex, for example, had an old quota of sixty-three and a half knights, but in 1245 service of just two knights was provided. The process by which the reductions were achieved remains obscure, but represents a striking success on the part of the baronage. Records of a muster in 1218 show that the new levels were, for the most part, acknowledged by then. In some cases in 1245 men voluntarily offered more than their formal obligation. Thus Robert de St John owed the service of three knights, but his contingent, including himself, numbered five. Peter of Savoy's traditional quota for the honour of Richmond was 140; he acknowledged an obligation to provide five knights, but actually campaigned with thirteen.[13] In practice, the army was only in small measure 'feudal'. All of the infantry would have been paid by the crown, as would the force of the king's household knights. The marcher lords, however, were expected to fight from their own resources.

The campaign of 1245 was supported from Ireland as well as from England, but although the plans were elaborate, the preparations were not all they should have been. Above all, food supplies ran short. A letter written from Degannwy describes cold, frightened men unable to pay the exorbitant prices being charged. A halfpenny loaf cost 5*d*.[14] Nevertheless, the English were able to begin the building of a new castle at Degannwy, and they demonstrated that they could push a substantial army a long way into north Wales. The expedition did not achieve all that was hoped, but the English position was greatly strengthened by the death of Dafydd in 1246. In the following year the Welsh under Owain and Llywelyn ap Gruffudd submitted in the treaty of Woodstock.

Now, in 1247, Henry III's dominance over Wales was acknowledged. The dependence of the Welsh princes was made clear. They were now tenants of the English crown, holding their lands in accordance with the obligations of fealty and homage. Military service might be demanded from them, and the English king claimed ultimate rights of jurisdiction over them. In territorial terms, there was a massive English expansion into north Wales. The Four Cantrefs of Rhos, Rhufuniog, Dyffryn Clwyd, and Tegeingl, which together made up the Perfeddwlad, went to the crown. The castles of Degannwy and Diserth protected this English expansion. In mid-Wales the crown held Montgomery and the lordship of Builth, while in the west it held Carmarthen and Cardigan. It has been suggested that Henry could have achieved even more than this had he wished, but there was no reason why he should have sought complete conquest.[15] The campaign of 1245 had shown the limitations, as well

---

[13] I. J. Sanders, *Feudal Military Service in England* (Oxford, 1956), 73, 110–14, 133, 145; M. C. Prestwich, *Armies and Warfare in the Middle Ages: The English Experience* (London, 1996), 68–70.

[14] Paris, *Chron. Maj.* iv. 481–4.

[15] D. A. Carpenter, *The Struggle for Mastery: Britain 1066–1284* (London, 2003), 364–5.

as the might, of the English army, and there would have been considerable risks in further military action. With the subjection of the Welsh princes in the treaty of 1247 Henry achieved all he wanted.

The scale of the English successes of the 1240s proved deceptive, and in the second half of the next decade the pendulum swung back as the Welsh acquired new leadership under Llywelyn ap Gruffudd. He was determined to resist partition, and was equally determined to revive the authority of his dynasty, treating other Welsh rulers as his vassals. English administration in the Four Cantrefs aroused much hostility, and royal instructions that the English were to use the established laws and customs did not ease the situation.[16] In 1254 the crown lands in Wales, along with Chester, were granted to the king's eldest son, Edward, as part of the massive appanage he received following his marriage. Edward's justice of Chester, Geoffrey de Langley, was even more unpopular than Alan la Zouche, who preceded him. A visit by Edward in the summer of 1256 did not improve the situation. Rebellion began in that year, and achieved rapid success, as it spread nationwide. An English army under Stephen Bauzan was defeated in the south in 1257 at Cymerau. Henry III's initial view that Wales was for his son Edward to deal with was misguided, and when he launched a campaign himself in the late summer of 1257, little was achieved even though the English forces reached Degannwy. By 1258 the political difficulties the king faced meant that there was no hope of mounting an effective campaign. In that year Llywelyn used the title of Prince of Wales for the first time.[17]

LLYWELYN AP GRUFFUDD

The political turmoil that England suffered from 1258 to 1265 presented Llywelyn ap Gruffudd with splendid opportunities, although at the same time the uncertainties made it impossible for him to reach the final settlement with the English that would secure his position. There were real dangers for him should he support what turned out to be the losing side in the English civil conflict. In 1259 he explained that he was ready to do homage to Henry III, and marry a royal niece, provided that he was accorded the position that Llywelyn ap Iorwerth had held. No settlement could be obtained from the English government, and by 1262 Llywelyn resorted to war, attacking the central marches. In December the bishop of Hereford wrote in alarm after one of Mortimer's castles surrendered to the Welsh. 'All this has given rise to

---

[16] For the following events, see Smith, *Llywelyn ap Gruffudd*, 77 ff., and Prestwich, *Edward I*, 17–19.
[17] *Littere Wallie*, ed. J. G. Edwards (Cardiff, 1940), 184–5.

rumours of treachery and the whole March is in terror. The Welsh have for the most part burned and plundered the lands of the March nearly to Weobley, Eardisley and the vale of Wigmore.' Early in 1263 a force of marchers had a limited success against part of a Welsh force, but the constable of Abergavenny feared a revenge attack. If this happened, 'they will destroy all the king's land as far as the Severn and the Wye'. Another letter, from John de Grey, expressed fears that 'Llywelyn had caused a great army to be collected from all directions in order to devastate and occupy the lands of the king and those loyal to the king.'[18] In the north Llywelyn's forces took Diserth and Degannwy, the two powerful symbols of the English advance towards the river Conwy.

Llywelyn's position became increasingly clear; he gave his backing to the Montfortians, and in 1265 he obtained in return full recognition of his position as Prince of Wales, and of the gains he had made. He remained properly cautious, and his forces did not take part directly in the campaign that led to Montfort's defeat and death at Evesham. That defeat was not a complete disaster for Llywelyn, for the English government was in no position to adopt an aggressive policy towards him. Rather, a peace settlement was needed. In 1267 the treaty of Montgomery was negotiated. In this, Llywelyn's title of Prince of Wales was acknowledged, and the other Welsh rulers (with one exception) became his tenants, owing him fealty and homage. He now had an acknowledged dominion over Powys and Deheubarth, in addition to his own Gwynedd. Most of the territorial gains he had made in the 1260s were conceded. There was a price to pay for all this. Llywelyn acknowledged that he owed fealty and homage to Henry III. In addition the Welsh prince agreed to pay 25,000 marks in yearly instalments. He also promised to restore the lands he had taken from his brother Dafydd when the latter had defected from his cause in 1263.[19]

A treaty was one thing, the reality of power might be quite another. Llywelyn was anxious to secure his lordship in the south. This threatened the marcher lords, of whom the most powerful was the earl of Gloucester. In 1268 the earl began to build a new castle at Caerffili, which Llywelyn destroyed in 1270. Llywelyn's own construction of a castle at Dolforwyn, close to Montgomery, was a serious issue in 1273. That was not all. A letter stated that 'Llywelyn's men have invaded Brecon, the land of Humphrey de Bohun, and other lands of his, laying them waste; they have also presumed to besiege and occupy his castles.'[20] From 1270 Llywelyn failed to make the payments due under the agreement of 1267, and he soon began to argue that he would resume payment only when the marchers returned lands that were rightly his. Once

---

[18] *Cal. Anc. Corr. Wales*, 15, 18, 53.   [19] *Littere Wallie*, 1–4.
[20] *Cal. Anc. Corr. Wales*, 57.

Edward returned to England from Gascony in 1274, a new element featured in the disputes, that of the homage and fealty that Llywelyn was due to perform. The Welsh prince did not attend Edward's coronation, and did not respond to repeated summonses from Edward. Even when the king went to Chester, Llywelyn still would not come. This failure to acknowledge Edward's feudal overlordship provides the formal explanation for the outbreak of war in 1276.

There were, of course, deeper reasons for the conflict. One was the plot to kill Llywelyn, hatched in 1274, in which Gruffudd ap Gwenwynwyn and his son conspired together with Llywelyn's brother Dafydd. When the details gradually emerged, the conspirators fled to England to be under Edward's protection. This naturally infuriated the Welsh prince. A second issue was Llywelyn's decision to marry Simon de Montfort's daughter Eleanor. No doubt this had been bruited as a possibility in the mid-1260s, but it was only in the aftermath of the plot against him that Llywelyn decided to go forward with the plan. For Edward, this was intolerable, and his delight can only be imagined at the news in 1275 that Eleanor had been captured at sea, on her way from France to Wales. The prospect that Llywelyn would produce an heir whose blood was that of Simon de Montfort was one that must have appalled Edward. Negotiations failed, despite the involvement of the archbishop of Canterbury.[21]

THE EDWARDIAN CONQUEST

The campaign of 1277 had been a long time coming. It was not a war of conquest; it fitted into the previous pattern of wars in Wales rather than being a precursor of the war of 1282–3. Commanders were appointed in the marches, and Edward was able to put quite substantial paid forces into action in the early part of the year; in the middle marches the knights of the royal household, together with forces under the command of the earl of Lincoln, numbered about 150 cavalry. The marchers served at their own expense. Paid forces in the south numbered about 120. Very considerable successes were achieved, even before the royal army had mustered. The garrison of Llywelyn's castle of Dolforwyn surrendered in April, marking the end of the prince's attempts to establish his power in the middle marches. The loyalty of the Welsh lords of this area, and of the south, to Llywelyn was paper-thin, and surrender followed surrender. Resentment at Llywelyn's rule had been simmering for years, and the weakness of the edifice he had constructed was now revealed. The Welsh

---

[21] The fullest account of the events leading to the war of 1277 is provided by Smith, *Llywelyn ap Gruffudd*, 338 ff. The war itself is fully analysed ibid. 414 ff. See also J. E. Morris, *The Welsh Wars of Edward I* (Oxford, 1901), 110–48, and Prestwich, *Edward I*, 177–82.

prince's technique of forcing loyalty by taking hostages from nobles in mid- and south Wales cannot have endeared him to them. Men such as Rhys ap Maredudd in the south had gained little from allegiance to Llewelyn, and were very willing to throw off the yoke of Gwynedd in favour of an English one.

Edward had issued a conventional feudal summons in December 1276, for a muster at Worcester the following July. This yielded service of 228 knights and 294 sergeants. Paid troops, combined with men serving at their own expense but not under a formal feudal obligation, probably brought the cavalry strength up to 800 or more. Arrangements were made for the recruitment of infantry; at its peak there would be about 15,500, of whom 9,000 were Welshmen drawn from the south. Steps to provide victuals for the army look to have been limited. Some supplies were requested from Ireland, and in July commissions were set up to buy grain in nine counties. There was little about this army that was novel; these were the methods of recruitment that were familiar from Henry III's reign.

The troops who mustered at Worcester marched swiftly north, to Chester. From there the royal army advanced rapidly to Flint, where a camp was established. The king then advanced to Rhuddlan, and on to Degannwy. Naval support was provided by the fleet of the Cinque Ports, and a force was sent to Anglesey, where the English collected the harvest. There is no record of any significant military action, though no doubt the English army caused much damage during its advance. Edward decided on negotiation rather than out-and-out conquest. It may well be that by early November he was running short of both supplies and men. This had never been intended as a campaign of conquest. He had set out his aims in late August. What he hoped to do was to extend the area of English rule, taking over the Four Cantrefs, and to oust Llewelyn, replacing him with his brothers Dafydd and Owain. Anglesey, Snowdonia, and other lands in the west were either to be divided up between himself and the two Welsh princes, or, if he so chose, Edward would retain Anglesey, and the other lands would be divided between Dafydd and Owain. What he achieved in the treaty of Aberconwy in November was more limited. The Four Cantrefs were retained by Edward, as were all other war gains with the exception of Anglesey, which Llewelyn was allowed to keep in return for an annual rent of 1,000 marks. Llewelyn was allowed to retain Dafydd's lands in Gwynedd; Dafydd would be compensated with land elsewhere. Owain was to be released from captivity. A massive indemnity of £50,000 was imposed on Llewelyn, though he was soon released from this obligation.[22]

The campaigns in Wales of Henry III's reign had been consolidated by castle-building, and Edward I continued this pattern. The campaign base at

---

[22] *Littere Wallie*, 103–4, 118–22; Smith, *Llywelyn ap Gruffudd*, 438–44.

Flint was further fortified with a fine castle, and rather than rebuild his father's castle at Diserth, Edward chose to build at Rhuddlan. Builth in mid-Wales and Aberystwyth on the west coast also saw the building of new royal castles. The diplomatic success of the treaty of Aberconwy was set in stones and mortar. To build these castles Edward first turned to Master Bertram, a Gascon engaged on building military machines at the Tower of London. The king, however, did not want to interrupt progress of the elaborate works at the Tower, and soon recruited Master James of St George from Savoy.[23] He first appears in the accounts for April 1278, and was the leading expert for the whole of the great building programme in Wales. The new castles were unusual. At Flint one of the four corner towers of the inner ward formed a free-standing donjon of remarkable form. In the way in which it is sited it resembles the Tour de Constance at Aigues Mortes, which Edward would have seen on his way to his crusade, but its plan, consisting of one drum inside another, was unique. At Rhuddlan the massive inner ward featured two twin-towered gatehouses, placed unconventionally at the angles, not mid-way along the curtain wall. An outer line of defences added considerably to the strength of castles, which the Welsh were scarcely in a position to challenge. Should they threaten a blockade, at both Flint and Rhuddlan care was taken to ensure that provisions could be easily supplied by sea, as could also be done at Aberystwyth. The fourth castle built after Edward's first Welsh war was at Builth, where an old motte-and-bailey site was refortified.[24]

In just five years the settlement of 1277 broke down completely. The English show of force had not been sufficient to quench the spirit of the Welsh, and in the aftermath of the war mismanagement and miscalculation goaded them into rebellion. English officialdom was good at being oppressive, and seized every opportunity to demonstrate this. The appointment of Reginald de Grey as constable of Chester in 1281 was particularly important, marking as it did the adoption of a particularly harsh and aggressive style of English rule. The way in which the volatile prince Dafydd was treated was perhaps the most serious error committed by the English. Dafydd had obtained less than he hoped for out of the war of 1277, and his entanglement in the complex processes of English law drove him into rebellion. A dispute between Dafydd and William de Venables over lands granted to the prince in 1277 provided an important test case. It had earlier been determined that these lands were Welsh and should be subjected to Welsh law, but Grey took a different view. Dafydd went

---

[23] A. J. Taylor, 'Master Bertram, *Ingeniator Regis*', in C. Harper-Bill, C. J. Holdsworth, and J. L. Nelson (eds.), *Studies in Medieval History Presented to R. Allen Brown* (Woodbridge, 1989), 289–304; A. J. Taylor, *Studies in Castles and Castle-Building* (London, 1985), 63–7.
[24] *KW* i. 293–9.

to the county court at Chester, and argued that he was under no obligation to answer there for land subject to Welsh law. The case was particularly important for Dafydd, since he was building a new castle, Caergwrle (Hope), on the disputed territory. In more general terms, Dafydd must have been very discontented at not receiving rewards for his support of Edward in the war of 1277 on the scale he must have expected.

The most celebrated issue was over Arwystli, and involved Llywelyn himself. The Welsh prince had taken this land from Gruffudd ap Gwenwynwyn of Powys in 1274. The problem was whether the case that resulted should be heard according to Welsh law, as Llywelyn demanded, or marcher law, as Gruffudd sought. This was a tricky matter, which the English met with all the prevarication of which they were capable. A commission that sat in 1281 to investigate the laws and customs of Wales was of little help, and the incessant delays suited Edward, since a decision in the case risked either alienating a loyal supporter in Gwenwynwyn, or antagonizing Llywelyn to such a degree that he would be forced into rebellion.

Law became central in these years to the rhetoric that the Welsh hurled at the English. It now appeared, as never in the past, as central to Welsh identity. 'All Christians have laws and customs in their own lands; even the Jews in England have laws among the English; we had our immutable laws and customs in our lands until the English took them away after the last war.'[25] For Edward, it was quite unacceptable that he should allow Welsh laws to be observed unless they were just and reasonable. Law was, of course, an important element in national identity, but the way in which it was elevated in these years suggests that Llywelyn deliberately chose to challenge Edward on this issue, even though it was not a matter over which the Welsh people necessarily felt very deeply. The position in Scotland makes an interesting comparison, for there law was never regarded as crucial to independence in the same way. What was at stake ultimately in Wales was not whether English legal customs were adopted in cases such as that over Arwystli, but the question of power and who was to exercise it.[26]

Edward's policies in the years after his first Welsh war do him little credit. He displayed no appreciation of the difficult position that Llywelyn and Dafydd were in, and showed no political subtlety in his management of the Welsh princes. It was not that he was unaware of the grievances of the Welsh, but rather that he did not consider that they were worth taking into account. What Edward managed to do as a result was to unite the Welsh in opposition to

---

[25] *The Welsh Assize Roll, 1277–1284*, ed. J. Conway Davies (Cardiff, 1940), 266.
[26] Prestwich, *Edward I*, 188; R. R. Davies, *The King of England and the Prince of Wales, 1277–84: Law, Politics and Power*, Kathleen Hughes Memorial Lectures, University of Cambridge (2003).

him. Given the past history of relations between Llywelyn and Dafydd, and of the hostility that existed in mid- and south Wales to the dynasty of Gwynedd, this was remarkable.

When the rebellion came, at Easter 1282, it was Dafydd who began it. The castles of Hawarden, Oswestry, Aberystwyth, Carreg Cennen, and Llandovery were all taken. Flint and Rhuddlan were attacked. The Welsh moves had come in remarkably coordinated fashion in the north, east, south, and west. For Edward I, there was now no option. This would be a war of conquest, not one simply intended to tame a difficult vassal. Llywelyn had almost certainly not intended to challenge Edward again in war, but the option of siding with the English against his brother can hardly have been imaginable. The death of his wife when giving birth to a daughter, it has been suggested, would have shattered his hopes for continuing his dynasty. In his despair, all he could do was to join in the rebellion, hopeless though the task must have seemed.[27]

The first step for the English was to set up commands in the marches.[28] Reginald de Grey's troops at Chester were swiftly reinforced with household knights. The main muster was set for Worcester, on 17 May; the magnates summoned there were asked to serve at the king's wages, a startling change from past practice. When the king reached Worcester, however, new summonses were issued, traditional in form, asking for feudal service, unpaid, with a muster at Rhuddlan on 2 August. The reasons for this late change of plan are not clear. One hypothesis is that the king was faced with objections from the magnates, who might have resented the subordination implied in accepting wages. The sources, however, do not even hint at any disagreement, and it is possible that the change was the king's own decision, intended as a way of boosting recruitment.[29]

Edward's march to Chester, and on to Flint and Rhuddlan, went smoothly, and further consolidation met with little resistance. The next objective was Anglesey. A force, commanded by Luke de Tany, sailed there in October. The plan was extraordinarily ambitious; Anglesey was to be linked to the mainland by a bridge of boats, so that Tany and his men could strike into the heart of Snowdonia. By the time that the bridge was ready, however, pressure was building for a settlement. The strategy had depended not only on Edward's own army advancing along well-known routes into north Wales, but also on the actions of English armies further south. There things went less well. Part of Gloucester's substantial army was defeated by the Welsh in June. Edward, always suspicious of the earl, removed Gloucester from command; Gloucester

[27] Smith, *Llywelyn ap Gruffudd*, 510.

[28] The fullest account of the war is given by Smith, ibid. 511 ff. See also Prestwich, *Edward I*, 182–201.

[29] Morris, *Welsh Wars*, 156–8; Prestwich, *Edward I*, 189.

promptly withdrew his troops. He was replaced in command by William de Valence, who conducted a raid that reached Aberystwyth but failed to engage the Welsh. In mid-Wales the death through natural causes of Roger Mortimer in October was a major setback for the English. The time was ripe for negotiations, and John Pecham, archbishop of Canterbury, attempted to mediate. There was little chance of success. Llywelyn could provide an impressive list of grievances, but offered no grounds for compromise, while Edward was insistent that the Welsh prince should submit unconditionally to his will. Pecham's attempt to find a route to peace was creditable, but as an English archbishop he was deeply distrusted by the Welsh. It is hardly surprising that he was treated with sarcasm and disdain.[30]

While the negotiations were still under way, news came of the dramatic defeat of Luke de Tany and his men on 6 November. The incredible engineering feat of constructing the pontoon bridge from Anglesey was successful. Tany crossed, and as he and his men returned from a brief raid on the mainland, they were ambushed by the Welsh. At least sixteen knights were slain. This must have given the Welsh new heart, and Llywelyn gave his final rejection to the peace proposals, which had included the secret suggestion that he would be given land in England if he surrendered all he held in Wales. Unexpectedly, he marched out of Snowdonia towards Builth in mid-Wales, possibly lured by the Mortimers by means of a bogus suggestion of an alliance, and possibly betrayed in some way by a few among his own men. On 11 December Llywelyn met an English force in battle, at a bridge over the river Irfon. Accounts of the battle are inconsistent one with another, but the central facts are clear, that an army led by the lords of the middle marches met the Welsh in battle, and that after what seems to have been a fierce fight, the Welsh prince was killed. This was not the end of the war; there was no realistic option for Prince Dafydd other than to continue to resist the might of the English war machine.

Edward took a bold decision. A winter campaign in the Welsh mountains was an enterprise full of risk, but the king was determined. He recruited fresh troops and in January marched into the Welsh heartland of Snowdonia. Dolwyddelan, apparently secure in a remote fastness, was taken, and its new English garrison equipped with winter camouflage. At much the same time Valence led a raid from Cardigan to Aberystwyth, and in April he moved into Meirionydd, and forced the surrender of Castell-y-Bere. These operations were of vital importance, complementing those of the king in the north, maintaining remorseless pressure on the Welsh.[31] In March the king moved

---

[30] For Pecham's negotiations, see D. Douie, *Archbishop Pecham* (Oxford, 1952), 234 ff.; Smith, *Llywelyn ap Gruffudd*, 530–6.

[31] R. F. Walker, 'William de Valence and the Army of West Wales, 1282–3', *Welsh History Review*, 18 (1997), 407–29.

his headquarters from Rhuddlan to Conwy, and all that remained was to hunt down Prince Dafydd. He was eventually captured on 21 June, through the treachery of his compatriots.

As already seen, castle-building was an important part of Edward's strategy. New castles were built at Harlech (Plate 4), Conwy, and Caernarfon (Plate 5), and new work took place at Criccieth. In addition, seigneurial castles were built at Denbigh, Holt, and Ruthin. Master James of St George, assisted by other Savoyards, was primarily responsible. At Harlech it is easy to see a further development of the type of castle built after the first Welsh war. A massive inner ward, with great twin-towered gatehouse providing accommodation as well as defence, dominated. A narrow outer ward with a much less formidable curtain wall followed the concentric principle. At Conwy and Caernarfon the sites demanded different treatment. In each case, a long site meant that the best solution was two linked wards. At Conwy there was no twin-towered gatehouse, but the entrance was nevertheless well guarded. One ward was marked out by watchtowers placed on the towers and characterized by magnificent suites of accommodation within it. Caernarfon was more grandiose still. It featured two splendid gatehouses, and an extra-large triple-turreted tower appears to have been intended to perform something of the function of a keep.

The Savoyard element in the castles can easily be demonstrated from the details of the architecture. The use of scaffolding spiralling up the towers, which can be seen from the holes left when the supporting beams were removed, was not an English technique. Full-centred round arches were a Savoyard element. The construction of latrine chutes at the re-entrant angle between towers and curtain walls was novel in English building, but very strikingly, the measurements of one such chute at Harlech are identical to one at St Georges d'Espéranche, the castle from which James took his name. The pay records for the process of castle-building reveals the presence not only of Master James but of other Savoyards as well. What this type of analysis fails to reveal, however, is who was responsible for the overall design of the castles. Is it likely that the king entrusted the whole process to James of St George, or did he and his military experts take a hand? The probable answer is that the design of the castles was the result of lengthy discussion between a number of people, of whom the king was surely one, along with other men of military experience, and the technical expert, Master James of St George.[32]

Whoever was primarily responsible for the design of the castles, the fact remains that these castles stand as a remarkable testimony to Edward I's

---

[32] A. J. Taylor, *Studies in Castles and Castle-Building* (London, 1985), 1–28; N. Coldstream, 'Architects, Advisers and Design at Edward I's Castles in Wales', *Architectural History*, 46 (2003), 19–36.

extraordinarily grandiose vision, which extended to seeing Caernarfon as a Welsh Constantinople. The polygonal towers and dark bands running through the masonry recall the Theodosian walls of the Byzantine capital; well-informed people would have appreciated the way in which Edward I was paying homage to the legend that saw the emperor Magnus Maximus, alleged father of Constantine, buried at Caernarfon: Edward had what he thought were Magnus Maximus' remains reburied in the church at Caernarfon in 1283.[33] The castles were a magnificent achievement and must have exemplified for the Welsh the astonishing scale of Edward's power. Yet it was hardly necessary to have built on quite so megalomaniac a scale to keep down a people who, for all their undoubted spirit, had such limited resources.

THE ORGANIZATION OF WAR

The war of 1282–3 saw the English state organized for war more intensively than ever before. The strategy may have resembled that of the 1277 campaign against Llywelyn, and even that of Henry III's 1245 expedition, while the component elements of the army were also similar. However, the magnitude of the financial commitment, and the scale of the logistic arrangements, marked out this war as a new and distinct stage in the development of the English military machine.

Despite the initial plans to summon men to serve for pay, the recruitment of cavalry followed traditional lines.[34] The record of the feudal muster lists just 123 knights and 190 sergeants, but this may not be all who responded. Paid cavalry probably numbered seven or eight hundred, while many magnates, particularly marcher lords, served at their own expense. Exceptionally, Geoffrey de Camville obtained letters from the king to ensure that no precedent would be made of this service.[35] There was a substantial contingent recruited from Gascony, numbering forty knights, 120 other cavalry, and up to 1,300 infantry. The crossbow was their specialized weapon. Pay rolls suggest that at any one time up to 8,000 infantry were employed by the crown, mostly drawn from the marches, and from counties adjacent to Wales. In addition, in April 1282 writs were sent out for the recruitment of 1,010 diggers and 345 carpenters, for there was a need to cut roads through the Welsh forests, and for the construction of fortifications of earth and timber.

Thought was given to every possible problem. There was a worry that there were not enough great horses, suitable for heavily armed knights, in England.

---

[33] *KW* i. 369–71.   [34] For the following section, see Prestwich, *Edward I*, 196 ff.
[35] *Calendar of Various Chancery Rolls: Supplementary Close Rolls, Welsh Rolls, Scutage Rolls 1277–1326* (London, 1912), 229.

One answer was to import them; the earl of Warwick and Walter de Beauchamp, for example, were given letters of safe conduct to bring thirty-six
horses to England. In May orders were issued that everyone with at least
£30 worth of land a year should have such a horse; that was not practicable,
and in June those who owed service but did not have an adequate horse were
allowed to pay fines in lieu of mustering in person.[36] Much equipment was
needed. Ready-made hurdles, to form palisades, were shipped from Chester.
Lead and iron were provided for the smiths. Sheaves of arrows and crossbow
bolts were bought in London. Lances were acquired to bear the king's banners.
Tents and pavilions were needed for Edward and his household.[37]

Provisioning was a vital element in the military preparations. When Edward
held his council at Devizes in mid-April, he decided to collect foodstuffs from
his overseas dominions. The seneschal of Ponthieu was to provide 2,000
quarters each of wheat and oats, with 300 quarters of beans and peas. Boars,
venison, and other salt meat were also to be sent. A sergeant was sent to
Ireland, with instructions to buy 2,000 quarters of wheat, 4,000 of oats, 500
of barley, 600 tuns of wine, and 1,000 salt salmon. From Gascony, the king
ordered 2,000 quarters of wheat, 1,000 of oats, 300 of beans and peas, 500 tuns
of wine, 20 tuns of honey, and 1,000 bacon pigs. The English counties from
which food supplies were requested were an unusual selection, given the
location of the campaign: 1,500 quarters of wheat and 2,000 of oats each
were requested from Essex, Surrey, Sussex, Kent, and Hampshire. The
intention was clearly to bring them by sea to Wales. In June William Bagot
was appointed to buy up provisions in Gloucestershire, Worcestershire,
Shropshire, and Staffordshire, and to take them to the army muster points.
He was commissioned again in November, when the collection of victuals from
Shropshire, Staffordshire, Nottinghamshire, Derbyshire, Worcestershire,
Herefordshire, Gloucestershire, Oxfordshire, Northamptonshire, Warwickshire, Leicestershire, and Lancashire was ordered.[38] A central victualling
depot was set up at Chester, and at Rhuddlan a mill was constructed to provide
flour for the army.

It was not just the crown that was concerned to provide sufficient foodstuffs
for the army. Magnates made their own arrangements. Theobald de Verdun's
men brought grain, wine, and other commodities from Ireland, and Roger de
Molis's men took supplies by ship from Bridgwater to their lord in Wales.
Roger Bigod made his own arrangements. Otto de Grandson sent men to Jersey
and Guernsey to buy victuals. In addition, private merchants were encouraged

---

[36] *Calendar of Various Chancery Rolls: Supplementary Close Rolls, Welsh Rolls, Scutage Rolls
1277–1326* (London, 1912), 217, 252–3.
[37] E 101/351/9.
[38] *Calendar of Various Chancery Rolls*, 214–17, 224, 245.

to take goods to Wales to sell to the troops. In May the king instructed the sheriffs of London and a number of counties to make proclamations requesting merchants to bring their goods to Chester, for sale to the army. By early June letters of protection were being issued to those taking advantage of this opportunity.[39]

All these arrangements were costly. It is not easy to separate military expenditure from other items in the accounts, but the total cost of the war, excluding that of castle-building, was probably at least £80,000. Much of this was spent in cash by the officials accompanying the army; £38,000 or more was taken to Chester, and other sums were sent to the forces operating further south. The main sources of the money were the customs revenues, which provided £23,000, the tax of a thirtieth granted in 1283, which produced over £36,000, and contributions taken from towns, monasteries, and a few individuals amounting to £16,500.[40]

SETTLEMENT AND REBELLION

Given the weight of resources that Edward I was able to deploy, his success in the war of 1282–3 is hardly surprising. The victory brought new problems. One was the destruction of the princely dynasty of Gwynedd. Dafydd was savagely executed by hanging, drawing, and quartering at Shrewsbury; no account was taken of his noble lineage. His sons were imprisoned at Bristol; his daughters, and Llywelyn's one daughter, were sent to distant nunneries. There were substantial rewards for the great men who had assisted the king. Earl Warenne, the earl of Lincoln, and Reginald de Grey all received major grants in north Wales. There was not the same opportunity to reshape the marches further south, but the Mortimers and John Giffard received due rewards. There were, however, some who may have felt understandable bitterness towards the king. The earls of Gloucester and Hereford made no substantial territorial gains as a result of the war, though it did reinforce their lordship in south Wales. Roger Bigod received 1,000 marks to cover his financial losses during the war, but no lands.[41] The king retained Snowdonia and Anglesey. New counties of Flint, Caernarfon, Merioneth, and Anglesey were created. This was done in the Statute of Wales, issued in 1284, which provided for the introduction of an English-style administration into the Welsh territory that was now annexed to the English crown. The statute was a considerable achievement. It did not seek to abolish Welsh law in all matters, but criminal law was brought into line with English practice. In administrative

[39] Ibid. 221 ff., 226, 250.   [40] Tout, *Chapters*, ii. 113–14.   [41] *CPR, 1281–92*, 149.

terms, the statute recognized the value of the existing units of cantrefs and commotes, though these were now to operate within the English county framework.[42]

Along with the castles, which stood as a vivid physical reminder of the English conquest, went the establishment of new towns. In 1284 charters were issued to Flint, Rhuddlan, Conwy, Caernarfon, Criccieth, Harlech, and Bere, while the new lords in the northern marches also created new urban settlements. The new towns were intended to be English enclaves, and were the clearest indication that colonization was following in the wake of conquest. The attitude of the new townsmen is indicated by the protest of those in Rhuddlan 'that so many Welsh are lodged near the town on the outside that they disturb the profit and the market of the English, and give voice to much treason among them'.[43]

Had it been Edward I's policy throughout to achieve the conquest of Wales, and did this fit with an overall imperial plan? There are no council minutes or other sources that suggest anything of the kind. Edward and his queen, however, did visit Glastonbury in 1278, and, demonstrating rare archaeological skill, excavated the tomb of King Arthur and his queen Guinevere.[44] Although there was no apparent overt link between this event and the recent Welsh campaign, it may be that Edward's interest in Arthur was because he wished to emulate the legendary British king and rule over all Britain. That desire was, however, entirely compatible with ensuring that Llywelyn ap Gruffudd performed his feudal duties towards Edward, and did not imply a full-scale conquest. It was the events of Easter 1282 that made the English king decide that there was no way in which he could continue to permit the continued rule in Wales of Llywelyn and his dynasty, and that conquest was the necessary course of action.

Inevitably, English rule in the aftermath of conquest was harsh. One effect of the war had been to heighten a sense of national identity on both sides. A chancery clerk in 1283 suggestively referred to the tricks and machinations of those of the Welsh tongue, as well as stressing the slaughter of the English at Welsh hands.[45] Archbishop Pecham, his prejudices exacerbated by war, set out an English view of the Welsh that condemned them in all aspects of life. They were treacherous, barbaric, idle, ignorant, and uncultured. Drunk and sexually incontinent, they were clearly wholly different from the English.[46] English officials continued after the war of conquest to take the same kind of aggressive

[42] L. B. Smith, 'The Statute of Wales, 1284', *Welsh History Review*, 10 (1980–1), 127–54.
[43] *Calendar of Ancient Petitions relating to Wales*, ed. W. Rees (Cardiff, 1975), 461.
[44] Prestwich, *Edward I*, 120.   [45] *Parl. Writs*, i. 15–16.
[46] Douie, *Pecham*, 250, 262.

approach towards the Welsh that had characterized their behaviour previously. The queen's officials in Hope and Maelor Saesneg were particularly hostile in their attitude. However, rebellion, when it came in 1287, took place in the south, not the north. It was primarily the result of the king's lack of generosity to Rhys ap Maredudd, who had supported his cause in the wars of 1277 and 1282–3.[47] This rising was a small-scale affair, marked by one disaster for the English, when a mine that they were constructing at Dryslwyn castle collapsed prematurely. Edmund of Cornwall, however, acting on behalf of the king, who was in Gascony, had little difficulty in dealing with the rising. The rebellion of 1294 was far more serious. It may well have been stirred up by the imposition of a tax of a fifteenth in 1292. The assessment was far more severe than was normal in England, and payment of a final instalment in the autumn of 1294 was probably the spark that ignited nationwide resistance to the English. The rebels were led in the north by Madog ap Llywelyn, a distant relative of Llywelyn ap Gruffudd, yet another man who was discontented at the way in which his earlier support for the English had been inadequately rewarded. Others led the rebellion elsewhere in Wales. This was a well-coordinated rising, which was carefully timed to take advantage of the king's preoccupation with his French war. In practice, however, what happened was that Edward was able to divert to Wales resources originally intended for Gascony.

The effort required to put down the rising of 1294–5 was of a similar order of magnitude to that needed to conquer Wales in 1282–3. The army was not summoned by means of a feudal muster; there had been trouble over using that method for a force intended to serve in Gascony. Many of the cavalry were paid, but as was normal a good many, especially those from the marches, served at their own expense. Huge numbers of infantry were employed, with up to 35,000 in all the various forces that were poured into Wales. The king's force marched from Chester to Conwy, where he was for a time besieged by the Welsh. Food and drink was running out, and the story went that Edward refused the small quantity of wine that had been kept back for him, insisting that it be shared out between the troops. In January the king conducted a remarkable raid, riding from Conwy to Nefyn, on the Lleyn peninsula, and back. In April he mounted an attack on Anglesey. He was concerned not to run out of drink there, and had sent an insistent message ordering all the brewers in Chester to brew as much ale as possible for himself and his army, to be shipped to the island.[48] It was not Edward's own forces, but the much smaller ones commanded by Warwick, that won a signal success. On 5 March they defeated Madog at the battle of Maes Moydog in mid-Wales. 'The Welshmen held their

---

[47] For the rebellions of 1287 and 1294–5 see Prestwich, *Edward I*, 218–26.
[48] *Cal. Anc. Corr. Wales*, 207.

ground well, and they were the best and bravest Welsh that anyone has ever seen' was the verdict of one newsletter. Nevertheless, Warwick's men, some 2,500 strong, won the battle, and there were other successes further south. The rebellion collapsed, but it had taken all the efforts of the considerable English war machine to defeat it. Funds that were much needed for the French war had to be spent on Wales, with about £55,500 in cash sent to the royal paymasters there. As usual, success was marked by castle-building, this time with James of St George laying out the symmetrical plan of the perfectly concentric castle at Beaumaris in Anglesey. The castle was never finally completed, but even as it stands today, its towers no higher than the curtain walls and one great gatehouse half-completed, it is possible to see that it marks the culmination of the type of plan seen earlier at Harlech.

ENGLISH ARMIES

To what extent were English armies transformed during the period of the Welsh wars? The view that Edward succeeded in transforming an incoherent feudal host into an efficient, paid military machine is seductive, but the evidence does not fully support such a hypothesis. For whatever reason, his plans for a purely paid force in 1282 were abandoned, and feudal summonses continued to be used, even though they produced inadequate forces for a limited forty-day period. Edward had a substantial paid cavalry force at his disposal in the form of the household knights, squires, and sergeants, and those who accompanied them. In 1277 the king had a force of forty knights and seventy sergeants immediately available to fight in Wales, before the rest of the army had been recruited. Shortly after the end of the second Welsh war there were fourteen bannerets and eighty-seven knights in receipt of the king's wages. Such a household force, however, was nothing new, though the numbers fluctuated considerably at different periods. The rest of the cavalry was provided by the magnates, and formed into retinues of varying size, but normally numbering between ten and fifteen. The infantry were organized in more logical fashion, in groups of twenties and hundreds. There is no evidence to suggest that the crown did much to provide the men with the equipment they needed, for that was the task of their local communities. Even in the first Welsh war the majority were described as archers; the proportion rose later, but it would not be correct to see Edward I as the father of the English longbow.

There is insufficient evidence to show clearly whether the battle tactics employed by Edward's armies were significantly novel. Neither of the main battles of the Welsh wars, Irfon Bridge in 1283 and Maes Moydog in 1295, involved very large English armies, or indeed, the king himself. The accounts of the former do not suggest anything particularly remarkable about the way in which the English fought. The manner in which, according to one account, the earl of Warwick at Maes Moydog interspersed men-at-arms with crossbowmen has been seen as an innovatory combination of horse and foot, a stage on the route towards the later victories at Crécy and Poitiers. The account, in Trevet's chronicle, is not corroborated, and one immediate problem is the emphasis on crossbowmen rather than archers. The payroll for Warwick's force in any case suggests that there were only thirteen footsoldiers, including both archers and crossbowmen, present. A newsletter from someone present at the battle suggests nothing innovatory about the English tactics, but notes the unexpected bravery of the Welsh, who for once were prepared to meet the English in the field, and held their ground well.[49]

The transformation that took place during Edward's Welsh wars was, in reality, quantitative more than qualitative. There is an immense contrast between the small, ineffective English campaigns of the 1220s and 1230s, and the great efforts made by Edward I, particularly in 1282–3 and 1294–5. It is easy to see why Edward was able to conquer Wales, such was the weight of resources he was able to mobilize. The numbers that participated in the campaigns in these two wars were among the largest forces mustered by the English in the whole medieval period, though, of course, they did not form one single army but were deployed in various contingents from the north to the south of Wales. The organization of these forces was an immense achievement for Edward's clerks and other officials. Perhaps most remarkable was the feat of bridging the Menai straits, involving as it did the commandeering of ships, the manufacture of a roadway to cross the pontoons, and the complex engineering of the whole structure so that it would resist the fierce tides. That was a spectacular achievement, but much more important was the far less glamorous business of building up sufficient stocks of food, providing the carts and packhorses to carry the supplies, and maintaining the supply bases. It was these successes in logistics that marked out Edward's campaigns as quite different from those of the past.

THE AFTERMATH

Edward I had conquered Wales. There were, of course, fears of further resistance, but what was striking under Edward II was the way in which some influential Welshmen, not members of the old aristocracy whose power had been broken, provided the crown with support. Gruffydd Llywd was particularly notable. Despite a period of imprisonment between 1316 and

---

[49] Morris, *Welsh Wars*, 256–7; Prestwich, *Edward I*, 223.

1318, he served Edward II well. No doubt Gruffydd appreciated the profit he could make from his office as sheriff of Merioneth; at the same time, he and men like him realized that supporting the crown was a way of limiting the growth of the power of the marcher lords, and notably that of Roger Mortimer. The danger that the Scottish invasion of Ireland would be extended into Wales came to nothing. There was, however, a significant rebellion in Glamorgan in 1316, led by Llywelyn Bren. This was in large part the result of the insensitivity of royal officials, particularly Payn Turberville, sent in to the lordship following the death of the earl of Gloucester at Bannockburn. Though short-lived, the rising was serious, and demonstrated the pressures that existed in a defeated Wales. For Edward II, however, the Welsh provided welcome support in 1322, and it was of course in Wales that he sought, but did not find, refuge in 1326.[50]

There were some echoes of the past as late as 1345. In that year Welsh troops recruited in Merioneth reached the river Conwy, but refused to go any further on their journey to fight in France. There were complaints from those who were prepared to go that they were not led by a Welshman, as they wished. In the same year there was panic when Henry de Shaldeford, the Black Prince's official and attorney, was murdered. The townspeople of Caernarfon informed the prince that they 'suffer daily from the malevolence and enmity of the Welsh, who seek to destroy the prince's English ministers and burgesses'. Those of Rhuddlan told him that the Englishmen living in Wales had never been in such a perilous plight; the castle had been attacked, several towns-people killed, and their cattle driven off. John de Weston, who went to Wales on behalf of the prince, 'found the country *molt merveillous et estrange*'.[51] Edward I may have conquered Wales, but it remained a distinct and separate country, with its own traditions and identity.

[50] J. B. Smith, 'Edward II and the Allegiance of Wales', *Welsh History Review*, 8 (1976), 139–71.
[51] *Cal. Anc. Corr. Wales*, 231–2, 239, 247–8.

CHAPTER 7

Political Crises, 1294–1311

In the early 1290s the years of success for Edward I came to an end. The men who had been the architects of the remarkable transformation of the English State in the first twenty years of the reign were no longer by his side, nor was his beloved Eleanor. The king's ambition to lead western Europe in a successful crusade had to be abandoned; instead, he was faced with a succession of expensive and difficult wars nearer home. The political unity that had been forged from the unpromising material presented by England in the aftermath of civil war could not be maintained under the pressures of war finance and military logistics.

THE DEMANDS OF WAR

The years from 1294 to 1298 were the most difficult.[1] War with the French began in 1294, and Gascony had to be defended throughout the period. In 1294–5 there was also the Welsh rebellion to be dealt with. The next year saw Edward conduct his successful campaign against the Scots, and in 1297 he took an army to Flanders, returning early in the following year. Troops had to be paid for and arrangements were required to provide them with the supplies they needed. Grasping foreign allies had to be paid subsidies to prevent them allying with the French. Home defences were needed. The total cost of warfare in this period has been calculated as roughly £750,000.

At the start of the French war there were some imaginative ideas, for which the treasurer, William March, was probably responsible, about how it might be financed.[2] Initially, the crown was in a relatively strong position, for the tax granted in 1290 had been exceptionally successful. Much more, however, was

---

[1] For a fuller account of these years, see Prestwich, *Edward I*, 401 ff.

[2] For convenient tables of the taxes of these years, see M. W. Ormrod, 'The Crown and the English Economy, 1290–1348', in B. M. S. Campbell (ed.), *Before the Black Death: Studies in the Crisis of the Early Fourteenth Century* (Manchester, 1991), 149–64. Tables are also to be found, compiled by Ormrod, at <http://www.le.ac.uk/hi/bon/ESFDB/frameset.html>.

needed. The first step was to try to fight the war from the backs of English sheep. In June 1294 the sheriffs were ordered to take forward a seizure of all the wool in the country, so as to prevent it from being exported to France. The magnates then agreed that wool confiscated in this way should be exported directly by the crown. The merchants would have been cut out, but they proposed instead that the king should levy a far heavier customs duty than that agreed in 1275. Forty shillings a sack became the rate, and between 1294 and 1297, the new duty, known as the *maltolt*, raised over £110,000.

An extraordinary action took place in June 1294, with a scrutiny and seizure of funds deposited in churches throughout the land. The excuse for this was a search for clipped and forged coin, but the money, over £10,000, that was taken was used to strengthen the king's financial position. Only about a fifth of the sum was ever repaid. There was also a seizure of sums that had been collected as crusade taxation, amounting to over £32,000. This was still not enough. Edward was initially reluctant to ask for a tax from the laity, for they were contributing manpower to the war. The Church, however, was put under severe pressure, and compelled to agree to pay a tax at the unprecedented rate of a half. This was collected on the basis of a recent assessment, made in 1291, that put the value of the Church at about £200,000. Still this was not regarded as sufficient, particularly when it became evident that a campaign would have to be fought against the Welsh rebellion.

Direct taxation, assessed on a valuation of people's movable goods, was an obvious measure with solid precedents. These years saw assessors and collectors coming annually to the counties. The level of taxation was unprecedented. In November 1294 a special gathering took place at which the magnates, with representatives of the shires, agreed to a tax of a tenth and a sixth, with the higher rate being paid by the towns and ancient demesne. This was assessed at over £81,000. In the following year an eleventh and seventh was granted, to be followed in 1296 by a twelfth and eighth. The assessment fell to almost £53,000 in 1295, and then to about £38,500 in 1296, reflecting both people's increasing skill in avoiding tax, and, perhaps, a sense on the part of the assessors of growing impoverishment. The clergy were more reluctant than the laity to offer taxes, but granted a tenth in 1295.

One method of financing war that had been successful in Wales could not be used in the 1290s. The Italian bankers, the Ricciardi, on whom Edward had relied so heavily, were effectively bankrupted in 1294. The reasons for this are not entirely clear. It is likely that Edward was angry because the firm failed to hand over in full the receipts of the crusading tenth that had been imposed on the Church by the papacy in 1274, and that was finally promised to Edward in 1291. The French moved against the firm because of its links with the English king. At the news of the Anglo-French war the Ricciardi's depositors in Italy sought to withdraw their funds. 'Everyone to whom we owed money ran to us and wanted to be paid.'[3] There was no company willing to come forward to take up the position that the Ricciardi had occupied. Forced loans, totalling almost £29,000 between 1294 and 1298, were no substitute for the willing cooperation of a company that had provided the king with considerable financial expertise.

The real difficulties came in 1297. The clergy had promised to answer the king's request for yet more funds in January. By then, however, Archbishop Winchelsey had received a papal bull, *Clericis Laicos*, in which the pope prohibited the Church from paying taxes to the lay power. Boniface VIII hoped by doing this to put pressure on the kings of England and France to come to terms. The king's response was to threaten the clergy with the removal of royal protection. When the seizure of all lay fees held by clerics was ordered on 12 February, Edward made it known that his protection could be bought by paying as a fine what would have been paid in taxation. Once the archbishop agreed that each should follow his own conscience, the fines began to flow in.

Edward could not ask the laity for a tax at the same time as the clergy, for their last grant had been made only in November 1296. By the summer of 1297, however, he was in desperate need. A grant was made of an eighth and fifth, and assessors were appointed on 30 July. This tax, however, was not agreed in a proper parliamentary assembly, with representatives present. One chronicler claimed, with a pardonable degree of exaggeration, that it was granted to the king by 'people standing around in his chamber'.[4]

Taxation was not the only important matter of concern by 1297. Military service had probably been an issue as early as 1294, when the king issued a feudal summons for troops to go to Gascony. The muster, however, was postponed and not reinstated, for events were overtaken by the news of the Welsh rising. There were objections in 1295 from a group of magnates asked to go to Gascony, even though they were to be paid wages. It was only when they were threatened with collection of the debts they owed to the crown that they agreed to go. Early in 1297 the issue of service in Gascony was the subject of debate in parliament at Salisbury. When the king asked for his magnates to go there, according to the chronicler Walter of Guisborough (who was good at inventing dialogue), discussion between the king and Roger Bigod, earl of Norfolk, became heated. 'By God, Sir Earl, either go or hang.' Bigod's accurate reply was that he would do neither.[5]

Seizures of goods were extremely unpopular. One type was intended to provide the crown with much-needed funds. The plan for a compulsory seizure of wool, abandoned in 1294, was revived in 1297. A prise, or seizure,

---

[3] Kaeuper, *Bankers to the Crown*, 209–29. The quotation is from p. 228.
[4] *Flores*, iii. 296.   [5] Guisborough, 290.

was ordered to take place at Easter. It did not go well, and only about 2,333 sacks were collected. This did not mean that the measure was any the less unpopular. To make matters worse, the council decided in July that the best way to raise money to pay the king's foreign allies was to seize a further 8,000 sacks of wool. Again, the measure was a failure, with records suggesting that a mere 799 sacks were collected and exported.

Another type of prise was intended to provide foodstuffs for the armies. Seizures had been at a high level in 1296, and in April 1297 the collection of 13,000 quarters of grain was ordered. This was followed in June by requests for at least 3,100 sides of bacon and 1,500 beef carcasses. In the course of the year at least 10,300 quarters of wheat, 6,700 of oats, 2,400 of barley and malt, and 1,000 of beans were seized by royal officials. In theory, men would eventually be repaid for what they had lost, but the theory was rarely put into practice.

The demands for money and supplies were rendered the more unpopular because these were years of real economic difficulty, with bad harvests. Wheat prices rose steadily and sharply year by year from 1294 to 1296. The war, combined with the *maltolt*, severely disrupted wool exports, and as a result growers were not receiving good prices.[6] The earl of Arundel complained to the king that his resources were insufficient to meet the costs he incurred as a result of the war; although he had been given permission to lease out some of his lands, at £100 a year, he could find no takers for it.[7] The travails of lesser men are not documented in the same way, but these were not comfortable times.

The problem by 1297 was not merely that the demands for money, men, and materials were excessive, but also that there was little support for the king's war aims. There were increasing worries that the situation in Scotland was deteriorating rapidly, and strong views that it was a mistake for the king to contemplate an expedition to Flanders. Edward, however, was a determined and obstinate man. He had not been in a position to lead an expedition to the Continent until this year, and the opportunity was not one he was prepared to pass up.

THE CRISIS OF 1297

The situation became increasingly explosive. It was made the more acute by the personal grievances of some of the leading actors. Gloucester, the most probable leader of opposition to Edward, had died in 1296. Two men now came to the fore. Neither had a history of heading resistance to the crown, but both had

---

[6] *Agrarian History*, ii. 790, 809.
[7] *Documents Illustrating the Crisis of 1297–8*, ed. Prestwich, 142.

reasons for resenting the king. Humphrey de Bohun, earl of Hereford, must have objected to the way he had been treated at the start of the decade, as a result of his feud with Gloucester. Roger Bigod, earl of Norfolk, had long-running arguments with the exchequer over debts he owed to the crown. His hereditary position as marshal had been ignored by the king in 1294, when Roger de Molis, a household knight, had been given the position on the Welsh campaign. In addition to these two earls, John de Ferrers, son of Robert Ferrers, earl of Derby, had a very obvious grievance, for in the aftermath of the civil war his family had been deprived of most of its lands along with the title. Robert Winchelsey, archbishop of Canterbury, had begun his tenure of his see by making it clear that he was swearing fealty only in respect of his temporalities, not his spiritualities. Edward demanded that Winchelsey pay off a debt to the crown of £3,568 within three years. This was not, however, a crisis born of private grievances; the key issues were those concerning the country as a whole, and there is no doubt that the king's opponents considered that they were acting in a wide national interest.

The lay and clerical opponents of the crown did not unite. The crisis began in January with the problem of the clergy's refusal to grant a tax and their subsequent outlawry. The February parliament saw the dispute with Bigod over military service in Gascony. It was not until early July, however, that the question of service overseas became acute. A novel form of summons was used to call men to muster in London. Everyone with at least £20 worth of land was to attend. Many did not respond. Bigod and Bohun, however, were present, but when asked by the king, in their roles as marshal and constable, to draw up lists of those present, they refused. The muster was not a normal feudal levy, because the summons did not use the correct language. The two men were promptly dismissed from their offices. Geoffrey de Geneville and Thomas Berkeley were appointed as replacements. Four days after the muster, on 11 July, the king achieved a major success when he reconciled himself with Winchelsey, and ordered the restoration of his lands. Negotiations with the earls were unsuccessful; later in July they drew up a lengthy statement of grievances, known as the Remonstrances. Edward drove his policies forward with little regard for the opposition. Preparations for the military campaign in Flanders went ahead; writs were issued on 28 July asking men to muster at Winchelsea to serve at royal wages. The tax of an eighth was set up; the new wool seizure went ahead. On 20 August Edward ordered the exchequer to proceed with the levy of a heavy tax on the Church, which would take the form either of a fifth on the value of all ecclesiastical property, or a third on that of the spiritualities. This tax had not been granted, and at a stroke the king undid what had been achieved when he had come to terms with Winchelsey.

On 22 August, when the king was about to embark for Flanders, Bigod and Bohun with a group of their followers appeared at the exchequer. Bohun took the lead. He emphasized the grievances that had been presented in the Remonstrances, and protested at the imposition of the eighth, and at the wool seizure. To impose a tax amounted to placing the people in servitude, and to disinheriting them. The king's reaction was to promise that the tax of an eighth would not become a precedent. As for the wool seizure, 'It seems to us that we should be as free as any man to buy wool in our land,' an arrogant and deliberately disingenuous comment.[8] Edward's departure for Flanders removed a major obstacle to political peace in England. Even with the king out of the country, however, there was still a possibility that the situation might deteriorate into civil war. The news of the English defeat in Scotland at Stirling Bridge on 11 September transformed the situation. The opposition had been proved right in arguments that they had put when they suggested that the situation in Scotland was too dangerous for Edward to risk going to Flanders. The defeat meant that both opposition and regency government in England were anxious to settle the political disputes so that attention could be turned to the problems in the north. Articles, known as *De Tallagio*, were presented. Taxes were not to be taken without consent. Goods were not to be seized without the owner's consent. The *maltolt* was to be abolished, and pardons were demanded for the leaders of the opposition. These concessions were envisaged as additional clauses to Magna Carta. The council was not prepared to go that far, but on 10 October agreed to the issue of the *Confirmatio Cartarum*, which did not add clauses to Magna Carta, but met the main opposition demands. No precedent would be made of the emergency fiscal measures, and seizures of goods, or prises, would not become customary. In future, 'aids, mises and prises' would not be taken without the common consent of the realm, and for the common benefit. The *maltolt* was abolished.[9] In return, a new tax of a ninth was granted, replacing the infamous eighth. It was also agreed that the boundaries of the royal forests should be surveyed, or perambulated. The agreement was reached without consultation with the king, who must have been angry at what had been done. He had no option, however, other than to issue the *Confirmatio* himself, on 5 November at Ghent in the Low Countries, and to provide the opposition leaders with pardons and assurances that they would not suffer for what they had done.

The crisis of 1297 was very different from that which began in 1258. It was above all the result of war and its demands, and it was not fuelled by deep-seated grievances about the way in which the country was governed. The Remonstrances were not a radical statement. They pointed out that the

---

[8] *Documents Illustrating the Crisis of 1297–8*, ed. Prestwich, 140.   [9] Ibid. 158–60.

military summons had not specified where the expedition was headed. If it was to go to Flanders, there was no precedent. In any case, a Flanders expedition was unwise in view of the situation in Scotland. England was impoverished by the king's demands. One version of the document ended with a clause that suggested that the various impositions—tallages, aids, mises, and prises—meant that the people were being treated as if they were unfree and placed in servitude. The elements of the document that did not relate directly to the war were complaints that men were being deprived of their franchisal rights, and that Magna Carta was being ignored. Forest law was arbitrary, and was being applied with a new harshness. *De Tallagio* did not take the argument much further, though it did state that consent for taxation should be obtained from the lay and ecclesiastical magnates, knights, burgesses, 'and other free men in our realm'.[10] The agreement in the *Confirmatio Cartarum* offered one new principle, stating that taxes and other impositions should be taken not only with common assent, but also for the common profit. It did not, however, attempt any definition of how assent was to be obtained, or who should give it. There was no question of any attempt to control the king in the ways familiar from Henry III's reign. Above all, there was no question of appointing a council or councillors.

It has been suggested that the arguments between the king and his opponents in 1297 were conducted within a framework defined by Roman and canon law in a way that had not been the case previously. It can be difficult to distinguish between a technical plea made in these terms, and a straightforward practical statement of the difficulties faced by the king. Did the argument that the king aimed 'to recover his rightful inheritance out of which he had been tricked by the king of France, and for the honour and common profit of his realm' amount to a justification of the war by scholastic criteria?[11] There certainly was usage of Roman law ideas in the king's dealings with the clergy. His justification for imposing new taxes on them made on 20 August was clearly couched in terms derived from current views on the rights of a ruler when there was an urgent necessity. As far as the earls were concerned, however, the Roman law background was far less significant.[12] For the country at large, the unprecedented level of the crown's demands mattered more than any constitutional principles.

It is more difficult to identify the composition of the opposition of 1297 than that which had faced Henry III, partly because the movement was so short-lived. The leading figures, Bigod, Bohun, and Winchelsey, are well known, and in Bigod's case a list reveals the identity of his immediate following. There was

[10] Ibid. 115–17, 154.   [11] Harris, *King, Parliament and Public Finance*, 63.
[12] *Documents Illustrating the Crisis of 1297–8*, ed. Prestwich, 28–30.

clearly very extensive backing for the opposition. The earls of Warwick and Arundel were certainly sympathetic, and the fact that an opposition gathering was held at Montgomery shows that there was strong support in the Welsh marches.[13] Local feeling was strong in Worcestershire, where the county community challenged royal officials who were trying to collect the tax of an eighth, arguing that it would not grant the money until it received the liberties to which Magna Carta entitled it.[14] The knights, alienated by the summons of £20 landowners, were very reluctant to answer the king's summons to muster at Winchelsea. Returns from three counties reveal only one name, and the accounts for the army in Flanders indicate that the total number that responded was a mere sixty-three.

THE AFTERMATH OF CRISIS

The crisis of 1297 did not end political argument. Rather, it marked the start of years of dissension and disagreement.[15] There was understandable concern that the king, on his return to England in 1298, might go back on the concessions he had agreed. Bigod and Bohun refused to participate in the Scottish expedition of 1298 unless the king guaranteed that he would confirm the concessions and would see to it that the boundaries of the royal forests were investigated. It was agreed that he would do this, if the campaign was successful. However, Edward did not do as the two earls wished. Archbishop Winchelsey, in a church council held in June 1298, took an aggressive line, ordering the excommunication of any official who seized goods without the consent of the owner. The residue of a tenth granted in the autumn of 1297 was not handed over to the crown, on the grounds that an English campaign in Scotland did not amount to an urgent necessity. A full judicial investigation of official wrongdoings at a local level did little to pacify the king's critics. In parliament in 1299 the king put off a promised further confirmation of the charters. Rather than give an answer, he left London in secret, saying that the air pollution there was bad for his health and that the council would respond. A new statute was produced, *De Finibus Levatis*. This made it clear that any investigation of forest boundaries would not be permitted to curtail royal rights, and that the Charter of the Forest was not to be confirmed in full. Riots were threatened, and eventually

---

[13] J. H. Denton, 'The Crisis of 1297 from the Evesham Chronicle', *EHR* 93 (1978), 576.

[14] Worcester Annals, 534.

[15] For the following section, see Prestwich, *Edward I*, 517 ff. H. Rothwell, 'Edward I and the Struggle for the Charters', in R. W. Hunt, W. A. Pantin, and R. W. Southern (eds.), *Studies in Medieval History Presented to F. M. Powicke* (Oxford, 1948), 319–32, also discusses the aftermath of the 1297 crisis.

Edward was forced to announce that the perambulation of the forest would begin at Michaelmas.

When parliament met in March 1300, the arguments were widened. At the start Winchelsey and Bigod requested the confirmation of the Charters. Separate lists of ecclesiastical and lay grievances were presented. The clerical articles covered familiar ground, and led to no concessions from the king, for the clergy were unwilling to make a grant of taxation as a quid pro quo. The lay complaints concerned prise, the jurisdiction of the king's household, the use of the privy seal to interfere with the course of legal proceedings, and the recent summons of £40 landholders to serve in Scotland. These complaints formed the basis of royal concessions, known as the *Articuli super Cartas*, which were the price the king paid for a grant of a twentieth. This document showed that the opposition had moved on a long way from its position in 1297. It covered a wide range of issues in detail, rather than attempting broad-brush solutions. The points made in the articles were picked up, though no mention was made of the military obligation of the £40 landholders. Some of Edward's previous measures were reinforced. The Statute of Winchester was to be read out publicly four times a year, and its terms maintained by three knights in each county. They were also to ensure that the terms of the Charters were kept. This emphasis on reform in the localities was taken further with perhaps the most remarkable clause in the document, one that provided for the local election of sheriffs. The Provisions of Westminster of 1259 had laid down a procedure whereby four men were to be elected in each county, one of whom would then be selected by the exchequer officials.[16] There were reasons why the issue had come to the fore again in 1300. The treasurer, Walter Langton, had misused his power to appoint sheriffs. In one example, he had compelled Richard Whitacre to become sheriff of Warwickshire and Leicestershire so as to have him 'in his power'. John of Broughton, sheriff of the same two counties, had been one of Langton's bailiffs.[17] What is particularly curious, however, is that it was only in Shropshire and Staffordshire that an election actually took place. Nor did the man selected, Richard de Harley, prove satisfactory.[18]

One argument has it that the *Articuli* of 1300 represent a significant success for Edward I, for the concessions that the king made were qualified by a savings clause: 'In each and all of the aforesaid things it is the king's will and the intention of him and his council and of all those who were present at the making of this ordinance that the right and lordship of his crown be saved.'

---

[16] *DBM* 154.

[17] J. R. Maddicott, ' "1258" and "1297": Some Comparisons and Contrasts', in *TCE* ix. 8–9.

[18] W. A. Morris, *The Medieval English Sheriff to 1300* (Manchester, 1927), 184–5.

Nor were the new concessions made in the *Confirmatio* of 1297 confirmed.[19] It could be added that the *Articuli* did not have the standing of a statute. The parliament of 1300, however, cannot be seen as a victory for the king. He had to make unwelcome concessions, and in the event did not even obtain the tax of a twentieth. A grant was made, but it was conditional. According to the Worcester annalist the magnates' position was 'When we have secure possession of our forests and of our liberties, often promised to us, then we will willingly give a twentieth, so that the folly of the Scots may be dealt with.'[20] It is probable that collection of the tax was made conditional upon the king agreeing to put into effect the verdicts of the perambulation of the forest, and that he was not prepared to do this.

By the time that parliament met at Lincoln early in 1301 the financial situation had become more acute. A fifteenth was demanded. In response, a Lancashire knight of the shire, Henry of Keighley, put forward a bill of complaint, which was then presented to the king on behalf of the whole community. It demanded adherence to the Charters, and asked that the perambulation of the forest should be completed. Offences against the *Articuli* of the previous year, particularly those relating to prises, should be dealt with. Increments added to the sheriffs' farms ought to be cancelled. In addition to this bill, there was a direct attack on Walter Langton, who was held responsible for the unpopular prises, and was thought to have overthrown the traditional customs of the exchequer. The king, furious, accused the magnates of wanting to reduce him to a servile condition, which echoed the arguments of 1297, when the charge was the other way round. He should be able to appoint his own servants, just as the magnates could do. The outcome of the arguments was that Langton remained in office, and that the grant of the fifteenth was agreed, provided that the Charters were maintained, and that the perambulation of the forest took place. In the autumn the magnates meeting in the course of the Scottish campaign agreed that the collection of the tax could go ahead.

The emphasis placed on the investigation of the forest boundaries no doubt derived in part from a genuine belief that the crown had illicitly extended them. In the case of the New Forest, the records of a forest eyre held in 1280 suggest that the bounds were much more extensive than they had been in the early thirteenth century.[21] What was probably more important was the way in which the perambulation became a clear test of the king's good faith. Whether or not the crown was putting into effect regulations about prise could be a

---

[19] Rothwell, 'Edward I and the Struggle for the Charters', in Hunt *et al.* (eds.), *Studies in Medieval History Presented to F. M. Powicke*, 327–8.

[20] Worcester Annals, 544.

[21] *A Calendar of New Forest Documents 1244–1334*, ed. D. J. Stagg, Hampshire Record Series, 3 (1979), 33–4.

matter of interpretation and argument, but there could be little doubt about the perambulations. Edward's attitude towards them can have left his critics in little doubt that he was an unreliable prevaricator. In December 1305 he obtained a papal bull absolving him from the concessions he had made. While it does not seem that the king intended to disregard all of them, it is clear that he did intend to use the bull to cancel the effects of the perambulation.[22]

In the years from 1301 until Edward's death there was far less political argument. One reason is that the leaders of the opposition of 1297 were either dead or neutralized. Humphrey de Bohun had died in 1298. His son married Edward's daughter Elizabeth in 1302, so linking the earldom of Hereford to the crown. Roger Bigod came to terms with the king in the same year, resolving his financial difficulties by making Edward his heir in return for £1,000 a year.[23] Winchelsey was neutralized in a quite different way. In 1305 a Gascon congenial to the king was elected pope as Clement V. Charges were brought against Winchelsey, who was suspended from office. In 1306 he left England to defend himself at the papal curia.

The Scottish war provides another reason for the relatively quiescent nature of politics. This was a conflict that had wide support, in contrast to Edward's Continental ambitions of the 1290s. Although the practice of prise continued, for the troops needed to be supplied, Edward did not impose unacceptable financial burdens on the country. A tax of a thirtieth was negotiated in 1306, but this was in lieu of a traditional feudal aid for the knighting of the king's eldest son, and so was rendered less objectionable. Additional customs duties were agreed in 1303. After negotiations with English merchants failed, the foreign traders operating in the country agreed to pay an additional 3s. 4d. on each sack of wool exported, together with duties on imported goods. This was in exchange for significant privileges, which placed them on far more equal terms with their English rivals than they had been in the past. Such a grant was not unpopular in the way that the infamous *maltolt* had been. Edward also benefited from papal taxes. The profits of a crusading tenth imposed by the pope in 1301 were shared with the king, who eventually received about £42,000 from this source. A new tax was negotiated with Clement V after his election in 1305. This too was ostensibly for the crusade, but it was agreed that all of the first year's receipts should go to Edward, with the second year's allocated to his son. By early in 1307 the exchequer had received over £25,000 from this tax.[24]

---

[22] J. H. Denton, *Robert Winchelsey and the Crown 1294–1313* (Cambridge, 1980), 237–8.
[23] M. Morris, 'The "Murder" of an English Earldom? Roger IV Bigod and Edward I', in *TCE* ix. 89–99.
[24] Prestwich, *Edward I*, 532–3.

It must have been very clear to his subjects that it was not worth antagonizing Edward. His techniques for managing the nobility had not changed since
he compelled Arundel and others to fight in Gascony in 1295. When Marmaduke Thweng abducted Lucy, the battered wife of William Latimer junior, in
1304, the king wrote to the exchequer:

We order you that if this same Marmaduke owes us any debt at our exchequer, then
collect it to our use as quickly and hastily as you reasonably can, without allowing him
any manner of grace or sufferance, until we know that he has fully repented the spite
and trespass which he has shown in this matter to the said William.[25]

There was a cost to political stability. By limiting the demands placed on the
country, Edward incurred an increasing load of debt. Attempts such as that
made in 1301 to persuade the sheriffs to pay their receipts in to the exchequer
in June rather than September did nothing to ease the fundamental problems.
There was no effective system of control of government expenditure. War
finance went through the household department of the wardrobe, and the
exchequer had no means of limiting the liabilities that were entered into. It
did not even prove possible to audit the wardrobe's annual accounts. Borrowing did not offer an effective way out. The company of the Frescobaldi of
Florence came to take the place occupied in the first half of the reign by the
Ricciardi. They had contributed to a forced loan taken from the Italians during
the war with France, and had advanced money to Edward in Flanders. By 1302
they had lent some £33,000, and in 1305 it was calculated that it would take
eighteen months to repay the firm out of the revenues of the customs. The
Frescobaldi were certainly useful to Edward, but their loans were not on the
same scale as those of the Ricciardi. Between November 1299 and April 1302,
for example, they advanced £9,555, as against receipts from the crown of
£3,352. Loans on this scale could not come near to filling the gap between
income and expenditure.[26]

By 1307 Edward was probably in debt by some £200,000. An accurate
calculation is not possible, but the figure of £60,000 which is often given
represents the king's debts as they stood not at the end of the reign, but in the
1320s. Those to whom money was owed ranged from his officials and bankers at
one end of the spectrum to infantry soldiers and workmen at the other. The
number of petitions presented in parliament in 1305 testifies to the scale of the
problem. In political terms, however, it proved better, at least in the short term,
to run up debts in this way than to burden the country with heavy taxation.

[25] E 159/77, m. 13; E 368/74, m. 39. For the background to this, see M. C. Prestwich, 'An
Every Day Story of Knightly Folk', in *TCE* ix. 151–62.
[26] R. W. Kaeuper, 'The Frescobaldi of Florence and the English Crown', *Studies in Medieval
and Renaissance History*, 10 (1973), 56–7; E 101/126/21.

These final years of Edward's reign did not see major administrative or legislative achievements that could be compared with the 1270s and 1280s. Problems of law and order were tackled in 1305, when the Ordinance of Trailbaston saw five judicial circuits set up to deal with cases of violent assault and similar offences. The name Trailbaston is said to derive from the staves, or bastons, that criminals carried. There was a further reform of the coinage in 1300. This was not a full recoinage like that of 1279. The problem was that there was a great deal of poor-quality coin circulating in England, which had been imported from the Low Countries. The pollards and crockards, as these foreign coins were termed, varied considerably in quality, some containing no more than half the amount of silver in a genuine coin. At Christmas 1299 they were declared to have a face value of a halfpenny, and at Easter they were fully demonetized. The crown made useful profits from buying up these coins and reminting them into good-quality sterling.[27] One effect of the recoinage was to transform the popularity of the sterling currency. Bullion flowed in from the Continent, and in the years up to about 1310 the mints were exceptionally active. The amount of coin in circulation may have risen to a level approaching £2 million, four times the probable figure for the mid-thirteenth century.[28]

The personality of Edward I is central to the character of his reign. In his final years he was a formidable figure. Physically impressive, with a wealth of experience, he was not someone people would have been ready to stand up to. In 1295 the dean of St Paul's approached the king to protest against the taxation of the clergy, and died on the spot as he began his speech. That was a somewhat extreme reaction, but it was noted later that after Archbishop Corbridge of York had been berated by the king, he went away so depressed that he died.[29] Edward was a man who could not be diverted from his purpose, as was shown in 1297 when he determinedly pursued his plan for a campaign in Flanders despite all his domestic problems. There was criticism of Edward. In his youth he had been compared to a leopard, brave and fierce like a *leo*, but at the same time unreliable and deceitful, like a *pard*.[30] The chronicler Langtoft contrasted him in maturity with King Arthur, and suggested that he feasted too much in the evenings, slept too long in bed in the mornings, gave his trust to criminals, showed too much compassion towards his enemies, acted according to his will without taking sufficient counsel, and failed to distribute conquered lands to his supporters as he should have done.[31] Edward was not a king loved

---

[27] Challis (ed.), *A New History of the Royal Mint*, 137–40.
[28] M. Allen, 'The Volume of the English Currency, 1158–1470', *EcHR* 54 (2001), 606–7.
[29] *Flores*, iii. 275–6; Guisborough, 359. [30] *Political Songs*, 93.
[31] Pierre de Langtoft, 401.

by his subjects, but he was respected, and even feared. The situation under his successor would be very different.

EDWARD II AND THE ORDINANCES

It must be doubtful whether a better training for kingship would have made Edward II a better ruler. He proved to be incorrigibly incompetent. Edward I had attempted to give him some responsibility, with command of one of the two armies that invaded Scotland in 1301. Significantly, the experiment was not repeated in 1303–4, but he was entrusted with a force in 1306. He had, however, no stomach for war. His political experience amounted to little more than quarrelling bitterly with his father and with Walter Langton, and suffering a six months period of exile from the royal court as a result. The title of Prince of Wales, granted to him in 1301, meant virtually nothing in practice. What was most significant about the years before his accession was the friendship he forged with a young Gascon, Piers Gaveston, son of a royal household knight. The relationship did not meet with the old king's approval. This was perhaps because Edward sought excessive favours for Piers, who was sent into exile in 1307.[32]

The new reign began on 7 July 1307 as the English army was on the brink of invading Scotland. The new king came north from London with some speed, but the expedition was quickly abandoned. The first major decision that Edward took was to take his revenge on Walter Langton, who was promptly arrested. Piers Gaveston returned from his exile in Ponthieu, and was granted the earldom of Cornwall in a charter issued on 6 August at Dumfries.[33] Edward had undone what he perceived as the injustices he had suffered as prince. Parliament was held at Northampton in the autumn. There was optimism, as a tax of a fifteenth was granted without argument, not because of any urgent necessity in Roman law terms, but so as to meet the costs of the forthcoming coronation and royal marriage. The first indication of discontent came when the king went to Boulogne in January 1308 for his marriage to the 12-year-old Isabella of France. There a group of magnates, all former councillors of Edward I, entered into a formal agreement. The wording was sufficiently vague for the document to carry a number of possible meanings. 'Things' had been done contrary to the king's honour and the rights of the crown. Those who sealed the document agreed that they should do all they could to put right

---

[32] Edward's early career is described by H. Johnstone, *Edward of Caernarvon 1284–1307* (Manchester, 1946). For a biography of Gaveston, see J. S. Hamilton, *Piers Gaveston, Earl of Cornwall 1307–1312* (Detroit, 1988).

[33] P. Chaplais, *Piers Gaveston, Edward II's Adoptive Brother* (Oxford, 1994).

the oppression of the people that had been, and still was, taking place. They also expressed their loyalty to the king. The document can be seen as a disguised attack on Gaveston, or it may be that the oppressions it mentioned were the established grievances of prises, household jurisdiction, and other matters that had led to the production of the *Articuli* of 1301. The approach of the authors of the agreement may have been that of moderate royalists seeking to protect Edward II from others with more radical views, or that of men loyal to the memory of the old king, appalled at the direction in which events were now going. Whatever interpretation is adopted, it is clear that there were significant political arguments taking place.[34]

Edward's coronation took place on 25 February 1308, at the hands of the bishop of Winchester, for Archbishop Winchelsey was still abroad. According to the annals of St Paul's, the English magnates together with the queen's uncles demanded Gaveston's exile, and threatened to delay the coronation when the king refused.[35] It may be that such arguments led to the addition of a new clause to the oath sworn by Edward when he was crowned. In this, he promised 'to maintain and preserve the laws and rightful customs which the community of your realm shall have chosen'. There has been much discussion and argument among historians about this.[36] Was the king in effect signing a blank cheque, and promising to agree to unspecified future decisions? It may be that there was alarm lest Edward should try to go back on promises he made, in the way that his father did when he obtained a papal bull revoking the concessions he had made. The terminology 'shall have chosen' (*aura eslu*) is somewhat confusing, for it is not absolutely clear whether it applies to past and future enactments, or simply to the former. The answer is probably that at the time, as later, the clause meant different things to different people.

Crisis soon followed the coronation. At the Easter parliament the earl of Lincoln presented a very threatening document. It pointed out that homage and allegiance was due to the crown, rather than to the person of the king. Gaveston, through extravagance, was impoverishing the crown. The new clause of the coronation oath was appealed to, in misquoted form. The king was asked to exile Gaveston, 'since he is bound by his coronation oath to keep the laws that the people shall choose'. Edward had no option other than to

---

[34] The Boulogne agreement is printed by J. R. S. Phillips, *Aymer de Valence, Earl of Pembroke 1307–1324* (Oxford, 1972), 316–17. For interpretations, see J. R. Maddicott, *Thomas of Lancaster 1307–1322* (Oxford, 1970), 72–3, and R. M. Haines, *King Edward II: Edward of Caernarfon, his Life, his Reign, and its Aftermath 1284–1330* (Montreal, 2003), 56–7.

[35] Pauline Annals, 260.

[36] H. G. Richardson, 'The English Coronation Oath', *Speculum*, 24 (1949), 44–75; B. Wilkinson, 'The Coronation Oath of Edward II', in J. G. Edwards, V. H. Galbraith, and E. F. Jacob (eds.), *Historical Essays in Honour of James Tait* (Manchester, 1933), 405–16; R. S. Hoyt, 'The Coronation Oath of 1308', *EHR* 71 (1956), 353–83.

agree, and Gaveston was forced to abjure the realm, going to Ireland. The depths of hostility to the king's favourite are hard to plumb. He does not appear to have sought to dominate politics. The evidence of charter witness lists is interesting here, for on average he witnessed no more than 5.7 per cent of royal charters, which stands in contrast to the young earl of Gloucester's 56.5 per cent, and the earl of Lincoln's 63.4 per cent.[37] His behaviour was, however, unacceptable in many ways. At the feast following the coronation, 'Piers, seeking not the king's glory but his own, as if contemptuous of the English, where the others were in cloth of gold, appeared in purple, decked with pearls, rode between the guests, as if worth more than the king.'[38] The English earls did not appreciate the nicknames he gave them. There was jealousy at his success in tournaments; in one, held at Wallingford, three or four earls were worsted by Piers and his followers.[39] There were also more serious matters. Gaveston was in a position to influence royal patronage. In a letter to his follower Robert Darcy he apologized for not obtaining a wardship and marriage for him; three days earlier it had gone to someone else.[40] Philip IV of France, Edward's father-in-law, was bitterly hostile to Gaveston, whom he regarded as his enemy. This was hardly surprising in view of Edward's open display of affection towards Gaveston at the time of the coronation, and his neglect of his young queen, but may also have been because Gaveston had designs upon the county of Ponthieu.[41]

Was hostility towards Gaveston also the result of distaste at a homosexual relationship between Edward and his favourite? The annals of St Paul's hint strongly at this in the early stages of the reign, reporting rumours that the king loved Gaveston more than his wife. One plausible suggestion is that Edward and Gaveston had entered into a pact of adoptive brotherhood, and that it is this that explains their closeness, rather than a sexual bond.[42] The two, however, are not necessarily mutually exclusive. No proof is possible, but it is most likely that the relationship between Edward and Gaveston was one of strong friendship, and that it was not homosexual in character. It is relevant that Edward had four children by his queen, and one illegitimate son; Gaveston had a daughter. Although Edward's relationship with Isabella broke down so disastrously, there are hints of earlier genuine affection, such as a letter in

---

[37] J. S. Hamilton, 'Charter Witness Lists for the Reign of Edward II', in N. Saul (ed.), *Fourteenth Century England*, i (Woodbridge, 2000), 5.

[38] Pauline Annals, 262.

[39] *Vita Edwardi*, 3.

[40] Maddicott, *Thomas of Lancaster*, 335.

[41] Chaplais, *Piers Gaveston*, 10.

[42] Pauline Annals, 262; Chaplais, *Piers Gaveston*, 7–8, 20–2.

which he addressed her as 'Dear heart'.[43] When a royal messenger was accused of making slanderous statements about the king in 1314, no mention was made of homosexuality.[44]

While for some the presence of Gaveston at Edward's court was wholly unacceptable, for others the Gascon favourite offered a convenient bargaining counter. The king could be allowed to have Gaveston back, provided that he agreed to reforms. In parliament in April and May 1309 grievances were presented. These covered familiar ground, taking arguments on from the *Articuli* of 1300. The main issues were purveyance, the jurisdiction of the royal household, and the abuse of royal writs of protection and of the privy seal. The new elements concerned the customs duties introduced in 1303, the debasement of the currency, the fact that not all petitions in parliament were being heard, and the way in which criminals were being granted pardons.[45] If these were met, then a grant of a twenty-fifth would be made. The next parliament was held at Stamford in July. The Statute of Stamford met the grievances of the previous parliament, and the collection of the tax duly went ahead. In addition, the price that the opposition paid for the statute was the return of Piers Gaveston. During the parliament Gaveston received a regrant of the earldom of Cornwall, on slightly different hereditary terms from those of the first grant in 1307.[46]

Gaveston had caused no problems during his exile in Ireland, but on his return to England showed that he had not learned his lesson. His waspish tongue continued to irritate. A dispute with Thomas, earl of Lancaster, was particularly serious. According to the *Vita* of the king, one of his retainers was thrown out of office at court at Piers' request. The statement presents historians with problems, for no such incident has been identified for 1309, although there is a case from 1311 which could fit.[47] Lancaster was the one earl who did not witness the regrant of the earldom of Cornwall to Gaveston, and his opposition to the royal favourite became increasingly crucial. The situation was becoming more and more difficult for Edward at a time when financial problems were becoming increasingly acute. There was growing reliance on the Frescobaldi; the debt to the firm in 1310 was calculated at £21,635.[48] Indebtedness, combined with the king's failure to take effective measures to deal with Robert Bruce's successes in Scotland, left the king with few options. Articles were duly presented in parliament early in 1310 by the magnates. The king had

---

[43] E 163/4/11, no. 5.
[44] H. Johnstone, 'The Eccentricities of Edward II', *EHR* 48 (1933), 264–7.
[45] *Rot. Parl.* i. 443–5; Maddicott, *Thomas of Lancaster*, 97–8.
[46] Chaplais, *Piers Gaveston*, 68.
[47] Maddicott, *Thomas of Lancaster*, 93, 117–18; Chaplais, *Piers Gaveston*, 69–71.
[48] Kaeuper, 'The Frescobaldi of Florence', 70.

accepted poor counsel, and had frittered his treasure so that he could neither maintain his household nor defend the land. Taxes had been wasted. Prises were heavier than ever. The petition argued that the situation could be rescued only by baronial ordinance. In March the king duly agreed to the appointment of a committee of Ordainers, with full power to reform the state of the realm and the royal household.[49] In exchange, the magnates agreed that the king's concession should not be made into a precedent for the future. Six preliminary ordinances were issued remarkably promptly in March, and confirmed in August. No grants were to be made without the consent of the Ordainers. Customs were to be paid into the exchequer and not handed over to foreigners, who were to be arrested. The provisions of Magna Carta were to be adhered to.[50]

Edward attempted to outflank the Ordainers by conducting, at long last, a campaign in Scotland. Military triumph would have brought with it political success, but victory over Robert Bruce was not to be achieved. The work of drafting the Ordinances was complex, and it was not until October 1311 that they were finally published. There were forty-one clauses in all, and the document as a whole can be seen as the climax to the arguments that had begun in the 1290s. Much that was in the Ordinances looked back to the *Articuli super Cartas* of 1300, and to the Statute of Stamford of 1309, while some of the abuses addressed were of very long standing.[51]

It is possible to divide the enactments into various groups. Some were directed against specific individuals: Gaveston, Henry de Beaumont and his sister Isabella de Vescy, and the Italian merchant banker Amerigo de Frescobaldi. Another group dealt with royal exactions. The new customs duties were to go, and all customs revenues were to be paid directly into the exchequer. Prises were limited to those that were 'ancient, rightful and due'. The exchequer was to cease demanding payment of debts when people had in fact got receipts to demonstrate that they had paid them off. There was a range of legal issues in the document. Parliament was to be held regularly, so that pleas would not be delayed. The jurisdiction of the exchequer was limited, as was that of the royal household. The privy seal should not be used to impede the processes of the common law. Pardons should be properly granted. Statute merchant, used for recovery of debt, should only be used between merchants.

---

[49] The Ordainers were: the archbishop of Canterbury; the bishops of London, Salisbury, St David's, and Llandaff; the earls of Gloucester, Lancaster, Lincoln, Hereford, Richmond, Pembroke, Warwick, and Arundel; Hugh de Courtenay, Robert FitzRoger, John de Grey, William le Marshal, William Martin, Hugh de Vere, barons. Robert Clifford replaced FitzRoger on the latter's death.

[50] Ann. Lond. 168–73.

[51] *SR* 156–67; M. C. Prestwich, 'The Ordinances of 1311 and the Politics of the Early Fourteenth Century', in J. Taylor and W. Childs (eds.), *Politics and Crisis in Fourteenth Century England* (Gloucester, 1990), 1–18.

Steps were taken to prevent malicious accusations being made in the courts. Measures were introduced to control royal officials. The most important were to be appointed with baronial agreement, in parliament. Sheriffs in future were to be appointed by the chancellor, treasurer, and members of the king's council. The activities of forest officials were to be investigated.

There were few new concepts in the Ordinances. One that has been seen as novel appeared in clauses four, eight, and ten. These stated that the king should live 'of his own' without taking any prises save traditional and rightful ones. This was a significant idea, which could be seen as a criticism of the way in which the crown was becoming increasingly dependent upon taxation. The idea, however, had already been expressed by Edward I, when he informed the clergy in 1298 that he did not propose to ask them for a tax as he intended to finance the Scottish campaign of that year of his own.[52]

What was quite new in the Ordinances was the way in which consent was to be obtained. In 1297 consent was to be given by the community of the realm, and this was not defined. In 1311 consent on a wide range of issues was to be provided by the baronage in parliament. Parliamentary consent was, of course, nothing new, but it had not been provided for in this way in the past, nor had it covered such a range of activities. These extended from the king's leaving the realm and making war to changes in the currency and the appointment of officials. Baronial consent in parliament was the main form of control of the king and government that was envisaged. The Ordinances did not echo the solutions of the 1250s and 1260s. No attempt was made to impose a council on the king, and there was no mechanism suggested for day-to-day supervision of government.

The Ordinances used to be interpreted as attacking the way in which the system of government through the royal household operated.[53] More recent views have emphasized the importance of hostility to prises, and to the desire to control royal patronage. It has also been argued that, increasingly, 'Fiscal and administrative reform took second place to personal and political demands...'[54] One of the difficulties in analysing the Ordinances is that there is very little information about the process of drawing up the document. One manuscript preserves what appears to be a draft version, but there is little else. This draft contains a clause that provided for a committee of five to survey

---

[52] B. P. Wolffe, *The Royal Demesne in English History* (London, 1971), 47–8; Prestwich, 'The Ordinances of 1311 and the Politics of the Early Fourteenth Century', 6.

[53] This was the view of Tout and J. C. Davies. See T. F. Tout, *The Place of the Reign of Edward II in English History* (Manchester, 1914), 92–3; J. C. Davies, *The Baronial Opposition to Edward II* (London, 1918), 372.

[54] Maddicott, *Thomas of Lancaster*, 106–8, 178; Harriss, *King, Parliament and Public Finance*, 168.

royal receipts. In addition, the keeper of the wardrobe was to present his accounts annually at the exchequer. The fact that this clause was not included in the final version is important, for it suggests that control of crown finance, and of the main household financial department, the wardrobe, was not a high priority for the Ordainers.[55] Personal and legal issues were more important. In the final version the committee of five was used to hear complaints against royal officials who contravened the terms of the Ordinances and did not have specific financial responsibilities.

The question of the royal household was not dealt with fully in the Ordinances, but a supplementary document was soon issued which did. This was very different in character from the main Ordinances. It was more informal in style, and concentrated on individuals. For example, a group of household knights were to be expelled from the household, and the relevant clause reads: 'Item, Sir John de Charlton, Sir John de la Beche, Sir William de Vaux, Sir John de Ockham, Sir Gerard Salveyn should be removed from office and command and put out of the king's service so that they should not come near to him.' There were no structural reforms suggested, but the purge was to be extensive, even extending to the carters responsible for the transport of the household. The document also revealed the difficulties that there were in implementing the provisions of the main Ordinances. Amerigo de Frescobaldi had not yet been banished. Piers Gaveston had been given royal protection and letters of attorney, which needed to be cancelled. Royal officials had not yet been appointed on the terms set out in the Ordinances.[56]

One criticism made by historians, if not contemporaries, of the Ordinances is that the document was thoroughly oligarchic. Consent was to be provided by the baronage in parliament, and there was no role allocated for the representatives of shires and boroughs.[57] The fact that no representatives had been summoned to the parliament of February 1310, in which the king agreed to the appointment of the Ordainers, helps to explain this. Nor should the point be exaggerated. There is no indication that the Ordainers intended to deny the representatives their function of providing consent to taxation. The parliaments that were summoned under their influence in 1311 had a full attendance of representatives. The provisions of the Ordinances were not obviously biased in a baronial direction. There is no evidence of any formal consultation with the knights in the shires, but it is likely that soundings were taken. A number of clauses, particularly those dealing with the law, reflected concerns far wider than those of the baronage. On the question of the appointment of sheriffs,

---

[55] M. C. Prestwich, 'A New Version of the Ordinances of 1311', *BIHR* 57 (1984), 189–203.

[56] Ann. Lond. 198–202. Of those named in the quotation, Ockham was a clerk, not a household knight.

[57] W. Stubbs, *Constitutional History of England*, 4th edn. (Oxford, 1906), ii. 346.

however, the Ordinances did not propose the radical route of local election that had featured in the *Articuli* of 1300.

The crisis of 1310–11 threw up few new ideas. The authors of the Ordinances built on the work of the past, and particularly the criticisms of government that had been voiced since the turn of the century. Was this because there was a strong degree of continuity in the personnel of opposition to the crown? Of the Ordainers, Archbishop Winchelsey was a notable survivor from 1297. Robert FitzRoger had accompanied Roger Bigod to the exchequer in 1297. The earl of Arundel no doubt resented the way in which Edward I had forced him to go to Gascony by threatening to foreclose on the debts he owed to the crown. Hugh de Courtenay had good reason to resent the way in which Edward I had deprived him of his inheritance. The earl of Hereford had, it was said, sworn to follow the political ideals of his father, the leader with Bigod of the secular opposition in 1297.[58] Much more striking, however, is the role of former loyal supporters of Edward I. The earls of Lincoln, Pembroke, and Richmond were all Ordainers, as was Robert Clifford.[59] This may help to explain the moderate tone of much of the Ordinances; the legal and financial provisions were scarcely radical. The Ordinances reflect a widespread consensus over what was needed. For Edward, however, the renewed demand for the exile of Gaveston, and the severe limitation that was placed on the exercise of royal patronage, were elements that rendered the Ordinances wholly and completely unacceptable. The publication of the Ordinances did not close a period of crisis, it opened one.

PARLIAMENT

These years were of great importance for the development of parliament. Its composition was not yet standardized. The king and his council were of course central to parliament, but beyond that there could be considerable variation. The number of those who received individual summonses might vary considerably. In November 1296, for example, thirty-six lay magnates were asked to attend, but for the Salisbury gathering in the following February, six earls and seventy-five barons were summoned. It became convenient for the chancery to use the same lists for both military and parliamentary summonses, with those for the final years of Edward I's reign deriving from an abortive attempt to recruit an army for Scotland in 1299. In 1301 nine earls and eighty barons were summoned, and thereafter numbers remained at around this level. The fact that men were summoned, however, did not mean that they attended. At the

---

[58] Trokelowe, 74.
[59] Prestwich, 'The Ordinances of 1311 and the Politics of the Early Fourteenth Century', 5.

Carlisle parliament in 1307 writs were sent out six weeks after proceedings had begun, requesting the personal attendance of the earls of Lancaster, Warwick, and Angus, and twenty-four other lay magnates. Even then, only half of these men responded.[60]

The representatives of shires, boroughs, and lower clergy were not summoned to all parliaments; they did not attend at Salisbury in 1297, or at any of the three parliaments of 1299, for there were no requests for grants of taxes at these assemblies. Their attendance, however, was more frequent in the years after 1294 than it had been previously. It was important that the representatives should have full authority to act on behalf of their communities, and the concept of *plena potestas*, or 'full power', which derived from Roman law, was employed to ensure this. In 1294 two sets of knights were summoned to parliament, one with full powers to provide consent, the other without such authority to do whatever was decided. In the following year the representatives were asked, in a simplified procedure, to come to what would much later become known as the Model Parliament, with full powers to do what should be ordained by common counsel.[61] The link between such powers and the granting of taxation seems obvious, but in 1306 when representatives were asked to come to 'treat, ordain and consent' so that the tax of a thirtieth and twentieth could be collected, there was no requirement on them to be armed with *plena potestas*.[62] This may have reflected the fact that this tax had, in part, the character of a feudal aid levied on the occasion of the knighting of the king's eldest son.

The business of parliaments was wide-ranging, extending as it did from the hearing of judicial cases and the hearing of petitions to the discussion of great affairs of state. Rolls that were kept of parliamentary assemblies contain little more than matters of legal record, but they were drawn up for that specific purpose. Parliaments were occasions for political discussion and debate. The development of the institution was transforming the way in which the political nation operated.

One striking change in the Ordinances, as compared to earlier documents, was the absence of reference to the community of the realm. In 1297 the earl of Hereford had put forward the Remonstrances on behalf of the 'prelates, earls, barons and the whole community of the land', and the *Confirmatio Cartarum* used the terminology of 'community of the realm'.[63] In 1301 and 1309 letters to the pope had been sealed by a number of barons 'as much for ourselves as for

---

[60] Prestwich, *Edward I*, 446–7.
[61] Edwards, 'The *Plena Potestas* of English Parliamentary Representatives', 136–49.
[62] *Parl. Writs*, i. 164.
[63] *Documents Illustrating the Crisis of 1297–8*, ed. Prestwich, 115, 159.

the whole community of England', but by 1311 it was clearly considered inappropriate for the barons to claim to speak on behalf of the community as a whole. The terminology that was adopted was that of 'common assent of the baronage and that in parliament'. It would not be long before it was recognized that it was the representatives in parliament, not the barons, who spoke for the community.[64]

The development of parliament showed one way in which the nature of politics was changing, but the tensions that were emerging in Edward II's first years on the throne were not to be resolved by debate and discussion. The Ordinances of 1311 suggested solutions for at least some of the difficulties that had vexed the country since the French war began in 1294, but without the agreement of the king these were unlikely to be effective. The problem presented by Piers Gaveston was not to be settled by compelling him to go into exile, as the Ordinances requested he should; the only permanent solution was to be a violent one. Matters were made more difficult by the fact that they were played out against a backdrop of continued failure in Scotland (this will be discussed in Chapter 9). Until the situation in the north was reversed, it would prove impossible to establish a stable regime in England. Politics in this period was intensely personal, and unstable. The best-informed commentator remarked, with some despair: 'See how often and abruptly great men change their sides. Those whom we regard as faithless in the North we find just the opposite in the South. The love of magnates is as a game of dice, and the desires of the rich like feathers.'[65]

---

[64] M. C. Prestwich, 'Parliament and the Community of the Realm in Fourteenth Century England', in A. Cosgrove and J. I. McGuire (eds.), *Parliament and Community* (Belfast, 1983), 5–6.

[65] *Vita Edwardi*, 7.

CHAPTER 8

Times of Trouble, 1311–1330

In 1312, on Blacklow Hill in Warwickshire, Piers Gaveston was brutally killed. One man ran him through with a sword, the other cut off his head. Politics had reached a new low. The succeeding years were to see crisis follow on crisis, with no evident way out. By 1327 the monarchy had reached its apparent nadir, with the deposition of Edward II; but the regime that came next, that of Queen Isabella and Roger Mortimer, proved quite as corrupt and incompetent. It is remarkable that a monarchy that had appeared so strong in the hands of Edward I should have collapsed in so dramatic a way.

THE DEATH OF GAVESTON

The death of Piers Gaveston in 1312 was a defining moment. Political argument had not deteriorated into open bloodshed since the 1260s; now, violence was on the agenda. The years between 1312 and 1322 were to be dominated by rivalry between the king and his cousin Thomas of Lancaster. The holder of no fewer than five earldoms, Lancaster was a man of unparalleled wealth. From his father he inherited Lancaster, Leicester, and Derby, while his marriage to Alice, daughter of the earl of Lincoln, brought him the earldoms of Lincoln and Salisbury. His lands brought him some £11,000 a year, almost double the revenue of the next richest of the earls, Gloucester. As Edward's cousin, his loyalty might have been expected, but Lancaster had no respect for the king. His wealth meant that he had little need of patronage from the king; he was even in a position to recruit a household to rival Edward's.

Gaveston had gone into exile briefly in the autumn of 1311, probably to Flanders. He was swiftly recalled by Edward II, who according to the well-informed author of his *Vita* was bitterly resentful at the demands made by the Ordainers to oust various members of his household.[1] Gaveston joined the king

---

[1] *Vita Edwardi*, 21. For discussion of this important chronicle, see C. Given-Wilson, *Chronicles: The Writing of History in Medieval England* (London, 2004), 165–74; id., '*Vita Edwardi Secundi*: Memoir or Journal?', in *TCE* vi. 165–76; W. Childs, 'Resistance and Treason in the *Vita Edwardi Secundi*', ibid. 177–91.

at York in January 1312. The situation was moving closer to civil war as the king and his favourite moved to Newcastle. The threat presented by baronial forces under the earl of Lancaster compelled the king and Gaveston to escape by sea to Scarborough. The king then left Gaveston there while he himself moved to York. It seems an act of inexplicable folly to have divided forces in this way. One possibility is that Gaveston was unwell; it seems unlikely that Scarborough was considered impregnable. The castle was duly besieged, and Gaveston soon came to terms. If no agreement was reached with the king, then Gaveston would return to the castle, which was not to be reinforced during what amounted to a period of truce. The earl of Pembroke guaranteed Gaveston's safety. On their way south, however, Pembroke left Gaveston at Deddington while he went to see his wife. The earl of Warwick seized the opportunity and captured Gaveston. It seems that a trial of sorts was held, and that Gaveston was sentenced to death on the basis of the Ordinances. His death, however, had little of the character of a judicial execution, and more that of a public lynching.[2]

Those responsible for Gaveston's death were the earls of Warwick, Lancaster, and Hereford. John Botetourt, a veteran knight of Edward I's household, gave his support in a formal letter to the group, along with Henry Percy.[3] Pembroke, who had guaranteed Gaveston's safety, joined the king's cause, as did Earl Warenne. It seemed almost certain that civil war would break out. The reasons why it did not are various. One was financial. The king was not in any position to finance a conflict on any scale. The Frescobaldi had been forced out of the country by the Ordainers, and ruined. It would take time for a successor to emerge. Another was that Lancaster and his associates had an important bargaining counter in their possession. When the king and Gaveston fled from Newcastle, they left behind horses, arms, and a sumptuous collection of jewels, gold, and silver. There was also a single ruby, set in gold, worth £1,000, which was found on Gaveston's person when he was seized at Deddington. The total value of the jewels and horses cannot be calculated, for many items are not valued, while for others the weight, rather than the price, is given.[4] They were, however, well worth recovering. A third reason is that on 13 November 1312 Queen Isabella gave birth to the future Edward III. This meant that whereas in the past the French had treated Edward II with understandable suspicion, relations between the two courts thawed rapidly. There were also powerful voices of moderation, notably that of the earl of Gloucester, whose sister Margaret had been married to Gaveston.

[2] Hamilton, *Piers Gaveston*, 91–9, discusses the final stages of Gaveston's career. The most detailed chronicle account is in the *Vita Edwardi*, 24–7.

[3] Hamilton, *Piers Gaveston*, 98, 165 n. 71.

[4] The list is printed by Chaplais, *Piers Gaveston*, 125–34.

Negotiations were complex and long-drawn-out.[5] The earls were insistent that the Ordinances should be maintained; they agreed in a draft of peace terms that, when parliament next met, they would do everything possible to ensure that a tax would be granted so as to further the Scottish war.[6] As time went on, new issues emerged. Lancaster was particularly concerned about a problem in the Welsh borders, where his retainer Gruffudd de la Pole was in dispute with the royalist John Charlton over the lordship of Powys. Early in 1313 the jewels and horses were finally returned to the king, but a final settlement was delayed until the following October. A royal visit to France was one reason for delay. The author of the *Vita* commented: 'But what do these incessant delays profit the king? Some say that he could force his opponents to waste their resources, or perhaps awaits the death of an earl whom he could not hope to conquer.'[7] The financial position was improving, but only slowly. The tax promised in the negotiations was finally granted in November, but the first instalment of this twentieth and fifteenth was not due to be paid until the following Easter. A Genoese merchant, Antonio Pessagno, had emerged as a successor of sorts to the Frescobaldi. He did not have financial resources behind him on the same scale as the Florentine merchants, but he was effective as a royal agent in raising loans from others, which he then advanced to the king. Early in 1314 he received the equivalent of £25,000 in florins from the pope, and by the following November was owed over £111,000 for the loans he had made to the crown.[8]

LANCASTER AND THE LINCOLN PARLIAMENT

The defeat at Bannockburn at midsummer 1314 is described in the next chapter. It was not just a calamity for English ambitions in Scotland. It also transformed domestic politics, for the battle could be seen as a verdict on Edward's mismanagement of affairs. In addition, the death of the earl of Gloucester in his suicidal charge on the Scots removed from the political scene an important force for moderation. Thomas of Lancaster and Guy of Warwick had played no part in the campaign, which in their view had not received consent as laid down in the Ordinances, and were therefore not discredited by it. At parliament in York in September 1314 Edward was in no position to resist the earls' demands. The maintenance of the Ordinances was requested, and conceded. A reshuffle of officials took place. The treasurer,

---

[5] For a full discussion, see Maddicott, *Thomas of Lancaster*, 130 ff.
[6] Ann. Lond., 211.   [7] *Vita Edwardi*, 42.
[8] N. Fryde, 'Antonio Pessagno of Genoa, King's Merchant of Edward II of England', in *Studi in Memoria di Federigo Melis* (Florence, 1978), ii. 165, 168–9, 171; *CPR 1313–17*, 203–6.

John Sandale, became chancellor, and Walter of Norwich, a safe pair of hands, took his place at the exchequer. The keeper of the wardrobe, the unpopular Ingelard Warley, was replaced by William Melton, a man of the utmost probity. Almost all the sheriffs were replaced. Demands that various individuals leave the royal court were deferred, with the exception of Hugh Despenser the elder, who had to go.[9]

The new regime fared little better than its predecessor. Initially, Warwick had been made the king's chief councillor, but he died in 1315, and this left Lancaster pre-eminent.[10] Every effort was made to adhere to the Ordinances. A number of grants made since 1310 were cancelled, and lands taken back by the crown. Lancaster was very unfortunate, in that his period of power coincided with the most disastrous economic conditions that the country had faced in recorded memory. The appalling weather and consequent bad harvests of 1315 and 1316 were problems that no government could have dealt with. Royal finances were hard hit, with customs revenues severely reduced as well as income from land. No government could have succeeded without dealing with the Scots, and conditions made it extremely difficult to mount an effective campaign. Even the failure of the Scottish siege of Carlisle in 1315 did little if anything to improve the position.

Relations between the king and his cousin Lancaster were not easy. A reply to the king from Lancaster, sent in October 1315, demonstrates this. The king had complained about baronial assemblies that had been held. Lancaster told Edward that he should not use force to prevent these, unless they were to the harm of king or kingdom. The treasurer had said that there was no money for the king to come north; the disingenuous reply was that 'it seems to the said earl that our lord the king will have the same expenses in the north as he does in the south'. Lancaster concluded by stating that he was prepared to stay in the north as had been agreed at Lincoln, although other magnates were not ready to do so.[11]

Lancaster himself faced a severe problem when one of his retainers, Adam Banaster, rebelled against the earl in Lancashire in the autumn of 1315. The reason for the rising is not clear, but it was probably the result of Banaster's hostility towards his brother-in-law Robert Holland, Lancaster's chief retainer. The rising distracted Lancaster from affairs of state, and in particular from the need to organize a Scottish campaign. Proceedings at the Lincoln parliament early in 1316 were delayed because he appeared a fortnight late. During the

---

[9] Maddicott, *Thomas of Lancaster*, 165; *Vita Edwardi*, 57. Despenser ceased witnessing royal charters at this time: *The Royal Charter Witness Lists of Edward II (1307–1326)*, ed. J. S. Hamilton (List and Index Society, 288, 2001), 79–80.

[10] *Ann. Lond.* 232.

[11] Davies, *Baronial Opposition*, app. 108.

session he was, however, formally appointed as head of the king's council; when he accepted the post which he had in practice occupied for some time, he stressed the need to maintain the Ordinances.

The record of the proceedings at the Lincoln parliament took, for the first time, a narrative form.[12] William Inge, chief justice of the common bench, made the opening speech on 28 January. It was decided to use the time before Lancaster and other magnates arrived to hear petitions, and committees of auditors were set up for this purpose. The prelates put forward a set of articles which, for the most part, summed up and made use of grievances dating back to Edward I's reign. The earl of Hereford responded on the king's behalf on 7 February; the issues that had not already been answered would be considered. Edward, fed up with waiting for Lancaster, left for a few days, leaving the bishops of Exeter and Norwich, with the earls of Richmond and Pembroke, to take charge on his behalf. Lancaster soon arrived, and on 12 February the full parliament began, with an exposition of the Scottish problem and a royal request for advice. On 14 February, after discussions, the decree that had been issued in 1315 setting maximum prices for foodstuffs was abolished (this was a time of famine and the decree had not worked), and a statute was enacted formalizing the method of appointing sheriffs that had been set out in the Ordinances. Lancaster's appointment as head of the council took place, no doubt after heated discussion, on 17 February. Three days later a grant of an unusual kind was made, of one footsoldier from each vill in England to go to fight in Scotland, for sixty days at local expense. The magnates agreed that the king should issue a normal summons of knight service as well. This was followed by a grant of a fifteenth by the knights of the shire and the burgesses, as their contribution to the war effort. The clergy made a separate grant of a tenth, on condition that Edward should go to Scotland and remain there on campaign. It would be wrong to think of parliament as solemn and well ordered. It was during this Lincoln parliament that Hugh Despenser the younger assaulted John de Ros, in the king's presence, in Lincoln cathedral. He was charged with 'striking him with his fist until he drew blood', but Hugh's account, predictably, was that 'he touched John on the face'. This bout of fisticuffs was over a private matter: John had allegedly arranged for the arrest of one of Hugh's knights.[13]

The author of the *Vita* thought that little was achieved at the Lincoln parliament.[14] His cynicism was typical of the age. Robert of Reading commen-

---

[12] *Rot. Parl.* i. 350–2; Sayles, *Functions of the Medieval Parliament*, 332–4; Davies, *Baronial Opposition*, 408–14.

[13] Sayles, *Functions of the Medieval Parliament*, 353.

[14] *Vita Edwardi*, 69.

ted on the 'ridiculous and deceitful' parliaments of Edward II's early years on the throne, in which fraudulent taxes were authorized, and from which wise men departed having failed to obtain the justice they sought.[15] However, the record of the Lincoln proceedings, for which William Airmyn was responsible, shows how parliament had developed as an institution. The range of business was considerable, with a clear priority naturally given to the major issues of policy. These were a matter for the magnates, lay and ecclesiastical, to discuss. There had been considerable changes to the list of those summoned in 1311, but from 1314 it was stabilized, with eighty-eight lay magnates asked to attend.[16] They were beginning to think of themselves as peers: in the negotiations that had followed Gaveston's death it had been stated that the great men would do all they could to ensure the grant of a tax 'when they will have their peers more fully with them, and the community'.[17] The parliament roll does not suggest that at Lincoln in 1316 the representatives had any major function, apart from making the grant of a fifteenth. In this period, however, they were playing a greater part than in the past in the business of petitioning. In the January 1315 parliament, for example, of 220 petitions nine were presented by the shires and fourteen by boroughs.[18] Analysis of the representatives who attended parliament in Edward II's reign shows that high politics appears to have played no part in their election. Some attended frequently, being re-elected up to a dozen times, though in any parliament it was normal for half the representatives to be attending for the first time.[19]

One achievement at Lincoln was a settlement over the issue of clerical grievances. There was a long history to these wide-ranging complaints. The central problem was the relationship between secular and church courts. There was a long-standing belief on the part of both the crown and the Church that the other was encroaching on their rightful sphere of activity. The story goes back to Edward I's reign and the lengthy statement of clerical grievances drawn up in 1280. Grievances, some old, some new, were put to Edward II in 1309. These included such issues as the need for electors to positions in the Church to be free from secular pressures, and a demand that lay judges should not hear cases of bigamy.[20] A long list of twenty-one grievances, which made full use of earlier documents, was drawn up and presented at the Lincoln parliament; a conciliatory reply promised joint consideration by prelates, magnates, and the

---

[15] *Flores*, iii. 143.

[16] J. E. Powell and K. Wallis, *The House of Lords in the Middle Ages* (London, 1968), 310.

[17] *Ann. Lond.* 211.

[18] Maddicott, 'Parliament and the Constituencies', 69.

[19] J. G. Edwards, 'The Personnel of the Commons in Parliament Under Edward I and Edward II', in Fryde and Miller (eds.), *Historical Studies of the English Parliament*, i. 150–67.

[20] *Councils and Synods*, ii, ed. Powicke and Cheney, 1269–74.

king's council. In November these consultations resulted in the issue of the
Articuli Cleri. This was a royal writ setting out thirteen clerical grievances with
the king's responses to them. The complaints did not follow those presented
earlier at the Lincoln parliament, though they drew on them extensively.
There were, for example, four clauses at Lincoln complaining about the
Statute of Mortmain and its use in cases where there was no potential loss to
a feudal lord. These were not included in the *Articuli*. There was no victory to
the clergy; the crown was not prepared to make significant concessions. This
was hardly surprising given the attitude of Archbishop Reynolds, a man with a
court background who was one of the king's councillors and who had no
evident sympathy for the cause of reform.[21] The *Articuli* did not represent a
significant advance; rather, it marked the closing of a chapter.

One indication of the position of the Church in this reign is provided by
statistics on taxation, which show that it paid a much higher proportion than it
had under Edward I. Lay taxes yielded, in all, some £250,000, while those on
the Church produced about £220,000. Of this sum, about £55,000 was derived
from direct grants by the clergy, while the remainder was derived from taxes
imposed by the pope, most of which were paid over to the crown. This compares
with figures for Edward I's reign that show about £500,000 received from direct
lay taxes and some £300,000 from ecclesiastic taxation. With Walter Reynolds, a
moderate man, as archbishop of Canterbury, and a papacy anxious to do all it
could to assist the king, Edward II had considerable advantages.

NEW FAVOURITES

After the Lincoln parliament matters soon began to go badly. A high-powered
commission, which included Lancaster, was appointed to see to the reform of
the household and the governance of the realm, but the king would not
cooperate with the outcome.[22] Lancaster finally withdrew from government
in August 1316. It may be that his move was prompted by the summons of £50
landholders to serve against the Scots, a summons that was redolent of Edward
I's techniques of 1297. He may have also have been angered by the form of
summons sent to him and the other magnates. This appeared to extend the
obligation of fealty and homage beyond the traditional feudal quotas, and made
unprecedented threats of confiscation of land in cases of non-compliance. A
third possibility is ill health.[23]

[21] J. H. Denton, 'The Making of the *Articuli Cleri* of 1316', *EHR* 101 (1987), 564–95.
[22] Murimuth, 272–3.
[23] Maddicott, *Thomas of Lancaster*, 187; M. C. Prestwich, 'Cavalry Service in Early Fourteenth
Century England', in J. Gillingham and J. C. Holt (eds.), *War and Government in the Middle Ages*
(Woodbridge, 1984), 154.

Both Lancaster and the king were building up their retinues of household knights, as the threat of a trial of strength loomed. In 1317 the king complained to Lancaster that he and his men 'had retained many people and seem likely to retain them without number and we are said to have made bonds thereon in disturbance of your peace and the destruction of your people'.[24] The king was doing precisely the same thing when he entered into a series of indentures in 1316 and 1317 with a number of magnates, some simply for military service and others for war and peace. They included Bartholomew Badlesmere, John Giffard, John de Mowbray, and even the earls of Pembroke and Hereford. At least sixteen men were involved. This was clearly an attempt to build up Edward's political and military power. In addition, twenty-one knights were admitted as members of the royal household in 1317.[25] More threatening still to the precarious political equilibrium was the emergence of a group of power-hungry courtiers, William de Montague, Hugh Audley, and Roger Damory, who were all three among the group of those who made indentures with the king. The chronicler Robert of Reading considered them to be worse that Piers Gaveston.[26] Montague became steward of the royal household in 1316, and in the following year Audley and Damory acquired immense landed wealth through their respective marriages to Margaret and Elizabeth, two of the earl of Gloucester's three sisters. Division of the Gloucester estates, which had been held up by the claim of the earl's widow that she was pregnant, finally took place shortly before the two weddings.[27] Hugh Despenser the younger was linked to the new group of favourites; he was the husband of the third Clare sister, Eleanor.

Any hope that the earl of Lancaster would acquiesce in the regime that was emerging was dashed when his wife, Alice de Lacy, was abducted by the royalist Earl Warenne in May 1317, almost certainly with the king's connivance.[28] Warenne had his own dispute with Lancaster, who had been blocking his attempts to obtain a divorce from his wife, Joan de Bar, but the matter was much more than a private quarrel. Negotiations between the king and Lancaster were rendered almost impossible by the acute distrust between them. Lancaster would not attend a council at Nottingham for fear of plots against him. Two cardinals, then in England, attempted mediation. At times it seemed

[24] Murimuth, 271–6.
[25] Phillips, *Aymer de Valence*, 312–14; M. C. Prestwich, 'The Unreliability of Royal Household Knights in the Early Fourteenth Century', in C. Given-Wilson (ed.), *Fourteenth Century England*, ii (Woodbridge, 2002), 4.
[26] *Flores*, iii. 178.
[27] Phillips, *Aymer de Valence*, 131–2.
[28] L. E. Mitchell, *Portraits of Medieval Women: Family, Marriage and Politics in England, 1225–1350* (Basingstoke, 2003), 109–13.

as if civil war was about to break out; it was only dissuasion by Pembroke that prevented the king from attacking Lancaster's castle at Pontefract.[29] In south Yorkshire attacks by Lancaster's retainers on Warenne's properties came very close to civil war. It was not until August 1318 that an agreement was eventually reached, in the so-called treaty of Leake. The negotiations that led to this are complex to reconstruct.[30] An important meeting took place at Leicester in April, attended by six prelates, Lancaster, Pembroke, and Hereford, and twenty-eight barons. The role of the bishops was central to the negotiations. It was agreed that the Ordinances should be maintained and Lancaster pardoned for any offences he might have committed. Lancaster promised to be loyal to the king and to attend parliament when required, but he reserved his right to continue to take action against Warenne. Eventually, after much hard bargaining, a treaty was agreed at Leake, in Nottinghamshire, a preliminary stage to the final agreement that was reached in the parliament at York held in October.

The treaty of Leake saw Lancaster and his men promised a pardon for any misdeeds, while Lancaster agreed not to bring any actions against anyone who had injured him, with the exception of Warenne. The Ordinances were to be maintained. These terms were predictable. What was novel in the Leake agreement was that a council of seventeen was nominated. This consisted of eight bishops, four earls, four barons, and one banneret to represent Lancaster. Five of these, including Lancaster's banneret, were always to be with the king in rotation, exercising control over all those matters that did not require parliamentary assent.[31] The idea of the council was Lancaster's, though the provision for him to be represented on it by a banneret was either a concession he made, or a means of preventing him from withdrawing his cooperation. For all that the arrangements for the council appear to look back to those made by Simon de Montfort in the aftermath of his triumph at Lewes, the settlement was in practice moderate, not a radical solution to the extreme difficulties that the country faced.

At the York parliament some ministerial changes took place. Montague was replaced as steward of the household by the moderate Bartholomew Badlesmere. The younger Despenser became chamberlain. A lengthy ordinance for the reform of the royal household was enacted, which set out the duties and perquisites of the officials in tedious detail.[32] A review of royal grants took place, and some were cancelled. The arrangements for the council, agreed at

---

[29] *Vita Edwardi*, 82.
[30] See Maddicott, *Thomas of Lancaster*, 213 ff.; Phillips, *Aymer de Valence*, 151 ff.; Haines, *King Edward II*, 109 ff.
[31] *Parl. Writs.* ii/2. 123–4; *CCR 1318–23*, 112–13.
[32] The ordinance was printed by Tout, *Place of Edward II*, 270–318.

Leake, were confirmed, with the addition of further personnel. Lancaster was paid off by the courtiers Damory, Audley, and Montague, who acknowledged that they owed him a total of just over £1,700. More importantly, Warenne handed over to Lancaster his property in Yorkshire and north Wales, and acknowledged, but did not pay, a debt of £50,000 to him.

The settlement achieved in 1318 at Leake and at York was fragile. Hardly surprisingly, it broke down in the following year. The government was successful in obtaining full consent, even from Lancaster, for an expedition to recapture Berwick, lost to the Scots in the previous year. It was, however, a recipe for disaster to have Lancaster, Edward, and the various royal favourites all present in the discomfort of the English siege lines. Gossip and rumour abounded, and there was deliberate misrepresentation of what was being said.[33] Lancaster was told that the king had said, 'When this wretched business is over, we will turn our hands to other matters. For I have not yet forgotten the wrong that was done to my brother Piers.'[34] To make matters worse, there were suspicions that Lancaster was acting in collaboration with the Scots. He abandoned the siege, and Edward was left with no option other than to do the same. There was no longer any possibility of maintaining the uncomfortable cooperation between Edward and Lancaster.

Inevitably, there were complex manoeuvrings at court as the various favourites competed for power. Montague died in 1319, and the man who came increasingly to the fore was Hugh Despenser the younger. His position as chamberlain perhaps gave him an advantage; he was also more unscrupulous, and more ambitious, than his rivals Damory and Audley. The evidence of the lists of those witnessing royal charters is indicative of his rise. In 1317–18 he witnessed no more than 5.7 per cent, but in the following year the figure was 35.5 per cent, in the next it was 68.6 per cent, and in 1320–1 it reached 78.8 per cent.[35] He was dissatisfied with his share of the Gloucester inheritance, and began to try to take some of Audley's lands late in 1317. In 1320 he was successful in acquiring Newport from Audley. The issue that led to civil war, however, was his attempt to gain the lordship of Gower. He persuaded the king in 1320 to take the lordship into his own hands, on the grounds that John de Mowbray had received it from his father-in-law, William de Braose, without royal licence. Braose had promised the lordship to various people, including Despenser, and had even accepted a deposit towards its purchase from the earl of Hereford. The crown's seizure of Gower, however, was seen as a direct threat to the traditional liberties of the Welsh marcher lords—in the marches

---

[33] Gesta Edwardi, 57.   [34] Vita Edwardi, 104.
[35] Hamilton, 'Charter Witness Lists for the Reign of Edward II', in Given-Wilson (ed.), Fourteenth Century England, i. 5.

there was no need to obtain a royal licence to alienate land, and the royal excuse for the seizure was seen as invalid.

THE CIVIL WAR OF 1321–1322

Matters moved quickly. The marcher lords—Hereford, the Mortimers, Clifford, Audley, Damory, and others, with Lancaster's backing—faced little serious opposition in Glamorgan in May 1321, when they took matters into their own hands. At the end of June an important meeting was held at Sherburn-in-Elmet, in Yorkshire, where the marchers met Lancaster, his retainers, and a number of northern magnates. A bill was produced setting out criticisms of the government. This indictment was not particularly impressive. Officials had been appointed contrary to the Ordinances; lords were being arbitrarily deprived of their inheritances (with a clear reference to the Gower issue); improper judicial inquiries into law and order offences had been set up; an eyre had been improperly held in London; so many serjeants-at-law were employed by the crown that it was impossible to hire lawyers; and the creation of a staple at Saint-Omer was damaging to merchants and the people as a whole.[36] These last complaints show that every attempt was being made to broaden the basis of complaint, but this was hardly convincing. There has been much argument about the document that was produced at this meeting, the so-called Sherburn Indenture. Several versions of the text survive, but there is no original. One sealed version at least did exist, for it is included in a list of Lancaster's documents seized in 1322. It had twenty-five seals. The document explained that Hereford and the marchers set out a case against the two Despensers, father and son, and recorded the assent of Lancaster's supporters to the cause. 'And it seems to all that Hugh the father and the son have imposed oppression daily on the people, which they are maliciously increasing and should be restrained.'[37] One interpretation of what happened is that the marchers first proposed a document to which all present at Sherburn would agree. The northerners, however, refused, and an amended version of the indenture was then presented to, and sealed by, Lancaster's retainers.[38] In that case, the document would have been kept by the marchers, and it is hard to see how it could have been found later among Lancaster's muniments. A simpler explanation seems possible. Indentures were normally divided into two, each party keeping the one sealed by the other. The version in Lancaster's

---

[36] Gesta Edwardi, 62–4.

[37] B. Wilkinson, 'The Sherburn Indenture and the Attack on the Despensers, 1321', EHR 62 (1948), 21.

[38] Maddicott, Thomas of Lancaster, 275.

archive was surely sealed by the marchers, while the marchers would have kept one sealed by Lancaster's retainers. Where the meeting at Sherburn failed was in persuading the northern magnates who were not linked to Lancaster by bonds of retainer to join in the enterprise.

The Sherburn Indenture did not name the most startling recruit to the baronial cause. Bartholomew Badlesmere was sent by the king to Sherburn to try to stop what was happening. Instead, he changed sides. This can be partly explained by his family connections to the marchers. Not only was he married to Roger Clifford's aunt, but in 1316 his daughter had married Roger Mortimer's eldest son. His political position had been that of a moderate royalist. He had been closely associated with the earl of Gloucester, was a member of the commission to reform realm and household set up in 1316, and after the treaty of Leake had been added to the council in the York parliament. Badlesmere provided intriguing information that was included in the indictment of the Despensers, initially drawn up at Sherburn. He claimed that the younger Despenser had used the baronial declaration of 1308, which stated that homage and allegiance was due to the crown, not the person of the king, in a plot against Edward II. The allegation was that Despenser had given the document to Richard de Grey and John Giffard, both household bannerets, and to another man.[39]

Parliament met at Westminster in July and August, under threat of force. It became known as the 'parliament of the white bend', for the baronial retinues were all equipped with a common uniform of green coats, with the right upper quarter yellow with a white bend.[40] The final version of the indictment was presented in parliament, and the Despensers were duly exiled. The king won a small concession, in that this was done not by statute, but by the slightly less formal process of an award, or judgement.

It was probably at around this time that a treatise was written setting out the alleged rights of the steward of England. This was an office that had come to Lancaster by hereditary right, as it appertained to the earldom of Leicester, and which had of course been claimed in the previous century by Simon de Montfort. Lancaster had put forward claims in 1317, and went so far as to demand the stewardship of the royal household as a result. The treatise argued among other things that the steward had a special duty to deal with evil councillors. Where there were doubts in the law, a committee of twenty-five should be selected by the steward and constable to determine the issue. The

---

[39] Ibid. 278–2; *Parliamentary Texts of the Later Middle Ages*, ed. N. Pronay and J. Taylor (Oxford, 1980), 157, 162–3. Grey, when questioned, stated that he had found the document in his bag, implying that it had been planted there.
[40] *The Brut*, ed. F. W. D. Brie (Early English Text Society, 1906), 213.

steward also had a duty to decide all cases in which plaintiffs could not obtain a proper remedy.[41] The treatise gives an idea of the power that Lancaster wished to exercise; but its ideas were never put into practice.

The baronial triumph was very short-lived. The autumn and spring of 1321–2 saw an astonishingly successful royal campaign in which the rebels were picked off in succession. The indecision and prevarication that had characterized the king's actions earlier in the reign were gone. There was no question of lengthy drawn-out negotiations as had taken place in the aftermath of Gaveston's death. The younger Despenser, after a brief piratical adventure, rejoined Edward. The first move was against Badlesmere. The queen, Isabella, had a claim to his castle of Leeds in Kent, and when she asked for admittance, was refused. This led to a full-scale siege in October. The barons offered their new ally no assistance; the marchers had wanted to help, but Lancaster forbade it. He had his own feud with Badlesmere, which had not ended with the latter's change of sides at Sherburn. At the end of December the next stage in the campaign began, directed not against Lancaster, but against his marcher allies. It was a very different matter to face an army led by the king in person from conducting a campaign against the Despenser castles in Glamorgan in the previous year. Surrenders came quickly. After some resistance at Bridgnorth, first the Mortimers came to terms, then Berkeley and others.[42] Hereford, with Audley, Damory, Clifford, and the rump of the marchers, fled to join Lancaster at Pontefract.

Lancaster had held a meeting at Doncaster at the start of December to try to rally support, but he was facing increasing difficulty. No fundamentally new arguments were put forward. Appeal was made to Magna Carta and the Ordinances, but the main part of the document prepared at Doncaster was a somewhat unspecific denunciation of the Despensers and other unnamed evil councillors. It rightly pointed out that there was an urgent need to deal with the defence of the north against the Scots. Support for Lancaster was beginning to drift away. In some desperation, he entered into negotiations with the Scots. This was a very high-risk strategy, which if it became public threatened to discredit him completely.[43]

The royal army mustered at Coventry at the end of February. Lancaster attempted to block its advance northwards at Burton upon Trent, but after some limited fighting he was outflanked when the royalists found a ford upstream to cross the river. Even Robert Holland, Lancaster's closest

---

[41] L. W. V. Harcourt, *His Grace the Steward and Trial of Peers* (London, 1907), 164–7.

[42] *Vita Edwardi*, 116, 119.

[43] Maddicott, *Thomas of Lancaster*, 297–301; G. L. Haskins, 'The Doncaster Petition, 1321', *EHR* 53 (1938), 483–5.

associate, abandoned his cause at this point. The baronial forces retreated to Lancaster's castle at Pontefract, and then fled northwards. At Boroughbridge they found their route blocked by forces under Andrew Harclay, who had come south from the Scottish border. The subsequent engagement hardly deserves to be called a battle. Hereford gallantly attempted to cross the bridge, but was slain. 'As the noble lord stood and fought upon the bridge, a thief, a ribald, skulked under the bridge, and fiercely with a spear smote the noble knight in the bottom, so that his bowels came out.'[44] An attempt to cross by a ford failed in the face of a hail of arrows. The following morning, after yet more desertions, Lancaster had no option other than to surrender. Escape proved impossible, though some tried to flee in disguise. The author of the *Vita* commented: 'O how monstrous! To see men recently dressed in purple and fine linen now attired in rags, bound and imprisoned in chains.'[45]

Thomas of Lancaster, like his cousin Edward II, was not worthy of the position that hereditary right gave him. There are no indications of the idealism that had, at least in part, motivated Simon de Montfort. His political ideas amounted to very little more than maintaining the Ordinances. No medieval magnate could afford to neglect his own interests, but Lancaster was all too ready to abandon national concerns in return for very substantial concessions from Earl Warenne. In 1313–14 he pursued his claims to Thorpe Waterville and two other midland manors with force as well as legal trickery, again at the expense of the wider political interest of the country as a whole.[46] He had a disturbing habit of withdrawing from public affairs, spending lengthy periods of time in his castles, above all at Pontefract. It is conceivable that illness may explain this; some physical incapacity may also explain his lack of enthusiasm for military matters. It was Hereford, not Lancaster, who tried to lead the troops across the fatal bridge at Boroughbridge. In more personal terms, there is little that seems attractive in Lancaster's personality; it seems likely that his wife, Alice de Lacy, positively welcomed her abduction in 1317. On the positive side, Lancaster was conventionally pious, and a generous patron of monastic houses. This, however, was not the calibre of man needed to lead an effective opposition movement, even against the incompetent Edward II. It was only in death that he became a popular and saintly hero.[47]

The defeat of Lancaster's rebellion was followed by a bloodbath. The earl himself was summarily tried and executed in his own castle of Pontefract. He was not permitted to answer the accusations against him, but was convicted on

---

[44] *The Brut*, 219.   [45] *Vita Edwardi*, 124–5.
[46] This affair is described by Maddicott, *Thomas of Lancaster*, 154–6, and Phillips, *Aymer de Valence*, 77–82.
[47] For a full and sympathetic summary of Lancaster's character, see Maddicott, *Thomas of Lancaster*, 318–34.

the king's record. A number of his associates were tried alongside him, and others at York on the next day. Executions took place at Gloucester, Bristol, Windsor, Cambridge, Canterbury, and Cardiff. These were horrific in their brutality. Lancaster himself was beheaded, in deference to his royal blood, but for the rest, hanging, drawing, and quartering was the order of the day.[48]

Bloodlust had been shown at Evesham, with the death of Simon de Montfort, but the aftermath of the royalist victory on that occasion was nothing like that of 1322. Change had begun under Edward I, who had punished the Welsh and Scots with savage executions. This extended to those of the highest rank, even to a prince in the case of Dafydd ap Gruffudd in 1283, and to an earl in the case of Atholl in 1306. The household knight Thomas Turberville, guilty of treasonable correspondence with the French in 1295, had been hanged, drawn, and quartered. Under Edward II another household knight, Gilbert de Middleton, had been similarly executed for treason after the notorious outrage in 1317 when he had kidnapped two cardinals and the bishop-elect of Durham as they were on their way to the latter's installation ceremony. The death of Piers Gaveston provides another explanation; with that deed the rules of the game had changed. Where in the past acts of clemency had encouraged further clemency, now the savagery of revenge encouraged further savagery.[49]

One interpretation of this period saw it in terms of the manoeuvrings of political parties. In particular, the treaty of Leake and the succeeding period of government were seen as the achievement of 'the middle party'.[50] The origins of this, it was suggested, lay in an embassy to the papal curia in 1317 led by the bishops of Norwich and Ely, the earl of Pembroke, Bartholomew Badlesmere, and Antonio Pessagno. An indenture drawn up later in the same year between Pembroke and Badlesmere on the one hand, and Roger Damory on the other, was seen as a cornerstone of the party, formalizing a political alliance. This view has been discredited. The indenture was not an agreement between equal partners, but between two moderate royalists on the one hand and a court favourite on the other. Detailed examination of the negotiations leading to the treaty of Leake suggests that the bishops played an important role in mediating between the king and Lancaster, but that the concept of a middle party does not fit.[51]

---

[48] Gesta Edwardi, 77–8; N. Fryde, The Tyranny and Fall of Edward II (Cambridge, 1979), 61.

[49] D. A. Carpenter, 'From King John to the First English Duke: 1215–1337', in R. Smith and J. S. Moore (eds.), The House of Lords: A Thousand Years of British Tradition (London, 1994), 29–35.

[50] Stubbs, Constitutional History of England, ii. 359, mentioned the 'middle party', but did not make as much of it as Tout, Place of Edward II, 111–21, or Davies, Baronial Opposition, 425–43, for whom it was a key element in their analysis.

[51] Phillips, Aymer de Valence, 136–77.

The fact that the middle party has proved to be a mirage does not mean that there were no attempts in this period to form political groupings. The agreement reached at Boulogne in 1308 provides an early example, and as the reign proceeded there were many other efforts. The agreements reached between the earls responsible for Gaveston's death provide one example, as do the bonds entered into in 1317 by the Despensers, father and son, together with Montague, Audley, and Damory, acknowledging that they owed each other £6,000.[52] The Sherburn Indenture is a clear example of an attempt to establish a formal political grouping. However, the very fact that it was thought necessary to cement political agreements by threat of excommunication (in the case of the Boulogne agreement) or by financial arrangements suggests their essential fragility. What is more striking than the establishment of political groupings is the volatility of politics in this period. The author of the *Vita* commented: 'See how often and abruptly great men change their sides. Those whom we regard as faithless in the North we find just the opposite in the South. The love of magnates is as a game of dice, and the desires of the rich like feathers.'[53]

A curious incident happened in 1317, when a woman dressed theatrically rode into the king's hall at Westminster during a banquet. After riding round, she approached the king's table and put a letter in front of him. It turned out that one of the household knights had put her up to this, and that the letter criticized the king for not treating his established knights properly and promoting worthless men in their place.[54] The criticism was understandable. Edward was recruiting household knights at this period on an exceptional scale, and it is hardly surprising that there should have been resentment among the older hands. William Latimer had an impeccable royalist background as the son of one of Edward I's household knights. He served in Edward II's household, but in 1319 an indenture records his entry into Lancaster's service. He had the political sagacity to desert his new lord in time to fight for the king at Boroughbridge; others were not as perceptive. John Giffard of Brimpsfield was one of the less fortunate. A household banneret in 1318, he was a marcher lord, and as such it is not surprising that he joined the rebels in 1321 and that he was executed in the aftermath of Boroughbridge.[55] While a good number of the king's household knights showed a lack of loyalty, the problem was still more acute for Lancaster. In the final crisis above all, his retainers displayed little loyalty towards their lord. The most notable defection was that of the earl's chief henchman and favourite, Robert Holland, but the list is a long one, including such important men as Peter de Maulay and John

---

[52] Ibid. 133.   [53] *Vita Edwardi*, 7.   [54] Trokelowe 98–9.
[55] M. C. Prestwich, 'The Unreliability of Royal Household Knights in the Early Fourteenth Century', in Given-Wilson (ed.), *Fourteenth Century England*, ii. 5–7.

de Clavering, who had been Lancaster's banneret on the council set up at Leake. There was little enthusiasm for taking up arms against the king.[56]

Thomas of Lancaster's revolt was not followed by inquiries on the scale of those that had followed the collapse of Simon de Montfort's regime. It is nevertheless possible to provide some analysis of the composition of his support. The geographical distribution shows that backing was derived largely from the Welsh marches, while the main region of Lancaster's own authority, the north midlands and south Yorkshire, did not make a very substantial contribution. Baronial support was limited. Out of the eighty-four barons summoned to parliament in 1318, only thirteen joined the rebel ranks. There was less knightly assistance for Lancaster than there had been for Montfort, and there was virtually no backing from the towns. As for gentry and peasant support, it seems likely that most of the lesser men who joined in the rising did so under pressure from their lords. In addition, and above all in areas close to the Welsh borders, there were a good many who simply seized the opportunity presented by the rebellion to pursue their own ends by violent means.[57] The difficulties involved in defining the rebels by region or lordship is suggested by the way that the rising divided families. Lancaster himself was not supported by his brother Henry. John and Robert de Sapy were royal household knights of long standing, yet John was one of the rebels in 1322. There are many other examples of families with split allegiances; it may even in some cases have been a deliberate strategy, aimed at ensuring that at least one member would end up on the victorious side.[58]

The rebellion of 1321–2 did not have a background of grievances over incessant royal demands for money and material, as did the crisis of 1297. Nor was there the ideological strength to the opposition movement that had been so important in the mid-thirteenth-century crisis. There was nothing that compared to the backing of the friars for Simon de Montfort, and no equivalent to the way in which the concept of the crusade had been manipulated by both sides in 1264–5. The programme of maintaining the Ordinances may have been laudable in its way, but it did not compare with the scale of commitment to reform at the local as well as national level that existed in the years following the Oxford parliament of 1258. The movement headed by Lancaster had much more limited aims and a far narrower basis of support. Its failure was scarcely surprising.

---

[56] Maddicott, *Thomas of Lancaster*, 295–6.
[57] The composition of the rebellion is examined by Valente, *Theory and Practice of Revolt*, 141–53.
[58] Prestwich, 'Unreliability of Household Knights', 6, 10; Fryde, *Tyranny and Fall*, 73.

THE RULE OF THE DESPENSERS

The crushing of Lancaster's rebellion was a triumph for the Despensers, and it was they who dominated government until the final act of Edward II's reign, his deposition. The brief period from 1322 to 1326 was most extraordinary. From a position of what appeared to be complete dominance after Borough-bridge, the regime collapsed totally in 1326. Part of the reason for this will be discussed in later chapters. The military success against Lancaster was rapidly followed by failure against the Scots, while an unsuccessful war with France in 1324–5 helped to the discredit the Despenser regime.[59]

This regime was characterized by astonishing greed and political folly, and yet it also witnessed a great deal of positive work done to reform government. The elder Hugh Despenser was a veteran of Edward I's reign, a thoroughgoing royalist. There is little in his earlier career that presaged what was to happen after Boroughbridge. It would be wrong to see him as a mere cipher in the hands of his grasping son; he was a man of considerable experience. The key figure, however, was the younger Despenser. 'This sir Hugh was full of evil and wrongdoing, and he was also greedy and covetous while he was in office. He was also proud and haughty, more inclined to wrongdoing than any other man.'[60] Closely associated with the Despensers were Robert Baldock, chancellor from 1323, and the earl of Arundel.

There was much to do after Boroughbridge. Parliament was held in May, at York, and there the Ordinances were annulled. Six clauses were, however, re-enacted. These covered the issues of household jurisdiction, the forest, the appointment of sheriffs, outlawries, appeals, and merchants. In condemning the Ordinances, the Statute of York went on to lay down the way in which legislation should be put through.

But the things which are to be provided for the estate of our lord the king and of his heirs and for the estate of the realm and the people, are to be discussed, agreed and ordained in parliaments by our lord the king and with the assent of the prelates, earls and barons and the community of the realm, as has been the custom in times past.

What was really important about the statute was its uncompromising annul-ment in perpetuity of anything that detracted from royal power. It did, however, apparently allocate the representatives in parliament a far larger role than they had ever in practice possessed, for by this date 'community of the realm' was coming to mean 'Commons'. In 1320, for example, a petition from the knights, citizens, and burgesses was described in the parliament roll as

---

[59] See below, 242–3; 303.   [60] *Anonimalle*, 92–3.

coming from the whole community of the realm.[61] In 1321, according to a Rochester chronicle, the magnates declared that 'they had the power, since they were peers of the realm, to promulgate and establish a new law in parliament in accordance with the custom of the realm'.[62] It may have been in reaction to such oligarchic views that the Statute of York included the assent of the community of the realm as being necessary for legislative measures. The authors of the statute are unlikely to have shared the radical view of an unofficial tract, almost certainly written at about this time, the *Modus Tenendi Parliamentum*, which declared that 'it is to be understood that two knights who come to parliament for the shire carry more weight in parliament in granting and refusing than the greatest earl in England'.[63]

The victors in the civil war needed to be rewarded, and the losers dealt with. The elder Despenser accordingly received the title of earl of Winchester; his son, surprisingly, did not claim the earldom of Gloucester through right of his wife as might have been expected. Andrew Harclay, victor of Boroughbridge, was given the title of earl of Carlisle. Land was more difficult to allocate than titles. Huge estates came into the crown's hands just from those executed in the aftermath of Boroughbridge. The Despensers gained much land. The father built up his estates in the midlands and the south, while the son increased his power in south Wales and the marches. There was, however, no general redistribution of land held by the Contrariants (as the rebels of 1321 were known); most of the estates that came into the crown's hands were retained in the hands of royal officials.[64] Financially, this may have made sense, but it also meant that there was no powerful vested interest created to support the new regime.

Fines were imposed on most of those supporters of Lancaster and the marchers who were not executed. Some of these were very substantial. For example, John de Willington was charged £3,000, Gilbert Talbot £2,000, Nicholas Stapleton 2,000 marks, Bogo de Knoville and Otto de Botrigan 1,000 marks each. The total came to some £17,000. It was not, however, intended that the entire sums should be paid off at once. Instalments were set out in some case. John de Willington was to pay off his huge fine at no more than £5 a year, and Nicholas Stapleton was to provide 2 tuns of wine a year.[65] It was clearly the intention to guarantee the future loyalty of the former rebels by ensuring that

---

[61] *Rot. Parl.* i. 371.
[62] *Parliamentary Texts of the Later Middle Ages*, ed. Pronay and Taylor, 168.
[63] Ibid. 77, 89. For the *Modus*, see the Appendix to this chapter.
[64] Fryde, *Tyranny and Fall*, 108–9.
[65] *Parl. Writs*, ii/2. 203–4; *Cal. Fine Rolls, 1319–27*, 154–5, 170; M. Buck, *Politics, Finance and the Church in the Reign of Edward II: Walter Stapledon, Treasurer of England* (Cambridge, 1983), 174.

they owed substantial sums to the crown. Given the intense resentment that was inevitably created, this was hardly a recipe for stable government.

The Despensers were not satisfied with the gains that they made in grants from the Contrariant estates. A particularly repugnant element in their policies was the way in which they pursued vulnerable widows and other women. Elizabeth de Clare, Roger Damory's widow, provides a good example, for she set out her story in a petition. Despenser wanted her estates of Usk, offering the far less valuable lordship of Gower in exchange. Once successful with this exchange, he recovered Gower by legal trickery. She was firstly imprisoned in Barking abbey, and under threat agreed to what was demanded of her. Part of her story reads as follows:

I took the road to York, and when I came there, the king took me in custody, removing my council and my following from me, until I sealed a quitclaim against my will regarding the land of Usk and all my inheritance in Wales, and in addition ordered me to seal another writing by which I was, and am still, obliged by my body and my lands, contrary to the law of the land, and because of the argument I had about sealing this writing some of my council were taken and imprisoned for a long time and I myself left the court much discomfited. And when I was five days journey from there, on my way to my castle of Clare, the king menacingly ordered me that if I did not return and seal the said document, I would never hold from him any of the lands which I do hold from him.[66]

Other widows of high status who suffered at the hands of the Despensers included Alice de Lacy. Even though she had been estranged from her husband for some years, she was forced to quitclaim most of her inheritance to the king. He then granted some of it back to her for life, with reversion to the younger Despenser. Her great lordship of Denbigh went to the elder Despenser. The widow of a Glamorgan lord, Stephen Baret, was so badly treated in prison, presumably as a means of obtaining her lands, that she went mad. It was not only the womenfolk of Contrariant lords who were targeted. Marie de Saint-Pol, widow of the earl of Pembroke, who had died in 1324, lost lands in south Wales. The heiress Elizabeth Comyn, Pembroke's niece, was held in custody and threatened with life imprisonment if she did not hand over some of her lands to the Despensers, and she made out an acknowledgement of debt to the elder Despenser in the huge sum of £10,000. John de Mowbray's widow was held in the Tower, and 'in fear of death and by force and duress of imprisonment' granted the reversion of her lands to the younger Despenser.[67] The

---

[66] G. A. Holmes, 'A Protest Against the Despensers, 1326', *Speculum*, 30 (1955), 211 (my translation).

[67] Fryde, *Tyranny and Fall*, 113–17; *CCR 1323–7*, 357; *Rot. Parl.* ii. 57–8; *Cal. Fine Rolls, 1327–37*, 221.

younger Despenser was quite clear about his objectives, which were 'that we may be rich and may attain our ends'.[68] His success in accumulating lands in the Welsh marches transformed the territorial structure of the region, and saw the creation of unparalleled landed authority there. He took Hereford's lordships of Brecon, Hay, and Huntingdon, the Giffard lordship, and the lands of Mortimer of Chirk. The grant of the wardship and marriage in 1325 of Laurence Hastings, heir to the earldom of Pembroke as well as to Abergavenny and Cilgerran, increased his strength still further.[69] The splendid fortifications of Caerfilli, where there were Despenser additions to the existing structure, were a demonstration of power. Holding vast estates, however, was no guarantee that this could be translated into active political and military support when needed.

These few years witnessed an astonishing spate of administrative reforms and changes in the royal household and at the exchequer. There were three major ordinances dealing with the exchequer, issued in 1323, 1324, and 1326. That of 1323 saw new appointments authorized, so as to speed up the writing of the pipe rolls and other records. Record-keeping was simplified. A range of steps were taken to hurry through the collection of debts due to the crown. Measures were taken to simplify the hearing of the keeper of the wardrobe's accounts. The most radical decision, taken in 1324, was to divide the exchequer into two, northern and southern, as a means of accelerating the hearing of accounts. Predictably, this met with hostility from the exchequer officials, but most of the reforming measures were carried through with some success.[70] The purpose of the exchequer reforms was not the simplification of office procedures as an end in itself. Rather, the aim was clearly to try to increase revenue from the traditional sources, and to develop more effective means of collecting debts owed to the crown.

The household had been the object of reform in 1318, but change continued after 1322. It had been opposition policy to rein in the department of the wardrobe; but it was the Despenser administration that achieved far more in this direction than had been possible earlier. The financial independence of the household was severely limited. The privy seal was put in the charge of keepers with chancery experience, not, as had been normally the case, men with long experience in the wardrobe.[71] An ordinance of 1323 set out instructions about when accounts were to be tendered, how purveyance was to take place, and what alms the king should give. In 1324 various departments that had

---

[68] SC 1/49/143. This is normally quoted from *Cal. Anc. Corr. Wales*, 219–20, as 'that Despenser may be rich and may attain his ends', but this is a calendar, not a translation.
[69] Davies, *Lordship and Society in the March of Wales*, 280–1.
[70] Buck, *Politics, Finance and the Church*, 163–96; Tout, *Place of Edward II*, 191–204.
[71] Tout, *Place of Edward II*, 167.

accounted through the wardrobe were ordered to account directly to the exchequer. The wardrobe was increasingly limited to its household role and deprived of wider responsibilities. The effect of this was seen in the figures. In 1325–6 wardrobe receipts totalled just over £6,000, whereas in 1319–20 they had been over £50,000.[72]

Walter Stapledon, bishop of Exeter and treasurer from 1320 to 1321 and again from 1322 to 1325, played a major role in the administrative changes of these years.[73] He was an outsider to royal administration. At the time of his first appointment he had served on several diplomatic missions, but had not been a significant participant in the domestic political upheavals of the reign. A calendar of documents relating to Gascony goes under his name, and was his responsibility; but his concerns went much further than that. The way in which accounting procedures were tightened up, and the determination with which debts owed to the crown were pursued, almost certainly owed much to Stapledon. It is not surprising that a man who worked so hard on the documents should have possessed a pair of spectacles.[74] Others had their parts to play. The plan to divide the exchequer was attributed by Robert of Reading to Roger Belers, baron of the exchequer. Belers, a former Lancastrian official, was another recruited from outside the ranks of the royal administration.[75]

The programme of financial reform, while carried through by the experts at the exchequer, was driven from above. Many letters testify to the close supervision and constant interference that took place. In the case of a poorly performing sheriff, 'we greatly wonder that you, who should be concerned about our and our people's profit, should allow such a man to be elected to such an office, and that you have allowed him to remain after you realised his inadequacy'. On a minor matter of someone presenting an account for a ship repair, 'we greatly marvel that you should have so negligibly and lightly passed his account without examining the matter more extensively'.[76] Such letters, and there were many, that came to the exchequer were all in the king's name, and one view is that it was indeed Edward II himself who was taking such an active interest in the working of the financial administration. One instruction, issued in 1323, asked for all accounts audited in the past three years to be scrutinized, and for all debts arising from them to be listed. The officials were asked 'to pay attention to it so that we become rich' ('mettez votre peine qe nous soioms riches'). The parallel to the younger Despenser's earlier

---

[72] Ibid. 178–9, 314–18; Tout, *Chapters*, vi. 84–5.
[73] His career is the subject of Buck's study *Politics, Finance and the Church*.
[74] *The Register of Walter de Stapledon, Bishop of Exeter*, ed. F. C. Hingeston-Randolph (London, 1892), 565 ('unum spectaculum cum duplici oculi').
[75] *Flores*, iii. 232.
[76] Cited by Buck, *Politics, Finance and the Church*, 166 nn. 26, 30.

instruction 'that we may be rich and may attain our ends' is suspiciously close.[77] It is difficult to believe that Edward, who had showed no signs of this kind of close attention to administrative business earlier in the reign, should have undergone a sudden conversion to the joys of bureaucracy. It cannot be proven, but it seems far more likely that the great majority of these instructions to the exchequer were the work of the younger Despenser, writing in the king's name.

Another example of the innovative approach to royal finance came with the Ordinance of Kenilworth, issued in 1326. This dealt with trade. Earlier in the reign the crown had adopted a staple policy under which all English merchants would export their wool to a single outlet. This meant that they could be better protected from potential attack, which was important at a period of Flemish hostility. The solution to the problem produced at Kenilworth was for the creation of English staples. English merchants would no longer have to risk taking their wool abroad; instead, they would take it to one of eleven specified English and Welsh ports, where foreign merchants would come to purchase it. Significantly, one of the ports was Despenser's own town of Cardiff. The measure had obvious merits, particularly for the middlemen of the wool trade, but was not given time to prove itself.[78]

In financial terms, the crown benefited in this period not only from efficient management at the exchequer and low expenditure in the household, but also from a successful tax of a tenth and sixth, agreed in 1322, which brought in about £40,000. In addition, a tenth for two years was granted to the king by the pope in 1322. Income from the confiscated estates of the Contrariants was estimated in 1324 at over £12,500. The outcome was that even though Edward II was unable to obtain any further grants of taxation, the financial situation in the final years of the reign was remarkably healthy. The 1324 estimate showed a total income of about £60,500. In 1325 the treasury contained almost £70,000 in gold and silver plate, and coin, and in the dying days of the regime in 1326 the figure was almost £62,000.[79] The crisis, when it came, was not a financial one.

Reform was not confined to the financial sphere. Military recruitment was another area of experimentation. In 1324 all knights were asked to attend a meeting at Westminster to discuss affairs of state, and orders were issued for a distraint of knighthood. Sheriffs drew up lists of all the knights and men-at-arms in their counties. This was clearly connected to the war in Gascony, and what seems to have been intended was recruitment of knights and men-at-arms by commissioners, in a similar way to that in which infantry were recruited.

---

[77] Above, 208.

[78] T. H. Lloyd, *The English Wool Trade in the Middle Ages* (Cambridge, 1977), 115–16.

[79] Fryde, *Tyranny and Fall of Edward II*, 97, 105; Buck, *Politics, Finance and the Church*, 170.

At the end of the reign, in 1326, attempts were being made to recruit military forces in this way. Had this been carried through effectively, there is no doubt that it would have been extremely unpopular.[80]

The political techniques used by the Despensers and their allies were those of blackmail and bullying, not reward and persuasion. The use of recognizances, which acknowledged that debts were owed, was extended far beyond the rebels of 1322. The sums involved were often far beyond the payment capabilities of the individuals concerned; these agreements were intended as a means of persuading men to toe the line, rather than as commercial arrangements. There were many recognizances to the younger Despenser. William de Braose made out a recognizance to him for £10,000. Hugh de Hastings, lord of Bergavenny, entered into an agreement whereby he acknowledged that he owed Despenser £4,000 while Despenser owed him £1,000. The bishop of Ely agreed that he owed Despenser £2,000, and the bishop of Winchester did the same. Even other members of the governing clique entered into recognizances with Despenser, for in 1324 Bishop Stapledon, the earl of Arundel, and three others agreed that they owed £6,000. It was not only great men who were brought into the net. The men of Sudbury in Suffolk acknowledged, under duress, a debt of 1,000 marks to Despenser.[81]

The use of recognizances might yield a sulky obedience, but was hardly a recipe for building effective political support. This was a regime with a very narrow power base. Arundel was the only earl who was solidly committed to it. Pembroke provided some valuable diplomatic expertise, but he died in 1324. The king's half-brothers Norfolk and Kent had no great loyalty to Edward II. Earl Warenne, despite being a bitter opponent of Lancaster, was no supporter of the Despensers. The one new earl to be created, apart from the elder Despenser as earl of Winchester, was Andrew Harclay, earl of Carlisle, but he was executed for treason in 1323. The numbers of lay magnates summoned to parliament were low; forty-nine in February 1324, and only thirty-eight in November 1325.[82]

The Despensers had their own household knights; it has been calculated that there were over two dozen of these in the 1320s. This, however, is no more than might be expected for magnates of their wealth. The reliability of some of these men must have been suspect, given that they had changed sides. John le Boteler, for example, had been a retainer of the Berkeley family, and Thomas Gobion had served the earl of Hereford. The severe economies imposed on the

[80] Prestwich, 'Cavalry Service in Early Fourteenth Century England', 155–6.

[81] *CCR 1321–7*, 174, 309, 325, 358, 537, 647. Earlier, in 1320–1, the Despensers had been involved in complex dealings with John de Cromwell, which had involved recognizances on both sides for the enormous sum of £40,000: *CCR 1318–23*, 346, 358, 368.

[82] Powell and Wallis, *History of the House of Lords*, 297.

royal household meant that there was no substantial force of royal household knights to call on, as there had been earlier in the reign. There was no concerted effort to ensure that officials at a local level, such as sheriffs, were loyal Despenser men. It was only in the case of the posts of castle constables that the Despensers tried to ensure the security of their power, for of the sixty-seven appointments made in this period, forty-two went to men associated with them or the royal household.[83]

The Church had provided an important buttress for Edward II for most of the reign. Archbishop Reynolds of Canterbury was a very different figure from his predecessor Winchelsey, and was not a man to oppose the crown. The *Articuli Cleri* of 1316 had closed a long chapter of clerical grievances. Papal support for Edward had been important, not least with successive grants of taxation. Now, in these final years of the reign, the regime faced enemies among the bishops. Adam Orleton, bishop of Hereford, John Droxford, bishop of Bath and Wells, and Henry Burghersh, bishop of Lincoln, were all involved in differing degrees in the rebellion of 1321–2. Orleton's appointment to his see in 1317 by the pope had been resented by the king, who considered that as a royal envoy he had behaved in Rome 'in a different way towards us than he should have done'. Orleton was associated with the Mortimers, and was put on trial in 1324.[84] When Rigaud d'Assier, bishop of Winchester, died at the papal curia in 1323, the right of appointment lay with the pope. Edward wanted the see for his close associate Robert Baldock, but the pope appointed John Stratford, a royal envoy currently at Avignon. Edward was furious, but could do nothing save protest. Stratford's opposition was inevitable when he returned to England.[85] William Airmyn presented a similar case. He was a loyal royal official until the pope appointed him to the see of Norwich in 1325, thinking he was doing the king a favour. Edward had wanted this see too for Baldock, and did not forgive Airmyn, whom he also blamed for the treaty with France of 1325.[86]

Hostility towards Edward and the Despensers in London was a serious problem. The city had been infuriated by the imposition of a judicial eyre in 1321, for which, rightly or wrongly, Bishop Stapledon was held responsible. Influential Londoners had been enmeshed in the complexities of recognizances to the Despensers and their friends. In 1323 the mayor, Hamo de Chigwell, had

---

[83] N. Saul, 'The Despensers and the Downfall of Edward II', *EHR* 99 (1984), 7–8, 12, 17, 29.

[84] R. M. Haines, *The Church and Politics in Fourteenth-Century England: The Career of Adam Orleton c.1275–1345* (Cambridge, 1978), 137, 144–51; *Calendar of Chancery Warrants*, i: *1244–1326*, 481.

[85] R. M. Haines, *Archbishop John Stratford, Political Revolutionary and Champion of the Liberties of the English Church c.1275/80–1348* (Toronto, 1986), 136–49.

[86] J. L. Grassi, 'William Airmyn and the Bishopric of Norwich', *EHR* 70 (1955), 550–61.

been removed from office, only to be restored later. He was prepared to collaborate with the regime, but the citizens as a whole did not follow his example. The atmosphere was tense; violence surfaced with a dispute between the goldsmiths and the weavers, and a little later a quarrel between the northerners and southerners among the apprentice lawyers ended with the deaths of many. By 1326 the city was seething with discontent.[87]

DEPOSITION

The victory at Boroughbridge had been crushing. There was some continued resistance as a few of the defeated engaged in sporadic local violence directed against Despenser estates. Some of this is hard to distinguish from mere lawlessness. The government panicked in 1322 when Robert Lewer, a former member of the royal household with something of a reputation as a desperado, rebelled. He was reported in many parts of the country, from the south to Wales, Lancashire, and Yorkshire, but was in the end captured without great difficulty. At least as serious was the unsuccessful attempt early in the next year to free Maurice de Berkeley from imprisonment at Wallingford.[88] Such incidents, however, did not seriously threaten the regime.

The real threat did not come from the many in England who were resentful at the way in which power was being misused. It came from a very different quarter, with the build-up of a powerful group of exiles in France. The first step was the dramatic escape of Roger Mortimer from the Tower in 1323. The story of the way in which the garrison was drugged at dinner, enabling an accomplice to release Roger, who made his way out of the Tower by using rope ladders, is astonishing, but not to be disbelieved. Soon Mortimer was in France.[89] In the following year war broke out between England and France over the foundation of the *bastide*, or fortified town, at Saint-Sardos; in such circumstances Charles IV was bound to treat Mortimer with honour. There was, however, little that Mortimer could do at this stage to oppose Edward. The next step was the decision in 1325 to send Queen Isabella to France to negotiate for peace, and, following that, to send her son Edward to perform homage to the French king. Bishop Stapledon, who had accompanied the prince to France, made a disastrous intervention, refusing to pay Isabella anything for her expenses unless she returned to England. Isabella would not come back, and in a famous speech, declared:

[87] G. A. Williams, *Medieval London from Commune to Capital* (London, 1963), 286–95; Pauline Annals, 307, 313.

[88] *Vita Edwardi*, 127–31; Fryde, *Tyranny and Fall of Edward II*, 154–6.

[89] I. Mortimer, *The Greatest Traitor: The Life of Sir Roger Mortimer* (London, 2003), 130–1; Trokelowe, 145–6.

I feel that marriage is a joining together of man and woman, maintaining the undivided habit of life, and that someone has come between my husband and myself trying to break this bond; I protest that I will not return until this intruder is removed, but, discarding my marriage garment, shall assume the robes of widowhood and mourning until I am avenged of this Pharisee.[90]

Quite what this refers to is a matter of guesswork. One possibility suggested is that Edward was having an affair with the younger Despenser's wife, his niece Eleanor. This accusation was levied by a Hainault chronicle, and there is circumstantial documentary support for it. An entry in a wardrobe account for 1319–20 showed medicines costing £5 12s. 4d. bought 'for the king and Eleanor la Despenser his niece, when ill', a curious linking of the two. Later, chamber accounts show sugar bought at the king's instructions to make sweets for Eleanor. Edward also gave her caged goldfinches, and on one brief visit to her the very substantial sum of 100 marks. Robert of Reading, writing near the end of the reign, condemned Edward for 'illicit and sinful unions', and for rejecting the 'sweet conjugal embraces' of Queen Isabella. This could be read as a reference to homosexuality, but it is at least as plausible that the 'illicit' union refers to a liaison with Eleanor. If there was such a liaison, Despenser must have been at least aware of what was happening, and it is conceivable that he encouraged it as a means of maintaining the control he exercised over the king. It has even been suggested that he and the king were engaged in wife-swapping.[91] For this, however, there is no shred of evidence. The obvious alternative explanation is that Isabella was alluding to a homosexual relationship between her husband and Despenser. The earliest explicit suggestion to this effect was made by Bishop Orleton in 1334, when he referred to the 'immoderate and inordinate love' that the king had for Despenser.[92] At that date, however, there were good reasons for Orleton to do all he could to denigrate Edward II's character. Whatever the truth was, there is no doubt that Isabella conceived a virulent hatred for Despenser.

Soon after Isabella's refusal to return to England, Mortimer joined her in Paris. There is nothing to prove that there had been any close relationship between the two before this, and it is hard to see what previous opportunity they could have had to start an affair. Isabella had intervened in 1323 to try to ensure that Lady Mortimer received the pay to which she was entitled during her imprisonment in the Tower, but this hardly suggests that she had a liaison

[90] Vita Edwardi, 143.
[91] Haines, King Edward II, 42–3; 170; Flores, iii. 229; P. C. Doherty, Isabella and the Strange Death of Edward II (2003), 101–2; P. C. Doherty, 'Isabella, Queen of England' (D.Phil. thesis, Oxford University 1978), 90; BL, Add. MS 17362, fo. 18; Society of Antiquaries of London, MS 122, fos. 15, 28, 40.
[92] Haines, Church and Politics, 168 n. 43.

with Roger Mortimer at that time.[93] Now, however, the two formed not only a scandalous union, but also the core of a party of exiles determined to destroy Despenser power. The earl of Kent was the most notable in rank. The group included Henry de Beaumont, the veteran John Botetourt, John Cromwell, John Maltravers, and William Trussel.[94]

Things did not go well for the exiles, for the French were unwilling to give them support in mounting an invasion. The count of Hainault, however, was prepared to take the risk, in return for the marriage of Edward, heir to the English throne, to his daughter Philippa. This had been mooted much earlier, in 1319, when a remarkable description of her was written by the English ambassadors. She met with their approval; she had a neat head, nice enough hair somewhere between blonde and brown. Her mouth was large, as were her lips, especially the lower. Her bottom teeth were a little behind the upper, but not by much. Her ears and chin were attractive, her shoulders, limbs, and all of her body of a reasonable size. She was neither too large nor too small. The ambassadors had thought that she would do.[95] Now, the marriage was vital, for without the Hainault alliance Isabella's cause was lost. The invasion force was small, certainly no larger than the 1,500 men estimated by the Pauline Annals.[96] The Hainault contingent was a vital element. The voyage was stormy, and according to the Hainault chronicler Jean le Bel, the sailors did not know where they were when they landed at Orwell in Suffolk.[97]

The Despenser regime collapsed like a building hit by an earthquake. Even before the invasion, along with preparation there had been panic. Now there was simply panic on the part of the king and the Despensers. Isabella's was a triumphant progress; the king fled westwards, presumably hoping to find support in the Despenser lands in the Welsh marches, and possibly even aiming for backing from Ireland. The elder Despenser was left to guard Bristol, while Edward II, the younger Despenser, and a dwindling band took to the sea, to go to south Wales. In some ways there was surprisingly little violence, for there was very little resistance to the invaders. One incident in London, however, showed that this was not to be a wholly peaceful revolution. Bishop Stapledon had been left in the city as its guardian, and on 15 October rode in from Enfield. Widespread rioting was taking place, and Stapledon fled to St Paul's to find sanctuary. Before he could enter, he was seized by the mob and beheaded with a bread-knife.[98] Not long afterwards, on 26 October, the

---

[93] SC 1/37/4.   [94] The exiles are listed by Haines, *King Edward II*, 174.
[95] *The Register of Walter de Stapledon, Bishop of Exeter, 1307–1326*, ed. F. C. Hingeston-Randolph (London, 1892), 169.
[96] Pauline Annals, 314.
[97] Le Bel, i. 18.
[98] Buck, *Politics, Finance and the Church*, 220.

elder Despenser was captured, summarily tried, and executed. Arundel was taken on 17 November, and also put to death. The party that had gone to Wales were soon discovered and taken. The younger Despenser was taken to Hereford, where he was sentenced to death on 24 November. He was drawn, hanged, eviscerated, beheaded, and quartered. There was no deference to his rank; he was made to suffer the full range of customary indignities.[99]

The rapid collapse of the government presented Isabella and Mortimer with a problem. The purpose of the invasion had been the removal of the Despensers. A document issued by the invaders on 21 November began, 'Isabel by the grace of God queen of England, lady of Ireland, countess of Ponthieu and we, Edward, eldest son to the noble king Edward of England, duke of Gascony, earl of Chester, of Ponthieu and of Montreuil'. It used the regnal year of Edward II for dating.[100] The document made the most of Isabella's and Edward's positions, but there was no challenge to the king in the formula. At some point, perhaps as late as Christmas 1326, the decision was taken to proceed to remove Edward from the throne.

Deposition was something new. There was no workable English precedent; chronicle tales taken from Geoffrey of Monmouth's fantasy Arthurian history may have told of kings being removed from office, but did not provide any details of how to do it. Historians have found much to argue about in the proceedings that were adopted, for the surviving sources are not wholly consistent, particularly in detail, and there is no formal official version.[101] The outline of events is reasonably clear. The first step was to send two bishops (Orleton and either Stratford or Bishop Gravesend of London) to Kenilworth, to ask the king to attend parliament. This he would not do, and on 12 January the bishops returned to London, where parliament had assembled on 7 January. A meeting of the magnates took place, which decided that deposition was the only option. Articles were probably produced at this stage. Strong pressure was coming from the Londoners, who initially demanded Edward II's deposition, and then got many of those present in parliament to swear to support Isabella and her son Edward. The crucial day was 13 January, when the assembly as a whole agreed that Edward II should be replaced by his eldest son. Mortimer made a speech, and Thomas Wake rose up, hands outstretched. 'I say for myself that he shall reign no more.' Sermons followed from Orleton,

---

[99] Gesta Edwardi, 87–9.   [100] SC 1/37/46.

[101] C. Valente, 'The Deposition and Abdication of Edward II', *EHR* 113 (1998), 871–5, argues that the *Forma Deposicionis*, found in a Canterbury chronicle, is an official version of events. However, it is not found in any official source. The dating clause is not in a style used in government documents, and though it takes the form of a memorandum, there is insufficient to imply that it was produced by the new regime of Isabella and Mortimer. The lack of copies (only two are known) would be surprising if it were an official text.

Stratford, and Archbishop Reynolds. At the conclusion of these proceedings it was determined that an embassy should go to Kenilworth to deal with Edward II himself. This was a large body, as representative in its composition as possible, with knights of the shire, Londoners, and men from the Cinque Ports as well as bishops, abbots, earls, and barons. At Kenilworth, Orleton acted as spokesman. Edward was faced with a choice of abdication or deposition. He seems to have agreed to the former, and certainly accepted the idea that his son should succeed him. William Trussell formally withdrew homage, and the steward of the royal household broke his staff of office. On 25 January the embassy reported back to parliament, and the new king's reign began formally on that date.[102]

The importance of parliament in the proceedings is striking; the assembly provided the context for the deposition, and Edward II's refusal to attend failed to prevent this happening. Remarkably, even the removal of the king from the throne did not mark the end of parliament; it continued in being until March. Another important context for the deposition was provided by the Londoners, whose pressure was crucial. Stapledon's murder had shown what might happen if events did not go the way they wanted. The citizens so frightened the archbishop of Canterbury that he gave them 50 tuns of wine.

Was any one individual primarily responsible for the deposition? Geoffrey le Baker, writing a hostile account many years later, singled out Adam Orleton, bishop of Hereford, together with Henry Burghersh, bishop of Lincoln.[103] Orleton certainly played a leading role, taking part in the first mission to Kenilworth, giving the first of the sermons in parliament, and acting as a spokesman on the second Kenilworth embassy. Orleton, however, claimed that the articles of deposition were drawn up by John Stratford, bishop of Winchester, and written down by his secretary.[104] It seems likely that among the bishops Orleton and Stratford took the lead, but the role of Isabella and Mortimer must also have been crucial.

There may have been no precedent in England for the deposition, but there were Continental parallels going back to Pope Gregory VII's declaration that the emperor Henry IV was deposed. The best route to have taken in 1327 might have been to get the pope to depose Edward, but there was no time for that. The recent deposition in Germany of Adolf of Nassau may have provided

---

[102] Valente, 'Deposition and Abdication of Edward II', 854–62, provides a helpful narrative. The main sources include *Lanercost*, 257–8; *Forma Deposicionis*, repr. in Fryde, *Tyranny and Fall of Edward II*, 233–5, and better by Haines, *King Edward II*, 343–5; *The French Chronicle of London*, ed. G. J. Aungier (Camden Society, 1844), 57–8; *Historia Roffensis*, in Haines, *King Edward II*, 344–5.

[103] Baker, 26–8.

[104] Haines, *Stratford*, 183.

a precedent; there were certainly similarities in the articles directed against Edward II and the charges against Adolf. That, however, could be explained in broader terms, in that there were generally accepted reasons for deposing kings. It was not a question of tyrannical behaviour, but rather of finding a ruler to be incapable, *inutilis*. Accepting evil counsel, wasting inherited lands, failing to maintain the peace, and overall incorrigibility were the types of accusation characteristic of depositions. Those responsible for removing Edward II from office, or certainly the churchmen among them, were undoubtedly well aware of the framework within which depositions had taken place in the past, such as those fulminated by Pope Innocent IV against the emperor Frederick II and King Sancho II of Portugal in 1245.[105]

To try to determine precisely how it was that Edward II was removed from the throne, whether by abdication, deposition, Roman legal theory, renunciation of homage, or parliamentary decision, is a futile task. What was necessary was to ensure that every conceivable means of removing the king was adopted, and the procedures combined all possible precedents.

Edward II had been a disastrous king. A number of chronicles recorded a curious incident in 1318 when the pretender John of Powderham appeared. He was said to be a tanner's son, and claimed to have been exchanged as a baby for the current king. He was clearly insane, but it was decided that he should be drawn and hanged. The story itself is inconsequential, but the incident was the occasion for much gossip, and its inclusion by chroniclers can be taken as a form of criticism of Edward II himself.[106] Tall and good-looking, Edward was kingly solely in appearance. The occasions on which he took some initiative and behaved as he should were so rare that they were remarked upon. Bishop Cobham noted the way in which, in 1320, the king was 'contrary to his former habit rising early and presenting a nobler and pleasant countenance to prelates and lords'. He was taking an active and positive role in parliament, and the bishop thought that there was hope that he had improved his ways.[107] Edward was capable of personal bravery when faced by extreme circumstances, as at Bannockburn, but the fact that he did not participate in tournaments suggests that he was no adept at feats of arms. Indolence and indecision were among Edward's leading characteristics, as the aftermath of Piers Gaveston's death shows. The one difficulty with this analysis is the evidence of the final years,

---

[105] E. Peters, *The Shadow King: Rex Inutilis in Medieval Law and Literature 751–1327* (New Haven, 1970), 232–41.

[106] *Anonimalle*, 94; *Gesta Edwardi*, 55; *Vita Edwardi*, 86–7; W. Childs, ' "Welcome, My Brother": Edward II, John of Powderham and the Chroniclers', in I. Wood and G. Loud (eds.), *Church and Chronicle in the Middle Ages: Essays Presented to John Taylor* (London, 1991), 149–63.

[107] Cited by Haines, *King Edward II*, 45.

with the evidence of royal letters showing an acute awareness both of the overall principles and of the details of government administration. It is conceivable that the king underwent a complete transformation in about 1320; but it is much more likely, as argued above, that these letters were in fact written in the king's name by the younger Despenser. The most curious feature of Edward's character was his taste for manual labour, and for the company of workmen, sailors, and others of low social rank. This was not just a matter of contemporary gossip; references in household accounts for purchases of iron, plaster, and other things 'for the private works of the king' provide strong documentary hints.[108] Entries in the accounts recording the dinners eaten in the royal chamber by sailors, such as Adam Cogg, are suggestive. Whether his documented taste for crabs and prawns was regarded as eccentric is not known.[109] These personal touches suggest that Edward was not simply 'one of the best examples of the brutal and brainless athlete, established on a throne'.[110] A brutal and brainless man would probably have done better as king; Edward's unconventional ways, combined with his lack of ability in politics and war, were disastrous in a king.

Edward did not long survive his deposition. He was taken from Kenilworth to Berkeley castle. An extraordinary group of conspirators led by a couple of disreputable friars, Stephen and Thomas Dunhead, appear to have succeeded briefly in rescuing Edward. After being recaptured, the former king was probably imprisoned for a time in Corfe castle before being taken back to Berkeley. The danger that he might escape again meant that there was only one possible solution. At Berkeley, Edward was murdered, very possibly by means of a red hot iron up his backside. Those responsible were John Maltravers, Thomas Gurney, and William Ogle, who were surely acting with the approval of Roger Mortimer, if not necessarily of Isabella as well.[111] There were, of course, stories that Edward survived. One of these, a tale told by a Genoese priest, Manuel Fieschi, recorded in considerable circumstantial detail the former king's travels following a dramatic escape, in which a murdered porter's body was substituted for Edward's. By this account, Edward ended his days as a hermit in northern Italy. This has caused intermittent excitement among historians ever since it was published in the late nineteenth century. While it cannot be disproved, it is highly improbable. It is, for example, unlikely that Edward could have gone to Avignon, to be honoured by the pope who kept him there in secret for a fortnight. The issue is little more than a curiosity; with a

---

[108] BL, Cotton MS Nero C. VIII, fo. 57.

[109] Society of Antiquaries of London, MS 122, pp. 4, 79.

[110] T. F. Tout, 'The Captivity and Death of Edward of Caernarvon', in his *Collected Papers* (Manchester, 1934), iii. 146.

[111] Tout, ibid. 145–90, provides a full account.

few exceptions, the most notable being the earl of Kent, it was generally believed by contemporaries that Edward died at Berkeley. If, remarkably, he did survive, he played no further part in the history of the country he had ruled so feebly.[112]

ISABELLA AND MORTIMER

In her petition against the Despensers, Elizabeth de Clare had looked forward to days when 'grace is more open, and the law of the land better maintained and equal for all'.[113] Expectations that those days would come with the accession of Edward III were sadly unfulfilled. The new king was a minor, and power lay with his mother, Isabella, and, above all, her lover Roger Mortimer. Things started well. Edward III was promptly crowned on 1 February. The assembly responsible for the deposition continued in being, and a council was set up consisting of four bishops, four earls, and four barons. This did not include Mortimer among its number. A mass of petitions were heard from those looking to have the injustices of the previous regime reversed.

The power base of the Despensers had been so narrow, and the collapse of their authority so total, that there was no blood bath as there had been in 1322. The Despensers and their leading supporters had been dealt with in 1326; there was no need for further revenge. There were, of course, some ministerial changes. Orleton became treasurer, though after a couple of months he was replaced by Henry Burghersh, bishop of Lincoln. Bishop Hotham of Ely became chancellor. There was, however, no extensive purge; many officials remained in office. Victims of the Despensers were restored. Queen Isabella wrote on behalf of one chancery official, William Thunnock, 'We having regard for the fact that the said Sir William is good and sufficient for the said chancery, and that he was maliciously removed from his position without cause, beg and charge you that not countermanding this command you should receive the said William and restore him to the same state, or better, that he used to have.'[114]

It was in the shires, rather than at Westminster, that the changes were most extensive, with most of the sheriffs and castle constables being replaced. Many of the experiments of the Despenser regime were done away with. The system

---

[112] The issue of Edward's alleged escape is discussed by G. P. Cuttino and T. W. Lyman, 'Where is Edward II?', *Speculum*, 53 (1978), 522–44; Haines, *Reign of Edward II*, 219–38; Mortimer, *The Greatest Traitor*, 244–64; Doherty, *Isabella*, 183–215. The last two works argue that Edward II did escape from Berkeley.

[113] Holmes, 'Protest Against the Despensers', 212 (my translation).

[114] Willard et al. (eds.), *English Government at Work*, i. 203 n. 3.

of home staples did not last long. The Despensers had introduced a structure of eight regional escheators; the old system of two, one to the north and one to the south of the Trent, was restored.[115] Parliaments met with what must have seemed unremitting frequency; there were no fewer than four in the course of 1328.

It was in the land settlement that the new regime revealed its political ineptitude. Isabella received a massive increase to her wealth, obtaining a grant of 20,000 marks a year, much of this coming from the estates of the younger Despenser. Kent and Norfolk benefited from the revolution, but while Mortimer did not get large grants immediately, very soon he had built up his position in the Welsh marches to a staggering extent. He acquired the lands of his cousins the Mortimers of Chirk. From the former Despenser lands came the great lordship of Denbigh, and from Arundel's forfeited estates Oswestry, Clun, and other lands. Grants of wardship and marriage gave him authority over the Hastings and Audley lands, and others. He held the royal castles of Builth and Montgomery. He also had the office of justiciar of north and south Wales. The younger Despenser had not sought to glorify his territorial position with a title; in 1328, however, Mortimer became earl of March, a brand new title.[116]

Roger Mortimer was a classic example of a man whose power went to his head.[117] There was nothing in his early career that presaged the extraordinary course that it would take from the time of his and Isabella's invasion of England in 1326. Through his marriage to Joan de Geneville he had acquired half of Meath and the lordship of Trim in Ireland, and half of the lordship of Ludlow in the Welsh march. In his own right, as lord of Wigmore, he was a substantial marcher lord. He had served as royal lieutenant in Ireland from 1317 to 1318, and as justiciar from 1319 to 1321. An avid enthusiast for tournaments, he appears a typical nobleman. The opportunities that presented themselves after 1327 showed that his greed paralleled that of the Despensers, and his political sensitivity that of Piers Gaveston.

The Scots provided the first failure for Isabella and Mortimer. The Weardale expedition failed to provide the military success that would have helped to give some justification for their rule. The logical next move of negotiation with the Scots, and concluding the so-called Shameful Peace of May 1328, compounded the situation.[118] At the same time a protest was made about the succession to the French throne of Philip VI of Valois and the passing over of Edward III's own claim. There were increasing financial problems, for although Edward II had left a full treasury, the costs of paying for the count

[115] Tout, *Chapters*, iii. 8–11. [116] Davies, *Lordship and Society in the March of Wales*, 281. [117] For his career, see Mortimer, *The Greatest Traitor*. [118] See below, 244.

of Hainault's assistance to Isabella and Mortimer were substantial, as were those of the Weardale campaign. A tax of a twentieth had been granted, but the situation had not been resolved. Later in 1328 the government faced a very serious threat from Henry, earl of Lancaster. Henry was Thomas's brother, but he had taken no part in the rebellion of 1322 and was in possession of much of the vast Lancaster inheritance. Among his supporters was Bishop Stratford of Winchester, who was forced to flee from parliament as he believed that Mortimer's men were out to kill him. Lancaster's grievances were straightforward. The king should live of his own, the council set up in 1327 should be advising him, and peace should be maintained in the realm. All that was new was the emphasis on the request that the king should live of his own, which received the reasonable answer made on behalf of Edward III that 'it was impossible for him to be any richer, since both he and his people were impoverished by the recent disturbances, but if any man knew how to make him richer, it would give him and his advisers great satisfaction'. Whereas in the Ordinances of 1311 the phrase 'live of his own' had been used in the context of prises, now it was used for crown finance. 'The King ought to have enough to live fitly, without oppressing the people, together with treasure for defending his land and people if need arose.'[119]

London gave the earl of Lancaster its full support. When parliament met at Salisbury in October and Mortimer was given his new title, Lancaster stayed at Winchester and would not attend. He then moved to the midlands, and there seemed a real threat of civil war. The earl, however, had insufficient support. Archbishop Simon Mepham demanded that instead of advancing in force on Lancaster, the principles of judgement of peers as set out in Magna Carta should apply.[120] The issues should be settled in parliament. A settlement was achieved in January 1329. The penalties were not exacted in blood, but in silver. Lancaster entered into a recognizance for £30,000, though this was never paid, and his leading supporters, Thomas Wake and Hugh Audley, entered into recognizances to the crown for £10,000 each. Thirty other men, who included the veteran John de Botetourt, made smaller acknowledgements of debt.[121] This was the technique of rule by indebtedness so familiar under the Despensers.

There were, naturally, elements in Henry of Lancaster's attempted rising that recalled the events of his brother's life. The murder of Robert Holland, who had deserted Earl Thomas, was one. Some of Henry's supporters, such as Hugh Audley, had fought earlier for Thomas. The earls of Norfolk and Kent, however, did not fall into this category, and earl Henry's programme, such as it

---

[119] *Cal. Plea and Mem. Rolls*, 68–9, 81–2.   [120] Ibid. 84.
[121] Haines, *Stratford*, 196–204; *CCR 1327–30*, 528–31.

was, had none of the familiar Lancastrian demands for the maintenance of the Ordinances. These were different times, and it would be wrong to try to see too much continuity in 'Lancastrian' opposition to the crown.

After Lancaster's failure, Mortimer seemed to be more strongly entrenched than ever. However, in March 1330 there was news of a new plot. The earl of Kent was arrested. He had been convinced that Edward II was still alive, partly lured into this by agents of Isabella and Mortimer. John Maltravers was later accused of being primarily responsible in that he knew full well that Edward II had been murdered but in an 'ingenious manner with false and wicked subtleties' persuaded the unfortunate earl that this was not the case. Kent confessed to the existence of a widespread plot, even implicating Archbishop Melton of York. Kent was duly executed, not without some difficulty as initially no one could be found to wield the axe.[122] The act, far from dissuading anyone from further moves against Mortimer, must have been significant in persuading some of the danger that the new earl of March presented to them. The new conspiracy that developed had a much more significant figure than Kent at its head.

In 1330 Edward III was 18. He had suffered humiliation on the Weardale campaign, and had been allowed no effective role in government. Mortimer treated him with contempt. Edward's position was all the more threatened in 1330 if there was truth in the rumours that Mortimer intended the throne first for himself, and then for the child Isabella was soon to have by him. With a small group of conspirators, Edward determined to act. The most important of his supporters was probably William Montague. He was the son of the William Montague who had played a prominent role in the politics of the central years of Edward II's reign, and who had been steward of the royal household from 1316 to 1318. William entered the household himself in 1320, and by 1328 he had the rank of banneret. It looks as if the plot to get rid of Mortimer had already been hatched by the time that Montague was sent with Bartholomew Burghersh on an embassy to Avignon in September 1329. Montague put Edward's problems to the pope, and a simple code was devised. Only letters that contained the words 'Pater Sancte' in the king's own handwriting were to be regarded by the pope as genuine.[123] In the event, there was no need to call on the pope for his help. News of the conspiracy reached Mortimer, and at Nottingham in October Edward and the chief suspects were questioned. Montague told the king that it would be better to eat the dog than to be eaten by the dog. The conspirators had to act. They met on the night of 19 October, about sixteen in number. Although more men had been expected, the

[122] Haines, *Stratford*, 211–12; *Rot. Parl.* i. 53.   [123] Tout, *Chapters*, iii. 27–8.

group went ahead. They had the help of William Eland, one of the officials of
Nottingham castle, who knew it like the back of his hand. He guided the band
through the tunnels that honeycombed the rock on which the keep stood. They
burst into the private quarters of the queen and Mortimer. Hugh Turplington,
steward of the household, was the one man of significance killed in a brief fight.
Isabella famously ran out of her chamber shouting, 'Good son, have pity on
noble Mortimer.'[124] Edward had no pity. The earl of March was taken for trial
and execution, the last bloody act in the series that had begun with the lynching
of Piers Gaveston on Blacklow Hill. With Edward III's personal rule, the
character of politics would change radically. The change in fortune for the
English crown would appear first in the king's dealings with the Scots; after
years of defeat and difficulty, success finally beckoned.

APPENDIX

The Modus Tenendi Parliamentum

The *Modus* is a much-discussed tract that most commentators have attributed to the
reign of Edward II; if this is correct, then it is important in demonstrating some of
the ideas that existed about parliament and how the institution might be improved.[125]
One view, however, strongly advocated by G. O. Sayles, is that the document is late
fourteenth-century in origin, and Irish; if this is right, then it has limited relevance to
the history of the English parliament.[126]

The text purports to describe parliament as it existed in the reign of Edward the
Confessor. Its most radical suggestion was that, in cases of discord, a committee of
twenty-five should be set up, and its most startling argument was that, in the context of
taxation, shire representatives 'have a greater voice in granting and denying than the
greatest earl in England'.[127] The dating is suggested not so much by such political
arguments as by the statement that the roll of parliament is said to be 10 inches wide, as
it was under Edward II, that it was to be delivered to the exchequer, not the chancery,
and that there is no set rate of payment specified for representatives, as was the case
before 1327. Sayles, however, was able to point to a list of fines to be levied upon

---

[124] C. Shenton, 'Edward III and the Coup of 1330', in Bothwell (ed.), *The Age of Edward III*,
13–34, discusses the coup and identifies the conspirators.
[125] *Parliamentary Texts of the Later Middle Ages*, ed. Pronay and Taylor, provides an edition of
the *Modus* and a summary of the orthodox view. See also M. C. Prestwich, 'The *Modus Tenendi
Parliamentum*', *Parliamentary History*, 1 (1982), 221–5.
[126] G. O. Sayles, '*Modus Tenendi Parliamentum*: Irish or English?', in J. Lydon (ed.), *England
and Ireland in the Later Middle Ages: Essays in Honour of Jocelyn Otway-Ruthven* (Dublin, 1981),
122–52.
[127] *Parliamentary Texts of the Later Middle Ages*, ed. Pronay and Taylor, 74–5, 77, 107–8, 113.

absentees from parliament, which reflects Irish not English practice, and he linked a section dealing with the king's absence from parliament with the inability of Roger Mortimer, royal lieutenant in Ireland, to attend the Irish parliament in 1382. The statement that there were two principal clerks of parliament might depict Irish late fourteenth-century practice; it was not the case in early fourteenth-century England. The arguments are not conclusive either way, but it is most probable that the work was written in the early fourteenth century. It was not, however, intended as an accurate description of parliament, and it contains puzzling elements. The statement that 'the king can hold Parliament with all the community of his kingdom, without bishops, earls and barons' does not fit any historical context. It is curious that there is no mention of the chief justice of Common Pleas, and the notion that an earldom was worth £400 a year finds no echo in other sources. The large number of parliamentary clerks specified, together with the emphasis on the written record, suggests that the treatise may well have been written by a clerk who served parliament. It is possible that the author had Lancastrian sympathies; there are obvious parallels between the committee of twenty-five and the provision in the Tract on the Steward drawn up for Thomas of Lancaster, which proposed a committee of twenty-five to deal with cases where the law was doubtful. Lancaster, too, had complained of parliament being held in private.[128] Yet the emphasis on the representatives, given a more important voice than the most important of the earls in granting or refusing taxes, hardly fits with a Lancastrian agenda.

Study of the manuscript versions of the *Modus* reveals a complex history, with three main groups, as well as an Irish adaptation, the latter probably being based on a French translation of a Latin original written in England. In some manuscripts the *Modus* is found together with the Tract on the Steward and a treatise on the rights of the Marshal; it is not consistently found in works of a legal character. A major problem is that none of the manuscripts is earlier than the late fourteenth century. While this does not prove that the text dates from that period, it makes it difficult to reach firm conclusions from the manuscripts about the ultimate origins of the work.

The *Modus* does not make its purpose clear. Its most recent editors see it as a legal tract, partly on the basis of its use by lawyers from the late fourteenth century onwards. It is certainly found in association with legal texts in a number of manuscripts, but this is not the only context in which it was copied. It was, for example, copied into a Durham cathedral priory register, along with the Tract on the Steward and that on the rights of the Marshal. Its stress on procedure, and its lack of reference to immediate contemporary problems, make it seem implausible that it was written as a political tract. It seems more likely that it was written by someone much concerned with the way in which parliaments were run and the way its records were kept. It is striking that the rate of expenses suggested for the clerks of parliament was a substantial mark a day.[129] Concern with ecclesiastical representation in parliament, and the requirement that clerical proctors should be elected by archdeaconries, suggest that the author was himself a cleric who did not go along with the way in which the Church preferred to

---

[128] Maddicott, *Thomas of Lancaster*, 289–92, argues the case for a Lancastrian connection.
[129] *Parliamentary Texts of the Later Middle Ages*, ed. Pronay and Taylor, 73–4, 106.

deal with the crown through convocations rather than parliaments.[130] Arguments have been put for a later date than the reign of Edward II, with the suggestion that the *Modus* springs from the same background of civil service desire for reform as Langland's *Piers Ploughman*, but while these are valuable in emphasizing the relative weakness of the case for dating the work from 1321, there are too many anachronisms for such a case to hold up.[131]

[130] The argument for a clerical background for the *Modus* was put by W. C. Weber, 'The Purposes of the English *Modus Tenendi Parliamentum*', *Parliamentary History*, 17 (1998), 149–77.

[131] K. Kerby-Fulton and S. Justice, 'Reformist Intellectual Culture in the English and Irish Civil Service: The *Modus Tenendi Parliamentum* and its Literary Relations', *Traditio*, 53 (1998), 149–202.

CHAPTER 9

Scotland

In March 1296 a small band of Scots crossed the Tweed at Pressen, near Wark. The village was surrounded and burned. Many of the inhabitants were killed, and others were taken away to Roxburgh castle. Those who were quick-witted enough to overhear and use the password which the Scots employed managed to escape.[1] This small-scale skirmish opened the Anglo-Scottish conflict, which dominated the years until the late 1330s. It provided Edward I and his successors on the throne with a far more severe test than the conquest of Wales, and contributed much to the increasing militarization of England. Although it was punctuated by truces and periods of inactivity, the frequency of campaigning, particularly in Edward I's later years and in the 1330s, was striking. The war was characterized not only by English invasions of Scotland, but also by Scottish raids into England. The consequent transformation of the north finds no parallel elsewhere in England; there were similarities to the devastation that would be wrought by English armies operating in France.

The war was not easy. There were few opportunities for heroic deeds of arms and little hope of profiting from plunder. The best description of campaigning was written by Jean le Bel, who accompanied the contingent of Hainaulters in 1327 on an expedition against the Scots who were raiding the north of England.[2] The Scots were hard to locate, though the smoke from burning farmsteads marked their route. The hilly terrain of Weardale was most unwelcoming to men used to the flat fields of the Low Countries. If the men chased a sign of movement, they would find that it was deer, not the Scots, that made the disturbance. The infantry could not keep up with the cavalry, and rations were low. Bread soaked in the sweat of the horses was all that was available after a hard pursuit. Nights spent in the open were acutely uncomfortable; when they found a village that the Scots had burned in which to sleep, 'it seemed to us like paradise'. When the Scots were located, they refused battle. The English thought that they had them cornered on a hilltop; but on the fourth day they vanished, and established themselves on another hill.

---

[1] Guisborough, 271–2.   [2] Le Bel, i. 53 ff.

For eighteen more miserable days the armies faced each other, until the Scots suddenly withdrew. The English army was in no fit state to pursue them; the men were cold and hungry and the horses were starving. This was not a glamorous war.

The course of the wars can be conveniently divided into distinct phases. The first, Edward I's war, concluded with the apparent subjugation of Scotland in 1304. The second, Robert Bruce's war, began with the murder by Bruce of John Comyn of Badenoch in the church at Dumfries in 1306, witnessed the triumph of the Scots in battle at Bannockburn in 1314, and saw the Scots make many serious inroads into the north of England. Edward III's campaigns of the 1330s form a third phase, one which began with major English successes at Dupplin Moor in 1332 and, above all, Halidon Hill in the following year. From 1337 the conflict with the Scots moved into a fourth phase, in which it formed a part of the wider war against Philip VI and John of France. A decisive point came in 1346 with the capture of the Scots king David II at the battle of Neville's Cross.[3]

ENGLAND AND SCOTLAND IN THE THIRTEENTH CENTURY

Many wars are the product of years of growing hostility. The Anglo-Scottish wars do not fit such a pattern. For most of the thirteenth century relations between the two countries were cordial, not marked by a pattern of bickering and argument. In contrast to Wales, Scotland had a strong and well-established monarchy. It had some archaic features, notably the form of inauguration using the Stone of Destiny, without coronation or anointment. The bureaucracy was not on the scale of that in England, but the structure of government, with earls and sheriffs, was not dissimilar. The Scottish monarchy had strong links with the English. Alexander II married King John's daughter Joan in 1221; his son Alexander III married Henry III's daughter Margaret in 1251. These marriages were far more important than the second marriages of the two Alexanders, to Marie de Coucy and Yolande de Dreux respectively.

The Scottish kings owed homage to the English monarchs. This created a similar position to that in which the English kings were subordinates of the French in respect of the lands they held in France. That relationship is seen as one of the fundamental reasons for Anglo-French hostility. In the case of the English and Scottish monarchies, however, it caused fewer problems, partly perhaps because the longevity of the kings meant that the issue came up rarely.

[3] For the history of Scotland in this period, see M. Brown, *The Wars of Scotland 1214–1371* (Edinburgh, 2004).

A crucial point was that the Scots argued that homage was owed only for those lands held by the Scottish kings in England. There was no question, from their point of view, of Scotland itself being subordinate to the English crown. Alexander II succeeded to the throne in 1214, and in 1216 did homage for his English lands not to King John, but to Louis of France. In the following year, however, he did homage to the young Henry III. Alexander III performed homage in 1251, at the time of his marriage, in respect of the lands he held in England. Suggestions that he should also do homage for Scotland were rejected.

Alexander II's relationship with his brother-in-law Henry III was not easy, but never seriously threatened to deteriorate into war. The Scottish king objected to the fact that his father's treaty with King John had not been put into full effect, and he laid claim to the counties of Northumberland, Cumberland, and Westmorland. He gave his support to Richard Marshal in the latter's revolt in 1234. In 1237 agreement was reached, under papal pressure, between Henry III and Alexander at York. In return for abandoning his claims, Alexander was granted lands in Northumberland and Cumberland valued at £200, notably Tynedale and Penrith.[4] This did not end tension. In 1244 Henry III was alarmed at Alexander II's activities. The Scottish king's marriage to Marie de Coucy in 1239 was seen as an aggressive move, while Henry's intervention on behalf of Walter Bisset, who had been exiled from Scotland, raised the prospect of English feudal overlordship in Scotland. The Scots were accused of fortifying the border, and English shipping was suffering from Scottish piracy. Henry paraded his strength with a summons of the feudal host to Newcastle. He also obtained assistance from the count of Flanders. Alexander marched south with his own army, but negotiations, not battle, were the order of the day. The king of Scots formally agreed not to make any alliances with Henry's enemies, and to keep the agreement that had been reached at York in 1237. Alexander's son was to marry Henry's daughter. The expedition to Newcastle cost Henry at least £4,000, most of it going to his Flemish troops.[5] War had never been likely, but this was a price worth paying to ensure peace.

The Scots were in no position to take advantage of the troubles that began in England in 1258.[6] Alexander II had died in 1249, when his son was not yet 8 years old. In 1251 a Scottish deputation representing the faction headed by

---

[4] F. M. Powicke, *The Thirteenth Century 1216–1307*, 2nd edn. (Oxford, 1962), 586–7.

[5] *Chron. Maj.* iv. 358–9, 381–2; Stacey, *Politics, Policy and Finance*, 245; Powicke, *Thirteenth Century*, 587–8.

[6] For Anglo-Scottish relations, M. Brown, 'Henry the Peaceable: Henry III, Alexander III and Royal Lordship in the British Isles, 1249–1272', in Weiler (ed.), *England and Europe in the Reign of Henry III*, 43–66. See also A. Young, *Robert the Bruce's Rivals: The Comyns, 1212–1314* (East Linton, 1997), 45–61.

the Comyn family asked Henry III to provide help. The opportunity was welcome. Henry arranged the marriage of the young Alexander III to his daughter Margaret, and ensured that the Scottish king did homage for his English lands. A new Comyn-led government in Scotland lasted until 1255. A regency council was then created, with English support. In 1258, following an attempted coup by the Comyn family, Henry III threatened to use force, but the political situation in England made that impossible. A conciliar government was set up in Scotland, which lasted until Alexander III established his full personal authority in 1261. The level of English interference in the Scottish minority should not be exaggerated, but it provided a limited precedent for Edward I's far more extensive intervention in the early 1290s.

Alexander III, once he came of age, was able to take some advantage from Henry III's difficulties in England, for example in establishing his rule over the Isle of Man, but he did not lend any support to Simon de Montfort. Some Scots were involved in the English civil war of 1264–5. John Comyn, John Balliol, and Robert Bruce all served in Henry III's army, and were captured at Lewes in 1264. William of Kilbride, in contrast, fought with Simon de Montfort. The limited scale of Scottish support for Montfort was significant, for it meant that when Edward I came to the throne, he had few scores to settle with the Scots, in contrast to the Welsh. Edward I did not appear to have been in any hurry to receive homage from Alexander III. The matter was not raised until 1278. The Scottish king demanded an extraordinarily impressive escort, to be headed by both English archbishops. He was not prepared to admit that his Scottish realm was held as a fief from Edward. 'No one has a right to homage for my kingdom of Scotland save God alone.' Although the English reserved their position, Edward appears to have been content to receive homage purely for the lands that Alexander held in England.[7] Relations thereafter between Edward and his brother-in-law Alexander III were remarkably untroubled. The friendly formalities of diplomatic interchanges can be misleading, but in this case seem to have been genuine. Edward was no doubt appreciative when Alexander enquired politely after his health in 1284, and sent him a present of four fine gerfalcons.[8]

EDWARD I'S INTERVENTION IN SCOTLAND

Crisis hit the Scottish crown in 1286, when Alexander III died when he fell from his horse as he rode through the night in a romantic dash to reach his new

---

[7] Prestwich, *Edward I*, 357; G. W. S. Barrow, *Robert Bruce and the Community of the Realm of Scotland* (London, 1965), 17.
[8] *CDS* ii, no. 253.

French queen. His heir was his granddaughter Margaret of Norway. This provided Edward I with a splendid opportunity, though his immediate priority lay in Gascony. A marriage of Margaret to his son Edward should ensure the peaceful acquisition of the Scottish kingdom. Negotiations were not easy, for the Guardians of Scotland were very well aware of English ambitions. The treaty of Birgham of 1290 provided that Scotland should remain separate after the marriage, with its own administration. Edward's actions, however, suggested that he had little time for such guarantees, and when he confirmed the treaty he also appointed Anthony Bek, bishop of Durham, to act on behalf of the young couple, Edward and Margaret, in Scotland. He was to 'administer justice and set the realm in order'. Edward did not get everything his own way, for the Norwegians were rightly suspicious of him. He wanted the young princess to sail direct to England, and even sent a lavishly equipped ship to fetch her, but this was in vain. In the end, she sailed for the Orkneys, where, tragically, she died.[9]

The death of the Maid of Norway dashed Edward's hopes of gaining Scotland for his son through marriage. He was not a man to abandon his ambitions, and in the disputed succession to the Scottish throne found another means to try to establish English lordship over the Scots. Genealogical accident meant there was no agreed heir to the Scottish throne on Margaret's death: in the end, there were to be fourteen claimants, though in reality the choice lay between John Balliol and Robert Bruce, grandfather of the future king. Edward was the obvious person to oversee the choice of a new king of Scots, and indeed received approaches from rival factions. He chose to use the opportunity to gain recognition for his dubious claim to be the superior lord of Scotland, rather than providing the independent arbitration that was looked for by the Scots. A very obvious military and naval presence gave unwelcome weight to his arguments. The Scots were not prepared to acknowledge Edward's overlordship, but he was able to extract recognition of it from the candidates. The castles of the kingdom were handed over to him, and for the duration of the legal hearings Scotland was formally in English hands. Edward was evidently not prepared to allow Scotland the degree of independence envisaged in the treaty of Birgham, and was ready to take every advantage he could of the weakness of the Scots.

The case to determine the succession, known to posterity as the Great Cause, was heard at Berwick. A decision could have been reached quite quickly, but there was a delay of ten months to allow one of the claimants, Florence, count of Holland, to provide documentary proof of his assertion to

[9] M. C. Prestwich, 'Edward I and the Maid of Norway', *Scottish Historical Review*, 69 (1990), 157–73.

be the rightful heir. He argued that David, earl of Huntingdon, had surrendered his rights, and those of his descendants, to the Scottish throne. If accepted, this would have nullified the claims of both Bruce and Balliol. Edward, there can be little doubt, was well pleased by the adjournments and delays in the case; the longer he could be seen to exercise his rights of direct lordship over Scotland, the stronger those rights would appear. There were arguments among the English over what should be done. The earl of Gloucester supported Robert Bruce, his brother-in-law, while Earl Warenne and the bishop of Durham backed John Balliol. In the autumn of 1292 the court reached its decision, in favour of John Balliol. This was the right decision in law; but it was also what Edward I wanted. The English had successfully manipulated the entire process.[10] The official record of the proceedings was drawn up a few years later by a public notary, John of Caen, probably in 1296–7. It was carefully slanted to demonstrate that Edward I was 'superior and direct lord' of Scotland, a claim that the Scots, rightly, had never accepted.[11]

John Balliol has gone down in history as a thoroughly ineffectual monarch. He faced extreme difficulties, and it is hardly surprising that he adopted policies of appeasement towards Edward. He acknowledged that he owed homage to the English king, not simply for the lands he held in England, but for all of Scotland. Edward was determined to show what his lordship meant in practice. A case brought by a Berwick burgess, Roger Bartholomew, was promptly taken to the English king's court on appeal. It was made clear that Edward did not regard himself as bound by promises made when the Scottish throne was vacant. Further appeals followed, notably that from Macduff, uncle of the earl of Fife, who claimed to have been deprived of his inheritance; Balliol was compelled to attend the English king's court in person. The summons of Balliol and a considerable number of Scottish magnates to provide feudal service for the English expedition to Gascony in 1294 was a further turn of the screw. It is unlikely that Edward was deliberately trying to provoke the Scots so that he would have an excuse to invade, but this was to be the outcome of his actions.

EDWARD I'S SCOTTISH WAR

The outbreak of war between England and France in 1294 transformed the situation for the Scots.[12] For Philip IV of France, Scotland was an obvious ally.

[10] For the records of the process, see E. L. G. Stones and G. G. Simpson (eds.), *Edward I and the Throne of Scotland, 1290–1296* (Oxford, 1978). *Scalacronica*, 120, reveals the different English views.

[11] A. A. M. Duncan, 'The Process of Norham', in *TCE* v. 207–30.

[12] For Edward I's Scottish wars, see F. Watson, *Under the Hammer: Edward I and Scotland, 1286–1306* (East Linton, 1998).

John Balliol, however, despite the way he had been treated by Edward I, was pro-English. In a rather mysterious coup, power was taken from his hands and a council of twelve set up in 1295. In October of that year Scots ambassadors negotiated a treaty with the French in Paris, and in the following February it was ratified in Scotland. Before that Edward I had issued a military summons for a muster at Newcastle on 1 March 1296. The war began with the Scottish raid at Pressen. The Scots also attacked in the west, where Carlisle was fortunate not to be captured when a Scottish spy succeeded in setting fire to the city. Edward I's operations started with the English siege and capture of Berwick, a brutal business. The resistance of the Flemish merchants in the town was particularly notable; they defended themselves to the death in the Red Hall. The English campaign was deceptively successful, culminating in the abject submission of John Balliol. The regalia of the Scottish kingdom were removed and taken to Westminster.

In 1297 the Scots rose under the combined leadership of William Wallace and Andrew Moray. Wallace's achievement was astonishing. He was a man of knightly origins, who must have possessed an extraordinary charisma to achieve the leadership role he rapidly assumed.[13] To the English, he became a terrifying figure, a man capable of horrific acts of cruelty. In September Wallace routed an English army under Earl Warenne at Stirling Bridge. He followed that up with a devastating raid into the north of England, which was halted not by defensive measures, but by poor weather. An effective riposte had to wait until Edward I's return from Flanders.

Edward I led massive expeditions north in 1298, 1300, 1301, and 1303, pouring resources into the war on a scale that the Scots could not possibly match. The king's strategy of employing overwhelming force worked in 1298, when the English army defeated Wallace's forces at Falkirk. The Scots cavalry fled at the outset. The stout Scottish defensive infantry formations, the schiltroms, were softened up by English archers and prised open by the cavalry. The battle demonstrated to the Scots the acute dangers involved in challenging the English on the battlefield, and not until 1314 did they attempt this again. They could fight the war effectively without major battles. The war was characterized not only by the great English expeditions northwards, but also by many smaller engagements and raids. A letter of 1299 from Robert Felton, constable of Lochmaben, sets the scene well. It brings out the importance of the fighting done by castle garrisons, the hope that a major campaign would end the war, and the personal hardships of those who fought for Edward. Felton complained that the garrison of the nearby castle of Caerlaverock, held by the Scot Robert Cunningham, had been doing much damage. In a

---

[13] For Wallace's career, see A. Fisher, *William Wallace* (Edinburgh, 1986).

fight between the two garrisons, however, the English had had the upper hand, and Cunningham's head now decorated the keep at Lochmaben. Felton noted that the news that the English had come to terms with the French (Edward I married the French princess Margaret in 1299) had greatly dispirited the Scots, and he encouraged the king to undertake a further campaign in Scotland. He added a request that he should be given the robes to which he was entitled, as a household knight, for he could not leave the castle to buy any.[14] The war did not all go the English way. Small English forces were vulnerable, as was demonstrated at Roslin in 1303, when John Segrave was defeated and John Manton, an important financial official, slain. Slowly, however, the Scottish will to resist was worn down.

Castles played an important part in the war. Those held by the English provided bases essential for a permanent occupation. Constables were ordered 'to spy and arrange spying for all the news they can of the enemies and their supporters'.[15] Roxburgh and Jedburgh dominated the border in the east; Lochmaben and Dumfries controlled the route into south-western Scotland. In 1302 plans were drawn up for building work to take place at Linlithgow and Selkirk. The reduction of Scottish castles by the English punctuated the war. In 1300 Caerlaverock fell, a meagre return for a major campaign. In the following year Bothwell was captured and Ayr was taken into English hands. The first Scottish castle to fall in Edward's campaign of 1303–4 was Brechin. Lochindorb, further north, was taken by siege, and Urquhart and Cromarty also came into English hands. The major prize was Stirling, where the final Scottish resistance took place. It was captured in July 1304 after a lengthy siege.

It was important for Edward to win as much support as possible within Scotland. He had the consistent backing of some of the great Anglo-Scottish nobles, notably Gilbert de Umfraville, earl of Angus, and Patrick, earl of Dunbar. Simon Fraser became a royal household knight in 1297, and the list also included Thomas de Morham and Reginald Crawford. In 1300 Herbert de Morham and Simon Lindsay were members of Edward's entourage.[16] These were not, however, men to rely on. Fraser and the Morhams joined the Scottish opposition to Edward, to the king's fury. In 1302 he wrote to the constable of the Tower of London saying that he was sending him Herbert de Morham, 'who has misbehaved towards us since he came to our peace. We order you that you are to receive him into a good, strong prison, and keep him in the Tower all by himself, without any companion, Scot or other.'[17] On the other hand, a great success for Edward came when Robert Bruce abandoned the Scottish cause

---

[14] *CDS* ii, no. 1101.   [15] E 101/7/10.
[16] BL, Add. MS 7965, fo. 60; *Liber Quotidianus*, 188, 190.   [17] E 101/4/10.
[18] Discussed by Barrow, *Robert Bruce*, 172–5.

early in 1302.[18] Alexander of Abernethy probably came over later in the same
year, and was certainly serving the English by early 1303.[19] As Edward's position
strengthened during his stay in Scotland in 1303–4, so more Scottish nobles
realized that the best way of preserving their estates was to come to terms.

In Wales, above all in the south, it had been possible to recruit many ordinary
people into the English armies. Scotland was very different. There was widespread popular hostility to the English. In 1297 Edward's demands for men and
money to support his war against France aroused the antagonism of the ordinary
people of Scotland. This underlay Wallace's rising, and gave the character of a
popular rebellion.[20] The English were aware of the need to win general support.
In 1301 John Kingston, constable of Edinburgh, and John de St John, com-
manding in the south-west, were authorized to receive the 'middle men' of
Scotland to the king's peace.[21] Records of English administrators in Scotland
show that it was possible to collect some revenues, but acceptance of their rule
was very limited. The overall impression given by the documents is that there
was very little cooperation from the Scots, and that men such as John of
Musselburgh, who guided John de Segrave and Robert Clifford through
Lothian in an unsuccessful search for William Wallace, were very rare.[22]

The war would not have begun had it not been for the alliance made by the
Scots with Philip IV of France, and as it continued it had its diplomatic
dimension. The Scots obtained support from the papacy, and in 1300 Archbishop Winchelsey journeyed to Scotland to give Edward a bull, *Scimus Fili*,
which informed him that 'the realm of Scotland belongs to the Roman church',
and that it was 'not lawful for him to dominate it by force'. Baldwin Bisset and
other Scottish envoys put a cogent and well-argued case to the pope in 1301,
but legal arguments could not divert the English sword, and Edward was
unmoved by papal pleas.[23] French backing for the Scots was more serious.
Edward received a report, probably in 1302, that 'The bishop of St Andrews is
showing the people a letter under the king of France's seal…It asserts that
there will be no peace between him and the king of France if the Scots are not
included. The people trust in this and the efforts of Master Baldwin, their
proctor at the court of Rome.'[24] In reality, it was unlikely that the French
would provide active military assistance to the Scots, but it was difficult for
Edward to bring the war to a conclusion before he reached agreement with

[19] *CDS* ii, no. 1694.
[20] See A. A. M. Duncan, *The Nation of Scots and the Declaration of Arbroath*, Historical
Association Pamphlet (1970), 14–16.
[21] *CDS* ii, no. 1244.
[22] BL, Add. MS 8835, fo. 42[v].
[23] Barrow, *Robert Bruce*, 165–8; Stones (ed.), *Anglo-Scottish Relations*, 81–117.
[24] *CDS* ii, no. 1431.

Philip IV. The startling French defeat at the hands of the Flemings at Courtrai in 1302 paved the way for Edward I and Philip IV to reach an accommodation. Effectively, Philip agreed to cease supporting the Scots if Edward gave up backing the Flemings. Peace was agreed in 1303, and the Scots were left friendless. Even Boniface VIII ceased to offer them words of support.[25]

Edward I achieved victory in 1304. The final triumph was the capture of Stirling castle, but by the time that took place in July, the leaders of the Scottish community had given up. In January and February 1304 John Comyn of Badenoch led surrender negotiations, acting in his capacity as the leading Guardian. He was anxious to ensure that the laws and customs that had existed in the time of Alexander III should be maintained, though envisaging that change might take place, on the advice of Edward I acting on the advice of the good people of the land. The most important aspect of the negotiations was that rights to land should be preserved as they had stood in 1296. Edward insisted on varying periods of exile for leading Scots; Comyn himself receiving a one-year sentence, and Simon Fraser three years.[26]

Peace in Scotland presented Edward with great difficulties. In reality, he had obtained the surrender of the powerful Comyn faction, rather than of the whole community of Scotland. The question of the Scottish crown was simply sidestepped. Edward did not claim the throne for himself, but exercised his rights of overlordship over what was now described as a land, rather than a realm. In 1305 an ordinance for the government of Scotland was produced after discussions between ten Scots and twenty of Edward's councillors. Edward's nephew John of Brittany was appointed as the king's lieutenant in Scotland. The chancellor and chamberlain were both English, but there was to be a council containing twenty-one Scots in addition to the officials. The great majority of the sheriffs outside the south-east were Scottish. Justices were to operate in pairs, one Scotsman and one Englishman. Edward and his advisers obviously thought that it would be possible for Scotland to be largely governed by Scots acting under English direction. A harsher reality to the settlement was revealed soon after the Ordinance was agreed. In terms reminiscent of the Dictum of Kenilworth, it was decided that the Scottish nobles should pay fines amounting to the value of their lands for varying number of years. This replaced the earlier imposition of periods of exile. The settlement of 1305 has received an undeservedly good press. 'Care was taken precisely to foster consensus and acquiescence at all levels of society.'[27] It certainly bears all

[25] Prestwich, *Edward I*, 397, 479.

[26] *Documents and Records Illustrating the History of Scotland*, ed. F. Palgrave (London, 1837), 27–88; see also Watson, *Under the Hammer*, 185–8.

[27] Watson, *Under the Hammer*, 220. See also Barrow, *Robert Bruce*, 189, for a more grudging acknowledgement of Edward's 'political wisdom'.

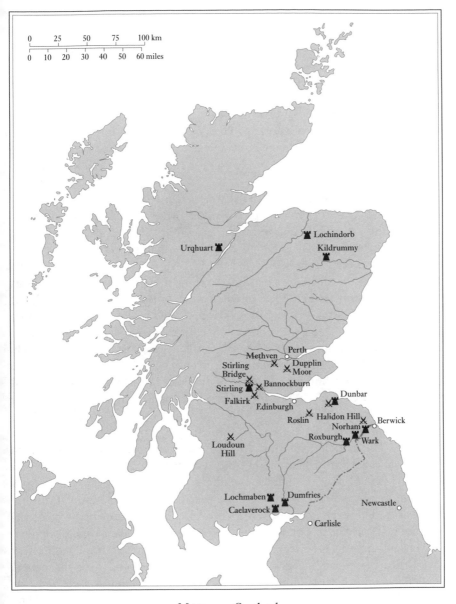

0   25   50   75   100 km

0   10   20   30   40   50   60 miles

Urqhuart

Lochindorb

Kildrummy

Methven   Perth

Stirling   Dupplin
Bridge   Moor

Stirling   Bannockburn
Falkirk   Dunbar
Edinburgh

Roslin   Halidon Hill   Berwick
Norham
Roxburgh   Wark
Loudoun
Hill

Lochmaben   Dumfries
Caelaverock   Newcastle

Carlisle

MAP 9.1. Scotland

the marks of compromise; like most compromises, it probably failed to
satisfy anyone. The Scots were punished more heavily with the fines for
their lands than had been anticipated at the time of the surrender of 1304.

The English had not obtained the expected rewards for trudging north on so many dreary campaigns. The fundamental question of the future status of Scotland, and above all of its crown, was fudged. The value of the settlement could only have been tested over time; and time was precisely what proved not to be available. The reality of Edward's attitude towards the Scots was displayed not so much in the settlement, but rather in the brutal execution of Wallace in 1305, hanged, drawn, burned, and quartered with all the vicious imagination of which men were capable. The man responsible for his capture was paid £20; John de Segrave was advanced 15s. to carry the four parts of the corpse to Scotland, where they would hang as an example to any who chose to oppose Edward.[28]

The evanescent nature of Edward's settlement of Scotland was quickly demonstrated. On 10 February 1306 Robert Bruce murdered John Comyn, author of the surrender of 1304, in the Greyfriars church in Dumfries. Six weeks later he was installed as king of Scots. Bruce had very obvious grievances against Edward. When he had joined the English in 1302, the agreement he made promised the king's support for his rights, though it is unlikely that this included the family claim to the Scottish throne. In the event, the surrender of 1304 meant that the rival faction in Scotland, headed by John Comyn, retained lands and influence. Legal moves threatened his extensive rights in Annandale. Bruce received nothing from Edward's settlement of Scotland, but merely continued to hold the sheriffdoms of Ayr and Lanark. He was one of the Scottish councillors, but was not a man of influence in the new regime. Edward had miscalculated badly in not rewarding Bruce sufficiently, and the price he paid was a very heavy one.

No one in 1306 could have predicted the failure of the English enterprise in Scotland. The gamble that Robert Bruce took very nearly failed. Aymer de Valence defeated him at Methven in June. Kildrummy castle fell in September, and the ladies of Bruce's entourage, including his queen and sister, fleeing from the siege, were captured. Bruce spent the winter of 1306–7 in hiding, probably in the Isles. However, when he returned to Scotland, success began to come. Valence was defeated at Loudoun Hill, and Bruce attracted ever more support. In May an English supporter wrote a letter that has often been quoted: 'I hear that Bruce never had the good will of his own followers or of the people generally so much with him as now. It appears that God is with him, for he has destroyed King Edward's power both among English and Scots. The people believe Bruce will carry all before him . . .'.[29]

---

[28] E 101/369/11, fo. 9ᵛ; E 101/367/16, fo. 4.
[29] *CDS* ii, no. 1926, trans. Barrow, *Robert Bruce*, 245.

Edward I's reaction to Bruce's seizure of the Scottish throne was to display an iron fist in a steel gauntlet. Bruce's Scottish lands were promptly promised to the earl of Hereford. The king congratulated Valence on burning Simon Fraser's lands in Selkirk Forest, and ordered him to 'burn, destroy and waste' the houses and lands of his Scottish enemies. Captives were to be put to death, apart from the leaders for whom Edward no doubt envisaged a grisly process of trial and execution.[30] Simon Fraser duly suffered hanging, drawing, and beheading, and many Scots were executed. Bruce's sister Mary and the countess of Buchan, who had enthroned Bruce, were imprisoned in public view, in specially constructed cages on the walls of the castles of Berwick and Roxburgh. This level of brutality was quite new, and ruled out any further compromise settlement on the lines of that of 1304–5. The policy of terror merely stiffened Scottish resolve. Their spirits must have been lifted when Edward I's slow advance northwards in 1307 came to an end with the king's death just across the border, at Burgh-by-Sands, on 7 July.

EDWARD II'S SCOTTISH WAR

The advent to the English throne of a new king provided Bruce and his followers with the time they needed. Edward II had none of his father's determination or qualities of leadership. The importance of individual leadership became very apparent with the startling change in the fortunes of war once Robert Bruce established himself in Scotland.[31] Although Bruce had none of the massive resources that were available to the English, both in physical and administrative terms, he was able to take the initiative in the war. English armies were at best ineffective in the field. The north of England and Ireland were opened to Scottish invasion. The former in particular suffered appalling damage at the hands of well-organized raiding bands.

The 1307 English expedition was soon abandoned, and it was not until 1310 that they mounted a significant military effort. The speed of Bruce's triumph within Scotland was remarkable. His first need was to defeat his Scottish opponents. The murder of John Comyn had not destroyed the powerful Comyn faction. Bruce brutally terrorized the Comyn earldom of Buchan, and opposition in Galloway was crushed. By 1309 the new king had won his civil war, and was able to hold his first parliament, at St Andrews. The Scottish clergy pronounced that the throne should have gone to Bruce's grandfather, rather than to John Balliol.[32]

[30] *CDS* ii, nos. 1757, 1782, 1787, 1790.
[31] For the Anglo-Scottish war during the reign of Robert I of Scotland, see C. McNamee, *The Wars of the Bruces: Scotland, England and Ireland, 1306–1328* (East Linton, 1997).
[32] Stones (ed.), *Anglo-Scottish Relations 1174–1328*, 140–2.

When Edward II at last mounted an expedition, in 1310, it achieved little. While the army was at Biggar, marching towards Glasgow, news came that Bruce was near Stirling, but it proved impossible to engage him in battle. The king wintered at Berwick, but resources were not sufficient for a further campaign in the following year. The optimism of one writer, who claimed in April 1311 that the Scots were daily coming over to Edward II, was completely misplaced.[33] Before Edward's campaign, the castles Bruce had taken had largely been in the north. The process gathered pace from 1311. Perth fell in 1313, and by the following year Linlithgow, Roxburgh, and Edinburgh were all in Scottish hands.

The Scots began to take the war to the English. Sword and firebrand were used systematically to destroy villages and farms. Those who wanted to be spared this treatment had to pay heavy tributes, which in turn sustained the Scottish war effort. The raiding began in 1311 with two attacks on Northumberland and a raid into Cumberland. In the following year Corbridge and Hexham were burned and Durham attacked. In 1313 Bruce's brother Edward invaded Cumberland. A pattern of raids and truces dominated the years until 1322. Defence of the north was not easy. The deaths of Robert Clifford in 1314 and of Henry Percy in the following year removed from the scene two of the men most capable of organizing resistance. The appointment of great magnates to take charge, with Pembroke in 1315 and Arundel in 1316, was an obvious step, as was the garrisoning of castles in the north by the crown, but too little was done too late. In the west Andrew Harclay, an ambitious and able local man, achieved prominence when the Scots were held off at the siege of Carlisle in 1315. He did good work using light cavalry to deter Scottish raiding.[34] Much responsibility was laid on the bishops. Archbishop Greenfield of York and Bishop Kellawe of Durham were not men of military experience, and the latter's policy of paying off the Scots did not commend itself to the king. Greenfield's successor, William Melton, was an experienced royal administrator, but the one field in which he failed totally to distinguish himself was that on which the battle of Myton was fought in 1319. One reason for the promotion of Louis de Beaumont to the Durham see in succession to Kellawe was to provide better for the defence of the north. An aristocrat, no doubt expected to follow in his brother Henry's distinguished military footsteps, Beaumont was a sad disappointment. His appointment had been sold to the king on the grounds that he would defend the north 'like a stone wall', but Edward condemned him for his 'default, negligence and lukewarmness'.[35]

---

[33] CDS iii, nos. 166, 204.

[34] Harclay's career is summarized by Summerson, Carlisle, i. 230–43.

[35] H. Schwyzer, 'Northern Bishops and the Anglo-Scottish War in the Reign of Edward II', in TCE vii. 243–54; Registrum Palatinum Dunelmense, ed. T. D. Hardy (RS, 1873), vol. i, pp. xxix–lxxx.

The English hoped that a large-scale campaign, led by the king in person, would achieve a notable victory. Instead, that of 1314 ended in totally unexpected disaster. In the spring of 1314 Bruce's brother Edward was besieging Stirling castle, and came to an agreement with the commander that the castle would be surrendered if no relieving force had come by the following midsummer.[36] This was a challenge that even Edward II could not refuse, and the scene was set for the English defeat at Bannockburn. Unfortunately, no pay accounts survive for the English army, but it was clearly very substantial. Edward and his commanders knew in advance that the Scots would meet them in battle close to Stirling, but their plans were woefully inadequate. The battle took place over two days. The Scots had prepared their position well. The boggy ground was highly unsuitable for English cavalry forces, but was well selected to suit infantry forces fighting defensively. Bruce's men were formed up in the traditional schiltroms. A dispute between the earls of Gloucester and Hereford over which of them had the right to lead the van typified the muddle and confusion in the English ranks.[37] This led to a suicidal charge into the Scottish ranks by Gloucester; his men, wisely, did not follow him, with the exception of the chivalric hero Giles of Argentein. He died a courageous and pointless death. The English had no way of breaking the Scottish infantry formations; the difficulties of the site made it difficult to manoeuvre their troops effectively, and no effective use was made of their archers. This was a calamitous defeat, celebrated by the Scots with taunts about Edward's unwarlike love of rowing.[38]

The Scots were rampant after Bannockburn. The siege of Carlisle in 1315 was one of their rare failures, but there was nothing to stop the incessant raiding of the north of England. The garrisons of the main English castles could not block the invasion routes. In 1316 the Scots reached Yorkshire. Particularly serious raids took place in 1318 and 1319; on the latter occasion a motley English force gathered together by the archbishop of York was routed at Myton-on-Swale. The English in Berwick had been reduced to sore straits by 1316. The garrison were deserting. All there was left to eat were the horses. The cavalrymen boiled and ate the flesh, leaving the infantry with the bones. 'Pity to see Christians living such a life', wrote Maurice de Berkeley.[39] Not surprisingly, Berwick was lost through treachery in 1318, and the castles of Wark, Harbottle, and Mitford also fell. Edward II mustered a large army in 1319. Such was the seriousness of the situation that the earl of Lancaster was

---

[36] See A. A. M. Duncan (ed.), *John Barbour, the Bruce* (Edinburgh, 1997), 402, for a convincing argument that this agreement was not made, as usually thought, in the summer of 1313.

[37] *Vita Edwardi*, 53. For a full description of the battle, and a convincing case as to where it was fought, Barrow, *Robert Bruce*, 290–332.

[38] *The Brut*, 208.

[39] *CDS* iii, no. 470.

persuaded to join in the expedition. Planning appears to have been negligible, for although the purpose was to recapture Berwick, insufficient care seems to have been taken to bring the siege equipment essential for success. Only after operations had begun were orders issued to bring siege engines from York.[40] Political dissension within the army, rather than Scottish action, brought the siege to a premature conclusion. There were suspicions that the earl of Lancaster had been bribed by the Scots to provide Bruce with secret assistance. According to Hugh Despenser the younger, 'By procurement and doing of the earl of Lancaster, the said earl did things so that the king left the place with all his army, to the great shame and grievous damage of us all.'[41] Once again, the English command structure had proved woefully inadequate.

In 1315 the Scots had taken the war to the English in Ireland.[42] Given the way in which Edward I had made as much use as possible of Irish resources in his wars against the Scots, recruiting men, raising money, and obtaining food supplies on a scale that exceeded his exploitation of England, this was an obvious move. Edward Bruce led what proved to be an over-ambitious enterprise. It was not easy to conduct war during a period of acute famine, and the Scots suffered considerably from food shortages. Fine words encouraged the Irish to join in what the Bruces regarded as a Celtic alliance against the English; but in the complex world of Irish politics it was not possible to create a unified force. For every ally Edward Bruce found, he also created an enemy. The Scots had their successes; at Ardscull in 1316 a force assembled by Anglo-Irish magnates was defeated, but Edward Bruce was unable to follow up the victory. In 1317 Robert Bruce himself went to Ireland, but the campaign achieved little save the destruction of territory. In October 1318 Edward Bruce was defeated and killed in the battle of Fochart, near Dundalk, by Anglo-Irish forces under John de Birmingham. This was a rare success, brought about more by Edward Bruce's carelessness and arrogance than by the skill of his opponents.

The last campaign Edward II led against the Scots took place in 1322. The English had no answer to a Scottish strategy of withdrawal. The army found a deserted, barren country on its march to Edinburgh. Supplies did not get through by sea, partly as a result of the action of Flemish pirates. The story told by the Scots was that the English found nothing to eat save one lame cow. 'This is the dearest beast I have ever seen; it must surely cost £1,000 or more,' joked Earl Warenne.[43] To make matters worse, when Edward retreated south, he was

---

[40] CDS iii, no. 663.

[41] Vita Edwardi, 97; Œuvres de Froissart, ed. de Lettenhove, xviii. 3.

[42] For the Bruce invasion of Ireland, R. Frame, 'The Bruces in Ireland, 1315–1318', Irish Historical Studies, 19 (1974), 3–37, and McNamee, The Wars of the Bruces, 166–99.

[43] M. C. Prestwich, 'Military Logistics: The Case of 1322', in M. Strickland (ed.), Armies, Chivalry and Warfare in Medieval Britain and France (Stamford, 1998), 276–88.

pursued by the Scots under Moray, and almost captured in an engagement near Byland in Yorkshire. There was much alarm at the news. In London the mayor and many of the citizens went to the Tower to try to get some news; the constable comforted them and assured them, mendaciously, that the king had gone elsewhere to raise troops to drive out the Scots.[44]

By 1322 it had become very clear that the English had no hope of winning the war by military means. Defence of the north was proving difficult. Edward wrote furious letters to the constables of Bamburgh, Warkworth, Dunstanburgh, and Alnwick, expressing his amazement at the way in which the Scots had taken ransoms and hostages from the neighbourhood of the castles and had got away without being challenged. He was astonished that they did not have proper intelligence. Another letter rebuked the bishop of Durham for not keeping Norham castle properly, and threatened him with confiscation of his lands.[45] There was a mood of despair in the north. Andrew Harclay, made earl of Carlisle after Boroughbridge, took matters into his own hands. He was authorized to make a truce, but in 1323 went much further and negotiated a peace with Robert Bruce. The agreement he made survives in two different versions. Both acknowledged Bruce as king of Scots, and recognized Scotland as an independent country. There was to be a commission of twelve, six Scots and six English, which in the 'English' version of the treaty was to have wide powers to take measures for the common good of both realms. The 'Scottish' version saw the twelve appointed as arbiters of the agreement, and promised that in the event of an invasion of England, Harclay's lands would be protected.[46] This was completely unacceptable to the king, and Harclay was duly tried, convicted of treason, and sentenced to be hanged, drawn, and quartered. It is remarkable that a man who had done so much to defend the north should have acted as Harclay did. He was arrogantly overconfident, and had many reasons to be dissatisfied with Edward's government. Since he had failed to come to the king's rescue at Byland in the previous year, he was not in the king's favour. He was probably also aware that the government under the Despensers was unlikely to put the necessary effort into the Scottish war. It is also possible that he had hopes of marrying one of Robert Bruce's sisters. His actions also undoubtedly reflected a widespread view in the north, especially among ordinary people, that peace was essential.[47]

After Harclay's execution the government proceeded to make a truce with the Scots, which it was intended should last thirteen years. In contrast to the

---

[44] SC 1/63/169.
[45] CDS iii, no. 783; E 163/4/11, no. 50.
[46] The texts are printed and discussed in *Regesta Regum Scottorum*, v: *The Acts of Robert I*, ed. A. A. M. Duncan (Edinburgh, 1988), 480–5.
[47] Summerson, *Carlisle*, 235–56.

agreement made by Harclay, however, there was no acknowledgement of Bruce's kingship. Edward II was not prepared to give way on this point. The Scottish king bitterly resented this lack of recognition. 'It was not in our mind to make a truce now where there is no more reference made to us than to the meanest of our realm,' he wrote in 1323.[48]

EDWARD III'S SCOTTISH WAR

The truce agreed in 1323 lasted only until 1327. Taking advantage of the political confusion in England, the Scots attacked Norham castle, and made known that they intended to annex Northumberland. The new English regime under Isabella and Mortimer recruited an army, which included a force from Hainault. With them was the chronicler Jean le Bel, whose description of the miserable campaign in Weardale provides such a highly realistic account of the realities of medieval warfare.[49] The Scots were far more mobile than the English. Rain and lack of proper food supplies severely hampered operations, and when the Scots were located, they refused battle. The young Edward III's first experience of war was deeply frustrating, and was followed by what was, from the English point of view, a thoroughly unsatisfactory peace. The terms agreed in 1328 were for the full recognition of the independent Scottish kingdom. Robert Bruce's son David was to marry Edward III's sister Joan, and the Scots would pay the English £20,000. Nothing was said about the claims of various English magnates to lands they had been granted, or to which they had rights, in Scotland.

It was these men, the so-called Disinherited, who renewed the war in 1332.[50] They launched a private expedition and invaded Scotland unexpectedly by sea, landing in Fife. They included Edward Balliol, son of the abject king John, who had been deposed in 1296, John de Beaumont, who claimed the earldom of Buchan through his wife, and the claimants to the earldoms of Atholl and Angus. At Dupplin Moor the little force, positioned with great tactical skill, routed the Scottish army. Edward Balliol was then crowned king at Scone. The success was too easy; the Scots drove out Balliol, who appealed for help to Edward III. In 1333 Edward began the siege of Berwick. A relieving Scottish army was mercilessly defeated at Halidon Hill, and Berwick once again became an English town. The pendulum of war had swung dramatically.

Edward III's policy towards Scotland was novel. Unlike his grandfather, he showed little respect for the boundaries of the northern kingdom. In 1332

---

[48] *Regesta Regum Scottorum*, v. 491.   [49] Le Bel, i. 53 ff.
[50] For accounts of Edward III's wars, R. Nicholson, *Edward III and the Scots* (Oxford, 1965); Brown, *The Wars of Scotland*, 232–54.

Edward Balliol acknowledged that Edward had feudal lordship over Scotland, and that he was obliged to provide military service. He also agreed to grant Edward land worth £2,000 in Scotland. In 1334 Balliol, who was in no position to argue, granted Edward much of southern Scotland. Most of the southern shore of the Firth of Forth was annexed to England, and in the south-west the border began at Wigtown. This was not just an extension of the existing border. It brought under English rule the regions dominated by the castles at Berwick, Roxburgh, Jedburgh, Edinburgh, Lochmaben, and Dumfries. It remained to be seen whether such a grant could be turned into reality.[51]

The past had shown that single victories did not win the war against the Scots, and Edward III found himself leading a succession of frustrating campaigns. A massive expedition in 1335, numbering some 15,000 men, failed to achieve the conquest that was hoped for. It persuaded David of Strathbogie, claimant to the earldom of Atholl, to change sides, but in the autumn of the same year he was killed in battle at Culblean. The war had its dramatic moment with the king's high-speed dash in 1336 to rescue the countess of Atholl at Lochindorb, but the reality of the conflict was a familiar one of English-held castles succumbing to Scottish assaults and sieges, and of ineffectual large-scale English campaigns.[52] There were fears that the French would invade in support of the Scots, and it was increasingly clear that the war could not be ended as long as the Scots had French support: the situation was a similar one in some ways to that at the start of the century. At the same time, increasing English preoccupation with the French war gave the Scots a breathing space. Edward III was unable to take advantage of the political divisions that existed in the competitive world of the Scottish aristocracy.

In 1341 the Scots captured Edinburgh castle, and the young David II, who had succeeded to the throne in 1329, returned from a seven-year exile in France.[53] In 1342 Stirling and Roxburgh fell. The tide of war was running strongly in the Scots' favour, but in 1346 they suffered a devastating reverse. The opportunity for David II to raid the north of England while Edward III was engaged on his campaign in France was too good to miss. On 17 October, however, the Scottish army was routed by a hastily gathered force of north-erners at Neville's Cross, just outside Durham. David himself was captured.[54]

---

[51] Nicholson, *Edward III and the Scots*, 98–9, 160.

[52] Though the countess was rescued, she felt aggrieved many years later, when in 1347 she put forward a petition in parliament that put her losses at 16,400 marks and those of her son at £4,800. She pointed out that the annuity, initially of 100 marks and subsequently of £100, granted her was substantially in arrears: *Rot. Parl.* ii. 181.

[53] For David II's career, M. Penman, *David II 1329–71* (East Linton, 2004).

[54] M. C. Prestwich, 'The English at the Battle of Neville's Cross', and A. Grant, 'Disaster at Neville's Cross: The Scottish Point of View', both in D. W. Rollason and M. C. Prestwich (eds.), *The Battle of Neville's Cross 1346* (Stamford, 1998), 1–35.

Negotiations for his ransom and release were extraordinarily protracted, complicated as they were by the questions raised by Anglo-French diplomacy. Edward III conducted one more campaign against the Scots, early in 1356. Berwick was swiftly retaken. The English troops, with the experience of France behind them, then engaged in such an orgy of destruction in Lothian that the expedition became known to the Scots as the Burnt Candlemas. Bad weather, however, dispersed the English victualling fleet, and Edward was forced to retreat. The Scots retaliated, achieving considerable successes in the south-west of the country, where they took Caerlaverock castle and re-established their authority in Galloway.[55] The difficulties Edward had faced in his campaign helped to persuade the English, and perhaps also the Scots, that it was time for serious negotiation. Balliol finally surrendered his crown to Edward III in 1356, and in the next year ransom negotiations were completed. David II returned to Scotland, in exchange for the promised payment of 100,000 marks in annual instalments of 10,000 marks. At Brétigny it was agreed that the French would cease their support of the Scots, and the way was open for a final peace with the Scots, though that, of course, was not to be achieved.

LAND AND PATRONAGE

A central issue in the Anglo-Scottish wars was land, and more specifically the need of the nobility to retain their ancestral estates and their desire to gain more. The peaceful years of the thirteenth century saw a relatively unusual situation, in which there was substantial cross-border landholding. In part this went back to the twelfth century and the advent of an Anglo-Norman nobility in Scotland. There were also marriage connections forged more recently; these brought lands with them. Marriage in the late twelfth century to illegitimate daughters of the Scottish king William the Lion brought Scottish estates to the families of de Ros and de Vescy. In the thirteenth century the marriages of the three daughters of Alan of Galloway were particularly significant. Helen, the eldest, married Roger de Quincy, earl of Winchester (1235–64). He came from a family that had held significant lands in both England and Scotland since the twelfth century; with the marriage he acquired the title of constable of Scotland and further Scottish estates. William de Forz, earl of Aumale (1241–60) through marriage to Alan's second daughter Christiana, briefly gained estates in Galloway, and also those in both England and Scotland held by her uncle John the Scot, earl of Chester. Christiana died childless in 1246, so the estates did not remain with the Forz family. The third daughter, Dervorguilla, married the Northumbrian magnate John Balliol in 1233, bring-

---

[55] J. Sumption, *The Hundred Years War II: Trial by Fire* (London, 1999), 187–90.

ing him extensive Scottish lands, and his family their claim to the Scottish throne. The earldom of Angus was acquired in 1243 by another Northumbrian magnate, Gilbert de Umfraville, again through marriage.

In addition to English magnates holding lands in Scotland, Scottish magnates held land in England. The earls of Dunbar possessed the barony of Beanley in Northumberland, and the earl of Strathearn gained a third of the barony of Wooler by marriage in 1250. Through marriage to the earl's daughters, the earl of Mar and Nicholas Graham acquired important interests in Wooler. The Comyns of Badenoch held much of Tynedale, while the Buchan branch of the family had many estates in England, mostly in the south. Simon Fraser had land in both Scotland and England. The Bruces were landowners in Cumberland, Essex, Huntingdon, and elsewhere; their English connections were emphasized by the story that the future king served in Edward I's household in the early 1290s. Religious houses also had cross-border connections. Coldingham in Scotland was a cell of Durham cathedral priory. Holm Cultram, Lanercost priory, Carlisle cathedral priory, and St Bees priory all had significant Scottish interests. These examples could be multiplied many times.[56]

While these cross-border connections made for stability in the thirteenth century, once war broke out they had a very different effect. As early as 1295 Edward I ordered the confiscation not only of John Balliol's lands, but also of the lands held in England by other Scots.[57] When confiscated lands or titles were redistributed, their new holders had a strong vested interest in the war. This applied on both sides of the border. At the York parliament of 1298 Edward announced a policy of expropriating his Scottish enemies, and of granting their lands to his supporters. There were difficulties in the process, which took place after the victory of Falkirk, since the earls of Norfolk and Hereford protested at the king's predictable lack of consultation. The full list of grantees is not known, but the earls of Warwick and Lincoln, Robert Clifford, Robert de Tony, and Adam Swinburn were among those who were promised Scottish lands. By 1302 a list of those granted lands in Scotland by Edward I contained fifty-one names. The settlement of 1304–5 created problems for Edward in that he had to return much of the land he had granted to his

[56] K. J. Stringer, 'Identities in Thirteenth-Century England: Frontier Society in the Far North', in C. Bjorn, A. Grant, and K. J. Stringer (eds.), *Social and Political Identities in Western History* (Copenhagen, 1994), 28–66; G. G. Simpson, 'The *Familia* of Roger de Quincy, Earl of Winchester and Constable of Scotland', in K. J. Stringer (ed.), *Essays on the Nobility of Medieval Scotland* (Edinburgh, 1985), 102–3; A. Young, 'Noble Families and Political Factions in the Reign of Alexander III', in N. Reid (ed.), *Scotland in the Reign of Alexander III* (Edinburgh, 1990), 17–22; *CDS* ii, no 952; for Bruce's role as 'a young bachelor in the chamber of King Edward', *Scalacronica*, 120.

[57] *CDS* ii, nos. 718, 723, 736.

followers to its original owners. Robert Hastang, for example, had been granted lands held by a dozen Scots worth 300 marks a year, but all save two estates were handed back to them.[58] In many cases this was probably not too painful a process, for most Englishmen had not been able to draw any significant revenues from lands north of the border. However, the earl of Lincoln was promised £4,000, and John de Bar £2,000, in compensation.[59]

The renewal of the war in 1306 saw the king start once again to grant out lands in Scotland, building up a vested interest in conquest. The earl of Hereford received a charter granting him Lochmaben castle and Bruce's lands in Annandale. The title of earl of Carrick went to Henry Percy. John Hastings was given the earldom of Menteith, before the true holder of the title had surrendered. Ralph de Monthermer, titular earl of Gloucester, became earl of Atholl. Some Scots received rewards: John of Menteith, who had captured William Wallace, was rewarded with the title of earl of Lennox and the castle and shrievalty of Dumbarton. As Edward I travelled slowly northwards, he was beset by so many requests for lands in Scotland that he promised to produce an ordinance dealing with the issue, though this was never done.[60]

The classic case of how Edward I's distribution of land in Scotland created antagonism is that of James Douglas. An account of his life was incorporated into John Barbour's *Bruce*, which was written in the 1370s. His father's lands had been granted to Robert Clifford, and in the hope of recovering them he joined Bruce. 'It troubles me wondrous sorely that the Clifford so peaceably enjoys and holds the lordship that should be mine.'[61] Given the strongly patriotic tone of Barbour's writings, the stress in this case on land rights is very striking. When Edward Balliol conceded control of southern Scotland to Edward II in 1334, the Douglas estates were again placed under threat. The only hope the family had of retaining them was continued support of the Scottish cause.

While the Douglases chose the Scottish cause, initially at least, to protect their lands, others saw success for the English as the only way to secure estates in Scotland. The remnant of the Comyn faction naturally fitted this pattern. The Disinherited who invaded Fife in 1332 had strong Comyn connections. The group included Henry de Beaumont. He had married Alice Comyn, one of

[58] *CDS* iii, no. 258.
[59] M. C. Prestwich, 'Colonial Scotland: The English in Scotland Under Edward I', in R. Mason (ed.), *Scotland and England 1286–1815* (Edinburgh, 1987), 8; Watson, *Under the Hammer*, 68, 209.
[60] Prestwich, 'Colonial Scotland', 10–11; *Documents and Records Illustrating the History of Scotland*, ed. Palgrave, 301–8.
[61] Duncan (ed.), *John Barbour, the Bruce*, 61, 85, 203 (my translation). See also M. Brown, *The Black Douglases* (East Linton, 1998), 15–17.

the co-heiresses of John Comyn, earl of Buchan, who had died in 1308. Her Scottish estates were forfeited in 1314, and distributed by Bruce to his supporters.[62] David of Strathbogie was married to a daughter of John Comyn of Badenoch, and supported the English until 1312, even though his father had been savagely executed in 1306 on Edward I's orders. He then changed sides, but reverted to the English cause on the eve of the battle of Bannockburn. His son, also David, claimed the earldom of Atholl, given to John Campbell in 1329, and he also claimed half of the lands of John Comyn of Badenoch through his mother. Richard Talbot claimed the other half, by marriage to another Comyn daughter. Gilbert de Umfraville sought the earldom of Angus, which Bruce had recently granted to John Stewart.[63]

Some Englishmen fought for the Scots. Marriage was one explanation. At the very start of the war Robert de Ros, lord of Wark, went over to the Scots because he wished to marry a Scottish lady.[64] Christopher Seton, who held lands in Yorkshire and Cumberland, married Robert Bruce's sister Christina, and his participation in the 1306 rising is therefore hardly surprising. John Seton, who was with Bruce at the murder of John Comyn, and who held Tibbers castle for the new Scottish king, was presumably a close relation of Christopher's.[65] In other cases, men saw profit in joining with the successful Scottish enterprise of raiding the north of England. Walter de Selby was an Englishman who clearly despaired of the situation in the north in the middle years of Edward II's reign. He joined with the Scots in their raid in April 1318, and was involved in the short-lived capture of the bishop of Durham. For a time, he held Mitford castle for the Scots, but surrendered it to the English under Robert de Umfraville, earl of Angus. He redeemed himself in the eyes of the English, but to the Scots he was a traitor. When the Scots captured him, during David II's ill-fated 1346 expedition, he was duly hanged as a traitor. William de Prendergast, who held lands at Cornhill-on-Tweed, was congratulated for his gallant service in the garrison at Jedburgh, but much later was accused of handing the castle over to the Scots. He certainly changed sides, and was killed fighting against the English at Halidon Hill. Some families were divided in their loyalties. Henry de Normanville sided with the Scots, as did his children. His brother Thomas, however, and his heir, Isabel, remained English in their allegiance.[66] At a lower level of society, Andrew Potter was accused in 1319 of riding with the Scots. He refused to recognize the authority

[62] Barrow, *Robert Bruce*, 385.
[63] Nicholson, *Edward III and the Scots*, 66. David of Strathbogie joined the Scots in 1334, but reverted to the English cause in 1335.
[64] Guisborough, 271.
[65] *CDS* ii, nos. 1811, 1910.
[66] *CDS* iii, nos. 70, 418, 610, 981, 1356, 1636.

of the jury appointed to try him, and was accordingly sentenced to die by *peine forte et dure*.[67] Not all who were accused of joining the Scots may have in fact done so. Many who took part in Gilbert de Middleton's rising in 1317, and in associated disturbances, were later accused of complicity with the Scots. It is more likely that they were acting on their own behalf, taking advantage of the confused and chaotic situation in the north to plunder as they chose.

THE ORGANIZATION OF WAR

The Anglo-Scottish conflict tested the English war machine in a way that the wars in Wales had not done. As a result, it saw changes in the way that the English fought, with the development of the systems of warfare that would prove to be astonishingly effective when Edward III deployed them against the French.

Edward I's methods built on his experiences in Wales. His armies were recruited by means of old-fashioned feudal summonses in 1300, 1303, and 1306, but in reality the cavalry forces were a mixture of men paid through the royal household, and others provided by the earls and great magnates at their own expense. The evidence of a heraldic poem, the *Song of Caerlaverock*, set against the pay records, shows this with especial clarity for the 1300 campaign: of eighty-seven bannerets named in the poem, only twenty-three served for pay. In all, there were probably some 3,000 heavily armed horsemen on this expedition, organized into retinues of varying size, but normally with between ten and fifteen men in each. Recruitment of cavalry did not take place without some political argument; a request that those who possessed £40 worth of land should serve at royal wages was issued in 1300, but following protests this was not used as a precedent for later campaigns. Instead, individual summonses were issued to 935 individuals, far more than was usual, in the following year.

Infantry were recruited by means of commissions of array, and were all paid by the crown. Recruitment was concentrated upon the northern shires, with no call made on counties south of Nottinghamshire and Derbyshire. Welsh troops were extensively employed, although in 1300 they were not called on. In their absence it proved impossible to pursue the Scots into rough country. In the field, the infantry was organized in groups of twenties and hundreds. Accounts show that about 25,700 infantry were on the English payroll at the battle of Falkirk in 1298. Numbers were not so high in the subsequent campaigns, but Edward had a maximum of about 9,000 infantry with him in 1300, and 7,500 in 1303. Desertion was a constant problem; it was difficult to retain large forces

---

[67] C. J. Neville, 'Local Sentiment and the "National" Enemy: Northern England in the Middle Ages', *Journal of British Studies*, 35 (1996), 426.

for the full duration of a campaign. A severe ordinance was promulgated in 1303. Those suspected of desertion were to be imprisoned, and wages they had received would be recovered by force.[68]

Massive victualling operations were required to ensure that the armies did not starve. Permanent bases were established at Berwick and at Skinburness, near Carlisle. In 1303 figures for the quantities collected at the two bases were as follows (qu. = quarters):

Flour	1,872 qu.	Salt	680 qu.
Wheat	6,431 qu.	Cattle	44
Rye etc.	276 qu.	Pork	447 carcases
Barley	143 qu.	Mutton	8 carcases
Malt	1,326 qu.	Venison	73 carcases
Oats	5,974 qu.	Stockfish	2,018
Beans	1,305 qu.	Salmon	380
Vetch	275 qu.	Cod	45
Wine	1,366 tuns		

In the following year the army had about 7,000 quarters of wheat and the same amount of oats available to it, together with 2,311 quarters of malt.[69] These supplies were not handed out free to the soldiers. On occasion they might receive food in lieu of pay, and gifts of food and drink might be made, but victuals were also sold to the men. The foodstuffs were acquired by purveyance, which amounted to compulsory purchase. This was inevitably unpopular, for it was open to all sorts of corruption, but it was only in 1301 that negotiations of any sort took place with the counties. Use of the system meant that Edward's armies were not forced by hunger to retreat; it was rare for supplies to run out as they did at Aberdeen in 1303, compelling the king to turn to merchants to provide him with foodstuffs on credit.

Substantial fleets were required, to take the supplies north to the bases and on to the armies. In 1301 over fifty vessels were employed on the east coast, while forty-seven supported operations in the west, and similar numbers were needed in other years. In 1303, in an operation similar to the bridging of the Menai Straits, prefabricated bridges were brought north from King's Lynn to enable the English army to cross the Firth of Forth; thirty-one ships were needed to act as pontoons to support the roadway. Not surprisingly, there was considerable hostility from the ports when their vessels and crews were requisitioned for duties that were dangerous and probably unprofitable.[70]

---

[68] Prestwich, *War, Politics and Finance*, 67–113.
[69] Ibid. 124, 126.
[70] Ibid. 145–6.

Surprisingly little is known about the battle tactics that the English employed in Scotland under Edward I. At Dunbar in 1296 and Stirling Bridge in the following year, battle began before the English under Earl Warenne were properly ready. At Falkirk in 1298 the English encountered, probably for the first time, the Scottish circular defensive formations known as schiltroms. Accounts of the battle are uninformative, but it seems likely that the English archers played a very important role in weakening the schiltroms, ready for the final hammer-blow from the cavalry. From 1298 to 1314 the Scots avoided large-scale battles. At what was not much more than a skirmish at Loudon Hill in 1306, however, Bruce showed how it was possible to defeat well-armed cavalry by careful choice and preparation of the terrain. A road with boggy ground on either side, with deep ditches dug at right angles to it, compelled the English to fight on a narrow front. Once the front English rank was driven back, the rest turned and fled.[71]

At Bannockburn in 1314 the Scots proved to Edward II's army that traditional methods of fighting were not to be relied on. The battle showed the weakness of heavy cavalry, and demonstrated the strength of a well-established defensive position. Thomas Gray explained that the English were not accustomed to dismount to fight, whereas the Scots followed the example of the Flemings, who had fought on foot with such success at Courtrai in 1302.[72] The defeat must have prompted many of those involved to think hard about what would be needed if the Scots were once again to be defeated. Accordingly, one idea was that the infantry should be much better armoured and equipped. A series of summonses over the next few years sought to ensure this; hauberks, basinets, and iron gauntlets were seen as advisable.[73] Such heavily armoured foot would no doubt have been useful in battle, but they lacked mobility, as was demonstrated on the 1322 campaign, when it proved impossible to engage the Scots.

More effective than the use of heavily armed infantry was the development of mobile forces, needed for pursuit, and for the raiding which was an increasingly dominant aspect of the war. Under Edward I there was some use of hobelars, or lightly armed cavalry. These appear to have been Irish in origin; certainly the first significant number of such troops appeared in the earl of Ulster's retinue in 1296.[74] There were five such soldiers in Lochmaben castle in 1299, one of them employed to spy out the comings and goings of the Scots by day and night.[75] These troops seem largely to have been used in this way, as a means of providing garrison forces with much-needed mobility. They were

---

[71] Duncan (ed.), *John Barbour, the Bruce*, 298–308.   [72] *Scalacronica*, 142.

[73] M. R. Powicke, *Military Obligation in Medieval England* (Oxford, 1962), 142 ff.

[74] Prestwich, *War, Politics and Finance Under Edward I*, 74.   [75] *CDS* ii, nos. 1084, 1089.

not extensively employed in Edward I's reign on larger raids, such as that led by John Botetourt in the south-west early in 1304. His force was conventionally composed, and included only eight hobelars.[76] Larger numbers of hobelars were found in English forces in the second decade of the fourteenth century. Edward II continued to recruit them from Ireland, while many were raised locally in the north. Andrew Harclay took 360 hobelars and 980 infantry to the siege of Berwick in 1319, and other military men from the northern marchers also supplied significant numbers of hobelars. By 1322 Harclay was able to muster almost 1,500 hobelars for the Scottish campaign.[77]

At the battle of Boroughbridge in 1322, where the king triumphed over the earl of Lancaster, Andrew Harclay drew up his forces in the Scottish fashion, on foot.[78] They were hardly tested by Lancaster's feeble resistance, but the incident is important as demonstrating the way in which the English were learning from the Scots how to fight. In 1327 orders went out before the campaign, informing all those involved that they would fight in battle on foot, and that light horses would be needed to pursue the Scots.[79] When it faced the Scots, the English army was duly arrayed in three battalions, all dismounted. The problem then was that the Scots did not engage them; no battle took place.[80] The tactics were tried again by the Disinherited at Dupplin Moor. Here the English took up position in a narrow defile. As the Scots pressed forward, many of them died of suffocation. Grim piles of the dead accumulated in front of the English line. At Halidon in the next year three English battalions, each flanked by wings of archers, fought the Scots on foot. Men-at-arms and archers complemented each other, the archers doing their deadly work from a distance of some 200 yards, and the dismounted men-at-arms fighting in most effective fashion in the close-quarters mêlée.

The last effective use of a feudal summons took place in 1327. For the largest army that Edward III led to Scotland, that of 1335, the royal household provided over 400 heavily armed cavalry, 250 mounted archers, and a small force of sixty foot archers. The magnates, who by this date expected to be paid for their service, provided retinues that totalled about 2,500 cavalry and some 650 mounted archers. Forces recruited by means of commissions of array numbered almost 9,000, over 2,000 of them being mounted archers.[81] The greater use of pay was one significant change from Edward I's day, but the major change was the appearance of the mounted archers, who provided English armies with a much-needed capacity for rapid movement. They

---

[76] E 101/11/19.
[77] McNamee, *Wars of the Bruces*, 48, 52, 155; *CDS* iii, no. 668; Summerson, *Carlisle*, 235.
[78] *Lanercost*, 243.   [79] *Rotuli Scotiae* (London, 1814), i. 208.   [80] Le Bel, i. 65.
[81] Nicholson, *Edward III and the Scots*, 198–200. There was to be one further feudal summons, in 1385.

could ride with the cavalry and dismounted to fight. Whether their adoption owed anything to the earlier use of hobelars is doubtful; the latter were light skirmishers who fought on horseback.

There was also a significant change to the composition of the retinues provided by the magnates. Until the 1330s there was no question of these consisting of anything other than heavily armed cavalry, knights, squires, and men-at-arms. In 1335 some of the cavalry leaders brought archers with them as part of their contingents, and the development of the 'mixed retinue' was important in creating, over time, a much more coherent and well-ordered army.[82] The bulk of the infantry were still recruited by commissions of array, but by this period many of the commissions were appointed not for a whole county, but for much smaller units. Where in the past commissioners had been ordered to recruit 'both within and without liberties', in many cases they were now specifically appointed for individual liberties. Thus in 1334 men were appointed to recruit troops in Yorkshire from the lordship of Wakefield, the honours of Richmond and Tickhill, and the franchises of Northallerton, Knaresborough, Ripon, Howden, Whitby, and Beverley, as well as from individual wapentakes in the county.[83] It seems likely that recruitment on this much more localized basis would result in a more careful selection of troops than in the past.

Sieges were an important element in the Scottish wars. There were major set-piece sieges, of which the most notable was the siege of Stirling in 1304, and very many smaller ones. The English approach was conventional, relying on the deployment of equipment such as trebuchets, great throwing engines, and movable siege towers. At Caerlaverock in 1300 assaults on the castle failed, but surrender came quickly once the English engineer Master Robert had ranged his throwing engines effectively. In the following year Bothwell fell when the English dragged a siege tower, or belfry, up to the walls. At Stirling, Edward had fifty carpenters build a huge siege machine, called the Warwolf. Regrettably, the sources do not reveal what it was, though it seems most likely that it was an enormous trebuchet. So frightening was it that, once it was ready, the garrison offered their surrender. Edward, anxious to see how the machine worked, refused to let them out of the castle until it had been tried out. Gunpowder was also used at this siege, but as an explosive rather than as a propellant.[84]

The Scots did not have the equipment to besiege castles in the same way as the English. When they did try to take Carlisle in 1315 with siege engines, the

---

[82] A. Ayton, 'English Armies in the Fourteenth Century', in A. Curry and M. Hughes (eds.), *Arms, Armies and Fortifications in the Hundred Years War* (Woodbridge, 1994), 32.

[83] *Rotuli Scotiae*, i. 303–4.

[84] Prestwich, *Edward I*, 487, 493, 498–9.

result was a miserable failure as their belfry sank immovably into the mud.[85]
Blockade was possible, but was very lengthy. It took most of the year for the
Scots to compel the garrison at Stirling to surrender late in 1299. According to
his son, Thomas Gray was besieged twice at Norham, once for seven months
and once for about a year.[86] The Scots proved to be masters at the capture of
castles, not by lengthy sieges but by surprise assaults. The years before
Bannockburn saw an astonishing series of successes. At Linlithgow a group
of Scots entered the castle hidden in a haycart. At Roxburgh, James Douglas
used specially designed rope ladders with ingenious clamps that held them
firm. At Edinburgh, William Francis led a party up a steep and unexpected
rock-climbing route into the castle. He had served as a young man in the castle,
and had used this way to go down into the town in search of amorous
adventure.[87] It was not that the castles were ill garrisoned. In 1311 Roxburgh
was defended by twenty-four men-at-arms, eighteen crossbowmen, seventeen
hobelars, and over fifty archers. What the English were not prepared for was an
attack by camouflaged men at night, when the garrison were celebrating Shrove
Tuesday. The position was increasingly desperate, and it was hardly surprising
that the Gascon commander at Edinburgh, Pierre Libaud, deserted to the
Scots when the castle fell.[88] The Scots were similarly successful in taking
English-held castles in the late 1330s and early 1340s. Their strategy of then
slighting and destroying castles deprived the English of bases that they could
use in the future as centres of occupation. At Bothwell only half of the great
thirteenth-century keep still stands, for half was cast down after Andrew
Moray took it in 1337.

In England the wars in the north made clear the need to provide better
physical defences. The great castles of an earlier period, such as Bamburgh,
Warkworth, Alnwick, and Newcastle, had their part to play, but could not
provide the depth of defence at a local level that was needed. The northern
border in the thirteenth century was far less well provided with castles than was
the Welsh in the same period. Castle garrisons could not control large tracts of
land, and were themselves highly vulnerable once they left the security of stone
walls and towers to make sorties. Yet there was no alternative method of
defence available. In the difficult years of the middle of Edward II's reign,
quite substantial forces were placed in the castles of the north. In 1316–17 the
crown paid out just over £17,000 in garrison wages, and about £10,500 in the
following year. At Cockermouth the cost of garrisoning the castle with 159 men
for three weeks in the summer of 1316 came to about £100. In 1322 five knights,

---

[85] *Lanercost*, 231.   [86] *Scalacronica*, 147.
[87] Duncan (ed.), *John Barbour, the Bruce*, 368–73, 378–85, 388–95.
[88] *CDS* iii. 406–7; Barrow, *Robert Bruce*, 277; *Scalacronica*, 140.

thirty-four men-at-arms, forty hobelars, and forty archers defended Carlisle castle. Warkworth held thirty-one men-at-arms and seventy hobelars.[89]

What was needed in the north was far more castles, which could offer security at a local level. According to a sixteenth-century note, in 1322 'le prior et sez homes fled al castle de Skipton pur feare des Scottes', and there must have been many more who wished for the security of stone walls.[90] One solution was to militarize existing halls and manorial buildings. In 1305 Robert de Reymes obtained a licence to crenellate Aydon and also Shortflatt. Haughton was converted from hall into castle at some point in the fourteenth century. The characteristic defence of the region was to be the 'tower house', a relatively simple but well-fortified dwelling, of which the Vicar's Pele at Corbridge is a fine example. These buildings are undated, but the earliest probably do not date from earlier than the 1340s, and most were probably built in the later fourteenth century. The time of real difficulty in the north, the second decade of the fourteenth century, saw very little building of new defences. It was only when the danger from the Scottish raids had largely passed that the gentry of the region found the resources to start building the castles that had been so badly needed decades before.[91]

Was the transformation of English armies and the way they fought the work of a single military genius? Andrew Harclay has been seen as one possible candidate and Henry de Beaumont as another.[92] The former was the hero of Boroughbridge, where he persuaded his men to fight in the Scottish manner; the latter had lengthy military experience dating back to the Flanders campaign of 1297, and was the senior military man at the battle of Dupplin Moor in 1332. Such men were no doubt wise in the ways of war, but the evidence is simply not sufficient for it to be possible to apportion responsiblity for what amounted to a military revolution. It is possible that the Hainaulters present in the army that struggled in the hills and valleys of Weardale in 1327 brought new ideas with them. One Hainaulter, Walter de Mauny, having fought on that campaign, was the only royal household knight present at Dupplin Moor in 1332,

---

[89] M. C. Prestwich, 'English Castles in the Reign of Edward II', *Journal of Medieval History*, 8 (1982), 163–4.

[90] *The Bolton Priory Compotus 1286–1325, Together with a Priory Account Roll for 1377–78*, ed. I. Kershaw and D. M. Smith, Yorkshire Archaeological Society Record Series, 154 (Woodbridge, 2000), 503.

[91] P. Dixon, '*Mota, Aula et Turris*: The Manor-Houses of the Anglo-Scottish Border', in G. Meirion Jones and M. Jones (eds.), *Manorial Domestic Buildings in England and Northern France*, Society of Antiquaries of London Occasional Papers, 15 (1993), 27–36; P. Dixon, 'From Hall to Tower: The Change in Seigneurial Houses on the Anglo-Scottish Border After c.1250', in *TCE* iv. 97–9.

[92] For Harclay, see J. E. Morris, 'Mounted Infantry in Medieval Warfare', *TRHS*, 3rd ser., 8 (1914), 77–102, and for Beaumont, see Nicholson, *Edward III and the Scots*, 133.

and as such may have been in a strong position to give advice.[93] Experienced soldiers such as Thomas Ughtred were also in a good position to provide advice on the best way to tackle a difficult foe.[94]

CASUALTIES AND RANSOMS

War brought casualties. There can be no doubt that a great many ordinary people lost their lives. Some will have died in battle; more, probably, died in the course of the savage burnings and plunderings committed by both English and Scots. Yet in the upper echelons of society the number of deaths in the fighting itself was surprisingly few.[95] At Stirling Bridge the only named English casualties were the unpopular stout official Hugh Cressingham, along with Robert Somerville and his son.[96] The wage account for the army that won the battle of Falkirk shows losses of some 3,000, but the only notable English casualties were the Master of the English Templars, Brian le Jay, and John of Sawtry, of the same order.[97] At Roslin in 1303 Ralph Manton, cofferer of the wardrobe, was a major loss for the English, but no one else of note was killed in the skirmish. There were massive English casualties at Bannockburn. One chronicler commented, 'So many fine noblemen and valiant youth, so many noble horses, so much military equipment, costly garments and gold plate—all lost in one unfortunate day, one fleeting hour.'[98] Yet in comparison to the battles of the Hundred Years War, it is surprising how relatively few nobles fell. Only one earl, Gloucester, was killed, and that was said to be because he was not bearing his coat of arms and so was not recognized. Giles de Argentine, Robert de Clifford, Payn Tibetot, and William Marshal were the only other casualties named by the author of the *Vita* of Edward II, who also noted that over 500 men thought to have been killed had in fact been taken prisoner and were held for ransom.[99] At Dupplin Moor and Halidon Hill, English casualties were at a very low level. Scottish noble casualties in the fighting were not high until Edward III's reign. The horrifyingly long list of Scots executed by Edward I contrasted strikingly with the limited number who died in battle in his reign. Dupplin Moor, in contrast, saw a high level of Scottish casualties,

---

[93] Nicholson, *Edward III and the Scots*, 80.
[94] A. Ayton, 'Sir Thomas Ughtred and the Edwardian Military Revolution', in Bothwell (ed.), *The Age of Edward III*, 107–32.
[95] A. King, ' "According to the Custom Used in French and Scottish Wars": Prisoners and Casualties on the Scottish Marches in the Fourteenth Century', *Journal of Medieval History*, 28 (2002), 263–90.
[96] Pierre de Langtoft, 388.
[97] Barrow, *Robert Bruce*, 145.
[98] *Vita Edwardi*, 56.
[99] Baker, 8; *Vita Edwardi*, 53–6.

including three earls. At Halidon Hill in the next year five Scottish earls died, as well as very large numbers of lesser men. The list of those killed at Neville's Cross included two earls as well as the marshal, constable, chancellor, and chamberlain of Scotland.[100]

There was a major difference in the attitude of the English and the Scots towards the war that helps to explain the level of casualties. For the English, particularly in the earlier stages of the conflict, the Scots were rebels. As a result, the English would have considered that normal laws of war should not apply. Edward's execution of so many Scots, including Wallace, Simon Fraser, the earl of Atholl, and Bruce's brothers Thomas and Alexander, is explicable in these terms. At the same time, they were the product of the malevolence of an angry elderly man. For the Scots, however, the position was very different. For them, the war was just, and was fought between two independent nations. On that basis, the laws of war did apply. Prisoners were to be properly treated, and ransomed, rather than executed. There were, of course, more practical considerations as well. A fear of what might happen if the wheel of fortune turned might well dissuade men from treating their enemies with excessive brutality.

For the Scots, the income to be obtained from ransoms was a further good reason for avoiding killing the wealthy among their opponents. Ralph Neville was held to ransom for 2,000 marks; John de Hesilrigg was ransomed for 200 marks, after a two-year period of imprisonment; Robert Clifford of Ellingham was ransomed for £100; John de Grimstede's ransom was set at 100 marks; Luke de Wharton, a minor figure, had to pay 44 marks.[101] The archbishop of York paid out 200 marks to help John Giffard pay his ransom, 100 marks to Baldwin Frivill, and £20 to Simon Ward.[102] In the case of the earl of Hereford, captured after Bannockburn, a valuable exchange was negotiated, which saw Robert Wishart, bishop of Glasgow, Bruce's queen, his sister and daughter, and Donald of Mar all returned to Scotland.[103] The figures for individual ransoms were low in comparison to those that were demanded later in France, particularly after the battle of Poitiers, but even so, they provided the Scots with a useful form of revenue.

Nor was it simply individual ransoms that the Scots obtained. They also extorted substantial payments from communities in return for periods of truce. Durham negotiated at least eight such periods, costing up to 1,000 marks each time, and paid in all a minimum of some £5,000 to the Scots. Northumberland paid £2,000 on two occasions and an unknown sum on a third. One

[100] Nicholson, Edward III and the Scots, 89, 137; Grant, 'Disaster at Neville's Cross', 33.
[101] CDS iii, nos. 527, 1031; Ancient Petitions relating to Northumberland, ed. C. M. Fraser (Surtees Society, 1966), 140–1, 160–2.
[102] Historical Papers and Letters from Northern Registers, ed. J. Raine (RS, 1873), 248.
[103] CDS iii, no. 393.

Cumberland truce cost 2,200 marks. As the Scottish invasions continued, so it became more difficult for county communities to organize the payment of tribute in this way, and demands were made of smaller units. Bamburgh was charged £270 for a short truce in 1315. The practice was extended further south by the Scots as their raids were extended. In 1318, for example, the inhabitants of Ripon agreed to pay £1,000. It is impossible to calculate how much the Scots raised in this way during Edward II's reign, but estimates of £20,000 do not exaggerate.[104] After 1313 Edward II was unable to raise taxes in the north of England; what money could be raised there was being paid to the Scots. Robert Bruce was able to finance his war from money collected not from his own subjects, but from the English.

THE SCOTS AND THE NORTH OF ENGLAND

The Scottish war had a major impact on the north of England. Above all during Edward II's miserable reign, the raids led by men such as William Douglas caused immense damage. 'And in the same time came the Scots again into England, and destroyed Northumberland and burned that land, and robbed it, and killed men and women and took children that lay in cradles.'[105] Nor was it purely a matter of damage done by the Scots. They had their English emulators. The rebellion of Gilbert de Middleton, a royal household knight, in 1317, had its origins partly in discontent at the failure of Edward II's government to provide properly for the defence of the north. Gilbert and his followers collected protection money from Durham, just like the Scots. Their 'schavaldours', lightly armed horsemen, ravaged and plundered at will. One group seized Aydon castle in Northumberland and held it for a month, during which time they attacked Corbridge.[106] The English keepers of castles oppressed the surrounding territory, imposed heavy charges if people wanted refuge, and even demanded equivalent sums to those requested by the Scots in return for truces.[107]

The war accelerated changes in the landholding structure of the north, as some families failed to meet the challenge of the times while others thrived. William de Ros, lord of Wark, granted the castle of Wark to the king in 1317, in exchange for 400 marks' worth of land south of the Tees. The tough and

---

[104] J. Scammell, 'Robert I and the North of England', *EHR* 73 (1958), 393–402; McNamee, *Wars of the Bruces*, 131–40.

[105] *The Brut*, 210.

[106] M. C. Prestwich, 'Gilbert de Middleton and the Attack on the Cardinals, 1317', in T. Reuter (ed.), *Warriors and Churchmen in the Middle Ages: Essays Presented to Karl Leyser* (London, 1992), 179–94; *A History of Northumberland*, x, ed. H. H. E. Craster (Newcastle, 1914), 84.

[107] *CDS* iii, nos. 458, 463; *Registrum Palatinum Dunelmense*, ed. Hardy, iv. 131.

dangerous conditions on the border had clearly become too much for him.[108] The family that had held Warkworth throughout the thirteenth century was another that did not thrive in the early fourteenth century. John of Clavering's interests were increasingly concentrated on his Essex, rather than his Northumberland, estates. When he died in 1332, Henry Percy, a man far more active in the war, acquired Warkworth. Nicholas de Huntercombe sold his half of the barony of Wooler in Northumberland to John de Lilburn in 1326. These were perhaps exceptional cases. The families that did badly as a result of the wars were primarily those such as the Umfravilles who had done well through cross-border landholding in the peaceful years of the thirteenth century.

Some did well out of the war. Grants in return for good service, and even wages, were more important than any possible profits from plunder and extortion. The Percys are the prime example of a family that owed much of its fortune to good service in the Scottish wars. Early in Edward II's reign Henry Percy acquired Alnwick from the bishop of Durham. His death in 1314 meant a short minority during which William de Felton received two-thirds of the Percy rents from the family's Yorkshire estates, but the fortunes of the Percys soon rose further under his son, also Henry. At about the same time that he acquired Warkworth, he was granted all the forfeited Northumberland lands of Patrick, earl of March.[109]

At a slightly lower level of society Thomas de Rokeby is an example of one who profited from the wars. His success was founded on a stroke of luck, for he was the first man to sight the Scots on the unsuccessful 1327 Weardale campaign. For this he was knighted, and received a grant of £100 a year. He received a further £60 a year in 1337–8. He went on to help defend the castles of Edinburgh and Stirling. He was sheriff of Yorkshire from 1342 to 1349, and played a notable part in the battle of Neville's Cross. In 1347 he was promised £200 a year out of the revenues of Yorkshire, to maintain his new status as a banneret. With success came property, in both England and Ireland, where he was appointed governor in 1349.[110] Another who did well as a result of Neville's Cross was John de Coupland, the man who captured David II. His ambition and acquisitiveness, however, was such that he was murdered in 1363 by a group of local Northumberland gentry.

---

[108] *CDS* iii, no. 577.

[109] R. A. Lomas, *North-East England in the Middle Ages* (Edinburgh, 1992), 66; *CDS* iii, no. 142; *Ancient Petitions relating to Northumberland*, ed. Fraser 137; W. P. Hedley, *Northumberland Families* (Newcastle, 1968, 1970), i. 39.

[110] *CDS* iii, nos. 936, 1241, 1269, 1479; R. F. Frame, 'Thomas Rokeby, Sheriff of Yorkshire, the Custodian of David II', in Rollason and Prestwich (eds.), *The Battle of Neville's Cross*, 50–6; id., 'Thomas Rokeby, Sheriff of Yorkshire, Justiciar of Ireland', *Peritia*, 10 (1996), 274–9.

At the same time as the success stories, and the failures, there were other families that managed to adjust to the changing circumstances, and showed resilience simply in survival. Such families as the Herons, the Swinburns, and the Ogles did well through successful marriages, acquiring lands and offices. At about the worst time in the north, in 1316, in the midst of Scottish raids and the horrors of the famine, Robert de Lucker was building a new hall in his manor at Lucker in Northumberland. Robert de Reymes, an Ipswich man, acquired half of the barony of Bolam just before the onset of war, in 1295. He faced enormous difficulties in Edward II's reign. In 1315 he claimed that he had lost horses and armour worth 100 marks, that he had to pay a 500 mark ransom to the Scots, and that his lands had been destroyed, at a loss of £1,000. His castle at Aydon was taken over by supporters of Gilbert de Middleton for a time in 1317. Yet he survived, and served as a knight of the shire for Northumberland in 1322. At his death his manor house at Bolam lay in ruins, and all the tenants and stock had gone. Shortflatt, which he also owned, was in similar plight. Yet his son, who died of the Black Death, did well, and like his father served in parliament, and as sheriff. The family continued, and was well integrated into the gentry society of Northumberland.[111]

The north of England, especially the far north, was reduced to a horrific state of devastation as a result of the Scottish raids. There are difficulties in assessing quite how serious this was. Men had an interest in exaggerating claims of destruction, so as to reduce demands for rent or taxation. Some of the problems were the result of famine and murrain, not war, and the pattern was not uniform, with some districts much less affected than others. Recovery was possible.[112] Yet despite this, the consistent weight of the evidence, particularly for the second decade of the fourteenth century, goes to show that the Scots inflicted damage of a kind not seen since at least the eleventh century.

Wallace's invasion of 1297 was a dreadful foretaste of what was to come. As a result of his depredations, records show that the mills of Norhamshire and Islandshire were destroyed, and the value of tithes fell to between a third and a half of their normal level. The parish church at Longhorsley was destroyed. In the west, records of ecclesiastical taxation for the diocese of Carlisle reveal that in 1301 fourteen parishes were exempted from tax, and sixty others had their burden reduced by a third, because of the damage that had been done. At Bolton in Allerdale the grange and two mills were destroyed and rental income badly affected.[113] At Embledon one of the two mills was burned and the value of the manor reduced from £48 to £36. The Tweed fisheries

[111] Hedley, *Northumberland Families*, ii. 23–5, 274; Dixon, 'From Hall to Tower', 97.
[112] Lomas, *North-East England in the Middle Ages*, 54–74.
[113] C. J. McNamee, 'William Wallace's Invasion of Northern England in 1297', *Northern History*, 26 (1990), 45, 49–50.

were halved in value.[114] The effects of even a short period of ravaging could be catastrophic.

Edward II's reign was the period when the north was put to the rack. There are many stories from these years of the misery caused by the war. Robert Blackburn served for twenty-two years in the war, and was taken prisoner when severely wounded at the fall of Berwick castle. He lost his brother and ten friends at Bannockburn. All his income from lands on the border, and from fishing rights in the Tweed, was gone.[115] Robert Clifford of Ellingham was captured at Bannockburn and had to pay a ransom of £100. He claimed that he had lost rents for six years, worth £100 a year, and that he had helped in the defence of Bamburgh at his own expense. The burgesses of Bamburgh successfully asked to be relieved of an annual payment of 26 marks, and arrears of a further 6 marks, since the place was completely burned by the Scots, and many of their neighbours, wives, and children taken into captivity.[116] At Prudhoe the castle and manor were 'wasted' by the Scots, as were the other possessions of Robert de Umfraville, earl of Angus.[117]

The regular Scottish raids of the second decade of the fourteenth century were extremely destructive. An inquisition taken in 1324 at Felton in Northumberland showed that the manorial centre, once valued at £5 a year, was worth nothing, and 260 acres of land, formerly worth 6d. an acre, were valueless, as were 18 acres of meadow. Rents from burgage tenants used to bring in £2 6s. and had fallen to 8s. Five cottagers were reduced in number to one. The watermill, in the past worth £6 13s. 4d., was now only worth £2. The forest and park were valueless as there were no animals left there. The tax records for 1296 show that Felton's inhabitants had been assessed at almost £20. In contrast, the 1336 record shows a value of £1. At Gunnerton an inquest made in 1325 revealed land that had been worth 8d. per acre lying waste and tenant holdings largely abandoned. East Swinburn saw fourteen men assessed for the tax of 1296, with a total valuation just over £21. The 1336 assessment listed five men and a valuation of 17s. 1d. Two of those five were shepherds; arable farming had been abandoned in favour of pastoral.[118]

The situation was no better in the west. The parish of Stanwix near Carlisle was said to be totally destroyed by 1318. The temporalities of Lanercost priory were so badly damaged as not to be worth assessing, and those of Wetherall priory had fallen from over £50 in 1291 to a mere £4. Burgh-by-Sands, worth £50 according to the 1291 valuation, was assessed at 50s.

[114] CIPM iii. 304–5.   [115] CDS iii, no. 624.

[116] Ancient Petitions relating to Northumberland, ed. Fraser, 161–2, 181–2.

[117] CIPM vi, no. 607.

[118] A History of Northumberland, 15 vols. (Newcastle upon Tyne, 1893–1940), vols. iv and vii, ed. J. C. Hodgson, iv. 306–8, 324; vii. 233–5.

There was considerable discontent with local officials. Some of the local gentry, such as Anthony de Lucy and John of Kirkbride, were bitterly opposed to Andrew Harclay and his brother John. The latter, as keeper of Carlisle castle, was said to have caused so much anger by his activities that all the influential people of Gilsland and Liddel had gone over to the Scots.[119]

Records of revaluations of ecclesiastical taxation also tell a sorry tale. By 1318 Northumberland was simply not included, for there was no income worth taxing. All the valuations in the diocese of Carlisle were reduced by at least half, and similar reductions were applied to parishes on the route through Yorkshire that the Scots had taken. Fountains abbey had been used by the Scots as a base, and it was said to have been so hard-hit, its granges and similar buildings burned and destroyed, that there was not enough to provide for the monks. In 1319 the exemption of the northern counties from lay taxation because of the Scottish raids was extended to include even Lancashire, so far-reaching was the damage.[120] Some religious houses in the north were dispersed in 1320, because they no longer had sufficient resources to provide for their residents. They included Rosedale, Marton, and Bolton priory.[121]

The case of Bolton illustrates some of the problems involved in assessing the real extent of damage from the Scottish raids. The letter from the archbishop of York asking other houses to accept canons from Bolton explained that the house had been severely affected by the cattle murrain as well as the raids. Nor was the economy of the monastery damaged beyond repair. The canons who left in 1320 were not gone for long. There were signs of some limited recovery by 1325. The house acquired a wealthy living in the early 1350s, and a substantial rebuilding programme began.[122] Bolton, however, lay in Yorkshire. Further north, in Northumberland, the relative impact of the Scots was surely much greater than that of the famine and the murrain. Even there, however, the capacity existed for recovery, though this continued to be hindered by Scottish raids in Edward III's reign. A letter described the way in which raiders in 1340 under the earls of Sutherland and March came within two miles of Bamburgh, taking 2,000 cattle, as well as some of the inhabitants for ransom. They then set their torches to the land.[123]

Despite the widespread destruction, this was a remarkably resilient society. Figures of Durham's tithe incomes in Northumberland show a catastrophic fall

[119] CDS iii, no. 675.
[120] McNamee, Wars of the Bruces, 87–8, 95; Historical Papers and Letters from Northern Registers, ed. Raine, 282.
[121] Historical Papers and Letters from Northern Registers, ed. Raine, 306–8, 318, 322–3.
[122] I. Kershaw, Bolton Priory: The Economy of a Northern Monastery 1286–1325 (Oxford, 1973), 16–17, 179–80.
[123] SC 1/54/30.

up to the years around 1320, but ten years later were up to about half the pre-war level. They rose from £2 in 1318/19 to £100 in 1329/30, and £186 in 1338/9. At Corbridge income from two watermills had been £24 in 1310; in 1352 it was £20.[124] It was possible to buy seed corn so as to bring fields back into cultivation, to buy or hire stock, and to persuade tenants to return. It was also possible to protect revenues to some extent by switching from arable farming to sheep. The raids were not so severe as to destroy settlements completely. Mortham in Yorkshire, which vanished after the 1316 raid, was a rare exception to this rule.[125] There was some rebuilding of manorial halls so as to provide better defences, and some new fortifications were created, though it was probably not until the later fourteenth century that there was widespread construction of tower houses in the north.[126]

CONCLUSION

The war at the beginning was brutal, and this does much to explain how attitudes were quickly set. The English sack of Berwick in 1296 was horrific, with the town put to the torch and its inhabitants to the sword. At the same time, the invasion of the district round Carlisle by a powerful group of Scottish earls brought the horrors of war across the border. Even worse was the raid to Corbridge and Hexham. There 200 schoolboys, it was alleged, were burned alive in their school. Women and children were savagely killed, according to the English propaganda.[127] The raids of Wallace's men in the following year saw yet more horrors perpetrated. He was said to have tied up old men, priests, and nuns, and thrown them off bridges, and to have forced naked men and women to sing for him. After Wallace's victory at Stirling Bridge in 1297, the body of the English treasurer of Scotland, Hugh Cressingham, was skinned to provide the Scots with trophies.[128] There were, of course, atrocities committed by the English in Scotland. In Edward II's reign Marmaduke Basset was so troubled by his conscience over what he had done (it is not known what this was) that he went to the papal curia to seek absolution. Indeed, he was so concerned when he returned to England from the curia without sufficient evidence of the absolution that he went back there once more to get it.[129]

[124] Lomas, *North-East England in the Middle Ages*, 59; *History of Northumberland*, x. 97.
[125] McNamee, *Wars of the Bruces*, 82.
[126] *CPR 1341–3*, 4, 179, 221; Dixon, 'From Hall to Tower', 85–107.
[127] Stones (ed.), *Anglo-Scottish Relations*, 106–7; *Documents and Records Illustrating the History of Scotland*, ed. Palgrave, 149.
[128] Guisborough, 296, 303; Rishanger, 226.
[129] *CPR 1317–21*, 399.

As the war continued, so national antagonisms acquired their own momentum. The English had little more than abuse to hurl against the untrustworthiness of the Scots. Bruce was accused of tyranny, and the familiar tale was told of burned villages, captured castles, the flow of innocent blood, and the damage to churches and their possessions.[130] The Scots responded with the splendid, simple eloquence of a call to freedom. 'Ah, freedom is a noble thing,' John Barbour would write later in his life of Robert Bruce.[131] The Declaration of Arbroath was a letter from the Scottish earls and barons sent to the pope in 1320, and fits into an established tradition of such letters. It used the conventional prose rhythm of the *cursus*. It aimed to justify Bruce's right to the Scottish throne, but what was particularly striking was the way that it stressed that the Scots were bound to their king 'for the maintaining of our freedom'. Stirringly, it declared that 'As long as a hundred of us remain alive, we will never on any conditions be subjected to the lordship of the English. For we fight not for glory, nor riches, nor honours, but for freedom alone, which no good man gives up except with his life.' This splendid terminology was lifted from Sallust's *Conspiracy of Catiline*. The freedom of the realm of Scotland had been emphasized before, notably in 1301, but the Declaration of 1320 suggested an identification of personal and national freedom.[132] The English opposition to Edward I in 1297 had suggested in strong terms that the king's policies would lead to servitude for his people. The Scots were saying something similar, but they said it far better.

[130] See e.g. *Historical Papers and Letters from Northern Registers*, ed. Raine, 220–3, 238, 240.

[131] Duncan (ed.), *John Barbour, the Bruce*, 57.

[132] E. J. Cowan, *'For Freedom Alone': The Declaration of Arbroath, 1320* (East Linton, 2003), 57–60, 146. See also the essays in G. W. S. Barrow (ed.), *The Declaration of Arbroath: History, Significance, Setting* (Edinburgh, 2003), which among other things explain (on p. 29) the difficulty that Americans may have in pronouncing 'Arbroath'.

CHAPTER 10

England under Edward III

With hindsight, it appears that there was a complete transformation of political life when Edward III came to power in 1330. At the time this cannot have seemed to be the case; here was yet another small clique of courtiers seizing power. Those responsible for the palace coup of 1330 had not built up any power in the localities, and had no obvious backing among the central administrators and officials. Edward was a young man with no experience and little to recommend him. Yet within a few years he had established a wide power base. He was much more than a highly successful war leader; he had political skills and the capacity to win the support of the nation he ruled.

THE RESTORATION OF ROYAL AUTHORITY

The difficult position in which the monarchy stood in 1330 was turned round in two main ways. Edward II had been inept in war and injudicious in his use of patronage; his son was quite the reverse. The victory over the Scots at Halidon Hill in 1333 transformed the prestige of the crown, even though it led, not to ultimate conquest, but to an exhausting series of further campaigns. Secondly, skilful use of patronage enabled Edward to retain the support of the existing elite, while at the same time building up backing among those rising in his service.[1] The war with France, which began in 1337, created problems resembling those that had faced Edward I forty years previously. Heavy taxation, prises of wool, and corruption in local government, combined with a lack of success abroad, led to political crisis, but the very different style of Edward III meant that this would not be a rerun of the events of 1297.

The amount of land that had been forfeited to the crown in the recent political upheavals, and especially Mortimer's fall, meant that Edward III was in a good position to reward those who had backed his coup in 1330. William Montague, for example, received the lordship of Denbigh and important lands

---

[1] For discussion of Edward's patronage, see J. S. Bothwell, 'Edward III and the "New Nobility": Largesse and Limitation in Fourteenth-Century England', *EHR* 112 (1997), 111–40.

in Wales in 1331. With Montague, Robert Ufford, William Clinton, and William Bohun were notable recipients of Edward's generosity, which peaked in 1337 when all four men were elevated to earldoms. Others involved in the events at Nottingham in 1330, such as Thomas Bradeston, received due rewards. The members of the little group were even given magnificent jackets of Aylesham red enhanced with purple velvet and gold thread.[2] Edward's brother John of Eltham was granted substantial estates that had been in Queen Isabella's hands; his death in 1336 again made land available to the king. Edward's patronage was not confined to a narrow group. Surprisingly, some grants went to previously disgraced families. The earl of Arundel, to whom Edward restored his title in 1330, received part of the forfeited Mortimer estate, and Hugh Despenser, son of the executed younger Despenser, also received some favours. There were even some who had played a part in Isabella and Mortimer's regime who continued in favour under Edward III. Gilbert Talbot, royal chamberlain in 1328, received one of Isabella's manors. John Darcy was another political survivor who, having supported Isabella and Mortimer, received some of their lands in the 1330s. Roger Swinnerton, one of Edward II's household knights, had been conspicuous in always finding himself on the winning side in every political dispute. It was at Edward III's hands that he received more rewards than he had done in the past.[3] Following the Ordinances of 1311, every attempt had been made to control and limit royal grants of land. The situation in the 1330s was rather different, in that the lands that Edward had at his disposal to grant out were not part of the hereditary estate of the crown, but were lands that had come his way largely by forfeiture. In 1337 the confiscation of the estates held by French religious houses (the 'alien priories') provided Edward with further lands that he could grant out. Even allowing for his different circumstances, Edward's policies were strikingly different from that of the past. Royal generosity was not limited to a narrow clique. Certainly the king rewarded his friends, but the spread of royal munificence was wide. Nor was Edward conspicuously careless with his resources. In many cases grants took the form of monetary payments, with land promised once it became available. There was some criticism. In 1340 Archbishop Stratford, by then Edward's opponent, not his chief minister, charged the king with making grants on such a scale that the royal treasury was exhausted. Thomas Gray, in his *Scalacronica*, commented on the way in

---

[2] C. Shenton, 'Edward III and the Coup of 1330', in Bothwell (ed.), *The Age of Edward III*, 32–3.
[3] For Edward's patronage in this period, J. S. Bothwell, 'Edward III, the English Peerage, and the 1337 Earls: Estate Distribution in Fourteenth-Century England', in Bothwell (ed.), *The Age of Edward III*, 35–52.

which so much land was granted out that the king had to live on subsidies, which were a considerable burden on the populace.[4]

Land was not the only means of patronage available to Edward III. Wardships and marriages could be granted to those he favoured. In 1343, for example, the king arranged for Thomas Dagworth, a notable military captain but a man of very limited means, to marry the widow of the earl of Ormond, a granddaughter of Edward I and a woman who controlled substantial dower lands.[5] On occasion the king might strike a bargain. In 1336 William de Montague paid 1,000 marks to have the lucrative wardship and marriage of Roger Mortimer; the details suggest that this was likely to prove a good investment for William.[6] Annuities, grants of money, were also important, offering a way of rewarding men without damaging the long-term resources of the crown. There was a balance to be struck, and the results suggest that Edward III struck it correctly.

The ranks of officialdom, particularly those at the centre of government, were not transformed following the coup of 1330. Experience was needed to provide efficient government. The keeper of the privy seal, Richard de Bury, was the one official who was party to Edward's coup in 1330. Naturally, he remained in office. The most important ministerial change was the appointment of John Stratford, bishop of Winchester, as chancellor; he was to be the dominant administrator during the 1330s. His brother Robert became chancellor of the exchequer in 1331, and would in time succeed John at the chancery. At the treasury, William Melton, archbishop of York, returned briefly to office in 1330, to be replaced after four months by another experienced man, William Airmyn, bishop of Norwich. There was little continuity in this office in the 1330s, however, with eight different men holding the post. As steward of the household, Hugh Turplington, killed in Edward's coup at Nottingham, was replaced by Ralph Neville of Raby. Likewise, the keepership of the wardrobe was held by five different men in the course of the 1330s. These changes, however, were not an indication of political instability. In the shires, change was more spectacular than at the centre, with a wholesale turnover of sheriffs and custodians of royal castles following the coup of 1330.[7]

These were not years of major administrative change; the frenetic pace of reform that had characterized Edward II's later years was not maintained. Much effort went into dealing with the problem of maintaining law and order. The system of home staples, introduced briefly in 1326, was revived

---

[4] Tout, Chapters, iii. 39 n. 3; Scalacronica, 167.
[5] Bothwell, 'Edward III and the "New Nobility"', 121.
[6] Cal. Fine Rolls, 1327–37, 488–9.
[7] For these changes, see Tout, Chapters, iii. 35–46.

in 1333, only to be abandoned again in 1334 at parliament's request.[8] The royal household revived as the administrative centre of government; it had been drastically cut back by the Despensers. Within the household, the department of the chamber became increasingly important, though the wardrobe still played a major role in the organization of war. The office of the privy seal became much more significant, especially with the appointment of Richard de Bury to its keepership. There was experimentation with the escheatorships, with eight local ones created in 1332, but a reversion to traditional practice in 1335.[9] The financing and organization of the Scottish wars meant that Edward had to make significant demands on his people. In 1332 he was granted a fifteenth and tenth, with the same in 1334 and 1336.

THE DEMANDS OF WAR

The French war, which began in 1337, created a very different situation from that with Scotland. Demands were on a much larger scale, and it was not long before Edward III was faced with a major, complex political crisis in 1340 and 1341. In some ways the position looked similar to that which had faced Edward I in 1297. The king entered into financial obligations that could not be met. Heavy taxes combined with seizures of wool and foodstuffs, combined with the corruption of local officials, led to widespread discontent in the localities. To make matters worse, the economic climate was extremely difficult. The autumn of 1338 saw heavy rains, and it was followed by a hard winter, which killed off autumn-sown crops. This led to a bad harvest in 1339, when wheat yields fell to levels not seen since the famine years of 1315–16.[10] The background was of a serious shortage of coin: there was probably well under £1 million in circulation, less than half the level of the initial years of the century. The government at home faced increasingly bitter criticism from the king and his associates abroad; they felt that they were trying to fight a war without receiving proper financial assistance. By 1340 Edward faced widespread popular discontent, combined with the opposition of an archbishop of Canterbury he had dismissed from his government.

In 1337 it was clear that major financial efforts were needed. Edward had not built up a treasure in the way that Edward I had at the start of his conflict with the French. Further taxation was needed, and in parliament the king obtained a generous grant of a fifteenth and tenth for three years. Since 1334 the assessment of these lay taxes had remained unchanged; a single tenth and fifteenth was assessed at about £38,000. In convocation, the clergy granted the king a

[8] Lloyd, *Wool Trade*, 121.   [9] See Tout, *Chapters*, iii. 49–53.
[10] Murimuth, 88–9; *Agrarian History*, i. 797.

tenth, also for three years, each of which raised about £15,000. These were substantial demands to make of the people, even greater than those of the 1290s:

> Now there runs every year in England
> The fifteenth penny, to everyone's damage
>
> .   .   .
>
> And makes ordinary folk sell their cows, utensils and clothes
> It does not please to pay the fifteenth to the last penny.[11]

The poet went on to complain that the collection of wool was an even bigger grievance. It was wool, the 'sovereign merchandise and jewel of the realm', that the government considered offered the best method of financing the war.[12] In September 1336 an assembly of merchants agreed to pay a subsidy of 20s. on each sack of wool exported, in addition to the customs of 6s. 8d. a sack agreed in 1275. In the following year, however, a new plan was produced, and agreed by the merchants: 30,000 sacks of wool would be collected; their sale at an overseas staple would yield about £200,000, which would be lent to the king. As time proceeded, so the situation became more difficult. Royal officials failed to collect the requisite quantities of wool in England, and the king become more and more frustrated. Wool that had been exported to Dordrecht was taken over by royal officials, when the merchants refused to advance £276,000, more than had been originally agreed. The failure of the scheme did not mean the end of wool levies. In 1340 a 'loan' of 20,000 sacks was imposed, though as it turned out it was not a severe burden, for it yielded fewer than 1,000 sacks. Records of the inquiries made into the activities of officials at a local level reveal that there was widespread corruption and extortion surrounding the prises of wool. Incorrect balances were used for weighing, and bribes were exacted.[13] Taking all the demands made by the crown from 1337 to 1341 together, including lay and clerical taxes, customs duties, and seizures of wool, one calculation is that the overall total in cash and kind amounted to about £665,000.[14] This was a massive burden.

Victuals were also taken, for provisioning the English military efforts in Scotland and the Low Countries. The techniques used by this period were rather different from the past. Instead of orders being given to sheriffs to

---

[11] *Political Songs*, 183 (my translation).   [12] *Rot. Parl.* i. 246.

[13] Lloyd, *Wool Trade*, 145–58; E. B. Fryde, *William de la Pole, Merchant and King's Banker* (London, 1988), 148; *The 1341 Royal Inquest in Lincolnshire*, ed. B. W. McLane (Lincoln Record Society, 1988), *passim*.

[14] Ormrod, 'The Crown and the English Economy', in Campbell (ed.), *Before the Black Death*, 183, and see the tables ibid. 153, 161. See also the tables in <http://www.le.ac.uk/hi/bon/ESFDB/frameset.html>.

provide specific quantities of foodstuffs, individuals were given commissions, extending widely, to collect grain and other goods. In 1338, for example, Thomas Dunstable was ordered to collect 3,600 quarters of wheat, 4,100 quarters of malt, 200 quarters of beans and peas, 1,340 sides of bacon, 400 of beef, 4,100 of mutton, 40 lasts of herring, and 5,900 stones of cheese in seventeen counties. Dunstable was accused of a great many offences, such as taking money to exempt places from prise, taking victuals for his own use, using false measures, and even falsely accusing men of rebellion and imprisoning them until they paid him fines. In Lincolnshire food had been taken to be sent on to Perth, but in several cases it had never left the county. In 1338 Dunstable was ordered to be arrested and brought to answer before the council, and in 1339 a commission was set up to investigate his activities.[15]

Demands for military service caused fewer problems than they had done in the 1290s, for there was no resentment on the part of those serving the king in Flanders, who were in receipt of his generous offer of double wages. A rare complaint came from Earl Warenne, who argued in 1338 that his lordship of Bromfield and Yale was more heavily burdened with a demand for a hundred men than neighbouring lordships, but orders to the commissioners of array should have resolved this issue.[16] There were, however, significant doubts about Edward's overall strategy. The earl of Salisbury, according to Thomas Gray in the *Scalacronica*, was so alarmed in 1338 at the cost of the continental alliances that he raised the issue in parliament.[17] However, his protest did not prevent him from participating in the king's campaigns in the Low Countries; quite unlike Roger Bigod in 1297, he was no opposition leader.

While the populace was aggrieved by the scale of the demands placed upon it by the government, the king was increasingly angry at the difficulties he faced in financing the war. Severe problems were evident as early as December 1337, when royal envoys demanded that the wool merchants should provide £276,000 by mid-Lent, and the latter said that they could afford to pay no more than 100,000 marks. Subsidies promised to foreign allies by the end of 1337 totalled £124,000. With insufficient income to match expenditure on troops, foreign allies, and all the other costs of war, Edward III had to turn to credit finance. The Florentine company of the Bardi had a long history of lending to the crown, though not on a very large scale, while the Peruzzi, also from Florence, had dealt with the younger Despenser as well as the government. At the start of the war, up to Michaelmas 1338, the two Italian

---

[15] *1341 Royal Inquest in Lincolnshire*, ed. McLane, xii. 2–3, 14, 72–3, 106, 127, and see index under Dunstable; J. R. Maddicott, *The English Peasantry and the Demands of the Crown, 1294–1341*, Past and Present, suppl. 1 (1975), 54; *CPR 1338–40*, 145, 283.
[16] *CCR 1337–9*, 452.
[17] *Scalacronica*, 168.

companies lent over £70,000. From then until early 1340 they lent a much smaller sum, just over £28,000. The two Italian companies were in increasing difficulty. The more they were involved with Edward III, the less their depositors put trust in them. The English king had to find other sources of loans. Paul de Monte Florum, an Italian operating in the Low Countries, raised much money for Edward from other Italians, such as the Portinari, who advanced just over £6,000. Monte Florum raised over £25,000 on the security of the king's great crown and other royal jewels and plate. Merchants in the Low Countries, however, charged extortionate sums in interest, and demanded solid guarantees of repayment. In 1340 the earls of Derby and Northampton were held as security for loans made to the English king.[18]

English merchants had not been in a position to offer assistance to Edward I, but now William de la Pole helped Edward III. By November 1338 he had provided over £33,000, and, as the Bardi and Peruzzi dropped out, so he came to take their place, advancing over £67,000 between December 1338 and September of the next year. Much of what he lent was raised by him from other English merchants.[19] Despite every effort, however, the king's ever-increasing obligations to his allies, combined with the sums he owed to his financial creditors, far outstripped what he could raise. One estimate is that by the time that Edward returned to England early in 1340 he owed over £100,000 to merchants and moneylenders, and over £200,000 to his allies. The king's view was that the government in England had failed him.

In 1338 arrangements for the government of England were set out in the Walton Ordinances, issued shortly before the king set sail for the Low Countries. These have been regarded by historians as 'elaborate machinery for ensuring that his [the king's] control was exercised from Brabant', and as 'the clearest exposition of the views of the high curialist party'.[20] They provided for much more effective royal control over the exchequer than in the past. Privy seal warrants were needed to authorize all save the most routine payments. The king was to be much better informed than he had been about the overall financial position. There were elements in the document that reflected the reforms of the Despenser years, such as the requirement that household expenditure was to be reviewed weekly and monthly. Yet there were also echoes of earlier measures inspired by the crown's opponents. The provision for local election of sheriffs, which was largely ineffective in practice, goes back to the Articuli super Cartas of 1300. It seems unlikely that, as was once suggested, Edward deliberately adopted a policy of local election of sheriffs so

---

[18] E. B. Fryde, Studies in Medieval Trade and Finance (London, 1983), vii. 1146–7, 1149, 1153–5, 1159, 1164.

[19] Ibid. vii. 1153, 1159–60, 1171–2.

[20] Harriss, King, Parliament and Public Finance, 241; Tout, Chapters, iii. 77, 144–50.

as 'to set off the lesser landed gentry of the shires and the commercial classes against the magnates of church and state, who were his natural critics'.[21] It is more probable that the measure was a sop to critics of the government. The arrangements for an audit committee are reminiscent of those set out in the draft version of the Ordinances of 1311, and would be surprising to find in a context of high curialism. The origins of other clauses may lie in criticisms of Edward III's policies. In a section dealing with royal patronage, the Walton Ordinances explain that those receiving grants should pay the full customary annual renders, so preventing the king from being as generous as he had been in the past. One clause stated that no debts should be paid off in instalments, or respited. That was hardly likely to be a popular measure, but it surely reflects criticism of the king's apparently profligate patronage policy. One clause required the treasurer to find out how much the king owed to merchants (the Bardi and Peruzzi were presumably intended), and how much in other large debts, and how much would be needed to acquit him of debt and maintain his position.[22] Again, this looks likely to have been the result of some censuring of Edward's policies, presumably in parliament. Unfortunately, the parliament rolls are missing for 1336 to 1339, apart from the survival of a few petitions, so this must remain a hypothesis. What the Walton Ordinances show, however, is that Edward III was sensitive to the situation.

The Walton Ordinances, however, did not work. It was impractical to try to exercise control from abroad by means of the privy seal; what happened was that the government in England was constantly hampered rather than helped by the instructions it received. Proper accountability was impossible to maintain, for in the case of many officials, 'as soon as orders are sent to them to render accounts, they cross the sea and remain under the protection of the men who are there'.[23] It made obvious sense to put the government in England on a proper footing with an effective regency. Archbishop Stratford had been engaged on diplomatic activity in France from July 1338 until October 1339. On his return to England he became principal councillor to the nominal regent, the king's 9-year-old son Edward.

THE CRISIS OF 1340–1341

Archbishop Stratford's task as chief councillor was impossible. In parliament in October he explained that the king was in debt to the tune of £300,000.[24] Although the magnates were prepared to offer a tenth, taken in kind on the

---

[21] Ibid. iii. 75.   [22] Ibid. iii. 144–50.   [23] Tout, *Chapters*, iii. 94–7.
[24] For these parliaments, see E. B. Fryde, 'Parliament and the French War, 1336–40', in his *Studies in Medieval Trade and Finance*, v. 255–69.

same basis as a clerical tithe, the representatives were not ready to make any grant, and asked for time to consult their local communities. Parliament in January 1340 was unhelpful. The magnates duly granted a tenth of produce, but the Commons offered a levy of 30,000 sacks of wool, on conditions that the council considered had to be referred to the king. In February Edward III himself returned to England. His presence in parliament at the end of March 1340 transformed the atmosphere, and the magnates and Commons together made a grant of a ninth for two years. Like the previous tenth, which it replaced, it was to be taken in the form of produce rather than coin. The grant was not unconditional. In a petition the representatives set out a number of demands. Magna Carta and the Charter of the Forest were to be maintained. Infringements of the liberties of the Church should be corrected in parliament. They asked that a council of magnates should be elected in parliament and made answerable there. It should have full authority in the king's absence on military business. Investigation of the taxes of recent years was needed, for it was suspected that there had been widespread corruption. Future taxes should be spent on the king's needs in war. There was also a demand, reminiscent of the Ordinances of 1311, for an inquiry into crown lands granted out since 1307; and a request for the resumption of grants.[25] Statutes were duly issued, and the demands were largely met, though there was no inquiry into grants of royal lands.

The new tax of a ninth did not transform royal finances as expected. One reason for making this unusual grant in kind was the serious shortage of coinage in the country. Since people had no cash, it appeared to make sense to take a tax in kind. However, the theory was that the goods would then be sold by the crown, but of course people had little money with which to buy them, and could not meet the prices that the crown had fixed. The ninth was expected to raise £100,000, with a similar sum in the next year when it was to be repeated, and by June 1340 no less than £190,000 had been assigned on it. However, in practice it yielded no more than about £15,000 by November 1340, though eventually it raised about £65,000. A forced loan of 20,000 sacks of wool was another failure, yielding fewer than 1,000 sacks. There were no new ideas; the government appeared bankrupt, both financially and intellectually. All it could do was to try to count sheep, an exercise in which it again failed dismally.[26]

There was not one royal administration at this time, but two, one in England and one in Flanders, where the king had his household officials. Most notable was the keeper of the privy seal, William Kilsby. Thomas Hatfield, receiver of

---

[25] Harris, *King, Parliament and Public Finance*, 518–20.
[26] Fryde, *William de la Pole*, 146–8, 50.

the chamber, was another important figure, a man who had been catapulted from nowhere into the higher ranks of officialdom. William Norwell, keeper of the wardrobe, also had a major role. Among laymen, there was John Darcy, steward of the household, and the influential, corrupt John Molyns, a chamber knight. These men, along with the king himself and military commanders such as the earl of Salisbury, were increasingly infuriated at the failure of the government in England to provide the funds that were so urgently needed for the war.[27]

There was an extraordinary atmosphere of malice and intrigue in 1340. The level of the king's fury can be seen by the accusations he levied against Archbishop Stratford at the papal curia. Stratford had apparently advised Edward to go abroad without proper supplies of horses or money, and had failed to send sufficient funds. 'I believe that the archbishop wished me, by lack of money, to be betrayed and killed.'[28] According to a London chronicler, one loyal official in England kept the king informed about the activities, and failures, of the government there. He urged Edward to return privately and to go to the Tower; if he did so, he would find sufficient treasure to continue the war and conquer his enemies. This advice was duly accepted, and in a dramatic move typical of the man, Edward unexpectedly sailed up the Thames, arriving at the Tower in the middle of the night of 30 November, to find the constable 'out of town'.[29] A rapid purge of the administration took place, far more dramatic than that conducted by Edward I on his return from Gascony in 1289.

The victims were headed by John Stratford's brother, the chancellor Robert Stratford. Roger Northburgh, the treasurer, was dismissed. The chief clerks of the chancery were all removed. John Stonor, chief justice of the King's Bench, and four justices of Common Pleas were dismissed. One of the justices, Richard Willoughby, was questioned for two full days by royal commissioners; he was so exhausted by this that his voice gave out.[30] The financiers William de la Pole, his brother Richard, and John Pulteney were among the others who were objects of the king's anger. John Stratford himself escaped from the king's clutches and took refuge in Canterbury. The government in England had come up against the most formidable of all possible opponents, the king himself.

The stage was set for a remarkable struggle between the king and his former leading minister, which showed the power both of propaganda and of parliament. Stratford in his initial case condemned the king for adhering, like Rehoboam, to the counsel of young men. The arrests of the officials were

[27] For these men, see Tout, *Chapters*, iii. 84 ff.
[28] *Calendar of Papal Letters*, ii. 584–5.
[29] *The French Chronicle of London*, ed. G. J. Aungier (Camden Society, 1844), 83–4.
[30] Ibid. 87.

contrary to the law of the land and Magna Carta. Edward was in danger of losing the hearts of his people, and should hold a parliament in which proper inquiries could be made about the way in which the war had been financed. Stratford himself was ready to submit to the judgement of his peers, 'saving always the estate of holy church'.[31] There was little that was novel in this, but what is interesting is the emphasis on the support of the people as a whole, and, above all, on parliament. The document was written in French, rather than Latin, and was obviously designed for wide circulation. Stratford followed this with further letters. One sent to his fellow bishops stressed the need to preserve the freedom of the Church, its rights and its liberties; Stratford was attempting to widen the whole basis of the dispute.[32]

A lengthy pamphlet, known as the *Libellus Famosus*, was written to justify the king's position. The chronicler Robert Avesbury attributed this to Adam Orleton, but this seems unlikely.[33] Its language shows that it was not intended for wide circulation, for it is in a somewhat ornate Latin. The core of the argument was that Stratford had failed to provide the king with the financial supplies he needed. He was guilty of malice and malpractice, and it was through his advice that the crown had earlier been so weakened by prodigal gifts and improper alienations. This provoked a lengthy self-justification from Stratford, who was able to answer the accusations against him point by point very effectively.[34]

The issues between king and archbishop were settled when parliament met in April 1341. According to a London chronicle, for a whole week Stratford, his brother Robert, and Roger of Northburgh were refused admittance to parliament, at Kilsby's instigation. Then Earl Warenne protested at the presence of Kilsby and the other officials. John Darcy, Kilsby, and others left without a word, and at the earl of Arundel's request Stratford was permitted to enter. Stratford's contemporary biography gave a more complex account, including a shouting match between the archbishop and John Darcy, and various negotiations between the parties.[35] In the end, no trial took place. Stratford humbled himself before the king, and he was restored to a degree of favour.

In many ways the petitions presented on behalf of the Commons were much more significant in this parliament than the dramatic dispute with Stratford. The magnates wanted assurance that they were entitled to trial by their peers in parliament. They also wanted to have responsibility for maintenance of the Charters; breaches of them should be reported in parliament, and those who

---

[31] Avesbury, 324–9.   [32] Haines, *Stratford*, 291–2.
[33] Haines, *Church and Politics*, 194–7. The text of the *Libellus* is in Avesbury, 330–6, and its contents are summarized by Haines, *Stratford*, 293–6.
[34] Haines, *Stratford*, 296–305.
[35] *French Chronicle of London*, ed. Aungier, 90; Haines, *Stratford*, 312–18.

transgressed their provisions should be punished by the peers. The joint requests of the representatives and the magnates asked for the Charters and the statute of 1340 to be observed. They asked for a committee to hear the accounts of officials since the war started. More seriously for the king, he was asked to appoint his chief ministers and officials by the advice of prelates, earls, and barons in parliament, as had been a requirement of the Ordinances of 1311. Edward was prepared to accept most of the demands made of him, but he was not prepared to dismiss his existing ministers. It was agreed that if any should leave office, then the advice of the lords and the council should be taken on their replacement. Ministers would be answerable in parliament. In return for the concessions, the king was granted 10,000 sacks of wool, in addition to the similar quantity which it had been agreed should replace the second year of the ninth.[36]

By the time that parliament ended in the spring of 1341, it must have appeared that the king had given in on virtually everything demanded of him. Stratford had not been disgraced; parliament had demonstrated its power by demanding significant concessions in exchange for taxation. Above all, the crisis had demonstrated the overriding political importance of parliament. The speed with which the king recovered his position was startling. In October Edward used a council of selected magnates as the occasion for revoking the statute agreed earlier in the year. There was a full reconciliation with Stratford. A parliament did not meet again until early in 1343. When it did, the Commons protested at the revocation of the 1341 statute, but the king met this with a blunt explanation that it had been 'against his oath and to the blemishment of his crown and his royalty, and against the law of the land in various points', but he did promise that it would be re-examined, and any valuable points re-enacted in a new statute. Edward, remarkably, had emerged from the crisis with his power and authority intact.

Edward had shown his discontent with his government in England in 1340 by the dismissal of his ministers; he did the same with the government in Ireland in the following year. Irish revenues had sunk to a very meagre level of no more than £1,240 in 1339–40, and the king's response early in 1341 was to replace most of the administration. In July he took a drastic measure he had refused to adopt in England, and cancelled all royal grants made in Ireland since 1307; lands were to be returned only if they were found to have been granted for good reasons. Not surprisingly, there were bitter protests, and early in 1342 the king backed down. The revocations of grants were cancelled, and remedies for abuses followed the lines suggested by the Anglo-Irish community.[37]

---

[36] *Rot. Parl.* ii. 128; Harris, *King, Parliament and Public Finance*, 298–302.
[37] R. F. Frame, *Ireland and Britain 1170–1450* (London, 1998), 113–29.

These were difficult years in England, and the crisis had been more acute because it took place at a time when the economic position was so serious. The inquiries into the tax of the ninth suggest that exploitation had reduced much of the country to a dreadful state by 1341. In Shropshire many tenants had simply left their villages because of their poverty, leaving the land uncultivated. Everyone in Ludlow was said to be impoverished and in no position to be taxed. The burden of various government levies had led some of the burgesses of Oxford to leave the city. Agriculture had suffered from the climate, with a cold winter followed by a dry summer. In Wiltshire it was reported that lambs were few and weak, that many sheep had died, and that wool had fetched low prices because of the lack of coin in circulation. Unseasonal storms were a further problem there. In some coastal districts flooding had destroyed both arable and pasture. Of course, in an inquiry intended to find out why a tax had not produced as much revenue as anticipated, some exaggeration was to be expected, but the bleak nature of the picture it revealed cannot be denied.[38] Fortunately for the king, much of the cost of his overseas venture was borne not by his English subjects, but by the Italian companies and others he borrowed from abroad.

The challenge to Edward III's kingship was a serious one in 1340–1, with vicious accusations hurled by both sides. In many ways it echoed the problems that Edward I had faced in 1297, for, as in that year, this was a crisis born out of the pressures of war. There were, however, major differences when compared to previous political crises. This one was not played out against a background of threats of civil war, and there was a far greater role for parliament. There was a new maturity to politics.

STABILITY, STATUTES, AND PARLIAMENT

The challenge that faced Edward in the aftermath of the political crisis in England was not to be dealt with quite so easily as that in Ireland. One of his reactions was a loss of faith in clerical ministers, and chancellors in particular. He did not appoint a churchman to the office of chancellor for five years, but the rapid turnover of laymen in this post suggests that they faced difficult problems. In particular, the reward mechanisms of the provision of church livings were not available to them. There was no question of their being any less conscientious than their clerical predecessors; the reverse was in fact the case. There was no general move, however, against clerical officials; there was a lay treasurer for a very brief period before the appointment of William Cusance, who had been keeper of the wardrobe. Stability came with the

---

[38] *Inquisitiones Nonarum* (London, 1807), 9, 11, 142, 165, 175, 191, 194, 366.

appointment of William Edington as treasurer in 1345, for he held the post for a dozen years. John Thoresby was in charge of the chancery from 1349 to 1356.[39] Importantly, the problems that had resulted from long-term separation of the government, with the household abroad with the king, and the main departments operating in England, were not to be repeated after the king's return from the Low Countries in 1340. When Edward was engaged on the siege of Calais in 1346–7, communication with the government at Westminster was quick and easy, and did not create problems.

The very different war strategies adopted from 1342 meant that the burdens placed on England were not as great as they had been in the late 1330s. Nor was it easy to criticize a war that brought success, notably in 1346 at Crécy. The problem of how to finance war did not, however, go away.[40] A subsidy was granted for two years in 1344, another in 1346, and one for three years in 1348. In 1352 there was another grant made for three years. In 1357 a single subsidy was agreed, and there was another conceded in 1359. Fifteenths and tenths had, therefore, become virtually an annual tax. There was no questioning of the king's right to levy taxation; where there was a clear necessity, it was acknowledged that a tax should be granted. That did not mean that there was no argument. In 1344 conditions were imposed to the effect that the receipts from the tax had to spent on the war in Brittany, and on defence against the Scots. A range of concessions, mostly relating to legal issues, were granted by the king, of his good grace. The king also promised that he would not impose any further 'mises or tallages'. In 1346 the representatives in parliament protested that, despite this promise, commissions of array had been set up to recruit troops, and customs had been levied at 40s. a sack. To make matters worse, these had not been agreed in parliament. Despite this, a fifteenth and tenth was granted for two years, on condition that if a truce was obtained, the second year's levy would be cancelled. The representatives then presented a lengthy list of grievances that they wished to see redressed, some of which received positive responses. On the question of the customs duty, however, Edward claimed that he had the consent of the magnates and the merchants for the 40s. duty, which he was not prepared to lift.[41]

In 1352 the parliament roll explicitly stated that the grant of a triennial fifteenth and tenth was made conditionally. A lengthy set of petitions followed. Many of the issues were the familiar ones. There should be no additional tallages or taxes. Purveyance was, as ever, a matter for complaint. A new element was the demand that the proceeds from fines, raised as result of the

[39] Full details are given by Tout, *Chapters*, iii. 151 ff.
[40] For a full discussion, see Harriss, *King, Parliament and Public Finance*, 313 ff.
[41] *Rot. Parl.* ii. 150, 159–63.

legislation fixing wages in the aftermath of the Black Death, should be paid into the subsidy. There was an interesting stress on Magna Carta, with particular clauses picked out. Clause thirty-nine, which promised that no one would be proceeded against save in accordance with the law of the land, was one. Clause forty, in which King John had promised not to sell justice, was raised in the context of the heavy charges imposed by the chancery. It was also claimed that clause thirty-five in Magna Carta, which required standardization of weights and measures, was being ignored.[42]

These arguments that centred around the grants of taxation never threatened to evolve into a major crisis. While there were hopes that the French war would come to an end, there was no fundamental disagreement with the king's policies. The magnates were wholeheartedly in support of the king, while the representatives must have realized that, while their power to grant taxes gave them a position of some strength, this was not such as to enable them to mount a serious challenge. Edward's political strategies, of giving soft answers to criticism and of conceding points on which he might well go back subsequently, were highly effective. What was also important is that there was effective financial management. There was no return to the days of Edward I, when the officials of the wardrobe had been able to run up debts without any real control being exercised by the exchequer. Although the wardrobe continued to be the department largely responsible for administering and financing royal campaigns, the exchequer was fully aware of the overall financial position.

Edward III's concentration on the war did not mean that domestic affairs were neglected. The character of politics was changing as parliament became increasingly important. By this period parliament nearly always met in the same place, Westminster. There, the initial meeting would take place in the Painted Chamber. The Lords then sat in the White Chamber, while the Commons normally used the Painted Chamber for their deliberations, although on occasion they might meet in the Chapter House of the abbey.[43] The status of the magnates as peers was fully recognized, and although the list of those summoned varied over the years up to 1360, the character of the peerage was stable. Edward acknowledged newly acquired wealth and prestige, and was very ready to see adjustments take place, as in 1348, when four men of great military reputation, Reginald Cobham, Thomas Bradeston, Thomas Dagworth, and Walter Mauny, all received summonses for the first time.[44] No parliaments were held at which representatives were not present; meetings held purely with the magnates had the status of great councils.

---

[42] *Rot. Parl.* ii. 238–43.
[43] J. G. Edwards, *The Second Century of the English Parliament* (Oxford, 1979), 3–11.
[44] See below, 370; Powell and Wallis, *House of Lords*, 355.

Edward faced no serious criticism from the magnates during this period. To a considerable extent this was due to the success of the war in France, in which so many of them were engaged. At the same time there were questions of promotion and patronage to be managed. In 1351 the king's loyal supporter and great general Henry of Lancaster was elevated to ducal rank.[45] This was more than just a matter of title, for Henry was accorded full palatine authority, something that had been done before only for the king's eldest son Edward. The move was remarkable, not only indicating the degree of favour in which the king held the new duke, but also demonstrating a readiness to devolve the highest authority of the State. Edward was not, however, prepared for the new palatinate to have the same degree of independence as those of Durham or Chester; Lancaster was to continue to send knights and burgesses to parliament. In the same parliament that saw Lancaster promoted, Ralph Stafford was appointed earl of Stafford, which recognized his status as husband of the heiress of Hugh Audley, earl of Gloucester.

It was not possible, even by the 1350s, to forget the problems that had been created by the executions and forfeitures of 1327 and 1330. In parliament in 1354 the judgments on the earl of Arundel and on Roger Mortimer, earl of March, were reversed.[46] Mortimer's grandson, now earl of March, began to recover the estates that had been distributed as part of Edward's patronage. In particular, he regained the great lordship of Denbigh from the earl of Salisbury, who was not regarded with the same degree of favour as Edward had shown to his father.[47] What were seen as old wrongs were undone, and the process was achieved, astonishingly, without creating fresh opposition.

The composition of what would become known as the House of Commons remained unpolitical. There is no evidence that attempts were made to ensure that representatives, once elected, would put forward a particular point of view. Neither crown nor magnates tried to pack parliament. When Edward III told the sheriff of Gloucestershire to find 'wiser and more sufficient' knights to represent the county in parliament, his desire should be taken literally, and not as an attempt at gerrymandering.[48] The social status of the county representatives did not increase with the growing authority of the Commons. Rather, the reverse was the case. It became increasingly normal to select men who, although usually of note in the localities, had not taken up knighthood. It has been calculated that of those elected from Warwickshire between 1332 and 1348, only about a quarter were knights. Analysis of those elected for

---

[45] *CPR, 1350–4*, 60.   [46] *Rot. Parl.* ii. 355–7.
[47] G. A. Holmes, *The Estates of the Higher Nobility in Fourteenth-Century England* (Cambridge, 1957), 14–16.
[48] W. M. Ormrod, *The Reign of Edward III: Crown and Political Society in England 1327–1377* (London, 1990), 164.

Gloucestershire shows that some of the representatives, particularly in the 1330s, were men who appear to have been of little consequences even in their localities, for they did not even hold a single manor. The lack of knights might be a matter of concern on occasion, and in 1340, and on some later occasions, instructions made it clear that belted knights were to be elected, not that these had much effect. Such men were required by the crown, as their military experience was obviously thought helpful in parliaments in which the war and its needs were especially high on the agenda. In 1351, when the plague and law and order issues were emphasized as the reason for assembling parliament, what was wanted was men 'of good faith, diligent in seeing to the public good'. A few of those who attended parliaments were lawyers; twenty-six have been identified over the whole of Edward III's reign. There were thought to be problems with this, and in the 1350s instructions went out that those elected 'be not pleaders, nor maintainers of quarrels nor such as live by pursuits of this kind, but responsible men of good faith, devoted to the general welfare'.[49] People were often re-elected. The proportions varied considerably, but normally at least half of the shire representatives had attended at least one parliament previously. In July 1340 about three-quarters had done so.[50] Re-election was also common with the boroughs: in Edward III's reign one man was returned no fewer than eighteen times for Yarmouth. There was therefore, in most parliaments, a fair degree of experience in the Commons just as there was among the peers.

A puzzling element in parliament is that of the attendance of representatives of the clergy. There was no question over the presence of the prelates as peers, but there was little point in obtaining the attendance of representatives of the lower clergy, when the Church made grants of taxation in meetings of convocation rather than in parliament. Stratford argued in 1341 that the clergy were not bound to attend parliament. Yet clerical representatives did continue to attend parliaments, though what advantage either king or Church obtained from this is unclear. There was a watershed in about 1340, marked by the crown's abandonment of separate writs sent to the archbishops to encourage attendance; after that date parliament was effectively a secular assembly.[51]

A very important change in the role of the representatives came with their involvement in the process of petitioning. Until 1327 there were very few

---

[49] K. Wood-Legh, 'Sheriffs, Lawyers and Belted Knights in the Parliaments of Edward III', *EHR* 46 (1931) 377, 384–7; Saul, *Knights and Esquires*, 120–1; Coss, *The Origins of the English Gentry*, 198–9.

[50] K. Wood-Legh, 'The Knights' Attendance in the Parliaments of Edward III', *EHR* 47 (1932), 398–413; McKisack, *Parliamentary Representation of the English Boroughs*, 42.

[51] J. H. Denton, 'The Clergy and Parliament in the Thirteenth and Fourteenth Centuries', in Davies and Denton (eds.), *The English Parliament in the Middle Ages*, 99–106.

general petitions from them, and it seems unlikely that many individual petitions were put forward by representatives on behalf of their constituents. In the first parliament of Edward III's reign a set of forty-one articles was presented from the community, with a request that they be put into statutory form.[52] Just what was meant by the *commune de la terre*, or community of the land, at this stage is not absolutely clear. It was even possible, at about this period, for an apparent distinction to be drawn between the knights of the shires and the *genz de la commune*, or representatives of the community.[53] It is clear, however, that by 1340 the language of community was clearly denoting the representatives in virtually every case, and that the common petitions of the following decades did indeed come from what can be termed the Commons. Legislation was normally drawn up in response to common petitions.

The Black Death might have been expected to have a destructive effect on the political consensus that was being established in the aftermath of the crisis of 1340–2. In practice, the reverse was the case. One immediate effect of the epidemic was that parliament did not meet from 1348 until 1351. When it did, government policy was accepted. The labour legislation enacted by ordinance in 1349, intended to keep wages down, was put into statutory form. It can be argued that one effect of the catastrophic loss of life in the Black Death was to persuade the knights and others representing the shires in parliament that their interests and those of the great magnates were similar; there was a pulling together of what might be called the establishment, both at the centre and in the localities, in order to try to preserve the status quo ante.[54] The great epidemic no doubt played its part, but the broad political consensus and stability of this period was also the result of a range of highly successful policies. Above all, success was achieved abroad in the war without subjecting the country to the kind of pressures which had been so damaging in the late 1330s. Management of the nobility by means of effective patronage was combined with political skill in managing the demands made through the Commons.

One notable piece of legislation in these years was the Statute of Treason of 1352. This demonstrated the king's sensitivity to the demands both of magnates and of commons. The statute provided a very limited definition of treasonable activity. Attacks on the persons of the king, queen, and their eldest children; making war on the king; killing the chancellor, treasurer, or royal justices; counterfeiting the royal seal or coinage, and importation of false coinage; these were the only offences now regarded as acts of treason. The

---

[52] *Rot. Parl.* ii. 7–11.   [53] Ibid. ii. 67, 69 (parliament in 1332).
[54] Ormrod, *Reign of Edward III*, 22–3; Harris, *King, Parliament and Public Finance*, 374.

statute would make it impossible to bandy charges of treason about as lightly as was done in the 1320s, and it can be seen as a final act of reconciliation with the baronage. It is striking that in the same parliament that saw the statute enacted, John Maltravers, who had been found guilty of treason for his role in the death of the earl of Kent twenty years earlier, was fully restored to favour.[55] The statute, however, also has to be seen in the context of the law-and-order campaign of recent years. Treason charges had been used inappropriately, and with the statute the king tacitly accepted the criticisms that representatives in parliament had made.[56]

There were many other developments in the law. The year 1346 saw the Ordinance of Justices, provisions intended to deal with the problems of judicial corruption. Procedures were altered: in January 1349 a proclamation was issued asking that people presenting petitions about common law issues should put them before to the chancellor. He, or the keeper of the privy seal, should also hear requests for royal favour.[57] The reason was that Edward III himself was busy with other more important matters. Though this was probably intended as a temporary expedient, it began a process that saw the chancery play an increasingly important part in the law, which accelerated in the 1370s. In various ways the 1350s and 1360s saw an apparent tightening of social control. It was easier to use writs of trespass to cover a wider range of wrongs than in the past. It became possible, for example, to sue doctors and horse-doctors for malpractice in a way not previously possible. After 1352 farriers could be sued for laming a horse.[58]

The traditional view of legal development in Edward III's reign is that it was largely the work of lawyers eager to please their clients by finding new ways of getting round the limitations of the law. There was, of course, some of that. Much, however, of the legal change of the 1350s should be credited to an active, innovatory, and thoroughly successful government, with Chief Justice Shareshull playing an important role. The need to maintain social order was a high priority, and the demographic disaster of the Black Death presented a threat to that order, though this was no more than one element in a multifaceted situation. There was throughout from Edward III and his government 'a commitment to reshaping the law and facilitating legal procedure'.[59]

---

[55] *SR* i. 320; *Rot. Parl.* ii. 239, 243.   [56] Below, 522.
[57] R. C. Palmer, *English Law in the Age of the Black Death* (Chapel Hill, NC, 1993), 108; *CCR, 1346–9*, 615.
[58] Palmer, *English Law in the Age of the Black Death*, 163–6, 185–96, 225.
[59] A. Musson, 'Second "English Justinian" or Pragmatic Opportunist? A Re-examination of the Legal Legislation of Edward III's Reign', in Bothwell (ed.), *The Age of Edward III*, 69–88. The quotation is from p. 86.

LEGISLATION AND THE CHURCH

These years saw, in the statutes of Provisors and Praemunire, the culmination of many years of protest over the exercise of papal patronage and jurisdiction in England. In Edward I's last parliament, that held at Carlisle in 1307, a petition put forward on behalf of the earls, barons, and community of the land had raised a number of issues, the most important of which was the provision of clerks, many of them foreigners, by the papacy to English benefices. In 1327 the community had asked that no one provided to a living in this way should be allowed to enter the land, under pain of losing life and limb.[60] The fourteenth century saw an increase in the scale of papal provisions. From 1265 the papacy claimed the right to make an appointment in cases where the previous holder died in the papal curia. This was later extended to cover those travelling to or from the curia, and in the fourteenth century there were many additions to the cases in which the right of appointment was reserved by the papacy. The provisions themselves might take different forms. The pope might make a grant of a specific vacant benefice, or he might make a promise of a benefice when it next became vacant. The system had its advantages; it provided a route for poor scholars to obtain benefices, and without papal provisions the proportion of university graduates building careers in the Church would almost certainly have been far lower than it was. It could also lead to serious disputes, such as that over the deanery of York, which became vacant in 1342. The chapter elected Thomas Sampson, but the pope provided Cardinal Talleyrand de Périgord. When this became known, the king put forward John Offord, and subsequently, in 1347, Philip de Weston. Eventually Talleyrand reached agreement with Weston, and was victorious in what had been a very long-running and bitter dispute.[61]

In parliament in 1343 the representatives claimed that Cardinal Talleyrand was 'the fiercest enemy that there was in the curia, and the most hostile to the king's affairs'. The country was losing, so it was alleged, 10,000 marks a year through the grant of benefices to him and another cardinal. The secrets of the land were exposed to foreigners. In general terms, the wishes of founders of ecclesiastical houses were being ignored, patrons were losing their rights to present to benefices, and resources were being lost to the realm. It all amounted to 'damage and depression of the people and subversion of the state'. The king responded with an ordinance which aimed to prevent anyone from bringing

---

[60] Prestwich, *Edward I*, 551–2; *Rot. Parl.* i. 9.
[61] For a convenient discussion of papal provisions, see A. D. M. Barrell, *The Papacy, Scotland and Northern England 1342–1378* (Cambridge, 1995), 79 ff., and 114–15 for the York dispute.

into England papal letters that were prejudicial to the king and the people.[62] The proctors appointed by the two cardinals were hauled up before the chancellor and royal justices, and told to leave the realm.[63] The hard line was not maintained for long, however, and by 1345 a compromise had been negotiated with the papacy. The issue continued to be raised in parliament; there was a lengthy protest in 1347, which included the argument that foreign clergy could not take services properly, as they knew no English. In 1351 it was claimed that the amount of money taken out of the realm every year by those provided to livings by the pope amounted to more than the king's own revenues, and that it was going into the hands of the French. English clergy were being ousted from livings they had held for a long time as a result of papal action.[64] The king responded with the Statute of Provisors.

The Statute of Provisors aimed to protect the rights of lay patrons to make appointments to church livings. Rights of free election to bishoprics were to be maintained. The statute also extended royal power, for if no appointment was made by a patron within six months of a vacancy occurring, and the bishop did not exercise his right within a further month, then the right would pass to the crown. Papal provisors were threatened with a fine and imprisonment.[65] The statute met the requirements of parliament, but in practice it was a dead letter, and very little use was made of it. The crown itself had quite sufficient weapons at its disposal without needing the statute. In 1346, employing the doctrine of necessity, Edward had seized all benefices held by foreigners into his own hands, a far more effective weapon than anything the statute of 1351 would provide.[66] From the king's point of view, it was better to use influence with the papacy to secure the appointment of appropriate bishops, rather than to risk the vagaries of electoral processes.

The Statute of Praemunire of 1353 dealt with the question of appeals to the papal curia. The Commons complained that cases were being brought against the king's subjects in courts other than his own, by which they meant in particular the papal curia.[67] The claim in the preamble of the statute was that cases that should be dealt with in the royal courts were being taken out of the realm, and the remedy was that anyone who appealed to courts outside royal jurisdiction should appear within two months to answer for what they had done, under threat of forfeiture and outlawry. In many cases appeals were over rights of appointment to benefices. The statute added a weapon to the armoury that the king had at his disposal, but it would be wrong to see it as marking a major shift in relations with the papacy. This statute, like that of Provisors,

---

[62] *Rot. Parl.* ii. 144–5. [63] Murimuth, 142–3. [64] *Rot. Parl.* ii. 173, 228.
[65] Ibid. ii. 232–3. [66] Barrell, *Papacy, Scotland and Northern England*, 139–41.
[67] *SR* i. 329; *Rot. Parl.* ii. 252.

shows how the king was very ready to introduce legislation to meet the popular demands expressed in parliament.

THE GOVERNMENT AND THE ECONOMY

The extent to which governments can influence economic issues is often questioned, but there can be no doubt of the importance of the decisions that Edward III and his ministers made in this period. The shortage of coin in the country had become a significant problem by the late 1330s, with about half the amount of coin in circulation that there had been earlier in the century. The inquisitions taken into the failure of the ninth had provided evidence of the difficulties that people faced when they did not have the physical means with which to make payments. The issue was discussed in parliament in 1343, and with the assistance of some merchants and goldsmiths, a solution was suggested. Analysis of the problem suggested that the root cause was the high value of gold florins. Wool was being sold in the Low Countries for florins, not silver, and as a result no silver was coming into England. The solution was for the gold coins circulating among merchants to be taken to the mints and replaced by a new English gold coinage. This would be used for international trade, and the export of silver would be prohibited.[68] Accordingly, the English mints began to produce gold coins in 1344. The first coinage was a complete failure, for the level of seignorage was so high that the coins were wholly uncompetitive. Subsequent adjustments reduced the profit to the crown, but produced coins that were acceptable to the market, particularly with the gold nobles coined from 1351. At that date the total value of the currency was probably only about £1 million.[69] It was not, of course, possible to reverse monetary trends in the way that parliament had intended. The gold coins were not confined to international trade, but circulated alongside silver in England. Downward adjustments were made to the weight of the silver penny, until in 1351, 300 pennies were coined from a pound of silver. In 1352 the Commons demanded that both gold and silver coins be maintained at their existing levels, which the king agreed. Further changes were not needed, for the standards proved effective, and in the 1350s England enjoyed a currency that was both stable and adequately plentiful. Between May and December 1353 almost £70,000 worth of silver coins were issued by the London mint, a level not seen since the early fourteenth century.[70] It is striking that Edward III accepted parliamentary advice over the currency. The issue had been raised in the

---

[68] *Rot. Parl.* ii. 137–8.
[69] Challis (ed.), *New History of the Royal Mint*, 163–8; Allen, 'Volume of the English Currency', 606.
[70] *Rot. Parl.* ii. 240; Challis (ed.), *New History of the Royal Mint*, 680.

Ordinances of 1311, at a time when it was suspected (wrongly) that the coinage was being debased, but this was an area that in the past had been regarded as an aspect of the royal prerogative.

The crown's manipulation of the wool trade had been a major issue in the difficult initial years of the war with France. The king did not abandon the use of wool as a means of financing war after the crisis of 1340–1.[71] A grant of 30,000 sacks of wool, made at Easter 1341, proved far more successful than any previous attempts by the crown to collect wool. Even military commanders were paid in wool, rather than cash. The heavy customs duties were continued, and the crown saw the way forward as lying with merchants who would advance money in exchange for a monopoly of exports through a staple at Bruges or elsewhere. The Commons wanted to gain effective control over the taxation of wool, and were highly suspicious of the monopoly arrangements that the crown favoured. In 1344 a request for free trade was one of the conditions set on the grant of fifteenths and tenths. Although a favourable answer was given to this, the crown continued with its policy of giving monopoly rights to merchant consortia. The customs were handed over to the merchants in exchange for a substantial £50,000 a year. The policy was not popular, particularly when it was combined with a levy of 20,000 sacks of wool in 1347, granted not by parliament but by a great council. Parliamentary protests were duly made.[72]

In 1353 the government introduced a new policy, and replaced the unpopular Bruges staple with a number of English staple ports. This was reminiscent of the Despensers' scheme of 1326. One explanation for the change is that the crown was responding to the protests of the growers and smaller merchants against the monopolies that had been controlled by small numbers of rich traders. Alternatively, it has been suggested that the reason lay in the nature of Anglo-Flemish relations. In 1351 the count of Flanders, Louis de Mâle, had abandoned his support of Edward III and had agreed a treaty with the French.[73] In those circumstances, the continuance of the Bruges staple was impossible, and home staples offered the best alternative. In practice, it seems that a number of pressures came together in 1353, and that the new policy could not have been implemented without the backing of the Commons, whose sole criticism of a measure that would be to their 'ease and relief' was that there were not as many staple towns as they wished to see.[74] Under the system of home staples, English merchants were not to export wool themselves; it was

---

[71] See, for the following, Harriss, *King, Parliament and Public Finance*, 443 ff.; Lloyd, *Wool Trade*, 158 ff.

[72] *Rot. Parl.* ii. 148, 151, 165–70.

[73] The second suggestion is that made by Lloyd, *Wool Trade*, 206–7.

[74] *Rot. Parl.* ii. 253

foreigners who carried the risks of shipwreck and piracy. In 1357, however, this prohibition was lifted, and two years later the staple policy was reversed, with the re-establishment of a short-lived staple at Bruges. In 1362 it was decided that the staple should be moved to Calais.

In purely financial terms, the taxation of wool was a great success for the crown. In 1353–4 income from the customs, astonishingly, came to about £113,400, and in the following year £83,900.[75] In the 1350s trade was booming, and Edward III was provided with the means to finance his military ambitions. It would be wrong to attribute all of this success to the wisdom of the policies adopted by the English government. Much was due to the way in which trading patterns favoured England, but at the same time, Edward's political acumen meant that he was able to extract large sums of money with surprisingly little difficulty.

In the case of the lay subsidies, the fifteenths and tenths, there was no option available to the king other than to negotiate with parliament. The position was less clear when it came to customs duties and wool levies, for it might be considered sufficient to negotiate simply with merchant assemblies. One important outcome of the complex arguments of the 1340s and 1350s was the effective triumph of parliament. In 1341 and 1342 Edward negotiated customs duties with merchant assemblies, while in 1346 and 1347 it was a great council, with no representative element, that made grants. In 1348 the Commons in parliament protested about the customs, that 'henceforth no such grant be made by the merchants, as this is simply a grievance and charge on the community, and not on the merchants who buy wool for less'.[76] In other words, the merchants were passing on the levy to the growers in the form of lower wool prices. Although it was not until 1362 that Edward III finally agreed, by statute, that subsidies on trade could not be levied without parliamentary consent, the principle applied in practice through the 1350s.

CONCLUSION: EDWARD III

Much of the credit for the remarkable successes of the thirty years from 1330 must go to the king himself. Edward's character is not easy to delineate, though it would be wrong to say that he was a complex individual. His main qualities are easy enough to discern. He was a man capable of acting impulsively; his dash to rescue the countess of Atholl from the siege at Lochindorb provides one example, and his night-time arrival at the Tower in November 1340 may be another. In broader policy terms, the risk that the king ran in incurring such huge debts in the Low Countries in the late 1330s is one that appears

[75] Ormrod, *The Reign of Edward III*, 207.   [76] *Rot. Parl.* i. 201.

indefensible. Nor can Edward have been unaware of what was happening, when even his very crown, as well as his top military commanders, had to be pledged against the desperately needed loans. Edward was not, however, a man who regarded his duties lightly. There is no doubt that he believed in exercising a tight control over his administrators; he was a hard-working man who was closely involved in decision-making. Council memoranda make it quite clear that issues were submitted to him, for him to conclude what should be done. He was not a man to indulge in favourites, as his father had done. Edward had his friends, such as William Montague, to whom he owed much—in Montague's case the throne itself, given the future earl of Salisbury's role in the Nottingham coup of 1330. He made sure that those on whom he relied received their rewards, but although his patronage was generous, it was also balanced. Edward was much more of a politician than his predecessors on the throne had been. His approach to political problems was very pragmatic. He was untroubled by any principles that might tell him not to give away royal rights; he was very ready to concede points to his opponents, in the full knowledge that he would be able to recover his position later. Yet although he broke promises, he did not acquire the sort of reputation for unreliability that his grandfather had attracted. He was not, and this was important, a man to bear grudges. The crisis of 1340–1 left no bitter aftertaste; Edward did not try to pursue his opponents. He was very ready to restore to favour families whom he might well have distrusted; there was no question of feuds in the way in which Edward I had pursued the Montforts.

Edward was devoted to his queen, Philippa, and her contribution to his success should not be underestimated. One very striking feature of his rule is his management of his own family. There were no jealousies and rivalries between his sons like those that had so bedevilled the reign of Henry II. Edward was fully prepared to delegate authority to his eldest son, the Black Prince, and his plans for the territorial endowment of his other sons did not create problems. He permitted the Black Prince to make what must have seemed a highly unsuitable marriage to Joan of Kent in 1361, and he allowed his daughters their own way rather than making use of them as diplomatic pawns, tempting though that must have been. By 1360 only one was married, Margaret, to the earl of Pembroke.[77]

In his religious attitudes Edward could hardly have been more conventional. There are no indications that he was influenced by new mystical approaches; he did not have psalters or fashionable books of hours made for his use. He showed a very normal devotion to the Virgin Mary; the commitment that he

---

[77] For a full analysis of Edward III's arrangements for his family, see W. M. Ormrod, 'Edward III and his Family', *Journal of British Studies*, 26 (1987), 398–442.

showed to English saints was perhaps as much political as devotional. Edward paid due and full attention to the ceremonies of the Church, notably funerals; he showed a concern to secure an easy passage in the afterlife that was typical of the period, by ensuring the saying of large numbers of masses. His new foundations, such as that of the Dominican nuns at Dartford and the house of St Mary Graces, close to the Tower of London, were not marked by the extravagant planning that had characterized Edward I's abbey of Vale Royal. His endowment of the King's Hall at the University of Cambridge was scarcely generous.[78]

There is every indication that Edward enjoyed being king, and that those in his court enjoyed being around him. Politics was a serious business, but the chivalric ideals, the frivolities of tournaments, and the splendid display of dress were also an important part of Edward's monarchical style. 'It is as it is' was one of the mottoes worn by the king, on a green velvet jacket. 'Hey, hey, the white swan, by God's soul I am thy man' is still more mystifying as a motto to be worn by the king and those of his court, but these embroideries testify to the sense of camaraderie that undoubtedly existed in the royal circle. There must have much jollity when the king appeared at one of the tournaments in 1348 dressed in an ingenious bird costume.[79] His human side emerges in Froissart's tale of the king aboard ship before the battle of Les Espagnols sur mer, when he wore a beaver hat and had much fun persuading John Chandos to sing to the latest German tune.[80]

---

[78] Ormrod, 'The Personal Religion of Edward III', *Speculum*, 64 (1989), 849–77; Cobban, *The King's Hall Within the University of Cambridge*, 93–4.

[79] Newton, *Fashion in the Age of the Black Prince*, 43; J. Vale, *Edward III and Chivalry* (Woodbridge, 1982), 71.

[80] Froissart, iv. 91.

CHAPTER 11

England and France

By the 1340s and 1350s England had become the most powerful military force in Europe, as the victories of Crécy and Poitiers confirmed. There had been intermittent wars between England and France through the thirteenth and early fourteenth centuries, which escalated in seriousness and scale in the reign of Edward III with the outbreak of the Hundred Years War in 1337. It is only with hindsight that this war is seen as a single entity, somehow different in kind from the Anglo-French disputes that had preceded it. Contemporaries did not see the war that started in 1337 in this way. It is certainly true that Anglo-French conflict intensified in the fourteenth century, but many if not all the issues between Edward III and Philip VI were the familiar ones from the past. The fact that the English kings held substantial lands in south-western France was an obstacle to the extension and strengthening of rule by the French monarchy. The relationship established in 1259 whereby the English held their French lands as vassals of the French king was never likely to be an easy one. By the end of the thirteenth century French support for the Scots was a significant issue, as was English backing for anti-French factions in the Low Countries. Rivalry and conflict between England and France, therefore, was a theme that ran through the whole period from the reign of Henry III to that of Edward III and beyond. Where the war that began in 1337 differed from its predecessors was in its long duration, and in the enthusiasm with which it was regarded by leaders of English military society.

THE CAUSES OF WAR

The roots of conflict were tangled. Much of the analysis by historians has concentrated above all on the question of the homage owed by the king of England for Gascony following the treaty of 1259. That was only one element; the wars need to be seen in a broader context of political and even commercial rivalry. The feudal relationship receives much attention in the documentary sources, for this was the kind of issue over which lawyers and diplomats could develop complex arguments. In reality the wars were about power and influence in a wide range of areas. Maintenance of English control of Gascony was certainly very important, but alongside that were the issues of Scotland and Flanders. Internal dissension in France was also important, as those opposed to the Capetian and above all Valois monarchies looked to England for assistance, much as the Scots looked to France for help.

Through descent from Henry II's queen, Eleanor, the kings of England were dukes of Aquitaine. This title covered rights extending from Poitou to the Pyrenees, the most important lands being those of the old duchy of Gascony, the region south of the Garonne, but also including the Agenais to the west and Saintonge to the north. In normal usage the terms 'Aquitaine' and 'Gascony' could be almost interchangeable, but interestingly it was suggested (although not agreed) early in Edward III's reign that the royal title should include both lord of Gascony and duke of Aquitaine.[1] The duchy of Gascony was all that the English held in France at the start of Henry III's personal rule. Normandy, Maine, Anjou, Touraine, and Brittany had been lost under King John, as had Poitou further south. Ironically, the links between Gascony and England were much weaker than those that had existed between England and Normandy. The Gascon dialect was very different from the French spoken in England, which was similar to that of Normandy and Picardy. The duchy was not easy to rule; the towns were anxious for independence, and the great nobles reluctant to accept anything more than nominal ducal authority.

Few Englishmen held lands in Gascony. Gascons were not particularly welcome in England, and the number who settled there was very small. Edward I on one occasion had to rebuke the exchequer officials for their treatment of his Gascon creditors, reminding them that they were also his subjects.[2] Gascony never became very English. There are a handful of place names redolent of the rule of Edward I. Baa, now vanished, was named after Bath, where Robert Burnell was bishop. Libourne preserves the name of Roger Leyburn, and Hastingues that of John de Hastings. The castle at Villandraut has a similar ground plan and overall appearance to Harlech in north Wales. But there was little substance to such links. English officials worked in Gascony, but often for no more than a few years. They did not put down roots, but returned to their homeland after service in the duchy. No large army of English functionaries operated there, and this was not an early parallel to British India. Nor was Gascony employed by the English crown as a source of lands to be used in patronage. It had not been conquered by the English, and so there was no ready supply of estates to be granted out as there was, to some extent at least, in Wales and in Ireland.

---

[1] Chaplais, *Medieval English Diplomatic Practice*, pt. i, i. 154.
[2] See E 159/75, mm. 59d, 62, for a case of Edward's intervention in favour of a Gascon merchant, and for his surprise that the customs had been taken away from the Gascons.

The economic connections between England and the duchy were centred on the wine trade. This reached its peak in the early fourteenth century. In 1308–9 almost 103,000 tuns were exported, at least a quarter of it to England. In 1329–30 the figure was over 93,000 tuns. The number of ships engaged in carrying wines to England varied from year to year, but might exceed 200.[3] The trade was important, but those engaged in it were not men of great political influence, and the preservation of England's wine imports was not the type of cause for which medieval governments went to war. English exports to the duchy included grain, cloth, and hides. The war that began in 1337 had a severe effect on Anglo-Gascon trade. Not only did the sea route to England become more hazardous, necessitating the introduction of a convoy system, but also, more seriously, wine production in the Gascon hinterland was severely damaged by the fighting and the destruction of territory that accompanied it.

How much was Gascony worth to the English crown? The Agenais was valued in 1261 at a mere 3,720 *livres tournois* a year, or rather less than £1,000. Accounts for 1306–7 suggest that the overall royal income in Gascony stood at about £17,000, most of it derived from the customs on wine. An estimate of royal revenue in 1324 put the clear receipt from Gascony at £13,000.[4] This was a significant sum, but profits from the duchy were not normally received by the exchequer in England. The money raised in Gascony was needed by the government in the duchy.

HENRY III AND FRANCE

In 1225 an expedition under the nominal command of the king's brother Richard of Cornwall, but in reality headed by the earl of Salisbury, sailed to Bordeaux to re-establish English rule in the duchy. Success was achieved with the capture of La Réole, but it proved impossible to extend English control into Poitou. This was what Henry III attempted to do in his campaigns of 1230 and 1242. In 1230, although Henry faced little resistance, the campaign as a whole was a failure. The immediate occasion of the expedition was the rebellion of Peter Mauclerc, count of Brittany, against the regency government headed by Blanche of Castile. Peter had come to England in the previous year, when he performed homage for Brittany to Henry. The English force landed at Saint-Malo, and engaged in what was little more than a march or progress to Poitou, with virtually no military action. Roger of Wendover, whose bitter pen is not always to be trusted, criticized the count of Brittany. When the force returned

---

[3] M. K. James, *Studies in the Wine Trade*, ed. E. M. Veale (Oxford, 1971), 10, 32, 35.
[4] *Gascon Register A*, ed. G. P. Cuttino (London, 1975), 531; M. W. Beresford, *New Towns of the Middle Ages* (London, 1967), 360; Harriss, *King, Parliament and Public Finance*, 523.

to Brittany from Poitou, 'the count, with Hubert the king's justiciar, would not allow them to move against the enemy, but enjoyed themselves with parties in the English manner, feasted and drank together as if they were celebrating Christmas'.[5] Illness, and a lack of adequate finance, compelled the king and much of the force to return to England; in the next year a truce was negotiated with the French. The English failed to maintain their position, for Peter Mauclerc changed sides once again in 1234.

The expedition of 1242 was prompted by the difficulties that followed the appointment of Alphonse, Louis IX's brother, to the county of Poitou in the previous year. Henry III's mother, Isabella of Angoulême, incited her second husband, Hugh of Lusignan, to rebel; it is said that she threatened to deprive him of his conjugal rights unless he did so.[6] Many Poitevin barons joined in the hostility to Alphonse. There were also hopes of support for the English from Raymond of Toulouse. In the event, Hugh de Lusignan had submitted to Louis IX before Henry arrived in Gascony, and Count Raymond proved totally unreliable. The English had no strategy other than to retreat in the face of French advances. They withdrew from Taillebourg, where the Poitevins failed to hold the bridge, and were defeated at Saintes. One chronicler tried to turn this into a triumph for the English, but it was nothing of the sort. Simon de Montfort, tactless as perhaps only he could be, told the king that after this disaster he deserved to be locked up like the worthless Carolingian ruler Charles the Simple after his defeat at Soissons.[7] Henry fled from Saintes to Blaye, with the remnants of his army starving. On the news that the French were advancing in his direction, he moved on to Bordeaux. Had it not been for an outbreak of disease in the French army, from which Louis IX himself suffered, the expedition could well have ended in total disaster. As it was, Henry had completely failed to regain any influence in Poitou. English control of Gascony was weakened by the king's display of impotence, but a truce was agreed with the French for five years.[8] Henry's expeditions had shown little indication of any effective strategic thinking, and demonstrated the ineffectiveness of English armies.

A different approach to the problems of Gascony was taken in 1248 when Simon de Montfort was sent to the duchy to impose English authority and to deal with the problem of external threats. He was successful with the latter, but

---

[5] Wendover, iii. 7.

[6] F. M. Powicke, *King Henry III and the Lord Edward* (Oxford, 1947), i. 188; N. Vincent, 'Isabella of Angoulême: John's Jezebel', in S. D. Church (ed.), *King John: New Interpretations* (Woodbridge, 1999), 211.

[7] Guisborough, 177–8; Maddicott, *Simon de Montfort*, 32.

[8] Paris, *Chron. Maj.* iv. 209–25.

his harsh rule provoked much hostility. He ignored traditional liberties, and failed to deal impartially with the feuding factions in Bordeaux. His methods were expensive, and in 1252 he was put on trial to answer the many complaints against him by the Gascons.[9]

In 1253 Henry III himself sailed for Gascony. There, a great magnate, Gaston de Béarn, was in revolt, and there was a threat of invasion from Alfonso X of Castile. Henry could rely on the support of the coastal towns, above all Bordeaux and Bayonne, but little more. He was unexpectedly successful in re-establishing his authority, although the town of La Réole held out determinedly. Negotiations with Castile led to a treaty, with a marriage alliance agreed. Edward, Henry III's son, duly married Eleanor of Castile in 1254, and a new regime was put in place in Gascony under his nominal authority.[10]

The position of Gascony was transformed, in legal terms, by the treaty of Paris of 1259. This treaty was not the product of a crisis in Anglo-French relations. There had been no English campaign on the Continent since 1242, but given the difficult domestic situation in England it was obviously desirable that there should be no problems abroad. The English negotiators appointed in 1257 were an impressive group of men. The bishop of Worcester, Hugh Bigod, and the friar Adam Marsh were all advocates of reform. They were to act with the advice of Simon de Montfort and Peter of Savoy. Montfort's experiences in Gascony no doubt gave him a special insight into the problems that resulted from the English possession of the duchy. Peter of Savoy was a major international figure, sympathetic to reform in England, with wide connections in France. The indications are that the leading role in determining the English line in the negotiations was taken by Simon de Montfort. The core of the agreement that was finalized at Paris in 1259 was that Henry III should give up his claims to Normandy, Anjou, Maine, Touraine, and Poitou, and that he should receive Gascony as a fief from the French king. Previously, Gascony had been held quite independently, without a superior lord. In addition, Louis IX gave Henry rights in the dioceses and cities of Limoges, Cahors, and Périgueux. Two questions were left undetermined, that of the status of the Agenais, to the east of Gascony, and that of Quercy, still further east.[11]

---

[9] Maddicott, *Simon de Montfort*, 106–15.

[10] J. P. Trabut-Cussac, *L'Administration anglaise en Gascogne sous Henry III et Edouard I de 1254 à 1307* (Geneva, 1972), pp. xxxi–xli; Parsons, *Eleanor of Castile*, 12–16. For a useful discussion of England and Gascony in the first half of the 13th century, J. R. Studd, 'Reconfiguring the Angevin Empire, 1224–1259', in Weiler (ed.), *England and Europe in the Reign of Henry III*, 31–41.

[11] The treaty is conveniently summarized in M. Vale, *The Origins of the Hundred Years War*, 2nd edn. (Oxford, 1996), 53–4.

1. A self-portrait of Matthew Paris

2. Henry III sailing to Brittany in 1242, drawn by Matthew Paris

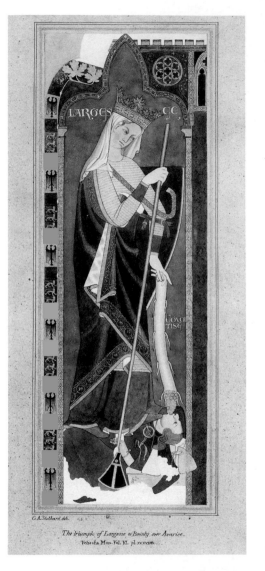

3. Figures from the Painted Chamber at Westminster,
copied by Charles Stothard in 1819

4. Harlech castle

5. The Eagle Tower at Caernarfon castle

6. Edward I creating his son prince of Wales in 1301

7. The Eleanor Cross at Hardingstone in Northamptonshire

8. Guisborough priory in North Yorkshire

Primeps Eduardo. non tua pancia caude.
In Scotos mota. p te fit Cambria nota.

9. The future Edward II

10. The King John Cup

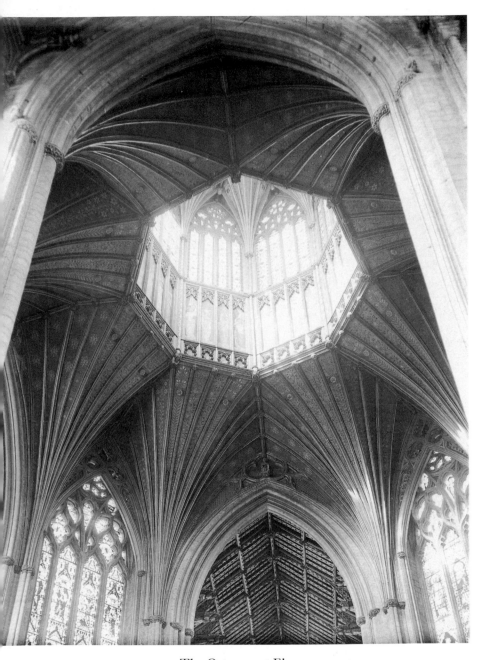

11. The Octagon at Ely

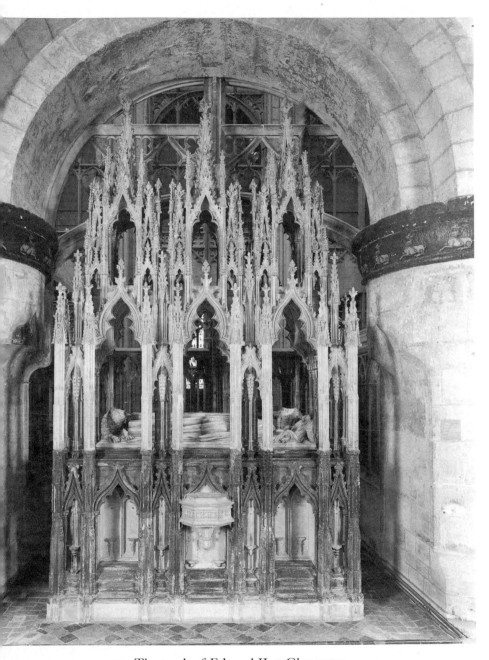

13. The tomb of Edward II at Gloucester

14. Markenfield Hall, North Yorkshire. The house; with, below, the piscina in the ch

15. Sir Geoffrey Luttrell, from the Luttrell Psalter

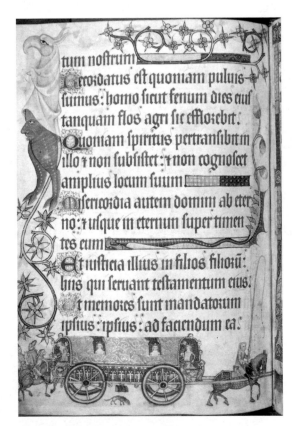

16. A page of the Luttrell Psalter, showing a queen in her coach

17. The battle of Poitiers in 1356

The treaty of Paris set Anglo-French relations on a different footing, and created a new agenda.[12] The fact that homage was required meant that there were potential difficulties every time that there was a new king in either country, for it would then have to be renewed. The way in which the French interpreted their overlordship would be very important. Would the king of England be expected to provide military service when it was summoned by the king of France? What rights did Gascons have to appeal to the court of their overlord, the king of France, against judgments of the king of England or his lieutenants? These were difficult questions. The position was hardly novel; kings of England had been vassals of the French king between the Conquest and the loss of Normandy, for their possessions in Normandy, Anjou, Maine, and Touraine. Indeed, Henry II had acknowledged that he held Gascony from the French king, but only because it was at that time part of the county of Poitou.[13] There was a parallel in England, in that the Scots king held lands in England as fiefs from the English crown, and accordingly owed homage. In terms of prestige it was obviously an awkward situation, but it was clearly one that Henry and the English negotiators were prepared to accept. Had it been as humiliating as has often been suggested for the king of England to do homage to his French counterpart, Henry III, a man very conscious of his dignity, would not have agreed to the terms. The question of homage would certainly be a point of friction in the future, but the alternative, that Henry should hold Gascony freely, was not acceptable to the French. From their point of view, the position was that the duchy had been forfeited by King John, had been granted to Arthur of Brittany, and on his death had escheated to the French crown. The English, however, would not forget the idea that Gascony was 'a free land where the king of England holds complete jurisdiction'; the claim was to be made by Edward I's negotiators in 1298.[14]

It is easy to condemn the treaty of Paris in the light of hindsight for creating difficulties that would lead to the Hundred Years War. It was, however, negotiated by a highly experienced group of men, and ushered in over thirty years of peace between England and France, an achievement that should not be ignored. Rather than condemn the treaty as containing within it the seeds of future conflict, it should be praised as bringing a period of peace.

---

[12] The most important account of Anglo–French relations is in the two articles by P. Chaplais 'Le Duché-Pairie de Guyenne', in his *Essays in Medieval Diplomacy and Administration* (London, 1981), chs. III and IV.

[13] Vale, *Origins of the Hundred Years War*, 61.

[14] Powicke, *Henry III*, 256; H. Rothwell, 'Edward I's Case Against Philip the Fair over Gascony in 1298', *EHR* 42 (1927), 574–6.

ENGLAND AND FRANCE UNDER EDWARD I AND EDWARD II

The importance of Gascony to Edward I was indicated when, on his return from crusade in 1273, he went to the duchy, rather than straight to England. This was largely to deal with internal difficulties, notably the activities of Gaston de Béarn. A major survey of feudal obligation was also undertaken. Relations with the French monarchy were not a major issue, although the king's support for the people of Limoges, north of Gascony, against the local vicomtesse, who was supported by the French, could have created greater difficulties than proved to be the case. Edward was not anxious to challenge Philip III, and was prepared to accept his jurisdiction in this instance.

In 1279 the outstanding difficulties between England and France, resulting from the treaty of 1259, were the subject of negotiations at Amiens. Philip III had taken possession of the Agenais, Quercy, and Saintonge. Now he conceded the Agenais and southern Saintonge. The English abandoned their claims to the dioceses of Limoges, Périgord, and Quercy. This settled some of the outstanding problems of the treaty of Paris, and there was little reason to suppose that relations between England and France would deteriorate. In the same year Edward's queen, Eleanor, acquired the county of Ponthieu in Picardy through inheritance. It was Eleanor, not Edward, who performed homage for it, and paid the relief, but this put the English crown into a further feudal relationship with the French monarchy.

In 1286 Edward went to Gascony once more. Rather than taking ship directly to the duchy, he travelled first to Paris. There, he performed homage to the new French king, Philip IV. Edward's chancellor, Robert Burnell, made a speech in which he explained that although the king had been advised to oppose the French demand for homage, he wished to perform it for the sake of peace. Edward duly declared that 'I become your man for the lands which I hold overseas, according to the terms of your peace made between our ancestors.'[15] A compromise was reached on the question of Quercy, and arrangements were made to delay any possible French intervention in the tricky business of appeals from Gascon jurisdiction to the French *parlement*. All the indications were that relations between England and France were good. No storm clouds were visible. The French, however, must have been suspicious of Edward I's intentions during his stay in Gascony, which lasted until 1289. His reorganization of government indicated a more active, interventionist line. The creation of an English appellate jurisdiction must have been

---

[15] Cited in Prestwich, *Edward I*, 323.

regarded as a threat to the rights of the French king, who was eager to see Gascon appeals brought to his court. In the early 1290s a significant number of appeals were brought to the Paris *parlement* by men who claimed that they had been denied justice by Edward I. This was a period when Philip and his advisers were eager to assert royal rights wherever possible, and the Gascon situation was clearly becoming more critical.

When war broke out in 1294, it had its immediate origins in naval rivalry between sailors from the English Cinque Ports and Breton mariners. The involvement of sailors from Bayonne gave Philip IV a reason to involve Gascony, and the status of the duchy was a key issue during the negotiations. The English attitude was conciliatory. Early in 1294 the king's brother Edmund was sent to make a final effort to agree terms. Interestingly, the widow of the late Philip III and Philip IV's own queen intervened on Edmund's behalf. A secret treaty was agreed, though it seems never to have been sealed and ratified. The terms were that various towns and castles in Gascony, along with twenty hostages, would be handed over to the French. Edward would announce publicly that he was handing over the whole of the duchy. The Gascon possessions, however, would be speedily returned to Edward. The summons to the French *parlement* would be withdrawn. Edward and Philip would meet, and Edward would marry the French king's sister Margaret. Gascony would be held by their children, who would owe fealty to the kings of England. Edmund of Lancaster must have been delighted with these terms, which would have resolved the outstanding problems arising from the 1259 treaty. What was lacking was a proper guarantee for the restoration of the duchy by the French. In the event, the handover of towns and castles by the English took place, but the French did not reciprocate. The summons to Edward was renewed, not withdrawn. There was no question of the marriage taking place. Edmund considered that he had been duped by the French. It is likely in fact that the ladies of Philip's court were acting in good faith, but had less influence than they, and Edmund, had thought.[16]

Some chroniclers put the story in romantic terms. Edward, it was suggested, was so overcome by his desire for the French princess (named as Blanche, not Margaret) that he acted without taking proper counsel. The agreement broke down because Blanche refused to marry someone as old as Edward. The story was an exaggeration, of course, but should not be dismissed out of hand. Edward did need a queen, and the proposed marriage alliance was an important element in the negotiations. The way in which Peter Langtoft told the story in part reflected the world of romance, as when messengers reported to Edward

[16] Vale, *Origins of the Hundred Years War*, 178–200, provides an excellent summary of the origins of the war.

that 'So beautiful a creature is not to be found in the whole world.' At the same time, the terms on which Gascony was to be held were set out by the chronicler in legal language of enfeoffment and issue, which suggests that his sources were more than idle gossip.[17]

Edward I, in complete contrast to his father, had a clear strategic plan for his French war. Although his primary aim was to recover and retain Gascony, it made much more sense to fight the war nearer home. The costs and ease of shipping troops across the Channel provide part of the explanation, but the main reason was that he intended to fight with the assistance of a massive coalition of allies. The concept was hardly new, for this was the strategy that had been used by Richard I and John. According to the chronicler Peter Langtoft, Anthony Bek, bishop of Durham, was the prime mover. He advised the king to put on his armour, mount his steed, and take his lance in his fist, and then to seek allies. The king of Germany, the archbishop of Cologne, the king of Aragon, and the count of Savoy were specified.[18] Edward had three means available to him to win support: money, wool, and daughters. Agreement was swiftly reached with Adolf of Nassau, king of Germany, and with the duke of Brabant, who was already married to Edward's daughter Margaret. Guelders and Holland were also soon drawn into the net. Flanders, however, was more difficult, and a plan for the marriage of Count Guy's daughter to Edward's son was foiled by the French, who demanded that the girl be handed over to their custody. The count of Holland's support was bought by Philip IV in 1296. He was then murdered by a pro-English faction, and was succeeded by his son, who married Edward's daughter Elizabeth early in 1297. The pressure of an English embargo on wool exports was telling on Flanders, and Count Guy was persuaded to join the English alliance. In addition to the allies in the Low Countries, Edward could count on the support of the count of Bar, who had married his daughter Eleanor in 1293, and on that of a group of Burgundian noblemen. In all, the allies were probably promised about £250,000, of which some £165,000 was actually paid.

The grand alliance proved to be a grand flop. Edward's plans for a Continental campaign were delayed by a Welsh rebellion in 1294–5 and a campaign in Scotland in 1296. The German king, possibly bribed by the French, but more probably because of internal difficulties, never joined in the campaign at all. An allied force was defeated by the French at the battle of Veurne shortly before Edward landed in Flanders in August 1297, and the town of Lille fell to Philip IV's forces. There was serious fighting when the English fleet arrived in

---

[17] Pierre de Langtoft, 260–2. See M. W. Ormrod, 'Love and War in 1294', in *TCE* viii. 143–52.
[18] Pierre de Langtoft, 266.

Flanders, but not with the enemy; the men of Yarmouth seized the opportunity to continue their long-standing feud with the Cinque Ports. Edward faced hostility from the local citizens of both Bruges and Ghent, and was extremely fortunate that Philip IV's sense of caution led him to avoid battle with a numerically vastly inferior English army. Edward had employed trickery so as to deceive the French into thinking his forces were greater than they were: footsoldiers were sent out in front of the army bearing cavalry banners. A truce was agreed by the two kings on 9 October. Meanwhile, English forces had been engaged in what was little more than a holding operation in Gascony. Defeat at Bellegarde early in 1297 was not so serious as to jeopardize the whole operation, but the English succeeded in holding onto little more than Bourg and Blaye in the north of the duchy, and Bayonne in the south. The French held the main city of Bordeaux.[19] This was an expensive war for the English, with the bill coming to roughly £400,000, of which about £140,000 went on the pay of Gascon troops. The war placed other burdens on England: in 1297 just over 12,000 quarters of grain were collected in East Anglia and sent in a fleet of sixteen ships to the duchy.[20]

The war of 1294 had its origins in naval rivalry, and Edward I took steps to provide England with the ships necessary to deal with the French threat. In 1294 he ordered the construction of thirty galleys each of 120 oars, with attendant barges. The advantages of galleys in warfare were obvious. They were fast, and could be easily manoeuvred, whereas sailing ships with their single square sail were highly dependent on a favourable wind. They were, however, flimsy vessels, in frequent need of repair. Eight of the galleys are known to have been built, and there may well have been more. The steps Edward took did not prevent the French galleys (which unlike the English were of Mediterranean type) from attacking Dover, Winchelsea, and Hythe in 1295. The galley built at Southampton, however, captured five French ships in 1297, and galleys were used for escort duty to both Gascony and Flanders. The main naval provision consisted of sailing vessels requisitioned for the purpose and the naval service provided by the Cinque Ports, usually some thirty ships for forty days. In 1296 the fleet that protected the area between King's Lynn and Harwich consisted of no less than ninety-four vessels, with a total complement of 3,578 men. Ships were also needed for the expeditions to Gascony and to Flanders. The latter required 305 vessels, and about 5,800 sailors.[21]

It was one thing to agree a truce in 1297, and quite another to negotiate a peace. The final treaty was not agreed until 1303. There were issues to be dealt with that

---

[19] Prestwich, *Edward I*, 381–400.
[20] Prestwich, *War, Politics and Finance*, 171–2; E 372/145, m. 20.
[21] E 159/68, m. 77^{r-v}; Prestwich, *War, Politics and Finance*, 138–42.

arose from the war itself: compensation for losses by merchants and others were not easy to settle. There was the question of what to do about the Scots and the Flemings. There were also the problems that arose from the 1259 treaty of Paris about the status of Gascony. Boniface VIII was invited to arbitrate, not as pope but as a private individual. The options that the English put were, firstly, that they should hold Gascony freely, and in exchange some lands would be handed over to the French. Secondly, if that were not acceptable, the French should renounce all rights to hear appeals from Gascon courts. Again, some lands would be handed over by the English. The third option was for the French to agree to exercise the right to hear appeals in moderation. The fourth, which was very different, was for Gascony to be held as a fief, not from the French king but from the papacy. The English, after so indecisive a war, were not in a strong position. Boniface's decree was that the duchy should revert to its pre-war status. Disputed lands should be handed over to the papacy. Future friendship between the two kings was to be ensured by the marriages of Edward I to Philip IV's sister Margaret, and of Prince Edward to Philip's daughter Isabella. The marriage of Edward and Margaret duly took place in 1299.

The marriage was not the end of the story of the peace negotiations. The French did not hand over territory to the papacy as they should have done, and further discussions at the papal curia came to nothing. What transformed the situation was the defeat of the French army by the Flemings in 1302 at the battle of Courtrai. After that Philip IV needed to concentrate all his forces on Flanders, and could not risk the possibility that the English might offer the Flemings assistance. After all the complex manoeuvres and the ingenuity of the arguments, the peace that was agreed in 1303 was simple: there should be a return to the pre-war situation. Of course, the clock could not easily be turned back. There were continuing issues. One was the performance of homage. Different plans were made for Edward, or his son acting in his place, to do homage to Philip IV; unsurprisingly, none were fulfilled. In the 'processes' of Montreuil in 1306 and Périgueux in 1311 lengthy negotiations took place over the question of reparations and compensation for war damages, to little effect. There was, however, no will on either side to go war, and early in Edward II's reign, in January 1308, the new king went to Boulogne to marry Philip IV's daughter Isabella, and to do homage to his father-in-law. Friction remained over Gascony. Among other issues, there were fears that the French would enter clandestinely and seize the *bastides* and other fortified places that had been the possession of the knightly order of the Temple, which had been suppressed in 1312, largely at Philip IV's instigation.[22] War, however, did not break out again until 1324.

---

[22] *Gascon Register A*, ed. Cuttino, 692.

The feudal position of Gascony was, predictably, an important part of the background to the brief war of 1324–5. As overlord, the French king claimed the right to hear appeals against the English king's courts there. The case of a notorious brawling Gascon noble, Jourdain de l'Isle, ended with his being hanged in Paris after a judgment by the French king's court. In March 1324 no less than thirty-seven Gascon appeals were recorded in the proceedings of the *parlement* of Paris. Edward II repeatedly put off going to France to perform homage to Charles IV. Some at least of the French king's advisers must have interpreted the postponements as refusals. The immediate cause of the war was the attempt by the abbot of Sarlat to found a new *bastide* at Saint-Sardos in the Agenais. A share in the new foundation was promised to the French king. On the day of the formal foundation in 1323 the French sergeant was found hanged on the stake that marked the site of the new settlement. The French laid blame, very possibly rightly, on the lord of Montpezat and Ralph Basset, the seneschal of Gascony, who refused to accept French jurisdiction. This led to war.[23]

The war of 1324–5 was one that the English wished to avoid, while French enthusiasm for it was limited. The major military action was the siege of La Réole, held by the king's brother, the earl of Kent, until he surrendered after a five-week siege. The French took control of the Agenais and most of Saintonge, but made little further progress. Bordeaux remained loyal to Edward II, in contrast to the war of 1294–7, when it had been in French hands. The Gascon nobility for the most part supported the English, though Amanieu d'Albret, who had served Edward I loyally, did not give his son the same support.[24] Peace was relatively easy to conclude. Family connections between the English and French monarchies provided the key. Isabella, Edward II's French queen, was in large part responsible. She had been infuriated by the way in which the English government had treated her as an alien, which had resulted in the seizure of her lands and the dismissal of the French members of her household, and was determined that peace should be restored. In March 1325 she was sent on an embassy to Paris, taking a far more direct role than was normal for a queen. The terms that were agreed were perhaps the best that could be achieved. Gascony was restored to its pre-war status, but English control of the Agenais was no longer assured, for Edward II's title to it was to be investigated by a special commission. It was initially intended that Edward should do homage to the French king, Charles IV, but in the event it was the future Edward III who did this on behalf of his father.

---

[23] Vale, *Origins of the Hundred Years War*, 229–36.

[24] The war of Saint-Sardos is conveniently summarized by Vale, *Origins of the Hundred Years War*, 232–41.

THE ORIGINS OF WAR IN 1337

For the first ten years of Edward III's reign the question of Gascony was a running sore. In 1325 one English official had argued that the English could claim to hold the duchy free of any French suzerainty, given the way in which Charles IV had acted. He had not behaved as he should to a tenant holding in fealty from him, and had allied himself with English traitors.[25] Such a line of argument might have had some validity in law, but could not be maintained. In 1329 Edward III paid homage to the new French king, the Valois Philip VI, placing his hands between Philip's and kissing him on the mouth. He thus accepted the feudal relationship, and in so doing prevented a French invasion of the duchy. Two years later he acknowledged that the homage he had done to Philip should be considered as liege homage. This was not enough to prevent the French from putting considerable pressure on the English administration in Gascony. There the usual issues over compensation for war losses to be dealt with, and some new problems. The Agenais was in French hands. French interference in the affairs of the duchy ran at a high level, and considerable pressure was put on local officials. The claim of the abbey of La Sauve-Majeure that it and its daughter houses were directly held from the French king carried echoes of the Saint-Sardos affair. Cases were heard by French officials which it was claimed lay within Edward's jurisdiction. The castle of Blanquefort, near Bordeaux, had been inherited by the count of Armagnac. Philip VI bought the right to it, and in 1336 granted it to the lord of Dufort in the Agenais, on terms that included garrisoning the castle against the English. In the same year Philip contracted with Gaston, count of Foix, for the provision of 100 men-at-arms and 500 infantry in case of war in Gascony. In such ways the English were goaded into war in 1337.

Gascony, however, was far from being the only reason for war in 1337. The question of Scotland was important. Alexander III's second queen had been French, and it was hardly surprising that during the war that began in 1294 the French should have looked to Scotland as a possible ally. In October 1295 a formal treaty was drawn up, providing for the Scots to invade England should Edward I take an expedition overseas against the French.[26] Though the French provided no troops to assist the Scots, their backing was important. Only when all French support for the Scots was withdrawn after the Anglo-French peace treaty of 1303 did Edward achieve what turned out to be very temporary success in Scotland, with its subjection in 1304.

---

[25] *The War of Saint-Sardos*, ed. Chaplais, 218.
[26] *Acts of the Parliament of Scotland*, ed. T. Thomson and C. Innes (Edinburgh, 1814), i. 451–3.

In the 1330s French support for the Scots again created problems for the English. Despite his initial triumph at Halidon Hill in 1333, Edward III failed to secure Scotland for his puppet king Edward Balliol. Robert Bruce's heir, David, went into exile in Normandy in 1334, and was well looked after by Philip VI of France. It was clear to Edward that final success in Scotland could not be achieved while the Scots could rely on French assistance. In negotiations the French made it very clear that, in any accommodation that might be made, Scotland had to be included. For at least some of Edward's advisers in the late 1330s, the main purpose of the war with France was to neutralize Philip VI's support for David Bruce and the nationalist cause in Scotland. With knowledge of what had happened under Edward I, it made sense to argue that only when French support for the Scots was withdrawn could Scotland be brought under English control.

Another element in the complex international jigsaw of Anglo-French relations was provided by the Low Countries. In formal terms, allegiance here was divided. Most of Flanders was held from the kings of France. Brabant, Hainault, Holland, Guelders, and Luxembourg were held from the German empire, as was the county of Jülich. The political influence of the empire was weak, and that of the kings of France strong. In economic terms, the region was heavily dependent on imports of fine English wool. This meant that, very broadly, the towns looked to England while the aristocracy looked to the French monarchy. Alliances in the Low Countries made by Edward I in the 1290s were a clear threat to French hegemony of the region, and the defeat of a major French army at the hands of Flemish urban levies at the battle of Courtrai in 1302 was a serious blow to Philip IV. However, the peace made with England in 1303 left Edward I a free hand to do as he wished in Scotland, while at the same time the English ceased to offer any support to the Flemings. The threat of further English intervention in the Low Countries was a significant element in the growing crisis of the early years of Edward III's reign. William de Deken of Bruges, a leading rebel against the French, suggested soon after Edward's accession that he should claim the French throne and overlordship of Flanders.[27] The Flemings were defeated by Philip VI at Cassel in 1328, and in the following years English and French diplomats jockeyed for advantage, building alliances among the princes of the Low Countries. The imposition of an English trade embargo on Flanders late in 1336 created a very difficult situation there, while the fact that the English had secured alliances with Hainault, Guelders, Holland, and Jülich must have been regarded with deep suspicion by Philip VI.

[27] H. S. Lucas, *The Low Countries and the Hundred Years War 1326–1347* (Ann Arbor, 1929), 81–2.

Naval rivalry was another element in Anglo-French tension. This had been very clear in the 1290s. Diplomats claimed in 1306 that the kings of England had 'from time out of mind had peaceable possession of the sovereign lordship of the English sea, and of the islands in it',[28] but such words had very little force behind them. English naval power was threatened in 1336, when with the abandonment of ambitious plans for a crusade, Philip VI transferred the fleet he had assembled at Marseilles to Normandy, in an obviously threatening move.

The failure of the intended crusade was a further element in the outbreak of war in 1337. From the outset of his reign Philip VI was anxious to lead Christendom in a campaign against the heathen. Initially, his plan was to do this in Spain, but by 1331 the Holy Land was the declared destination. Edward III was very ready to go along with these plans. The memory of Richard I was a powerful stimulant. The English may also have considered that if Philip was engaged on a crusade, he would not be in a position to create difficulties for them in Scotland or Gascony. Edward never went so far as to take the cross himself, but he declared that he would participate in Philip's expedition, provided that he received satisfaction over Gascony. There have to be doubts over Edward's sincerity; he was using the crusade as a lever to obtain concessions from Philip. The French king would not play. Given the impossibility of establishing an effective peace in Europe, it is no surprise that in 1336 Pope Benedict XII cancelled the crusade. Philip was angry, and must have felt that Edward had considerable responsibility for the abandonment of the plans.

For Philip VI, the backing that Edward III gave to Robert of Artois was an important factor in the outbreak of war, while the chronicler Jean le Bel considered that it was because of the advice Edward III received from Robert of Artois that 'the said king undertook the war against the kingdom of France, which has been the cause of so many evils'.[29] Robert was brother-in-law to Philip VI, and had supported him strongly during the initial years of his reign. He had a claim to the county of Artois, which had been inherited by his aunt Mahaut, and clearly expected Philip to back him. The story is bizarre. Robert had documents forged in support of his claim, and when this device failed it was alleged that he resorted to poison, murdering both his aunt and her daughter. When cited to appear before the *parlement* over the forgery, he fled from France to Brabant. He began to plot the downfall of Philip VI by every possible and impossible means, the latter including the use of magical red and black writings, and pins stuck into wax images of the French king and queen. In 1334 Robert, finding life ever more dangerous in the Low Countries, fled to England. Here he found favour in Edward's court. In 1337 he was given an

---

[28] Chaplais, *English Medieval Diplomatic Practice*, pt. 1, i. 367.   [29] Le Bel, i. 100.

annual pension of 1,200 marks and entrusted with the custody of three castles. There is no doubt that Philip was furious. In December 1336 he had requested that the seneschal of Gascony should return Robert to France. When he declared Gascony forfeit in the following year, he laid great emphasis on the case of Robert of Artois. The view that this explains the outbreak of the war is, not surprisingly, not to be found in English chronicles.[30]

EDWARD III'S WAR AIMS

In a curious poem, *The Vows of the Heron*, the tale is told of a banquet in the late 1330s. Robert of Artois entered and presented the king with a nicely roasted heron. 'I will give it to the greatest coward who is, or ever was, alive: that is Edward Louis, disinherited from the noble country of France of which he is the rightful heir.' Edward then swore an oath on the heron that he would pursue his rights.[31] This question of Edward III's claim to the French throne was a very different issue in the conflict that started in 1337 from those that had underlain earlier Anglo-French wars. It was, however, not a significant factor in the immediate origins of the war. When Edward wrote to his subjects to set out his reasons for going to war, he stressed first of all the various offers that he had made of marriage alliances with the French. He also explained his willingness to go on crusade with Philip VI, provided that the French king was prepared to do justice on Edward's claims to lands in France. French naval activity was another reason for war, while much emphasis was laid on the support that the French had offered to the Scots. Neither the question of Robert of Artois, on which Philip VI laid such stress, nor the claim to the French throne were mentioned.[32] Edward had, however, a good claim, for he was the son of Isabella, daughter of Philip IV. Philip VI was descended from Charles of Valois, son of Philip III; his father was a mere count. On the other hand, when he did homage to Philip VI in 1329, Edward had acknowledged the Valois right to the throne, and in doing so had tacitly abandoned his own claim.

Edward III used the title of king of France for the first time in October 1337, when he issued letters appointing the duke of Brabant and others to act on his behalf in France. It is not clear that these letters were delivered; the English

---

[30] *Œuvres de Froissart*, ed. de Lettenhove, xviii. 34–7; Lucas, *The Low Countries and the Hundred Years War*, 113–14, 177; J. Sumption, *The Hundred Years War*, i: *Trial by Battle* (London, 1990), 171–2.

[31] The poem was printed by T. Wright, in his *Political Poems and Songs relating to English History* (RS, 1859), i. 1–25. The case for its being satirical was put by B. J. Whiting, 'The Vows of the Heron', *Speculum*, 20 (1952), 261–78. The fact that it was written in a northern French dialect suggests that its author's allegiance was to the Valois not the Plantagenet monarchy.

[32] *Foedera*, ii/2. 994–5.

diplomats may well have kept them in their possession. The situation changed in 1340. On 22 January flags with the English and French coats of arms quartered were bought at Antwerp for 27s. 3d. Four days later, in the market place at Ghent, Edward formally received homage from Guy, the half-brother of the count of Flanders. The civic authorities of Ghent, Bruges, and Ypres acclaimed Edward as king of France, and Edward swore to maintain their privileges and provide them with protection.[33] For all the pomp of the ceremony, there was no coronation. In correspondence with Continental rulers Edward usually used the title 'Edward by grace of God king of France and England and lord of Ireland', putting France before England. Edward promised to rule France well as its king. He would respect the laws of St Louis, would cease the practice of currency debasement, and would not take taxes to which he was not entitled. Liberties were to be respected, and he promised that he would follow the counsel of the peers and prelates of France. He also promised to further the cause of the crusade. This was an attractive, if impractical, political agenda. In England, Edward made it absolutely clear in March 1340 that the fact that he claimed the French throne did not mean that there was any question of the subjection of the realm to France.[34]

The purpose of the ceremony in 1340, and the formal assumption of the title of king of France, had a clear purpose. Edward III wanted to strengthen his system of alliances. His supporters in the Low Countries would be in a stronger position if they could claim that they were supporting the legitimate king of France, rather than appearing as rebels against the Valois king Philip. One argument is that the claim was, from Edward's point of view, a convenient diplomatic ploy. Not only did it suit his allies; it was also a bargaining counter. The English could offer the French the prospect of Edward's abandoning his claim in return for holding Gascony and other lands in France in full sovereignty. It has, however, been argued to the contrary, that Edward seriously intended to make himself king of France, and that this was a fundamental aim of his military strategy.[35] In England, Edward did not make very much of his claim to the French throne. He was careful to call himself king of England and France there, whereas across the Channel he put the realms the other way round in his title. There was little propaganda emphasis in England on Edward's right to the French kingship; there must have been suspicions that his English subjects would not have been particularly sympathetic to a war fought to place their king on a foreign throne. The many newsletters that were

---

[33] Lucas, Low Countries and the Hundred Years War, 364–5; Sumption, Hundred Years War, i: 302.

[34] Foedera, ii/2. 1111; Œuvres de Froissart, ed. de Lettenhove, xviii. 129–30.

[35] The case is put by J. Le Patourel, 'Edward III and the Kingdom of France', in C. J. Rogers (ed.), The Wars of Edward III: Sources and Interpretations (Woodbridge, 1999), 247–64.

sent home from campaign laid no stress on Edward as king of France. No doubt Edward hoped that his claim to the French throne would succeed, but the retention and extension of the English lands in France were more fundamental to his war aims.

A further argument over Edward's aims in the war is over how he intended to fight. The conventional view is that medieval generals believed in attaining their objectives without, if possible, risking battle. Even the legendary Richard Lionheart fought no more than two or three true battles during his long military career, and his rival Philip Augustus one. The advice of the late classical theorist Vegetius, whose work was widely circulated in the middle ages, was to avoid battle save as a last resort.[36] The alternative to battle was a war of attrition, in which the enemy would be brought to its knees by the besieging of castles and the destruction of towns, villages, orchards, and fields. Under Edward III's leadership the *chevauchée*, or mounted raid, proved to be a highly effective means of doing this. Savage raids would destroy the country-side, and with it the capacity of its inhabitants to pay taxes. The French would be forced to the negotiating table. 'The intention, and sometimes the effect as well, was to achieve an element of demoralisation and a spirit of criticism of the administration among the French king's subjects; this was the way by which the war was to be won. The regular battle on a major scale was seen to be only the death-blow at the end of the process.'[37]

An alternative analysis suggests that the English strategy was a battle-seeking one.[38] The public statements that were made by Edward III expressed the clear view that the aim of his campaigns was to bring the French to battle. 'When we saw that our enemies did not want to come and give battle, we therefore had the surrounding lands burned and laid waste' was how the king described part of the 1346 campaign.[39] In the following year the French army approached Calais, and Edward was able to write that 'we can see their tents and lodgings from our said host, so that we hope that with the aid of our lord Jesus Christ we will soon have a good battle according to our just quarrel, to the honour of us and all our realm'.[40] Destruction of territory was not the best way for Edward to establish his right to the French throne; it would hardly endear him to those he wished to make his subjects. Battle, on the other hand, was a

---

[36] J. Gillingham, 'Richard I and the Science of War in the Middle Ages', in J. Gillingham and J. C. Holt (eds.), *War and Government in the Middle Ages* (Woodbridge,1984), 80–2.

[37] C. T. Allmand, *Society at War: The Experience of England and France During the Hundred Years War* (Edinburgh, 1973), 2.

[38] C. Rogers, *War Cruel and Sharp: English Strategy Under Edward III, 1327–1360* (Woodbridge, 2000), provides a valuable antidote to the conventional view.

[39] Rogers (ed.), *The Wars of Edward III*, 130.

[40] *Œuvres de Froissart*, ed. de Lettenhove, xviii. 302, trans. Rogers, *War Cruel and Sharp*, 279.

form of trial before God, and victory would provide a demonstration of divine approval for his cause. It is also relevant that siege warfare was difficult for the English in France. Equipment was difficult to ship. In 1342 one great siege engine was taken from the Tower of London to Sandwich to send to France, but there were insufficient ships and equipment for the task, so it had to be returned to London.[41] The length of time involved in sieges also presented problems for armies operating far from home. It would prove possible to besiege Calais in 1346–7, given the short Channel crossing, but major sieges further afield presented considerable difficulties. Battle was the better option for the English. The problem in the French war was that it made sense for Philip VI and his son John to avoid battle, for the English normally had far more to gain and the French far more to lose. Once the French had experienced the sharp points of the English arrowheads and the tempered blades of the English swords, it is hardly surprising if they adopted battle-avoiding strategies.

THE GRAND STRATEGY

The war that began in 1337 was very different from that of 1324–5. Edward III consciously looked back to the strategy adopted by his grandfather in the 1290s. In the years leading up to the final breach with France, English envoys such as John de Thrandeston (a German in Edward's service), John de Montgomery, and John Wawayn had been exceptionally busy creating a new alliance, similar to that which Edward I had built. The duke of Brabant, the count of Hainault and Holland, and the count of Guelders, together with the count palatine of the Rhine and other German magnates, were all brought into the network. The margrave of Jülich was an important ally, and the emperor Ludwig of Bavaria added prestige if little real power. At a grand meeting in Koblenz, held in 1338, king and emperor held a splendid joint ceremony, formalizing a relationship in which Edward was Ludwig's deputy. In Flanders the English cause was strongly supported by the townspeople of Bruges, Ghent, and Ypres, who were desperate for English wool. The grand alliance was extremely expensive, for the king promised his Continental supporters over £200,000.[42]

The strategy of fighting a war with the aid of a grand alliance had not worked particularly well in the 1290s, and it fared little better in the late 1330s. The plan was for English forces in Gascony to maintain their position, while the major assault on the French would come from the north. A small-scale raid in 1337 on the island of Cadzand by Walter Mauny saw considerable slaughter

---

[41] *Foedera*, ii/2. 1213, 1215.
[42] Knighton, 8–11; Fryde, *Studies in Medieval Finance and Trade*, ch. VII, p. 1180.

and some important prisoners taken. Edward himself sailed for Flanders in the next year. His army was small, and he was heavily reliant on his allies. They were rightly suspicious that the English would not be able to produce the promised subsidies. This was a phoney war, until October 1339, when Edward invaded French territory, burning and laying waste the area around Cambrai. The army advanced on a 20-mile-wide front, burning and destroying defenceless villages. The region was so hard-hit that Pope Benedict XII later made a grant to alleviate the suffering of those who were left there.[43] Near Buirenfosse the French and English armies faced each other for a day without fighting. The French wisely chose not to attack the allies, who had established a strong defensive position. Edward could not risk advancing his own troops. From a propaganda point of view it was important that Edward had been on French soil; but beyond misery for the inhabitants of the Cambrésis and the Thiérache, the campaign had achieved very little, at great financial cost. Edward was facing bankruptcy and increasing political difficulties at home.

The English cause in Gascony was ably sustained by Oliver Ingham, the seneschal. In 1338 the French invaded, and took Saint-Macaire and Blaye. Ingham achieved a considerable success in the following year, when he detached the lord of Albret from the French cause and with his help conducted a raid into French territory. In 1340 the pendulum of war swung to and fro in Gascony, with skirmishes and sieges proving ultimately indecisive. Both sides faced heavy expenditure, and must have welcomed the truce that came in September.

Edward III, meanwhile, was concentrating all his efforts on attacking the French from the north. In 1340 things began badly. Edward had returned to England in February, in order to obtain further financial support and to deal with the growing political difficulties there. His queen was left behind in Flanders, a clear indication that Edward intended to come back promptly. In April the earls of Salisbury and Suffolk were both captured because of their 'stupid bravery'. Only the persuasion of the king of Bohemia, John of Luxembourg, prevented Philip VI from executing them.[44]

In the summer the course of the war was dramatically shifted. Edward sailed from England on 22 June, and on the next day arrived off the Zwyn estuary. He was clearly determined to fight. The massive French fleet could be seen off the port of Sluys, moored in a defensive formation, 'like a line of castles', linked by a chain. On 24 June the French sailed about a mile towards the English. They were possibly tricked into doing this when they saw what appeared to be an English withdrawal. In the late afternoon, with the wind and sun behind them

[43] H. J. Hewitt, *The Organisation of War Under Edward III* (Manchester, 1966), 124–6.
[44] Murimuth, 104–5.

and the tide with them, the English attacked. Two out of the three French squadrons were defeated, and to the English delight three ships taken earlier in the war were recaptured. French casualties were heavy, more through drowning than from the fighting itself. A mere four English knights lost their lives, along with a more significant number of sailors. The joke told by the English was that if God had given fish the power of speech, after they had eaten the dead at Sluys, they would have spoken French.[45]

The victory at Sluys did much to secure the coasts of England from any further French raids, and meant that English expeditions to the Low Countries and France would be in far less danger than in the past from French naval activity. French morale was hit hard. The victory did not, however, ensure success for Edward's land-based campaigning. Robert of Artois suffered defeat, described by English chroniclers as a victory, at Saint-Omer. The major objective for Edward and his allies was Tournai. The siege was a massive undertaking. Siege engines, including guns, did little to damage the defences, and although famine threatened the defenders, they held out stubbornly. Assaults on the walls were driven off. The arrival of Philip VI and his army nearby at Bouvines did not result in battle; as at Buirenfosse in 1339, no engagement took place. Edward challenged the French king to settle the issues between them by single combat, or if that was not acceptable, between a hundred men from each side, but this was done more to make a point than in the hope that Philip would agree.[46] Edward's allies were increasingly dispirited. Funds were short, and the difficulties that the English faced in meeting their treaty obligations were more and more evident. Edward's debts were mounting daily. In late September 1340 the truce of Esplechin was agreed. There was to be a nine-month cessation of hostilities on all fronts, including Scotland and Gascony.

YEARS OF TRIUMPH

The truce of Esplechin ended the first phase of the Hundred Years War. The cost, both financial and political, of the strategy that Edward had adopted had been immense. Expensive alliances could not be afforded, and allies could not be relied upon. If the war was to continue once the truce was over, it would have to be fought on a very different basis. The English were presented with a new opportunity to take the war to the French by a succession dispute in

---

[45] Murimuth, 106–7; Avesbury, 312; Baker, 68–9; *Anonimalle*, 16; *Melsa*, iii. 45; Knighton, 28–31. N. Rogers, *The Safeguard of the Sea: A Naval History of Britain*, i: *660–1649* (London, 1997), 99, suggests that the sun was behind the English as they attacked in the morning, but the sources make it clear that it was in the afternoon that the battle began.
[46] *Œuvres de Froissart*, ed. de Lettenhove, xviii. 170–1.

Brittany. When Duke John III died in 1341, he had no direct heir, and the succession was disputed between his niece Jeanne de Penthièvre and his half-brother John de Montfort. John had the better claim, for he was the closest male relation of the previous duke. Jeanne, however, was married to Philip VI's nephew Charles of Blois. Influence, if not law, placed the duchy in Charles's hands. John de Montfort's only recourse was to arms and an alliance with Edward III. Things went badly for Montfort in the first half of the year. Nantes was surrendered, and he himself was imprisoned in Paris. The fortunes of his cause rested with his wife. Edward III was reluctant to commit himself. A small English force under Walter Mauny was sent out, but was able to do little. Jeanne de Montfort held out gallantly in Hennebont, and then moved to Brest, which was besieged by the French. Finally, in August 1342 an English force under the earl of Northampton arrived. At the end of September it engaged Charles of Blois at Morlaix. Victory was achieved, though this was only a minor engagement, which did little to alter the course of the war.

Edward III himself landed in Brittany in October 1342. He moved quickly to besiege Vannes, 'which is the best town in Brittany after the town of Nantes'. The army was well supplied, for 'the land is very abundant in corn and meat'. There was the usual problem, as the king explained in a letter to his son: 'But ever, dear son, it behoves you to stir up our chancellor and our treasurer to send money to us, for they are well aware of our estate.' Things may have looked good at that stage, but they did not continue well. Robert of Artois was wounded and died. Vannes held out, though Philip VI with his relieving army once again did not choose to give battle. In January 1343, thanks to the intervention of two cardinals, a truce was agreed at Malestroit, which was set to last until 1346.[47] Intervention in the Brittany succession dispute had been useful for Edward, providing him with new allies within France, and coastal strongholds that would help to secure the sea route to Gascony. In practice, the English armies were not sufficiently strong, nor adequately equipped for siege warfare, for more than a limited achievement.[48]

The war was punctuated by diplomacy. The truces of Esplechin in 1340, and of Malestroit in 1343, were no more than temporary halts to the fighting. In 1344, a year of diplomacy more than war, the new pope, Clement VI, attempted to negotiate a peace. Edward III sent various missions to Avignon. Henry, earl of Derby, achieved nothing in private discussions. Bishop Bateman of Norwich, the king's clerk John Offord, Nicolas de Luca, and Hugh Neville, knight, were then sent on a formal embassy. Had Edward been in earnest about concluding the war, perhaps a more formidable group would have been used. The intention was that Clement VI should resolve the disputes by arbitrating,

---

[47] Avesbury, 340–51.   [48] M. Jones, *Ducal Brittany 1364–1399* (Oxford, 1970), 8–14.

not as pope, but as a private person. The arguments used by both sides were predictable. The French were insistent that Gascony was held as a fief from the French crown. They were not prepared to discuss Edward's claim to the French throne, while the English were not prepared to give it up. The arguments used to support Edward's case were carefully worked out, with precedents from Roman law cited to show that any limitation on women exercising public office would have no impact on the rights of their sons. It does seem that the English ambassadors were prepared to envisage Edward giving up the claim, provided that in exchange he would hold Gascony in full sovereignty, independent of the French crown. This, however, was not acceptable to the French. The negotiations failed.[49]

For the English at least, further campaigning was necessary if worthwhile gains were to be achieved. In 1345 the transformation of the course of the war began, and a period of spectacular English success opened. That year three fleets were prepared, one to take the earl of Lancaster to Gascony, another to take Northampton to Brittany, and the third to take the king to Flanders. This was an overambitious plan. Success on all three fronts was hardly likely. Lancaster and Northampton were both given very full powers, both military and civil, to act in the king's name, as his lieutenant. Lancaster was astonishingly successful.[50] He moved rapidly to besiege and take Bergerac on 24 August. He failed to capture Périgueux, but then won a remarkable victory over a French force that was besieging Auberoche. This was achieved by a surprise night attack, rather than by the normal English tactic of fighting in a strong defensive formation. The shooting by the English archers was particularly devastating. An impressive number of prisoners were taken, both at Bergerac and at Auberoche. Lancaster followed up his victory with the capture of La Réole. The earl then wintered in Gascony. He and his men worked hard to bring the Agenais back into English hands. The town of Aiguillon, situated where the Lot and Garonne join, surrendered to Ralph Stafford. The following April saw a major French attempt to recover the town, with a siege led by the duke of Normandy. The achievements of the previous year were seriously threatened, and there was an urgent need, as Lancaster made clear to the king, to provide him with assistance.

Northampton's expedition to Brittany was not so successful. Thomas Dagworth had an initial striking success against Charles of Blois, but the

[49] For details of the negotiations, Œuvres de Froissart, ed. de Lettenhove, xviii. 202–56; C. Taylor, 'Edward III and the Plantagenet Claim to the French Throne', in Bothwell (ed.), The Age of Edward III, 155–69.

[50] For Lancaster, see K. Fowler, The King's Lieutenant: Henry of Grosmont, First Duke of Lancaster, 1310–1361 (London, 1969).

siege of Quimper failed. John de Montfort himself fell ill and died. His son was only 5, and was hardly an effective figurehead for the English cause in the duchy. The king's own expedition to Flanders went even worse. The fleet arrived at Sluys, but the men and horses were not disembarked. Unsatisfactory negotiations took place. Disastrously, one of Edward's main supporters in Flanders, Jacques van Artevelde, was killed in a riot in Ghent. Edward then returned to Sandwich. A council was held at London, with those present no doubt in a very depressed state of mind. It would have been hard indeed to organize a new expedition. It was therefore decided, as one chronicler has it, to devote the autumn to hunting and relaxation.[51] This was typical of Edward, a man who knew when he should take his chances and when he should not.

In the next year Edward assembled a substantial fleet at Portsmouth and an army perhaps some 14,000 strong. Great care was taken not to reveal the destination, though the belief was that it was Gascony, so that Aiguillon could be relieved. The fleet sailed at the end of June, only to be forced back by contrary winds. It finally left two weeks later, on 11 July. Edward set course for Normandy. Whether this had been the intention all along, or whether it represented a late change of mind forced on the king by the capriciousness of the winds, is not clear. Bartholomew Burghersh, writing to the archbishop of Canterbury, certainly thought that the weather had forced a change of plan. Edward was an opportunist, and it seems very possible that the decision to make for Normandy was made very late. It made such good strategic sense, however, that it is very difficult to see it as the product of mere accident. The chronicler Jean le Bel, whom Froissart followed in his chronicle, thought that the advice of a renegade Norman noble, Godfrey de Harcourt, had been influential. He pointed out the wealth of Normandy, and its vulnerability at a time when most of the military were at the siege of Aiguillon.[52] The attack on Normandy was a bold choice. It involved making a landing in hostile territory, which the English had not attempted previously with a full army. There were no local allies, as in the Low Countries or Gascony. It did, however, offer the advantage of complete surprise; a landing in Gascony would have met with opposition from significant naval forces recruited by Philip VI from Genoa.

According to the Norman chronicle, Edward first considered a landing at Cherbourg, but the port was too strongly defended. The fleet then moved east round the peninsula, and made an easy landing at Saint-Vaast-la-Hougue.[53] The campaign that followed was successful beyond any possible expectations,

[51] Murimuth, 170.   [52] Ibid. 200; Froissart, iii. 131; Le Bel, ii. 70.
[53] *Chronique normande du XIVe siècle*, ed. A. and É. Molinier (Paris, 1882), 75.

and was recorded in a number of triumphant newsletters and a remarkable campaign diary, the *Acta Bellicosa*.[54] The first to write home was Bartholomew Burghersh:

And the town of Barfleur is taken. And my lord of Warwick jousted at war with the enemy, and had a good and honourable day; and my lord John de Beauchamp and many other knights and squires have had to do with the enemy, both riding and in other ways, and there has been no halt to this kind of thing. The armed men of the country have retreated to their castles and fortified towns, and the commons of the land are all coming to the obedience of our lord the king.[55]

The first major engagement came when Caen was taken and brutally plundered. The capture of the count of Eu by Thomas Holland, 'a noble knight who had only one eye',[56] and that of the lord of Tancarville by Thomas Daniel, provided a foretaste of the great profits to be obtained from ransoms later in the war. Burghersh put the French casualties at some 5,000.

Edward's plan was to march northwards, to join up eventually with his Flemish allies; a force under Hugh Hastings had been sent to Flanders. The English faced two major difficulties. One was the French army under Philip VI. The other was geographical. If Edward was to combine forces with the Flemings, he would have to cross two major rivers, first the Seine, and then the Somme. His plans were partly revealed in a letter he wrote from Caen, in which he asked for reinforcements to be sent to Le Crotoy, at the mouth of the Somme, though this does not make it clear where, or how, he intended to cross the Seine.[57] The English army was forced to march up the Seine valley as each successive bridge was either too strongly defended, or broken. The English reached Poissy, within a day's march of Paris, again to find the bridge broken. Carpenters began to construct a temporary structure using the existing piers. Philip VI appears to have been distracted by the operations of English troops burning and pillaging villages near Paris. He also sent the bishop of Meaux to Edward, to challenge him to meet the French army on the field of battle. It is hard to know how seriously to take such challenges, which were a common feature of the war. It may be that on this occasion Philip considered that

---

[54] Conveniently translated in *The Life and Campaigns of the Black Prince*, ed. R. Barber (Woodbridge, 1979), 26–40.

[55] Murimuth, 200. The 1346 campaign has been subjected to frequent analysis. See in particular J. Viard, 'La Campagne de juillet–août 1346', *Le Moyen Âge*, 2 ser., 27 (1926), 1–84; A. H. Burne, *The Crécy War* (London, 1955), 136–203; Sumption, *Hundred Years War*, i: 497–534; Rogers, *War Cruel and Sharp*, 238–72.

[56] Le Bel, ii. 82.

[57] K. Fowler, 'News from the Front: Letters and Despatches of the Fourteenth Century', in P. Contamine, C. Giry-Deloison, and M. H. Keen (eds.), *Guerre et société en France, en Angleterre et en Bourgogne XIVe–XVe siècle* (Villeneuve d'Ascq, 1991), 78–9, 84.

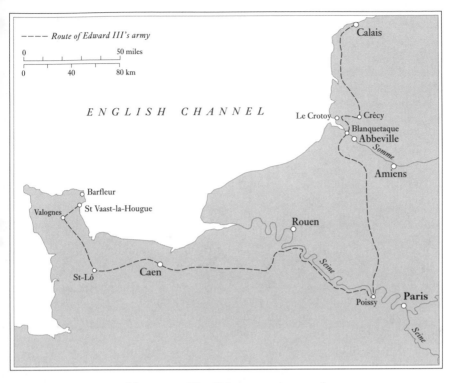

MAP 11.1. The Crécy campaign, 1346

Edward had no option other than to fight, and it is also possible, as the Norman chronicle has it, that the English king gave his rival the impression that he would indeed accept the challenge. The English certainly delayed at Poissy, waiting in vain for the French to attack. Part of a letter from Edward to Philip is revealing. He expressed his readiness to fight, but added that 'We shall never be dictated to by you, nor will we accept a day and place for battle on the conditions which you have named.' The English then slipped across the reconstructed bridge, and marched north towards the Somme, burning and pillaging as they went. As Edward put it to Philip, 'We decided to continue further into our kingdom, to comfort our loyal friends and punish rebels, whom you wrongly claim as your subjects.'[58]

The crossing of the Somme was achieved at the ford of Blanquetaque, between Saint-Valéry and Abbeville. One account has it that a Yorkshireman long resident in those parts showed the English where it was; others that a

---

[58] *Chronique normande*, ed. A. and É. Molinier, 78; *Life and Campaigns of the Black Prince*, ed. Barber, 38–9; see also the version of this letter in Rogers, *War Cruel and Sharp*, 260.

prisoner was bribed to reveal his local knowledge. The ford was defended, but the English archers and men-at-arms succeeded in forcing a crossing. They then advanced to Crécy through the forest. On 26 August Edward drew up his men in battle array, on well-chosen ground between the villages of Crécy and Wadicourt. It is at first sight surprising that he chose to fight at this stage of the campaign. His troops must have been tired by the march from the Seine to the Somme. At Crécy, however, he had the opportunity to fight on ground of his choosing. Further, Crécy was in the county of Ponthieu, which the English had acquired in 1279; it gave the English a certain moral advantage to fight on what could be regarded as home territory. Edward had, almost certainly, been keen throughout the campaign to meet the French in battle, but only if he had an evident advantage. At Crécy, at long last, he did.

There were bitter arguments in Philip's camp over whether or not to fight at Crécy, and whether the battle should be delayed until the French army was properly assembled and arrayed. This initial confusion undoubtedly helped the English considerably. There are many chronicle accounts of what happened, and no fully consistent story emerges. It is clear that an advance by Genoese crossbowmen was halted by English archery. French cavalry charges in the early stages of the fighting suffered badly from the storm of vicious bodkin-headed arrows; the horses were maddened and the scene was chaotic. In the hand-to-hand fighting that followed, there was a moment when the Black Prince, fighting in the front line, was in real danger, but the English triumphed. The battle was savage, with massive casualties on the French side. The normal chivalric conventions, which made excellent business sense, of capturing prisoners to hold them to ransom were abandoned when the French unfurled their sacred battle standard, the *Oriflamme*. The list of noble and distinguished dead was headed by John of Luxembourg, king of Bohemia, and included the duke of Lorraine, the counts of Flanders, Blois, and Alençon, and the archbishop of Sens.[59] The victory was astonishing. It was to be followed a few weeks later by the decisive defeat of David II of Scotland, one of Philip VI's allies, at the battle of Neville's Cross.

In the south the siege of Aiguillon by the French was abandoned on 20 August, a week before Crécy. In September Lancaster conducted a raid northwards, through the Agenais and Saintonge, and sacked the town of Poitiers. This was a most successful *chevauchée*, which saw the English troops burn and plunder at will. Meanwhile, in the north Edward marched towards Calais. His strategic intention was clear. The town was strongly defended, and would provide an ideal bridgehead for future invasions. The siege was not easy,

---

[59] For a fuller discussion, see the analyses in A. Ayton (ed.), *The Battle of Crécy* (Woodbridge, forthcoming).

and lasted eleven months. Disease and desertion dogged the English army, but Edward's patience eventually won the day. The French succeeded in bringing in supplies by sea on several occasions, but by April 1347 the blockade of the town was complete. Philip VI eventually succeeding in mustering an army to try to effect a relief in July, but as so often, the French and English forces faced each other without doing battle. Challenges and negotiations came to nothing; the French were understandably reluctant to fight after the disasters of the previous year. Dysentery inflicted heavy losses on the English troops, and the royal wardrobe, the administrative headquarters, suffered a serious fire. Yet the siege continued. The English even had time to hold hearings on disputes about heraldic insignia as they waited for the inevitable conclusion. The exhausted and starving townspeople of Calais had no option other than to surrender, in what seems to have been a carefully staged ceremony. The king, after a show of fierceness, agreed after an intercession by the queen to pardon the towns-people.[60] There was one other significant triumph in this spectacular period of the war. In May 1347 Thomas Dagworth defeated Charles of Blois at La Roche-Derrien in Brittany, after a bold night march. Charles himself was captured; many French noblemen were killed in a very hard fight.

Good planning, and a substantial pinch of good fortune, had thoroughly vindicated Edward's strategy in 1346–7. The successes, however, were not followed up. In part this was because of the Black Death, which first appeared in England in the summer of 1348. Even without the epidemic, it would have been difficult to mount a further major military effort, for the financial strains imposed by the campaigns of 1346–7 had been considerable. Success brought problems. The acquisition of Calais provided the English with a new base from which expeditions could be launched; no longer would it be necessary to negotiate with the rulers of Flanders and Brabant. In practice, however, Calais proved to be an expensive distraction, a fortress that needed to be garrisoned and held at considerable cost. The French were naturally very anxious to regain it, and late in 1349 Geoffroi de Charny negotiated with an Italian member of the garrison, Amerigo of Pavia. In return for 20,000 gold écus, Amerigo was to admit the French troops. Amerigo, however, revealed the plot to Edward III. When the French advanced to the space between the inner and outer walls of Calais, a trap was sprung. The French were defeated, their leaders taken prisoner. Calais was safe.[61]

Fighting continued around Calais and elsewhere, but there were no major campaigns. In 1350 a naval battle took place, in which Edward himself was

---

[60] The siege is fully described by Sumption, *Hundred Years War*, i: 535–8, 557–8, 568–70, 576–82. For the hearings, A. R. Wagner, *Heralds and Heraldry in the Middle Ages*, 2nd edn. (Oxford, 1956), 23.
[61] Baker, 103–8, has an elaborate account of these events.

involved. Castile was an ally of France, and a Castilian fleet in the Channel was a major threat to the important English wool export trade. The Castilian ships, sailing south from Flanders, took a course very close to the English coast, and were intercepted by the king's fleet off Winchelsea. Edward had a remarkable number of nobles with him: Lancaster, Northampton, Warwick, Salisbury, Arundel, Huntingdon, and Gloucester. The ships crashed into each other, the Spanish vessels towering above the English. As in land battles, English archery played an important part, but the battle soon turned to a hand-to-hand fight. Accounts of the number of Castilian ships vary, from forty-four to half that number. This was not a major victory as Sluys had been, and certainly not the major triumph that the chroniclers claimed, but it must have demonstrated to the French and their allies the continuing danger that was presented by English fleets.[62]

In 1353 serious moves to negotiate a peace took place. Discussions at Guînes yielded no more than a truce, but it is clear that significant proposals were put forward. In the autumn Edward explained his aims to parliament. He was prepared to abandon his claim to the French throne in return for the duchy of Aquitaine (interpreted in the most generous sense), Brittany, Normandy, Flanders, and Ponthieu, all to be held in full sovereignty.[63] In April 1354 a draft treaty was drawn up at Guînes, which envisaged that Edward would hold Aquitaine, Poitou, Limoges, Maine, Anjou, Touraine, Ponthieu, and the area around Calais, all in full sovereignty. In contrast to the proposals of the previous year, there was no mention of Brittany or Normandy. Edward III in return would give up his claim to the French throne. In the following autumn a most impressive embassy was sent by Edward to Avignon, to finalize the peace. It was headed by the earls of Lancaster and Arundel, and included the veteran diplomat Bishop Bateman of Norwich as well as Bartholomew Burghersh, Guy Brian, and Michael Northburgh. They went with careful instructions concerning how far they might yield in return for peace. The key issue was that of how much land the French would be prepared to hand over in full sovereignty. Normandy was expendable, as were Cahors, Quercy, and Angoulême, although the latter three were not if it were proved that they were part of the ancient duchy of Aquitaine. If it was not possible to retain Angoulême, then other lands should be handed over in compensation. The negotiations failed. The English claimed that this was because the French would not agree to surrender sovereignty, but one chronicler, Henry Knighton, states that the earl of Lancaster refused to abandon Edward III's claim to the French throne. There is, however, good evidence to suggest that it was in fact the French who wrecked the treaty.[64] The truth of the matter cannot be finally determined;

---

[62] Baker, 110; Avesbury, 412.   [63] *Rot. Parl.* ii. 251–2.

[64] Knighton, 126–7; C. J. Rogers, 'The Anglo–French Peace Negotiations of 1354–1360 Reconsidered', in Bothwell (ed.), *The Age of Edward III*, 195–6; Fowler, *The King's Lieutenant*,

the answer may be simple, that neither party was yet convinced that they could not get more by continuing the war.

THE BLACK PRINCE'S WAR

In 1355 the war entered a new phase, with a fresh English offensive. The peace negotiations had failed, and it was decided in a council at Westminster to send two expeditions, one under the prince of Wales to Gascony, and the other under Henry of Lancaster to Normandy, where it was hoped he would work together with Charles of Navarre, count of Évreux. Subsequently, the king himself joined the fleet, but contrary winds forced a return to Portsmouth. In September Lancaster's plans were altered, and he was given a new command in Brittany. However, his fleet failed to get further than the Isle of Wight because of continued contrary winds. There were also long delays in getting the prince's expedition under way, and it was not until September that it sailed. It is likely that the plan was for the prince to march north, to join forces with Lancaster, but that was not practicable so late in the year.

In October 1355 the prince led a great raid from Bordeaux right across to the Mediterranean coast at Narbonne. The aim was to retaliate against the count of Armagnac, who had conducted damaging raids into Gascon territory. There was no sophisticated strategy in this; the objective was to do as much destruction as possible, and to bring the count to battle. A detailed day-to-day diary of the campaign survives. It is a record of burning and pillaging, not of fighting. Montgiscard was burned, with twelve windmills outside it. At Avignonet, stormed by the English, twenty mills were burned. The emphasis on the destruction of mills reveals how keen the prince's men were to destroy the economic infrastructure. At Carcassonne the citizens made a tempting offer reported as 250,000 gold écus so that the town would be spared, but the prince declared that he had come for justice, not for gold. The English duly set light to the place, and departed. They were very well aware of what they were doing. John Wingfield reported that records had been found that showed just how much had been raised in taxes in support of the French war effort from the areas destroyed. What the prince's army was not able to do was to engage the French in battle, as it is clear that they had hoped to do. They approached close to Toulouse, where the count of Armagnac was, and waited there two days. Later in the campaign there was news that the enemy were pursuing the English to fight them. 'We turned to face them, and thought we would have a battle in the next three days. But once we turned towards them, they returned to Toulouse.'[65]

129–44. The instruction to the ambassadors are printed in Chaplais, *English Medieval Diplomatic Practice*, pt. I, i. 189–91.

[65] Baker, 128–39; Avesbury, 434–45.

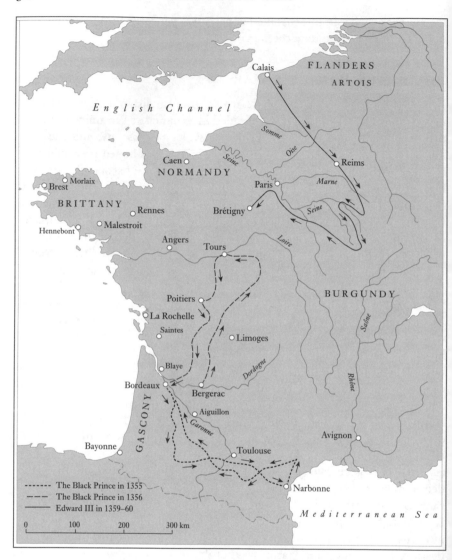

MAP 11.2. English campaigns, 1355–60

In 1355 Edward III was far less successful than his son. Following the failure of the fleets in the summer to leave English waters, he decided to take a host himself to Calais in the autumn, as there was news that French forces were massing.[66] On 2 November the army, a substantial one, made a destructive

[66] *Rot. Parl.* ii. 264.

march towards Saint-Omer. Jean de Boucicaut, a noted French knight who had been taken prisoner and was now on parole, went to Edward and told him that he thought the French king John was at Amiens. 'By St Mary, why is he waiting for me there, when he has strong forces with him, and sees his lands being burned and emptied by so few men?'[67] Edward was clearly seeking battle, but John withdrew his own forces, emptying the countryside as they went so as to make it impossible for the English to live off the land. One chronicler reported that the English troops were reduced to such desperation by this tactic that they had nothing to drink save water for three days; clearly a great hardship. On 11 November Edward's army returned to Calais. Negotiations took place with the French to agree a day and a place for a battle, or even single combat between the two kings. The negotiations proved difficult; no agreement was reached. Both sides probably wished to fight, but naturally neither wanted to give any tactical advantage to the other. The English claimed, rightly or wrongly, that they had waited until the specified day but that no French had appeared.[68]

The English strategy in 1355 of multiple expeditions had been overambitious, but Edward persisted with similar planning for the following year. Lancaster's destination was once again changed, this time from Brittany to Normandy.[69] King John had arrested Charles of Navarre, whose power base was in Normandy. This provoked Charles's brother Philip to rebel, and Edward, ever the opportunist, responded to his appeal by sending the earl of Lancaster to Normandy. As with the prince's campaign of the previous year, a day-to-day diary of the expedition survives. This does not emphasize the destruction of the countryside; as this was an expedition in support of the Navarrese cause, such tactics were inappropriate. After Lancaster took Verneuil, he began to march back towards the coast. The French army, under the king, approached. The usual interchange took place. French heralds pointed out that the earl's delay at Verneuil, where he had spent four days, suggested that he was ready for battle. Lancaster's response was 'that he come to those parts to do certain business, which, thanks to God, he had completed. If King John of France wished to disturb him from his route, he would be willing to meet him.'[70] In this case, the English were not anxious to fight. Lancaster did not have a large army, and marched swiftly back to the Cotentin peninsula. The campaign had achieved its purpose. It had demonstrated the strength of English military power, relieving important strongholds. It gave new heart to the Navarrese cause; Philip of Navarre fully acknowledged Edward's claim to the French throne, and to the duchy of Normandy.

[67] Le Bel, ii. 213; see also Froissart, iii. 144–5.
[68] Avesbury, 429–30. For discussion, see Rogers, *War Cruel and Sharp*, 301–4.
[69] For Lancaster's military role in this period, see Fowler, *King's Lieutenant*, 147 ff.
[70] Avesbury, 464.

From Normandy, Lancaster moved to take up his command in Brittany, where he arrived early in August. The plans of the previous year could now be reactivated. Hopes, however, that the king would be able to take yet another army to France came to nothing. Preparations began too late, and there were fears of naval attacks on the south coast of England. The strategy therefore centred on the prince of Wales and the duke of Lancaster. The prince had marched from Bordeaux to La Réole in July, causing panic that he would repeat his raid across to the Mediterranean coast. Instead he moved north, to Bergerac, and by 6 August was at Périgueux. He then marched further northwards. According to his own account he hoped to find and engage the count of Poitiers, King John's son, at Bourges.[71] The army reached the Loire near Tours; the hope was to join forces with Lancaster. However, it proved impossible to cross the Loire, for the bridges were broken and the river was running too high to be fordable. When Lancaster arrived at the river, further west at Les Ponts-de-Cé, he too failed to force a crossing. The optimistic strategy of joining forces had failed.

The prince then marched south, back towards Gascony. His own account is quite clear. He had rebuffed an earlier attempt by Cardinal Talleyrand of Périgord to negotiate a truce, and was anxious to meet King John in battle. When, eventually, scouts found the French army drawn up in battle array near Poitiers, the English prepared to meet them. Lengthy negotiations preceded the battle. Cardinal Talleyrand did all he could to try to prevent the fight. He was clearly convinced that the English would lose, in view of their inferior numbers and strength. A truce for a year, or one until Christmas, was suggested. The compromises suggested by the cardinal were not acceptable to either side. The English must have been alarmed that during the delays the numbers of French troops were steadily increasing. According to Knighton, supplies were running short, giving the English little option other than to fight.[72]

The battle of Poitiers was hard-fought, but ended in total triumph for the English. The English army, drawn up as was normal in three main divisions, had the advantage of fighting from a defensive position that was protected by a hedge and other natural obstacles. The French, advised by William Douglas, fought for the most part on foot, in the English style. They did not, however, have the immense advantage that the English longbowmen provided, and ironically in the final stages of the battle it was a cavalry charge led by the Gascon Captal de Buch that gave the *coup de grâce* to the French host.[73] The triumph, however, belonged to the Black Prince.

---

[71] *Life and Campaigns of the Black Prince*, ed. Barber, 57–9.
[72] Knighton, 142–3.
[73] D. Green, *The Battle of Poitiers 1356* (Stroud, 2002), 49–69.

DIPLOMACY AND WAR

In contrast to the battle of Crécy, an extraordinary number of prisoners were taken at Poitiers, chief of whom was the French king John. His capture transformed the issues between England and France, and placed a bargaining counter of immense value in Edward III's hands. It also created problems. It would be very hard to find a way to release King John for a substantial ransom and major territorial concessions without acknowledging that he was king of France. In the negotiations the English were able to extract good terms from John himself, in exchange for Edward III's abandonment of his claim to the French throne. The problem was whether they would be acceptable in Paris. In 1357 the draft terms were for the French to hand over a ransom of 4 million écus (about £666,666), and Gascony, the Agenais, the Limousin, Angoulême, Quercy, and Poitou, with Ponthieu and Calais in the north, all to be held in full sovereignty by the English. In addition, Edward III was to hold those lands in Normandy that he had been given by Godfrey of Harcourt. Full agreement was reached between the two kings in 1358 in the first treaty of London.

The French, however, did not implement the treaty. The first instalment of the ransom payments was not forthcoming. The country was in turmoil, with revolution in Paris and chaos in the countryside. The peace, the French claimed with some justification, was threatened by the activities of English mercenary captains. In March 1359 an increasingly desperate King John agreed to new proposals in the second treaty of London. This went even further than the first treaty, and promised Edward all of Brittany, Normandy, Maine, Anjou, and Touraine, in full sovereignty, in addition to the lands already agreed. The ransom remained at 4 million écus, but 1 million was to be pardoned. It is hardly surprising that this treaty did not prove acceptable to the French. The Estates urged the Dauphin to reject it, and he needed little persuasion.

Different interpretations can be put on the negotiations of 1357–9. It is possible that the English deliberately set their sights very high in the full expectation that the French would find them unacceptable. Edward would then have been able to take advantage of the confused and desperate state that France was in, and have been able to mount an invasion and take the throne. It could, on the other hand, be the case that King John and those with him miscalculated, and misled the English in good faith. It is possible that they believed that the proposals would find acceptance in France. There is no direct evidence of what Edward and his councillors thought, but even though their demands were very heavy, it seems unlikely that the negotiations were simply a sham, intended to provide a means to justify the renewal of the war. There was no need for such a level of duplicity, and it may be that the English simply underestimated French hostility to the proposals.[74]

The failure of the negotiations meant that Edward had to adopt the alternative strategy and fight one more campaign. The 1359 expedition was intended to achieve the final victory and culminate in his coronation as king of France. The timing seemed right, for France was in a state of chaos, ravaged by the peasant uprising of the Jacquerie and torn apart by the activities of mercenary captains loosely linked to the English cause. The country was desperate, and even the dramatic reconciliation of Charles of Navarre to the Dauphin Charles did little to reinforce the French position.

The English army marched out from Calais in three columns on 4 November. The aim was clear: Edward was to have his coronation as king of France. Reims was reached early in December. This was where the kings of France were, by tradition, crowned. The English army encamped around the city. Neither soft words nor hard assaults persuaded the citizens to open the gates. The huge English host soon exhausted all available supplies, and after five fruitless weeks Edward had to abandon his hopes of achieving a triumphant coronation in France. His army swept east and south through Burgundy, and then swung round to the south of Paris. It is most unlikely that Edward intended to try to capture the city; his hope now was that the Dauphin would meet him in battle. This was a risk the French would not take. On 13 April disaster struck the English army. A violent storm struck, with vast hailstones and rain such that no one could remember. Many horses, already starving, died. Baggage carts had to be abandoned. The balance between continuing the campaign and negotiating was sharply shifted. One suggestion is that the king may have regarded the storm as a divine verdict on the campaign, and that it was this, rather than a changed strategic situation, that led him to the negotiating table.[75] It is more likely that he saw the storm as divine confirmation of a decision that was imposed by the military reality of the campaign. In May terms were agreed at Brétigny.

The fact that there had already been extensive, if futile, negotiations must have simplified the dealings at Brétigny. The basis of the agreement was quickly reached. Edward would hold Gascony and the surrounding territories, including Poitou, the Angoumois, Périgord, the Limousin, and Quercy in full sovereignty. In the north all he would have was Calais and its march, and the county of Ponthieu. The ransom sum was reduced to 3 million écus. Edward would surrender his claim to the throne. He may not have achieved all he had hoped for, but when compared to the position he had been in at the start of the

---

[74] The negotiations are discussed by Rogers, 'The Anglo-French Peace Negotiations of 1354–1360 Reconsidered', 193–213.
[75] Ibid. 212–13.

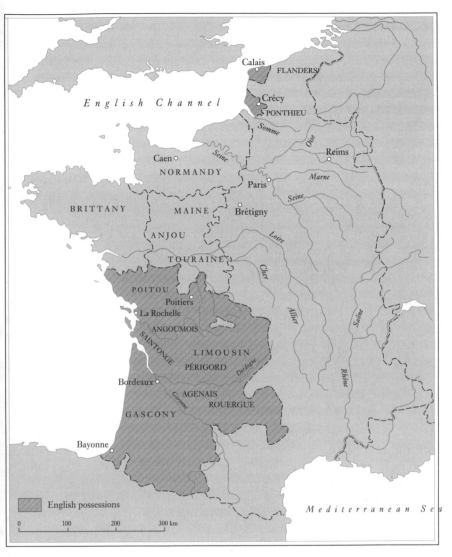

MAP 11.3. Lands ceded to Edward III by the treaty of Brétigny, 1360

war, the gains were astonishing. The eventual outcome of the negotiations at Brétigny was predictable, in view of events since the war started. The treaty would founder on detailed questions of its implementation, particularly the renunciations of territory. Far from a permanent peace, all that was achieved was a nine-year truce. The rulers of England and France were better at making war, with all its attendant horrors, than at making peace.

CHAPTER 12

The Armies of Edward III's French War

Even at the outset of the Hundred Years War, English armies were formidable. The chronicler Jean le Bel commented that the English had no reputation at the start of Edward III's reign for prowess or bravery, and that their armour and equipment were then completely out of date. By the late 1330s they had learned well, and were, the chronicler claimed, most noble and redoubtable warriors.[1] The Scottish wars had seen important developments such as the appearance of mixed retinues of cavalry and archers. The advent of mounted archers enabled forces to move with impressive speed. Military tactics had been developed that had proved highly effective against the Scots at Dupplin Moor and Halidon Hill, and a cadre of experienced soldiers knew how to exercise command. Royal officials were practised in the vital tasks of recruiting men, and of organizing victualling and the shipping of supplies.

RECRUITMENT

At the start of the war there were worries about recruitment. Edward I had had difficulties in persuading men to go to Flanders to fight, and there was no reason why attitudes should be different in 1337. The cavalry were accordingly offered double the normal wage rates between July 1338 and November 1339. When their horses were valued, so that compensation could be given if they were killed, high figures were allowed by the royal clerks. Such generosity could not be afforded for long, but in the mid-1340s wages began to be supplemented by payment of the regard, a quarterly bonus normally paid at the rate of 100 marks for the service of thirty men-at-arms. Particularly notable service might bring greater financial reward. The Black Prince granted Robert Neville £100 a year for service in Gascony and at Poitiers, while Baldwin Botetourt, one of his knights, was given £40 a year for what he did at Poitiers.

---

[1] Le Bel, i. 155–6.

Roger de Cotesford received 40 marks a year, and the prince's standard-bearers obtained similar rewards.[2]

During Edward III's French wars it was common to recruit men by negotiating a contract of service with them. It was, indeed, once claimed that 'The "Indenture" system of military service is the most important, and the most neglected, factor in the development of the English army in the later Middle Ages.'[3] The system was a simple one, whereby commanders of retinues contracted with the crown to provide contingents of an agreed size. There were obvious advantages in this, for the crown would know how many men it was getting, while those entering into contracts would be quite clear about the terms on which they were serving. More importantly, the system was simple to administer. This was why it was used. It was not that this was a far superior method of organizing armies; it was driven by administrative necessity. When the king himself headed a campaign, as in 1346–7 and 1359–60, there was no need to draw up contracts of this sort. The administrative machinery of the royal household was there to carry out the tasks of paying troops in the way that it had done in the past. When, however, expeditions were sent to Scotland or France under other commanders, they did not have the same administrative resources present to support them. It therefore made sense to use a system of contracts. This was nothing new; Edward I had contracted with the earls of Lancaster, Lincoln, and Cornwall for their expeditions to Gascony in the 1290s.[4] The first time that an entire army was recruited by means of contract was the Scottish expedition of 1337, an experiment that was not wholly successful as some of the contingents failed to reach the expected numbers and desertion thinned the ranks. In the French wars the system worked far better. There are many examples of contract service. In 1346 Thomas Dagworth agreed to hold Brittany for 2,500 marks, with wages and regard in addition for his force of 300 men-at-arms and 600 mounted archers. In 1347 Thomas Ughtred contracted to serve for a year with twenty men-at-arms, of whom six, himself included, would be knights. He was also to provide twenty mounted archers. There was a fee of £200, in addition to wages, and the king agreed to provide Ughtred with shipping both to and from France.[5] In July

---

[2] *The Black Prince's Register*, ed. M. C. B. Dawes, 4 vols. (London, 1930–3), i. 196, 203, 215, 219; A. Ayton, *Knights and Warhorses: Military Service and the English Aristocracy Under Edward III* (Woodbridge, 1994), 50–120.

[3] A. E. Prince, 'The Indenture System Under Edward III', in J. G. Edwards, V. H. Galbraith, and E. F. Jacob (eds.), *Historical Essays Presented to James Tait* (Manchester, 1933), 283.

[4] Prestwich, *War, Politics and Finance*, 76.

[5] Prestwich, *Armies and Warfare*, 85, 92–3; E 101/25/19; E 101/25/33; A. E. Prince, 'The Strength of English Armies in the Reign of Edward III', *EHR* 46 (1931), 370–1, prints a slightly earlier indenture with Dagworth.

1348 the earl of Warwick arranged to serve the king with 100 men-at-arms, in return for a very substantial annual fee of 1,000 marks, and he and his men would also receive both wages and regard.[6]

One of the problems with pay was that it was often not forthcoming. An account drawn up in the late 1340s shows that there were substantial arrears. The list was headed by two debts to the earl of Northampton, one of £782 and the other of £1,237. Arrears of war wages to the earl of Oxford totalled £349, and those to Ralph de Stafford £621.[7] It was only by disallowing items totalling some £8,000 that the exchequer was able to balance its accounts with John Chandos in the early 1360s.[8]

Pay was only a minor element among the inducements that led men to fight for Edward III. Jean le Bel noted in 1339 that 'there was a great quantity of lords, of knights, barons and others, who so loved the king that they wished to serve him at their own expense, and did not want to take any wages or payment at court'.[9] Ransoms and booty were to be won in France. As the English marched through Normandy in 1346 and sacked the city of Caen, they found rich pickings, and the same was true of other campaigns. Arrangements set out how such profits were to be shared. Normally, in the years up to 1360, the principle was one of equal division. When Geoffrey Walsh made an indenture for life service with the earl of Salisbury, it was agreed that ransoms and other gains were to be shared equally between lord and man. When, however, the earl of Northampton agreed in 1356 to take command in Brittany, with extensive powers, the agreement with the king specified that it was only necessary to report prisoners to the king if they were worth over £500.[10]

Despite the evident enthusiasm on the part of many to serve in France, the crown did not abandon the concept of obligatory service easily. In the 1320s Edward II's government had ordered the sheriffs to draw up lists of the knights and men-at-arms in their counties, and for the war of Saint-Sardos commissioners were appointed to array not just the infantry, but also knights, squires, and men-at-arms. It seems clear that the introduction of a new form of military obligation was being attempted. The precedent was tempting. In 1344 Edward III introduced a graduated scale by which men were to be assessed for their contribution to the army. Everyone with an income of at least £5 a year was to be included, and all were to find troops in proportion to their wealth. A £5 landholder would provide a mounted archer; a £25 landholder a man-at-arms. In 1345 orders went out to recruit men on this basis, a move that was highly unpopular. There were protests in parliament, and the king promised that no precedent was intended. Eventually, in 1352,

<hr>

[6] E 101/509/12.   [7] E 101/391/1, fo. 1.   [8] E 10128/10.
[9] Le Bel, i. 155.   [10] E 101/68/3, no. 66; E 101/68/4, no. 72.

Edward conceded that no one should be obliged to provide military service save by common consent given in parliament.[11]

In practice, there was little difficulty in recruiting cavalry troops, and obligation was not needed. Enthusiasm for the war replaced compulsion. Individual agreements were more important than general summonses. According to Jean le Bel, all the knights, squires, and men of honour between the ages of 20 and 40 flocked to join the host that sailed for France in 1359.[12] The evidence suggests that over 3,000 cavalry served, of whom over 700 were bannerets and knights.[13] The latter figure probably represents about half of the knights in England, and demonstrates the depth of commitment to the war. Orders for distraint of knighthood continued to be issued, but the evidence does not suggest that there were many men wealthy enough to be knights who did not accept the honour. John Colby was returned in 1347 as having not taken up knighthood, but he got the king to issue a privy seal writ stating that he had indeed been knighted on the battlefield at Crécy.[14]

The cavalry were normally expected to provide their own armour and equipment. By the end of the thirteenth century some elements, such as cuisses, or thigh-pieces, and gauntlets were of already of plate, while a will of 1325 refers to a 'pair of plates', which provided body protection. In the French war plate armour became more common, and bacinets with visors replaced the earlier and more clumsy style of helmet. Calculations are difficult, but a full set of equipment for man and horse might cost £10 or more. Horses were expensive; the average assessed value of those taken on the Brittany campaign of 1342–3 was over £14. Although the crown offered repayment for those lost in war, this provision applied to no more than one animal. A knight would be expected to take at least four on campaign.[15]

Archers, mounted and dismounted, were recruited partly as members of magnate retinues and partly by means of commissions of array. In 1338 about 1,000 archers served as members of retinues, while some 3,000, including Welsh troops, were listed separately in the accounts. By 1359 the proportion of those in retinues had risen markedly, with about 4,500 archers in this

---

[11] M. R. Powicke, *Military Obligation in Medieval England* (Oxford, 1962), 195–9; Prestwich, *Armies and Warfare*, 80.
[12] Le Bel, ii. 298.
[13] A. Ayton, 'English Armies in the Fourteenth Century', in A. Curry and M. Hughes (eds.), *Arms, Armies and Fortifications in the Hundred Years War* (Woodbridge, 1994), 28.
[14] E 159/121, m. 228.
[15] F. Lachaud, 'Armour and Military Dress in Thirteenth- and Early Fourteenth-Century England', in M. Strickland (ed.), *Armies, Chivalry and Warfare in Medieval Britain and France* (Stamford, 1998), 344–69; A. Ayton, *Knights and Warhorses*, 215; Prestwich, *Armies and Warfare*, 24–6.

category and just over 2,000 not listed in this way.[16] Care was taken over the selection and equipment of troops. On one occasion, around 1340, 200 north Welsh were recruited, but it was decided that it would be better to take just eighty of them to France, making sure that they were properly equipped and clothed, with proper coats and mantles.[17] Welsh contingents came to the wars complete with chaplains, interpreters, standard-bearers, and even doctors.[18] In 1345 the archers recruited from London were all equipped with coats and hoods of striped red-and-white cloth.[19] Details of a couple of local arrays in Suffolk in the mid-1340s show very few men were armed with bows. The majority had billhooks (gisarmes) and knives, or simply a stave and a knife. Lists of Norwich men arrayed in 1359 show a proportion of archers (with bow, arrows, sword, and knife), but the majority armed with staves, knives, and hatchets.[20] To convert such men into archers, the crown had to provide them with the right equipment. There is no evidence of formal training, though practice at archery butts was encouraged. A good many men may have needed little training in fighting, for the practice of emptying the country's gaols in order to fill the armies, which had begun in Edward I's reign, continued; about 8 per cent of the infantry raised for an expedition in 1344 were recruited in this way. Over 1,800 pardons were issued to men who took part in the 1346–7 campaign. The violent behaviour that had led to many of them being convicted was used to terrorize the inhabitants of France.[21]

In the past, in wars in Wales and Scotland, desertion had been a major problem. With wars in France this was no longer the case; the account for a contingent of 420 Welsh troops from November 1359 to January 1360 shows that numbers remained unchanged, apart from two men who went absent without leave for a week. The distance from home and the English Channel were perhaps too much of a deterrent to would-be deserters, while the riches of the French countryside were a temptation to stay overseas.

The government had the administrative capability to put quite as many men into the field as Edward I had done, but it was rare for large armies to be sent to France. Transport problems provided one reason for this. Nor would large numbers of relatively untrained footsoldiers, such as those whom Edward I had marched north, have been of much value in France. Smaller, better-equipped armies with a high proportion of mounted troops were what was needed for the fast-moving campaigns such as those led by the Black Prince. The exception

[16] *Wardrobe Book of William de Norwell*, ed. Lyon *et al.*, 356–62; E 101/393/11, fos. 115^{r-v}.
[17] *Cal. Anc. Corr. Wales*, 192–3.   [18] E 101/23/22; see also E 101/393/11, fo. 115^v.
[19] *Cal. Plea and Mem. Rolls*, 222.
[20] C 47/2/58; W. H. Hudson, 'Norwich Militia in the Fourteenth Century', *Norfolk and Norwich Archaeological Society*, 14 (1901), 263–320.
[21] E 101/17/3.

was the force needed for the capture of Calais. Detailed accounts for the 1346–7 campaign do not survive, but a summary suggests that a total of some 32,000 men were recruited for the siege. The 1359–60 host was also exceptionally large; when it marched out of Calais it probably numbered about 10,000. A good estimate is that it contained about 4,000 knights and men-at-arms, 5,000 mounted archers, and about 1,000 other troops.[22] In contrast, on the 1339 campaign Edward III's English troops numbered roughly 1,600 men-at-arms, 1,500 mounted archers, and 1,650 footsoldiers. One estimate is that the Black Prince's army at Poitiers, excluding the Gascon troops, numbered no more than about 2,600 men in all. Contemporaries usually exaggerated; on this occasion Bartholomew Burghersh reported in more realistic terms that the prince had in all 3,000 men-at-arms, 2,000 archers, and 1,000 sergeants with him.[23] If the numbers of men were not very great, the quantity of horses was very considerable. Conventionally, it was expected that each knight should have four, each squire three, and each mounted archer two.[24] There might, however, be difficulties in taking quite so many to France. Ralph, earl Stafford's account for his expedition to Gascony in 1352 shows that they had to stay in England for some time for want of sufficient shipping, and could not take all their horses to Gascony for the same reason. It cost £686 to buy substitutes in the duchy after their arrival.[25] The great horses were highly valued, being worth up to £100 and more. They had grand names, such as Grisel King or Morel de Salisbury. Some of the names celebrated notable captains, such as Lyard Audley, Baiard Burghersh, or Lyard Coupland.[26]

Even a relatively small expedition demanded a considerable effort to put it into the field. Lancaster took a force of about 2,000 men to Bordeaux in 1345. His account shows that he retained in his personal retinue seven bannerets, ninety-two knights, 150 men-at-arms, and 250 horse archers, with 300 Welsh infantry in addition. They received a regard as well as wages. Forty-two horses were lost, and compensation paid for them. The cost in wages and other expenses came to £38,574, very considerably in excess of receipts, which totalled £20,845. It took a fleet of 152 ships to take the total force of 2,000

---

[22] Ayton, 'English Armies in the Fourteenth Century', 31. The account book dealing with this campaign, E 101/393/11, is not organized in a way that makes calculation easy. A. E. Prince, 'The Strength of English Armies Under Edward III', *EHR* 46 (1931), 368, gives a total of about 11,900, which includes foreign troops.

[23] Prince, 'The Strength of English Armies', 361, 366; *Œuvres de Froissart*, ed. de Lettenhove, xviii. 387. Green, *Poitiers*, 61, estimates that the English army consisted of '3,000–4,000 men-at-arms, 2,500–3,000 archers and 1,000 other light troops'.

[24] E 101/28/70.

[25] E 101/26/25.

[26] *Black Prince's Register*, ed. Dawes, i. 15, 28.

men to Bordeaux; the crews totalled 2,484 sailors with 306 boys, and the voyage took twenty-four days.[27]

THE NAVY

Lancaster's 1345 account brings out very clearly the immense importance of the English navy in Edward's war effort. Evidence of the planning that went into the war shows that the government fully appreciated this. One memorandum from early in the war details the provisions that were needed for the fleets from the Thames to the north, and from the Thames to the west respectively, for a four-month period, carefully calculated. Another council memorandum on naval matters noted that it would be necessary to speak to the king concerning whether the whole fleet should assemble at Portsmouth or not; Edward was closely involved in decision-making.[28] Another document set out a decision that 2,000 well-armed men equipped with lances and bacinets should be arrayed at Portsmouth, ready to go abroad, along with 4,000 archers and 4,000 Welshmen. Of the Welsh, two-thirds were to be archers and the remainder armed with lances. A large fleet of ships of over 30 tons was to be gathered from all the ports of England, from the Humber in the east to Chester in the west. Commissioners were named who were to impress the ships.[29]

The demands on the country's shipping resources were therefore very heavy. In 1338 the king used 361 ships to transport his small force to the Low Countries and maintain it there; far more sailors, about 12,500, were used in the operation than were troops. A force assembled between April and July 1344 at Portsmouth consisted of 290 horse, with 1,789 infantry. They needed eighty ships for transport, manned by 1,600 sailors.[30] The expedition that culminated in the battle of Crécy and the siege of Calais required the services of 738 ships and about 15,000 sailors.[31] Delays due to lack of shipping were a common feature of the war, while there was also much resentment at the way in which the king's demands for ships might lead to vessels being tied up for long periods waiting for troops to assemble. In addition to their unglamorous role of providing transport, naval forces were responsible for two of the victories of Edward III's French war, Sluys in 1340 and Les Espagnols sur mer a decade later.

Fleets were also needed for defence. This was emphasized by some damaging French raids in the early stages of the war, notably with the destruction of much of Southampton in 1338 and a raid on Hastings in the next year. The capture of five English ships, including some owned by the king himself, at

[27] E 101/25/9.   [28] C 47/2/29, 31.   [29] C 47/2/31.
[30] E 101/17/3.   [31] Prestwich, *Armies and Warfare*, 273–5.

harbour in the Low Countries was another blow. The dangers of losing control of the seaways were further illustrated by a raid on the Isle of Wight and Plymouth in the summer of 1340. In 1349 a damaging naval attack on Poitou culminated in a small-scale naval battle in which some English ships were lost to a Franco-Castilian fleet. In 1360 a French naval raid culminated in a serious attack on Winchelsea.

SUPPLIES

English armies in France could live off the land in a way that had not been possible for the forces that had been sent to Wales and Scotland, while the fact that most of them were relatively small also reduced the demand for victuals. The accounts show that purveyance was no longer on as massive a scale as it had been in Edward I's reign. The accounts of William Dunstable, a hated official in charge of purveyance in seventeen counties in 1338, show that he collected about 2,000 quarters of wheat, 2,400 quarters of malt, 220 quarters of beans and peas, 120 cattle, and 650 sheep, along with other miscellaneous supplies. The effort involved in the operation was considerable, involving as it did the hiring of granaries in Great Yarmouth, King's Lynn, and elsewhere, but it did not match that which had been made by the victuallers at Berwick and Carlisle at the start of the fourteenth century.[32] Supplies might be bought from merchants, as well as being purveyed by the sheriffs. An account of victuals and other supplies taken from England to the king in Brabant in the same period detailed flour made from 481 quarters of wheat, 75 beef carcases, 3,000 horseshoes, and 30,000 horseshoe nails provided by three London merchants.[33] With relatively small forces in the Low Countries at that time, needs were not all that great. Bigger efforts were made in 1346. The accounts of William de Kelleseye, receiver of victuals from ten eastern counties, show that he had charge of almost 3,000 quarters of wheat, 1,000 quarters of oats, and 330 quarters of beans and peas, together with quantities of beef, pork, mutton, and cheese.[34] Following the capture of Calais, the town needed regular supplies of victuals from England. Fleets could not live off the land as armies did; a memorandum from early in the French war specified that the 4,050 men in the fleet from the Thames to the north would need 5,400 quarters of wheat, 8,250 quarters of malt, 2,400 quarters of beans and peas, together with substantial quantities of meat and fish, for a four-month period.[35]

---

[32] E 101/21/4.   [33] *Wardrobe Book of William de Norwell*, ed. Lyon *et al.*, 413.
[34] H. J. Hewitt, *The Organisation of War Under Edward III* (Manchester, 1966), 55.
[35] C 47/2/31.

Armies needed more than food. Whereas little had been done under Edward I to provide men with the equipment they needed, the government under his grandson made great efforts to ensure that there were sufficient archery supplies, as well as such specialized equipment as guns. Orders for the collection of bows and arrows were regularly issued, and sizeable quantities of bows were accumulated at the Tower for distribution to the troops. In 1360 the stock totalled over 15,000 bows, 4,000 bow staves, and over 560,000 arrows.[36] The Tower was also where guns and gunpowder was stored. In 1345–6 guns known as ribalds were manufactured there, together with the quarrels they fired, at a cost of £124. Ten guns, two of them large, were sent from the Tower to assist in the siege of Calais. Large quantities of sulphur and saltpetre were collected and sent to France.[37] Much other work was needed to prepare an expedition. Carpenters, tailors, and stitchers were needed to make the tents.[38] Banners needed to be made: an account from 1342 lists a wonderful display of these. Six carried the arms of St Edmund, one those of St Edward. There were eighteen standards with the king's arms. Three banners displayed the cross of St George, as did 1,000 pennons.[39]

COMMAND AND TACTICS

Contemporaries could give no good explanation for the successes of Edward III's armies. Divine approval for the king's cause was, of course, frequently cited, and was perhaps a more plausible explanation than the French explanation that the failure of their armies might be attributed to wearing short-cut clothes.[40] For the most part the many newsletters and other correspondence from France simply reported English successes without real explanation. Part of a report of Lancaster's *chevauchée* in Brittany in 1356 gives a typical flavour:

And on Tuesday my lord moved to Carentan. And on Wednesday he came to Montebourg, in the Cotentin peninsula. On that day, when my lord first came to the peninsula, Robert Knollys with seven men-at-arms rode ahead of him, to find lodgings for him and his men, and suddenly encountered 120 men-at-arms, crossbowmen, lightly armed soldiers, and Frenchmen, who had made a sortie from a castle nearby, in order to plunder and burn a town which is in our power. And the said Robert and the seven men-at-arms killed all of them, apart from three who were taken to be ransomed.

---

[36] Tout, *Chapters*, iv. 469.
[37] T. F. Tout, 'Firearms in England in the Fourteenth Century', in his *Collected Papers*, ii. 238–41.
[38] *Black Prince's Register*, ed. Dawes, i. 14.
[39] E 101/16/5.
[40] *The Chronicle of Jean de Venette*, trans. J. Birdsall, ed. R. A. Newhall (New York, 1953), 34.

Each of the towns where my lord stayed was a fine town, large and rich, and each day the men captured various castles and a very great quantity of prisoners and booty; and when they returned they brought with them 2,000 of the enemy's horses.[41]

There were many reasons for the English triumphs. The quality of command was important. Edward himself had great qualities of leadership, as did his son the Black Prince. Where possible, command generally went to members of the highest aristocracy. There were good reasons for this. A council memorandum noted that the earl of Arundel should be given a naval command as admiral, 'for no one could be that unless he was a great man', capable of leading men and disciplining them.[42] The intangible qualities of prestige that came with high rank were important, but at the same time it was important that these men were capable of bearing the burden of command that their status entitled them to. Edward III had nobles of the right ability, in part because he had had the opportunity to create a new aristocracy. Unlike Edward I, he had no shortage of earls to lead Continental campaigns. In Henry of Grosmont, earl of Derby and then earl and duke of Lancaster, he had a quite exceptional lieutenant, a man of charisma and ability. Salisbury, Northampton, and Warwick all proved themselves to be excellent soldiers well worthy of command. Command, however, was not the exclusive preserve of the highest-born. Ability was recognized, though good connections doubtless helped. Thomas Dagworth was a Suffolk knight who had the good fortune to marry the sister of the earls of Hereford and Northampton. The latter made Dagworth his deputy in Brittany, and as the English success at La Roche-Derrien proved, it was an excellent choice. The Hainaulter Walter Mauny was a man who by sheer military ability came to play a leading part in Edward III's wars. Walter Bentley was an adventurer, a Yorkshire knight who achieved much on his own account in Brittany as well as on the king's. Marriage to a wealthy Breton dowager brought him wealth; Edward III was ready to recognize the ability of a thrusting individual by giving him command as Dagworth's successor.[43]

There was immense experience in the English forces. Edward III's Scottish wars must have provided many with familiarity with the problems of campaigning. Thomas Ughtred has been singled out for note. A Yorkshire knight, he fought in the disasters of Bannockburn and Byland in Edward II's reign, and then campaigned successfully in the 1330s in Scotland. He was present at Dupplin Moor and Halidon Hill. On the Crécy campaign he acted as the earl of Warwick's lieutenant and as sub-marshal; he was a man of influence. He ended

---

[41] Avesbury, 465 (my translation).   [42] C 47/2/29.
[43] For Dagworth, see Sumption, *Hundred Years War*, i. 572–5, and for Bentley, id., *The Hundred Years War*, ii. 30.

his military career with the campaign of 1359–60.[44] Long military careers such as Ughtred's were not unusual. John de Sully, as an old man of 105 by his optimistic reckoning, could recall fighting at Halidon Hill, Crécy, Les Espagnols sur mer, Poitiers, and Najera in 1367.[45] Examples could be multiplied; from the next generation such men as Audley, Calveley, Knollys, and Chandos stand out as commanders whose skill was born of many years' campaigning.

Commanders took good care to have proper intelligence. In 1336 a remarkable report set out the preparations that the French were making for the coming war, giving details of proposed support for the Scots, and of planned landings by French forces at Portsmouth and in Fife. The accounts for the late 1330s provide details of the way in which men were employed to spy out French naval activity. At the same time, care was taken not to reveal English intentions. The plans for the Normandy landing in 1346 were kept secret with as much care as were those of 1944. On the campaign itself, the information provided about the ford across the river Somme was vital, enabling Edward's army to escape from being trapped by the French, and allowing it to advance northwards to Crécy.[46]

The English had developed tactics in the Scottish wars that served them superbly in France. The basic concept was simple, though its execution might be complex. The men-at-arms should fight on foot, in a strong defensive line. Archers positioned on the flanks would break up cavalry charges; by the time that any enemy reached the English line, their formations would be shattered. The English would mount their horses only in the final stages of battle, in order to pursue and hunt down those they had defeated. It was probably at Buirenfosse in 1339 that the French first saw the English drawn up ready to fight on foot, but it was not until Morlaix in 1342 that they experienced the effectiveness of the tactic. There, successive cavalry charges were decimated; casualties were massive among the French.[47]

There are difficulties in interpreting how the tactics at Crécy worked. The English probably drew up their three divisions one behind the other, but it is not impossible that they were side by side. There has been much argument about the way the archers were organized. Froissart used the term *en herse* to describe their formations, a term that has led to much ultimately futile

[44] A. Ayton, 'Sir Thomas Ughtred and the Edwardian Military Revolution', in Bothwell (ed.), *The Age of Edward III*, 107–9.

[45] Richard Scrope, *The Scrope and Grosvenor Controversy*, ed. N. H. Nicholas (n.d.), i. 74.

[46] Prestwich, *Armies and Warfare*, 212–14; J. R. Alban and C. T. Allmand, 'Spies and Spying in the Fourteenth Century', in Allmand (ed.), *War, Literature and Politics in the Late Middle Ages* (Liverpool, 1976).

[47] T. F. Tout, 'The Tactics of the Battles of Boroughbridge and Morlaix', in his *Collected Papers*, ii. 223–5; K. DeVries, *Infantry Warfare in the Early Fourteenth Century* (Woodbridge, 1996), 137–44.

argument. It is most likely that they were triangular or wedge-shaped, like the type of candelabrum known as a hearse used in Holy Week. The way in which these formations were deployed is not entirely clear; if the army was in three divisions side by side, they may have flanked each division, or may have been positioned to the sides of the army as a whole. A novelty, as far as the English were concerned, was the way in which the baggage train was placed within a defensive formation of carts to the rear of the army. It is likely that it was here that some at least of the guns were placed. The battle was fought on ground ideally suited to the English tactics. Edward and his army were drawn up on a slope overlooking a valley. Opposite them was a short, steep bank or escarpment, some 6 feet in height, which severely limited the French range of manoeuvre, and which turned the valley into a killing ground once the battle began.

At Poitiers the English again relied upon dismounted men-at-arms with archers in support. The French had appreciated the devastating effect of archery on cavalry, and so advanced on foot. Again, however, the impact of the archers was vital in breaking the initial thrust of the French. The battle showed, in its final stages, that cavalry were still a force to be reckoned with, for a charge by Captal de Buch was the decisive blow. The English were not rigid in the tactics that they used, but they showed great skill in using their forces to the best possible advantage.

It would be wrong, however, to place too much emphasis on the battle tactics employed by the English. They can help to explain some of the victories, notably Mauron, Crécy, and Poitiers. In other cases, such as Henry of Lancaster's success at Auberoche, the tactics employed were rather different. There was also a great deal of fighting that did not take the form of major set-piece battles. Many skirmishes took place on a small scale. The war in Brittany provides numerous examples, and as the war expanded in the late 1350s into the state of general disorder affecting most of France, bodies of English troops, often acting in their own interest rather than their king's, were involved in a multitude of small-scale actions. In these experience and morale were perhaps more important than the application of particular tried tactical methods. As the war proceeded, the English must have gained an extraordinary self-confidence, a belief in their own invincibility.

CHIVALRY AND PROPAGANDA

The chivalric ideology of those who fought for Edward III has to be an element in the explanation of English success, but the issue is not straightforward, for the concepts were fully shared with the French. Indeed, one of the greatest exponents of chivalry was the French knight Geoffroi de Charny, a man of international renown, bearer of the sacred *Oriflamme* and author of the *Book of Chivalry*, who was killed at Poitiers.[48] Chivalry was the gloss that rendered the rough realities of war acceptable. The fourteenth century appears in many ways to have been a golden age of chivalry, but this is to be explained in part because of the surviving sources. Far more was written about chivalry then than in previous periods. That does not necessarily imply that war was in practice fought in a more chivalrous style than in earlier periods. 'It is better that chivalry should be done on horseback and not on foot,' said Thomas Gray, but much of the fighting in the Hundred Years War took place on foot.[49]

The way in which feats of arms redounded to the honour of the participants was important in encouraging men to fight. Incidents were many. There was the 1351 Fight of the Thirty in Brittany, a challenge made and accepted. Thirty on the English side, which included Bretons and Germans, fought thirty Frenchmen, and lost. This was told as a splendid example to encourage all young knights, even though many of the thirty were killed and others captured for ransom.[50] Stories were told of Edward III's own prowess, how he had fought Eustace de Ribemont outside Calais, doing so incognito, under the arms of Walter Mauny.[51] The many anecdotes about splendid individual and collective feats of arms colour other narratives as well as Froissart's. The *Anonimalle Chronicle* records a challenge to single combat issued by a French knight soon after the English had crossed the Somme in 1346. Each knight should fight for the love of his lady. Thomas Colville met the challenge, and they ran two jousts before deciding that a third would be too dangerous since the French knight's shield was broken. The two men then swore to became good friends.[52] On the 1359–60 campaign a group of thirty young English knights rode up to the gates of Paris seeking an encounter in which they might perform fine deeds of arms. Sixty French spearmen came out, perhaps hardly a fair match, but of course, since the story is from an English chronicle, the English knights won the day.[53] It was characteristic of chivalric culture to lay stress on acts of individual bravery. Eustace d'Aubrichecourt was at Carcassonne on the 1355 raid. The streets of the town were blocked with chains hung across them. With his sword in his hand, the athletic Eustace jumped one chain, fought the Frenchmen there, and then jumped four further chains, one

---

[48] *The Book of Chivalry of Geoffroi de Charny*, ed. R. W. Kaeuper and E. Kennedy (Philadelphia, 1996).
[49] *Scalacronica*, 146.
[50] Froissart, iii. 110–15.
[51] Ibid. iv. 80.
[52] *Anon. Chron.* 22. *Gesta Abbatum Monasterii Sancti Albani: A Thoma Walsingham*, ed. H. T. Riley (RS, 1867), ii. 376–7, has a version of the story in which Colville killed his opponent.
[53] Knighton, 176–7.

after another.[54] The swearing of vows to perform deeds of valour in the wars was a common practice. The acceptance of favours from a lady-love by those going off to fight is not unique to a chivalric culture, but was a significant element of it.[55]

Edward III worked hard to encourage the culture of chivalry. How far this was in a deliberate attempt to build up enthusiasm for his military ventures is impossible to say; it is just as likely that his encouragement of tournaments and foundation of the Order of the Garter was a genuine reflection of his own tastes. The value of tournaments as providing practice for war was questionable, for tournaments were becoming more stylized and conventional, with equipment specially designed for the purpose. They were, however, occasions for men to get together and encourage each other in the enterprises of chivalry. Many notable tournaments were held under royal patronage. Early in 1342 there were contests between English and Scots on the border, held with the king's approval. In the spring there was a great tournament at Dunstable, one of several in which the king took part as an ordinary knight (it is hard to believe that he was not in fact recognized), along with the earls of Derby, Warwick, Northampton, Pembroke, Oxford, and Suffolk. This was followed by more royal jousting at Northampton, and yet another tournament, this time at Eltham.[56] One of the great tournaments of the reign was that at Windsor in January 1344. This was widely advertised, both at home and abroad. The festivities included a special banquet for all the ladies who had been invited, headed by two queens and nine countesses; the only men allowed to be present were two French knights. There was jousting for three days, in which the king and nineteen companions challenged all comers. Not surprisingly, Edward III himself was among the prizewinners.[57]

This Windsor tournament was the occasion for Edward's announcement that he was founding a round table. The round house in which the table was to be placed had a diameter of 200 feet, but although a good deal of work was done on it, it was never finished.[58] The high point of chivalric romanticism came with the foundation of the Order of the Garter in 1348, and its formal establishment in the following year. This has been the subject of much discussion and analysis. The king's original ambitious plan for a round table of 300 knights had, of course, strong Arthurian echoes. Its replacement, the Garter, was also based at Windsor, but was conceived on a much smaller and

---

[54] Froissart, iv. 166.
[55] In more recent times tokens are said to take the form of articles of female underclothing, frequently worn under a helmet.
[56] Murimuth, 123–4.
[57] Ibid. 155.
[58] Barker, *The Tournament in England*, 92–3.

less expensive scale, and did not draw so overtly on the legendary past. It was following the triumph of Crécy and the capture of Calais that the idea for the Garter seems to have been developed, perhaps in the course of the six tournaments the king held in 1348. At one of them, held at Eltham, the king wore a robe decorated with a dozen garters. Why the garter was chosen as an emblem is a mystery; equally, the reasons for the use of the motto 'Honi soit qui mal y pense' are unknown. The new order was composed of twenty-six knights, and it has been shown that they were nearly all heroes of Crécy, and formed two groups, one that had fought with the king at the battle, and the other with the Black Prince. The knights of the Garter were not all of the highest rank; they were representative of all ranks of knighthood, from simple knights bachelor to earls. Nor were they all English; they included the Gascon Jean de Grailly, the Frenchman Sanchet d'Aubrichecourt, and the German Henry Eam. Curiously, none of the earls created in 1337 were among the original Garter knights. The order was linked with St George's chapel, and support was to be provided for an equal number of poor knights. The order is especially well known simply because it has survived; it is less clear quite how important it was in the mid-fourteenth century. The chronicler Geoffrey le Baker thought that what was significant about it was the institution of an almshouse to look after impoverished knights, not the glorification of the warriors who had won the victory at Crécy.[59]

There were differing views of chivalry. The *Scalacronica* was written by a hardened northern knight, Thomas Gray. This chronicle is no paean of praise for chivalry. Gray recorded the story of how William Marmion went to Norham castle to fulfil a vow made to his lady that he would make the helmet she gave him famous in the most dangerous place in Britain. Once he had charged on horseback into the Scottish ranks, Gray's father had to rescue him, with the garrison fighting on foot. Marmion is made fun of, bedecked as he was with gold and silver. Gray described the 1359 expedition at some length. He noted that Bartholomew Burghersh took part in 'jousts of war by agreement with the French' outside Reims, but made nothing of this, though he took great pride in English feats of arms, particularly when small numbers of Englishmen defeated larger French forces. Chivalry for Gray was a practical code, a set of conventions that provided a framework for the business of war. He may not have made vows to beautiful ladies, or won prizes at tournaments, but he esteemed honour and bravery.[60] A poem in French, *The Vows of the Heron*,

---

[59] Vale, *Edward III and Chivalry*, 76–91; D'A. J. D. Boulton, *The Knights of the Crown: The Monarchical Orders of Knighthood in Later Medieval Europe 1325–1520* (Woodbridge, 1987), 96–130.

[60] A. King, 'A Helm with a Crest of Gold: The Order of Chivalry in Thomas Gray's *Scalacronica*', in N. Saul (ed.), *Fourteenth Century England*, i (Woodbridge, 2000), 21–35.

preserves what purports to be the vows made in 1338 by Edward III and his companions to pursue the war in France. The vows are, however, odd. The earl of Salisbury promised not to open one eye when he fought in France: the earl, however, had already lost the use of an eye in a tournament, and the vow seems pointless. John of Valkenburg vowed to set the Cambrésis alight, not even sparing churches or pregnant women, hardly a chivalric offer. Queen Philippa implausibly vowed that if she was not taken across the Channel, she would kill herself and her unborn child with a great steel knife. Nor are these the only curious features of the poem. On a superficial reading it appears to fit the chivalric pretensions of Edward's court, but the more closely it is examined, the more it emerges as a critical satire.[61] It seems likely, however, that it mocked a genuine occasion, for the swearing of oaths to perform valiant deeds was common. John de Fauconberge vowed in 1343 that he would not bear arms anywhere until he had armed himself in the Holy Land against the enemies of God. He had fought previously against the Scots and in Flanders, but presumably felt that he could not be a true knight until he had fulfilled the highest purpose of knighthood. He was duly given a licence to go to the East, and returned in time to die of the Black Death.[62]

Women had an important place in chivalric culture. It was often claimed that it was for love that men performed their feats of arms. The celebrated picture in the Luttrell Psalter of Sir Geoffrey Luttrell shows the knight being encouraged to go off to fight by his womenfolk, perhaps in much the way that Marmion was urged on by his lady-love. One London squire promised his adored that he would take a crossbow bolt from each tower when Edward III besieged a town in France. Accordingly, he rode past each tower of Tournai during the siege in 1340, and for his pains was shot by a crossbowman. He succeeded in making it back to the English camp, and went to the king's tent. There, he pulled the bolt from his body, and died. The bolt was duly sent back to his beloved lady in London.[63] At Hennebont in Brittany in 1342 it was for love of the countess of Brittany that, according to Jean le Bel, Walter Mauny decided to stand and fight when on a sortie from the besieged castle.[64] Eustace d'Aubrichecourt, a hardened soldier, was sent letters and tokens by Isabel de Juliers, widow of the earl of Kent, to encourage him in his exploits. It may be that all this is no more than literary flummery, but it seems very likely that

[61] The Vows of the Heron (Les Vœux du héron): A Middle French Vowing Poem, ed. J. L. Grigsby and N. J. Lacy (New York, 1992). Whiting, 'The Vows of the Heron', 261–78, sets out the evidence for seeing the poem as satirical.
[62] CPR 1343–5, 6.
[63] K. DeVries, 'Contemporary Views of Edward III's Failure at the Siege of Tournai, 1340', Nottingham Medieval Studies, 39 (1995), 102.
[64] Le Bel, i. 317.

there was indeed a culture among women of high birth that taught them to persuade their men that they should go off to war. They would have known little of the hardships and miseries, but would have been well versed in the absurdities of the romantic fiction of the day. They might also participate in the more pleasant side of chivalric activities; 288 special headdresses were made for the ladies who took part in a tournament at Lichfield in 1348.[65]

The ideology of chivalry provides an important part of the explanation of why men were willing to fight in wars, particularly in Edward III's French war. For individuals, it was no doubt part of a complex mesh of motivation. In the case of John de Lisle there was probably a complicated mix of loyalty to a king who provided favour and patronage, and a sense of religious duty that may have combined with chivalric ideals. After the death of John's mother in 1339 his father became a friar, and in 1342 John took over his lands, at the age of about 24. He already had military experience, for he had fought in Scotland in 1338 and was present at the abortive battle in the Low Countries at Buirenfosse in the following year. In 1341 he had campaigned in Gascony, and in 1342 he was in Brittany. In 1345 he was with Henry of Lancaster in Gascony, and in the following year he took part in the battle of Crécy. He had a retinue of six knights, eleven squires, and twenty-three archers on that campaign, and was rewarded for his efforts by promotion to the rank of banneret. He also received a grant of £200 a year to enable him to maintain his new status. He was present at the siege of Calais, and was one of the first members of the new Order of the Garter. At a tournament at Eltham he was one of four men who were given splendid hoods by the king, who also had one for himself. They were white, embroidered with dancing men in blue, with pearl buttons. A little later Edward gave him a harness of white taffeta with a blue border. New responsibilities followed the favours. Lisle was summoned to parliament from 1350, and in the next year became sheriff of Cambridgeshire and Huntingdonshire. Like his father, he was a pious man. In 1352 he received papal permission to choose a confessor and to take two or three priests with him when he went overseas. At about the same date his wife, whom he had married when he was about 14, took the veil and entered a convent of minoresses accompanied, according to the licence she received, by two honest matrons. Despite Lisle's piety, he was responsible for the death of John Goys, a knight, for which he was duly pardoned. His last campaign came in 1355, when he was with the Black Prince on his raid to Narbonne. He was one of the few English knights to be killed on this expedition.[66]

---

[65] Vale, *Edward III and Chivalry*, 70.
[66] *Complete Peerage*, viii. 73–6; Fowler, *King's Lieutenant*, 104.

There were practical rewards to be gained from chivalric warfare, with the profits from taking prisoners and ransoming them. In warfare in Wales and Scotland there was little opportunity for the English to make substantial gains this way, but fourteenth-century France was a very different matter. In the early stages there were few prisoners taken. Walter Mauny's raid on Cadzand in 1338 yielded him the half-brother of the count of Flanders, but Edward III soon set him free. The 1346 campaign must have opened the eyes of many to the profits that could be made from war. Not only was there vast plunder to be taken in Normandy, but at Caen the count of Eu was taken prisoner, along with the lord of Tancarville and many lesser knights. There was a trade in prisoners, and the count was later sold to the king by his one-eyed captor, Thomas Holland, for an astonishing 20,000 marks. At Crécy, however, the French unfurled the *Oriflamme*, and Edward the English dragon emblem. Orders were given on both sides that prisoners were not to be taken. This instruction was not followed to the letter, but it helps to explain the surprisingly high level of aristocratic casualties. There were no members of the high nobility taken prisoner in the battle and brought back to England to be ransomed. Thomas Dagworth took Charles of Blois in the next year, and was granted a reward of £4,900 by Edward III. Eventually, in 1356, Charles agreed to pay Edward III a ransom of over £100,000, but no more than about £17,000 was ever actually paid.

It was at Poitiers that the English scooped the ransom jackpot. Huge numbers of captives were taken, many to be quickly released on parole. The ransom for King John was to transform English royal finances in the 1360s. One estimate is that, excluding King John and his son, the total receipts from ransoms came to some £300,000. The Black Prince sold three prisoners to the king for £20,000. Robert de Clinton obtained £1,000 from the king for a quarter of the ransom of the archbishop of Le Mans, but subsequently remitted 400 marks of that in return for three manors and other rights in Ireland. Reginald de Cobham obtained about £1,250 for part of the ransom of the count of Longueville. The archbishop of Sens was worth about £8,000 to his captor, the earl of Warwick. There were, of course, great difficulties in obtaining full payment of the sums agreed, and it is not possible to produce a definitive total.[67] What is abundantly clear, however, is that the English had large and justified expectations that the war would yield them rich pickings. Places as well as people could be ransomed and sold. Eustace d'Aubrichecourt profited greatly from his plundering, burning, and looting on the 1359

---

[67] C. Given-Wilson and F. Bériac, 'Edward III's Prisoners of War: The Battle of Poitiers and its Context', *EHR* 116 (2001), 802–33; Murimuth, 80–1; Le Bel, ii. 81–3; *CPR 1345–8*, 337, 538, 550; *CPR 1358–61*, 167, 300, 440; *CPR 1361–4*, 323; *Foedera*, iii/i. 170; Sumption, *Hundred Years War*, ii. 248.

campaign, selling Autry to the duke of Bar for 7,000 florins, and obtaining 25,000 gold deniers from the count of Flanders for two other places.[68]

The war in France was not always fought in the best chivalric manner. In part this was because the chivalric code was loosely defined. It could be adopted when it suited, and abandoned at other times. Nor was it shared by, or extended to, common soldiers or ordinary civilians. The English archer who slid a dagger through the gaps in knightly plate armour was not contravening any conventions of war. Alongside chivalry more primitive customs of war continued. Rape and slaughter following the capture of a town was only to be expected. Examples are many. In 1338 Walter Mauny's capture of the island of Cadzand was followed up by horrific slaughter of the inhabitants. The firing of the villages and townships of the Cambrésis in 1339 by Edward's troops was intended to appal, and it did. There is a celebrated story that Geoffrey le Scrope took a French cardinal up a church tower to see the flames for 15 miles around. 'My lord, do you not see that the silken cord which surrounds France is now broken?'[69] Caen in 1346 saw horrific scenes of violence once the English entered, and it is hard to believe that all were the work of the common soldiers. Ransoming was not always a pleasant and gentlemanly business. According to Froissart, on the Black Prince's 1355 raid men of bourgeois or even peasant status were held for ransom, and 'they did physical mischief to anyone who did not agree to be ransomed'.[70] Discipline was difficult to maintain at the best of times. Captains of semi-independent companies made their living from the war, and chivalrous behaviour was often incompatible with financial necessity.

It was important that enthusiasm for the king's cause was maintained, not merely among those who fought for him, but also among those who supported the war by paying taxes and providing supplies. Royal writs ordering the recruitment of troops, or the collection of wool or other goods, would naturally often provide some explanation of the king's needs. One in 1338 began by stating:

Since in many of our parliaments and councils held before now it was ordained and agreed by common assent and counsel of the prelates, earls, barons and communities of our realm that we should go in our own person, in force, overseas for the defence and salvation of our realm, Holy Church, and of our people and the rights of our crown to act against our alien enemies, who attempt to pursue and attack us and our people by land and sea.[71]

Those who received such writs may well have regarded such phraseology as little more than common form. The many newsletters written, recording the

---

[68] Fowler, *King's Lieutenant*, 204. [69] Baker, 60, 65. [70] Froissart, iv. 164.
[71] *Treaty Rolls*, ii: *1337–1339*, ed. J. Ferguson (London, 1972), 220.

triumphs of the English campaigns, were probably far more influential. Many of them were clearly intended for public consumption, and were included in the chronicles compiled by Adam Murimuth and Robert of Avesbury. Bartholomew Burghersh, on the 1346 campaign, sent two letters to the archbishop of Canterbury. Michael Northburgh, a senior royal official and the king's confessor, sent letters home from the same campaign reporting their news. There was a more official letter written in the king's name at Caen in 1346, reporting the initial successes of the expedition. The Crécy campaign, perhaps because it was so very successful, was exceptionally well reported, but there were many other letters sent back to England on other occasions. The diary of the Black Prince's campaign of 1355 was circulated in a similar fashion.[72] The accounts that were given of events were straightforward, but it was the story of English victories that was told. This was not a cynically concocted propaganda campaign by the king and his supporters, but it was more than a simple matter of people sending news to their friends. Another technique was the use of renowned soldiers, heroes of the war, to address parliament. Bartholomew Burghersh explained the war in Brittany and the truce of Malestroit to Lords and Commons in 1343, and he made another speech to the same audience in 1353. In the following year parliament was addressed by Walter Mauny.[73] It was not just by providing good news that people were persuaded that the war was worth fighting. The French attacks on English coastal ports warned that war might be more than an English export to France. The discovery in Caen, when the city was captured in 1346, of a French invasion plan that dated from 1338 was a splendid propaganda coup, so convenient that it is impossible to avoid wondering if it was an ingenious English fabrication.[74]

The Church provided a useful means of conveying the message that the king needed support in his enterprise. Edward I had instructed his clergy to say prayers and hold processions so as to obtain divine support for his wars, and under Edward III such requests were systematically used to build backing for the war. Prayers, sermons, masses, and processions paid lip-service to the cause of peace, but in reality offered a way of popularizing the king's military ambitions and making what was happening far more widely known that would otherwise have been possible.[75]

[72] Fowler, 'News from the Front', 76–8.   [73] Rot. Parl. ii. 136, 252, 264.
[74] Murimuth, 205–8.
[75] A. K. McHardy, 'Some Reflections on Edward III's Use of Propaganda', in Bothwell (ed.), The Age of Edward III, 171–89.

WAR AND THE ECONOMY

One final controversy needs to be examined, that relating to the overall economic impact of the war.[76] One argument has it that the war was thoroughly successful, bringing in substantial profits in the form of ransoms and plunder; the alternative is that, despite such gains, the overall cost to the country was high. It is not possible to calculate a precise balance sheet, but it is clear that in this period the pattern was not consistent. The early years of the war, up to 1340, saw the government effectively bankrupted by the costs. In many cases, however, the money that Edward III paid out, notably to his allies, was money raised abroad from Italian and other merchants. Very little English coin was exported in support of the military and diplomatic efforts, in contrast to Edward I's war in the 1290s. Soldiers' wages were not paid promptly, if at all, and in many cases must have been handed over in England, with the money remaining in the country. The government's complex dealings in wool, however, meant that money that would have been brought back into England by English traders was spent instead by government agents on payments to allies in the Low Countries, and on other costs incurred abroad. However, much of the cost of the war in these early stages was met by Italian and other merchants, who were never repaid. Quite unintentionally, Edward III was conducting a foreign war at considerable foreign expense.

As the war proceeded, England gained at France's expense in terms of ransoms and plunder. While it is unlikely, however, that very large sums flowed into England from the trade in ransoms in the period before 1360, in the following decade the story would be a different one, with the huge ransom of the French king John filling Edward III's coffers. The profits of plunder in more general terms are incalculable, but it is clear that in 1346 there were very rich pickings to be had in Normandy, in particular from the capture of Caen. Many an English household was the richer for items of French finery after that campaign was over.

The French suffered far more from English invasions than did the English from French naval raids and Scottish incursions. There was, however, a cost to England. French raids on the English coasts were not frequent, but they could be damaging. The attack on Southampton in 1338 was particularly serious; the town had not recovered from it by the time that it was hit by the Black Death. Of the two disasters, the evidence suggests that the French raid was the more serious. In the north, while Scottish raiding was by no means as serious and

[76] See K. B. McFarlane, 'England and the Hundred Years War', *Past and Present*, 22 (1962), 3–13; M. M. Postan, 'The Costs of the Hundred Years War', *Past and Present*, 27 (1964), 34–53.

damaging as it had been in Edward II's reign, the extent of recovery was seriously limited by continuing military activity. The major invasion of 1346 ended in the English triumph at Neville's Cross, but even so, was responsible for considerable damage.

The war had its effect on trade. The main market for English wool was in the Low Countries, where the great cloth-producing towns were badly affected. The manipulation of the wool trade in the late 1330s by the English government, and the imposition of very heavy customs duties, also had a serious impact on wool exports. Furthermore, the war had a direct impact on English shipping. In many years ships were tied up in harbour for long periods waiting for troops to embark and for the weather to be favourable. When they were at sea, they were carrying men and supplies to the campaigns, not valuable exports and imports. The picture, however, was not all dark: there was money to be made from the wool trade, and the home staple policy of the 1350s benefited English exports.[77]

A crude economic test of whether England was gaining or losing from the war is provided by the state of the currency and the activity of the mints. At the start of the war the country was desperately short of silver. In 1338 the wages of the porter at the London mint were reduced from 3d. to 1d. a day when it was realized he had virtually nothing to do.[78] There was, however, some gold coinage, mostly French écus, in use in England. The introduction of an English gold coinage in 1344 began to transform the situation, and in the 1350s output recovered strikingly, with the mint pouring out both gold and silver coinage.[79] The French war was not the cause of the way in which the coinage recovered, but it had its part to play. No longer was Edward III running up huge overseas debts, nor was he exporting huge quantities of coin in support of the war effort. Had the war been a severe drain on the English economy in these years, there would surely have been a coinage famine, whereas the reverse was the case.

A final balance sheet on the war, even in the relatively short period of 1337 to 1360, is not easy to draw up. Change in these years should not all be attributed to the effects of the war; the Black Death had a major impact on the economy. However, there were considerable costs to bear: taxation was heavy, and war undoubtedly hindered trade in several ways. The direct advantages won from ransoms and plunder are unlikely to have outweighed these. Nevertheless, there were benefits from this war, and for some, such as William de la Pole, there were fortunes to be made. For others, with names that have gone down in history, there was lasting fame and renown.

---

[77] See below, 494.   [78] Challis, *New History of the Royal Mint*, 144.
[79] See above, 287.

PART III

Society and People

CHAPTER 13

The Great Lords

Society in medieval England was highly stratified, but the distinctions between different groups were not always as clear-cut as historians might like. Wealth, lineage, and status might define a man beyond possible doubt, but it was possible for a baron to be wealthier than an earl, while a knight might possess a more distinguished lineage than a baron. Status might not equate with economic power. Terms such as 'gentry' provide convenient shorthand, but are not always easy to map onto the reality of medieval society. In the following chapters a division is made between the great lords, lay and ecclesiastical, the knights, the peasantry, and the merchants. These distinctions are convenient, but should not be regarded as definitive; social standing was made up of multiple elements, which were not always consistent.[1]

The normal terminology used in government documents to define the members of the higher nobility was 'prelates, earls and barons'. During the period of famine that afflicted England in 1315–16, regulations were drawn up that were aimed at reducing the extravagance of 'the great lords'. They were not to be served more than two courses, with four types of meat. The prelates, earls, and barons, however, were to be permitted an additional 'entremet'; they formed an especially privileged group. Another phrase that could be used was 'magnates and nobles'. Chroniclers might refer to men of the highest rank as 'the magnates'. Walter of Guisborough, for example, wrote about the king's request in 1296 that 'certain magnates' should go to fight in Gascony, and described how in 1297 'all the magnates present' performed fealty to the heir to the throne, while 'the people' raised their right hands. Bartholomew Cotton described how, after its confirmation in 1297, Magna Carta was read out in the presence of the king's son Edward and 'the earls, barons and magnates'.[2]

---

[1] For an extensive discussion of the problems of social structure, see S. H. Rigby, *English Society in the Later Middle Ages: Class, Status and Gender* (Basingstoke, 1995), 181–205 and *passim*.
[2] *Ann. Lond.* 238–9; *Select Charters*, ed. Stubbs, 472; Guisborough, 290–1; Cotton, 327.

There is no problem in knowing who the earls and the bishops were. There are, however, problems in defining the abbots and priors who can be counted as magnates. The heads of the major monastic houses, numbering about thirty, clearly came into this category, but there is no easy line to be drawn between them and those of the next rank. The term 'baron' presents even greater difficulties. It was not always used with great precision. It was applied to the heads of roughly a hundred families of wealth and influence, below the rank of earl, who possessed baronies. To be a baron did not confer any special rights or powers, and men were not necessarily anxious to be barons. Thomas Furnival was treated as a baron, and was frequently summoned by Edward I and his son to parliament, but in 1326 he complained that he had been fined by the exchequer as if he were a baron, whereas in fact he held no land by baronial tenure. This claim was accepted.[3] The only adequate definition of a baron in this period was that he held his land from the king by baronial tenure, and paid a relief at the baronial rate of £100 (100 marks after 1297). If a barony was divided, then the holders of all the parts had baronial status. In many cases, however, uncertainty remains. There were some estates called baronies that did not pay baronial reliefs. The fullest study of the problem identified 135 baronies and a further seventy-two 'probables'.[4] What mattered, however, was who considered themselves, and were thought of by others, as barons. The term was not widely used as a form of individual identification. The lords of Stafford styled themselves Baron Stafford, but this was rare. Nor did it mean much; in the case of Baron Helton, the family did not hold any land of baronial status.[5] Most barons simply described themselves as 'lord' (*dominus*), and were not easily distinguishable from knights. In war it was the banneret, a military rank, who was marked out by use of a rectangular banner, not the baron.

THE EARLS

There is no doubt that the earls were the elite among the nobility; in 1300 there were just nine in England. The title itself was largely honorific, for there were few specific duties associated with it. There was no question of an earl being expected to preside in the county court, and the traditional right to receive the 'third penny' from his county amounted in practice to very little. In 1230, for example, Earl Warenne received £10 from Surrey, Hubert de Burgh £50 from Kent, Humphrey de Bohun £20 from Herefordshire, Roger Bigod 50 marks from Norfolk; none were very significant amounts.[6] Later, the sums would be

---

[3] T. Madox, *History and Antiquities of the Exchequer* (London, 1769; repr. 1969), i. 533–8.
[4] I. J. Sanders, *English Baronies: A Study of their Origin and Descent 1086–1327* (Oxford, 1960).
[5] D. Crouch, *The Image of Aristocracy in Britain 1000–1300* (London, 1992), 113.
[6] *Pipe Roll 14 Henry III*, ed. C. Robinson (Pipe Roll Society, 1927), 7, 110, 216, 337.

standardized to £20 a year. There were some hereditary duties associated with particular earldoms. These might be largely formal, such as the bearing of ceremonial swords at the coronation ceremony. In 1308, for example, when Edward II was crowned, Lancaster carried the sword known as Curtana, and other swords were borne by the earls of Lincoln and Warwick. Edward II's request that Piers Gaveston should carry Edward the Confessor's crown in the ceremony was not well received; tradition was important, and innovation unwelcome.[7] More important than formal duties such as those at the coronation were the military offices of marshal and constable, held for much of the period by the Bigod earls of Norfolk and Bohun earls of Hereford. The marshal had some responsibility for discipline in the army, helped to register feudal service, and had a role in command. The constable shared some of the marshal's duties, but had a particular responsibility for infantry troops.

To be an earl was to possess dignity and status. Earls were probably normally addressed by their title, though this might not represent their real power base. The earls of Gloucester had significant estates in Kent and East Anglia, but their most important lands lay in Glamorgan and the Welsh march. The earls of Oxford held nothing in Oxfordshire; the bulk of their limited landed estate lay in eastern England. The earls of Surrey possessed major estates in south Yorkshire, and preferred to use the title of Warenne. Edward II insisted that Piers Gaveston be known as earl of Cornwall, while Roger Mortimer demanded that he be addressed as earl of March. Great offence was caused when Piers Gaveston, himself an earl, used rude nicknames such as 'Burstbelly' for the earl of Lincoln and 'Whoreson' for Gloucester. Lancaster was termed 'Churl'.[8] Earls did not like to have their dignity punctured. Some clearly made much of their status. The bishop of Exeter complained in 1338 that the recently elevated Hugh de Courtenay was announcing that as earl of Devon he was equal to the king, that he could make law and judge it, that the wisdom of the realm lay in his person, and that the business of the kingdom depended chiefly on him.[9]

The wealth of the earls varied very considerably. Thomas of Lancaster, with his five earldoms, had annual receipts in the region of £12,000. The earl of Gloucester's income was half that, but he was probably the second richest earl in the land. In 1314 Earl Gilbert held over 160 manors in England and Wales, with some 19,000 acres in demesne. The earls of Oxford, in contrast, were very poorly endowed with land; their revenues were counted in hundreds, not

[7] J. H. Round, *The King's Serjeants and Officers of State* (London, 1911), 340–2; Pauline Annals, 261.

[8] *Vita Edwardi*, 3; *The Brut*, i. 207.

[9] *The Register of John de Grandisson, Bishop of Exeter*, pt. 1: *1327–30*, ed. F. C. Hingeston-Randolph (London, 1894), 290–5.

thousands, of pounds. Thomas, earl of Warwick, who died in 1242, suffered because much of his family property was in the hands of his stepmother as a result of the marriage settlement she had received. Thomas had to sell lands in a vain attempt to maintain his position. By 1315, however, Earl Guy of Warwick held almost 15,000 acres in demesne, in about a hundred manors.[10] In Edward I's reign the earl of Arundel wrote to the king in 1297 complaining that he was too poor to be able to campaign overseas. Promises of lands in Scotland had come to nothing, and he claimed that his English estates were worth only £500 a year.[11] His son Edmund, in the crisis at the end of Edward II's reign, was better off, for he was able to place £524 in Chichester cathedral, along with some plate, for safe keeping.[12] Edmund was executed, but his son succeeded to his estates and built a very substantial fortune. He added the Warenne estates to his own through inheritance in 1347, but much of his success was due to his own business sense and ability. His wealth was not simply based on land; in 1350 he invested money with a London merchant, 'to traffic therewith for the earl's profit'. He was one of the very few who profited from the risky business of lending to the crown. At his death in 1376 he left over £70,000 in cash in hand, movable goods, and debts due to him.[13] New earls had to be provided with lands or money so that they could maintain their position; the allocations made to them can be regarded as a minimum level of wealth that was appropriate. When Andrew Harclay was made earl of Carlisle in 1322, he was granted land worth 1,000 marks a year. The same sum was given when in 1337 Edward III promoted the four leading bannerets in his household to earldoms, apart from the poorest, who was promised land worth £1,000 a year.[14]

When a new earl was created, the king used a sword to symbolize his earldom. Letters of 1329 appointing Maurice FitzThomas as earl of Desmond in Ireland stated that 'we have girded him with a sword'.[15] When Earl Warenne, according to the story, waved a rusty sword at the royal justices in the *quo warranto* inquiries under Edward I, he was stressing his status as an earl as well as claiming to hold his lands by right of conquest. Coronets began to be worn by earls in the fourteenth century, and were not used by those of lower ranks. One was referred to in the inventory made of the earl of Pembroke's

---

[10] B. M. S. Campbell, *English Seigniorial Agriculture 1250–1450* (Cambridge, 2000), 61; D. Crouch, 'The Local Influence of the Earls of Warwick, 1088–1242: A Study in Decline and Resourcefulness', *Midland History*, 21 (1996), 13.

[11] SC 1/17/64.

[12] *CPR 1324–7*, 339.

[13] C. J. Given-Wilson, 'Wealth and Credit, Public and Private: The Earl of Arundel 1306–1397', *EHR* 106 (1991), 1–26.

[14] *Cal. Ch. Rolls, 1300–27*, 442–3; *CPR 1334–8*, 409–10, 415, 426.

[15] 'Sur ce nous li avoms ceinte despe': *Complete Peerage*, iv. 327 n.

possessions on his death in 1324, but no fewer than seven, along with eleven gold circlets, were among the earl of Derby's jewels and plate handed over to Italian merchants as a pledge in 1339.[16] The display that nobles were able to project emphasized their exalted position in society. Legislation of 1363 makes it clear that only the grandest in the land should wear cloth of gold and silver, and have ermine trimmings.[17] Heraldic symbols were very significant; the chevrons of the Clares, for example, were a proud part of their heritage. Even small household objects would be decorated with the arms of their owner; the Valence arms on a fine jewel box link it to the early fourteenth-century earl of Pembroke or his father.[18] The complexity of noble arms was such that professional expertise became required; Simon de Montfort's barber, Nicholas, was described as being expert in the recognition of arms.[19]

The seal used to authenticate documents was important. In the 1220s the practice of showing the earl mounted and armed on one side, with his arms on a shield on the other, began to be adopted. Seals became steadily more elaborate. The mid-thirteenth-century seal of John de Warenne showed his horse wearing a trapper with the chequered pattern of the earl's arms. The triangular shield on the other side was surrounded by eight cusps and tendrils of ivy. In the early fourteenth century the next John, Earl Warenne's seal showed his shield against a splendid background of a river and woodland, with swans, stags, and other animals. There was a visual pun on the earl's name, for rabbits are shown in their warren.[20] Charters granted to an earl might be finely decorated by the recipient; two letters to Warenne have a resemblance to his seal, showing hunting scenes. That which elevated Piers Gaveston to the earldom of Cornwall shows the royal shield, as well as those of the Gaveston and Clare families, the latter in honour of Piers's wife, Margaret de Clare. Cornish choughs naturally featured in the design. These embellishments to charters were added by the donees.[21]

The standing of an earl meant that he was expected to attend the king when required. The earls were invariably summoned to parliaments and great councils, and they headed the lists of those who received individual summonses to campaigns. They would witness charters when present at court—that which

---

[16] Crouch, *Image of Aristocracy*, 195, 210; *Wardrobe Book of William de Norwell*, ed. Lyon *et al.*, 408–9.
[17] *SR* i. 378–83.
[18] Woolgar, *The Great Household in Late Medieval England*, 54.
[19] Guisborough, 200.
[20] T. A. Heslop, 'English Seals in the Thirteenth and Fourteenth Centuries', in Alexander and Binski (eds.), *Age of Chivalry* (London, 1987), 117.
[21] E. Danbury, 'The Decoration and Illumination of Royal Charters in England, 1250–1509: An Introduction', in M. Jones and M. Vale (eds.), *England and her Neighbours 1066–1453* (London, 1989), 161; Chaplais, *Piers Gaveston*, 31–3.

elevated Gaveston to the earldom of Cornwall had no witnesses other than earls. William Bohun, earl of Northampton from 1337, witnessed over half of the charters issued by the royal chancery.[22] The extent of their influence in counselling the king is largely impossible to determine, but it is very clear that, for example, Henry de Lacy, earl of Lincoln, was a very influential figure in Edward I's immediate circle. The earls may well have considered that they were in a special position to advise and influence the king. Bracton had stated that 'kings associate themselves with such persons for consultation and to govern the people of God',[23] but this was not a constitutionally established right.

There were almost thirty comital titles in England between 1225 and 1360, and a striking lack of stability in their descent. The largest number of earls at any one time was seventeen, at the start of the period; the smallest was at the end of Edward I's reign, when there were only seven men who held earldoms in their own right. That tiny figure included the heir to the throne, who held the title of earl of Chester. At the beginning of Edward III's reign the situation was little better, for there were then only eight English earls, and in 1360 there were only a dozen. No earldom was held in direct line of succession from father to son throughout this period. The one that displayed the greatest continuity was the most obscure, that of Oxford. There was a very brief period when the earldom was forfeited in 1265, and in 1331 it passed from uncle to nephew, rather than from father to son. In contrast, the shortest-lived was that of Carlisle, which existed for slightly less than twelve months in 1322–3. Accidents of descent might mean that one man held several earldoms; in Edward II's reign Thomas, earl of Lancaster, also held the earldoms of Derby, Leicester, Lincoln, and Salisbury, through a mixture of descent and marriage.[24]

The contemporary author of the *Vita* of Edward II was well aware of the problem. 'The magnates of the land either fall in battle, or die without a son, or heiresses divide the inheritance, and the name of their father perishes for ever.'[25] Death at an early age from battle wounds explains just two cases of the failure of the direct line of descent, those of Richard Marshal, earl of Pembroke, in 1234 and of Gilbert de Clare, earl of Gloucester, in 1314. A surprising number of earls proved bad at reproduction, dying with no direct male heir. About 35 per cent of them, a high proportion, came into this

[22] C. Given-Wilson, 'Royal Charter Witness Lists 1327–1399', *Medieval Prosopography*, 12 (1991), 65–8. See ibid. 36–53 for a discussion of the reliability of these witness lists.
[23] Cited by Crouch, *Image of Aristocracy*, 61.
[24] The English earldoms are conveniently tabulated in *Handbook of British Chronology*, ed. E. B. Fryde, D. E. Greenaway, S. Porter, and I. Roy, 3rd edn. (1986), 448–89. Fuller details of the careers of the earls are to be conveniently found in the *Complete Peerage*.
[25] *Vita Edwardi*, 57.

category. The most astonishing failure was that of the family of William Marshal, earl of Pembroke, who died in 1219 leaving five sons. Each in turn died leaving no son to succeed him, an extraordinary circumstance that led to the division of the estates of the earldom between co-heiresses. Roger de Quincy, earl of Winchester, had no children at his death in 1264. Edmund, earl of Cornwall, died in 1300 leaving no children; he had separated from his wife in 1294. Roger Bigod, earl of Norfolk, likewise died childless in 1306, as did Aymer de Valence, earl of Pembroke, in 1324. John de Warenne, earl of Surrey, who died in 1347, had sons, but not by his wife, Joan de Bar, whom he spent many years attempting to divorce. Hugh Audley, earl of Gloucester, died in the same year, again with no male heir. The extinction rate was at its highest in the period 1225–49 and in the first half of the fourteenth century; in the final quarter of thirteenth, no earl died without leaving a son or grandson. Such variations are to be expected with a small sample. The extinction rate for a wider sample, the parliamentary peerage over the period 1300–1500, was about 27 per cent, a very significantly lower figure. A similar figure for cases where there was no direct male heir is produced by taking families recorded in inquisitions post mortem for the period from 1236 to the outbreak of the Black Death.[26] Table 13.1 does not count as extinctions cases such as that of Simon de Montfort or Robert Ferrers, who had heirs but who did not inherit their father's earldom; it counts only cases where there was no male heir.

An earldom was not necessarily extinguished when the family that held it died out in the direct male line of descent. Joan, niece of one of the five sons of William Marshal, was often styled countess of Pembroke. Her husband, William de Valence, was never given the title of earl, but their son Aymer de Valence was created earl in 1307. He died without a male heir in 1324, but

TABLE 13.1. *Extinctions in the direct male line in English comital families, 1225–1349*

	1225–49	1250–74	1275–99	1300–24	1325–49
Families at start of period	18	14	11	10	8
New families	2	1	2	5	15
Total no. of families	20	15	13	16	23
Extinctions	11	4	0	8	10
Extinction rate (%)	55	26	0	50	43

[26] McFarlane, *Nobility of Later Medieval England*, 146; S. J. Payling, 'Social Mobility, Demographic Change, and Landed Society in Late Medieval England', *EcHR* 45 (1992), 55. See also A. Grant, 'Extinction of Direct Male Lines Among Scottish Noble Families in the Fourteenth and Fifteenth Centuries', in K. J. Stringer (ed.), *Essays on the Nobility of Medieval Scotland* (Edinburgh, 1985), 210–16.

Edward III allowed the earldom to pass to Aymer's nephew Laurence Hastings in 1339. Interestingly, this was on the grounds that he was descended from Earl Aymer's eldest sister, ignoring the principle that female inheritance was partible.[27] Hugh d'Aubigny, earl of Arundel, died in 1243, and his lands were divided between the families of his four sisters. In 1291 Edward I recognized the claim to the earldom of Richard FitzAlan, the son of one of these co-heiresses. The death of the young earl of Gloucester, Gilbert de Clare, killed at Bannockburn in 1314, meant the temporary end of his earldom. The estates were divided between his three sisters, and in due course, in 1337, Hugh Audley, husband to one of them, was elevated to the earldom. As he died without heirs in 1347, however, the earldom was not perpetuated for long.

After the death of Simon de Montfort his earldom of Leicester was not extinguished as might have been expected. Instead, it was granted to the king's son Edmund of Lancaster. Nor was this the only earldom that Edmund acquired. The earl of Derby, Robert Ferrers, had a violent and controversial career during the Barons' Wars. There was a bitter feud between him and the king's son Edward, perhaps because Ferrers' lands had been in Edward's hands during his minority, and perhaps also because the two were in dispute over the Peak in Derbyshire. In the campaigning that preceded the battle of Lewes, Edward attacked Ferrers' castle of Tutbury and ravaged his lands. After the battle Ferrers conducted a vicious campaign against Edward's lands in Derbyshire and Cheshire. His ambitions ran counter to Simon de Montfort's own plans to take over Chester and the Peak. The outcome was the arrest of the young earl and his imprisonment in the Tower. In 1269 he was made to acknowledge a debt of £50,000 to Edmund of Lancaster, effectively as a fine for his release from custody. Edmund forced him to agree to hand over his lands if he could not raise the money. The earldom of Derby, and the great majority of the Ferrers estates, was in consequence combined with the earldoms of Lancaster and Leicester.[28] Interestingly, during the political crisis of 1297 draft opposition documents listed Robert Ferrers's son John alongside the two earls Roger Bigod of Norfolk and Humphrey de Bohun of Hereford. There was clearly a sense that he was still entitled to the status of an earl.[29]

While it was difficult to extinguish titles, it was not easy in the thirteenth century to create new ones. There was, no doubt, considerable conservatism about this. Henry III revived the earldom of Cornwall in 1227 for his brother Richard, and in 1267 the one wholly new earldom of the reign, Lancaster, was created for his second son, Edmund. Henry's Lusignan half-brothers gained

[27] *Complete Peerage*, iv. 680.
[28] Prestwich, *Edward I*, 42–3, 61; Maddicott, *Simon de Montfort*, 322–3.
[29] *Documents Illustrating the Crisis of 1297–8*, ed. Prestwich, 154–5.

much from him, but not, surprisingly, earldoms. He did not even accord William de Valence the title of earl of Pembroke, even though William could have been regarded as entitled to it by marriage. Henry was slow to give Simon de Montfort the title of earl of Leicester. Simon did homage for the Leicester lands in 1231, but did not receive the title until 1239, after his marriage to the king's sister Eleanor.

ROYAL POLICY

The question of whether the crown had a 'policy' toward the earls has been asked in the specific context of Edward I's reign.[30] Edward had been made only too aware in his youth of the potential problems that a powerful earl might pose during the struggle with Simon de Montfort. He had no obvious favourites, and did not face the problem of needing to find titles for his sons. The future Edward II was the only son from his first marriage to survive to adulthood, and his two sons by his second queen were too young for it to be necessary to make provision for them.[31] It would be wrong to view Edward as anxious to extinguish earldoms, but, conservative in many of his attitudes, he did not create any new ones, though he did allow Richard FitzAlan to become earl of Arundel in 1291, even though the title had been vacant since 1243, and in 1306 he created John of Brittany earl of Richmond. In both cases, however, the new earls had a strong hereditary claim.

Edward was eager to link the earldoms by blood to the crown, and this was surely a deliberate policy. Members of the royal family already held the earldoms of Lancaster and Cornwall. Two of the king's daughters were married to earls, Joan to Gloucester, and Elizabeth to Hereford. The earl of Lincoln's daughter was married to the king's nephew Thomas of Lancaster. Arrangements were made to ensure that should Alice die childless (as she did), her lands would come to Edward I's descendants, rather than to collateral members of her family.

Edward tried to put an end to the earldom of Devon, not for political reasons, but to provide him with more lands with which to endow his family. The dowager countess was persuaded, on her deathbed, to sell the Isle of Wight and three manors to the king in return for 6,000 marks. The rightful heir to the earldom, the somewhat distantly related Hugh de Courtenay, was not permitted by Edward I or Edward II to use the title. This does not seem to have greatly concerned Hugh; what he wanted was to be allowed to inherit the

---

[30] K. B. McFarlane, 'Did Edward I Have a "Policy" towards the Earls?', in his *Nobility of Later Medieval England*, 248–67.
[31] Edward II made Thomas of Brotherton earl of Norfolk in 1312, and Edmund of Woodstock earl of Kent in 1321.

countess's broad acres. When he petitioned Edward II in 1315, no mention was made of the earldom. However, in 1335 argument over whether he was entitled to the third penny of the county was resolved by Edward III, with an instruction that he should use the title of earl of Devon.[32]

Edward I struck a rather different deal with Roger Bigod, earl of Norfolk. He was elderly and childless when in 1302 he surrendered his lands and earldom to the king. He received them back on terms that ensured that on his death they would come to the crown, rather than go to a collateral heir. The purpose of such a policy and such arrangements was not so much political as dynastic, and suited both parties. Edward was doing the best he could to ensure that his descendants would have lavish landed endowments, while Bigod was promised £1,000 worth of lands and revenues.[33] In due course the earldom went to Thomas of Brotherton, one of Edward's sons by his second marriage.

Edward II marked a change of practice in dramatic fashion at the outset of his reign when, with the very first charter he issued, he promoted his Gascon favourite Piers Gaveston to the earldom of Cornwall.[34] According to the *Vita* of the king, there was much argument about this. Could the earldom be separated from the crown? The earl of Lincoln argued that it could, as two previous kings had done so.[35] There must also have been hostility to the move, as by birth Gaveston was at best no more in status than a minor noble, and an alien to boot. Equally startling, in some ways, was the creation of Andrew Harclay as earl of Carlisle in 1322, as a reward for the part that he had played in the defeat of the earl of Lancaster at Boroughbridge. This was a wholly new title, and Harclay was not a man of noble lineage. There was a precedent for this: Edward had earlier made John de Bermingham earl of Louth, as an acknowledgement of his victory over Edward Bruce at Faughart in Ireland in 1318. Like the earldom of Winchester, created in John's reign, the name of Harclay's new earldom was taken from a town, not a county; there was presumably a realization that the traditional link between earldoms and counties had become largely meaningless. Interestingly and innovatively, the earldom was created in tail male; that is, it was to descend in strict male succession.[36]

Edward's next new earldom (also named after a town) was created two months later. The earldom of Winchester was given to Hugh Despenser the elder, father of the king's favourite, and was forfeited when Despenser was executed in 1326. With the new regime that deposed Edward II in 1327 came a

---

[32] *Rot. Parl.* i. 334; *Complete Peerage*, iv. 324, 660.

[33] M. Morris, 'The "Murder" of an English Earldom? Roger IV Bigod and Edward I', in *TCE* ix. 89–99.

[34] P. Chaplais, *Piers Gaveston, Edward II's Adoptive Brother* (Oxford, 1994), 27–34.

[35] *Vita Edwardi*, 1.

[36] *Complete Peerage*, iv. 663.

new title, earl of March, accorded to Roger Mortimer, Queen Isabella's accomplice and lover. Given Mortimer's territorial strength in the Welsh marches, the title made sense; it was presumably the earl's personal choice not to attempt a revival of an older earldom. It was, however, striking that the earldom was named neither after a county or a town.

It had been noted that Edward I was not accompanied by any earls when he went to Flanders in 1297. The author of the *Vita* of Edward II remarked that 'Formerly when the kings of England raised their standard against the enemy, fifteen earls and more followed them to war; but now only five or six bring aid to our king.'[37] The prestige of a ruler was naturally enhanced if his entourage was sufficiently impressive, and Edward III was well aware of the lessons of the reign of his father and grandfather. It was in the context of his war preparations that Edward took a bold step in 1337. In parliament in March he created no fewer than six new earls. He took the four leading men in his household, William Montague, William Bohun, William Clinton, and Robert Ufford, and gave them the titles of Salisbury, Northampton, Huntingdon, and Suffolk respectively. In addition, he made Henry of Grosmont, son of Henry, earl of Lancaster, earl of Derby, and Hugh Audley, husband to one of the Clare co-heiresses, earl of Gloucester. Edward explained his actions:

Among the marks of royalty we consider it to be the chief that, through a due distribution of positions, dignities and offices, it is buttressed by wise counsels and fortified by mighty powers. Yet because many hereditary ranks have come into the hands of the king, partly by hereditary descent to co-heirs and co-parceners according to our laws, and partly through failure of issue and other events, this realm has long suffered a serious decline in names, honours and ranks of dignity.[38]

Of the new creations, Suffolk was a wholly new title; the others were revivals. Bohun was a younger brother of the earl of Hereford, and to have two earls in one family was most exceptional. The case of Henry of Grosmont was somewhat similar; it ran counter to the normal convention to give the title of earl to an earl's son during the father's lifetime. This startling expansion of the number of earls did not provoke criticism; the elevation in particular of William Clinton, a younger son of an undistinguished knight, might have been expected to arouse some hostility. Clinton, however, was a man of some means, as a result of his marriage to the twice-widowed Juliana de Leyburn. In creating the new earls Edward III claimed to be acting in response to a request from parliament, and he emphasized that he had the consent of the magnates. What was also important was that the elevations were not accompanied by excessive grants: Salisbury, Huntingdon, Suffolk, and Derby were promised

---

[37] Pierre de Langtoft, i. 385; *Vita Edwardi*, 62.
[38] Quoted by Powell and Wallis, *House of Lords in the Middle Ages*, 326.

1,000 marks each, and Northampton £1,000. There is no indication that the new men were looked down upon by the existing earls, or regarded as being of less than equal status.

Edward's generosity in creating new titles in 1337 did not continue on the same scale. In 1340 he revived the twelfth-century earldom of Cambridge for his ally William, count of Jülich (or Juliers). In 1351 Ralph de Stafford was made earl of Stafford. He was married to the only daughter of Hugh Audley, earl of Gloucester, who died in 1347, which explains his elevation. The title of earl of March, held by Queen Isabella's lover, was revived for his grandson Roger Mortimer in 1354. This recognized both his hereditary right and his excellent service in Edward's wars.

The king also had his family to consider. He had given his eldest son, Edward, the earldom of Chester in 1333; the earldom had been used in this way since 1254. The startling innovation came in 1337, when Edward was promoted to the title of duke of Cornwall. This was a title previously unknown in England, though it was claimed that dukes had ruled the county in the distant past.[39] Of Edward's other sons, Lionel of Antwerp acquired the earldom of Ulster in 1342 through marriage to the previous earl's daughter. In the same year John of Gaunt was made earl of Richmond; the earldom had become available with the death of the childless John of Brittany in the previous year. Edward III's other sons who survived to adulthood, Edmund of Langley and Thomas of Woodstock, received earldoms in 1362 and 1377 respectively.

COUNTESSES

Countesses were not as important as their husbands, but were far from being mere ciphers. The sources, regrettably, often fail to reveal the important role they must often have played. Simon de Montfort's wife, Eleanor, for example, is likely to have had a far greater influence on her husband's career than emerges from the chronicles. Women were very capable of independent action. Edward I's daughter Joan was first married to the earl of Gloucester, who died in 1295. She was clearly a self-willed and determined young woman, and two years later she married Ralph de Monthermer, a squire in her household. The king was furious; apart from anything else, he must have had hopes of using Joan again to forge a further politically useful marriage alliance. There was, however, nothing Edward could do, and Ralph was known as earl of Gloucester until Joan's son Gilbert came of age in 1307. In contrast, the career of Alice de Lacy suggests that even for a very great heiress, choices might be limited. She was the sole heiress to the earl of Lincoln, Henry de Lacy. When about 13, she

[39] Powell and Wallis, *House of Lords in the Middle Ages*, 327.

was married to Thomas of Lancaster. The marriage was not successful. It was childless, and Alice appears to have spent long periods of time away from her husband, notably at Pickering castle. In 1317 John, Earl Warenne, abducted her, very probably with her consent. This was the product of a personal feud between the two earls; Lancaster had done his successful best to block Warenne's attempt to divorce his wife, to whom Lancaster was related.[40] After Lancaster's execution in 1322, she was imprisoned, and was even threatened with death by burning; the Despensers suggested, on no good grounds, that she was the real cause of her husband's death. She was terrorized into making over most of her lands to the king.[41] Alice remarried after her release from prison, choosing as her husband a lame squire from her entourage, Eblo Lestrange, in what was clearly a love-match. The final dramatic turn in Alice's extraordinary career came after Eblo's death. She took vows of chastity, but then was seized in her own castle of Bolingbroke in 1336, abducted, and raped by Hugh de Frene. Alice was a wealthy widow in her fifties, and a splendid prize for such a man. He and Alice were arrested and briefly confined; they escaped, and married.[42] There is little indication in all of her complex story that Alice was able to do much to influence what happened to her, apart from her choice of second husband. One of the wealthiest women in England, her marriages deprived her of the independence that the great dowagers possessed.

Dowagers might have a very significant role to play, particularly when an earldom failed in the male line. Matilda, sister to the five Marshal brothers, was through marriage countess of both Warenne and Norfolk. On the death of the last of her brothers, Anselm, she took the title of marshal of England, which she added to her two earldoms.[43] A much more significant figure was Isabella de Forz, the widow of William de Forz, earl of Aumale, who died in 1260. On the death of his son Thomas some nine years later, the Aumale title came fully to Isabella. As sister to Baldwin de Redvers, who died childless in 1262, she was also countess of Devon. Isabella possessed great estates, and in consequence considerable power, for some thirty years. Margaret Marshal, daughter of Thomas of Brotherton, earl of Norfolk, succeeded to her father's estates on his death in 1338. She was not accorded the title of countess of Norfolk until 1377, and her two husbands, John de Segrave and Walter Mauny, were not given the title of earl. She nevertheless controlled a very significant estate for many years, and was a lady of great importance. She did not die until 1399.

---

[40] Maddicott, *Thomas of Lancaster*, 197–8.
[41] Fryde, *Tyranny and Fall of Edward II*, 113, 255.
[42] *Select Cases in the Court of King's Bench, Edward III*, ed. G. O. Sayles, v (Selden Society, 1958), 90–1; *Complete Peerage*, v. 572–4.
[43] Crouch, *Image of Aristocracy*, 77.

Marie de St Pol, countess of Pembroke, and Elizabeth de Burgh, one of the Gloucester co-heiresses, had long and, it seems, contented careers as dowagers.[44] Marie had been briefly married to Aymer de Valence, earl of Pembroke, who died in 1324 leaving no heir. She survived her husband for many years. A strongly religious lady, she founded a house for the minoresses at Denny, Cambridgeshire, in 1342. She was also responsible for the foundation of Pembroke College and Clare College, Cambridge. In the latter case she acted jointly with her friend Elizabeth de Burgh, about whom much is known. She ran through three husbands between 1308 and 1322, and then lived out a contented widowhood until her death in 1360. Her income was very substantial, reaching £3,000 a year; she had a massive landed inheritance. Her household was large and lavish: a livery roll from 1343 lists 250 people who received robes and furs from her. She lived a life of considerable luxury, and entertained her many friends and family in grandiose style. She was notably pious, but not without extravagance, for her clerks had magnificent embroidered vestments and her chapel was filled with gold and silver reliquaries, chalices, censers, and other equipment. She had parrots as pets. These two great ladies, Marie and Elizabeth, had very considerable status. Their immediate power over their households and their estates was as great as that of any other major landowner. What they could not do, however, was exercise the sort of influence and authority in political affairs that their male counterparts, Edward III's earls, could.

BARONS

Below the rank of the earls came the barons. There was a constant process of change as baronies fell prey to the accidents of family history and politics. Roger Bertram, lord of Mitford in Northumberland, was a determined supporter of Simon de Montfort and his cause. He had been taken prisoner early in the civil war, at Northampton, but had been released in time to fight at Lewes. In the aftermath Roger was reduced to poverty. He sold much of his land, and made extensive grants to the religious houses of Brinkburn, Newminster, and Tynemouth. By the time of his death in 1272, he was heavily indebted to Jewish moneylenders. The fact that he had no male heir probably contributed to his decision to part with his patrimony, but his career shows the way in which the outcome of rebellion might be disastrous for individuals.[45]

---

[44] For their careers, see F. A. Underhill, *For Her Good Estate: The Life of Elizabeth de Burgh* (London, 1999); J. C. Ward, *English Noblewomen in the Later Middle Ages* (London, 1992); P. R. Coss, *The Lady in Medieval England 1000–1500* (London, 1998), 59–63.

[45] *Complete Peerage*, ii. 160.

The Beauchamp family held the barony of Bedford. William de Beauchamp died in 1260. His eldest son and granddaughter died soon after him, and the barony went to his brother William, only for him to die in 1262. His other brother John was killed at Evesham in 1265. 'Who could contain their tears at the death of John of Beauchamp?', wrote Thomas Wykes.[46] The barony was then divided between their three sisters. Maud, the eldest, married Roger Mowbray, who died in 1266. She then married Roger Lestrange, who lived until 1311. On his death the lands went to John Mowbray, her grandson. He was executed after the battle of Boroughbridge, but his son John was restored to the estates in 1327 and died in 1361. Beatrice, the second of the Beauchamp sisters, on her death left only a daughter, Maud, who married John Botetourt. In 1328 the lands were settled on Maud's daughter Elizabeth, wife first of William Latimer and second of Robert Ufford. Ela, the third Beauchamp sister, left three daughters, so her third portion of the original barony was divided into ninths.[47] The story illustrates the complexities that might follow a failure of the direct male line of descent. The Derbyshire barony of Horsley had an even more involved fate in the thirteenth century on the death of William de Briwerre in 1233, for the lands were then divided between his five sisters and their descendants. One of the sisters in turn had five daughters, so that a fifth of the barony was itself divided into five parts.[48]

The case of John ap Adam shows how rapid a rise and fall was possible as a result of the workings of marriage and wardship. John married Elizabeth, daughter and heiress of John Gurnay of Beverstone in Gloucestershire. This gave him baronial status, and he was summoned to parliaments between 1297 and 1309. His son Thomas was about 2 when he died; he did homage for the lands in 1325. During his minority, wrongdoers broke into Beverstone castle and did a great deal of damage. Most seriously, forty charters and thirty letters of obligation were stolen; without proper title, the estates were at serious risk. When Thomas came of age, he began to dispose of his property. He granted Beverstone to Thomas de Berkeley in 1330, in a deal that shows an unsuccessful family giving way to a successful one. Thomas ap Adam also suffered from what must have been a family feud, because in 1331 Thomas Gurnay and others abducted his wife, Margery, and would not return her. It is no surprise that the ap Adams failed to maintain their briefly held baronial status.[49]

While old baronies might suffer division and decline, in some cases the fragments formed a part of a substantial new lordship. John Botetourt, who married Maud de Beauchamp, was a highly successful household banneret in

---

[46] Wykes, 174.   [47] *VCH Bedfordshire*, iii. 12–14; Sanders, *English Baronies*, 11–12.
[48] Sanders, *English Baronies*, 123.
[49] *Complete Peerage*, i. 179–80; *CPR 1324–7*, 237; *CPR 1330–4*, 204.

Edward I's service. No doubt his marriage helped to give him baronial status, for Maud not only inherited a third of the Bedford barony, but also possessed the lordship of Mendlesham through her first marriage. With his estates in Suffolk and elsewhere, Botetourt was of undoubted baronial status. He was one of those who sealed the barons' letter to the pope in 1301, and played a significant part in the politics of Edward II's reign.[50] The reconstruction of the Welsh march after Edward I's second Welsh war created opportunities. John de Grey was an Essex man of no very great note, though he was sheriff in 1233. His son Reginald's career began in the mid-1260s, when he was sheriff of Nottingham and Derby, and constable of Nottingham castle. He played a major role in Edward I's Welsh wars, and in 1282 was granted Ruthin and became lord of Dyffryn Clwyd. From this, the family became known as barons of Ruthin. A tough man, Grey served as justice of Chester, and headed the council in England during Edward's absence in Flanders in 1297. At his death in 1308 he left a widespread estate to his son John.[51]

There were other striking examples of social mobility. The Holland family alone provides two. Robert Holland owed his rise to the support of Thomas, earl of Lancaster. The family had risen steadily but unspectacularly during the thirteenth century to be among the leading Lancashire gentry. Robert first appeared in Lancaster's service in 1298, and was knighted by him a few years later. He became the earl's most important councillor, and received many estates from him in a series of complex deals. The value of these lands has been estimated at about £550, whereas his inheritance had been worth only about £40. In addition, it was through Lancaster's influence that he married one of Alan de la Zouche's co-heiresses, in a match that brought him lands worth probably about £720. He had become one of the wealthiest barons in the land. His fall was abrupt. Realizing that Lancaster's cause was doomed, he abandoned the earl shortly before the battle of Boroughbridge in 1322, but nevertheless suffered imprisonment and loss of his estates. The regime under Isabella and Mortimer ordered restitution of them in 1327, but he did not enjoy them for long. He was murdered in 1328, almost certainly by Lancastrian supporters who had bitter memories of the way he had deserted their cause.[52]

Robert Holland's elder son, Robert, had an undistinguished career. His younger brother, Thomas, on the other hand, made his way in the entourage of William Montague, earl of Salisbury. The French war was the making of him, along with his marriage. His capture of the count of Eu at Caen in 1346,

[50] Botetourt's career is summarized by C. Moor, *Knights of Edward I* (Harleian Society, 1929–32), i. 122–3.

[51] Moor, *Knights of Edward I*, ii. 151–2.

[52] J. R. Maddicott, 'Thomas of Lancaster and Sir Robert Holland: A Study in Noble Patronage', *EHR* 86 (1971), 449–72.

and the subsequent sale of his captive to the king, was one element in the making of his fortune. The second was his marriage to Joan of Kent, daughter of Edmund, earl of Kent. This took place in a private, even secret, ceremony when she was about 12, an age when it cannot have been clear that she would grow to be the most notable beauty in England. While he was away on crusade in Prussia, Joan's family, possibly acting in ignorance of her marriage, organized her marriage to the earl of Salisbury's son William. This took place in the winter of 1340–1. In 1347 Holland took his case to the papal curia, and succeeded in obtaining a verdict in his favour. On the death of John, earl of Kent, in 1352 without direct heirs, his lands came to Joan. Holland, now not only famous but also rich, was summoned to parliament as a baron. His grandson would rise to be a duke, if only briefly.[53]

The baronage had a voice in parliament; in the Ordinances of 1311 consent for many matters was to be provided by 'the baronage in parliament'. Not all barons received individual summonses, and the lists of those who did varied very considerably. Nor can all of those summoned be shown to have held land by baronial tenure, though it is reasonable to assume that they were considered to be of baronial standing. Witness lists for the confirmations of Magna Carta in 1225 and 1237 show twenty-three and eighteen barons respectively to have been present.[54] In 1242, according to Matthew Paris, Henry III summoned 'all the earls and almost all the barons of England' to a meeting at Westminster, along with the bishops, abbots, and priors.[55] Unfortunately no lists survive to reveal which barons were summoned on this occasion, but two years later Henry summoned seventy-two barons individually to muster at Newcastle for a projected Scottish campaign.[56] It is likely that similar numbers were summoned to parliamentary occasions, for later, under Edward I, the chancery used common lists for both parliamentary and military summonses. Under Edward I there was a considerable variation in the number of men below the rank of earl who received individual summonses. In 1295 fifty-three were asked to attend parliament in August. Forty-one were summoned for the following November. A year later, in November 1296, the number was down to thirty-six. For the Salisbury parliament of February 1297 seventy-five were listed, as well as nine described as knights. Thereafter numbers became more stable. By 1307 eighty-six men below the rank of earl received individual summonses. Each list would usually be based on the previous one, but in 1309 a new one, containing eighty-one names, was used, which included nine wholly new

---

[53] Joan's marriages are discussed by K. P. Wentersdorf, 'The Clandestine Marriages of the Fair Maid of Kent', *Journal of Medieval History*, 5 (1979), 203–31.
[54] Maddicott, 'An Infinite Multitude of Nobles', in *TCE* vii. 19–20.
[55] Paris, *Chron. Maj.* iv. 185.
[56] *Close Rolls (Supplementary) of the Reign of Henry III, 1244–66* (London, 1975), 1–3.

names. The clerks had not done all their research properly, for one of the new men, Henry Bodrigan, had died nine months before the writ summoning him was issued.[57] Changes continued, and following the problems of the civil war of 1321–2 which saw many names vanish, the list by the end of Edward II's reign was down to thirty-eight.

Numbers continued to vary under Edward III. In 1332 sixty-seven were summoned; in 1348 only thirty, but in 1349 the number increased to fifty-six. Though in most cases son succeeded father in receiving a summons, this was not invariably the case. Some men were summoned to parliament just once, for example Thomas de Brewose in 1348, and Robert de Benhale in 1360. William de Cantilupe was summoned from 1299 until his death in 1308. His elder son, also William, was never summoned, but his brother Nicholas, who succeeded him in 1320, was called to parliament by Edward III from 1336 until his death in 1355. Receipt of a summons was not always welcomed. James Audley of Heleigh's arrest was ordered in 1348 because he had not come to parliament when summoned, and five years later he obtained a life exemption from attendance.[58]

THE HIGHER CLERGY

The ecclesiastical elite consisted of the archbishops, bishops, and the greater abbots. The social origins of the higher clergy were very varied. Some were of aristocratic birth. Aymer de Valence, bishop of Winchester under Henry III, was the king's half-brother, while Louis de Beaumont, provided to the see of Durham in 1317, was related to the queen. Few great churchmen were drawn from the major comital families; Bogo de Clare, brother of Gilbert, earl of Gloucester, was one exception. Lesser aristocratic families provided several bishops, such as Walter Cantilupe of Worcester, Thomas Cantilupe of Hereford, and Anthony Bek of Durham. James Berkeley, briefly bishop of Exeter in 1327, was brother of Maurice Berkeley. Thomas Cobham, who was passed over in 1313 for the see of Canterbury in favour of Walter Reynolds, but who later became bishop of Worcester, came from a baronial family. His background was in his favour for one commentator, for he was described as 'the very flower of Kent, of noble stock; he had lectured in arts and on canon law'. The same author, however, thought little of the aristocratic Henry Burghersh, appointed to Lincoln in 1320, and commented that 'breeding and natural aptitude are looked for in a prince, but virtue and knowledge are required of a bishop'. In

---

[57] *Complete Peerage*, ii. 199.

[58] Powell and Wallis, *History of the House of Lords*, 225, 229, 251, 309, 310, 317, 355; *Complete Peerage*, ii. 111–13, 115–16, 308.

fact, Burghersh was university educated, and served both Church and State with some distinction.[59] Men such as Robert Grosseteste, bishop of Lincoln under Henry III, Robert Winchelsey, archbishop of Canterbury in the next reign, and William Melton, archbishop of York from 1316 to 1340, came from humble backgrounds. Analysis of the social origins of the bishops under Edward II shows that in over half the cases they were not of noble or gentry stock. Richard Kellawe at Durham was a monk from the cathedral priory whose father was a local burgess. John Stratford's father was likewise a townsman from Stratford upon Avon. A significant proportion of the bishops, normally about a quarter, had been in the king's service in some way before their elevation; for such men, their ultimate social origins were less significant than their experience in royal government.[60] A new force in the thirteenth-century Church was that of the friars; in Robert Killwardby and John Pecham they provided two archbishops of Canterbury. For the most part, however, bishops were drawn from the secular clergy.

The greatest of the bishops were immensely wealthy. The richest see was that of Winchester, with vast estates in Hampshire and others as far afield as Taunton in Somerset and Adderbury in Oxfordshire. There were almost sixty manors and ten boroughs. In 1301–2 the bishop's gross receipts came to almost £5,200, of which £2,405 was paid into his central treasury. Just over £3,000 came from the sale of produce from the manors, and over £1,500 was from rents. Profits from courts came to about £570. The net annual value of the archbishop of Canterbury's estates in the late thirteenth century ranged from £3,000 to £2,500. The bishop of Ely's revenue at the end of the century was perhaps £3,500 gross and £2,500 net. When the bishopric was vacant in the late 1330s, it was farmed for £2,000 a year.[61] Such levels of income placed these great bishops alongside the earls in terms of wealth, although other sees, such as those of Rochester or Exeter, were far poorer.

The abbots of the major monastic houses, which numbered about thirty, were men of some consequence, though with few exceptions their political function was limited. They were summoned to parliament as prelates, but because of their monastic role did not play as great a role in affairs of state as did the bishops. Edward II, however, informed the pope in 1320 that the abbot of

[59] *Vita Edwardi*, 45, 105; *The Registers of Bishop Henry Burghersh 1320–1340*, i, ed. N. Bennett (Lincoln Record Society, 1999), pp. xi–xvii.

[60] K. Edwards, 'The Social Origins and Provenance of the English Bishops During the Reign of Edward II', *TRHS*, 5th ser., 9 (1959), 51–79; J. R. L. Highfield, 'The English Hierarchy in the Reign of Edward III', *TRHS*, 5th ser., 6 (1956), 115–38.

[61] *The Pipe Roll of the Bishopric of Winchester 1301–2*, ed. M. Page, Hampshire Record Series, 14 (Winchester, 1996), pp. xx–xxii; F. R. H. Du Boulay, *The Lordship of Canterbury* (London, 1966), 243; Miller, *Abbey and Bishopric of Ely*, 81.

St Albans 'is one of the great ones of the realm and the king cannot dispense with his counsel without a great setback to his business'.[62] Most abbots showed little enthusiasm to attend parliament. When the abbot of St James without Northampton was summoned in 1319, there were vigorous protests, including a petition to the abbey's patron, the earl of Lancaster. After some argument the summons was withdrawn. In 1295 almost a hundred abbots had been asked to come to parliament, but numbers were much lower later in Edward I's reign. Under Edward II about fifty were summoned when representatives of the lower clergy were also asked to attend, but on other occasions the number was about thirty. By 1344 the number stood at twenty-eight, mostly drawn from old and well-established Benedictine houses. Thomas de la Mare, abbot of St Albans from 1349 until 1396, was an exception among abbots in being of high birth; it was surely at least in part because of this that Edward III made him a member of his council.[63]

The great abbots controlled considerable wealth. Calculations are difficult; the ecclesiastical tax assessment of 1291 bore little relationship to economic realities. The way in which income was, in the larger houses, divided between different officials makes it hard to provide convincing totals. Houses such as St Albans, Bury St Edmunds, and Glastonbury were major landholders; the revenues of Westminster abbey in the early fourteenth century were about £1,600 a year, while St Albans in the later fourteenth century saw receipts of some £900 a year. Durham's income was later put at over 5,000 marks a year.[64] Cistercian houses were run on a highly commercial basis, using a system of granges to run their widespread estates. In recording the deeds of abbots, monastic chronicles stressed their role as managers. The Meaux chronicle began its account of Roger of Driffield's abbacy with the near-disastrous financial consequences of his decision in 1286 to lease some property, and then buy it back at an eventual cost of over £1,000. Roger's successor, Adam, though more secular than religious in his interests, was praised for his management of the estates. Abbot Hugh, who took over in 1339, faced considerable difficulties, not least from the loss of land as the sea flooded the flat plains around the Humber estuary. Expensive investments in acquiring two churches did not produce the expected yields, and at the time of Hugh's death from the plague in 1349, debts stood at £500. At St Albans, Abbot Hugh, whose period of office coincided with Edward II's reign, was a disaster. He was educated at Oxford, but regretted spending time studying mathematics, astronomy, and

[62] *Calendar of Chancery Warrants*, i: *1244–1326*, 505.

[63] *Parl. Writs*, ii/2. 199–200; Powell and Wallis, *History of the House of Lords*, 221, 317, 351; *Gesta Abbatum Monasterii Sancti Albani*, ed. Riley, ii. 371, 390.

[64] A. Levett, *Studies in Manorial History* (Oxford, 1938), 66; B. Harvey, *Westminster Abbey and its Estates in the Middle Ages* (Oxford, 1977), 63; Durham cathedral muniments, 1.7 Pont. 8.

music rather than theology. As abbot, he incurred substantial debts, burdened the abbey with paying costly pensions, and was in the regrettable habit of entertaining ladies. He mortgaged much of the abbey's property. His successor, Richard, abbot from 1326 to 1334, was in contrast greatly praised for paying off the debts of his predecessors and doing all he could to recover rights lost by the abbey. He was a man of scientific bent, responsible for making an astronomical instrument, and skilled as a weather-forecaster. Henry of Eastry, at the Benedictine Canterbury cathedral priory from 1298 to 1331, transformed the management of the house, developing effective financial controls and making significant profits.[65]

Some other members of the higher clergy had substantial means and aristocratic tastes. Andrew Kilkenny, dean of Exeter, who died in 1302, left an estate valued at over £900. His books alone were worth £66. His potential annual income stood at about £300 a year. Kilkenny was no pluralist; Bogo de Clare, brother of the earl of Gloucester, was. Bogo built an income from the innumerable church livings he held of some £1,500 a year, but, as was perhaps right for a man who displayed no piety, he never acquired a bishopric.[66]

HOUSEHOLDS AND RETINUES

The great did not have a single, fixed abode. They lived in households rather than buildings. As they travelled, so did the household, packed into carts and carried on sumpter horses. The household provided for domestic needs, and was a complex institution. Households were divided into different departments. One early thirteenth-century agreement detailed the hall, chamber, pantry, buttery, marshalsea, and doorkeeping. The various functions are also demonstrated in the ordinance drawn up for Robert Willoughby of Eresby in the first half of the fourteenth century. Though he was not a baron, his wealth was equivalent to many who were of that status. In his household there was a steward, who had two assistants, and a wardrober, who also served as chief auditor. The clerk of the offices, or departments, had a controller or treasurer, who drew up a duplicate account roll. There was a chaplain and an almoner. Provision of food was a major undertaking, and there was a chief purchaser, two pantlers in charge of the bread, two butlers in charge of drink, with two grooms, two cooks and two larderers, again with two grooms, a saucerer, a poulterer, a baker, and a brewer, with a groom, two ushers, two chandlers,

[65] *Melsa*, ii. 183–6, 313; iii. 37; *Gesta Abbatum Monasterii Sancti Albani: A Thomas Walsingham*, ii. 177–83, 201–2, 207; J. Burton, *Monastic and Religious Orders in Britain, 1000–1300* (Cambridge, 1994), 251–2.
[66] D. Lepine and N. Orme, *Death and Memory in Medieval Exeter* (Exeter, 2003), 133–4; M. Altschul, *A Baronial Family in Medieval England: The Clares* (Baltimore, 1965), 176–87.

a porter, two farriers with a groom, and a laundress with her helper. The total staff was about twenty-five. This substantial establishment was the household of a Lincolnshire man of no great national standing.[67] A list of the household of Thomas of Brotherton, earl of Norfolk, in 1337 was much longer. It detailed a steward of the estates, and one of the household itself. There were nine clerks, six men in charge of the household departments, ten squires (including three for the countess), three ladies in waiting, seventeen valets, a dozen boys, and a laundry staff of ten. In all, there were sixty-eight people concerned to meet the domestic needs of the earl and countess.[68] Larger households might also include minstrels to provide entertainment. The list of payments to minstrels present at the Feast of the Swans in 1306 included eighteen to men retained by magnates and knights; the number included trumpeters, harpers, fiddlers, and a psaltery player.[69] There would also be huntsmen to manage what was the main leisure activity for many nobles.

The character of a well-run household was explained in the *Rules* drawn up for the countess of Lincoln in the early 1240s and based on instructions set out by Bishop Grosseteste of Lincoln. The knights and gentlemen, for example, were to wear the same livery every day, 'and not old surcoats, and soiled cloaks, and cut-off coats'. Ale should not be put on the table, but under it, while wine should only be put on side tables. The lord or lady's own dish was to be well filled, so that tasty morsels could be distributed to the others sitting nearby. Household officials were to be given as little leave as possible to visit their homes; if they grumbled, then others could be found to take their places.[70]

The size of magnate households is not easy to determine, in the absence of lists of the full establishments. The sixty-eight listed for Thomas of Brotherton did not include the knights he retained, or the huntsmen, carters, and other essential personnel. The average number of people employed probably increased significantly in the period covered by this book. When the earl of Gloucester and his countess visited her brother Prince Edward in 1293, they came with a following of over 200. The size of the earl of Lincoln's household at the end of Edward I's reign has been estimated from the accounts of food consumption at 184. Hugh Audley, a few years later, had a household just under 100 strong, according to similar calculations. The same method puts the

---

[67] F. M. Stenton, *The First Century of English Feudalism* (Oxford, 1932), 70–1; Woolgar, *The Great Household in Late Medieval England*, 17–18; N. Denholm-Young, *Seignorial Administration in England* (Oxford, 1937), 7. The ordinance is partially printed in Davies, *Baronial Opposition*, 569.

[68] C 49/7/4.

[69] C. Bullock-Davies, *Menestrellorum Multitudo: Minstrels at a Royal Feast* (Cardiff, 1978), 11.

[70] *Walter of Henley and Other Treatises on Estate Management and Accounting*, ed. D. Oschinsky (Oxford, 1971), 402–5.

total size of the earl of Lancaster's household in Edward II's reign at just over 700.[71] That was, however, highly exceptional; Lancaster's following bore more comparison with that of the king than of his fellow earls and barons. The number of knights he retained in his household was on a par with those who took fees and robes from Edward II. Great ecclesiastics also had substantial households. Walter de Wenlock, abbot of Westminster, had a permanent strength of around twenty-five, but it might rise well above that; on one occasion in 1291 his horses numbered eighty-seven.[72]

The household provided for the lord's domestic needs. The retinue of knights and squires was closely related to it, and was vitally important as a means of demonstrating and exercising power. The chronicler Bartholomew Cotton recorded the numbers of knights brought by magnates to the splendid wedding of Edward I's daughter Margaret to the duke of Brabant in 1290. Gloucester had 103, Cornwall 100, Bigod of Norfolk and Earl Warenne each had forty-eight, and Lincoln thirty-six.[73] A list of Bigod's retinue at the end of the thirteenth century names five bannerets, nine knights, seventeen squires, four men-at-arms, three major clerics, and four minor ones. One of the bannerets, John de Segrave, was to come with five knights and ten squires, and the other bannerets and knights would all have brought their own followings with them; the total number of men at Bigod's disposal would have been very considerable. The contract he made to serve with 130 men-at-arms in the winter of 1297–8 gives another indication of the scale of military resources at his disposal. A few years later the earl of Lincoln provided robes for his men in quantities that suggest a retinue of at least twenty-five knights and up to sixty men-at-arms.[74] Thomas of Lancaster's retinue in the second decade of the fourteenth century was larger still. In 1313–14 he paid out about £620 in fees, with a further £150 assigned out of the income of particular estates. Five years later he was in a position to summon one earl, Atholl, and twenty-seven knights, all members of his household, to serve with him. In all, he probably called on some fifty-five knights at different times in the year 1318–19. Overall numbers were higher still as at least some of the knights would have brought their own retinues into the earl's service.[75] All of these figures, however, show retinues swollen for some particular purpose of display, war, or politics. In

[71] Altschul, *A Baronial Family in Medieval England*, 236; Maddicott, *Thomas of Lancaster*, 45; Woolgar, *The Great Household in Late Medieval England*, 11–15.
[72] B. Harvey, 'The Aristocratic Consumer in England in the Long Thirteenth Century', in *TCE* vi. 29.
[73] Cotton, 177.
[74] Prestwich, *War, Politics and Finance*, 63–4; *Documents Illustrating the Crisis of 1297–8*, ed. Prestwich, 157–8.
[75] Lancaster's retinue is fully discussed by Maddicott, *Thomas of Lancaster*, 40–66.

normal conditions, numbers would not have been so high. Careful analysis of William de Valence's following in the mid-thirteenth century has yielded the names of no more than twenty-seven knights who served him between 1247 and 1272. In any given year it is difficult to identify more than half a dozen men in his following, though some of these would doubtless have brought their own men with them.[76]

By the late thirteenth century knights and others were normally retained by means of indentures, either for life or for a limited period.[77] The terms varied, but usually the lord would offer fees and robes, with wages for periods of active service. Saddles might also be provided. The standard of the robes varied with the standing of the recipient. Most of Bogo de Clare's retinue in the mid-1280s had robes of striped burnet, with a hood trimmed with budge (lambskin), but those his knights received were of better cloth. In some cases robes might bear the lord's coat of arms.[78] The nature of service might be specified; it could, for example, include or exclude appearance at tournaments or parliament. In the case of an agreement for life, the retainer might be assigned revenues from a particular estate, but where it was for a short term, payment would be made from the lord's household. A copy of the indenture Roger Bigod, earl of Norfolk, made with John de Segrave in 1297 survives. Segrave would receive robes and an annual fee from the earl, and would be provided for when he was with him. Special provisions were made for service with twenty fully armed horses in wartime. This was an agreement for life, and in return for his service Segrave was promised the revenues of the Norfolk manor of Lodden. In this case, Bigod did formally enfeoff Segrave with the manor, but the terms of the service the latter was to provide, as set out in the indenture, were quite different from the formal obligations that arose from enfeoffment.[79]

Household and estate officials, such as receivers, stewards, and auditors, were usually retained by means of contracts or charters (rather than indentures), which promised them rents or annuities, though a range of other benefits was possible. Clerics, for example, might be appointed to benefices in return for their services. It was also common practice to pay regular fees, and to give robes, to judges, lawyers, and officials. Justice Bereford and his wife

[76] H. Ridgeway, 'William de Valence and his *Familiares*', *Historical Research*, 65 (1992), 243.

[77] An indenture was drawn up in two copies. These would be written on a single sheet of parchment, which was then divided with an indented, or zig-zag, cut. Each party to an agreement would keep one copy. 'Private Indentures for Life Service in Peace and War 1278–1476', ed. M. Jones and S. Walker, *Camden Miscellany XXXII*, Camden 5th ser., 3 (1994), is an important collection of these documents.

[78] M. S. Giuseppi, 'The Wardrobe and Household Accounts of Bogo de Clare, A.D. 1284–6', *Archaeologia*, 70 (1920), 37; Denholm-Young, *Seignorial Administration*, 25.

[79] *Documents Illustrating the Crisis of 1297–8*, ed. Prestwich, 157–8; Denholm-Young, *Seignorial Administration*, 167.

received robes from Thomas of Lancaster in 1318–19.[80] Thomas de Berkeley, it was claimed in about 1330, gave fees and robes to the sheriff, bailiffs, and all other royal officials in Gloucestershire.[81]

Although many indentures and contracts were for life service, in practice men might move from one lord to another. A letter of recommendation survives, in which John de Champvent wrote to Aymer de Valence on behalf of Edmund of Martlesham, who had been with him for four years. He was good at writing letters in Latin, knew about accounting, was an excellent councillor, good company, and of good moral character.[82] Professional administrators might change lords several times in the course of their careers, and might alternate between royal and baronial employment. John La Ware was Earl Warenne's steward in the early 1260s. An ardent supporter of Simon de Montfort, he served as constable of Bristol in 1265, and was one of the Kenilworth garrison. In 1268 he entered Isabella de Forz's service as steward, remaining in office until 1274, when he became sheriff of Herefordshire. Four of Isabella's other stewards had almost certainly held similar posts with other magnates. In the 1260s Hamo Hautein was twice sheriff of Lincolnshire, and served as a royal escheator and as a royal wardrobe official, as well as being the earl of Gloucester's steward in 1268.[83]

As a result of the practice of retaining, manors might be encumbered with a number of payments. At North Cadbury, which belonged to Nicholas de Moeles in the early fourteenth century, there were regular charges to be met of 25 marks a year to Walter de Thornhill, along with robes for him, his wife, and groom, a pension of £2 to Elias de Godele, with a robe for him, and in addition a payment of 6s. 6d. to the local sheriff.[84] In Thornhill's case, it is likely that he had handed his lands over to de Moeles in return for adequate provision for him and his small entourage for life. The earl of Hereford recruited William de Merk as one of his squires by means of such a bargain in 1312, and in 1321 William de la Haye handed over his manor of Greenstead to Hugh Audley in return for a shilling a day, robes twice a year, and keep when William attended in his lord's household.[85]

Historians have adopted the somewhat unfortunate term of 'bastard feudalism' to describe this practice whereby lords retained knights, estate officials,

[80] J. R. Maddicott, *Law and Lordship: Royal Justices as Retainers in Thirteenth- and Fourteenth-Century England*, *Past and Present*, suppl. 4 (1978), 16.

[81] Saul, *Knights and Esquires*, 152, 266.

[82] SC 147/192.

[83] Denholm-Young, *Seignorial Administration*, 70, 75–6; Altschul, *A Baronial Family in Medieval England*, 228.

[84] *CCR 1313–18*, 275.

[85] G. A. Holmes, *The Estates of the Higher Nobility in* XIV *Century England* (Cambridge, 1957), 73–4; *CCR 1318–23*, 655.

and others in their service largely by means of cash payments. It is unfortunate, not simply because it may seem to imply that it is in some way a debased form of feudalism, but also because it implies that it succeeded feudalism. Much ink has been spilt over the chronology and origins of this means by which lords built up their retinues. The system was initially described for the fifteenth century and then pushed back into the fourteenth, but recent argument has centred on the late twelfth and early thirteenth centuries as the crucial period.[86]

One way of identifying the period of transition is to look for early evidence for retaining by means of cash payment and grants of robes. The earliest indentures survive from the late thirteenth century, but they do not mark the beginning of the practice. There is evidence from as early as the third quarter of the twelfth century for a grant of robes and sustenance in the lord's household for life.[87] A court action in 1220 sought payment of the arrears of an annuity granted in King John's reign.[88] In about 1250 William de Preston agreed to pay his steward 40s. a year, clearly as a fee. Two charters of 1278 show that William de Swinburn was retaining men for 20s. a year each, in return for their counsel and advice. Seventy legal cases from the years 1220–1300 have been identified in which there was a dispute over annual payments for life.[89] It is clear that the practice of retaining was widespread. The formal documents recording the bargains by which men agreed to serve lords developed and changed in the course of the thirteenth century; it is not, however, clear that modification of the documents reflected substantial change in the reality of retaining.

Another way to look at the problem is to see what evidence there is for lords continuing to use traditional feudal ties to create their followings. The normal terms of feudal land tenure did not extend to serving in the lord's household or as a member of his retinue on a permanent basis. In the twelfth century, however, there were cases where household officials were granted lands to hold in fee; in one example the earl of Chester granted out a manor quit of service as long as the tenant exercised his office of butler.[90] Such arrangements would have been unusual in the thirteenth century, when lords turned to professional administrators for their officials. Nor were household knights

[86] See in particular P. R. Coss, 'Bastard Feudalism Revised', *Past and Present*, 125 (1989), 27–64; D. Crouch, D. A. Carpenter, and P. R. Coss, 'Debate: Bastard Feudalism Revised', *Past and Present*, 131 (1991), 165–203.

[87] J. M. W. Bean, *From Lord to Patron: Lordship in Late Medieval England* (Philadelphia, 1989), 144.

[88] S. L. Waugh, 'Tenure to Contract: Lordship and Clientage in Thirteenth-Century England', *EHR* 101 (1986), 823, 829.

[89] Ibid. 819; 'Private Indentures for Life Service in Peace and War', ed. Jones and Walker, 35–6.

[90] Stenton, *First Century of English Feudalism*, 104.

often recruited from the feudal tenants. Only two out a sample of thirty of Thomas of Lancaster's knights were his tenants.[91] The inquisitions made after the civil war of the 1260s contain little direct evidence to suggest that men followed the course set by their landlords. Nicholas de Gymeges was reported to hold his land from Anselm Basset, but he was a member of the bishop of Winchester's household. There are few mentions of lordship of any sort in these returns. Miles de Hastings was 'of the following' of the younger Simon de Montfort, as was John Fortin for a time—he received a robe from Simon. Hugh Wake was 'of the household of Richard Trussell'. James Appleby was 'in the service of Sir Nicholas de Segrave'. 'Andrew de Tatton followed Brian [de Gouice] as his servant.'[92] Analysis of Simon de Montfort's support has shown that two of his tenants were especially prominent in his following, but that most of his backing came from his neighbours, rather than from those who held land from him.[93] There were, however, cases where feudal allegiance was claimed to be significant. Richard Vernon stated in 1275 that 'in the time of war he stood with his lord, Robert Ferrers, earl of Derby, from whom he held his lands and to whom he had done homage'.[94] The knights of the honour of Peterborough claimed that they were led to the baronial defeat at Northampton in 1264 by their lord, the abbot of Peterborough. This, however, was probably little more than an attempt to excuse their conduct.[95]

Further evidence comes from witness lists to charters. The charters issued by Roger de Quincy, earl of Winchester, show that of his five major tenants, only two were members of the earl's household, and they were not in the inner circle. The earls of Warwick in the early thirteenth century do not appear to have looked to their feudal tenants as the source from which to recruit their retainers. The feudal honour of Warwick has been described as 'little more than a fiscal survival by the 1190s'. It has been shown that of the eighteen knights known to have served William Marshal, earl of Pembroke, who died in 1219, twelve were not his tenants.[96]

The recruitment of retinues should not be seen in simple alternatives of either making use of feudal links, or using contracts involving the payment of fees and issue of robes. Family and neighbourhood connections were important, and links were not always cemented by means of written documents.

---

[91] Maddicott, *Thomas of Lancaster*, 58.   [92] *CIM* i, nos. 216, 627, 632, 646, 656, 695.
[93] Maddicott, *Simon de Montfort*, 61–2.
[94] D. A. Carpenter, 'The Second Century of English Feudalism', *Past and Present*, 168 (2000), 66.
[95] E. King, *Peterborough Abbey 1086–1310* (Cambridge, 1973), 96.
[96] G. G. Simpson, 'The Familia of Roger de Quincy, Earl of Winchester and Constable of Scotland', in Stringer (ed.), *Essays on the Nobility of Medieval Scotland*, 121; D. Crouch, *William Marshal* (London, 1990), 138; id., 'The Local Influence of the Earls of Warwick', 12–13.

About a dozen knightly retainers of Maurice de Berkeley in the early fourteenth century can be identified. They included Thomas de Berkeley junior and John de Berkeley. Men who lived fairly close to Berkeley castle formed the bulk of the retinue; only three men could not have been described as neighbours. Thomas de Bradestone was very close to the Berkeleys, particularly to Maurice, who may well have been his brother-in-arms. There is, however, no evidence that Thomas was bound by any formal indenture to the Berkeleys.[97]

The way in which the household was structured, and the way in which the retinue was formed, were important aspects of the lordship that great men exercised. There were other elements. Lords had important rights over their feudal tenants. The latter were expected to perform homage, to pay a relief when they took over their estate, to attend their lord's court, and to pay an aid when the lord's eldest son was knighted and his eldest daughter married. Most importantly, if the tenant's heir was under age when his father died, the lord would exercise rights of wardship. In many cases this relationship was one that created friction between lord and man, rather than loyalty. The performance, or non-performance, of suit of court was a significant issue in the heady days of reform, 1258 and the succeeding years, and the relationship between lord and tenant was a theme that ran through several of Edward I's statutes. The Provisions of the Barons had much to say about the relationship between lords and tenants. For example, in many cases tenants were no longer coming to their lord's court to perform suit of court. This may well have had a symbolic significance, with tenants resentful about the subordination that this duty implied. There was an issue when an estate was divided; in such a case, only one suit of court should remain due. The matter was followed up at length in the Provisions of Westminster of October 1259. The legislation was even-handed; it imposed severe measures on lords who unjustly tried to compel men to do suit of court that they did not owe. The Provisions also dealt with such issues as abuses of wardship by lords, where the latter refused to allow a rightful heir to take up his inheritance.[98] Under Edward I legislation dealt with the measures that lords were entitled to take in order to compel their tenants to perform services, while tenants were also given protection against unjust demands.

Despite the difficulties and tensions that undoubtedly existed, it is also the case that the traditions of service could be powerful, and that feudal lordship provided people with a sense of identity and loyalty. One indication of this is the way in which tenants might adopt, in modified form, the heraldic motifs

---

[97] Saul, *Knights and Esquires*, 69–71, 77.
[98] *DBM* 122–7, 138–45. For discussion, Brand, *Kings, Barons and Justices*, 43–53.

used by their lords.[99] There were regional differences in the scale of feudal lordship. In the Welsh marches the sense of territorial lordship was particularly strong, though it must be stressed that there, as elsewhere, 'lordship was far from being a uniform institution; it comprehended a vast range of differing powers, varied in their origin and changing with the passage of time'.[100] In the great liberties of the march, where the king's writ did not run, lordship was especially powerful, comprising as it did both profitable rights of jurisdiction, services and renders of various kinds, and the economic power of the landlord. For the earls of Gloucester, the lordship that they exercised in their East Anglian honour of Clare was very different from the all-embracing authority that they possessed in Glamorgan. The way in which the crown made use of the lordships, or liberties, of the north as units from which to recruit infantry troops provides one demonstration of their significance in another part of the country.

Little attention has been given to the question of how many knights remained outside the structures of lordship that saw men enter service in return for fees and robes. The sources make it hard to answer this; the numbers of surviving indentures are small, and it is not possible to reconstruct the retinues of more than a few great men. The Buckinghamshire 1322 returns, however, provide some evidence. Out of thirty-two men, three were reported to be in the king's company and one was with the queen. Two were in Stephen Segrave's retinue, though one of these was ill. One was with John de Beauchamp, and one with the earl of Pembroke. Eight men were too old or ill. That left seventeen who were not members of retinues. That return suggests that a high proportion of knights remained independent, and were not part of the mesh of aristocratic clientage. On the other hand, the sheriff of Cambridgeshire reported the names of a mere five knights who were not in retinues, of whom four were elderly and one was in prison. The equivalent Huntingdonshire list consisted of the names of two knights, one of them an old man.[101] It is unlikely that the situation in these counties was in reality as different as these returns suggest, and it is probable that the careful Buckinghamshire return was a relatively realistic one, and those from Cambridgeshire and Huntingdonshire the work of lazy or incompetent officials. There must have been a good many knights who were not formally bound to a great magnate, though they might enter contracts to provide military service for individual campaigns.

Historians have drawn attention to various factors that drove change in the ways in which lordship operated. Monetary inflation was one. In a changing

---

[99] Carpenter, 'The Second Century of English Feudalism', 30–71.
[100] Davies, *Lordship and Society in the March of Wales*, 130.
[101] *Parl. Writs*, ii/2. 507, 609–11.

economic climate that offered great opportunities to increase revenues from estates, it made little sense to grant land out in return for service. It was wiser to retain men by assigning rents to them, or by paying them in cash. Secondly, feudal lordship was weakening as changes in the law strengthened the position of tenants, enhancing their rights. Subdivision of holdings, and multiple lordships, were elements that reduced the importance of feudal tenure as a means of obtaining service.[102] The growth of royal power, and in particular the way in which the crown was establishing direct links with the localities and with knightly society, prompted lords to find new ways to assert their own authority.[103] Least satisfactory are arguments that stress the importance of the Statute of *Quia Emptores* of 1290. Since it made subinfeudation difficult, it has been suggested that the statute encouraged lords to find other ways of rewarding their followers. The chronology simply does not fit such an interpretation, nor did the statute prevent lords from rewarding their followers with grants of land. Indeed, the 1297 indenture between Roger Bigod and John de Segrave makes it clear that Bigod was rewarded with land granted by enfeoffment.[104] It is wrong to assign a single cause to a complex process of gradual change, and it remains to be shown whether feudal lordship was ever as powerful a force as the historians who argue for a clear transition to 'bastard feudalism' have supposed it to have been. A recent description of the magnate affinities of King Stephen's reign suggests that they were not very different from those of 150 years later.[105] There were various ways in which the groupings around magnates were formed. Family and neighbourhood connections were probably as important as formal contracts, and the natural desire to obtain the protection that a great lord could provide was another element. Shared interests led to sensible local alliances and the construction of networks of lordship and influence. There was no simple progression from a 'feudal' to a 'bastard feudal' structure; different methods of retaining overlapped and merged in complex ways. There were pressures driving men to use contracts and fees, and to record these in formal documents, though it must be stressed that the process of change was gradual. The essential nature of lordship was not transformed in the course of the thirteenth and fourteenth centuries.

CASTLES

In physical terms, castles were a powerful expression of lordship. There was no restriction in terms of status on who might build castles, but there is no doubt

---

[102] Waugh, 'Tenure to Contract', 812–15.   [103] Coss, 'Bastard Feudalism Revised', 45.
[104] Bean, *From Lord to Patron*, 125; Denholm-Young, *Seignorial Administration*, 168.
[105] D. Crouch, *The Reign of King Stephen 1135–1154* (London, 2000), 166–7.

that a grand castle, or a fine manor house, was an overt expression of power, wealth, and success. In the thirteenth century the nobility were swift to adopt the most up-to-date style where they could. The new Lacy castle at Boling-broke in Lincolnshire, built in the 1220s, was in the most modern fashion. It was polygonal in form. There was no keep, but round towers at the angles and twin towers controlling the gate gave the castle ample strength. Whitecastle in the southern Welsh marches provides another example of this theme, and probably dates, in its present form, from the 1270s, the work of Edmund of Lancaster. Caerffili in south Wales, largely constructed by Gilbert de Clare, earl of Gloucester, in the 1270s and 1280s, met an obvious military need in providing defence for the lordship of Glamorgan. At the same time, with its ample water defences, two gatehouses, and concentric lines of defence, it made a forthright statement about the earl's power. This was not lost on Edward I. Chepstow was an old castle, but the work done there by Roger Bigod, earl of Norfolk, again in the later thirteenth century, both provided defence for an important marcher lordship and emphasized the earl's authority. Thomas of Lancaster's building programme was extensive, with works at Pontefract, Pickering, Tutbury, and Kenilworth. He started a new castle on a majestic scale at Dunstanburgh, and contributed lavishly towards the castle built by his retainer Robert Holland at Melbourne in Derbyshire.[106] There was, however, no sense in which a grand, up-to-date castle was seen as a sine qua non for an earl. None of the new earls created in 1337 built on a notably impressive scale.

The castles built by the nobility were increasingly comfortable. The military structures, the towers and curtain walls, are what dominate the remains that still stand. The more domestic structures were not so massively built, and indeed were sometimes constructed from wood. At Whitecastle, reconstructed in the third quarter of the thirteenth century, the defensive enceinte survives in good condition, but there are little more than hints of what the domestic buildings consisted of. Sufficient survives, however, at other sites to show just how much attention was paid to comfort and privacy. At Chepstow, Roger Bigod built a new tower, Marten's Tower. Ample fenestration on the courtyard side reveals its residential purpose. A new hall was the main element in a grand set of buildings, which incorporated a kitchen and a chamber block.[107] Goodrich in Herefordshire was extensively reconstructed in the late thirteenth century. The small twelfth-century keep was preserved, but stands almost dwarfed by the two halls and solar block that surround it. The castle is characterized by its quite separate suites of accommodation all within the one defensive shell; it was perhaps constructed so as to house more than one

---

[106] Maddicott, *Thomas of Lancaster*, 25–6.
[107] S. Toy, *The Castles of Great Britain*, 4th edn. (1966), 139–40.

household. One thing all would have had to share was the single latrine tower, with its triple row of garderobe chambers.[108] Goodrich was a Valence castle; so was Bampton in Oxfordshire, built by Aymer de Valence, earl of Pembroke, in the second decade of the fourteenth century. Bampton must have impressed in terms of the area it occupied. A relatively flimsy curtain wall, with turrets and corner towers, formed a square with sides about 110 metres long, enclosing the hall and other domestic buildings. There were gatehouses on two, and perhaps even four, sides. Maxstoke in Warwickshire was built by William Clinton, first earl of Huntingdon, and similarly offers an imposing appearance, though it covers much less ground. It had fine apartments, but lacked military strength, though with moat, crenellated towers, and walls the castle made a splendid show.[109]

DEATH

Death, burial, and memorial were very important to the rich and powerful. The associated ceremonies and symbols provided an important means by which families emphasized their position in society. Funerals were often splendid occasions. Ralph Neville set out his preferred arrangements in his will in 1355. His body was to be borne in a cortège of eight horses, and taken into the nave of the church at Durham. At mass on the next day the horses were to be given in alms. Four of them should be equipped for war, with four armed men and all their equipment, and four for peacetime. Three splendid gold cloths were to be presented to the church, and 950 pounds of wax candles, with sixty torches, all to be placed around the body. Ralph's son John would buy back the four best horses for 100 marks, and the prior and convent would sell the other horses, with one gold cloth and a dozen torches, for another 100 marks. Ralph's widow was to send £120 for the upkeep of the fabric of the church, and 20s. was promised to each monk of Durham. Among other provisions, the sacrist was to have 300 pounds of wax, with fifty torches, and magnificent new capes were to be made for him from one of the gold cloths.[110] Today the austere Norman magnificence of Durham cathedral is jolted by the extravagant splendour of the multicoloured late fourteenth-century Neville monument.

Burial was not always straightforward. While most corpses were interred whole, some people might be buried in more than one place. Marriage might make for complex problems about where someone was to be buried,

---

[108] Woolgar, *The Great Household in Late Medieval England*, 51–9.

[109] *VCH Oxfordshire*, 13 (1996), 23–4; J. Blair, *Bampton Castle*, Bampton Research Paper 1 (1988); C. Coulson, *Castles in Medieval Society* (Oxford, 2003), 200.

[110] *Richard d'Aungerville of Bury*, ed. the dean of Durham (Surtees Society, 1910), 266.

particularly if a woman was married more than once. Isabella, daughter of William Marshal, was married first to Gilbert de Clare, earl of Gloucester, and then to Richard, earl of Cornwall. A three-way argument over where she should be buried was settled by placing parts of her in different places. Her body went to Beaulieu, her heart to Tewkesbury, and her entrails to Missenden.[111] Other cases of divided burial were more straightforward. Edward I's queen Eleanor's entrails were buried at Lincoln, her heart at Blackfriars in London, and what was left in Westminster abbey. This was not the product of argument, but more of a desire to spread the influence of the late queen. Divided bodies did, however, present problems for the anticipated bodily resurrection, and some attempts were made at reassembly. Andrew Harclay, earl of Carlisle, was executed for treason in 1323, and his body quartered. Five years later his sister collected the pieces together for proper Christian burial.[112]

Tradition was important in death as in life, and members of great families tended to be buried in the same church for generations. Hubert de Burgh, a 'new man', had no family convention behind him, and could therefore choose to be buried in the church of the London Blackfriars which he had founded. The friars were very anxious to get business in the form of burials, but it was exceptional that in 1298 the earl of Warwick should have chosen to be buried in the local friary at Worcester, rather than in the cathedral church alongside his ancestors. This was not altogether surprising, for relations between the Beauchamp family and the cathedral priory had not been good. The earl's father had been buried in the cathedral, but in 1276 there were rumours that his body had been thrown out. The son had the tomb opened to check if this was true, which it was not, and was excommunicated as a result.[113] Far more normal was the type of tradition that was established by the Clare family in the thirteenth century, when Tewkesbury became their favoured place of burial. Later, Hugh Despenser the younger began the conversion of the east end of the abbey into a grand mausoleum. Stained-glass windows commissioned by his widow, Eleanor de Clare, depicted the Clare earls of Gloucester and her own two husbands.[114]

Death, the funeral, and burial were far from the end of the story. For the deceased, there was the unappealing prospect of that uncomfortable waiting room, purgatory, and the hope of ultimate salvation. For those still living, there were obligations to help those who had died. It was not enough simply to hope

---

[111] B. Golding, 'Burials and Benefactions: An Aspect of Monastic Patronage in Thirteenth-Century England', in Ormrod (ed.), *England in the Thirteenth Century*, 64–75.

[112] Summerson, *Carlisle*, 242.

[113] Golding, 'Burials and Benefactions', 65.

[114] P. Coss, 'Knighthood, Heraldry and Social Exclusion in Edwardian England', in Coss and Keen (eds.), *Heraldry, Pageantry and Social Display*, 48–9.

that family and friends would say prayers for the soul of a deceased person. Arrangements that would ensure as brief as possible a stay in purgatory needed to be set up with care. William Ferrers, earl of Derby, persuaded the king to pardon him 100 marks which he owed, and used the money to set up a permanent chaplaincy so that services could be held for his soul.[115] William Montague, on his elevation to the rank of earl in 1337, founded a new Augustinian priory at Bisham in Berkshire. He obtained permission from the crown to alienate as much as £300 worth in lands and rents to the new house. Bisham became a family mausoleum; the earl left 500 marks for building works that were to include a magnificent tomb for himself, his parents, and his son. William Clinton planned a chantry in 1330, but his plans became more elaborate and he founded an Augustinian house at Maxstoke in 1336, the year before he was elevated to the earldom of Huntingdon. He endowed it generously, and was buried there. No doubt he was reassured about the quality of the prayers that would be sung for him by the careful provisions he made to ensure that all the canons had good voices. Thomas Wake was another who was anxious to be well provided for in the afterlife. He planned a new Augustinian house at Cottingham in Yorkshire, but then moved it to Haltemprice. He obtained a royal licence, which allowed the new foundation to acquire lands and rent worth £20 a year. Between 1331 and 1342 he steadily increased the endowment, and as his grants became more generous, so new licences, one for a further £20 and one for £40, were obtained. He was, of course, buried in his own foundation.[116] Henry of Grosmont, earl and duke of Lancaster, converted the hospital founded by his father in Leicester in 1331 into a college of secular canons. This was done in 1355, when the new foundation received a major endowment from the earl. Special sung services were to be performed on the anniversaries of the deaths of Henry's parents, and of his own death. There were to be daily prayers for the royal family, but no other people were to be remembered in services in the college.[117]

The memorial was important. The obvious purpose of this was to commemorate the individual it depicted, but there were in addition more complex messages to be communicated. A lavish effigy was a statement of family wealth and status; representation of someone in the latest form of armour made a statement about his martial skills. Memorials provided opportunities to display coats of arms, and to celebrate a family as well as an individual. Placing them in the chancel, rather than the nave or a side-chapel, was a way of differentiating firstly the higher nobility, then by the fourteenth century the gentry as well, from those of lower rank. A chantry chapel might become a family mausoleum. Extinction of a family in the male line, such as that of Brian FitzAlan of Bedale

---

[115] *CPR 1232–47*, 501.   [116] Ibid. 61–5.   [117] Fowler, *King's Lieutenant*, 188–91.

in 1306, might prompt a particularly grand memorial.[118] Memorials might take the form of a full effigy, or be two-dimensional in form. Fashion changed; in the thirteenth and early fourteenth centuries knights were frequently depicted in lively manner with legs elegantly crossed, often with their right hand on the hilt of their sword, as if about to fight. In contrast, the brightly coloured effigy of Reginald Cobham, who died in 1361, lies on his tomb stiffly, on its back, in full armour, with hands joined in prayer. As a cheaper option to a full three-dimensional effigy, an incised slab could be used, with various forms of inlay used to give emphasis to figures and inscriptions. Increasingly, from the later thirteenth century, brass, or latten as it was known, was employed, inset into the stone. The lost brass of the bishop of London, Henry of Sandwich, who died in 1273, was one of the earliest examples in England. Thomas Cantilupe, bishop of Hereford, was commemorated with a brass by 1287. It is likely that brasses were being produced in significant numbers in London by the 1280s. Designs followed standardized patterns, and initially successful regional workshops went out of business by the mid-fourteenth century as London dominated this business, as it did so much else.[119]

CONCLUSION

Given the great contrasts between the individual careers of members of the higher nobility, it would be risky to attempt to generalize about their abilities and attitudes. The author of the *Vita* of Edward II took the risk. The great men were unreliable: 'The love of magnates is as a game of dice, and the desires of the rich like feathers.' They were greedy:

Observe how the earls and other magnates of the land, who could live according to their station on their inheritance, regard all their time as wasted, unless they double or treble their patrimony; wherefore they pester their poorer neighbours to sell what they have inherited, and those who will not be persuaded they plague in many ways, until they are so straitened that they perhaps offer for a song what they could earlier have sold for a good price.

The chronicle is filled with distrust and dislike of the earls and great men.[120]

The caricature of the medieval higher nobility as a set of boneheaded brawlers occasionally still recurs. One notable French historian described William Marshal, earl of Pembroke, who died in 1219, as 'blessed with a

---

[118] For a more extended discussion, see B. and M. Gittos, 'Motivation and Choice: The Selection of Medieval Secular Effigies', in Coss and Keen (eds.), *Heraldry, Pageantry and Social Display*, 143–67.
[119] N. Saul, *Death, Art and Memory in Medieval England* (Oxford, 2001), 63–9, 75–7, 149–50.
[120] *Vita Edwardi*, 7, 99–100.

brain too small to impede the natural vigour of a big, powerful and tireless physique'.[121] In practice, of course, the earls included among their number men of very different character and ability. Robert Ferrers, earl of Derby, was one man who did fit the stereotype; his career in the Barons' Wars suggests that he was an unintelligent and violent young man. Other earls were very different. Richard, earl of Arundel, under Edward III, was a man with a fine financial brain, one of the few people in the medieval period to make money out of lending to the crown.[122] Henry of Grosmont, earl of Derby and then of Lancaster, was not only a distinguished general, but also a cultivated and sensitive man, the author of a remarkable religious treatise written in French, the *Livres des seyntes medicines*.[123] The earl of Warwick, who died in 1315, was responsible, to a considerable extent, for the death of Piers Gaveston. Although as a result often regarded as an unruly politician, he was also an intelligent and educated man who possessed a substantial library. Some are hard to assess. Thomas, earl of Lancaster, is a puzzling figure. He was certainly no bruiser; his career displays distaste for campaigning. He showed little political imagination and scant energy. It may have been ill health that led to his spending long winter months brooding in Pontefract castle. It is difficult not to conclude that his role leading opposition to Edward II came to him as a result of his immense wealth, rather than of his ability.[124] The earl of Hereford for much of Edward III's reign, Humphrey de Bohun, was highly untypical in that he did not participate in war. This may have been due to some physical incapacity; at least it provided him with time to exercise literary patronage. More examples would simply serve to make the obvious point that the nobles were a group of distinctive and very different individuals, not a group to be condemned or praised with facile generalizations.

[121] G. Duby, trans. in J. Gillingham, 'War and Chivalry in the History of William the Marshal', in *TCE* ii. 6.

[122] C. Given-Wilson, 'Wealth and Credit, Public and Private: The Earl of Arundel 1306–1397', *EHR* 106 (1991), 1–26.

[123] K. Fowler, *The King's Lieutenant: Henry of Grosmont, First Duke of Lancaster, 1310–1361* (London, 1969), 193–6.

[124] Maddicott, *Thomas of Lancaster*, provides much the best analysis.

CHAPTER 14

The Knights and the Gentry

Sir Geoffrey Luttrell was a knight of no very great distinction, but his is one of the most celebrated images of knighthood. On a page of the Luttrell Psalter he is shown mounted, encased in an elaborate high saddle, his surcoat, aillettes, crest, and pennon all bear his arms, *azure a bend between six martlets argent*, as does his horse's trapper and crest. His dappled grey horse is still, head bent down, but his bared teeth express a warlike character. Geoffrey's wife, Agnes, hands him his gilded helm, and holds his lance, which bears a triangular pennon. Geoffrey's daughter-in-law Beatrice Scrope waits to hand him his shield. Both ladies wear gowns embroidered both with the Luttrell arms and with those of their fathers. The military character of knighthood stands out from the picture—the lance has the point used in war, rather than tournament. The emblems of knighthood were warlike, and the close association of chivalry with horses made it right that Geoffrey should be shown mounted. Pride in family is very evident, with the emphasis on the links that the Luttrells had made through marriage. Though Geoffrey is mounted, while Agnes and Beatrice stand, the importance of the support provided by the womenfolk is very clear.[1] (See Plate 15.)

A knight is easier to define than a baron, but issues concerning the number of knights, and their rise or decline, have led historians into almost impenetrable thickets of tangled evidence. Unlike a baron, there is no doubt about what a knight was. He was someone who had been through a formal process of being knighted, and would be addressed as *dominus*, or lord. Knighthood in England was not hereditary, but there was an expectation that the son of a knight would himself take up knighthood. The rank was military in origin, and a knight was expected to be capable of bearing arms. However, this was not always the case, and in the 1320s it was reported that John Stonor 'is a man of arms, but he has never used them at all, and he is a royal justice'.[2] The pretence of military

---

[1] M. Camille, *Mirror in Parchment: The Luttreu Psalter and the Making of Medieval England* (London, 1998), 51–4, 60, pl. 29.
[2] *Parl. Writs*, ii/2. 611.

capability had to be observed. There was surprisingly little to distinguish a knight from a man-at-arms in war. He was mounted, and would have a triangular pennon on his lance, which marked him out from the rest of the cavalry and would bear a coat of arms; though perhaps as early as the late thirteenth century, and certainly by the mid-fourteenth, squires also began to do this. He would be paid in war at double the rate of a squire.

The great majority of knights campaigned in war, though some had a much more limited experience of active service than others. For most, the demands of administrative and legal work in their county were probably more onerous than those of service in war. The knights were the leading members of the county court. They were frequently called upon to serve as members of juries. They took part regularly in assizes and inquisitions. Increasingly, they demanded, and obtained, a significant role in the business of imposing law and order. In order to meet the various obligations and expectations placed on them, knights had to be significantly wealthy. The image of the landless knight of the twelfth century had little place in the thirteenth or the fourteenth. Knighthood, however, was not simply a question of economic status. In one sense, the concept of knighthood was closely bound up with ideas of chivalry, and knights were part of a very particular cultural world. It is always tempting to use the term 'class' in the context of a group in society such as the knights. It is wrong to do so. There were many who met the wealth criteria for knighthood who did not take it up. There were squires who were the social equals of many knights. Society did not fall into easy patterns of classifications.

COUNTING KNIGHTS

Knights are not as easy to count as sheep. Taking all the references to knights who served in administrative capacities in King John's reign, one scholar calculated a total of 3,453. Not all knights did serve in this way, however, and her estimate of the full total was 4,500. Yet one much-quoted estimate for the number of knights in the mid-thirteenth century was 1,250, of whom 500 were 'fighting knights'. A calculation based on the lists of knights serving on grand assize juries in the first half of the thirteenth century yielded the conclusion that there were probably about 1,000–2,000 knights involved in local administration at that period, and that 'it is difficult to believe that there could have been much more than 2,000 knights in England at any one time'. This conclusion, however, was based on a limited range of sources, and made no allowance for changes in the numbers of knights over the period.[3] The first

[3] K. Faulkner, 'The Transformation of Knighthood in Early Thirteenth-Century England', *EHR* 111 (1996), 7–9, 23; N. Denholm-Young, 'Feudal Society in the Thirteenth Century: The

half of the thirteenth century appears to have been a particularly difficult period, when numbers fell fast. It has been calculated that whereas forty-one knights took part in grand assize proceedings in Shropshire in 1221, the number was reduced to seventeen in 1256. In Warwickshire the number fell from forty-seven in 1221 to twenty-nine in 1262.[4] This suggests an overall fall from perhaps 4,000 or more in 1220 to under half that figure by the middle of the century. Thereafter, numbers look to have been steadier.

Some indication of knightly numbers at the start of the fourteenth century is provided by 935 individual summonses to men of knightly standing, all possessing at least £40 of land, sent out in 1301 for the Scottish campaign. It is not known how this list was drawn up, but it was presumably based on some record of military service, and can be taken as a list of the most active knights in the land. A different sort of list was drawn up in about 1310. The so-called Parliamentary Roll of Arms is a heraldic document. The body of the list is set out county by county. In all, it gives details of 1,110 blazons. Great men (the king, the earls, and major bannerets) number 169. There are therefore 941 knights listed.[5] Lists drawn up in 1324 produce a remarkably similar total. The government was attempting to transform the system of military obligation, and asked the sheriffs for the names of all the knights and men-at-arms in their counties. The returns are unfortunately incomplete for some counties. As they stand, they list about 1,150 knights. Some men, however, were returned for more than one county, and the total of individuals named was about 860. Making allowance for damage to the manuscripts, a very rough estimate of 1,000 for the total originally listed is perhaps reasonable.[6] All of these various totals might suggest that there were roughly 1,000 active knights in the country.

This evidence is not quite as satisfactory as it at first seems. The 1324 lists can be compared with others made in 1322. Taking Buckinghamshire as an example, an initial inquiry provided the names of twenty-seven knights. A second, later in the year, produced a list of four barons and twenty-eight knights. This compares with twenty-three knights returned in 1324. The numbers are not dissimilar, but no more than twelve names are common to

Knights', in his *Collected Papers on Medieval Subjects*, 61; J. Quick, 'The Number and Distribution of Knights in Thirteenth Century England: The Evidence of the Grand Assize Lists', in *TCE* i. 114–19.

[4] P. Coss, *The Knight in Medieval England 1000–1400* (London, 1993), 70.
[5] *Parl. Writs*, i. 410–20.
[6] M. C. Prestwich, 'Cavalry Service in Early Fourteenth-Century England', in Gillingham and Holt (eds.), *War and Government in the Middle Ages*, 155; id., *War, Politics and Finance*, 89; N. Denholm-Young, *The Country Gentry in the Fourteenth Century* (Oxford, 1969), 18. The lists are published in *Parl. Writs*, ii/2. 609–11, 636–58.

all three lists. In all, the names of forty-seven knights were given to the central authorities by the sheriff between 1322 and 1324. Of these, eight were over 60, and four too ill to be of any use. In Bedfordshire the 1324 list gave the names of fifteen resident knights and thirty-two non-residents. Eleven of the residents had been listed in 1322, when the names of twenty-seven knights in all had been returned.[7] The Gloucestershire return for 1324 listed about fifty knights, over half of whom were also returned under other counties. Four knights known to have lived in the county were omitted.[8] All of this suggests that the real number of knights was substantially higher than any one list suggests, and that a realistic estimate would be about 1,500.

There is no similar evidence for knightly numbers in the mid-fourteenth century. Inquiries in the mid-1340s asked for names in wealth bands (£5, £10, £25, and up to £1,000), and do not distinguish social rank. But there are no indications that there was any downwards change since the 1320s; it is possible that one effect of the successful war in France was to encourage rather more men to take up knighthood. The overall pattern, therefore, seems to have been that knightly numbers declined rapidly in the first half of the thirteenth century, when they fell by some 50 per cent. Thereafter they were steadier. No doubt there were fluctuations, but the sources are not sufficient for these to be accurately detected.

FALLING NUMBERS

The reasons for the decline in knightly numbers in the first half of the thirteenth century have been much debated. The period was not one of widespread economic difficulties; these were years of a rising population, and prosperity for great landlords. Was it the case that the knights were for some reason not in a position to take advantage of these conditions, and suffered an economic crisis? It has been suggested that they were not able to benefit from the process of taking land out of leasehold and into direct management in the way that larger landlords could. This is a difficult argument to sustain. Knights were not a class. The range of variation in wealth was too great to fit them all into a simple category. Some might be as wealthy as barons, certainly lesser barons. They might hold estates in several counties. Others might possess no more than a single manor. Evidence is much fuller for the great ecclesiastical estates than for secular lordships, though the Hundred Rolls of 1279 and the many inquisitions post mortem do give snapshots of a great many lay manors. The smaller landholders largely relied on paid rather than obligatory labour, but that was not necessarily a disadvantage in the circumstances of the

---

[7] *Parl. Writs*, ii/2. 587–8, 609–11, 654–5.   [8] Saul, *Knights and Esquires*, 32–3.

thirteenth century, with a high population and low wage levels.[9] The Hundred Rolls show that it was possible for small lay lords who took their rent in cash rather than labour to set very high levels. The business thrust of a small estate was inevitably rather different from that of a large one. The commercial imperative was stronger, with a considerable emphasis on production for the market. Demesnes were relatively large, enabling lords to sell a substantial proportion of what they produced. Evidence from the first half of the fourteenth century shows that small landowners were just as capable of keeping efficient accounts as their larger counterparts, and there is no reason to suppose that their thirteenth-century predecessors were not also effective managers. There is no hard evidence to demonstrate that the holders of small estates or even single manors were less able to take advantage of the economic conditions of the thirteenth century than the great landholders.[10]

There is no doubt that some knights did get into severe difficulties. Stephen Chenduit was well connected, for he was close to Richard, earl of Cornwall. Normally, service with a rich patron brought profits, but in Stephen's case he became increasingly heavily indebted to Jewish moneylenders. He sold three manors to Walter de Merton, the chancellor, who made a practice of buying up estates that were heavily encumbered with debt in order to provide his new Oxford college with an appropriate endowment.[11] Roger le Peytevin inherited his four manors after a minority, during which they probably suffered from mismanagement. When he came of age in the early 1250s, he began to borrow extensively, largely from Jews, though also from his aunt. He soon mortgaged, and then sold, his manor of Towton to her husband, and disposed of other property to the Hospitallers. He tried various means to recover Towton, even trying to invalidate the mortgage deed by attempting to have the seal on it destroyed. Like many in similar positions, he sided with the Montfortians in order to try to extricate himself from his financial plight, but this proved a major error. He had lost most of his lands by the late 1260s.[12] John Fitz Saer's father died in about 1250, with a debt of £80 to Benedict Crispin, a Jewish moneylender, and one of 50 marks to the exchequer. John continued to borrow from Benedict, and in the late 1250s sold most of his estate to Adam Stratton. He supported Simon de Montfort, like many indebted knights, and recovered

---

[9] E. A. Kosminsky, *Studies in the Agrarian History of England in the Thirteenth Century* (Oxford, 1956), 256–82.

[10] S. Raban, 'Landlord Return on Villein Rents in North Huntingdonshire in the Thirteenth Century', *Historical Research*, 66 (1993), 21–34; R. H. Britnell, 'Minor Landlords in England and Medieval Agrarian Capitalism', *Past and Present*, 89 (1980), 3–22.

[11] P. D. A. Harvey, *A Medieval Oxfordshire Village: Cuxham 1240 to 1400* (Oxford, 1965), 5–6.

[12] D. W. Sutherland, 'Peytevin v. La Lynde: A Case in the Medieval Land Law', *Law Quarterly Review*, 83 (1967), 527–9.

his main estate in Hertfordshire. Montfort's defeat spelled disaster for John, and in 1268 Stratton once again took over his lands.[13] An even more miserable story must lie behind an inquisition held in Edward I's reign into Compton Durville in Somerset. Eustace de Durville held the manor, which was assessed at a whole knight's fee in the previous reign, but he sold everything apart from annual rents of 6*d*., a pound of cumin, and a pair of white gloves. He died on the gallows, accused and found guilty of felony.[14]

Analysis of the records of Peterborough abbey has shown that the abbey, a highly successful enterprise in economic terms, was acquiring lands from knights. Of seven families with whom the monks had dealings, five can be shown to have lost out.[15] Evidence from Yorkshire shows that many knightly families, particularly the poorer ones, were selling or giving up advowsons, their rights to the patronage of churches. In some cases men may have sold these rights for good reasons, to raise money for land purchases, while at the same time some new knightly families, mostly with crown or other patronage behind them, were acquiring advowsons.[16] The evidence does, however, suggest that many knights were finding times hard. The small house of the canons of Malton spent almost £500 in fourteen years in the mid-thirteenth century buying up property largely from impoverished knights.[17]

Such evidence is not sufficient to demonstrate that there was a real crisis of the 'knightly class'. It is important not to treat the normal ebb and flow of affairs as if it were a flood tide. There were individuals and families doing well; those who enjoyed the patronage of the crown were perhaps most prominent among them, while some local offices brought profits. A careful and massively footnoted study of Oxfordshire families suggested that there was no general impoverishment of the knights taking place. The number who were forced to sell out as a result of financial pressure was small; the pattern was one in which those with very little land did badly, while some of the wealthy and middling knights gained land, and others lost some. A sample of fifty families in 1220, holding about ninety manors, showed thirty-one surviving to 1300. Nine failed through lack of male heirs; six at most sold out. Buckinghamshire has also been studied, with a sample of seventy-two families. Twenty-two died out in the male line in the course of the thirteenth century, while a further eleven

---

[13] P. R. Coss, 'Sir Geoffrey de Langley and the Crisis of the Knightly Class in Thirteenth Century England', *Past and Present*, 68 (1975), 33–4.

[14] *CIM* i, no. 1201.

[15] E. King, 'Large and Small Landowners in Thirteenth-Century England', *Past and Present*, 47 (1970), 26–50.

[16] J. E. Newman, 'Greater and Lesser Landowners and Parochial Patronage in Yorkshire in the Thirteenth Century', *EHR* 92 (1977), 280–308.

[17] R. Graham, *English Ecclesiastical Studies* (London, 1929), 256.

vanished for unknown reasons. Half of the knightly families, therefore, failed to survive. Only sixteen of those which did survive continued to be of knightly standing.[18] Calculations have also been produced for Warwickshire, based on sixty-two families, of which thirty-three survived into the fourteenth century. Between seven and thirteen sold out, while sixteen failed in the male line. The patterns are similar, and suggest that the chances of survival for these families were rather better than those of their social superiors. What did happen is that some of the families that had produced knights in the early thirteenth century ceased to do so by 1300, even though their economic position did not decline.[19] Knighthood was becoming more exclusive as fewer people took it up.

Why was it that some families that had in the past been of knightly standing were finding it increasingly difficult or burdensome to maintain that status? One suggestion is that the growing cost of military equipment was the problem. Armour was becoming more complex, and horses more expensive.[20] The evidence does not provide strong support for this hypothesis; armour and other military equipment fell in price in the thirteenth century, while the switch from chain mail to plate took place in the early fourteenth century.[21] It would be wrong to read too much into the cost of the most expensive horses. There is, however, evidence of a sharp rise in knightly wages in the second decade of the thirteenth century, with an increase from 1s. to 2s. a day.[22] That probably reflects the greater costs of knighthood at a period when it is likely that the numbers of knights were declining most sharply. An agreement made in 1272 between Roger Darcy and Ingram of Oldcotes for the knighting of the latter reveals what might be expected for a knight in the second half of the thirteenth century. Roger agreed to provide Ingram with all necessities of clothing, specifically two robes, two capes or their equivalent, and one tabard every year. Roger would also supply three horses, with all their harness and saddles, and would maintain a squire and two servants for Ingram. This was a considerable burden, and it is not surprising that the deal failed.[23] Later, in

---

[18] A. Polden, 'A Crisis of the Knightly Class? Inheritance and Office Among the Gentry of Thirteenth-Century Buckinghamshire', in P. Fleming, A. Gross, and J. R. Lander (eds.), *Regionalism and Revision: The Crown and its Provinces in England 1250–1650* (London, 1998), 30, 36–7, 52.

[19] D. A. Carpenter, 'Was there a Crisis of the Knightly Class in the Thirteenth Century? The Oxfordshire Evidence', in his *Reign of Henry III*, 348–80; P. R. Coss, *Lordship, Knighthood and Locality: A Study in English Society, c.1180–c.1280* (Cambridge, 1991), 294–304.

[20] Denholm-Young, 'Feudal Society in the Thirteenth Century', 63.

[21] This has been studied in detail by R. Storey, 'Technology and Military Policy in Medieval England, c.1250–1359' (Ph.D. thesis, Reading University, 2003).

[22] Faulkner, 'The Transformation of Knighthood', 20.

[23] P. Brand, 'Oldcotes v. Darcy', in R. F. Hunnisett and J. B. Post (eds.), *Medieval Legal Records* (London, 1978), 71, 104. In return for being knighted and maintained as a knight, Ingram agreed to hand over all his lands to Roger.

Edward II's reign, the grant of £100 by the king to John of Norwich to help him maintain his recently acquired knightly status gives some impression of the costs of knighthood.[24]

There is evidence to show that the cost of the knighting ceremony was a disincentive. John de Carun in 1243 had to borrow from a Jewish moneylender in order to cover the costs of his being knighted and of serving in Gascony. Knighting of his eldest son was, however, one of the occasions when a lord was entitled to ask for an aid from his tenants, so the whole burden of paying for a feast and ceremonial clothing was not borne by the new knight's family. The fortunate were those who were given the clothes and equipment by the king; the fact that this was done is a further indication of the cost of the ceremony.[25] Another way of avoiding the cost was to be knighted on the eve of battle, but this practice looks to have been more common in the fourteenth century than the thirteenth.

It is very likely that, as knightly numbers declined, so the burden of being a knight in civil society increased. Grants of exemption suggest this, showing that men were anxious to avoid the work their status entailed. For example, on 30 August 1247 William de Albini and Geoffrey Aiguilon were freed from the obligation to attend courts, from the local to the county level, and were no longer to be required for assizes, juries, or recognitions.[26] Exemptions might also extend to serving the crown as sheriff, coroner, forester, or similar officer. Between 1233 and the end of his reign Henry III made over 1,200 grants exempting men from their obligations.[27] Grants on this scale caused real difficulties in local government, and in 1258 the reformers made provision for men to take part in grand assizes, investigations of boundaries, or some legal cases, irrespective of the terms of the exemptions they had received from the crown.[28] The shortage of knights was a significant problem for local administration. The potential duties laid upon local knights became more considerable as the thirteenth century proceeded. The range of activities increased with the developments of Edward I's reign, and the growing pressures of war and of systems of justice. Knights were not simply burdened with suit at the county court and service on juries, but were expected to undertake wider duties, such as hearing oyer and terminer inquiries, or acting as tax assessors or collectors, or as commissioners of array, recruiting infantry troops. They might attend

---

[24] BL, Add. MS 9951, fo. 21ᵛ.

[25] Coss, *Knight in Medieval England*, 66–7; S. L. Waugh, 'Reluctant Knights and Jurors: Respites, Exemptions, and Public Obligations in the Reign of Henry III', *Speculum*, 58 (1983), 958.

[26] *CPR 1232–47*, 509.

[27] Waugh, 'Reluctant Knights and Jurors', 966.

[28] *DBM* 142–3.

parliament as knights of the shire. It is hardly surprising that many men were reluctant to become knights, since to do so would mean that they had to embrace not just a code of chivalric behaviour, but also a set of obligations to accept public office and responsibility.

The structures and changes of this period were complex. Patterns of inheritance meant that estates divided and coalesced into new forms as they evolved in response to the vagaries of family history. New families emerged to take the place of those that failed. Many of the successful newcomers had an official background, and either profited from positions in government or benefited from royal patronage. Matthew Paris singled out Paul Pever for notice. According to the chronicler, Paul began life with no more than two carucates; by his death he had at least fifty, acquired by licit and illicit means. His manor at Toddington was like a palace, with fine chambers with roofs covered with lead, surrounded by orchards and parks. Paul was a knight of the king's household, and steward of the royal household from 1244 to his death in 1251; he also held the sheriffdoms of Oxfordshire and Buckinghamshire for a time. Such a man was well positioned to make his way in society.[29] Geoffrey de Langley was a thrusting royal official. The details of his acquisitions of land have been used to show how some knightly families declined in fortune in face of his aggressive acquisitiveness;[30] at the same time his story demonstrates how a new man could establish himself as a wealthy knight through efficient service to the crown. Royal service could also provide a route for an apparently failing family to reverse its fortunes. The Belmeis family of Shropshire provides one example. This was a significant knightly family in the twelfth century, but the elder branch died out and its lands went by marriage to the Zouche family. The younger branch did not prosper, and when Roger de Belmeis inherited the lands in 1256, he bought a respite from knighthood. Nor did his son Robert become a knight. The burdens of responsibility in the county cost money. Roger and Robert both served in the royal household, receiving rewards above all in the form of wardships. Robert's son Hugh was also in royal service, and by 1292 had become a knight. The family had regained the status that it had lost.[31]

The first half of the thirteenth century, therefore, saw a transformation of the knights. As their numbers fell, so the dignity of knighthood became more exclusive. There was a shift in what was expected of a knight, with more responsibility in local affairs. In addition there was, very possibly, an increased emphasis on their chivalric character. There is no indication that families that had once been of knightly status resented their apparent drop in standing; what

---

[29] Paris, *Chron. Maj.* v. 242; Polden, 'A Crisis of the Knightly Class?', 41.
[30] Coss, 'Sir Geoffrey de Langley and the Crisis of the Knightly Class in Thirteenth Century England', 3–37.
[31] Waugh, 'Reluctant Knights and Jurors', 979.

is much clearer is the reluctance on the part of many to accept an honour that brought with it expenses and hard work in the public interest. Of course those who saw their wealth declining were bitter; it is clear that Simon de Montfort and the other opponents of the crown in the 1260s were able to win support from knights and others who, like Roger le Peytevin, had fallen heavily into debt.

SUCCESSFUL KNIGHTS

From the third quarter of the thirteenth century the environment for knightly families was more favourable. The decline in the capacity of the Jews to lend money, followed by their expulsion from the realm in 1290, probably meant that it was not quite so easy as it had been to become heavily encumbered with debt. The Statute of Mortmain of 1279 made it much harder for the great ecclesiastical institutions to buy up knightly land. The burden of local administration was increasingly shared with others; as the legal system changed and evolved, so elements such as the grand assize, which demanded a jury made up solely of knights, diminished. Men who were knighted in war, usually on the eve of battle, did not face the costs of an expensive ceremony. Examples of declining knights are much less common than earlier; suspicions that historians have not looked for them so hard seem unjustified. The question has been looked at in detail for Gloucestershire. The evidence suggests that the knights and smaller landowners were quicker than the greater landlords to abandon the use of labour services, and were substantially reliant on wage labour for the farming of their demesnes. If this is so, then they were relatively well placed to deal with the economic difficulties of the early fourteenth century. There is no reason to suppose that this caused them problems before 1348; the higher wages that came with the fall in population due to the Black Death would, however, create difficulties for anyone dependent on hired labour.[32]

There were many routes to success. The Thorpes rose from villein status at the start of the thirteenth century through service to Peterborough abbey and the law. The family seem to have risen steadily in the thirteenth century to become substantial freeholders in the village of Longthorpe, where they built a manor house. Robert Thorpe became steward of the Peterborough estates in 1309. He marked his rise in status by adding a fine three-storeyed tower to the manor house. His son became a judge, and his grandson a wealthy and corrupt chief justice. The family were slow to acquire knightly status; the chief justice was the first to do so.[33] The Scrope family provides another example of those

---

[32] Saul, *Knights and Esquires*, 205–35.
[33] King, 'Large and Small Landowners', 44–5; Maddicott, *Law and Lordship*, 49–51.

who rose to knightly status through success in the law. The law has always been profitable for its practitioners, if not for those who have recourse to it. John Stonor was the son of a reasonably well-to-do Oxfordshire man, of gentry but not knightly status. His three younger brothers all looked to the Church for their advancement; as a layman, John turned to the legal profession. He was a very able lawyer who became a serjeant in 1311 and a king's serjeant four year later. He became a justice of Common Pleas in 1320, becoming chief justice in 1329 as well as chief baron of the exchequer. The crisis of 1340–1 saw him dismissed from office, but he was rapidly restored to favour in 1342. He died in 1354. His main source of income was undoubtedly the fees and retainers he received from his clients. The abbot of Westminster, for example, put him on his payroll in 1319. Later in his career he was a member of the Black Prince's council. He did not accept all offers; in 1335 the priory of Christ Church Canterbury offered him the position of steward, 'for as you well know it is advisable to have some great man to maintain our right', but Stonor was in sufficient demand for him to be able to turn this position down. An ordinance of 1346, which prohibited justices from taking fees or robes, probably had little effect on his income; an increase of £40 in what he was paid by the crown was insufficient to change long-established habits.

Stonor invested his profits in land, particularly during the early part of his career. In 1317 he acquired Didcot in Oxfordshire, paying off the seller's debts of £740. In all, he bought eleven manors and fifteen other estates, as well as property in London and Westminster. The total value is impossible to calculate accurately, but his landed income was probably between £200 and £300 a year. In all, his income was probably over £600 a year. His purchases look to have been very shrewd, and his management of his estates expert. He was well aware that sheep were highly profitable, and all of his lands were in regions where pasture was good and wool of high quality. Interestingly, he believed in the virtues of direct management of his estates, and did not rely on renting out manors for his income. His case is particularly interesting since he did not acquire wealth, as so many did, through marriage. Rather, he built up his estate through his own ability as a lawyer and as a manager. He needed to do so if he was to provide properly for his family of six sons and five daughters.[34]

Edward III was skilled in the art of patronage, and many knights whose fame was due to their personal prowess owed their fortunes to the king. Those who were associated with the king's successful coup of 1330 against Roger Mortimer benefited very significantly. Edward was in a fortunate position since

---

[34] P. J. Jefferies, 'Profitable Fourteenth-Century Legal Practice and Landed Investment: The Case of Judge Stonor, c.1281 to 1354', *Southern History*, 15 (1993), 18–35; Maddicott, *Law and Lordship*, 37–8.

events after 1326 had brought a windfall of lands to the crown. The Despenser estates alone provided a great boost to royal patronage, and the estates accumulated by Isabella and Mortimer were a further major source of land to be distributed. Four leading household knights benefited greatly from Edward's patronage even before their creation as earls in 1337, namely Montague, Clinton, Ufford, and Bohun. At a slightly lower level, Thomas Bradeston also did very well in the 1330s. John Neville of Hornby was present at Mortimer's capture in Nottingham castle, and was granted three manors that had belonged to John Maltravers and one Despenser manor.[35] John de Coupland had the good fortune to capture David, king of Scots, at Neville's Cross in 1346. His reward was to be created a knight banneret, and to receive a grant of £500 a year for life, initially charged to the customs at London and Newcastle. He also received an additional £100 to serve the king with twenty men-at-arms. Very curiously, however, Coupland does not appear to have actually taken up knighthood. After receiving this grant, he was referred to as a king's yeoman, and he later paid a fine for respite of knighthood.[36] This is puzzling; there is nothing in his career to suggest that Coupland was a modest man, and inverted snobbery was not likely in the fourteenth century.

Edward III's patronage might on occasion be adequate, rather than generous. It was not possible to maintain the reward system on the scale of the 1330s, as sufficient resources were simply not there. John Ward, captain of the king's household archers in the 1330s, was promoted to knighthood in about 1343. He served with a small following at Crécy. In 1347 he was granted 2s. a day to maintain himself as a knight; his landed resources were inadequate for the purpose. He never became a significant member of the county community; his small estate at Sproston in Cheshire was not enough to provide him with the necessary wealth or standing.[37]

Royal patronage has received much attention from historians, partly because of the wealth of sources available. Other forms of patronage were also important. It is less easy to trace the way in which families rose in magnate service, but analysis of Thomas of Lancaster's retinue has shown how extensive the earl's patronage was. Men such as William Latimer and Nicholas de Segrave prospered in the earl's service. Some of those who served him went on, after the debacle of 1322, to do the same for his brother and successor, Henry of Lancaster. The indenture between Roger Bigod and John de Segrave shows that Segrave acquired the manor of Lodden in return for his service, and in a

[35] CPR 1330–4, 82, 166.
[36] CPR 1345–8, 226, 425, 561; CPR 1358–61, 121.
[37] M. C. Prestwich, 'Miles in Armis Strenuus: The Knight at War', TRHS, 6th ser., 5 (1995), 219.

multiplicity of other cases grants of lands, rents, or wardships accompanied the issue of fees and robes that were the overt signs of the relationship between lord and retainer.

Of course, there were failures that need to be set against the success stories. The Gascelyns of Sheldon in Wiltshire provide a remarkable case study of a family in decline in the fourteenth century. In the thirteenth century the Gascelyns had been successful. Geoffrey, who died in 1282, had served Henry III as a household knight. His son Edmund was retained by Roger Bigod, earl of Norfolk; his son in turn, also Edmund, was one of the earl of Pembroke's retinue. The family income was substantial, at about £200 a year. Geoffrey Gascelyn, who succeeded Edmund in 1337, was a complete contrast to his ancestors. He did not become a knight, and appears to have campaigned only once. He added nothing to the manor house at Sheldon. In 1351 he agreed to hand over most of his lands for seven years to Thomas de Berkeley in return for maintenance as a squire in Thomas's household and an annual rent. In 1358 a new bargain was struck. Geoffrey could stay in the household for a further five years or take an annuity of 10 marks. He was to have an acre of meadow and an acre in the spring field at Sheldon that could be sown with oats. The story, however, is one of an ineffectual individual, and not of a failing class.[38]

Richard Damory provides another example of the difficulties that knights might face, but his career also shows that it was possible to recover, at least partially, from apparent disaster. Richard's father had been steward of the king's household in the later years of Edward II's reign. His inheritance was substantial, with lands in Oxfordshire and Devon, but they may have suffered during his seven-year minority. Richard fought in Scotland, and in France on the Crécy campaign. Where campaigning brought some men wealth, in Richard's case it seems to have brought debt. He began to dispose of rights and lands in Devon in the mid-1340s, and in 1350 reached an arrangement with Otto de Holland, which involved his acknowledgment that he owed Otto £2,000, while Otto in return stated that he owed Damory £1,000. In the next year he sold more of his property. In 1352 disaster struck. He was briefly imprisoned in the Fleet for debts of £2,000 owed to the king. He claimed he had evidence that he had paid these off, but could not produce it. As a result, he agreed to grant all his lands to the king; Edward III then instructed him to give them all to John Chandos. In 1356 a quarrel he had with the university of Oxford over jurisdiction in the hundred outside the Northgate was settled in the university's favour. By 1360, however, Damory's affairs were in much better shape. It was agreed that he had fulfilled the terms of the agreements he

[38] N. Saul, 'A "Rising" Lord and a "Declining" Esquire: Sir Thomas de Berkeley III and Geoffrey Gascelyn of Sheldon', *Historical Research*, 61 (1988), 345–56.

had made, and the recognizance of £2,000 to the king was duly cancelled. Chandos regranted his properties back to Damory.[39]

MAINTAINING NUMBERS

The crown was concerned about knightly numbers. A lack of knights threatened not only the country's military capacity, but also the provision of good government in the localities. Henry III's government took to ordering 'distraint of knighthood', that is, ordering men who possessed an appropriate amount of land to become knights. The use of this technique is a clear indication that there were worries about the number of knights in the country; the decline was clearly evident at the time. In 1224 all who possessed at least one knight's fee had to be knighted if they had not already undergone the ceremony. The purpose of the measure was clear. An expedition to Gascony was planned, and this was a way of strengthening the army. Further distraints coincided with subsequent campaigns. In 1241 an important innovation was that those who had at least £20 of land were asked to become knights. This set the qualification in terms of wealth, not tenure. The process of discovering who fell within the net was not always easy. Men might hold land in several counties. Valuations could be inaccurate. Officials were often open to bribes. There might be political hostility to distraint; this was almost certainly the case in the mid-1250s. These orders, though their prime purpose was military, also offered a way to bring in money. In 1252, and on subsequent occasions, the government offered to take fines, at the rate of half a mark of gold, from those who did not want to be knighted. In 1256, when the level was lowered to £15 of land, at least 370 respites from knighthood were bought from the king. There must have been many who neither paid fines nor became knights. In Northamptonshire in 1279 only fifteen out of eighty-one men of appropriate wealth became knights as instructed.[40]

Distraint of knighthood continued to be used by the crown. In 1278 Edward I set out the rules for exemption from knighthood in the Statute De Militibus, making it clear, for example, that those under 21 did not have to be knighted. Men who held by socage on royal demesne manors, and those who held by burgage tenure, were exempt. The document demonstrates that the purpose of distraint was still seen primarily in terms of increasing the number of knights

[39] CCR 1349–54, 209, 483; CCR 1354–60, 56; CPR 1343–6, 205, 266; CPR 1345–8, 495; CPR 1350–4, 100, 181; CPR 1354–8, 372, 424–5, 447.
[40] S. L. Waugh, 'Reluctant Knights and Jurors', 941–55. This article revises some of the conclusions reached by Powicke, Military Obligation in Medieval England, 63–81. See also F. M. Nichols, 'On Feudal and Obligatory Knighthood', Archaeologia, 39 (1863), 202–15.

available for campaigning.[41] Edward relaxed the wealth requirement to £100 in 1285, as an expression of gratitude for the service he had received in his Welsh war, but in 1292 the level was lowered to £40, which became the normal benchmark. Further distraints were issued on five occasions under Edward II and seven times by Edward III. Increasingly, the motive looks to have been as much financial as military. Returns suggest that by Edward III's reign there were no longer many men with £40 worth of land who had not taken up knighthood. In 1333 the sheriffs reported the names of about 150 men, and in 1366 those of 170 men.[42]

There were other ways in which the king could encourage men to become knights. Mass knightings took place on various occasions. In 1241 Peter of Savoy and fifteen others were knighted in a single ceremony. Twenty new knights were created when Henry's daughter married Alexander II of Scotland in 1251. Ten years later eighty were knighted together with John of Brittany and two of Simon de Montfort's sons. The grandest by far of these ceremonies came in 1306 when Edward I's son was knighted along with some 250 young men.[43] The accounts for Edward III's army reveal that many squires were knighted in Flanders on 23 October 1339; this was the day of the abortive battle at Buironfosse.[44]

ESQUIRES

Many smaller landholders were not knights. They included many who might be described as aspirant knights, as well as minor manorial lords. To call them members of the gentry is to apply a construct from a later age, but one that is in many ways appropriate.[45] The use of the word *gentiz* implied that men were of gentle, rather than common, birth. It was used in the 1240s in the household instructions drawn up for the countess of Lincoln, which referred to 'your knights and your gentlemen', in French 'gentis hommes'.[46] An indenture drawn up in 1328 between Henry Percy and Ralph Neville made a distinction between the *gentiz gentz*, a term comprising the knights and men-at-arms whom Neville was to provide, and his servants.[47] Use of the term 'esquire' to describe men of a particular social group was part of this process of social

---

[41] *SR* i. 229.
[42] Powicke, *Military Obligation in Medieval England*, 109–10, 170, 173–4.
[43] N. Denholm-Young, *History and Heraldry 1254 to 1310* (Oxford, 1965), 25, 49.
[44] *The Wardrobe Book of William de Norwell*, ed. Lyon *et al.*, 343–6.
[45] For discussion of the gentry, and its definition, P. R. Coss, *The Origins of the English Gentry* (Cambridge, 2003), *passim*.
[46] *Walter of Henley and Other Treatises*, ed. Oschinsky, 402–3.
[47] 'Private Indentures for Life Service in Peace and War 1278–1476', ed. Jones and Walker, 68.

delineation, and dates very roughly from the mid-fourteenth century. The sumptuary legislation of 1363 spoke of esquires and *gentils gents*, and divided them into groups with incomes up to £100, and up to £200.[48] Contemporary Latin terminology used the terms 'esquire' (*scutifer*), 'man-at-arms' (*armiger* and *homo ad arma*), and 'valet' (*valettus*). Other terms, such as 'bachelor', and in a military context 'serjeant', might also be used. There was no great clarity in the use of these words.[49] In early fourteenth-century indentures between magnates and their men, the latter were often termed valets, yet in royal household accounts they were normally called esquires. The terms could be synonymous.[50] In 1338 Robert de Benhale, knight, had a retinue of six with him in Flanders. In the same entry they are first described as men-at-arms, and then as squires. There are even entries that talk of squire-men-at-arms (*scutiferi homines ad arma*).[51] It was of course possible for men to be promoted from this group to knightly status. When Ralph Basset of Drayton retained Philip Chetwynd as an esquire in 1319 for a year's service, the terms of the indenture were to be renegotiated should Chetwynd become a knight, although in fact he did not do so.[52]

Tax returns provide one way of identifying this gentry group; it is very common to find one individual in a village assessed at a level ten or twenty times the average.[53] However, there is regrettably insufficient evidence to make possible any realistic estimate of the number of men who might be classified as gentry in the thirteenth and fourteenth centuries. The sheriff's returns of 1324 provide lists of men-at-arms as well as of knights, but these are very unsatisfactory. The lists are incomplete, and the sheriffs did not use identical criteria. Evidence from the composition of armies would suggest that there was roughly a ratio of 1:3 between knights and esquires or men-at-arms. It is likely that a higher proportion of knights than esquires went on campaign, and a reasonable estimate might be that there were four or five times as many esquires and other members of the gentry than knights.

---

[48] Saul, *Knights and Esquires*, 11–29.

[49] See P. R. Coss, 'Knights, Esquires and the Origins of Social Gradation in England', *TRHS*, 6th ser., 5 (1995), 156–68, for a full discussion.

[50] In 1300 Walter Beauchamp junior had three esquires with him, but sent two valets to see to his accounts: *Liber Quotidianus*, 204.

[51] *Wardrobe Book of William de Norwell*, ed. Lyon *et al.*, 334, 341. For a particularly confusing entry, see Norwell's own account, ibid. 335, in which the *scutiferi* are paid less than the *homines ad arma*, though six of the latter are also termed *scutiferi*. An indenture between the younger Despenser and Hugh Neville equated valet and esquire: 'Private Indentures for Life Service in Peace and War', ed. Jones and Walker, 62.

[52] 'Private Indentures for Life Service in Peace and War', ed. Jones and Walker, 63.

[53] See e.g. *Hertfordshire Lay Subsidy Rolls 1307 and 1334*, ed. J. Booker and S. Flood (Hertfordshire Record Society, 1988).

There was no very clear economic distinction between esquires and the knights. In military terms the position was straightforward, for knights were paid at double the rate that applied to esquires and men-at-arms. In the shires, however, differences in what tasks and duties were expected diminished as it became more difficult to find knights to serve on juries and as officials. John de la Lee, appointed sheriff of Essex and Hertfordshire in 1299, was not a knight.[54] Walter de Meriet was given exemption in 1318, at the request of Thomas of Lancaster, from serving on assizes, juries, or recognitions, and from the offices of sheriff, coroner, forester, regarder, or other function as a royal official. Although Meriet was from a knightly family, he does not appear to have himself been knighted.[55] Those elected to parliament by the shires were normally knights in the thirteenth century, but might well not be in the fourteenth. In 1334, for example, Richard de la Hale, who was a bailiff and constable of the peace, was elected as a knight of the shire for Gloucestershire, and in 1338 William de Cheltenham, Maurice de Berkeley's steward, was member for the same county.[56] In 1340 this was considered to be a problem on such a scale that a special instruction was issued to try to ensure that the representatives were to be proper belted knights. In practice, by this period, coroners, escheators, tax-collectors, commissioners of the peace, and other royal officials were simply drawn from the county elite, irrespective of whether they had actually been knighted or not. It may well be that the many campaigns of the 1330s and 1340s, first in Scotland and then in France, so reduced the pool of knights available for official duty in the shires that there was no alternative to using other men.

COMMUNITY

Some historians have laid considerable stress on the county community as an important focus for the knights and gentry.[57] The county is seen as providing unifying horizontal links in society, in contrast to the vertical connections offered by government and lordship. The medieval term *communitas* was used for the body of county society, and its translation as 'community' carries dangers of anachronistic overtones of identity and unity. Viewed from a

---

[54] *Liber Quotidianus*, 76, does not refer to him as *dominus*.   [55] *CPR 1317–21*, 398.

[56] Saul, *Knights and Esquires*, 147, 153.

[57] For a general discussion, though one focusing on a slightly later period, see C. Carpenter, 'Gentry and Community in Medieval England', *Journal of British Studies*, 33 (1994), 340–8. Stress on the county community was laid by J. R. Maddicott, 'The County Community and the Making of Public Opinion in Fourteenth-Century England', *TRHS*, 5th ser., 28 (1978), 27–43; id., 'Magna Carta and the Local Community 1215–1259', *Past and Present*, 102 (1984), 25–65. See also Coss, *Origins of the English Gentry*, 209–15.

governmental perspective, the county was of immeasurable importance. The sheriff was the king's representative at a local level. Taxation was carried out on a county basis. So too was the recruitment of troops and the purveyance of supplies. In the field of justice, too, the county was an essential building block, though by the fourteenth century the county courts were declining in importance.[58] Statutes were distributed to the counties, and it was in the county courts that major royal documents were publicized. In 1258, for example, Henry III's October proclamation accepting the programme of reform, and the Ordinance of Sheriffs, were read out in the county courts.[59] Counties were represented in parliament, and petitions brought forward from the communities of the counties. There were men who formed a local elite and regularly undertook offices, both administrative and judicial, at county level. It was from their numbers that the parliamentary representatives were normally selected, and it was they who provided the impetus for the use of knights as keepers of the peace.

Counties were not simply tools of central government. They were capable of resisting the demands made by sheriffs. In 1269, for example, the community of Northumberland complained that they had been made to attend court sessions contrary to their understanding of Magna Carta, and in 1297 the community of Worcestershire challenged royal tax-collectors, stating that the money would not be granted until they had the liberties to which the Charter entitled them. The number of such instances, however, is not large. Petitions in parliament from county communities tended to concentrate on issues of official malpractice, rather than on broader political issues. When Edward I chose to negotiate a levy of foodstuffs for the army with the county communities in 1301, in every case there was agreement to provide what was requested. These communities were not powerhouses of political protest.[60]

The structures of lordship and of landownership do not map neatly onto county boundaries, and this must have weakened the sense of identity provided by county communities and courts. Marriage might lead men to have connections across counties. Thus William Latimer, household knight of Edward I and lord of Scampston in Yorkshire, became lord of Corby in Northamptonshire through his wife.

The returns made by the sheriffs to the inquiries into knightly numbers in 1322 and 1324 reveal that many knights held land in more than one county.

[58] R. C. Palmer, *The County Courts of Medieval England, 1150–1350* (Princeton, 1982), 297–306.

[59] *DBM* 116–22.

[60] J. R. Maddicott, 'Magna Carta and the Local Community 1215–1259', *Past and Present*, 102 (1984), 42; M. C. Prestwich, *English Politics in the Thirteenth Century* (Basingstoke, 1990), 56–9. See, for further arguments, P. Coss, 'Knighthood and the Early Thirteenth-Century County Court', in *TCE* iii. 45–7.

Those for Bedfordshire and Buckinghamshire also display startling differences between one list and the next, suggesting that there was little clarity in the minds of the sheriff and his officials about who the leading members of the county communities were.[61] The way in which men might sit as representatives in parliament for different counties also suggests that there was often no very strong sense of county identity. In the early fourteenth century, for example, Gerard of Braybrook was elected for Buckinghamshire, Bedfordshire, and Hertfordshire.[62]

Ties of lordship might take different forms, but were also very significant. The continuing sense of identity among the tenants of a great feudal honour, such as the lordship of Richmond, should not be underestimated. On the Ferrers honour in the mid-thirteenth century, two great courts were held a year, and a predominance of tenants among those who witnessed Robert Ferrers's charters in the early 1260s further suggests that there was a genuine honorial community.[63] The links represented by grants of fees and robes, discussed in the previous chapter, were also important, even though significant numbers of knights were not brought within the scope of aristocratic affinities in this way.

Locality might be important at a lower level than the county. There is no way in which a full reconstruction of the complex networks of friendship and association can be made, though an interesting examination of the deeds of Philip Chetwynd, one of the Staffordshire gentry at the start of the fourteenth century, is highly suggestive in the emphasis placed on locality and kinship. Lordship does not emerge strongly from these deeds, though Philip's son is the Philip Chetwynd who became a retainer of Ralph Basset of Drayton in 1319.[64] Henry de Bray, a minor Northamptonshire landlord, kept a remarkable memorandum book in the early fourteenth century. It shows a keen interest not only in his own genealogy, but also in those of his neighbours. The book begins with a brief description of the continents of the world and their provinces, and lists of the counties and bishoprics of England, together with the kings of England. Henry's real connections and interests, however, were confined to his own corner of Northamptonshire, to his relations, his neighbours, and his tenants.[65]

---

[61] See above, 391–2.

[62] J. G. Edwards, 'The Personnel of the Commons in Parliament Under Edward I and Edward II', in E. B. Fryde and E. Miller (eds.), *Historical Studies of the English Parliament*, i (Cambridge, 1970), 158.

[63] Carpenter, 'The Second Century of English Feudalism', *Past and Present*, 168 (2000), 52–3.

[64] Carpenter, 'Gentry and Community', 369–72; 'Private Indentures for Life Service in Peace and War', ed. Jones and Walker, 63.

[65] *The Estate Book of Henry de Bray*, ed. D. Willis, Camden 3rd ser., 27 (1916), 3–5, 28–30, 62–3, 125.

SYMBOLS OF KNIGHTHOOD

How did knights and members of the gentry identify themselves as members of a social elite? Names and heraldic insignia were as important to knights as they were to the earls. In the 1250s Agnes, the daughter of Geoffrey de Neville of Raby, widow of Richard de Percy and wife of John Deincourt, had a seal that showed her in a dress embroidered with the Deincourt arms. She is shown holding up two shields, one with the Percy arms and one with the Neville. The pride in these family symbols is very clear. It was made clearer still by her son Edmund Deincourt. He was very concerned that after his death his surname and arms would be lost from memory as his immediate heir was his daughter Isabella. In 1314 he made a land settlement to ensure that the succession would go to his grandson William. The name and arms were duly perpetuated.[66] The history of the Burnell family demonstrates the importance of name. They were of insignificant origins in Shropshire, but Edward I's chancellor Robert Burnell had a keen sense of family. This was in part exhibited through the fathering of sons who were inevitably, given his clerical status, illegitimate. As so often happened, the family, whose main seat was Acton Burnell in Shropshire, died out in the direct male line. In 1348 Nicholas Haudlo, whose mother was sister and heir to Edward Burnell, succeeded to the estate, and promptly took the name Burnell for himself.[67]

Increasingly during this period the coat of arms was a crucial symbol. It would be displayed on the shield, on the small shield-shaped *aillettes* worn on the shoulder, on the trapper born by a warhorse, and might be embroidered onto clothes. Much of the evidence for the use of heraldry comes from the rolls of arms, which give long lists of knights with their coat armour. The earliest such heraldic roll survives from the mid-thirteenth century; Glover's Roll lists 211 coats of arms, the majority of which belonged to the royal family and the baronage. St George's Roll, named after a sixteenth-century owner, dates from the 1280s. It is very much longer, containing 677 blazons. Some are historical; it includes the earls of Salisbury, Kent, and Winchester, but the great majority of those listed were barons and knights. There is a bias towards the Welsh march: the roll was almost certainly drawn up by a herald employed by the Mortimer family.[68] There are about 2,100 people mentioned in the various rolls of arms produced in Edward I's reign. That number includes some foreigners and a few mythical figures, but it demonstrates that by this time effectively all the knightly families in England possessed arms. The so-called Parliamentary

---

[66] *Complete Peerage*, iv. 118; *CPR 1313–17*, 89, 651–2.   [67] *Complete Peerage*, ii. 434.

[68] Denholm-Young, *History and Heraldry*, 41–5, 90–3; C. S. Percival, 'Two Rolls of Arms of the Reign of King Edward the First', *Archaeologia*, 39 (1863), 418–40.

Roll of Arms, drawn up in about 1310, gives details of 1,110 blazons.[69] Coats of arms could tell intriguing stories. Alianore Lovaine's seal depicted a shield with the arms of her own family and those of her first husband, William Ferrers of Groby. About the shield were three eagles, a reference to the arms of her final husband, William Bagot. What she did not include was any reference to the arms of William Douglas, who abducted her in 1289 and who was allowed to marry her in return for a fine of £100.[70]

Those below the rank of knight did not feature on the rolls of arms of this period, but this does not mean that they did not possess, and use, their own arms. In 1292 the Statute of Arms declared that esquires could only use the arms of their knightly lord; this suggests that some esquires had started to use their own insignia. It became increasingly common to use heraldic emblems, rather than other symbols, on seals, and by the 1320s some esquires had seals with their own personal coat of arms.[71] If they were using their arms on seals, then they were probably also using them on their shields and clothing, and must have been increasingly hard to distinguish from the knights.

Knightly and gentry dwellings may not have left their mark on the landscape as obviously as the castles of the great nobles, but they served in their own way to impress. William of Caverswall, sheriff of Staffordshire, built a small rectangular courtyard castle at Caverswall in about 1275. He was so proud of it that his memorial brass recorded that he had built a castle with houses, moats, and masonry.[72] William Cantilupe's Bedfordshire house at Eaton Bray does not survive, but was fully described in 1273. It lay within an enclosure wall and had a moat with two drawbridges. There was a hall, with two chambers at the ends; that which lay beyond the pantry and buttery had a tiled roof. There was a great chamber, a foreign chamber, a chapel, a granary, and a garderobe. Outside the enclosure there were tiled stables for sixty horses, a grange, cowsheds, pigsties, and other agricultural buildings. There were two gardens and an associated park of 20 acres of woodland.[73] Stokesay castle in Shropshire was built by the great wool merchant Laurence of Ludlow as he attempted to establish his credentials as a member of the gentry. It is a fine example of a manorial complex, with the hall extended by building a remarkable tower, surely intended more as a status symbol than as a defensive

---

[69] G. J. Brault, *Rolls of Arms, Edward I (1272–1307)* (Woodbridge, 1997), i. 40; *Parl. Writs*, i. 410–20.

[70] *Complete Peerage*, v. 338–9.

[71] Coss, 'Knights, Esquires and the Origins of Social Gradation in England', 175; P. D. A. Harvey and A. McGuinness, *A Guide to British Medieval Seals* (London, 1996), 56–7.

[72] C. Coulson, 'Some Analysis of the Castle of Bodiam, East Sussex', in C. Harper-Bill and R. Harvey (eds.), *The Ideals and Practice of Medieval Knighthood*, iv (Woodbridge, 1992), 84.

[73] *VCH Bedfordshire*, iii. 370.

structure. Aydon castle in Northumberland is an exceptionally well-preserved example of a manor house, which was fortified and extended in the fourteenth century. It demonstrates the basic elements of a hall, with solar block, kitchens and offices, and a courtyard. Aydon was built by Robert de Reymes, whose father bought the property in the mid-1290s. His was a merchant family that held land near Ipswich, and Aydon was clearly built in order to enhance its prestige.[74] Markenfield Hall in Yorkshire (built by a royal official, rather than a knight) provides another example of an early fourteenth-century fortified manor, complete with moat (see plate 14). William Kerdiston, a successful soldier under Edward III, built a moated brick courtyard castle at Claxton in Lincolnshire, obtaining a licence for it in 1340. A road was diverted, and a chapel founded in association with the castle. There was a deer-park and a warren, while commercial development was encouraged by Kerdiston's acquisition of grants of a weekly market and an annual fair.[75] The complex, which was not particularly large, transformed the locality and emphasized the status Kerdiston had achieved. Robert Thorpe's tower at Longthorpe is not impressive from the outside. Within, however, it has the finest set of secular wall-paintings to survive from the medieval period, and it gives an impression of the way in which many knightly homes must have been decorated. Every possible surface was painted, with a wide variety of subjects. Heraldic emblems were important, and carefully drawn birds provide a strong naturalistic touch. Less realistic is the mythical bonnacon, a beast that defended itself by defecating over its enemies. This is appropriately placed over the chamber doorway as a humorous deterrent to unwanted guests.[76]

The moated site was typical of a knightly dwelling, particularly in eastern England and the west midlands. It is estimated that about 70 per cent of the sites that have been identified date from between 1200 and 1325, though it is often very hard to fix them to an accurate timescale. The number is far greater than the number of knightly families, for there were more than 5,000. They are particularly common in areas where forest clearance was taking place.[77] Most were roughly rectangular, and mark the site of manorial buildings. They are usually on the edge of village settlements, though some are found in parks. They were not, of course, the sole preserve of the knights, but do represent the remains of a common form of knightly residence. Why moats were so popular can only be guessed at. It may be that they provided a limited form of defence

[74] P. Dixon, *Aydon Castle* (London, 1988), 7–8.
[75] R. Liddiard, *'Landscapes of Lordship': Norman Castles and the Countryside in Medieval Norfolk, 1066–1200*, British Archaeological Reports, British Series, 309 (2000), 115–17.
[76] A. Emery, *Greater Medieval Houses of England and Wales*, ii (Cambridge, 2000), 272–4.
[77] Cantor (ed.), *The English Medieval Landscape*, 137–43.

against local marauders and criminals, and even straying animals. The fish in the moat were no doubt an attractive addition to a tedious diet. Above all, however, the moat marked out the site clearly from the rest of the village, and was a clear declaration of superiority. The evidence of the building activity undertaken by the knights and gentry helps to demonstrate that they were a thriving, prosperous group.

Wealthy knights lived lives of some luxury. An inventory survives of some of the possessions of Osbert de Spaldington, who served briefly as a royal household knight in the 1290s, but was disgraced early in 1298. He possessed splendid sets of robes, one striped, one in a rich blue cloth, and a white one for summer use. His bed had a magnificent coverlet, with fur lined with blue-green cloth. There was in addition a linen canopy to go over the bed. He possessed quantities of fine bedlinen and tablecloths, and a *banquer*, a comfortable cushion to sit on. His table was graced with four silver goblets, eighteen plates, seventeen saucers, two silver candlesticks, and other items, including a splendid knife with an ivory handle.[78]

The cultural world that knights occupied was little different from that of the aristocratic superiors. Knights were certainly not boneheaded. Illiteracy was rare among their number. A Norfolk inquiry in 1297 into the date of Robert de Tony's birth twenty-one years previously shows that, of the thirteen jurors questioned, ten said that they had read the entry in a local chronicle where it was noted down. A lawsuit of about 1300 in which a knight turned out to be unable to read was exceptional.[79] The copy of the romance *Perlesvaus*, owned by Brian FitzAlan, survives. An inventory of some of James Audley of Heighley's possessions showed that he owned a book of romances, while his wife possessed three.[80] Knights did not, as a rule, have the time to write books themselves, but Thomas Gray was given the opportunity to start writing his substantial chronicle, the *Scalacronica*, when a prisoner of war in Edinburgh in the 1360s. The Luttrell Psalter, with which this chapter began, bears witness to the value that a knightly family might place on a book that was also a splendid work of art.

How pious knights and gentry were is difficult to say. For Thomas Gray, to judge by his *Scalacronica*, religion was of no more than conventional concern, but for Geoffrey Luttrell it was of fundamental importance. For at least the wealthier knights and gentry there was a tendency for religion to become an increasingly individual matter. Private confessors, usually friars, became more common; Geoffrey Luttrell had both a confessor and a chaplain. Manor houses

[78] F. Lachaud, 'An Aristocratic Wardrobe of the Late Thirteenth Century: The Confiscation of the Goods of Osbert de Spaldington in 1298', *Historical Research*, 67 (1994), 91–100.
[79] M. T. Clanchy, *From Memory to Written Record: England 1066–1307* (1979), 175–6, 222–3.
[80] Denholm-Young, *History and Heraldry*, 23; *CIM* iii, no. 109.

might feature private chapels, such as that which survives at Markenfield Hall in Yorkshire. In 1235 Geoffrey Esturmy agreed with the rector of Burbage in Wiltshire that he could have his own chapel, provided that he attended the village church on the five main feast days.[81] Books such as the Luttrell Psalter and the Holkham Picture Bible Book provide further evidence of private devotion.

Knightly interests might be reflected in popular cults. It is striking that one of the first miracles attributed to Thomas Cantilupe, bishop of Hereford, after his death was the cure of Miles Pichard, a Herefordshire knight, from injuries he had suffered in a tournament. A Cornish knight had cause to be grateful to the same saint, for he achieved the recovery of a prized falcon, which the knight's horse had trodden on.[82]

Crusading was, at least for some, an expression of piety. The numbers of those involved in crusading cannot be calculated with any precision. In 1240, however, separate expeditions set out, one under the command of Richard of Cornwall and William Longspée, another under Simon de Montfort, and a third under William de Forz, earl of Aumale. Almost twenty English bannerets went with these commanders, and there must have been a substantial number of knights. About 200 knights were reported as going with Longspée on a subsequent crusade in 1249. Crusaders took the cross for a variety of reasons, but Gerard de Fancourt's motives were surely genuinely religious. He went to Santiago de Compostela on pilgrimage in 1261, and in 1270 was a crusader alongside Prince Edward. His widow was taken into the fraternity by the prior of Belvoir.[83]

The ceremonies and memorials associated with death were, naturally, as important and as symbolic for knightly families as for those of great magnates. In his will Geoffrey Luttrell provided £20 for poor men to pray for him on the anniversary of his death, as well as 100 marks a year for five years to go to twenty chaplains who were to sing masses for him in the church at Irnham in Norfolk. The anniversary of the death of Eustacia, Gerard de Fancourt's widow, was celebrated with a solemn sung mass. Forty paupers were each given a loaf and two herrings.[84] Men would make grants of lands so that prayers could be properly endowed. Usually, they would ask for prayers for other members of their family, often their wife, their parents, and ancestors. The

---

[81] A. Brown, *Popular Piety in Late Medieval England: The Diocese of Salisbury 1250–1550* (Oxford, 1995), 76, 205.

[82] R. C. Finucane, 'Cantilupe as Thaumaturge: Pilgrims and their "Miracles" ', in M. Jancey (ed.), *St Thomas Cantilupe, Bishop of Hereford: Essays in his Honour* (Hereford, 1982), 138–9, 143.

[83] S. D. Lloyd, *English Society and the Crusade 1216–1307* (Oxford, 1988), 83–4; *The Thurgarton Cartulary*, ed. T. Foulds (Stamford, 1994), p. cxxxi.

[84] *Complete Peerage*, viii. 287; *The Thurgarton Cartulary*, ed. Foulds, pp. cxxxiii–iv.

crown had to give permission for land to be granted to the Church for this purpose, and not surprisingly, as the fourteenth century proceeded, it became more common to include requests for prayers for the royal family. Chantries, many of them very small, became the most favoured form of patronage to the Church. In 1299 Joan, widow of Robert de Grey, set one up with four chaplains, who were to celebrate mass for her soul and those of her ancestors. In addition, thirteen of the poor were to be given food and drink daily, and on the anniversary of Joan's death there was to be a distribution of 5 quarters of wheat and 5 of beans to the poor.[85] The number of chantries increased rapidly, with a notably high rate of foundation in the second quarter of the fourteenth century.[86] Effigies and brasses provided permanent memorials to members of knightly families, filling up churches with visual statements that were more about power than purgatory.

Some contemporaries were critical of knights, and concluded that things were no longer as they should be. The author of the *Vita* of Edward II thought little of those who had been promoted by Piers Gaveston, from the stable to the chamber. He complained about social climbers, squires who tried to outdo their betters, knights who tried to emulate barons.[87] Earls, barons, and knights were criticized in the *Simonie*, an early fourteenth-century poem. They should go on crusade, but instead were 'lions in the hall, and hares in the field'. Knights should wear the clothes appropriate to their station, but instead they wore such varied garments that a knight could not be distinguished from a minstrel. 'Thus is the order of knighthood turned upside down.' Now, any boy who could break a spear was made a knight. The order that should be good and gentle had become poisoned by bad blood.[88] The criticisms are understandable, if not justified, in terms of the social changes that took place. In many cases in the fourteenth century esquires were coming to take the place in society that had earlier been occupied by knights. Many tasks in local government that had been the exclusive preserve of knights in the thirteenth century came, in the fourteenth, to be handed over to men who did not enjoy that status. Together, however, knights and esquires, linked by ties of marriage, lordship, and locality, came to form the English gentry.

[85] *A Calendar of the Feet of Fines for Buckinghamshire 1259–1307*, ed. A. Travers (Buckinghamshire Record Society, 25, 1989), 81.

[86] J. T. Rosenthal, *The Purchase of Paradise: Gift Giving and the Aristocracy, 1307–1485* (London, 1972), 14–20, 32.

[87] *Vita Edwardi*, 29, 57.

[88] *Political Songs*, 334–5.

CHAPTER 15

Landownership and the Law

Broad acres of arable and pasture provided the aristocracy with their wealth; wide forests provided them with sport. Land and the right to inherit it were central to the workings of medieval society, from the highest down to the lowest. The law provided a framework for acquiring and passing on estates. Knowledge of how it operated, and how it might be manipulated, was essential for success. Relationships between lords and tenants, and family disputes, frequently led to the courts, with their formalized procedures. This was an age of litigation.

THE ACQUISITION OF LAND

Land could be acquired in various ways. Marriage was one; grants from the crown another. Purchase offered another possibility. Of these, perhaps the easiest was the first. Examples of men who acquired huge estates as a result of making a good marriage are many. When Simon de Montfort struck a deal by which he obtained half of the old honour of Leicester, he did not gain the resources appropriate to his new status of an earl. Marriage to a rich heiress was essential for him, and the king's sister Eleanor, widow of the earl marshal, was a tempting, if controversial, choice. Many of the Savoyard relations of Henry III's queen Eleanor, and their adherents, did well through marriage. Through the king's favour, Peter and Ebles of Geneva, Geoffrey de Geneville, and Ebles des Montz were all married to wealthy English heiresses or widows. In a slightly later period the match between Thomas, earl of Lancaster, and Alice, daughter of Henry de Lacy, earl of Lincoln, made an already wealthy man into a super-magnate when his father-in-law died in 1311. Lancaster himself used marriage as one way in which to reward his henchman Robert Holland, when he arranged his marriage to Maud, co-heiress of Alan de la Zouche.[1] Wealthy heiresses were very desirable. The death of Gilbert, earl of Gloucester, at Bannockburn in 1314 put two of his three sisters in a highly

---

[1] Maddicott, 'Thomas of Lancaster and Sir Robert Holland', 457.

marketable position (one, Eleanor, was already married to Hugh Despenser the younger). Margaret was the widow of Piers Gaveston, and Elizabeth the widow of John de Burgh, son of the earl of Ulster. The king arranged Margaret's marriage to Hugh Audley, a household knight and royal favourite of no great wealth, who would eventually become earl of Gloucester. Elizabeth fell prey to Theobald de Verdun, who married her in 1316 without royal licence. His expectations of great wealth were dashed by his death in the same year. A new marriage was then arranged for her, to Roger Damory, another royal favourite, providing a further demonstration that the easiest way to climb the ladder of wealth was by marriage. Damory did not enjoy his fortune for long as he was executed in 1322. Elizabeth did not remarry, but enjoyed a long widowhood until her eventual death in 1360.[2]

Marriages often involved complex land settlements. In the early thirteenth century it was normal practice for the father of a bride to give the groom land as *maritagium*, while the groom endowed his bride with land as her dower. By mid-century money paid as a marriage portion was replacing *maritagium*, and soon jointures were created in addition to dower. With a jointure, the newly married couple would settle land on themselves jointly, perhaps creating an entail, ensuring the estates would pass to their children in a direct line of descent.[3] Many examples could be given; one may suffice. In 1316 Robert FitzPayn agreed that his son Robert should marry Maud, daughter of Bartholomew Badlesmere. It was agreed that Robert should provide Maud with a dower of 200 marks' worth of land. Robert agreed that he would not grant out any of his land, save £200 worth, without Badlesmere's permission, and that the estates should be held in jointure by Robert junior and Maud, his wife, descending from them in the male line. Robert entered into a recognizance to Badlesmere in 20,000 marks to guarantee this, and Badlesmere agreed to pay Robert 1,200 marks in instalments as the marriage portion. Maud, who was under age, was to remain in her father's custody for a year after the marriage. A possible reason why Badlesmere took such care in this case was that Robert was Robert FitzPayn's son by his first marriage. Robert had subsequently remarried, and might well have wished to see much of his land go to children of the second marriage.[4]

Royal favour might bring with it grants of land, though those fortunate enough to obtain these might find that they were not always as secure as they must have hoped. It was generally acknowledged that the traditional royal

---

[2] Altschul, *A Baronial Family in Medieval England*, 168–9.
[3] This is a very brief summary of a complex issue, for which, see J. Biancalana, *The Fee Tail and the Common Recovery in Medieval England 1176–1502* (Cambridge, 2001), 142–60.
[4] *Complete Peerage*, v. 451–2.

demesne lands should not be granted away. That meant that what was available to the king was land acquired by conquest, or by forfeiture. The distribution of land that followed Edward I's second Welsh war saw major gains for Earl Warenne, for the earl of Lincoln, Reginald de Grey, and the Mortimers, as huge swathes of land in the marches were granted to those who had served the king well and loyally in the war.[5] The political upheavals of the 1320s made land available to the crown on a quite exceptional scale.

The fate of one of Edward I's new marcher lordships, that of Denbigh in north Wales, illustrates some of the vicissitudes that might follow from the distribution of land by the crown. Denbigh was granted to the earl of Lincoln, and on his death in 1311 it went, quite correctly, to his son-in-law Thomas, earl of Lancaster. On Lancaster's execution in 1322 Denbigh was forfeited to the crown, and it then went to the elder Despenser. His tenure was rudely ended by his execution in 1326, and the lordship was then granted to the queen's lover Roger Mortimer. His execution in 1330 meant that Denbigh, which was valued at about £1,000, was once more available to the royal patronage machine, and in 1331 Edward III granted it to William Montague, one of those responsible for the astonishing coup of the previous year. There were problems with previous claimants; in particular, Thomas of Lancaster's widow, Alice de Lacy, might well have expected to regain the lordship which she had lost in 1322. Montague paid her off with £200. Hugh Despenser's son and heir received compensation with a much larger sum, £1,000, while his mother was given 350 marks.[6] Nor did the Montague tenure of Denbigh prove secure. William's son inherited his father's earldom of Salisbury, but not the king's favour. In 1354 Roger Mortimer, grandson of the Mortimer executed in 1330, was successful in a lawsuit to recover Denbigh. This was largely due to the direct intervention of the king.[7]

Another way of gaining land was through purchase. Gilbert de Clare, earl of Gloucester in the later thirteenth century, engaged in a major programme of land purchase, particularly in the decade after Edward I's first Welsh war, in 1277. He acquired some whole manors, and also bought smaller parcels of land to round out existing holdings.[8] Humphrey de Bohun, earl of Hereford, who died at Boroughbridge in 1322, was constantly active in purchasing land in order to round out his estates. His near-contemporary Guy de Beauchamp, earl of Warwick, bought many small parcels of land.[9] Henry Percy bought the

[5] Davies, *Lordship and Society in the March of Wales*, 26–9; Prestwich, *Edward I*, 204.

[6] Davies, *Lordship and Society*, 50.

[7] G. A. Holmes, *The Estates of the Higher Nobility in* XIV *Century England* (Cambridge, 1957), 15–16.

[8] Altschul, *A Baronial Family in Medieval England*, 211–13.

[9] Holmes, *The Estates of the Higher Nobility*, 113–14.

entire barony of Alnwick from the bishop of Durham in 1309–10. Newcomers
to the landed elite were naturally keen purchasers. John Stonor, royal justice
under Edward III, built up a substantial estate very largely by purchase.
Religious houses were active in the land market, particularly in the thirteenth
century. Right through society, down to the level of the peasantry, land was
bought, sold, and leased.

Some methods of purchase were especially unpopular. In the thirteenth
century Jewish moneylenders played an important part in the land market.
Although they were not keen to acquire lands themselves, those who borrowed
from them were very ready to mortgage their estates in order to obtain loans. It
was then possible for religious houses or others to pay off the debts, in
exchange for the lands. There was an intriguing set of double standards at
work, as the Church simultaneously profited from Jewish business skills and
took up a position bitterly hostile to the Jews. Christ Church Canterbury, and
the royal officials Walter de Merton and Geoffrey de Langley, provide prominent examples of those who profited from this practice. Many others could be
cited. Those families that found it hard to maintain knightly status were
particularly vulnerable, as were those who faced high expenditure for some
reason. Gerard de Fancourt went on crusade with Prince Edward in 1270, and
to pay his expenses mortgaged his lands to Master Elias, a Jewish moneylender.
Thurgarton Priory then acquired the gage, and paid off Elias. What appears
from Gerard's charters to have been a pious grant was in fact a purchase by a
prospering religious house.[10] The crown acquired many Jewish debts. A significant number were then granted by Edward I to his queen, Eleanor of Castile.
She promptly foreclosed on the debts, and gained a good many properties as a
result.[11] As the position of the Jews in England became more and more difficult,
there was a shift as Jewish lending moved down the social scale. People
contracted to repay debts in commodities, particularly grain, and the impact
of lending on the land market declined, until the Jews were finally expelled in
1290.[12]

Purchase was not always straightforward. One technique was to buy rever-
sions, paying the owner for land that would come to the purchaser after the
former's death. In Edward II's reign Bartholomew Badlesmere appears to have
been something of a specialist in this technique. He purchased the reversion of
the barony of Castle Combe, acquired that of Chilham, and was granted that of

[10] *The Thurgarton Cartulary*, ed. Foulds 330.
[11] R. R. Mundill, *England's Jewish Solution: Experiment and Expulsion, 1262–1290* (Cambridge,
1998), 37–40, 62–3; J. C. Parsons, *Eleanor of Castile: Queen and Society in Thirteenth Century
England* (New York, 1995), 126–9.
[12] Mundill, *England's Jewish Solution*, 246.

Chatham by the king.[13] He also engaged in complex dealings with John FitzBernard. Badlesmere bought the reversion of some of FitzBernard's land, so that, should FitzBernard die without direct heirs, the estates would come to Badlesmere. In the event, it was Badlesmere who died first, on the gallows after Boroughbridge in 1322, though FitzBernard died in the same year. His widow was able to recover the lands, arguing that she had not consented to the grant to Badlesmere, and that she and her husband had held the land jointly.[14]

What amounted to a form of purchase was created by legislation on debt. In 1283 the Statute of Acton Burnell introduced new procedures for the registration and enforcement of debt. This was refined in the Statute of Merchants issued two years later. Debts could be registered in various towns, and if they were not paid off promptly, debtors could be imprisoned and given three months to raise the money. If they failed to do so, their creditors could receive all their lands and goods, to be held by a new form of tenure until the debt was fully paid. The legislation had been prompted by a case between two merchants, but the advantages of the procedures soon became evident. Edward I's treasurer, Walter Langton, was particularly notorious for the way in which he acquired much land by use of Statute Merchant in a series of complicated deals.[15] It is hardly surprising that the Ordinances of 1311 decreed that henceforth the procedure of the statute should only be applied to dealings between merchants.

Hunger for land was not always satisfied by legitimate means. This was particularly the case during Edward II's reign. The complex case of Thorpe Waterville is a good illustration of the problems. The manor, with two others, had been acquired by Walter Langton in 1300, in a questionable deal with William Tuchet. When Langton was arrested in 1307, these lands came to the crown. In 1312 they were granted to the earl of Pembroke, though Langton, now restored to a measure of favour, had not forgotten his interest. Nor had Tuchet abandoned his claims; at the instigation of his lord, the earl of Lancaster, he resorted to force, and seized Thorpe Waterville. The king bought out Langton's interest in the property at a high price of 3,500 marks, together with a promise of a grant of lands and advowsons for life. The intention was then to grant them to Pembroke. Eventually, the issue was settled in 1314, when Pembroke agreed to exchange Thorpe Waterville and the other manors with Lancaster, receiving lands in Monmouthshire in their place. Tuchet received his reward with a grant from Lancaster.[16] The complex story reveals the way in

---

[13] Sanders, *English Baronies*, 28, 32, 111.   [14] *Complete Peerage*, v. 400–3.

[15] A. Beardwood, *The Trial of Walter Langton, Bishop of Lichfield 1307–1312*, Transactions of the American Philosophical Society (1964), 28–31.

[16] Maddicott, *Thomas of Lancaster*, 154–6.

which questionable legal methods, unacceptable use of force, and political influence were all brought to bear in a way that was extraordinarily divisive. Much worse was to come later in Edward II's reign. The methods that the Despensers used, particularly after the defeat of Thomas of Lancaster in 1322, are a particularly horrific demonstration of the way in which force and fraud could be used to obtain title to lands. Wealthy widows, such as Alice de Lacy and Elizabeth de Burgh, were particular targets. Bullying, imprisonment, and even physical violence were used to force them to hand over their estates, as shown in Chapter 8. Nor did the Despensers confine their attention to widows. The younger Despenser bluntly requested that the elderly John Botetourt should hand over a manor, part of his wife's inheritance, to redeem an alleged wrong. He had, the letter indicated threateningly, spoken to the king about this.[17] The law provided their victims with no protection; rather, it was used by the Despensers as a tool with which to obtain their ends.

LEGISLATION

The way in which land was held, inherited, bought, and sold created many difficult legal issues. There were also many problems that were created as a result of the tensions in relationships between landlords and tenants. Great landlords needed the expertise provided by lawyers if they wished to maintain and expand their estates. In the late 1290s Westminster abbey had at least two, and probably four, royal justices on its payroll, along with two high exchequer officials, one attorney, and at least one pleader. In the same decade the earl of Gloucester employed a number of attorneys, some of them professional lawyers.[18] If resources would not allow for the permanent retaining of an impressive body of lawyers, then they might be hired for short periods. Without such backing, there was an ever-present danger that land might be lost. Every advantage had to be taken of the opportunities presented by the law, both to protect ownership and tenure of estates, and to maintain rights to services.

The Articles of the Barons of 1258 show the importance of legal issues in the reform programme. The first clause dealt with the problem of heirs and how they could make good their inheritance. Lords, the document demanded, should not make 'waste, destruction, sale or alienation of houses or of woods, stewponds, parks, or men holding in villeinage'. The Provisions of Westminster provided an appropriate remedy for this, and for many other problems.[19]

[17] SC 1/37/5.
[18] Maddicott, *Law and Lordship*, 17; Altschul, *A Baronial Family in Medieval England*, 238.
[19] *DBM* 77–9, 142–3.

The Provisions marked in many ways the start of a great process of adjustment and change to the law, which was continued in Edward I's statutes.

The relative simplicity of the legal actions made available by Henry II, which established quick means by which land could be recovered, contrasts with the increasing complexity of the law in the thirteenth and fourteenth centuries. *Novel disseisin* protected immediate possession of land, and provided a quick remedy for anyone whose property was seized by another. It did not, however, meet all eventualities. In 1275 Edward I, in his first Statute of Westminster, made it possible for the heirs of the original injured party to bring actions. Damages were to be paid if the disseisin had been violent, and these were doubled if the guilty party was a royal official. Further legislation in the Statute of Gloucester of 1278 and in the Statute of Westminster II of 1285 continued to revise the process. Plaintiffs were entitled to costs as well as damages. The scope of the action was extended so that it could be used in the case of lands held as a means of recovering a debt. Plaintiffs and defendants could not excuse themselves from attending court, and the use of ingenious but essentially bogus arguments was punished with double damages. The Statute of Joint Tenants of 1306 dealt with cases where the defence was that the land was not held by the defendant, but jointly with his wife or another. The refinements of the process all made sense; they also demonstrate the growing complexity of the land law.[20] It had been intended that actions such as *novel disseisin* should determine not ultimate right to land, but rather the simple question of its occupation. Inevitably, however, *novel disseisin* came to be used in questions of right. The alternatives of the grand assize, a jury of twelve knights, or even the use of champions to fight a trial by battle, were time-consuming and unreliable.

There were various ways in which title to land could be proved. Possession of a charter was the simplest, but even that could be challenged if it could be shown that a grant had been made under duress. An increasingly common and effective method of conveyancing land and establishing title was to bring a fictitious dispute to court. The court would then agree a settlement with the parties, which would be recorded in a final concord, known as a fine. Each party, and the court itself, would keep a copy. Since the agreement had been reached in court, it had a special binding quality. The practice began in the late twelfth century, and became extremely common in the thirteenth. A special action was developed, *de fine facto*, to deal with any violations of these agreements, and the system of fines was strengthened by statute in 1299.[21]

A major change to the land market came with the Statute of *Quia Emptores* of 1290. The question of protecting the rights of lords underlay this. They were

---

[20] Prestwich, *Edward I*, 271–2; D. W. Sutherland, *The Assize of Novel Disseisin* (Oxford, 1973).
[21] Fines are explained in Pollock and Maitland, *The History of English Law*, 94–103.

suffering potential losses of feudal income and authority if a tenant sold his land to another and did this by making the purchaser his feudal tenant (subinfeudation). The statute cut through the issues very neatly. If someone wished to sell land, he might do so, but he could not make the new holder his sub-tenant. He could only sell by substitution, not subinfeudation. That meant that the new holder of the land would take the place of the seller, and hold the land directly from the overlord. The implications of this legislation were far-reaching, even though the terms of the statute did not cover land held on conditional terms. It prevented the growing complexity of tenurial networks, but did not hamper the operations of the land market. It encouraged men to find different ways of making grants of land. It made more sense to reward a follower by giving him, say, the income from a particular manor for life than by granting him the land in fee.[22]

Another way in which lords might suffer was if land was granted to the Church. Since the Church did not die, and was never under age, reliefs were not paid, and there was no possibility of profiting from wardships. The lord would suffer a loss of income as a result. The second reissue of Magna Carta, in 1217, included a clause to prevent men from granting land to the Church and then receiving it back, a device that would leave the overlord with few effective rights. In an ordinance of 1228 the crown protected its position. Tenants-in-chief were forbidden to make such grants to the Church. The tenants-in-chief, however, did not have any equivalent protection should their sub-tenants hand land over to the Church. Records of religious houses show that they were indeed acquiring land during the thirteenth century at a very significant rate. In some cases grants were made for genuinely pious reasons, but there is no doubt that wealthy monasteries were actively engaged in the land market, profiting from the misfortunes of families less able to cope with the changing economic conditions of the thirteenth century. The Petition of the Barons of 1258 asked that monks should not be allowed to take over lands without the consent of the lord, who would lose rights such as wardship and marriage as a result. The response came in the Provisions of Westminster of 1259, which stated that 'Monks shall not be allowed to enter the fee of anyone without the permission of the chief lord, from whom that property is held.'[23]

The legislation of 1259 was one part of the work of reform that survived the defeat of Simon de Montfort. Most of the measures were re-enacted in the Statute of Marlborough of 1267, but the prohibition on the grant of lands to monasteries was not among them, nor had it been included in the reissue of

---

[22] The statute is fully discussed by T. F. T. Plucknett, *Legislation of Edward I* (Oxford, 1949), 102–8.
[23] *DBM* 80–1, 144–5.

1263.[24] The courts, however, continued to treat it as valid. In one case, the master of the Temple challenged this, and asked that his case be postponed until the king's will was known. In 1279 Edward I, very probably in response to this, enacted the Statute of Mortmain, which duly forbade the grant of land to the Church. It remained, of course, possible to obtain a licence from the crown to make such grants, but the interests of lords were much better protected as a result of the legislation. It was necessary to hold an inquest *ad quod damnum* before a licence to alienate land in mortmain could be issued, to ensure that the implications were fully assessed.[25] The legislation both met the requirement of the lords, and provided the crown with new powers. At the same time, the way that the statute operated in practice did not disadvantage the Church as much as might be expected. From 1299 a system was introduced of levying fines for alienation into mortmain, and the number of licences issued by the crown steadily increased until it peaked in the 1330s.[26]

A difficult problem resulted from people's understandable desire to impose conditions on grants they made. Donors were naturally concerned that land granted when a marriage took place should remain in the family. It was, however, very difficult to make such terms hold. Traditionally, it was held that once a child was born, the person to whom the land had been granted could do as he wished with it, and alienate or sell it. In a case in 1281 land was given to a couple whose children predeceased them. A claim that the land should then revert to the donor because the conditions of the grant had not been fulfilled failed. Edward I took steps in the first clause of the Statute of Westminster II of 1285, known as *de donis conditionalibus*, to deal with this issue. The king's intention was that the conditions attached to a gift of land should be observed. Writs were made available to enable the donor to recover the land if the conditions were not adhered to. The clause was awkwardly drafted, and it was argued that the conditions restricted the original grantee, and that for subsequent generations a gift would become absolute.[27] In 1311, however, Chief Justice Bereford stated that he knew what had been intended, which was that the conditions should hold until the third heir had succeeded.[28] Although not all justices accepted Bereford's view, this legislation made entails effective; land that was held in tail could only be inherited in the direct line of descent. If it was in tail male, then it should go in the direct male

---

[24] Brand, *Kings, Barons and Justices*, 191.

[25] P. A. Brand, 'The Control of Mortmain Alienation in England, 1200–1300', in J. H. Baker (ed.), *Legal Records and the Historian* (London, 1980), 29–40; Prestwich, *Edward I*, 251–2, 274; Plucknett, *Legislation of Edward I*, 94–101.

[26] S. Raban, *Mortmain Legislation and the English Church, 1279–1500* (Cambridge, 1982), 60, 155–6.

[27] Biancalana, *The Fee Tail and the Common Recovery in Medieval England*, 31–2, 87–8.

[28] Plucknett, *Legislation of Edward I*, 131–3; *SR* i. 71–2.

line. If that line failed, then the land would revert to the donor. *De donis*, therefore, in time made the entail effective as a means of controlling the way in which land was inherited.

ENTAILS, JOINTURES, AND USES

Landlords were naturally eager to make sure that their wishes for the future of their families were fulfilled. Various devices were developed to make it possible for men to settle their lands as they wished. Land could be granted to feoffees, who would then grant it back on different terms. One way that this was useful was to create a jointure. This was where a husband and wife held land jointly. Should either die, the survivor would continue to hold the land. This was an effective means of providing a widow with a secure dower estate. Widows had always been entitled to a third of their husband's lands as dower, but a jointure was much more secure. The use of feoffees in this way also made it possible to avoid feudal incidents such as relief and wardship. While widows gained, rightful heirs might lose out as a result of this technique. Piers Corbet, who died in 1322, had most of his lands jointly enfeoffed to him and his wife. She remarried, and retained the Corbet lands. This left John Corbet, Piers's half-brother, in a difficult and impoverished position.[29]

It was not easy with inherited land held in fee to make provision for younger sons, but here again techniques making use of feoffees were developed which made this possible. In 1332 and again in 1338 Adam de Everingham set up a complex series of arrangements that effectively put his lands in trust and ensured that each of his five sons would have property to inherit. Part of his estate was put in the joint ownership of himself and his wife (so creating a jointure), so that she would have sufficient land as a widow.[30] This is just one example of what was a very common practice by the fourteenth century. Such arrangements were quite different from what was allowed by the straightforward rules of male primogeniture. Also, while lords were keen to see the services due to them performed, there was an equally understandable enthusiasm to find ways of evading the services they owed to others. These needs led to developments that freed up the land market and saw a decline in the importance of feudal services and incidents.

It was also possible to use feoffees to make sure that lands would go to a lord's chosen descendants. In 1343 Bartholomew Burghersh enfeoffed John Thoresby and Ralph de Buck, both clerics, with three manors, a hundred, and an advowson in Wiltshire. They were to grant this back to Bartholomew for life, and after his death the lands were remaindered firstly to his son Bartholomew, secondly to

---

[29] *Complete Peerage*, iii. 417.   [30] Ibid. v. 187–8.

Henry, his second son, thirdly to his last son, Thomas. The ultimate remainder was to Bartholomew's eventual heirs.[31] That is a straightforward example. John de Grey faced a more difficult problem. In 1311 he bought a licence to grant Ruthin castle and most of his other lands to John Damory and another feoffee. They were to grant the estate back to him for life. It was then to go to his son Roger and the heirs of his body. The point of the transaction was that Roger was the son of a second marriage; what John was doing was depriving his elder son Henry of much of his inheritance.[32] Richard, earl of Arundel, obtained a licence in 1347 to grant his lands to two feoffees. He was to hold the lands for life, and on his death they were to go to his widow, Eleanor, and on her death to the male heirs of their marriage. Should there be no heirs, then Richard Arundel the younger would obtain them.[33] The implication of the technique of entailing land in tale mail was that the division of land between co-heiresses was prevented. If someone died leaving only daughters, with the land entailed in tail male, then the inheritance would go not to the daughters, but to the nearest male relative. The integrity of the estate would be preserved.

Historians have made much of the development of uses in this period. A use was created when lands were granted to feoffees, who would continue to hold it rather than grant it back under different conditions. What they would do instead was to allow the original owner the continued use of the land. On his death, they would follow his wishes and allow whomsoever he had designated as his heir to enjoy the use. By employing this device, men were able to avoid the rigid rules of inheritance that applied to land held in fee. They also avoided the feudal incidents of wardship and relief.[34] There are a very few examples from the early thirteenth century of these techniques. Crusaders were among those who found it useful to hand their lands over to feoffees.[35] The technique was also a means of providing property to the friars, whose own rules prohibited them from owning anything. Examples of enfeoffment to use remained relatively uncommon, however, until the 1360s and 1370s. The first great magnate to employ the technique on a large scale was Thomas de Beauchamp, earl of Warwick, in a complex settlement of his affairs in the mid-1340s. He was clearly worried about the prospect of death while campaigning in France, and set up feoffees so as to provide dowries for his daughters. In 1349, before sailing

---

[31] *CPR 1343–5*, 118.
[32] C. Given-Wilson, *The English Nobility in the Late Middle Ages* (London, 1987), 145.
[33] *CPR 1345–8*, 328.
[34] For a clear explanation of entails, jointures, and uses, see Given-Wilson, *The English Nobility in the Late Middle Ages*, 138–42.
[35] J. M. W. Bean, *The Decline of English Feudalism 1215–1540* (Manchester, 1968), 107, 109–10; Lloyd, *English Society and the Crusade*, 173–4. For a specific example, see *Civil Pleas of the Wiltshire Eyre*, ed. M. T. Clanchy (Wiltshire Record Society, 1971), no. 69.

for Gascony, Henry of Lancaster set up feoffees to serve for a twelve-year period. They received lands worth £1,000 a year, and were to spend the proceeds in ways he set out.[36] It was not chance that the examples before 1360 coincided with the French war. Like the crusaders of the thirteenth century, those going to fight in France in the fourteenth century had a very understandable desire to settle their affairs properly before they departed.

Entails, jointures, and uses were not created by royal legislation, but the crown tacitly approved the changes in the way in which inheritance was governed. De donis facilitated the development of entails, while complex arrangements involving the grant of land to feoffees, and the regrant of it by them under different terms, were made easier by quia emptores. The development of mechanisms involving feoffees could not have happened without royal approval. Tenants-in-chief could not grant their lands to feoffees without royal licence, and this was readily forthcoming, for a fee. The changes were in the interest of most great landowners, and that included the king himself.

The use of feoffees was open to abuse. In 1343 John Berenger handed over his small estate to feoffees. They held it for a week before, and a week after, his death. They then granted it to John's widow, with remainder to his heir, in accordance with his instructions. The royal escheator was suspicious and took the estate into the king's hands. There were serious questions concerning whether the lands really had been given to the feoffees.[37] This was the kind of case that was in the magnate's minds when in 1339 they made a request that 'remedy be ordained in this parliament concerning men who when dying make alienation of their lands and have themselves carried out of their manors, by fraud to deprive the chief lords of the ward of the same'.[38] There were worries about the way in which grants, presumably to feoffees, were used as a way of evading some of the consequences of lordship, but significantly no legislative action was taken to meet the complaint.

Edward III needed the support of his magnates for the war, and this was probably a key factor in the increasing number of licences to grant lands to feoffees that were issued from the 1340s. There were possible disadvantages for the crown, in that it might lose the profits from marriages if the right of co-heiresses to inherit was limited. Rights of wardship might be lost as a result of grants to feoffees. The benefits, however, in terms of the backing that the king received from his magnates more than outweighed such disadvantages. The scale of the loss of rights was very limited. In practice, there appears to have been only one case before 1360 in which there was an under-age heir, and the

---

[36] CPR 1348–50, 347. Bean, Decline of English Feudalism, 116–18, discusses the early examples of enfeoffment to use.

[37] CPR 1343–5, 180.

[38] Rot. Parl. i. 104, trans. Bean, Decline of English Feudalism, 195.

crown did not exercise rights of wardship because the estates had been granted to feoffees.[39] A study of nine great inheritances showed that in the first half of the fourteenth century uses played no part, and jointures a significant role only in one case. Examples such as those of the earl of Pembroke, Aymer de Valence, who died in 1324, the earl of Devon, Hugh de Courtenay, who died in 1340, and Laurence Hastings, who died in 1348, show no use of feoffees, uses, or re-enfeoffments.[40]

The land law, as it developed in the thirteenth and fourteenth centuries, was a splendid achievement in many ways. It is, however, difficult to assess how effective it was in practice. The procedures available to both plaintiffs and defendants in land disputes over time became more in number and greater in complexity. Litigation was expensive, and often appeared profitable only to the lawyers. Cases might drag on, in different forms, for decades or even centuries. One argument is that this was beneficial. No one could ever lose hope altogether, and instead of resorting to force to recover property, there was always another writ to apply for, another form of action to use.[41] This is questionable; it is surely more likely that it was fear of the crown's likely reaction that discouraged men from taking the law into their own hands, rather than hope of eventually winning a case in the courts. It was, however, the case that some disputes over land were extraordinarily long-drawn-out. The case of the lordship of Gower in south Wales is particularly striking. This was the subject of bitter dispute in the early 1320s, when William de Braose's attempts to dispose of it attracted the attention of the Despensers. Eventual success in the 1350s went not to any of the claimants of the 1320s, but to the earl of Warwick, whose family had not held Gower for well over a century.[42]

The legal foundations of the English landholding structure were transformed during the thirteenth and fourteenth centuries. Some of the issues may have been technical, but they were of fundamental importance, with the great age of change coming in the first half of Edward I's reign. Later, significant shifts came as lawyers developed mechanisms such as uses, which enabled landlords to avoid the rigorous simplicity of primogeniture. Successful landowners had to be adept in employing the law to their best advantage. This was not all they needed, for they also had to have the skill to ensure that their estates were managed effectively so as to take advantage of changing economic circumstances.

---

[39] Bean, *Decline of English Feudalism*, 211.
[40] Holmes, *Estates of the Higher Nobility*, 49–50.
[41] R. C. Palmer, *The Whilton Dispute, 1264–1380: A Social–Legal Study of Dispute Settlement in Medieval England* (Princeton, 1984).
[42] R. R. Davies, *Lordship and Society in the March of Wales 1282–1400* (Oxford, 1978), 272.

CHAPTER 16

The Management of Land

If profits were to be made from estates, they had to be effectively managed. There were two main ways of doing this. The manors could be rented out, and a fixed sum received. Leases could vary in length, but were usually fairly long. Alternatively, manors could be administered directly. Paid officials would run them, and the landlord would take the proceeds. There would still be a rental income from the tenants on a directly run manor, but the lord or his officials would take the proceeds of the demesne lands directly. A rental system offered a stable income, whereas under direct management there was a much greater potential for taking advantage of improving economic circumstances, and also, of course, a greater risk when times were not good. In periods of inflation, it made little sense to settle for fixed rents, which would steadily decline in real terms; direct management was the wiser option.

HIGH FARMING

The late twelfth century saw the beginning of a rapid movement away from a rental system and towards direct management, or high farming. The pattern was similar in virtually all the great estates where the process can be documented. Various causes have been suggested for this change. Particular stress has been laid on monetary inflation.[1] The evidence for prices suggests that a particularly sharp rise was taking place around 1200. The hundred years from 1220 saw a steady rise, with considerable short-term fluctuations. The early fourteenth century, for example, witnessed a period of inflation fuelled by a sharp increase in the quantity of coin in circulation. The price of oxen rose from about 8s. in the 1220s to around 16s. in the decade 1310–20. Grain prices over the same period increased by over 50 per cent. The evidence for this has been painstakingly collected from account rolls, particularly those of the

---

[1] P. D. A. Harvey, 'The Pipe Rolls and the Adoption of Demesne Farming in England', *EcHR*, 2nd ser., 26 (1973), 345–59; id., 'The English Inflation of 1180–1220, *Past and Present*, 61 (1973), 4–9.

Winchester estates.[2] There is an undoubted bias in the evidence towards the south of England, but there are no indications that the experience of other parts of the country was very different. Inflation did not, however, affect wages as it did prices; with the population rising, the costs of labour were low. The combination of high prices with low wages favoured direct management. There has to be some doubt, however, about how far contemporaries were sufficiently aware of long-term price changes for these to have influenced the decisions they made about the management of their estates. The short-term fluctuations that reflected the fortunes of individual harvests would have masked the underlying trends. It seems likely that what drove the adoption of direct management was a broad sense of increasing economic prosperity and potential, to which rising prices contributed.

The fear of losing land, or the rent due from it, provides another explanation. Changes in the law gave increased protection to tenants, and the argument is that landlords were increasingly reluctant to rent land out in case they lost control of it. Religious houses found it hard to recover lands that had been leased in the twelfth century. It was with considerable difficulty that the monks of Westminster in 1238 recovered half of the manor of Longdon, which had been farmed out in the previous century.[3] In the Huntingdonshire eyre of 1286 the master of the Temple in England brought a case against John de Lay of Paxton. He claimed that John held a messuage and two virgates of land, for 12s. a year. This rent was four years in arrears.[4] In this case, the rent was recovered, but it may have been seen as simpler to keep land under direct management than to have to pursue recalcitrant tenants through the courts.

In the case of ecclesiastical estates, directives from church authorities to stop leasing had a role. Such orders were issued by the papacy as early as 1179. In 1199 Innocent III gave specific instructions to the archbishop of Canterbury. In the 1270s Archbishop Pecham gave strong encouragement to the prior of Christ Church Canterbury when he brought the monastic lands into direct management. In this case the problem was that the lands had been farmed out to members of the monastic community itself. These monks then took up residence on the manors. Monastic discipline was lost: one of these monk–farmers even used the opportunity to seduce the local women. As Pecham stated, 'a monk without his cloister is like a fish without water'.[5]

[2] D. A. Farmer, 'Prices and Wages', in *Agrarian History*, ii. 715–817.

[3] Harvey, *Westminster Abbey and its Estates*, 166, 414–15.

[4] A. R. DeWindt and E. B. DeWindt (eds.), *Royal Justice and the Medieval English Countryside: The Huntingdon Eyre of 1286, the Ramsey Abbey Banlieu Court of 1287, and the Assizes of 1287–88* (Toronto, 1981), vol. i, no. 30.

[5] M. Mate, 'The Farming Out of Manors: A New Look at the Evidence from Canterbury Cathedral Priory', *Journal of Medieval History*, 9 (1983), 335; F. R. H. du Boulay, *The Lordship of Canterbury* (London, 1966), 205.

A further explanation is that direct management was a product of the developed market economy of the thirteenth century. Grain and animals could easily be sold, and profits made. Of course some grain was kept back to sow in the following year, to distribute to the manorial servants, and for animal fodder, but the manorial economy did not aim at mere self-sufficiency. On the Canterbury estates in the 1290s the policy was to sell grain in the market, even if this meant that the manors could not send the customary quantities to the monks. In the same period on the earl of Cornwall's Wiltshire manor of Mere, there was not even sufficient kept back to provide seedcorn for the next year; 113 quarters of wheat were sold, and 21 quarters had to be bought as seed.[6]

Another reason for the shift to direct management was that it became increasingly easy for landlords to run their estates directly, as stewards and bailiffs developed new skills. A management revolution took place. There is an extensive literature which shows that the methods of estate management were widely disseminated, and that they were taught in a systematic way.[7] The earliest were produced in the mid-thirteenth century. Bishop Robert Grosseteste of Lincoln wrote a set of rules in Latin for the use of his own officials. This was expanded in a French version, written for the countess of Lincoln, who died in 1243. Part of this dealt with the management of the household, part with the estate. It was a thoroughly practical work: 'If you know how many acres have to be sown with each type of corn, then enquire how much seedcorn each type of soil requires, reckon this in acres and by the number of quarters of seed you ought to know the yield of the seed and what ought to be left.'[8] The *Seneschaucy* was probably written towards the end of the third quarter of the thirteenth century. It was a straightforward guide to the duties of the various officials, from the steward down to the dairymaid, with chapters on the auditors and the lord himself added at the end. The *Husbandry* is another late thirteenth-century treatise. This was a practical guide written for the use of auditors. The best-known work on estate management was written by Walter of Henley, a man of whom nothing is known for certain apart from his name. He may have been a knight who became a Dominican late in life, and his work was probably written in the 1280s. As was appropriate in a friar's work, the treatise took the form of a didactic sermon. It is enlivened with homely proverbs, and was clearly intended for a student audience. Walter

[6] R. H. Britnell, *The Commercialisation of English Society 1000–1500*, 2nd edn. (Manchester, 1996), 110; *Ministers' Accounts of the Earldom of Cornwall*, ed. L. M. Midgley, Camden 3rd ser., 66, 67 (1942, 1945), i. 62, 65.
[7] For this literature, and the following section, see *Walter of Henley and Other Treatises*, ed. Oschinsky.
[8] Ibid. 397.

provided wise advice on many topics; he was very clear, for example, about the importance of dung.

This literature was highly practical, but it was not simply a matter of providing useful tips for farmers. The importance of proper information, and of planning, was stressed. The treatises set out ways of making proper calculation. Walter of Henley explained how to work out the different costs of using oxen or horses for ploughing. Land should be marled and dunged. Traditional practices, such as the use of heaped (and therefore inaccurate) measures were condemned. Profit was important, but more stress was laid on ways of ensuring that the lord was not cheated by his officials. The *Husbandry* provided a set of yardsticks by which the performance of bailiffs and reeves could be tested. Fourteen gallons of cow's milk, for example, should give a stone of cheese and 2 pounds of butter. The suggestions for animal husbandry were for the most part practical and sensible, and again seem to have been adopted. In matters on which the treatises were silent, such as sowing rates or the use of legumes, practice seems to have been far less consistent, with very considerable local variation taking place.[9] There is evidence to show that the precepts of this literature were followed, though it is not always easy to be sure that practice was following the advice in the tracts; the tracts may have simply reflected normal good farming methods.

The treatises that explain farming practice have, not surprisingly, received more attention than those that set out accounting procedures.[10] The latter, however, were much more important in setting yardsticks and creating standardized systems essential for the effective direct management of estates. The earliest dates from about 1225; the genre flourished above all in the late thirteenth and early fourteenth centuries. Some derive from, and were written for, large ecclesiastical estates, but others, such as that written by Robert Carpenter, were secular in origin. The treatises compared the two main different methods of accounting, Winchester and Westminster form: the main difference between the two was in the treatment of arrears. Sample accounts were provided. Most important, because of its wide circulation, was the *Forma Compoti*, written around 1300, which set out the best accounting procedures for small knightly estates.

The surviving manorial and estate accounts are remarkably standardized; different estates, both lay and ecclesiastical, in quite different parts of the country all used the same basic methods, with relatively minor variations. Accounts showed the cash inflow and outflow, and detailed the stock and

---

[9] M. Mate, 'Medieval Agrarian Practice: The Determining Factors?', *Agricultural History Review*, 33 (1985), 22–31.

[10] They are discussed in *Walter of Henley and Other Treatises*, ed. Oschinsky, 212–57, with substantial extracts given on pp. 459–78.

grain in full detail. They were well designed to provide a proper check on bailiffs. The earliest are from Winchester, and date from 1208–9, but it was probably not until the middle of the thirteenth century that the use of written accounts became widespread.[11]

A specific example of a manorial account is that for Crondal in Hampshire in 1248. First, the account dealt with the receipts. There was a small sum paid of £2 10s. 5½d. for arrears from the previous year. Then there were the fixed rents, with some small increments, which came to £45 17s. 11¾d., but after various acquittances the total of £39 15s. 2¾d. was reached. Miscellaneous sales, such as hides of dead cattle and 102 lambskins (the flocks had suffered from murrain), together with sales of some services, came to £23 13s. 3½d. Sale of cereal crops, mostly wheat, came to £26 0s. 3½d. Court profits, together with a tallage on the villagers, amounted to £33 5s. 2d. The total receipt for the manor, therefore, was £123 14s. 9¾d. There were a great many miscellaneous items of expenditure. Steel had to be bought for new ploughshares, needed because the ground was hard from a dry summer. Four horses and sixteen oxen were acquired; 1,115 pots of dung were spread on the fields, and there was the cost of transporting 1,856 pots of marl. Much fencing was done, and the roof of the manorial hall and chamber needed repair. There were costs involved in getting the crops in; grain had to be winnowed and ground, apples had to be picked. The total of expenditure on the manor came to £28 3s. 6½d. External expenses included the costs of visits from the lord, the prior of St Swithun's, Winchester. Preparations for a feast on the Nativity of the Virgin Mary included the purchase of twenty-four geese and eighty chickens. The total of these various expenses came to £11 16s. 4d. Various payments, mostly to St Swithun's itself, came to £67 3s. 8½d. The total of all payments amounted to £107 3s. 2¾d. This left the manorial officials still owing £16 11s. 2¾d. The account then went on to give details of grain production, and of stock. This was a bad year for sheep. Sixty-three out of a total of 417 died of murrain, while of the 296 lambs, 109 were stillborn. The account provides an extraordinary level of detail, for example specifying how much seed was used to sow particular fields, and the cost of a rope for the well. Every item of income and expenditure was carefully recorded.[12]

It was, however, no use having robust accounting methods if it was not possible to take effective action against corrupt or fraudulent officials. The process of setting up proper mechanisms began with the Provisions of Westminster of 1259, one clause of which dealt with bailiffs who absconded, and was

---

[11] P. D. A. Harvey, *Manorial Records* (British Records Association, 1984), 25–35.

[12] *A Collection of Records and Documents relating to the Hundred and Manor of Crondal*, pt. 1, ed. F. J. Baigent (London, 1891), 51–72.

continued in the Statute of Marlborough of 1267 and Edward I's Statute of Westminster II. Unreliable bailiffs could be imprisoned at the request of the auditors, their accounts could be submitted to the expert judgement of the exchequer, and they could be outlawed. The procedure was effective if unpopular; the earl of Gloucester had two of his officials, who owed over £800 between them, imprisoned. Relatively small inconsistencies in accounts could be detected. In 1330 the bailiff of Billingham was arrested when he was found to have defrauded Durham cathedral priory; among other things, he had deliberately miscounted the number of cattle, and had sold two without accounting for them.[13]

The accounting systems were not designed to show profit. It was, however, possible to calculate the profitability both of manors as a whole and of demesne agriculture from the evidence they provided. At Canterbury the profitability of some manors was being worked out as early as the mid-1220s, and from the middle of the century there is good evidence from the accounts of Norwich cathedral priory of quite sophisticated profit-and-loss accounting. At Malton priory in the same period balance sheets were produced, enabling an easy comparison to be made of one year's performance against another's. There are many more examples of profit calculation from the second half of the thirteenth century, particularly from the 1290s.[14]

The development of high farming led to the appearance of a group of highly trained and expert estate managers. Many of these men had careers that took them from aristocratic employment into royal administration. Hervey de Borham was steward of the honour of Clare in 1259, but served the Montfortian administration in 1264–5. He was appointed a keeper of the peace in 1266, and then reverted to service with the earl of Gloucester in the late 1260s. He was a royal itinerant justice in the 1270s. Hamo Hautein was another of the Gloucester stewards, serving in 1268. He also had a career as sheriff of Lincoln, Norfolk, and Suffolk, and as an escheator in 1261; in addition, he held a post in the royal household in 1263.[15] John la Warre was steward to Earl Warenne in 1261. He was an ardent Montfortian supporter, and was one of the heroes of the ill-fated defence of Kenilworth in 1266. He became steward of Isabella de Forz, countess of Devon, in 1268, and remained in her service until 1274, when he was appointed sheriff of Herefordshire. Many other examples could be

---

[13] *DBM* 146–7; Brand, *Kings, Barons and Justices*, 65–6; *SR* i. 80–1; Prestwich, *Edward I*, 275; Durham cathedral muniments, Billingham, 1330.

[14] E. Stone, 'Profit-and-Loss Accountancy at Norwich Cathedral Priory', *TRHS*, 5th ser., 12 (1962), 25–48; R. Graham, *English Ecclesiastical Studies* (London, 1929), 255; D. Postles, 'The Perception of Profit Before the Leasing of Demesnes', *Agricultural History Review*, 34 (1986), 12–16.

[15] Altschul, *A Baronial Family in Medieval England*, 227–8.

given. The most notorious is that of Adam Stratton, exchequer official and moneylender, who controlled the Forz estates in the late 1270s and 1280s. He, however, was untypical, for he did not hold the actual title of steward. He dominated the countess's administration, operating more as a financier than as the type of official described in the *Seneschaucy*.[16]

Historians have, very rightly, stressed that the thirteenth century was an age of direct management. Yet there were estates that did not follow this general trend. Just as the Provisions of Westminster of 1259 deal with the problem of bailiffs who did not render their accounts, so it also dealt with those who leased lands and engaged in asset-stripping.[17] This shows that leasing was still common. One great landlord, the crown, found it much the easiest way to run its estates. For all its administrative resources, the crown did not have the capacity to engage in the direct management of demesnes, and crown lands were leased out. A brief experiment took place in 1275, when three stewards were appointed to run these estates. A few manors were taken into direct management, but the scheme foundered. The stewards faced great difficulties, not least because of the non-cooperation of many sheriffs, and the system was abandoned in 1282.[18] Some estates belonging to the abbey of Bec were leased out in the mid-thirteenth century, and St Paul's in London consistently farmed out its manors, using members of the monastic community as farmers.[19] Canterbury cathedral priory used a similar system, and the manors remained leased, mostly to individual monks, until 1282. A change to direct management was prompted by the view of Archbishop Pecham, rather than by economic considerations. The monks who farmed the demesnes had to be brought back into the community. Interestingly, after the change the manors yielded less than they had before.[20]

One alternative approach to direct management was to try to increase rents. At some point in the first half of the thirteenth century the earl of Oxford compelled his villeins at Whitchurch in Buckinghamshire to rent the manor from him for £49 a year, for a fifteen-year term. Since the manor was valued at £23 15s. 10d., it is not surprising that this deal was against their will.[21] Two proofs of age taken in 1297 saw men recall a date because it was then that they agreed to take land on leases, in one case of sixteen years, and in the other

---

[16] Denholm-Young, *Seigneurial Administration*, 75–85. [17] *DBM* 146–7.
[18] Prestwich, *Edward I*, 103.
[19] M. Morgan, *The English Lands of the Abbey of Bec* (Oxford, 1946), 44–5; A. Jones, 'Caddington, Kensworth, and Dunstable in 1297', *EcHR*, 2nd ser., 32 (1979), 317–18.
[20] Mate, 'The Farming Out of Manors', 335–6.
[21] *CIM* i, no. 629.

twenty.[22] The accounts for the earl of Cornwall's estates for 1296/7 show many manors under direct management, but also Ilchester (Somerset) farmed out for £19 10s., Hambleden (Bucks.) for £60, Whitchurch (Oxon.) for £30, Stratton (Cornwall) for £27 10s. 1¾d., and Carhayes (Cornwall) for £27 2d. Elsewhere on the Cornwall estates, demesnes had been leased; at Tewington, it had even been possible to lease 46 acres of wasteland for a six-year term.[23]

The evidence of the money that men received from land suggests that the thirteenth century was a period of rising revenues and profits, and that the fourteenth in contrast saw stable or declining incomes. Comparisons are inevitably difficult to make since they involve using sources of different types. At Westminster, the abbey's net income in the late twelfth century has been estimated at £739 a year. At the end of the thirteenth century the figure was about £1,641.[24] For Ely, estimates suggest an income of £920 about 1170, £1,930 in the 1250s, and £2,550 by the end of the thirteenth century.[25] Profit calculations suggest that it was rare to make a loss, but that there was considerable volatility in the figures.[26] Such increases in the thirteenth century reflect an increase in the size of the estates, through purchase and other means. Inflation also provides a reason for the increase. Was it also the case that the direct management of estates led to better farming, and so increased incomes?

FARMING METHODS

There is an impressive quantity of evidence about the way in which thirteenth-century demesnes were farmed. There were considerable variations in different parts of the country. Cropping systems, for example, were adopted that suited particular terrains. The north and west saw a concentration upon oats, while in Norfolk much barley was grown.[27] Taken as a whole, the evidence can be interpreted in different ways. One scenario is that the thirteenth century saw arable farming extended so far that, under the pressure of a rising population, increasingly poor soil was brought under cultivation in highly marginal areas. The effects of this, combined with soil exhaustion on lands that had been long under the plough, was that yields deteriorated. 'People found that they had reached the limits of the land's productivity; not only because they were reclaiming new, poor soils, but also because they had been cultivating old

---

[22] *CIPM* iii, nos. 432, 435.
[23] *Ministers' Accounts of the Earldom of Cornwall*, ed. Midgley, i. 78, 91, 99; ii. 243–4, 247.
[24] Harvey, *Westminster Abbey and its Estates*, 63.
[25] E. Miller, *The Abbey and Bishopric of Ely* (Cambridge, 1951), 94.
[26] Postles, 'The Perception of Profit Before the Leasing of Demesnes', 19–21.
[27] Campbell, *English Seigniorial Agriculture*, 249–305, analyses cropping systems in detail.

land for too long.'[28] An alternative view is that the pressure of population drove people to find ways of improving the productivity of the land by adopting more intensive methods of agriculture. This suggests that, at least in some parts of the country, notably in parts of Kent and East Anglia, the thirteenth century saw the development of progressive, intensive methods of agriculture, well adjusted to meet the challenges of the age. Increased specialization and commercialization, together with some diversification, meant that the challenges were not insuperable.[29]

One measure that might demonstrate an intensification of agriculture in the thirteenth century is a move from a two-field rotation, which saw 50 per cent of the land left fallow each year, to a three-field, with one-third fallow. 'The change to a three-field system was a symptom of population pressure and the need for more grain,' wrote one historian.[30] In fact, there are only ten known cases of this change occurring before 1350. The different systems were characteristic of different regions of England, and there was little shift from one to the other. Nor, since the more intensive three-field system was likely to produce lower yields per acre, was there necessarily a major advantage to it.[31] The basic field structures changed little, though there is no doubt that the thirteenth century saw more and more land put under the plough.

The evidence for investment by landlords in their estates suggests that exploitation, rather than improvement, was the normal policy. Relatively little was spent on new manorial buildings such as barns and mills, on land reclamation, on new farming equipment, or even purchase of stock. Figures, admittedly somewhat crude, suggest that such capital expenditure was unlikely to rise above 5 per cent on great estates. It was markedly lower that that on the earl of Cornwall's manors in 1296. Nor do the estate treatises such as the *Seneschaucy* or that by Walter of Henley suggest that landlords should invest in order to improve their lands.[32] Purchase of new lands was seen as a better investment than improvement of existing ones. A summary of the expenditure for which Henry of Eastry was responsible, as prior of Canterbury cathedral priory from 1285 to 1331, may not be entirely typical, but provides an interesting example. £1,343 went on purchase of lands, rents, meadows, and mills; £360 went on land reclamation and protection from the sea; just £111 was

---

[28] M. M. Postan, *Essays on Medieval Agriculture and General Problems of the Medieval Economy* (Cambridge, 1973), 15.

[29] J. Hatcher and M. Bailey, *Modelling the Middle Ages* (Oxford, 2001), 21–65, 121–56, discusses these alternative models.

[30] H. E. Hallam, *Rural England 1066–1348* (Glasgow, 1981), 117.

[31] H. S. A. Fox, 'The Alleged Transformation from Two-Field to Three-Field Systems in Medieval England', *EcHR*, 2nd ser., 39 (1986), 526–48.

[32] R. H. Hilton, *The English Peasantry in the Later Middle Ages* (Oxford, 1975), 178–80, 184–90.

spent on marling so as to improve the land. Repairs to manorial buildings came to a much more impressive figure, £3,739. Royal taxation of various kinds took £4,611, and costs of litigation at Rome and in courts in England and Ireland a similar sum, £4,624.[33]

Capital investment was not necessarily required for land to be profitable. The estates of Isabella de Forz, countess of Devon, provide a good case study. Between 1260 and 1292 her estates were efficiently and effectively run. Although there were no major investments, buildings were maintained, ditches were dug, and fences were repaired. Manuring and marling took place regularly. On some of her manors up to a fifth of the acreage was given over to peas and beans. Large sheep flocks meant that in 1277 almost half her income came from the sale of wool. There were effective controls on the estate officials, and opportunities were taken to increase income from the peasantry in the form of entry fines and other charges.[34] The results of effective management at Isabella's manor of Little Humber were particularly striking. There, much attention was paid to spreading the manure from the many sheep. Legumes replaced oats as one of the main crops. Wheat yields responded remarkably, rising to over sixteen times the amount of seed sown in 1287, three and a half times as much as on the Winchester estates. That was exceptional.[35] Not all estates were well run, however. John de Barham sent a report to the king in 1300 about the lands of the recently deceased earl of Hereford in south Wales. 'There is a very fine and great lordship in those places, and, if well managed, they would be worth not less than 2,000 marks a year, but there have been bad and disloyal stewards and bailiffs, and the earl was lax.'[36] Development was very uneven, with parts of the country showing real signs of innovation, and others, away from the eastern counties, remaining conservative in agricultural method.

The extent to which horses were used in preference to oxen is an interesting indicator of agricultural advancement. By using horses for ploughing and carting farmers were able to reduce their costs. In East Anglia, on lay demesnes, horses made up 44 per cent of the working animals, the remainder being oxen, whereas the figure for the west midlands was 11 per cent, and that for the north 14 per cent. Of course, in some places oxen were at an advantage because they survive better than horses on rough pasture, but in broad terms the superior speed and stamina of horses meant that they were more efficient. There is an observable connection between an intensification of agriculture and

---

[33] Knowles, *Religious Orders*, i. 324–5.
[34] M. Mate, 'Profit and Productivity on the Estates of Isabella de Forz (1260–92), *EcHR*, 2nd ser., 33 (1980), 326–34.
[35] Ibid. 332.
[36] *CIM* i, no. 1870.

the greater use of horses. In this as in other ways, innovation and change came first to eastern England.[37]

Historians have paid most attention to the cultivation of arable, yet livestock farming was also of very great importance. The cattle and sheep of medieval England were of poor quality. Annual milk yields have been calculated at about 100–30 gallons per cow.[38] This is similar to the level produced by indigenous African cattle, and less than a tenth of what would be expected in modern Europe or America. Sheep were important as producers above all of wool, but also of milk and meat. As with cattle, the yield from each animal was very low, each sheep probably providing no more than a pound or two of wool. Improvement was possible. At Rimpton in Somerset only half the cows produced calves each year in the early thirteenth century, but by the second quarter of the fourteenth, the figure stood at almost nine out of ten. The number of piglets produced by each sow rose from an average of about seven and half in the second quarter of the thirteenth century to almost thirteen a century later. There were also improvements in the animal mortality rates on this manor. More efficient farming methods, with the construction of special sheep-houses and the establishment of specialized fattening pastures, were among the reasons for the improvement. The development of cheese-making showed how the estate was responding to market pressures.[39]

On large estates high farming made specialization possible. This was particularly the case with cattle and sheep. The earl of Lincoln operated vaccaries, units largely devoted to beef and dairy farming, in Lancashire.[40] The great Yorkshire Cistercian houses were able to specialize in wool production, and the Forz estates had their major sheep-farming operation in Holderness. Where a landlord had many manors, it was possible to move stock around. Thus in 1296/7 all of the cattle on the earl of Cornwall's Essex manor of Newport were transferred to Berkhamsted. On the Peterborough estates some manors concentrated on breeding cattle, then transferring animals to other manors.[41] Similar strategies might be applied to sheep. In the 1270s, for example, the abbey of Crowland introduced a system whereby the sheep on all the manors of

[37] J. Langdon, *Horses, Oxen and Technological Innovation: The Use of Draught Animals in English Farming from 1066 to 1500* (Cambridge, 1986), 93, 159–64, 268, 281.

[38] K. Biddick, *The Other Economy: Pastoral Economy on a Medieval Estate* (Berkeley and Los Angeles, 1989), 94–5.

[39] C. Thornton, 'Efficiency in Medieval Livestock Farming: The Fertility and Mortality of Herds and Flocks at Rimpton, Somerset, 1208–1349', in *TCE* iv. 31, 33–4, 43–6.

[40] M. A. Atkin, 'Land Use and Management in the Upland Demesne of the De Lacy Estate of Blackburnshire *c.* 1300', *Agricultural History Review*, 42 (1994), 1–19.

[41] *Ministers' Accounts of the Earldom of Cornwall*, ed. Midgley, ii. 25, 52. Biddick, *The Other Economy: Pastoral Economy on a Medieval Estate*, 84–6, discusses the movement of cattle on the Peterborough abbey estates.

the estate were centrally managed, and the Forz estates in Holderness operated along similar lines. Numbers might be very large. In the late thirteenth century Isabella de Forz had some 7,000 sheep on her Holderness estates. On one manor alone on the Crowland estates, that of Langtoft, there were about 2,000 sheep in the 1270s. The assessment of the ecclesiastical tax of 1291 indicates that Abbey Dore had 2,790 sheep, Tintern abbey 3,260, Neath abbey 4,204, and Margam abbey 5,244. The small house of Bolton priory had 1,215 sheep on its manors in the late 1290s, rising to over 3,500 by 1310. By that date Crowland abbey had approaching 7,000 sheep on its manors.[42]

Sheep and cattle, however, were very vulnerable to a range of diseases. In 1258 at Wellingborough in Northamptonshire sixty out of seventy-six sheep died, and mortality was high on the other Crowland manors. An outbreak of murrain that began in the mid-1270s and continued into the 1280s was very serious. One contemporary view was that it had its origins in the import of a sick Spanish sheep. One suggestion is that it was sheep scab, which destroys the fleece and eventually kills the animal. Declining average fleece weights were one consequence of the disease.[43] Purchases of various ointments are unlikely to have been of much value as a preventive. On the great Holderness sheep farms mortality was about 55 per cent, and there was a similar story elsewhere.[44] The disease was said to have plagued England for twenty-eight years; once it had passed, fleece weights began to recover rapidly. With wool exports booming, the first years of the fourteenth century were good for sheep-farming. Difficult times for animal husbandry came in the aftermath of the famine years of 1315–16, when flocks and herds were ravaged by disease. Sheep were affected nationally by what was very possibly liver-fluke. At Bolton it reduced the flocks to fewer than 1,000. However, a fairly swift recovery was possible, and by 1324 numbers had increased to just over 2,000. It was perhaps because of this vulnerability to disease, and the consequent high level of risk involved in large-scale sheep-farming, that the managers at Crowland abbey decided to abandon the enterprise in 1314, leaving no more than a few sheep on the central estate and none on the outlying manors. Cattle also succumbed to disease, thought to be rinderpest, on a massive scale between 1319 and 1321. At Broughton on the Ramsey abbey estates forty-eight cattle died in 1319–20,

---

[42] Denholm-Young, *Seignorial Administration*, 59; F. M. Page, ' "Bidentes Hoylandie" (A Mediæval Sheep-Farm)', *Economic History*, 1 (1926–9), 605, 611; *Taxatio Ecclesiastica Angliae et Walliae auctoritate P. Nicholai IV*, ed. J. Caley (London, 1802), 174, 282–4; M. J. Stephenson, 'Wool Yields in the Medieval Economy', *EcHR*, 2nd ser., 41 (1988), 385.

[43] Stephenson, 'Wool Yields', 381; Rishanger, 84.

[44] *Wellingborough Manorial Accounts*, ed. F. M. Page (Northamptonshire Record Society, 1936), 3, 36–7, 57; Page, 'Bidentes Hoylandie', 609; Denholm-Young, *Seignorial Administration*, 60–1; *Agrarian History*, ii. 410.

leaving six alive. Twenty per cent of the herd was lost at Clipstone in Nottinghamshire in 1318–19, and 40 per cent in the following year. In the next year twenty-three out of twenty-five cows at Sheen succumbed to the disease.[45]

THE FOURTEENTH CENTURY

The relatively buoyant conditions of the thirteenth century did not last. Times began to change in the 1290s. Poor harvests were partly to blame, but heavy war taxation and purveyance were also significant elements. In the second decade of the fourteenth century the heavy rains of 1315–16, followed by the severe murrains affecting both cattle and sheep, made matters far worse. The monetary situation was difficult. There had been a rapid burst of inflation in the first decade of the fourteenth century, fuelled by imports of silver coin in payment for massive wool exports, but in the following years imports dried up and there was an increasing shortage of coin.[46] It is clear that in some places there was a measure of recovery in the 1320s and 1330s, but thereafter war with France meant renewed heavy taxation and other burdens on the countryside.

One suggestion is that the thirteenth-century expansion of agriculture had gone so far that land was beginning to be exhausted. Grain yields provide one possible way to measure the decline in agricultural productivity. These have been worked out in exhaustive detail for the Winchester estates. There were great differences between individual manors, but the averages reveal a decline by 1300 from the levels attained seventy years previously. It was very rare to get a return of five times the quantity of seed sown.[47] Figures for the early fourteenth century were severely affected by the famine years of 1315–16, but if they are ignored, there was no major change in that period to productivity on the Winchester estates. Evidence from Norfolk and Suffolk does not suggest falling yields, and in the south-west, on the Tavistock estates, yields in the years before the Black Death were excellent. However, there are cases of individual manors where the land exhaustion hypothesis is more persuasive. At Cuxham in Oxfordshire there was a perceptible decline between 1300 and 1350. Detailed modelling of the likely effect of medieval agriculture on the soil there, taking due account of such variables as the amount of dung produced by

---

[45] I. Kershaw, *Bolton Priory: The Economy of a Northern Monastery 1286–1325* (Oxford, 1973), 80; Page, 'Bidentes Hoylandie', 608; I. Kershaw, 'The Agrarian Crisis in England 1315–1322', *Past and Present*, 59 (1973), 24–5.

[46] M. Mate, 'High Prices in Early Fourteenth-Century England: Causes and Consequences', *EcHR*, 2nd ser., 28 (1975), 1–16.

[47] J. Z. Titow, *Winchester Yields: A Study in Medieval Agricultural Productivity* (Cambridge, 1972); D. L. Farmer, 'Prices and Wages', in *Agrarian History*, ii. 721–3, 738.

medieval cattle and the quantity of nitrogen fixed by legumes, has suggested that it is likely that the land suffered from a phosphorus deficiency, with a resultant effect on the growth of cereal crops.[48] Accounts for the lay manor of Bourchier Hall in Essex are also suggestive. There, the land cultivated under a three-course rotation of wheat, oats, and fallow was showing clear signs of exhaustion. In 1339, for example, oats were sown on top of winter wheat that failed to grow. In the early 1350s yields were at appallingly low levels for both wheat and oats. In response, the manorial officials left much of the better land fallow to give it time to recover, and sowed oats on poorer land that had been used for pasture. In the mid-1350s the traditional rotation was abandoned. The acreage sown fell from 253 acres around 1340 to 137 acres in the 1350s.[49] It seems likely that there was considerable regional and even local variation, with the midlands particularly badly affected.

Further evidence for soil exhaustion comes from the inquiries into the failure of the tax of 1341, the so-called Inquisitions of the Ninth. The jurors in Ivinghoe in Buckinghamshire reported that over 400 acres were not cultivated 'because of the debility of the land'. In Stokehamond 30 acres that used to be ploughed now lay uncultivated. At Mulbrook in Bedfordshire half the land was not ploughed because it was sandy and could only grow rye at best. Poor soil, however, was not the only reason given. In some cases it was said to be because of the poverty of the tenants that the land was not tilled. The geographical distribution of abandoned land was curious: Sussex, Bedfordshire, Buckinghamshire, Cambridgeshire, Shropshire, and the North Riding.[50] It may be that for some reason it was only in those regions that the commissioners were ready to accept this particular excuse for the low receipts from the tax from local jurors, and that the inquiries do not reflect the true distribution of abandoned land. The inquiries do suggest that there was a widespread belief that much land was so debilitated that it was no longer fit for cultivation, even though the statistics for grain yields do not support the view that there was a major shift in productivity.

In the circumstances of the first half of the fourteenth century it began to make sense to move away from direct management of the demesnes to a system where they were farmed out. Landlords, faced by what they saw as unfavour-

---

[48] *Agrarian History*, ii. 292, 394; E. I. N. Newman and P. D. A. Harvey, 'Did Soil Fertility Decline in Medieval English Farms? Evidence from Cuxham, Oxfordshire, 1320–1340', *Agricultural History Review*, 45 (1997), 119–36.

[49] R. H. Britnell, 'Agricultural Technology and the Margin of Cultivation in the Fourteenth Century', *EcHR*, 2nd ser., 30 (1977), 53–66.

[50] *Nonarum Inquisitiones* (London, 1807), 11, 14, 326, 337; A. H. R. Baker, 'Evidence in the "Nonarum Inquisitiones" of Contracting Arable Lands in England During the Early Fourteenth Century', *EcHR*, 2nd ser., 19 (1966), 518–32.

able conditions, might prefer to settle for the relative security of fixed rents rather than taking the risks involved in direct management. Yet the position was not clear-cut. If it had been, the change would have been both swifter and more universal. Landlords and tenants needed to have very different assumptions for it to take place. The former would calculate that his likely revenues would be higher if he farmed out a manor for rent; at the same time, the latter would have to estimate that he was likely to make a profit after paying the agreed farm. This clearly happened in the case of the Merton College manor of Ibstone. In 1299/1300 the manor made no profit. In the next year it made £7 17s. 11¾d. From 1303/4 Ibstone was farmed out for £10 a year.[51]

The date of the change from direct farming to leasing was very different on different estates. At Durham six estates were leased in the 1290s, and of the priory's twenty-two manors, only eight were continuously under direct management in the years 1290–1325.[52] At Worcester the bishopric estates were surveyed in about 1290, and an attempt made to calculate the profitability of the demesnes. Worries were not alleviated by the results, and a reduction in the number of ploughs was recommended. More dramatic measures were taken in 1312, when the bishop ordered the leasing of barren and inconveniently sited demesnes. Even then, change took time. The first Worcester manor was not leased out until 1318, and it was not until 1339 that a large manor went the same way.[53] At Christ Church Canterbury, where direct management had been introduced very late, it was not until the mid-1350s that many manors were leased, and in many cases they were taken back into demesne in the next decade.[54] At Westminster the first lease of a manor took place in 1352/3, for a twenty-year period, but it was not clear until the 1370s that a fundamental change was taking place. On the estates of the archbishop of Canterbury the switch to leasing did not take place until the last twenty years of the fourteenth century.[55] The evidence is not confined to ecclesiastical estates, though they do provide the bulk of it. Thomas of Lancaster's accounts for 1313/14 show evidence of extensive leasing. On the honour of Tutbury, for example, it was only at Tutbury itself that the demesne was run directly.[56] On the Clare estates, on the other hand, leasing of the demesnes did not begin until the 1360s.[57]

[51] Postles, 'The Perception of Profit Before the Leasing of Demesnes', 21.
[52] R. A. Lomas, 'The Priory of Durham and its Demesnes in the Fourteenth and Fifteenth Centuries', *EcHR*, 2nd ser., 31 (1978), 341, 345.
[53] C. Dyer, *Lords and Peasants in a Changing Society: The Estates of the Bishopric of Worcester, 680–1540* (Cambridge, 1980), 82.
[54] Mate, 'The Farming Out of Manors', 337.
[55] Harvey, *Westminster Abbey and its Estates*, 150–1; du Boulay, *Lordship of Canterbury*, 220–1.
[56] Maddicott, *Thomas of Lancaster*, 31.
[57] Holmes, *Estates of the Higher Nobility*, 92.

A small Derbyshire landlord, Henry of Kniveton, began leasing parcels of land in the late thirteenth century, with the process accelerating after 1300. In his case, he was probably driven by debt. It is striking that his later leases were often for long terms, in two cases forty years, which suggests that he was not optimistic that times would improve.[58] In broad terms the change to farming out reflects a slowing down, or reverse, of the process of economic expansion. It is also possible that improved accounting methods, themselves a product of direct management, contributed to its decline as they made it simpler for lords to work out that they were not making profits on the scale they expected.

Some landlords found the changed conditions of the fourteenth century difficult, but in most cases they proved able to adjust, keeping revenues at a reasonable level. Indeed, in some cases, such as Christ Church Canterbury, there were significant profits to be made from the high grain prices of the famine years. At Ely the temporalities were valued for taxation purposes at £2000 a year in 1291, exactly the same figure at which the vacant see was farmed in 1337, which suggests that no great change had taken place. Calculations from the vacancy accounts of 1298/9, however, indicate that there was then a net income of about £2,500, so there may well have been some decline in the early years of the fourteenth century.[59] Beaulieu abbey took the unpopular step of enclosing some wasteland in the New Forest in the 1320s, a move that shows that the house was trying to increase its income by a policy of expanding the area under cultivation.[60] Many lay estates saw steps taken to deal with a declining income from arable land: on the Clare estates a clear decision was taken in the 1330s to develop sheep-farming. Accounts for the late 1330s show that there were healthy profits to be made.[61] The Berkeleys switched the emphasis of much of their estate activity from arable to sheep pasture from the 1330s. By the middle of the century the earl of Arundel had 6,549 sheep on his estates in the Welsh marches, and 8,625 in Sussex.[62] In the great lordships of Wales and the marches, landlords were able to bring in substantially increased incomes. Sheep and cattle were profitable, but it was above all by increasing the level of judicial activity that lords were able to push up their revenues. In the 1340s about 20 per cent of the revenues from the earl of Arundel's lordship of Chirk came in this way. A range of arbitrarily imposed local taxes provided another means by which the Welsh tenantry were

[58] *The Kniveton Ledger*, ed. A. Saltman (London, 1977), pp. xxiv, 225–72. Nos. 496 and 516 were for forty years.
[59] Miller, *Abbey and Bishopric of Ely*, 81.
[60] *CPR 1324–7*, 67.
[61] Holmes, *Estates of the Higher Nobility*, 89–90, 145–7.
[62] Given-Wilson, *English Nobility in the Later Middle Ages*, 125–6.

exploited unmercifully. In 1350 the men of Chirk were fined just over £100 for breaking into their lord's park, a huge sum for such an offence.[63]

The Black Death transformed the economic situation. Labour costs rose sharply in the short term, despite the attempts of the government to hold them down, and patterns of demand shifted radically as a result of the fall in population. Prices for manufactured goods rose. The new circumstances were more difficult for landlords. Yet there is every indication that they were able to develop effective stratagems to ensure that their incomes were not much affected. One was what has been termed a 'feudal reaction', a reimposition of labour services, which had, in most cases, been long since commuted for cash payments. Such a policy could not be maintained in the long term, but might prove effective in the immediate circumstances of the 1350s. Another technique was to raise the level of fines imposed in the manorial courts. Every effort was made to maintain the level of rents. Entry fines charged on new tenants were a useful source of revenue. One estimate is that by the 1370s income was not even as much as 10 per cent lower than it had been in the 1340s.[64] What made most sense, especially in the longer term, was to lease out lands, and more and more landlords turned to this. The position of the great landlords was threatened, but they proved well capable of adjusting to the new conditions of the world after the Black Death. This was an astonishingly resilient society, and one in which the established order was hard to change. In the longer term, however, the effects of the epidemic of 1348 and the subsequent outbreaks would be immense.

[63] Davies, *Conquest, Coexistence and Change*, 402–3; Davies, *Lordship and Society in the March of Wales*, 124–5.
[64] Holmes, *Estates of the Higher Nobility*, 114.

CHAPTER 17

The Peasantry

According to Robert Mannyng of Brunne, admittedly a biased witness, ordinary Englishmen, given good food and drink, were as handsome as the nobility. They had excellent fair, clear complexions, and had an attractive smell.[1] The great majority of such ordinary people in this period were peasants. They were the bedrock of the economy. It was they who were the producers, growing the corn, tending the herds and the flocks. Their labours were the basis of the economic growth of the thirteenth century, and in the fourteenth it was they who were in the front line, facing the problems of famine, animal murrain, and plague. It would be wrong, however, to idealize them. For the most part, the records suggest that they were ungenerous, suspicious, highly litigious, as well as downtrodden. Theirs was a miserable existence. Farming was difficult. Crops produced very poor yields, and animals were all too liable to disease. It would have been hard enough to scratch a living from a peasant holding without any additional burdens, but exactions in the form of labour services and money payments added to the hardship.[2]

Broadly speaking, peasants lived in villages, worked on manors, and worshipped in parishes. In many instances village, manor, and parish were effectively one and the same, but this was not invariably the case. Manors in different parts of the country were very different things. In some instances there were two or even three manors in one village. Linwood and South Carlton, small Lincolnshire villages, for example, each had two manors. In contrast, the west midland manor of Halesowen contained twelve separate settlements. The great Yorkshire manor of Wakefield was divided into eleven units, geographically dispersed into four separate groups.[3] The village appears

---

[1] Quoted by T. Summerfield, *The Matter of Kings' Lives* (Amsterdam, 1998), 269 n. 30.

[2] For a general discussion of the peasantry, P. R. Schofield, *Peasant and Community in Medieval England 1200–1500* (Basingstoke, 2003).

[3] P. L. Everson, C. C. Taylor, and C. J. Dunn, *Change and Continuity: Rural Settlement in North-West Lincolnshire* (London, 1991), 68, 127; Z. Razi, *Life, Marriage and Death in a Medieval Parish: Economy, Society and Demography in Halesowen 1270–1400* (Cambridge, 1980), 5–6; *The Court Rolls of the Manor of Wakefield from October 1331 to September 1333*, ed. S. S. Walker (Yorkshire Archaeological Society, 1983), p. xiv and map between pp. xvii and xviii.

in much less sharp a focus from the sources than does the manor. Villages did not have privileges like those of towns, but the village community was nonetheless important. Within the manor of Wakefield the individual villages had their own meetings, and made their own by-laws, which were needed to organize the communal system of farming. Equally, where a village contained several manors, the village community might meet as a whole. For certain matters, notably the recruitment of infantry troops and the collection of taxes, the crown dealt with villages rather than with manors.[4] The parish structure of England was largely fixed by the twelfth century. Some might be very large, such as the Berkshire parish of Sonning, 11 miles in length. This meant that many villages might be provided for by a dependent chapel, rather than a parish church.[5]

The peasant household was usually small; this was not a society in which large extended families lived together. This is not the traditional conclusion; it used to be commonly thought that households contained extended families, with three generations living under the same roof, but few historians would now support such a view. Evidence is scant and often difficult to interpret, but it largely points to a norm of two-generational families, of a couple with three or perhaps four children. Spalding priory provides some unique evidence, for it conducted inquiries in the mid-thirteenth century into the villein population, which sought details of the children. An entry for the village of Weston reads: 'John Wisman had two daughters and two sons, namely Thomas and Richard, who hold land, Beta who is married in Spalding, and Elena who is a vagabond.' There has been argument over whether these lists are censuses or genealogies; they do not fit either description accurately. They do, however, show an average of 3.54 children for each couple, and strongly suggest that households did not comprise extended families.[6] Legal records point in the same direction. In the 1240s criminals went to the houses of Walter and Hugh Wyk in Littleton Pannell, Wiltshire. Walter and Hugh were killed, as were their wives. Walter had two children, Hugh one. A similar attack on Richard and Agnes Bat in Warminster resulted in the death of the couple's daughter; this was a household of three. In Melksham, Nicholas Cok, his wife, and two daughters were all found murdered in their house.[7] The household in most cases was the same as

---

[4] C. Dyer, 'The English Medieval Village Community and its Decline', *Journal of British Studies*, 33 (1994), 407–16; W. O. Ault, *Open Field Farming in Medieval England* (London, 1972), 66.

[5] R. Bartlett, *England Under the Norman and Angevin Kings 1075–1225* (Oxford, 2000), 378–84; A. D. Brown, *Popular Piety in Late Medieval England: The Diocese of Salisbury 1250–1550* (Oxford, 1995), 68–70.

[6] E. D. Jones, 'Death by Document: A Re-appraisal of Spalding Priory's Census Evidence for the 1260s', *Nottingham Medieval Studies*, 39 (1995), 66.

[7] *Crown Pleas of the Wiltshire Eyre*, ed. Meekings, nos. 176, 211, 444.

the family, with a mean size of about four and a half to five, though some wealthier peasants might have servants living with them.[8] Evidence of people receiving criminals also suggests that some peasants, particularly widows, may have taken in lodgers.

FREE AND UNFREE

The peasantry was not an undifferentiated group. One fundamental distinction was between the free and unfree. To be unfree was to be a villein, liable to perform labour services for a lord. There were also distinctions based on the size and type of holding. Thus there were virgaters, who held a virgate, and cottars, who held a cottage tenement. The *famuli* were peasants who worked on the demesne, largely in return for renders of food, and who often held no land worth speaking of.[9] These were not the only landless men; there were many who eked out a precarious living working when they could for pay or other rewards. If the peasant community is analysed in terms of wealth, then there was a very great variation between the wealthiest in a village and the poorest. There were, inevitably, also substantial regional variations. Most striking was Kent, where villeinage was effectively unknown. In broad terms, eastern England saw far more freedom among the peasantry than did the midland and southern counties.

An analysis that relies on distinctions in terms of wealth fits uneasily with one that emphasizes legal status, for many villeins were better off than free-holders. Nor does the performance of labour services provide a clear differentiation, for many villeins were able to commute their services for a cash payment. Some historians therefore lay little stress on the question of freedom and villeinage, or unfreedom.[10] In theory, however, the disadvantages of being unfree were immense. A villein was his lord's chattel, to be disposed of as he willed. He was bound to the soil, and if his tenement was sold, he was sold with it. His property was his lord's property. Villeins, said the abbot of Burton in 1280, could own nothing except their bellies.[11] Accordingly, villeins could not sell the land they occupied without the lord's consent. If their land was passed on to their heir, then a death duty, known as heriot, was to be paid. This was

[8] Schofield, *Peasant and Community*, 83–4.

[9] M. M. Postan, *The Famulus: The Estate Labourer in the xiith and xiiith Centuries*, Economic History Review, suppl. 2 (1954).

[10] See e.g. J. A. Raftis, *Peasant Economic Development Within the English Manorial System* (Stroud, 1997), where discussion on pp. 96 and 126–7 implies that the question is of no great importance.

[11] P. R. Hyams, *Kings, Lords and Peasants in Medieval England* (Oxford, 1980), 19. This discussion of the legal position of villeins relies heavily on this important book. See also E. B. Fryde, *Peasants and Landlords in Later Medieval England* (Stroud, 1996), 17–25.

paid out of the deceased's goods; the incoming tenant would have to pay an entry fine before he could take over the holding. A fine, merchet, had to be paid for a villein to obtain permission for his daughter to marry. Villeins could not bring cases before the royal courts, but were subject solely to their lord's jurisdiction. There were other restrictions: normally, villeins were compelled to take their corn to the lord's mill, rather than using their own handmills. There was also a social stigma attached to the unfree. The tenants of East and West Rainton in County Durham were forbidden from calling any of their number a serf under pain of payment of a fine of £1.[12]

There could, however, be advantages to holding land as a villein. Population pressure in the thirteenth century meant that many holdings were subdivided. This, however, was easier to do in the case of free land than where land was held by villein tenure. On some ecclesiastical estates in particular, unfree holdings were not subjected to the same fragmentation and division as other land. In Cambridgeshire and on lay estates in Huntingdonshire in 1279 only about 10 per cent of villeins held 20 acres or more, whereas on ecclesiastical estates in the latter county about 30 per cent of villeins fell into this category. Customary rents paid by villeins might be lower than those paid by free tenants. In such ways some villeins were protected to an extent from the stresses of market forces.[13]

There were many complexities that resulted from the legal distinction that existed between personal servile status and servile tenure. It was even possible for serfs to acquire free landholdings. Marriage between people of free and servile status could create legal tangles. On lands categorized as ancient demesne, meaning that the crown had held them at the time of Domesday Book, servile tenants had far greater rights, including access to the king's courts, than serfs had elsewhere.

Although villeinage was not always as severe in practice as in theory, it undoubtedly mattered. The many cases that came up in court in which men tried to prove that they were free demonstrate this all too clearly. The line between free and villein was often difficult to draw, for there was no single easy test. Lords could bring an action of naifty to try to prove that someone was a villein. The alleged villein could counter this by obtaining a writ of *monstravit*. The issue would be determined by demonstrating the status of the man's relations, or the nature of the services performed. Although a villein could not bring cases in the royal courts, it was possible for him to start an action.

---

[12] *Halmota Prioratus Dunelmensis*, ed. W. H. Longstaffe and J. Booth (Surtees Society, 82, 1889), 33.
[13] J. Kanzaka, 'Villein Rents in Thirteenth-Century England: An Analysis of the Hundred Rolls of 1279–1280', *EcHR* 55 (2002), 593–618.

The lord would then claim him as a villein, and the court would determine whether or not he was of free status.

Petty restrictions on the unfree were often evaded. One enterprising early fourteenth-century Suffolk villein even erected his own mill in his garden, for the use of himself and his neighbours.[14] Villeins were not excluded from all public life. Serfdom was not slavery; a villein was unfree in relation to his lord, but not with regard to other people. They were protected by the criminal law. They may not have been able to sue in royal courts, but they served on coroner's juries, and on assizes of weights and measures. They frequently appeared in royal courts as defendants and as pledges. They were recruited to serve in royal armies, though there was no question of their being able to attain knightly status like the unfree *ministeriales* of Germany. Court rolls show that the restrictions on villein mobility could be circumvented. There was significant immigration and emigration. On the estates of Ramsey abbey it was normal practice to allow villeins to move elsewhere, provided they paid an annual fine of two chickens.[15] The effects of this policy have been analysed for the village of Broughton, where the results show, not surprisingly, that most connections were with other villages within a few miles. Ten per cent of Broughton's incomers, however, came from over 25 miles away.[16]

The lives of the peasantry were carefully regulated, partly by their lords and the officials who represented them, partly by the Church, and partly by their own communal actions and decisions. The cultivation of the great open fields of, above all, the midland counties demanded cooperation rather than individualism. The business of manorial courts, which varied in the extent of their jurisdiction and the frequency of their meetings, was carefully recorded, and the rolls that were produced provide a remarkable insight into the lives of the humble.[17] Although a great many manorial court records survive, they are no more than a very small fraction of the total that were drawn up. There is much disagreement among historians over how these rolls can be used. To use them merely as a source of anecdotes lacks rigour, but as a source of figures for statistical analysis the rolls leave much to be desired. It cannot be assumed that they were drawn up in the same way over long periods of time, for manorial officials and policies changed over the years. The kinds of cases that came up in

[14] M. Bailey, *A Marginal Economy? East Anglian Breckland in the Later Middle Ages* (Cambridge, 1989), 136.
[15] J. A. Raftis, *Tenure and Mobility: Studies in the Social History of the Medieval English Village* (Toronto, 1964), 139–41.
[16] E. Britton, *The Community of the Vill: A Study in the History of the Family and Village Life in Fourteenth-Century England* (Toronto, 1977), 180–3.
[17] For selections of cases from these courts, see *Select Pleas in Manorial and Other Seignorial Courts*, i, ed. F. W. Maitland (Selden Society, 2, 1888); *Select Cases in Manorial Courts 1250–1550*, ed. L. R. Poos and L. Bonfield (Selden Society, 114, 1997).

these courts ranged widely. Many related to the inheritance or sale of land. People might be fined if their animals were found on the lord's land: in 1340 at Walsham le Willows in Suffolk 6*d*. was levied from Robert Walpole as his pigs had trespassed in this way. One entry recorded a fine of a penny on Robert Payn the shoemaker, for unlawfully keeping a penny that belonged to Walter Cooper. Cooper was likewise fined as he had kept a penny that belonged to Payn. For defaming the reeve, the culprit was fined 6*d*. The reeve himself was fined 3*s*. 4*d*. for removing 3*d*. worth of straw from the lord's mill to his own house.[18]

Very substantial tracts of land were subject to forest law, and this imposed further limitations on the activities of those of the peasantry who lived within the bounds of the forest. The forest offered opportunities, such as those for cutting and selling wood, but very many were fined for doing this illicitly. Over 300, for example, were charged with these offences in Wychwood Forest in 1272, and fines totalled £27 8*s*. 4*d*. Assarting, or clearing land within the forest, was widely practised by the peasantry, who were duly fined. Poaching was, for many peasants, no doubt a temptation, but for some it may well have been a necessity, which was likely to bring them into court. It is clear that the lives of those who lived in the forest were closely supervised, but whether the opportunities presented by the forest outweighed the heavy hand of the law as applied by forest officials is impossible to determine.[19]

The labour services that villeins owed varied with local custom. Ploughing, sowing, harvesting, and carrying were central to the obligations. Additional boon works were usually requested at critical times of the year, and were normally rewarded with food. Work might be set in terms of days, or in terms of given amounts of work, *opera*. At Halesowen, where services were light, tenants had to plough for six days and sow for ten days a year. They also had to provide one day of boon work. At Crondal in Hampshire a range of duties were set out. Making heaps of manure, providing fencing around the manorial complex, carrying building materials, and supervising reapers were all required in addition to the normal ploughing, sowing, and reaping. The work did not all have to be done personally. One wealthy villein, Warren de Aula, who had a holding of over 60 acres, was to provide a dozen men for weeding, two men for loading carts, and three men at harvest.[20] On one manor on the St Albans estates the tenants had to collect mulberries as a boon work, and were given in return a feast that consisted of twenty-two white loaves, an oatmeal

---

[18] M. Bailey, (ed.), *The English Manor c.1200–c.1500* (Manchester, 2002), 199–200.
[19] J. Birrell, 'Forest Law and the Peasantry in the Later Thirteenth Century', in *TCE* ii. 149–63.
[20] *Hundred and Manor of Crondal*, pt. 1, ed. Baigent, 84–135.

dish, one sheep, and a dish of salt to flavour the food.[21] At Hartest, an Ely manor, a smallholder with 1 acre had to work on his lord's land every Monday save for red-letter days, weeding, reaping, ditching, digging, and doing other tasks, but not ploughing or harrowing. He also owed a hen at Christmas and an egg at Easter.[22] There was often little correlation between the size of a peasant holding and the level of services demanded. On the estates of Crowland abbey there was a great variation in service, and in many cases those with smallholdings owed much more than the wealthier peasants.[23] It was easier to exploit the weak than the strong. One unusual way of evading service was used in 1300 by Richard Eme, on the Winchester manor of Cheriton: he won his release in a game of chance. As reeve, he was in a favoured position.[24]

It was possible to substitute money payments for services; in many cases it made much more sense to hire labourers, rather than compel unwilling villagers to do labour services. If Warren de Aula did not want to supervise reaping in person, he could pay 1s. Robert de Brambesshate, another Crondal tenant, was to pay 2s in lieu of ploughing 4 acres in winter. At Lent he would pay 8d., instead of ploughing 2 acres.[25] At Battle abbey in 1310 calculations were made of the money value of services, making it possible to work out whether it was better to commute services and hire labourers with the money, or to continue to demand work from the tenants. In some cases the value of the meals provided to the tenants was so great that it was very clear that the lord was losing out significantly.[26] It was also the case that hired labourers worked more efficiently than did unwilling men performing customary services.[27]

The process of commuting services did not happen at an even pace across the country, nor did it take place steadily. There were periods when lords decided that services, once commuted, should be reimposed.[28] At Battle abbey during the thirteenth century there was some increase in services, but at the same time there was a tendency to commute them. On the manor of Marley, newly created by the abbey in the early fourteenth century, it was decided to

---

[21] A. E. Levett, *Studies in Manorial History* (Oxford, 1938), 195.

[22] Bailey (ed.), *English Manor*, 57.

[23] E. D. Jones, 'The Exploitation of its Serfs by Spalding Priory Before the Black Death', *Nottingham Medieval Studies*, 43 (1999), 149–50.

[24] *The Pipe Roll of the Bishopric of Winchester 1301–2*, ed. Page, 311–12.

[25] *Hundred and Manor of Crondal*, pt. 1, ed. Baigent, 95, 120, 125.

[26] E. Searle, *Lordship and Community: Battle Abbey and its Banlieu 1066–1538* (Toronto, 1974), 176–9.

[27] D. Stone, 'The Productivity of Hired and Customary Labour: Evidence from Wisbech Barton in the Fourteenth Century', *EcHR* 50 (1997), 640–55.

[28] M. M. Postan, 'The Chronology of Labour Services', in his *Essays on Medieval Agriculture and General Problems of the Medieval Economy* (Cambridge, 1978), 89–106, set out the general problems.

pay wages to all the labourers and to commute all labour services.[29] The Black Death of 1348 transformed relations between landlords and peasants, and while in some cases there was a short-term reaction with attempts to maintain or even reimpose labour services, the overall trend was to abandon such services.

THE LAND MARKET, WOMEN, AND THE LANDLESS

Inheritance customs varied in different parts of the country. Primogeniture, or inheritance by the eldest son, was used, as was ultimogeniture, known as 'borough English', where the youngest son took his father's land. Such rigid systems did not meet the needs of families, but partible inheritance was relatively uncommon. The strictness of inheritance customs meant that many villeins had to buy, sell, and lease land if they were to make a decent living. In 1282 the court roll of the manor of Crondal in Hampshire shows ten men making payments to the lord, in this case the monks of St Swithun's, Winchester, to have parcels of land of up to 5 acres, which had formed a single holding in the hands of one Richard Wisdom. The roll shows an active land market in operation, and vividly demonstrates the way in which single holdings were subdivided in the thirteenth century.[30] The legal framework within which the peasant land market operated was increasingly sophisticated. The manorial courts were strongly influenced by the way in which royal courts operated. It is striking how quickly arrangements similar to those envisaged in the clause *de donis* of Edward I's second Statute of Westminster came to be seen in manorial courts. The same is true of *Quia Emptores*. Forms of land tenure such as entails and joint tenancies, familiar from the land transactions of the nobility, find parallels in the hands of the peasantry.[31] It was, however, by custom rather than written law that these courts operated. That custom is hard to define. It comprised all the various practices that were agreed among the community, but might be governed by a sense of what was right in terms of those practices, rather than being determined purely by precedent.

There is much argument among historians about the detailed working of the peasant land market, but there is ample evidence that it was very active.[32] It was often in the interest of lords that peasants should buy, sell, and lease land.

---

[29] Searle, *Lordship and Community*, 167–80, 269.
[30] *Hundred and Manor of Crondal*, pt. 1, ed. Baigent, 145–6, 152–3.
[31] R. M. Smith, 'Women's Property Rights Under Customary Law: Some Developments in the Thirteenth and Fourteenth Centuries', *TRHS*, 5th ser., 36 (1986), 188; P. R. Hyams, 'What did Edwardian Villagers Understand by Law?' in Z. Razi and R. M. Smith (eds.), *Medieval Society and the Manor Court* (Oxford, 1996), 81.
[32] See P. D. A. Harvey's introduction to his edited volume *The Peasant Land Market in Medieval England* (Oxford, 1984), 1–28.

Profits were to be obtained from entry fines, and a vigorous land market meant that those who were most capable of paying rents and meeting their obligations acquired and enlarged holdings. Lords might, however, be reluctant to allow the disintegration of holdings that owed labour services. Despite this, the pressures of a rising population in the thirteenth century were inescapable, compelling peasants to buy land and divide holdings where they could so as to provide for increased numbers. One remarkable piece of evidence for the peasant land market survives in a Peterborough record, known as the *Carte Nativorum*, a collection of peasant charters of the mid- to late thirteenth century. These show both freehold and villein land being sold and leased.[33] By the mid-thirteenth century some villeins possessed seals, enabling them to authenticate their dealings in land.[34] Twelfth-century peasant holdings were often standardized in size; in many manors these were fragmented in the thirteenth through the operation of the land market, though the chronology of the break-up varied in different parts of the country. East Anglia appears to have witnessed the earliest development of a peasant land market, and it was there that the standard holdings can be most difficult to discern in the complex patchwork of late thirteenth-century land tenure.

The question of who bought and who sold land is complex.[35] The need to provide for younger sons was significant; fathers might buy land for this purpose. It may be that sellers were often those who did not have a substantial family to provide for. It is also likely that those with smallholdings who found it difficult to make ends meet were under pressure to sell. There tended, as a result, to be more sales in years when the harvest was bad. At Redgrave in Suffolk land transactions peaked in 1295 and in 1316–17, years of exceptionally low yields and high prices.[36] What is clear is that the effect of the land market in the thirteenth century was to build up a few big holdings and subdivide a large number of smaller ones.

The surviving sources inevitably reveal most about those peasants who held land. The majority of these were men; there is as a result less evidence about women than men. Peasant women were far from downtrodden, but widows and single women had greater legal independence than their married counterparts.

---

[33] '*Carta Nativorum*': *A Peterborough Abbey Cartulary of the Fourteenth Century*, ed. C. N. L. Brooke and M. M. Postan (Northamptonshire Record Society, 1960). Postan's introduction is reprinted in his *Essays on Medieval Agriculture*, 107–49.

[34] Hyams, *Kings, Lords and Peasants*, 47.

[35] For discussion, see R. M. Smith, 'Families and their Property in Rural England 1250–1688', in R. M. Smith (ed.), *Land, Kinship and Life-Cycle* (Cambridge, 1984), 6–21.

[36] R. M. Smith, 'Families and their Land in an Area of Partible Inheritance: Redgrave, Suffolk 1260–1320', in Smith (ed.), *Land, Kinship and Life-Cycle*, 154–5.

Widows were often able to maintain the family tenement, and there are even cases where wives appear to have been able to keep their own land, independently from their husbands. Gender had a marked effect on occupation. One important activity, brewing, was normally dominated by women. At Broughton in Huntingdonshire an alewife featured in 45 per cent of families in the late thirteenth and early fourteenth centuries. Tasks such as baking and butchering were usually a male preserve. An analysis of coroners' rolls suggests, from examining the evidence of accidental death, the unsurprising conclusion that women were more domestic than men in their activities and preoccupations, or at least that the most dangerous activities for women were those of a domestic nature. Women were more likely to have accidents when drawing water, men when carting.[37] Agricultural work was normally done by men, though at some times of the year women were hard at work in the fields. At Bearpark, not far from Durham, 136 women were paid 1d. for haymaking in 1340.[38] Gleaning was a task often undertaken by women. One extraordinary case from Kent in 1330 appears to suggest a very low regard for women, or alternatively a high regard for pigs, but was almost certainly in reality a dispute over work as a domestic servant. John Page and Agnes, his wife, sued John Pistor, complaining that Agnes had bought John's wife, Matilda, in exchange for a pig worth 3s. John was apparently initially pleased with the bargain, but later sought to reclaim his wife, offering 2s. for her. He did not pay up, but the jury found against him. Wife-selling was not a normal feature of medieval life.[39]

Those who held no land at all appear rarely in the records, and the existence of such an underclass has to be more a matter of deduction. These were people who worked as agricultural labourers, often hired by the wealthier peasantry. They were the most oppressed of all the village population, too poor to find a distinctive voice in the records that survive. They might live in humble shacks, or be taken in as servants to the wealthier peasantry, eking out what must have been a miserable existence. The court rolls of Glastonbury abbey are among the few that provide a record of these landless people, for they list the payment, known as chevage, with which they were charged. On one substantial manor no less than about 160 were listed in the early fourteenth century. Those who owed labour services might recruit these landless labourers to do their work for

---

[37] Britton, *The Community of the Vill*, 20–6; H. Graham, ' "A Woman's Work ...": Labour and Gender in the Late Medieval Countryside', in P. J. P. Goldberg (ed.), *Women in Medieval English Society* (Stroud, 1997), 126–48; B. Hanawalt, *The Ties that Bound: Peasant Families in Medieval England* (Oxford, 1986), 127, 145. For some criticisms of Hanawalt's methodology, see P. J. P. Goldberg, 'The Public and the Private: Women in the Pre-Plague Economy', in *TCE* iii. 76–81.

[38] Durham cathedral muniments, manorial accounts, Bearpark 1340.

[39] R. C. Palmer, *English Law in the Age of the Black Death, 1348–1381* (Chapel Hill, NC, 1993), 65 n.

them. The successful peasants, with substantial holdings of perhaps 30 acres, would also use them to work on their own lands. At peak times of the year, such as harvest, there was no doubt ample opportunity for able-bodied men to find paid work.[40] Provision for the poorest in society was very limited. One suggestion was that the crown's almsgiving made a substantial contribution to resolving the problem of poverty. On occasion alms were given to large numbers of poor men; in 1300, 1,700 received 2*d*. each on the future Edward II's seventeenth birthday, and over the whole year the king spent about £650 on gifts to some 66,000 poor. The numbers were impressive, but were hardly such as to make much difference on a national scale. Assistance to the poor was also provided by at least some noble households; almsgiving was a religious obligation. Joan de Valence normally provided for twenty or more poor men on a regular basis. Gifts to the poor also featured in some wills. Geoffrey Luttrell wanted 40 quarters of wheat to be distributed to them at his funeral, and he also provided £20 for the poor praying for him on the anniversary of his death. Henry Percy left 100 marks to be distributed to the poor on the day of his funeral.[41] Such evidence shows that poverty was a real and acknowledged problem, but the numbers of those who received help can have represented little more than the tip of an iceberg.

LIVING STANDARDS

A key question about the peasantry is whether they profited from the economic expansion of the thirteenth century, or whether the period was one of increased exploitation and hardship. There is little doubt that successful lords managed to increase their incomes very significantly, but was this at the expense of the peasantry, or was increased wealth shared through society? Or was it the case that the population was expanding faster than the means of production, with the result that people had to live on fewer and fewer resources?[42] No one measure can give a clear answer, and no doubt there were very different experiences in different parts of the country.

---

[40] H. S. A. Fox, 'Exploitation of the Landless by Lords and Tenants in Early Medieval England', in Razi and Smith (eds.), *Medieval Society and the Manor Court*, 518–68.
[41] *Liber Quotidianus*, 20, 25; H. Johnstone, 'Poor Relief in Royal Households of Thirteenth-Century England', *Speculum*, 4 (1929), 165–6; M. C. Prestwich, 'The Piety of Edward I', in Ormrod (ed.), *England in the Thirteenth Century*, 122; Woolgar, *The Great Household in Late Medieval England*, 54; *Complete Peerage*, viii. 287; *Testamenta Eboracensia*, pt. 1, ed. J. Raine (Surtees Society, 2, 1836), 57; C. Dyer, *Standards of Living in the Later Middle Ages: Social Change in England c. 1200–1520* (Cambridge, 1989) 324–57.
[42] This classic view was presented by M. M. Postan, *The Medieval Economy and Society* (London, 1972).

Entry fines have been seen as one possible indicator. At Halesowen, for example, the customary rate charged for taking over a virgate doubled in the thirteenth century, to 13*s*. 4*d*. Where the incoming tenant had no right of inheritance, levels were higher, with the fine for one half-virgate in 1294 set at £6 13*s*. 4*d*.[43] A celebrated example is that of very high entry fines paid at Taunton, where the highest fine was £40 and many were over £10.[44] Of course, high fines could be an indication of acute land hunger and successful exploitation by lords; they could also be an indication of the high profits that men expected to make from their newly acquired lands.

The land market also provides evidence. At Hinderclay in Suffolk court rolls show that there was a high level of activity in the mid-1290s. These were years of particular difficulty, with high grain prices in 1293–5, and heavy levels of taxation and purveyance from 1294 to 1297. The number of cases in which peasants attempted to recover debts peaked in 1295. It is plain that the high level of land sales, mostly involving small amounts, was the result of the impoverishment of many peasants in the village.[45]

The dwindling size of most peasant holdings offers further clues. Norfolk provides startling evidence. At Martham in about 1220, 18 per cent of the tenants held less than 1 acre; by 1292 that figure had risen to 60 per cent. Nineteen per cent had held between 10 and 20 acres in about 1220; the figure was reduced to 3 per cent by 1292. The 104 holdings of the early thirteenth century had disintegrated into a mosaic of over 900 units. In this case, the practice of partible inheritance encouraged the division of holdings. Where holdings became smaller, so peasants must have found it ever harder to make a living. Evidence of this type demonstrates the increasing pressure on the peasantry by the late thirteenth century. This pressure was not felt evenly. Many analyses of village communities reveal that, just as happened higher up the social hierarchy, some families did well, while others did badly. There is a pattern of a small number of wealthy peasants who managed to increase the size of their holdings at the expense of the majority. Martin Suvel, in the Norfolk village of Sedgeford, inherited 3 acres of land, and by 1282 had built up a holding of over 35 acres.[46] This meant that holdings varied greatly in size. At Hinderclay, in about 1300, the average size of a holding was 7 acres, but this figure disguises a considerable range. One holding was of 30 acres, another 20, while eight were of 2 acres or less.[47] One remarkable success story is provided

---

[43] Razi, *Life, Marriage and Death*, 9, 30.
[44] J. Z. Titow, *English Rural Society 1200–1350* (London, 1969), 75.
[45] P. R. Schofield, 'Dearth, Debt and the Land Market', *Agricultural History Review*, 45 (1997), 1–17; J. Williamson, 'Norfolk: Thirteenth Century', in Harvey (ed.), *The Peasant Land Market in Medieval England*, 95.
[46] Williamson, 'Norfolk', 69–70, 95.
[47] Schofield, 'Dearth, Debt and the Land Market', 3–4.

by John de Heworth, a Durham priory tenant, who built up a huge holding between 1315 and 1345. He accumulated over 280 acres, not all of it with proper authority. There must have been many who suffered as a result of his success. He was a man of sufficient importance to have been appointed to lead a force of almost 200 mounted archers on the Scottish expedition of 1335.[48]

What is more evident than any overall rise or decline in the position of the peasantry during the thirteenth century is the increased social differentiation that took place. This was the case not only within but also between villages, and between regions. Villages where the peasantry enjoyed exceptional freedom, often because they were classified as part of the crown's ancient demesne, tended to do well, while those where the seigneurial regime was harsh naturally suffered. Peasants in eastern England were, for the most part, in a better position than those elsewhere.

A major difficulty in determining how the conditions of the peasantry changed is the absence of any accounts for peasant farming. It is often assumed that the productivity of peasant holdings was much the same as that of demesne lands, for which there is so much evidence. Farming appears so carefully governed by a host of by-laws that it seems that individual initiative must have been smothered.[49] Peasants did not simply produce food for their own consumption. They grew crops, and kept animals, which they marketed. The active and innovatory agriculture of eastern England, and of East Anglia in particular, probably owed much more to the inventiveness of the peasantry than to their lords. Throughout England most of the work of extending the area under cultivation was the work of the peasantry. In some cases individuals might do this, but schemes for draining the fens and levels were often the collective responsibility of lively and ambitious communities.

It is likely that peasants paid more attention to their own strips than to those of the lord's demesne; there was a much greater inducement to work for themselves. Even care devoted to simple tasks such as weeding could have improved crop yields. Some individuals can be identified from the records as managing to do well. Peter Fezaunt, a Huntingdonshire man, was fined in 1287 for enclosing his croft with a ditch and hedge, so making it separate even at the open and fallow seasons from the main field where it was sited. He also mowed his small meadow twice, not once as was customary. This suggests a man of initiative, determined to make his little holding yield as much as was possible.[50] John de Heworth in County Durham has already been mentioned. In one deal

---

[48] *Halmota Prioratus Dunelmensis*, ed. Longstaffe and Booth, 14–16; BL, Cotton MS Nero C. VIII, fo. 258.

[49] By-laws are discussed by Ault, *Open-Field Farming in Medieval England*.

[50] *The Court Rolls of Ramsey, Hepmangrove and Bury, 1268–1600*, ed. E. B. DeWindt (Toronto, 1990), m. 1, p. 16.

in 1329 he agreed to take over a 9-acre holding, paying 6*d*. an acre for the first two years, 8*d*. for the next two, and 1*s*. after that. This suggests that he thought that he could increase the profitability of the land substantially.[51] At Wakefield in the 1330s one group of six tenants paid 40*d*. in order to enclose 18 acres of arable within a hedge. By creating this enclosure, they would be able to farm more efficiently.[52]

One way in which peasants may have been able to run their own holdings more effectively than those of the demesnes was by using horses. There is evidence to suggest that, relatively, peasants used twice as many horses as demesne farms. This, however, was in part a reflection of the size of holdings; the larger the holding, the more likely it was that oxen would be used. Very probably it was the versatility of the horse that made it attractive to peasants, rather than the prospect of improved yields or higher profits. The smaller the holding, the more important this versatility was.[53]

Attempts have been made to work out typical peasant budgets, but while this is an interesting academic exercise, it may not bear much relationship to harsh reality. One attempt took a tenant with his wife and three children. This man was a yardlander, holding 30 acres. In a normal year—1299 was suggested—he would have enough for subsistence, and would probably make a cash surplus of up to £2 11*s*. A half-yardlander with 15 acres would have found it, according to these calculations, much harder to make ends meet. Another scholar constructed a different model of a peasant budget, and found that a holding of 18 acres was the minimum to ensure subsistence and a cash surplus of about £2.[54] The detail of such calculations can of course be questioned, but enough is known about the productivity of land in this period to suggest that they are of the right order of magnitude. Yet in practice, holdings of this size were larger than most. The many peasants who held 10 acres or less must have found life very hard, and it is difficult to imagine how families survived on smallholdings of a single acre or less.

A rare inventory from 1329 of the possessions of a villein, William Lene, who lived in Walsham le Willows in Norfolk, gives an impression of his lifestyle. He held 37 acres of arable, with just over an acre of meadow and a similar amount of woodland. He was married with two young sons and two daughters; he also had an illegitimate son. In his house he had five brass pots and pans, a jug and basin, a trestle-table with three benches, and one chair. For cooking there was a griddle, a

[51] *Halmota Prioratus Dunelmensis*, ed. Longstaffe and Booth, 14–16.
[52] *Court Rolls of the Manor of Wakefield 1331–1333*, ed. Walker, 130.
[53] J. Langdon, *Horses, Oxen and Technological Innovation*, 187–9, 228.
[54] Dyer, *Standards of Living in the Later Middle Ages*, 110–17; H. Kitsikopoulos, 'Standards of Living and Capital Formation in Pre-Plague England: A Peasant Budget Model', *EcHR* 53 (2000), 237–61.

tripod, a mortar and pestle, and an iron pan. He also possessed sheets, bedcovers, and a couple of tablecloths. He had 7s. 8d. in cash, and was owed 27s. 8d. He had a couple of oxen, eight cows, a bullock, three calves, and two horses, a mare and a filly. His sheep numbered about 120; he had a castrated pig, a sow, and eight piglets. There were also some geese and chickens. His granary was separate from his main house, and held 5 quarters of wheat, 4 of barley and 4 of oats, with smaller quantities of rye, beans, and peas. He had two ploughs (only one of them iron-shod), and a cart.[55] William was clearly comfortably off, his land quite sufficient to support himself and his family.

There were, of course, many opportunities available to peasant communities in addition to agriculture. Fishing could provide a way of supplementing a meagre and monotonous diet, and no doubt some food supplies were acquired by poaching. Building required unskilled labour as well as skilled. Many smallholders combined farming their limited plot with a trade. There were many required by rural communities, of which the most prominent in the records was brewing, generally the preserve of women. Baking was also important. Cloth production moved from the towns into the countryside, and that meant a demand for spinning, fulling, and other elements of a complex process. Tailors were needed in villages as much as in towns. Smiths and carpenters were in demand, as were tanners and potters. There was work for bowyers and fletchers, particularly during the years when Edward III's armies were active in France.

Despite the evidence for peasant enterprise and energy, it seems likely that, in general terms, the lower orders of society did not benefit as much from the economic expansion of the thirteenth century as did the elite groups. The balance was weighted too heavily in favour of the lords. It is not possible to produce definitive calculations, but the growth in the population was probably greater than the increased productive capacity of the economy. It was the poorest who suffered the most as a result. The corpses found lying frozen in the fields in the hard winter of 1257–8 showed vividly how close was the margin where life became unsustainable.

While life was hard in the thirteenth century, it became harder in the early fourteenth. The peasants' own voices are not often heard, but poets depicted the misery they suffered in Edward II's reign in a way that suggests personal experience. One emphasized the effects of taxation. He described a man driven into poverty who, to make matters worse, 'has a heap of girls sitting around his floor'. The wealthy, on the other hand, got away lightly.[56] Another poet

---

[55] *The Court Rolls of Walsham le Willows 1303–1350*, ed. R. Lock (Suffolk Records Society, 41, 1998), 133–5.
[56] *Political Songs*, 337.

explained that 'Good years and corn both have gone.' Taxation meant that every fourth penny was due to the king. Local officials, haywards, bailiffs, and woodwards robbed the poor. Demands for bribery, in the form of roast chickens, lampreys, and salmon, burdened the peasant, who was 'hunted as a hound does a hare'. The peasant had to sell his mare and his seedcorn; he could not plough or sow, and his land lay fallow. Even the rye was rotten before it could be reaped.[57] There was perhaps some exaggeration in this picture, but there can be no doubt that life was extremely difficult, above all in the famine years of 1315 and 1316.

The famine was the result of appalling weather, which led to disastrous harvests in successive years. The situation was particularly bad on heavy clay soils, which normally provided good yields. Wheat yields on the Winchester estates were 60 per cent of the normal level in 1315, and 55 per cent in the following year, while the figures for Bolton priory in Yorkshire were much worse, falling to 19 per cent of the average. In the summer of 1316 wheat prices were as high as 26s. 8d. a quarter. This, however, represents the selling price as shown in manorial accounts; buying prices rose to much higher levels, reaching 44s. according to a Leicester chronicle. Some people may have been able to store sufficient surplus to deal with a single bad harvest; no one would have had enough to cope adequately with consecutive disastrous years. The murrains of cattle and sheep which came in the wake of the famine are well documented for manorial demesnes; peasant animals must have been just as hard-hit. Some great landlords, notably the monks of Winchester, were able to ride the bad times, and even to profit from them as they sold grain at inflated prices. For the peasantry, however, these were disastrous years. Mortality is impossible to calculate, as the very poorest, who will have been hardest-hit, do not feature in the records. What the manorial evidence does show is a high level of activity in the land market, as men were forced to sell their holdings. On the estates of the honour of Tutbury rents dropped by 30 per cent in the eight years from 1313, as land was simply abandoned.[58]

In the long run, the fall in population caused by the Black Death of 1348 and subsequent epidemics would do much to transform the position of the peasantry. The shortage of labour would spell the end of villeinage and see wages and living standards rise. There would be more opportunities for women. The changes were complex and far-reaching. Despite the labour legislation of 1349 and 1351, which restricted the workings of the labour market, and the attempts by some landlords to reimpose labour services rather than abandoning villeinage, the direction of change was already becoming very evident by 1360.

[57] Ibid. 149-52. The references to bad weather in this poem strongly suggest a date around 1315-16.
[58] Kershaw, 'The Agrarian Crisis in England 1315-1322', 12, 19, 41, and *passim*.

RESISTANCE

The manorial regime was onerous, and it is a reflection of the stability of society that there was not much more protest, particularly given the economic circumstances under which the peasantry laboured. Manorial court records contain many examples of resistance, but these rarely led to success.[59] Withdrawal of labour was one tactic. On the St Albans manor of Park a dozen tenants were fined for not providing two men each to assist in haymaking. Nineteen tenants were fined for not doing their services in 1265, and in 1314 twenty-seven men refused. At Abbot's Langley in 1282 the whole village community refused to come to the harvest, and a fine of 18s. was levied. On the Ramsey manor of Broughton in 1291 the tenants went on strike, refusing to do their autumn boon works, saying that they had not received the bread to which they were entitled. They were offered 3 farthings' worth of bread between two men, but said that this was not sufficient. This was regarded seriously, and the manor court imposed a fine of 40s.[60] In 1317 the abbot of St Augustine's, Canterbury, was attacked by a large group at Salmstone in Kent. They broke up his ploughs and cut down his trees. At another of his granges, at Cliff's End, one of the monks was imprisoned and eventually ransomed by the same mob. It looks as if economic grievances, much to the fore in the aftermath of famine, explain these actions.[61] In 1332 at the manor of Great and Little Ogbourne on the Bec Hellouin estate in Wiltshire, the peasants resisted the manorial officials for three years.[62] At Thornbury in Gloucestershire, a manor held by Hugh Audley, there was extensive refusal to perform labour services in the early 1330s. The 191 cases where service was not performed represent determined opposition to a grasping landlord. The changed circumstances after the Black Death might lead to protest. One peasant group in Durham in 1350 took an unusual step when 'they maliciously and with malice aforethought surrendered their ploughshares to the lord at Auckland', so declaring their unwillingness to perform labour services.[63]

The peasantry might have recourse to the courts in their struggles. In 1297 the customary tenants at Bury on the Ramsey estates were not performing the weekly ploughing duties that it was claimed they owed. The matter came

[59] R. H. Hilton, 'Peasant Movements in England Before 1381', in E. M. Carus-Wilson (ed.), *Essays in Economic History*, ii (London, 1962), 73–90.

[60] Raftis, *Tenure and Mobility*, 108.

[61] *CPR 1317-24*, 98, 172, 275.   [62] *CIM* ii, no. 1269.

[63] P. Franklin, 'Politics in Manorial Court Rolls: The Tactics, Social Composition, and Aims of a Pre-1381 Peasant Movement', in Razi and Smith (eds.), *Medieval Society and the Manor Court*, 162–98; *The Black Death*, ed. R. Horrox (Manchester, 1994), 327.

before the manorial court; the outcome of the dispute was unfortunately not recorded. The St Albans peasants were very sophisticated in the way they opposed their lord, even bringing in expert lawyers in the 1270s to help them fight for the right to convey land by charter.[64] A village community might well turn against the officials set in charge of the demesne farm. In 1308 on the abbey of Bec's manor of Preston, the villagers brought a series of complaints against Henry of Bereford, their bailiff. He had ploughed the lord's land, but failed to sow it in good time. He had taken land from tenants, and not given them what he had promised by way of exchange.[65] In a dispute between the men of Darnell and Over in Cheshire against the abbot of Vale Royal, the former brought cases in court, petitioned the justice of Chester, petitioned Edward III in parliament, appealed to him directly at Windsor, and also put their case to Queen Philippa. When all of these expedients failed, they resorted to violence, clearly putting themselves in the wrong. The abbot finally won the day.[66] In the 1350s the peasants at Wawne claimed that they were not villeins of the nearby abbey of Meaux. The ringleaders were imprisoned by the abbot, but one, Richard Cellarer, succeeded in escaping. His claim that he belonged to the royal manor of Easington, near Spurn Head, was accepted by the royal escheator. Lengthy legal proceedings followed, in which the abbey was eventually successful. The abbey's chronicler noted that all the king's officials had been hostile, with the exception of the chancellor. The presents he had received from the abbot had the desired effect on him. What is striking about the case is how Cellarer and the other villeins were able to take their case forward, obtaining influential support and using the mechanisms of the law with considerable success until the very end.[67]

VILLAGE LIFE

The manorial court rolls give a vivid picture of village life, with its squabbles and inconveniences. There are considerable methodological problems in simply selecting cases more or less at random, but individual examples can bring the past to life more effectively than columns of statistics. At Littleport in Cambridgeshire one man puts dung in the common lane so that people can hardly pass by. Another fishes at night in other people's fisheries. One gossipy woman slanders another; one man calls a woman a whore, and she calls him a thief. A book borrowed from the local Hospitallers was not returned. The

[64] Levett, *Studies in Manorial History*, 192, 203–4; *Court Rolls of Ramsey, Hepmangrove and Bury*, ed. DeWindt, m. 1, p. 90.
[65] M. Morgan, *The English Lands of the Abbey of Bec* (Oxford, 1946), 65–6.
[66] *Agrarian History*, ii. 846–8.
[67] *Melsa*, iii. 127–42.

vicar's dog is found to be chasing hares.[68] Feuds broke out, often for unexplained reasons. At Cottenham, also in Cambridgeshire, Andrew Noteman
dragged Matilda, daughter of Roger the thatcher, out of her house by her ears.
Later, each raised the hue and cry against the other. Andrew accused Matilda
of breaking down his hedges, but a jury found her not guilty.[69] These were
small, intolerant communities. On the Ramsey estates in 1298 the arrest was
ordered of Philip Noseles, a shoemaker, because he had been eavesdropping on
conversations and ran away when anyone saw him. In 1316 a man was fined 6d.
for receiving Joan, 'who is of bad reputation and unworthy of residing in the
vill'. No one was to take her in, under threat of a 40s. fine. At Walsham le
Willows in 1328 John Fraunceys claimed 2s. in damages because Avice Deve-
neys had accused his wife of wearing her short jacket before Easter.[70] The
peasant community was not comfortable for those who chose not to conform.
'Matilda Crane is in the habit of taking chickens of her neighbours and other
small things, and is not suitable to live among her neighbours etc. And
therefore it is ordered that no one henceforth receive her under serious
penalty.'[71] This case from the 1318 court roll of Wistow in Cambridgeshire
shows how difficult it was to deal with a persistent offender; in the end the
solution had to be expulsion from the village. In one exceptional case, at
Ricknall in Durham in 1350, the bishop of Durham's tenants found one of
the villagers, William Standupryght, to be so objectionable and quarrelsome
that it was they who left the village.[72]

Records of church courts provide a further perspective. Relatively few
survive, but there is a remarkable series covering a number of places in
Lincolnshire between 1336 and 1349. In 1347 Roger Sweatinbed of
Friesthorpe was accused of fornication with Letitia Bat. Both appeared, and
purged themselves of the offence. Such cases were extremely common. In some
instances it appears that the courts were trying to formalize and control
marriage customs. In the same year John de Wotton was accused of fornication
and secret marriage with Matilda Brown, and William Witlak, accused of
sleeping with Alice of Torkesey, was ordered to marry her if he repeated the
offence. A standard punishment was to be whipped three or more times around
the church, and around the marketplace, while fines were also levied. The

[68] F. W. Maitland and W. P. Baildon (eds.), *The Court Baron* (Selden Society, 4, 1891), 124,
125, 130–1, 133.
[69] F. M. Page, *The Estates of Crowland Abbey* (Cambridge, 1934), 142.
[70] *Court Rolls of Ramsey, Hepmangrove and Bury*, ed. DeWindt, m. 1, pp. 60, 205; *Court Rolls of
Walsham le Willows*, ed. Lock, 117.
[71] Raftis, *Tenure and Mobility*, 134.
[72] R. H. Britnell, 'Feudal Reaction After the Black Death in Durham', *Past and Present*, 128
(1990), 40.

efficacy of such punishments is questionable. Between 1336 and 1344 Legia Frere appeared eight times before the church courts accused of fornication, though not with as many different partners as Isabella Fox, who was accused of sleeping with at least five different men in the same period. For these women at least, penance and small fines seem to have had little effect.[73]

Religion was, no doubt, important to the peasantry, not least because the ecclesiastical calendar provided a cycle of holidays and celebrations focused on the parish and the Church. The fourth Lateran Council had aimed to improve and regulate the pastoral care provided to the laity, and much was done in England to implement its decisions. The injunctions issued by John Pecham, archbishop of Canterbury, were particularly important, with orders that priests should administer the sacraments and hear confessions regularly. Much, at a local level, must have depended on the quality of the priesthood. The author of a lengthy poem, the *Simonie*, commented that 'There be so many priests, they may not all be good.' He condemned their financial exactions as well as their incontinence 'when the candle is out'.[74] The practice whereby many landlords appropriated parochial revenues, and then appointed a salaried vicar or chaplain, probably did little for standards. Much, however, was done to try to improve the pastoral care that was provided. Works such as William of Pagula's *Oculus Sacerdotium*, written in the 1320s, provided priests with manuals to guide them. In 1357 Archbishop Thoresby of York produced a *Lay Folk's Catechism* as a guide to religious practice.

Specific cults might be important for the peasantry: St Walstan of Bawburgh, an obscure Anglo-Saxon figure, had an obvious appeal, for prayers to him were thought to ensure a good harvest, and might cure sick cattle. On occasion, sudden enthusiasms might erupt. In 1287 the bishop of Hereford had Thomas Cantilupe's bones moved into a new tomb. Miracles were encouraged, and until early in the next century, considerable numbers were apparently performed. Cantilupe's aristocratic background did not put off peasants; indeed, very few of the pilgrims who flocked to his shrine shared his social origins. Votive offerings were presented, and according to an inventory made in 1307, these included 1,200 wax representations of parts of the body.[75] Not all cults were encouraged, however, in the way that Cantilupe's was. There might be alarm at popular fervour which had distinct undertones of pagan worship. In 1295 the bishop of Winchester forbade the worship of stones, woods, trees, and wells, and in 1299 the bishop of Lincoln was anxious to stop large numbers

---

[73] *Lower Ecclesiastical Jurisdiction in Late-Medieval England*, ed. L. R. Poos (Oxford, 2001), 6, 14, 24, 121, 126, 149, 165, 167, 169, 177, 185, 193, 199, 215, 221.

[74] *Political Songs*, 326–9.

[75] R. C. Finucane, *Miracles and Pilgrims: Popular Beliefs in Medieval England*, 2nd edn. (Basingstoke, 1995), 98, 181–7.

of people flocking to worship at a well in Buckinghamshire.[76] In 1313 people
crowded to the parish church at Foston-on-the-Wolds in Yorkshire to worship
a statue of the Virgin Mary that had recently been put there. The statue was
one of the spoils of war, for it had been brought from Scotland by Thomas de
Poynton and placed in a chapel at Fraisthorpe. On his death, his widow had
sold it to the parson of Foston. The archbishop of York did his best to put an
end to the cult.[77] John Schorne, a Buckinghamshire priest, who died in 1315,
became the object of widespread adoration, and was regarded as a saint. He had
the distinction of having succeeded in conjuring the Devil into a boot, and
rather more practically helped to discover a spring whose water cured gout. In
1351 the bishop of Exeter denounced the cult of an image in one Devon village
as little more than the worship of an idol. There might be other reasons for
concern about popular cults. In 1359 a series of miracles occurred at the tomb
of the rector of Whitstone in Cornwall, a man popularly thought of as a saint.
The bishop of Exeter was alarmed, for every Saturday crowds from a wide area
flocked to his burial place, engaging in feasting, drinking, and taking part in
'unlawful and shameful acts'.[78]

WAR AND POLITICS

The perspective of many peasants was, no doubt, limited to the fields that
surrounded their village, and to the nearby markets. Wider considerations,
however, affected the lives of some, notably those of war. For the fortunate few,
there were profits to be made from fighting, particularly in France, but it is not
possible to relate the evidence from military payrolls to that from manorial
court rolls. No individual peasant can be identified as bringing back gains from
the wars, which were then fed into the local village economy. No doubt,
however, some peasants were able to bring back war booty to their villages,
particularly from France. Some peasant wives may have added articles of
French finery to their limited wardrobes. There is, regrettably, no way in
which the effects of war on wealth and social mobility within village communities can be assessed.

The negative effects of war surely outweighed the positive. With the largest
number of infantrymen recruited standing at perhaps 24,000 for the 1298
campaign in Scotland, and numbers substantially lower during the Hundred
Years War, only a small proportion of the total population was asked to fight.
Recruitment, however, burdened some parts of the country much more than

[76] A. Brown, *Church and Society in England 1000–1500* (Basingstoke, 2003), 52–3, 75, 82.
[77] K. Kamerick, *Popular Piety and Art in the Late Middle Ages: Image Worship and Idolatry in
England, 1350–1500* (London, 2002), 107–12.
[78] D. Webb, *Pilgrimage in Medieval England* (London, 2000), 154–6.

others. Cheshire, Yorkshire, Nottinghamshire, Derbyshire, and Lincolnshire were particularly affected, as were the Welsh marches. Much more onerous than the provision of manpower were the associated charges on villages. Men had to be equipped with appropriate weapons, and needed to be given expenses to cover their costs in travelling to the muster point. The burden on the village communities might be substantial. The hundred of Launditch in Norfolk faced a bill of just over £50 in 1295 for providing 187 men with their equipment and expenses.[79] Costs were relatively low under Edward I, but rose as the crown demanded better military equipment. In 1338 the men of Hatfield selected two men to serve as hobelars, and paid expenses for them of £3 3s. 4d.[80] In addition, corrupt officials might impose quite improper charges on villagers. In 1294 the under-sheriff of Lincolnshire charged Ingoldsmells 4s. to excuse them from sending men to fight in Wales. In the same county the vill of Kirby and Laythorpe was charged 10s. to equip two men who were recruited. In 1334 the men of Bassingham were threatened with service in Scotland until they paid a fine of 13s. 4d.[81]

More serious still were the demands for food to supply the armies. The burden was not shared equitably; not surprisingly, the crown tended to demand supplies from the counties that were best situated to meet its needs. This meant that eastern England and the east midlands were most heavily afflicted, as it was relatively easy to ship grain and other commodities from there to Newcastle and Berwick for the Scottish wars. It has been calculated that in 1297 the crown took the produce of about 2,700 acres in Lincolnshire, and of about 4,900 acres in Kent.[82] Records of the inquiries of 1297 and 1341 reveal a great number of complaints against the purveyors who took men's grain to feed the king's armies. This is not surprising. The process was wide open to abuse and corruption, and it meant that men were deprived of the provisions that they depended on for their subsistence. It was a much greater blow to lose a quarter of grain than to pay its value in taxation. It is hardly surprising that in 1311 the fear was expressed in the Ordinances that compulsory purchases of foodstuffs might cause 'the people of the land' to rise.[83]

The demands of the crown on the peasantry were particularly heavy in two periods, the mid-1290s and the late 1330s, when the government was attempting to put particularly ambitious diplomatic and military plans into operation. In the 1290s there were minimum levels of wealth set, below which people

[79] Prestwich, War, Politics and Finance, 101.
[80] Maddicott, English Peasantry and the Crown, 40.
[81] A Lincolnshire Assize Roll for 1298, ed. W. S. Thomson (Lincoln Record Society, 1944), 59, 79; The 1341 Royal Inquest in Lincolnshire, ed. McLane, 67.
[82] Maddicott, English Peasantry and the Crown, 31.
[83] SR 156–67, Ordinances, clause 10.

would not be taxed, but after 1334 even the poorest were not protected in this
way. The sums demanded in taxation were not obviously excessive, but the
requests for taxation coincided with those for purveyance. They were deeply
resented. The corruption associated with the processes of assessment and
collection made matters worse. A poem, the 'Song Against the King's
Taxes', which dates from the late 1330s, emphasized the way in which the
weight of taxation and collection of wool affected the ordinary people of the
land, and the author suggested that if they had a leader, they would rise in
rebellion. Other poems expressed peasant grievances in terms that suggest that
their authors had first-hand knowledge of the difficulties faced by the poorest
in society. In the 'Song of the Husbandman', which dates from Edward II's
reign, blame is placed on the demands made by all the various officials,
hayward, bailiff, and woodward, and stresses the burden of a corrupt tax
system. 'Ever the fourth penny must go the king' and 'To seek silver for the
king I need to sell my seed' are two of the lines that have a ring of truth about
them.[84] Detailed analysis of the records of the manor of Thornbury in Gloucestershire, set against the tax assessment of 1327, has shown the inequitable
nature of the tax burden. Fifty-one taxpayers can be identified as rich peasants,
nineteen as middle-ranking, and twenty-six as poor. The poor paid as much as
the middle-ranking group, and half as much as the rich. The goods of the lord
of the manor, Hugh Audley, were clearly substantially under-assessed.[85] Petitions to parliament in 1347 show continued grievances over taxation. At Wide-
combe in Devon heavy taxation had driven all but five poor tenants away from
the village. At Marshfield in Gloucestershire, a place that had suffered four
fires in six years, the surviving tenants had nothing left to live on, and begged
for a fair assessment.[86] The many burdens under which the peasantry groaned
seem more than sufficient to justify popular rebellion. Yet it was not until 1381,
when circumstances were very different, that the peasants rose up en masse.
Acquiescence, no doubt resentful, was the order of the day.

It was not that the peasantry were unaware of political events. In the difficult
days of the civil war of the 1260s, village communities were swift to take
advantage of events. Opportunities to settle old scores were not to be missed.
There is ample indication that the lands of particular royalists were targeted.
The estates of John Mansel were hard-hit in what were probably coordinated
attacks: of all the clerks who served Henry III, Mansel had probably built up
the largest fortune.[87] The lands of royalist sheriffs and justices were obvious

---

[84] *Political Songs*, 149, 152, 182–7.
[85] P. Franklin, *The Taxpayers of Medieval Gloucestershire: An Analysis of the 1327 Lay Subsidy Roll with a New Edition of its Text* (Gloucester, 1993), 15–18.
[86] *Rot. Parl.* ii. 189.
[87] E. F. Jacob, *Studies in the Period of Baronial Reform and Rebellion* (Oxford, 1925), 225.

targets. While many inquisitions merely note that attacks were the work of 'unknown men', some individual peasants can be identified. In some cases people claimed that they had sided with the rebels under duress from Montfort's officials and agents, but it is likely that political conviction played its part. This is clear from one celebrated case. In 1265, just after the battle of Evesham, the men of Peatling Magna in Leicestershire, a strongly pro-baronial region, rioted when a cart belonging to a royalist, Peter de Neville, was driven through the village. The carter was attacked, and the villagers accused Neville and his men of treason, 'because they were against the community of the realm and against the barons'.[88] In 1296 the king's treasurer, Walter Langton, was riding through Weston, north of Newark, when he and his men were attacked by some thirty villagers. The latter raised the hue and cry and chased Langton for a mile down the road. There were many reasons why they might have taken exception to the king's treasurer, for he was responsible for highly unpopular exactions, but, unlike the Peatling Magna case, the record does not explain the motives of the villagers. What is apparent is that this protest involved not just the poor, but also the leaders of the village community. The ringleader was Laurence, a younger son of a knight, Richard de Weston, and charters show that some of the others involved were men of standing in the village.[89] That even a villein might have strong political sympathies is shown by the account of funeral and other expenses for William Lene of Walsham le Willows in 1329, for this included the payment of someone to go to the shrine of Thomas of Lancaster.[90] There is, however, no indication that the peasantry ever even attempted concerted action to deal with political problems. No one in this period emerged, as they would in 1381, to provide the necessary leadership.

[88] *Select Cases of Procedure Without Writ Under Henry III*, ed. H. G. Richardson and G. O. Sayles (Selden Society 60, 1941), 43. This incident is discussed by D. A. Carpenter, 'English Peasants in Politics, 1258–1267', in his *Reign of Henry III*, 309, 339, 347–8.

[89] D. Crook, ' "Thieves and Plunderers": An Anti-ministerial Protest of 1296', *Historical Research*, 67 (1994), 327–35.

[90] *Court Rolls of Walsham le Willows*, ed. Lock, 135.

CHAPTER 18

The Towns

In 1283 Edward I founded what was intended to be an ideal thirteenth-century town at Conwy in north Wales. It had a fine site at the mouth of an estuary, making transport and communication by sea easy. It was defended by a magnificent castle, and by an equally splendid town wall, which provided a clear line of demarcation between the urban settlement and the surrounding countryside. Within the walls, the town was carefully planned, with its streets laid out on a grid pattern, and the oblong tenements equally spaced in fine geometric order. Conwy received a charter from the king in 1284, in which he conferred full burghal rights on the inhabitants. By 1295, 112 plots of land were occupied; ten years later a survey reveals that there were twelve shops in the marketplace, and two butcher's stalls.[1] It was not a place that would grow spectacularly, but in concept it shows what a thirteenth-century town should be.

NUMBERS AND CHARACTERISTICS

There can be no doubt about Conwy's status as a town, but in other cases definition is not so clear. Warenmouth in Northumberland received the same rights as Newcastle upon Tyne in 1247, and was in legal terms a town, yet in 1296 no more than three inhabitants had sufficient wealth for them to be taxed. In 1328, presumably as a result of Scottish raids, the place was said to be completely burned. Its site can no longer be traced. In contrast, Boston in Lincolnshire was both taxed as a village and listed as such in other sources. However, it had a guild merchant, and was the most important port for wool exports after London. In terms of taxable value, it was the fifth wealthiest place in England in 1334. It would be absurd to argue that Warenmouth was a town and that Boston was not, yet that is the logic if possession of a charter is used as the criterion. This admittedly extreme example shows how hard it is to say how many towns there were.

---

[1] M. W. Beresford, *New Towns of the Middle Ages* (London, 1967), 42–3, 445–6.

There are very different possible definitions of what towns were.[2] They can be thought of in terms of their legal status, or their economic functions, or their cultural identity, and within those categories there are different elements to be considered. It makes most sense to think in terms of what contemporaries regarded as towns, but unfortunately they were not always as clear as they might have been. Places were categorized in different ways at different times. One criterion is to consider which were asked to send representatives to parliament. The writs of summons simply asked the sheriffs to send two citizens and two burgesses from every city and borough. It was up to the sheriffs to identify the towns. In 1295, 115 towns sent men to Edward I's parliament. This does not represent a complete census of English towns; in all, 166 towns are known to have been represented in various parliaments in the course of the reign. The average number was around eighty.[3] The figures give little more than a general idea of the number of settlements considered by contemporaries to have been significant towns, but the order of magnitude is reasonable. It fits reasonably well with other evidence, such as the number of places that paid at the higher rate when taxes on movable goods such as fifteenths and tenths were collected. However, the difficulty of using summonses to parliament as a definite criterion is shown by the case of the sheriff of Bedfordshire and Buckinghamshire, who claimed in 1320 that Bedford was the only town in his counties, although in 1316 Amersham, Aylesbury, Marlow, Wendover, and Wycombe had all sent representatives.[4]

A different approach is to adopt a legal criterion, and to identify as towns places where tenements were held by burgage tenure. This carried no obligations to perform labour services, and holdings could be bought, sold, and inherited. Those who held tenements on this basis were free, and normally owed a money rent. Using burgage tenure as the basis of a definition, the number of towns in England by the end of the thirteenth century was probably about 600.[5] Yet in many cases places where burgage tenure existed were undoubtedly villages, not towns. They were essentially rural and agricultural in character.

Economic function provides another test. Towns were places where produce was brought in from the countryside, goods were exchanged, and where articles were manufactured, providing essential services to a hinterland. For

---

[2] For discussion of many of the problems presented by medieval English towns, see S. Reynolds, *An Introduction to the History of English Medieval Towns* (Oxford, 1977); R. Holt and G. Rosser (eds.), *The Medieval Town: A Reader in English Urban History 1200–1540* (London, 1990), 1–18.

[3] McKisack, *Parliamentary Representation of the English Boroughs*, 8, 11.

[4] Pollock and Maitland, *History of English Law*, i. 641.

[5] *The Cambridge Urban History of Britain*. i: 600–1540, ed. D. M. Palliser (Cambridge, 2000), 506.

somewhere to count as a town, the majority of the population should be involved in these activities, not in agriculture. It is possible to construct an economic model, with large towns at the top of a hierarchy, serving a large area, and with smaller towns below them. Such concepts, while they may provide a convenient theory, are not always easy to apply in practice. One problem is that marketing and manufacture were not confined to urban centres in medieval England, but could take place in a rural setting. It is also the case that some townspeople engaged in farming, for they provided a convenient source of labour for the surrounding rural economy. The clear demarcation line drawn by town walls could prove surprisingly permeable. It is, nevertheless, possible to argue on the basis of economic function that there were some 600 small towns in England by 1300, none with a population of over 2,000.[6]

The most difficult criterion for a town is that of the inhabitants' sense of identity. Self-government, which took very different forms in different places, will have contributed to this, but the question needs to be answered in wider terms. Larger towns in particular were complex, with multi-layered identities. A multiplicity of churches, friaries, fraternities, and guilds all provided different foci for the inhabitants, which came together to create a specifically urban culture.

Taking the various criteria together, it makes most sense to think in terms of a figure of very roughly 100, or perhaps 150, towns in England, with in addition 'more than 500 places with some urban characteristics in 1300', but numbers can be varied according to the definition adopted.[7] Even taking the lower figure, of about 100, towns varied enormously in size, from London, 'the mirror and exemplar of the whole land',[8] a city of international standing in a quite different class from any other English town, to such places of little more than local importance as Ottery St Mary or Mildenhall. Taking the tax assessment of 1334 as a guide, the ten wealthiest towns in the realm were: London, Bristol, York, Newcastle upon Tyne, Boston, Norwich, Yarmouth, Oxford, Lincoln, and Coventry. Of these, London was assessed at £11,000 and Coventry at £750.[9] Even this list is open to question, for, as already suggested, it is possible to argue that Boston fails to qualify as a town on various criteria. The tax assessment also throws up the remarkable anomaly of an undoubted village, Bampton in Oxfordshire, assessed at a startling £969.[10]

[6] C. Dyer, 'The Importance of Small Towns in England 1000–1540', *Historical Research*, 75 (2002), 1–24.
[7] E. Miller and J. Hatcher, *Medieval England: Towns, Commerce and Crafts 1086–1349* (London, 1995), 275.
[8] *Cal. Plea and Mem. Rolls*, 107.
[9] See the table given in *Cambridge Urban History*, i. 755.
[10] J. Masschaele, *Peasants, Merchants and Markets: Inland Trade in Medieval England, 1150–1350* (New York, 1997), 79–80.

The number of towns was not static, for there were many new foundations in the thirteenth century. For landlords, towns represented money. A successful town would bring in income in the form of rents and tolls. The early thirteenth century was a great age for new town foundation, with ten in the 1220s; as the century progressed, the country became more saturated with urban settlements, and success became less easy to achieve. Skinburness in Cumberland was a significant victualling base for Edward I's Scottish campaigns, and in 1301 it made obvious sense to grant it urban status. By 1305, however, the waves had washed it away. In all, calculations suggest that there were over fifty new towns established in England in the thirteenth century. In the less optimistic times of the fourteenth century, it was clear that there was no point in attempting to create new towns, given the difficulty of attracting the necessary settlers. After 1310 numbers of new foundations were negligible.

A celebrated example of a highly successful thirteenth-century new town is that of New Salisbury. The site known as Old Sarum was unsuitable in various ways; it was crowded within a massive earthwork on an elevated site, and relations between cathedral and castle were tricky. Papal approval for construction of a new cathedral came in 1219; in 1225 the bishop granted a charter to the new borough itself, and this was soon confirmed by the king. The new town grew rapidly. Old Sarum declined in face of the competition, despite the grant of a new fair in 1246. Nearby Wilton suffered equally. New Salisbury was much better situated for trade, and no doubt the cathedral helped to bring in economic prosperity.

Some new towns were created by the crown, notably in the exceptional circumstances of newly conquered Wales in 1284, or of Gascony, where *bastides*, strongly defended urban settlements, were part of a defensive strategy. Edward I also founded New Winchelsea in 1288, as a replacement for the old town, which was proving too vulnerable to the Channel tides and storms. He also created Kingston upon Hull, acquiring the site from Meaux abbey in 1293. Two markets and a fair were authorized, and in 1299 the town obtained its royal charter. It was a success from the first, bringing in an average annual revenue of £113.[11]

An unusual example of the organic growth of a new town is provided by one not far from Hull, which today lies under the waves of the North Sea. The men of Grimsby explained the history of their rival Ravenserodd in 1290. An island appeared in the Humber estuary in Henry III's day, and in about 1240 a ship was wrecked there. An enterprising man built a hut from the timbers and set up a business, providing food and drink to sailors. After ten years there were four houses on the island; after that the settlement expanded rapidly. Ravenserodd

[11] Beresford, *New Towns*, 328, 416, 506–8, 511–12.

soon began to take trade away from Grimsby, for it was nearer to the sea. There was no proper market day there, but the inhabitants traded every day, and persuaded merchants that they could offer much better prices than could be had in Grimsby. As its lord, the earl of Aumale obtained a charter for a market and fair at Ravenserodd in 1251, but it was not until 1299 that the town received a royal charter, which was issued on the same day as the grant to Hull.[12]

Much archaeological work helps to reveal the physical characteristics of towns and of the houses within them. Increasingly, sophisticated features once thought to be late medieval or even sixteenth-century in date are found to go back to the thirteenth century. There was, inevitably, great variety in building. The so-called 'Rows' at Chester provide a particularly notable example of urban housing, dating from the late thirteenth century. Vaulted undercrofts immediately fronting onto the street formed warehouses and wine cellars; they may have been let separately from the shops and houses above them. A covered walkway forming a kind of arcade above them gave access to shops, while above that were rooms and chambers providing accommodation. Southampton provides further examples of fine stone undercrofts, many of which served as shops or provided storage. Above them were complex storeyed buildings, stretching back along the relatively narrow tenements. Jettied upper storeys, known in London from the mid-thirteenth century, became increasingly common by about 1300. The housing of the urban poor has left few traces, and there is a danger that historians may be seduced by the relative splendour of the buildings that can be identified. The evidence, however, increasingly suggests that town buildings were well planned and substantial.[13] At Norwich in the early fourteenth century, however, where there was substantial immigration of the poor, the living standards of many were very low. Where there were thirty-six men and an unknown number of women and children living in twenty-seven properties in 1311, by 1333 the number of men had risen to 112. Many of the incomers to the city appear to have lived in simple clay-walled thatched dwellings.[14]

Town walls were hardly new in the thirteenth century, but evidence from murage grants, first recorded in 1220, shows that it was then that many towns acquired walls for the first time. There was a clear relationship with disorder and cross-border threats. Townsmen on the Welsh border were keen to have stone defences behind which they could shelter, and in the north, grants between 1310 and 1320 to Richmond, Durham, Hartlepool, and Lancaster

---

[12] *CIM* i, no. 1512; Beresford, *New Towns*, 513.

[13] J. Schofield and A. Vince, *Medieval Towns* (Leicester, 1994), 63–98; C. Platt, *Medieval Southampton: The Port and Trading Community, A.D. 1000–1600* (London, 1973), 99.

[14] C. Rawcliffe, *Medicine for the Soul* (Stroud, 1999), 15–16.

resulted from the Scottish threat. There was, however, a view that walls were not needed solely in regions under immediate threat, for military purposes. In 1360 Edward III wrote to the citizens of Gloucester expressing alarm since he had heard that the town's defences were in a ruinous condition. Although a truce had been agreed in the French war, the citizens were to see to the repair of the walls, 'because it is advisable that the town should be well fortified in time of peace as of war'.[15] Town walls, like those of castles, were much more than defensive fortifications. They were an expression of urban pride, an indication of superior and separate status.

TOWNSPEOPLE

The size of the urban population cannot be calculated with any accuracy; there is far less evidence than there is for the rural populace. London was the one English city that could compare in size with the great cities of continental Europe. Estimates for its size in about 1300, when the population probably peaked, vary from 40,000 to 100,000, but there is no solid evidence on which they can be based. A figure of about 70,000 may not be unreasonable, but is little more than the product of knowledgeable guesswork.[16] The evidence for other towns is even less satisfactory, but large provincial towns such as Norwich, Bristol, or Newcastle upon Tyne may have had populations as high as about 20,000, though many towns were a tenth of that size. Calculations based on the number of townspeople who paid tax suggest that Shrewsbury may have had a population of about 5,000.[17] Any estimates of the overall proportion of the population that lived in towns are open to such extensive qualifications as to be largely worthless.[18]

Where did the townspeople come from? It is normally, and logically, assumed that towns were less healthy than the countryside, with people living cheek by jowl in unsanitary conditions. This would have meant higher death rates in towns, so that the growth of population could not have been self-sustaining, but would have depended on immigration from the country. Analysis of personal names helps to demonstrate this. In the case of Stratford upon Avon, founded in 1196, most of the populace in the first half of the thirteenth century came from relatively close, within a 6- to 8-mile radius.

[15] H. L. Turner, *Town Defences in England and Wales* (London, 1970), 75–6, 78, 82.

[16] G. A. Williams, *Medieval London: From Commune to Capital* (London, 1963), 317; P. Nightingale, 'The Growth of London in the Medieval English Economy', in R. H. Britnell and J. Hatcher (eds.), *Progress and Problems in Medieval England* (Cambridge, 1996), 89–96.

[17] *Wealth of Shrewsbury*, ed. Cromarty and Cromarty, 28–9.

[18] An extreme example is provided by G. Rosser, with an estimate that 'one in five people in late medieval England … lived in a town': *Cambridge Urban History*, i. 337.

Ninety per cent came from within 16 miles. Patterns were similar elsewhere. In the early fourteenth century Winchester and Leicester were drawing people in from no more than 10 miles around. For Norwich and York the catchment area was larger, 20 miles around the cities, while for Bristol it was wider still. There, 42 per cent of identifiable immigrants came from places 40 miles or more away.[19] London, of course, had massive drawing power, with most of its immigrants coming from within a 40-mile radius. The east midlands and East Anglia were also important recruiting grounds for populating London.[20]

The structure and character of the urban population was quite different from the rural. As was normal in northern Europe, knights and greater nobles did not live in towns, though a number of aristocrats possessed town houses in London. There were no villeins or unfree people in towns; conventionally, residence for a year and a day conferred freedom. There was, of course, a huge range of wealth in urban society, from the great merchants, through the traders and artisans, down to the very poorest. The gradation of wealth within towns varied somewhat, but normally there was a small wealthy group which dominated, both economically and politically. Contemporaries normally thought of the urban population as being divided into three groups, the great men, those of middling status, and the poor, though these groupings were not formalized in any way. There was also considerable variation between towns, some being far richer than others. Tax assessments show major differences in average wealth on a per capita basis in different towns. In 1327, for example, the average tax paid in Coventry was 4s. a head. For Shrewsbury, the figure was similar at 3s. 7d. Warwick was lower, at 3s., Stafford 2s. 6d., Worcester 2s., and Lichfield a paltry 1s. 6d.[21]

There was a very much greater variety of occupations among townspeople than was the case with rural dwellers, with perhaps thirty or more different trades being practised in a medium-sized town. Food and drink provided the largest source of employment. Baking, brewing, and butchery were invariably important. A set of ordinances for the city of York, drawn up at the start of the fourteenth century, gives a good impression of the range of activities concerned with food. In 1304 lists were produced of those who had not obeyed the regulations. These give an idea of the numbers involved in the various trades. There were thirty-six bakers, twenty-six taverners, thirty-five cooks, forty-nine butchers, fifty fishmongers, seventy brewers, thirty-seven poult-

[19] E. Carus-Wilson, 'The First Half-Century of the Borough of Stratford-upon-Avon', *EcHR*, 2nd ser., 18 (1965), 54; *Cambridge Urban History*, i. 459; S. Penn, 'The Origins of Bristol Migrants in the Early Fourteenth Century: The Surname Evidence', *Transactions of the Bristol and Gloucestershire Archaeological Society*, 101 (1983), 122.

[20] D. Keene, 'Medieval London and its Region', *London Journal*, 14 (1989), 103.

[21] *Wealth of Shrewsbury*, ed. Cromarty and Cromarty, 29.

erers, nine forestallers (or retailers) of fish, twenty-seven regrators (or middlemen), and forty-five hostellers. After food, clothing trades were usually the
most significant. At York, other trades covered in the ordinances included
those of tanners, tailors, clothiers, skinners, prostitutes, physicians, doctors,
and apothecaries. In the lists, there were many women among the brewers
and regrators, or resellers, but as in the countryside, tasks such as baking and
butchery were male preserves.[22] Tax records provide another way of identifying occupations. Those for Shrewsbury suggest a similar pattern to York where
food trades were concerned, with the addition of spicers, but these documents
indicate a wider range of crafts, with various metal trades featuring alongside
the furriers, skinners, and mercers, as well as occasional chandlers, dyers,
wheelwrights, and others.[23] At Bristol no less than 122 different trades have
been identified from early fourteenth-century tax records.[24] Hitchin in Hertfordshire was distinguished as a small town from the nearby villages by the
number of occupations indicated by surname evidence from tax lists. In 1307
there were two linen-drapers, a spicer, a vintner, a miller, a tanner, smiths, a
merchant, and a 'smeremonger'. Two shepherds show that some rural occupations survived in the urban settlement.[25] Archaeological evidence gives an
interestingly different pattern of occupations, for activities such as those in the
leather trades, or even cloth, have left little material record. In contrast, there is
much archaeological evidence for the pottery industry, for which there is little
documentary trace.

The Jews were an urban people in medieval England, and in the first decades
of the thirteenth century some of them were very wealthy and successful. The
communities of York, London, and Oxford were the three wealthiest, to judge
by the tax paid in 1241. Money lending was the key to their success. They had
the capacity to advance money to landowners who needed capital at a time of
rapid economic expansion, and were also in a position to take advantage of the
difficulties that some knightly families faced. In the 1240s the position of
the Jews worsened rapidly as a result of heavy royal taxation, starting with
the tallage of 1241, when they had to pay 20,000 marks. They had begun the
march on the road that would lead to expulsion in 1290.[26]

[22] M. C. Prestwich, *York Civic Ordinances, 1301*, Borthwick Papers, 49 (York, 1976), 7, 10–18.
[23] *Wealth of Shrewsbury*, ed. Cromarty and Cromarty, 46–52.
[24] E. A. Fuller, 'The Tallage of 1312 and the Bristol Riots', *Transactions of the Bristol and Gloucestershire Archaeological Society*, 19 (1894–5), 217.
[25] *Hertfordshire Lay Subsidy Rolls 1307 and 1334*, ed. J. Brooker and S. Flood (Hertfordshire Record Society, 1998), 105–7.
[26] R. C. Stacey, 'The English Jews Under Henry III', in P. Skinner (ed.), *The Jews in Medieval Britain* (Woodbridge, 2003), 41–54.

Within towns the Jews formed quite distinct communities. In cultural terms, the reputation of the well-educated English Jews was considerable, at least in the first half of the thirteenth century. It is, however, unlikely that they contributed much to the cultural identity of the other townspeople, so separate were they. In a very different and wholly regrettable sense, their presence on occasion might provoke outbreaks of racial and religious hatred. Lincoln was one important Jewish centre, and it was the scene of one of the most notorious alleged atrocities committed by the Jews. In 1255 a boy called Hugh was said to have been kidnapped, tortured, and sacrificed by crucifixion. Ninety-two Jews were imprisoned in the Tower, and eighteen who refused to accept a jury that contained no Jews were executed. A large number of houses in Lincoln belonging to Jews were confiscated, though many were then acquired by one of the Lincoln Jews, Hagin, in return for a fine paid to the king. The affair of Little St Hugh of Lincoln, as the boy became known, was an appalling example of religious hysteria and racial hatred, and it forms part of the background to the eventual expulsion of the entire Jewish community from England. When that happened, in 1290, there were sixty-six Jews in Lincoln, who were owed money or goods to a total value of about £2,200.[27]

URBAN GOVERNMENT

Towns aspired to, and often achieved, self-government, particularly if the king was the lord. A typical example is Lincoln, where the early thirteenth century saw the emergence of the office of mayor, replacing the earlier alderman. There were also two bailiffs, four coroners, and four beadles, along with two clerks. There was a council of twenty-four to advise the mayor; its members were drawn from the wealthy oligarchy of the city.[28] In some cases the existing guild merchant could take on the responsibility of urban government; in others, a new mayor and council (usually of twelve or twenty-four) might appear. The period of Richard I and John's reigns had been particularly important, with the grant of charters to many royal towns, allowing them to pay a fixed annual sum (fee-farm) to the exchequer, and giving them other privileges. By 1300 about fifty towns enjoyed the right to pay their fee-farm, a right that gave them financial independence from the sheriff. Privileged towns might have the right of return of writ. As Henry III's grant of 1256 to Southampton put it, this was 'so that no sheriff or bailiff or other servant of ours hereafter shall intermeddle concerning the making of summonses of this kind or attachments or distraints in the aforesaid town except by default of the said burgesses or bailiffs of the

---

[27] J. W. F. Hill, *Medieval Lincoln* (Cambridge, 1948), 224–8, 237.   [28] Ibid. 196, 293–4.

said town'.[29] The burgesses had the right to elect their own coroners, and cases concerning urban property were heard in the town's courts. They could not be hauled before the courts of shire or hundred for internal urban matters.

Royal towns, in general terms, enjoyed greater liberties and rights of self-government than did others. However, the attitude of the crown towards towns was not always beneficent. It was always possible to take the liberties of a town back, and to place it under direct control. In 1280 both York and Canterbury were taken into royal hands. Lincoln's government was suspended from 1291 until 1301. The major example of intervention by Edward I came in 1285 when London was taken into the king's hands, the result of royal alarm at the state of public order and in particular at the murder of Laurence Duket, found hanged in a church where he had gone for sanctuary. For no less than twelve years the city's rights of self-government were suspended, and it was only as a result of the national political crisis in 1297 that they were eventually restored.[30] When in 1281 the mayor of Sandwich and three other townspeople mistreated a messenger bearing a royal writ, the outcome was gaol for the individuals and loss of liberties for the town.[31] In 1329 justices in eyre sat at Northampton. The liberties of the town were challenged, and Chief Justice Scrope declared that all the offices of the town were forfeit. New royal officials were to be appointed. On 1 December Robert of Arderne was appointed as keeper of the town. The confiscation did not last long; in return for payment of a fine of £20, the mayoralty was restored on 3 August 1330.[32] Examples could be multiplied. There were changes over time in royal policy; Edward III was less high-handed than his predecessors, especially his grandfather; cooperation replaced aggression.

About half the towns in England were under the control of lords, lay and ecclesiastical. Leicester, for example, was held from the earl of Leicester, and after the effective demise of that earldom, from Lancaster. Some major towns had monastic lords, as was the case at Bury St Edmunds and St Albans. Most lords were more reluctant than the crown to concede rights, no doubt fearing the consequences of a diminution of their authority. At Leicester the town had no right of fee-farm, nor any right to elect its own officials. Yet it possessed a considerable degree of self-government, which developed out of the twelfth-century guild merchant. From the mid-thirteenth century there was a mayor, two aldermen, and financial officials. Although the earl of Lancaster's steward exercised a supervisory role on occasion, the guild records show that

---

[29] Platt, *Medieval Southampton*, 57.
[30] Williams, *Medieval London*, 255–60; Prestwich, *Edward I*, 265.
[31] C. R. Young, *The English Borough and Royal Administration, 1130–1307* (Durham, NC, 1961), 15.
[32] *The Eyre of Northamptonshire*, ed. Sutherland, 52, 60.

self-government was the normal situation. It was the guild that controlled the town's communal finances. In the early fourteenth century it controlled funds that normally stood at about £20–40 a year, but which rose in 1316–17 to £82 after the lord of the town, Thomas of Lancaster, had imposed a heavy tallage. At times a subtle distinction between the community of the guild and of the town could be observed, but this became increasingly blurred.[33] In other cases, however, seigneurial power prevented the emergence of self-governing communities. Boston, for all that it was one of the richest places in England, remained under the control of the honour of Richmond, and was treated as if it were manorial rather than urban. All of the town officials were appointed by the earls of Richmond, rather than being elected.[34]

Those towns unfortunate enough to have monastic lords, such as Bury St Edmunds or St Albans, were often at loggerheads with them. In 1287 some of the townspeople of Bury complained to the king about the abbot's unreasonable demands and the arbitrary character of his court. Three years later the townspeople attacked a new dam built on behalf of the abbey as part of the process of land reclamation. In the late 1290s there was trouble when two leading townsmen read out copies of charters which set out, among other things, the rights of the burgesses. After royal intervention, they had to buy back the abbot's goodwill. Matters were more serious still in 1327, when there was a major conflict in Bury. By the townsmen's account, the monks refused to let a number of women and children leave their church after a service. The burgesses came to demand their release, and the monks assaulted them 'with arrows, stones and engines of war'. The townsmen rose in rebellion, and burnt much of the abbey, though they spared the church itself, and sought the fraternal assistance of the Londoners in their quarrel. The abbot was seized by a group of rebels, hauled off to London, and then taken overseas, where he was kept in custody for three months.[35]

The powerful influence of a great abbey was very clear in the case of one of the many disputes between the townspeople of St Albans and the monks of the abbey there. John of Cambridge was the abbot's steward, but nonetheless he was appointed one of two justices appointed to deliver the town gaol. He took the opportunity to free the abbot's men who languished there following their indictment for involvement in a riot in 1328, which had seen the death of an important townsman. In 1331 Cambridge was on a trailbaston commission in the town. He was well entertained by the abbot, who also made sure that the

[33] *Records of the Borough of Leicester*, ed. Bateson, pp. xxvii–xlix, 295, 300, 302.

[34] S. H. Rigby, 'Boston and Grimsby in the Middle Ages: An Administrative Contrast', *Journal of Medieval History*, 10 (1984), 57–61.

[35] A. Gransden, 'John de Northwold, Abbot of Bury St Edmunds', in *TCE* iii. 104, 108–9; *Cal. Plea and Mem. Rolls*, 35; Knowles, *Religious Orders*, i. 267.

jury that heard the case against the townspeople was packed with his men. Not surprisingly, at the end of a lengthy dispute, the abbot won hands down against the townspeople.[36] As so often with the history of towns, generalizations are dangerous, for there were places, such as Westminster and Durham, where conflict between monastery and townspeople was avoided.

Quarrels with secular lords were less common, but some did occur. In 1313 John de Montalt, lord of part of the town of Lynn, was assaulted when he came to collect dues and tolls to which he claimed he was entitled. He and his men were chased to an inn, where he was captured. Under threat of death he was forced to agree that the townspeople should appoint a bailiff to collect his dues, and that for the next twenty-one years the money should be paid to him. He was made to stand on a market stall and agree to a written document which set out a penalty of £2,000 should he not honour the agreement.[37]

CONFLICT

Conflict within towns took many forms, and can be interpreted in many ways. In some cases, class rivalries were of key importance, but in others, clashes were far more personal in character. London politics was very complex, and many disputes cannot be analysed in straightforward terms of class, or of rivalry between different types of guilds.[38] In 1311, with John de Gisors as mayor, a popular movement took control of the city, and in 1313 this culminated with a short-lived triumph for the craft guilds. A backlash followed under John de Wengrave as mayor in 1316, when increasing reliance was placed on the city's established professional administrators. In 1319 there was a further revolution, led by a fishmonger, Hamo de Chigwell. A new charter was obtained for the city, at a price of 1,000 marks. This made the power of the community of the city a reality. City officials were to be elected, and could be removed by the community. Aldermen were not to serve for consecutive terms. The triumph was brief. The crown showed its muscle by imposing a judicial eyre on the city in 1321, and in the years of Despenser rule Chigwell trod a difficult tightrope, attempting to ingratiate himself with the government while trying to retain the support of the community of London. A little later an alderman was said to have declared that Hamo de Chigwell 'was the worst worm that had come to London for twenty years, that there would be no peace in the City so long as he was alive, and that it would be a good thing if his head was cut off'. In 1326 the city rose in support of Mortimer and Isabella, with

[36] Maddicott, *Law and Lordship*, 35–6.
[37] R.W. Kaeuper, 'Law and Order in Fourteenth-Century England: The Evidence of Special Commissions of Oyer and Terminer', *Speculum*, 54 (1979), 775.
[38] For the following discussion of London politics, see Williams, *Medieval London*, 270–306.

wild popular enthusiasm. Chigwell was removed from the mayoralty, and with
the new regime in power in 1327 London received a new, all-embracing
charter. The old rivalries and ambitions, however, were not forgotten. When
in 1328 an electoral assembly took place, the recorder announced that Chigwell
had been elected. Some then shouted for Benedict de Fulsham, in the past a
supporter of John de Gisors, and others for Chigwell. There was much
confusion, and eventually both candidates were persuaded to withdraw, in
the interests of peace. John de Grantham was then elected without dissent.[39]

At Bristol, in Edward II's reign, there was a complex situation that resulted
in a lengthy period of rebellion, when the city was effectively beyond royal
control for several years. One of the issues was the presence in Bristol of a royal
castle. The constable was Bartholomew Badlesmere, and he and his men took a
much more aggressive line towards the citizens than the previous constable,
Nicholas Fermbaud, had done. Badlesmere found support among the urban
oligarchy, but this ruling group of fourteen was extremely unpopular, partly
because of their claims to receive market dues and tolls. A revolution took place
in the city, and a popular mayor, John le Taverner, was elected in 1312. The
rebellion was also in part a protest against the tallage imposed in 1312. It lasted
until 1316, when it took a full-scale siege to end the citizens' resistance.[40]

In many cases disputes took place between the wealthy oligarchy and the rest
of the townspeople. In 1290 a case inspired by the poor, who were allegedly
oppressed with unfair distraints and tallages, was brought against some members of the Lincoln oligarchy. The city was taken into the king's hands, where
it remained until 1301.[41] In York a convivial fraternity founded in 1301 rapidly
developed into a well-organized guild, which effectively dominated the government of the city. In 1306 a case was brought against the guild, which was
duly dissolved. The action of the royal justices was clearly inspired by the
poorer elements in York society. Newcastle upon Tyne had its troubles in the
same period. In 1305 the court of the Exchequer heard a case brought by some
'poor burgesses' against over thirty 'rich burgesses'. The rich had, allegedly,
hindered the trading opportunities available to the poor. In particular, they
were not allowed to sell retail any cloth made in their homes, nor to sell wine by
the tun, nor any kind of grocery. The poor could buy only hides of young
animals for tanning and selling. The wealthy had formed themselves into a
guild, and were trying to establish a stranglehold over commercial activities in
the town. Judgment went against the rich; the poor were burgesses just as they

---

[39] *Cal. Plea and Mem. Rolls*, 69, 72–3.
[40] *Vita Edwardi*, 70–4; E. A. Fuller, 'The Tallage of 1312 and the Bristol Riots', *Transactions of the Bristol and Gloucestershire Archaeological Society*, 19 (1894–5), 174–88.
[41] Hill, *Medieval Lincoln*, 213–14.

were, and entitled to the same privileges.[42] There are many other indications of class conflict and jealousy. At Lincoln there were complaints in the 1320s from those who described themselves as middle citizens. The bailiffs were oppressing them in various ways, including fining them for not undertaking watch duty, while they spared the rich and took the money for themselves.[43]

ECONOMY

Towns were a driving force in the medieval economy. They were, of course, very diverse in size, structure, and role; there was an immense contrast between a major international port, such as Boston, and a local thriving market town such as Stratford upon Avon. Interestingly, there was no evident connection between success in obtaining and exercising rights of self-government, and economic prosperity. The case of Boston, where the townspeople had no powers to rule themselves, provides one demonstration of this. It was a port that did extremely well out of the prosperous English export trade in wool.

Specialization in manufacturing, marketing, and distribution was provided by towns, albeit at very different levels. It was once suggested, in a neat but profoundly unhelpful phrase, that they were 'non-feudal islands in a sea of feudalism'.[44] They were in practice a fully integrated and essential element of a complex economic system. One way in which towns stimulated the economy of their hinterlands was by consuming the food that was grown there. London is an exceptional example. Study of the way in which the city was provided with grain at the end of the thirteenth century shows a heavy dependence on markets at Henley upon Thames, and at Faversham. Eighty per cent of the places with which London cornmongers can be linked were within 60 miles of the city. The fact that water transport was cheap and easy in contrast with land meant that London did not draw its supplies from an area easily defined by distance, but it is clear that the city had a profound influence on local economies extending from the Wash and East Anglia to the upper Thames valley. One calculation is that London's production hinterland could have been as high as 11,800 square miles.[45] Similar work has not been done for other cities, but the hinterland of large places such as Norwich must equally have been extensive. The impetus given to agriculture by the need to feed the urban

[42] Prestwich, *York Civic Ordinances*, 7; C. M. Fraser, 'Medieval Trading Restrictions in the North East', *Archaeologia Aeliana*, 4th ser., 39 (1961), 138–9.

[43] *CPR 1324–7*, 236.

[44] Postan, *Medieval Economy and Society*, 212.

[45] B. M. S. Campbell, J. A. Galloway, D. Keene, and M. Murphy, *A Medieval Capital and its Grain Supply: Agrarian Production and Distribution in the London Region c.1300*, Historical Geography Research Series, 30 (Institute of British Geographers, 1993), 47, 49, 77.

populace, even if it was only somewhere between 5 and 10 per cent of the total population, was significant.

Equally, manufacture of an extensive variety of products was important. Towns had no monopoly of making things, but it was only in an urban setting that complex specialization occurred, and only there that a wide range of stalls and shops was available to sell what was produced. In Stratford upon Avon, an undistinguished yet prosperous mid-thirteenth century town, there were tanners, glovemakers, shoemakers, weavers, dyers, fullers, tailors, smiths, a locksmith, a carpenter, tilers, coopers, a wheelwright, and a rope-maker. Most of the personal names from St Albans in 1307 were not occupational, but those that were show the following occupations: tiler, smith, tanner, cooper, limeburner, tailor, barber, vintner, and baker.[46]

Fairs were the great trading occasions for a number of towns. It has been calculated that the number of fairs rose from 146 in 1200 to 1,620 a century later, but these varied greatly in importance.[47] Fairs were normally held annually, and a few, such as those at Winchester, Westminster, Northampton, Bury St Edmunds, Stamford, and St Ives (Hunts.), were of international significance. They were important for the sale of wool to foreign merchants, and provided opportunities for trade in luxury and specialized goods. By the late thirteenth century, however, fairs were becoming less important, as London and major provincial towns were seeing the development of year-round trading activity. At Westminster the monks received a charter from Henry III in 1245 allowing them to hold a three-day fair twice a year. The October fair was soon extended to a fortnight, and by the end of the thirteenth century to a month. Westminster abbey made significant profits by renting out stalls, bringing in an income of about £100 a year by 1300. Substantial as this was, it was only about a third of the proceeds of the great fair at Boston. By the mid-fourteenth century, however, Westminster fair, like the other major fairs, had declined steeply in importance. By then, the abbey's income from this source was no more than a third of what it had once been.[48]

Much normal buying and selling took place in markets, many of which were held in towns. The right to hold a market was a right conceded by charter, and just as the number of new towns increased, so did the number of markets, from an estimated 356 in 1200 to 1,746 a hundred years later. This huge expansion of markets in the thirteenth century caused inevitable problems, as lords with

---

[46] Carus-Wilson, 'Stratford-upon-Avon', 56; *Hertfordshire Lay Subsidy Rolls*, ed. Brooker and Flood, 126–8.

[47] The figures for numbers of fairs and markets are provided by the Gazetteer of Markets and Fairs in England and Wales to 1516, to be found at <http://www.history.ac.uk/cmh/gaz/gazweb2.html>.

[48] G. Rosser, *Medieval Westminster 1200–1540* (Oxford, 1989), 97–111.

established markets feared the effects of competition from new foundations. In 1240, for example, William Longespée and his wife obtained a charter for a new market at Swaton in Lincolnshire. Gilbert de Gaunt feared that it would damage his market at Folkingham, about 5 miles away. There were also fears for the market at Sleaford, 6 miles distant. Inquiries were held by the sheriff, and the new market was allowed to go ahead.[49] Grants continued to be made in the fourteenth century, but in many cases the new foundations failed to take off, while the position of others became more difficult. Market rights limited sales to a particular place, day, and time. There was some control of prices, and there were attempts by the crown to prevent the practice of 'regrating'. This was where a trader set himself up as a middleman, buying goods from peasants and other producers before they reached the market, so lengthening the supply chain and putting up prices. In 1337, for example, Geoffrey Pecok went out of London to meet cattle merchants and buy their beasts, as a result of which it was claimed that he was putting up prices by up to a third. He admitted his offence, but a group of six men charged with forestalling oysters, and with mixing stinking, putrid oysters with fresh ones, were found not guilty.[50] At the start of Edward II's reign forestalling became an offence under statutory law.[51]

The economic fortunes of English towns were not all positive in this period. In the early thirteenth century cloth production was very important, with some towns such as Lincoln, York, and Winchester the homes of an industry that made very high-standard woollen cloth, notably scarlets. The market for this declined with competition from silks. The efficient Flemish cloth industry outpaced the English, reducing the export market for English cloth. Within England urban weavers found their products challenged by cloth made by rural producers, who were able to cut prices. The weavers of York complained as early as 1227 about the cloth being made outside the city. A technological argument suggested that the advent of fulling mills, which mechanized one stage of cloth production, was another element in the decline of the urban industry, for it was in the countryside that the fast-flowing streams were to be found that powered these mills. Attractive as this explanation is, the number of such mills that are known to have been constructed suggests that it has very limited validity. The effect of the various factors was the collapse of the urban cloth industry, and with it the failure of the weavers' guilds, which had played a very important role in the towns of the twelfth century. In 1290 there were only seven weavers in Oxford, where there had once been sixty. By 1309 the arrears due from the weavers of York for an annual payment of £10 to the exchequer

[49] Masschaele, *Peasants, Merchants and Markets*, 66.
[50] *Cal. Plea and Mem. Rolls*, 143, 145.
[51] Britnell, *Commercialisation of English Society*, 92–3.

stood at £790. At Lincoln the weavers continued to pay their £6 a year until 1321, but from that date the craft had no members within the city, though there were a few spinners in the 1330s and 1340s.[52]

Overall, in economic terms, there were both winners and losers among English towns. Broadly, ports thrived compared to inland towns, demonstrating the importance of long-distance trade. Newcastle upon Tyne was assessed for the tallage of 1252 at £67, and for the tax of 1336 at £133. York's figures are £333 for 1252, and £162 for 1334.[53] Elsewhere, however, the contrast was not so striking, and some qualification is needed. Southampton was a port that did badly as a result of the French sack of the town in 1338, while Edward III's demands for ships had a damaging effect on others. The story of new towns is mixed. Earlier foundations tended to prosper as compared to later ones. Salisbury is a prime example, as is Stratford upon Avon on a smaller scale. New Winchelsea, on the other hand, founded in 1288, was badly affected by French raids and the silting-up of the estuary on which it was sited. The dangers of generalization are demonstrated, however, by Hull, which, with royal patronage behind it, did well, even though Edward I did not acquire it until 1293. Wardour in Sussex, founded in the 1260s, though a port, never seems to have taken off at all.[54]

London provides a special case. The economic dominance of London was already established by the end of the twelfth century, but the thirteenth saw its position become still more pre-eminent. Figures show that about 16 per cent of English trade went through London at the start of the thirteenth century; by the end of the century that figure had doubled.[55] One reason for this was, of course, that success bred success. Another was that foreign merchants tended to congregate in one place, and London was the most obvious. A further element was the development of London as England's capital city. There were periods during the Scottish wars when the exchequer and law courts were moved to York; this was certainly unpopular with at least one of Edward I's officials, Philip Willoughby, who wrote disdainfully of 'this profane city of York'.[56] There was little likelihood of a permanent move north, as government

[52] Miller and Hatcher, *Medieval England*, 107–11; Hill, *Medieval Lincoln*, 326. For the argument about fulling mills, see E. Carus-Wilson, *Medieval Merchant Venturers*, 2nd edn. (London, 1967), 183–209.

[53] J. F. Hadwin, 'The Medieval Lay Subsidies and Economic History', *EcHR*, 2nd ser., 36 (1983), 217.

[54] Beresford, *New Towns*, 497.

[55] Williams, *Medieval London*, 106.

[56] SC 1/8/112a. The periods when the exchequer and courts were at York were 1298–1304, 1319–20, 1322–3, 1327, 1333–8. See W. M. Ormrod, 'Competing "Capitals": York and London in the Fourteenth Century', in S. Rees Jones, R. Marks, and A. J. Minnis (eds.), *Courts and Regions in Medieval Europe* (Woodbridge, 2000), 80.

business was increasingly concentrated upon Westminster and London. Parliament always met more often at Westminster than anywhere else; from 1339 it was invariably summoned to Westminster. This brought people thronging to London, as did the activities of the exchequer, chancery, and above all the law courts. One department was particularly important for many London merchants. From the later years of Edward I's reign the department of the great wardrobe had a permanent presence in London, where a house was rented. In 1328 property in Lombard Street was bought from the Bardi for this department, through which the crown bought cloth, spices, and other articles for the royal household in impressive quantities.[57]

GUILDS AND FRATERNITIES

Guilds provided a framework for the economic organization of many towns, but unfortunately there is often very little evidence about them. The chronology of guild foundation is often obscure, but it seems likely that many had their origins in the later fourteenth century. At the start of the thirteenth century most towns had a guild merchant, and in many there was a weaver's guild. At Leicester the guild merchant dominated urban government in the thirteenth century, and attempted to keep a tight control not only over trade, but also over the town's weavers and fullers. In Norwich craft guilds had appeared by the late thirteenth century. The cobblers, saddlers, and fullers were all fined small sums in 1292 for having guilds in contravention of the charter granted to the city by Henry III.[58] At Lincoln guild certificates of 1389 suggest that most of the city's guilds were fourteenth-century foundations. The one exception was that of the weavers, which had been powerful in the twelfth century, the great days of the production of Lincoln scarlet, one of Europe's most prized cloths. At Newcastle there were twelve guilds in the 1340s, but it is not clear when they began.[59] In many cases town governments resented the guilds, which were seen as a threat to existing authority.

There is much more evidence about guilds from London than is the case for other towns. There was a precocious development of guilds in the twelfth century; in 1179–80 eighteen unlicensed ones were fined by the crown. These included the goldsmiths, pepperers, the clothworkers, and the butchers alongside bridge guilds and others of unknown purpose. In the thirteenth century the craft ordinances of the lorimers were set down in 1261, and those of the

[57] Tout, *Chapters*, iv. 397–405; T. F. Tout, 'The Beginnings of a Modern Capital: London and Westminster in the Fourteenth Century', in his *Collected Papers*, iii. 249–75.
[58] *Leet Jurisdiction in the City of Norwich*, ed. W. Hudson (Selden Society, 1892), pp. lxxxviii–lxxxix, 42–3.
[59] Hill, *Medieval Lincoln*, 327; Miller and Hatcher, *Medieval England*, 361–5.

cordwainers two years later. These guilds, however, were formally suppressed in 1274. The fishmongers were almost certainly a guild in the 1260s, long before their ordinances were formally approved in 1279–80. In the early fourteenth century large numbers of London craft guilds obtained full recognition.[60] The purpose of these guilds was protectionist and regulatory. They aimed to maintain standards, and to ensure that there was no threat from outsiders to their livelihood. Competition was strictly limited; patterns for apprenticeship were firmly laid down. A difficult question is how far the guilds had their origins in religious fraternities. If it is accepted that the latter type of organization 'was essentially a secret association, which had every reason for withdrawing its existence and its regulations as much as possible from public notice', then it is unlikely that the question can be answered. It is most probable, however, that the craft guilds were formed for economic reasons, and it was only in a few cases that they were linked to a religious fraternity by 1300.[61]

The guilds had a long fight for recognition. They represented a threat to the existing power structure of London, with its wards and its aldermen. When Thomas FitzThomas was mayor, from 1261 to 1265, he provided strong support for the crafts, and the same line was taken by Walter Hervey in 1272–3. Hervey's successor, Henry le Waleys, took the opposing view, and in 1274 the charters that the craft guilds had received were annulled. The conflict can be interpreted in terms of the hostility of the great merchants, like le Waleys, for the crafts that, with their restrictive practices, threatened to put up prices. It is, however, dangerous to interpret what happened in strict class terms, of middling craftsmen against rich oligarchs, for many of those identified with the crafts were themselves wealthy merchants. By the fourteenth century, however, success went to the craft guilds.

Guilds and fraternities might provide a social focus, as well as protecting trades and crafts. One short-lived London fraternity, known as the Puy, has left a unique record of some of its proceedings. Its head was a prince, chosen each year. A feast was held when the new prince was installed. Ballads were presented in a form of talent show, with a crown awarded to the best. After the feast, the members of the Puy would ride through the city, escorting their new prince to his house, where they would perform a dance.[62]

[60] E. Veale, 'The "Great Twelve": Mistery and Fraternity in Thirteenth-Century London', *Historical Research*, 64 (1991), 239–41; *Cambridge Urban History*, i. 207; Williams, *Medieval London*, 178, 193.

[61] G. Unwin, *The Guilds and Companies of London* (London, 1908), 97; Veale, 'The "Great Twelve"', 237–63.

[62] Unwin, *Guilds and Companies of London*, 98–9; Veale, 'The "Great Twelve"', 260–1.

URBAN LIFE

Medieval towns were crowded places, in which many aspects of life had to be closely regulated. London jurors in 1276 produced a long list of complaints about buildings that had infringed the city's rules. Solars overhanging the road were a problem. The earl of Gloucester built a drain or gutter through his kitchen, which made a smell outside and was therefore ordered to be shut off. The objection to the four privies built by the earl of Norfolk was presumably similar. Steps were built blocking the roadway; even a vine planted by Ascelina de la Boche was held to be a nuisance.[63] In Norwich in 1295 John de Scotia was fined because he had built windows overhanging the roadway, which obstructed riders as they went past his house. In 1299 John the tailor was fined because he had made a privy.[64] There was a range of other problems. As in more recent times in London, pigeons were a nuisance, but in 1327 it proved necessary to forbid people to shoot them, since the arrows and stones broke windows and injured passers-by.[65] Muck was a constant issue. There were some arrangements for cleaning the London streets; in 1332 Richard Tailleboys, beadle of Cripplegate ward, was assaulted, and his cart taken from him, while he was doing this.[66] At Norwich in 1292 Richard de Seething was fined for having 'a noxious muck-heap', and in 1312 Christine Avenant was fined for blocking a gutter so that putrid filth ran out to the annoyance of her neighbours.[67] Just as in rural communities, scolding by women was seen as a problem. In Halesowen in 1300 Margery la Leche was sent to the pillory for declaring that Nicholas Sutor's wife was a whore, 'or if she had not been married she would have been one'. Scolding perhaps ran in the family, for two years later Scholacia la Leche accused John the Tanner of being like a woman in stature and manner.[68]

Public order needed to be maintained. Attitudes could be stringent; those in authority considered that urban communities should be well controlled. In London juries had suspicious minds. In 1340 one declared 'that Walter Walteshelf, Gracian le Palmer and John Walssh are nightwalkers, well dressed and lavish of their money', though no one knows how they get their living, and that these people, if they had their opportunity, would sooner consort with

---

[63] *The London Eyre of 1276*, ed. M. Weinbaum (London Record Society, 1976), nos. 349, 350, 357, 437, 456.

[64] *Leet Jurisdiction in the City of Norwich*, ed. Hudson 47, 52.

[65] *Cal. Plea and Mem. Rolls*, 36.

[66] Ibid. 99; Barron, *London in the Later Middle Ages*, 261–2.

[67] *Leet Jurisdiction in the City of Norwich*, ed. Hudson, 45, 56.

[68] R. H. Hilton, 'Small Town Society in England Before the Black Death', *Past and Present*, 105 (1984), 71–2.

bad characters and disturbers of the peace than with men of good report'.[69] Far more serious, however, in the same year was a riot between the Fishmongers and the Skinners, which even involved a direct assault on the mayor, who was seized by the throat. Two of those responsible for the violence were promptly hanged, but the man responsible for starting the affray was simply imprisoned for a year.[70]

Prostitution was a particularly urban problem. It was especially common in London. In the early 1260s two men, Henry and Roger, went to a brothel in London, in which Notekina Hoggenhore and five other prostitutes lived. They found some foreign merchants there, and a quarrel broke out. Both Englishmen were killed. Another brothel, in Bishopsgate ward, had four resident prostitutes.[71] Some brothels might provide specialized services: in 1338 a Londoner was accused of keeping 'a house of ill-fame to which married women and their paramours and other bad characters resorted'.[72] Attempts, no doubt unsuccessful, were made to ban prostitution from some towns. The first mention of one of the greatest intellectual figures of the age, Robert Grosseteste, in an Oxford context was an order of 1234 requiring him, along with the chancellor of the university, to oversee the arrest of all the prostitutes in the city, who had refused to obey a royal mandate that they should leave the town.[73] The York Ordinances of 1301 deliberately juxtaposed pigs and prostitutes, and forbade both. Driving prostitutes out was not always popular: in 1312 a Norwich man, presumably a satisfied customer, assaulted the bailiffs in an unsuccessful rescue attempt as they were escorting a group from the town.[74]

Urban life was not just a matter of muck, crime, and prostitution. Towns offered a remarkable intensity of religious life. Stamford in Lincolnshire, despite its importance as one of the major English centres for the marketing of wool, was not a large town. Yet by 1300 it possessed no less than fourteen parish churches, six chapels, a monastery, a nunnery, and at least three friaries, as well as hospitals.[75] York at this period had a remarkable forty-five parishes, and Winchester no fewer than fifty-four.[76] Religious fraternities were a feature of urban life. The establishment of the feast of Corpus Christi in 1264 was important, as it provided a particularly popular focus for urban religion, with many guilds and lay fraternities dedicated to it, but there were other important cults. There was a Fraternity of the Holy Cross at Stratford upon Avon from the

[69] *Cal. Plea and Mem. Rolls*, 126.   [70] Ibid. 128–9.
[71] *The London Eyre of 1276*, ed. Weinbaum, nos. 119, 134.
[72] *Cal. Plea and Mem. Rolls*, 167.   [73] Southern, *Grosseteste*, 71.
[74] Prestwich, *York Civic Ordinances*, 16–17; *Leet Jurisdiction in the City of Norwich*, ed. Hudson, 59.
[75] D. Roffe, *Stamford in the Thirteenth Century* (Stamford, 1994), 5–6.
[76] *Cambridge Urban History*, i. 461.

first half of the thirteenth century. At Boston the guild of the Virgin Mary was founded in 1250; no doubt it helped to provide the sense of corporate identity that the town's form of government could not provide. In 1350 the Corpus Christi guild at Lincoln was founded 'by folks of common and middling rank'. The guild brethren were anxious to exclude those of high rank from their numbers, unless they were 'of humble good and honest conversation'.[77] Most of the evidence for such fraternities and guilds comes from the late fourteenth or fifteenth centuries, but there is little doubt that groupings of townspeople were formed much earlier to provide support for particular churches or cults.

The friars were a particularly distinctive element in towns, and were radically different from the established religious orders. The first to arrive in England were the Dominicans in 1221, with the Franciscans coming three years later.[78] They interpreted the Christian message in a new way, adopting a life of poverty, preaching, and learning. Towns were important to them, as it was there that they could reach the greatest number of people. The friars homed in with a clear strategic sense on the cathedral cities of England, the county towns, and major commercial centres. They also concentrated their attentions on the intellectual hothouses of Oxford and Cambridge. In 1300 there were nine towns in England, including London, where houses for all four major orders of friars (Dominicans, Franciscans, Carmelites, and Austin Friars) were to be found. Twenty-seven towns had houses for both Dominicans and Franciscans. London, where the friars enjoyed considerable patronage from wealthy citizens, had no less than eight mendicant houses.[79] The Dominicans in particular were great preachers. The friars possessed greater pastoral skills than did the average parish clergy, and filled roles such as that of confessor with alacrity. They operated within society, rather than at arm's length from it as monks did, and soon gained great popularity. Out of 119 wills from Carlisle, over half contain bequests to the friars.[80] One attraction of the friars was that they came cheap. They were far less acquisitive than Benedictine or Cistercian monks, and in the early stages resisted the possession of property. Although by the later thirteenth century they were engaged in building houses on a significant scale, friars were never costly to endow. At Southampton plans by the townspeople to provide the Franciscans with a stone house in the 1230s failed, when the buildings were demolished on the

---

[77] Carus-Wilson, 'Stratford-upon-Avon', 62; Rigby, 'Boston and Grimsby', 61; Hill, *Medieval Lincoln*, 298.

[78] For a discussion of the friars in the 13th century, see J. Burton, *Monastic and Religious Orders in Britain 1000–1300* (Cambridge, 1994), 109–30.

[79] *Cambridge Urban History*, i. 144; J. Röhrkasten, 'Mendicants in the Metropolis: The Londoners and the Development of the London Friaries', in *TCE* vi. 61–75.

[80] Summerson, *Carlisle*, i. 360.

instructions of the order. In 1280, however, a major building project began, with stone church, dormitory, and chapter house.[81] As was almost invariably the case with movements of religious reform, the initial zeal and purity did not last.

The friars did not serve the towns solely in religious terms. As pioneers of water supply and drainage they worked to improve the environment. They built an aqueduct in London in 1255, one in Oxford in about 1280, and one in Cambridge, which even today supplies the water for the fountain in Trinity Great Court. In 1304 at Southampton the friars began a major project to bring piped water to their house. When Ralph Stafford provided the funding for a new friary just outside Stafford, the deal was that he should provide them with 5 acres of land, and they should provide it with an aqueduct.[82]

One of the themes of this book is that of the impact of war on England. Its direct effect on the great majority of inland towns was relatively limited. Recruitment of soldiers took place primarily in the countryside. London provided troops for Simon de Montfort in 1264, but their performance at the battle of Lewes demonstrated their inexperience. It was exceptional for the borough of Leicester to be asked to provide ten heavily armed footsoldiers and thirty archers in 1315–16; even the dozen provided in 1322 was out of the ordinary.[83] Seaports, on the other hand, were burdened by frequent requests to supply ships and sailors, particularly in the fourteenth century. The Cinque Ports were in a special situation, for they owed formal service, provided whenever there was a feudal summons; other ports saw their ships seized by royal commissioners so that troops and supplies could be transported to France. Problems on the east coast were emphasized when royal commissioners went to Dunwich in 1354. Much of the town had been submerged since Edward I's day. At the start of the French war there had been sixteen 'farships', twenty 'kreyers', and twenty-four fishing boats. These, with 500 men, had been destroyed, with a loss of goods worth £2,000. Now, there were only two 'kreyers' and ten fishing boats. Where there used to be 2,000 inhabitants paying 'scot and lot', there were now only forty-seven.[84] In addition, there were problems caused by French raids. Southampton suffered very badly from the raid of 1338. In 1360 the French attacked Winchelsea, and 'took away with them nine beautiful women from the town, and violated them in a manner horrible to relate'.[85]

---

[81] C. Platt, *Medieval Southampton*, 64.
[82] Ibid. 65, 68; J. R. H. Moorman, *The Franciscans in England* (London, 1974), 32–3; *CPR 1343–5*, 321.
[83] *Records of the Borough of Leicester*, ed. Bateson, 302–3, 340–1.
[84] *CIM* iii, no. 156.
[85] Knighton, 174–5.

CHAPTER 19

Trade and Merchants

The fleece from the backs of English sheep, once it was sorted, packed into woolsacks, and exported to be spun and woven in the Low Countries, underlay many of the successes of this period. At the peak of this trade, in the early fourteenth century, about 40,000 or more sacks were sent abroad each year. Some 10 million sheep had to be sheared to produce such a quantity. The value of exports on this scale came to roughly £250,000. It was hardly surprising that Edward I's opponents in 1297 claimed that wool amounted to half the wealth of England. While the wool trade was dominant, commerce in wine from Gascony was also important, and a wide range of other commodities were imported and exported. Within England, trade at a more local level, much of it taking place in markets, was essential to the health of an increasingly commercial economy. For the government, from Edward I's reign, the taxation of trade provided an essential source of revenue, while the loans provided by merchants gave a much-needed flexibility to crown finance. Trading rivalries might have very serious consequences; the Anglo-French war of 1294 had its origins in an unofficial naval conflict in the previous year between English and French sailors, with the former aided by men from Bayonne, and Normans.

Statistics for English trade are lacking for the period before 1275, when the wool custom was introduced. It is likely, however, that wool exports rose substantially under Henry III. The civil war of 1264–5 undoubtedly disrupted trade, and to make matters worse, in 1270 what amounted to a trade war broke out between England and Flanders. Average wool exports in the 1280s stood at about 26,750 sacks a year. The figure was low, for this was a period when epidemics were severely hitting wool production. The heavy taxation of wool from 1294 to 1297 undoubtedly affected exports severely, but in spite of this, in the year to Michaelmas 1298 over 26,000 sacks were exported. In 1299/1300 the figure was over 31,500. The early fourteenth century saw a boom on a spectacular scale, with over 46,000 sacks exported in 1304/5, and over 41,000 for the following two years. Such levels were not maintained, and by the period 1323–9 the average annual export had fallen back to under 24,000, rising again in the years 1329–36 to almost 31,000. During the French war the complexities of heavy royal taxation of wool exports, seizures, and the difficulties faced by the consumers in the Low Countries had their inevitable effect on the export trade. Even so, in the year from Michaelmas 1350 almost 36,000 sacks of wool were exported, a figure that includes more than a single year's production. In the ten years from 1353, a period characterized by a relative lack of restrictions, the annual average exports stood at an impressive figure, over 33,000 sacks a year.[1]

The excellence of the data for wool exports has meant that less attention has been paid by historians to other trades. England's trade extended from the north, from Norway and the Baltic region, south through Germany and France, to the Iberian peninsula and the Mediterranean. The range of commodities traded was immense; it would be an oversimplification to suggest that England was primarily an exporter of raw materials and an importer of manufactured items. Some cloth was exported, though much more came the other way; in the early fourteenth century about 12,000 cloths a year, woven abroad from English wool, were imported.[2] Dyestuffs, particularly woad, were much needed in England. Timber was both imported and exported. In 1304/5 over 25,000 boards and wainscots, 600 empty barrels, and almost 8,000 bowstaves along with other items were brought to Hull from the Baltic region.[3] Tin and lead were significant English exports, while iron was brought in from Spain. Food and drink were major elements. Imports of wine were substantial: in 1308/9, 7,300 tuns were brought into London alone. Exports of grain were significant; a petition from Edward II's reign complained, no doubt with a measure of exaggeration, that in one year German merchants had exported over 60,000 quarters of grain from Lynn since Candlemas, and that thirteen cogs were currently in the port loading a further 8,000 quarters.[4] Fish was imported, notably dried cod, known as stockfish, while cured herrings and other fish were exported. Spices and other luxury items were imported; salt came from the salt pans of the French Atlantic coast.

Of these various trades, that in wine is the best documented, and possibly the most important. The volume of wine imported from Gascony cannot be calculated in the same way as wool exports, but it is clear that there were considerable fluctuations, with a peak in the early fourteenth century of perhaps 20,000 tuns imported a year, out of total Gascon exports which may

---

[1] Lloyd, *Wool Trade*, 63, 97, 99, 123, 204, 215. For a convenient graph, see E. M. Carus-Wilson and O. Coleman, *England's Export Trade 1275–1547* (Oxford, 1963), 122.

[2] For cloth exports, see W. Childs, 'The English Export Trade in Cloth', in Britnell and Hatcher (eds.), *Progress and Problems in Medieval England* (Cambridge, 1996), 121–47.

[3] J. Kermode, *Medieval Merchants: York, Beverley and Hull in the Later Middle Ages* (Cambridge, 1998), 181.

[4] T. H. Lloyd, *Alien Merchants in England in the High Middle Ages* (Brighton, 1982), 109.

have reached as much as 100,000 tuns. The appalling weather of 1315–16, which hit grain production in England so hard, also hit wine production in south-western France. In the year from July 1315 only 129 wine ships came to England, whereas in 1317/18 there were 232. The war of Saint-Sardos halved the wine trade in the short term in the mid-1320s. Just as with the wool trade, there was a very marked shift as the wine trade was increasingly dominated by English merchants. The combined effects of war in south-western France and the Black Death meant that levels of imports fell sharply in the mid-1340s, and did not recover. In 1350–1 imports stood at no more than 8,350 tuns, less than half the high levels of the early fourteenth century.[5]

TRADE AND GOVERNMENT

Merchants had the ear of kings. Memoranda on financial policy and the taxation of trade survive, written by merchants and presented to Edward I and his son.[6] Others were surely written for the consideration of Edward III's government. They were close to the levers of power, literally so in the case of Orlandino da Pogio of the company of the Ricciardi, who according to the household ordinance of 1279 was one of the eight people allowed to sleep in the wardrobe.[7] The Genoese merchant Antonio Pessagno was high in Edward II's favour for a time, dominating the court.

The wool trade, given its value and importance, was particularly subject to government regulation and interference. England had a virtual monopoly of the supply of wool to the great weaving towns of the Low Countries, and one weapon in times of difficulty was to place embargoes on exports. For much of the thirteenth century the export trade in English wool was dominated by Flemish merchants; privileges were granted to the men of Ypres, Ghent, Saint-Omer, and Douai. Problems began in the mid-1260s, when wool was seized from Flemings by the Montfortian government. By 1270 the countess of Flanders was increasingly aggrieved at the English failure to compensate Flemish merchants for their losses, and at the non-payment of the annual pension due to her. She accordingly ordered a seizure of English goods in Flanders, and the English responded in kind. A ban on exports to Flanders was imposed. The hope was that the Flemings would come to terms when their

[5] M. K. James, 'The Fluctuations of the Anglo–Gascon Wine Trade During the Fourteenth Century', in Carus-Wilson (ed.), *Essays in Economic History*, ii. 125–45.

[6] C. V. Langlois, 'Project for Taxation Presented to Edward I', *EHR* 4 (1889), 517–21; M. W. Ormrod, 'Political Theory in Practice: The Forced Loan on English Overseas Trade of 1317–18', *Historical Research*, 64 (1991), 204–15.

[7] Tout, *Chapters*, ii. 163.

cloth industry was deprived of its main source of wool, as they did when a treaty was secured in 1274.[8]

The crown had an obligation to provide protection for its subjects as they engaged in trade, and this had significant diplomatic implications. The middle years of Edward II's reign, for example, saw much difficulty following an attack by English sailors in 1310 on a Flemish fleet in Brittany. The Flemings retaliated in kind. In 1317, among others, Stephen Alard of Winchelsea complained that his ship, *La Johanette*, laden with corn, had been captured, and the *Cog St Marie*, a wine ship also from Winchelsea, was taken by Flemings. Such actions led to the seizures of Flemish goods in England, and a truce was eventually agreed in 1323.[9]

A more practical measure than a total embargo, which was hard to enforce, was to direct all exports to a particular place, a staple, where it could be sold. It was easier to protect English merchants if their activities were confined in this way, and it provided a useful diplomatic weapon for the crown. Antwerp and Bruges were often used as staples, and in the 1290s Edward I channelled exports first to Dordrecht, and then to Malines. It was also possible to use English towns in this way, as was attempted in 1326, in an experiment that did not outlast Isabella and Mortimer's invasion. There were interesting arguments in 1328, when a body claiming to represent the community of English merchants argued that a foreign staple was the best solution, and that if it were adopted, the country would benefit to the tune of 20s. on each sack of wool exported, presumably because it was thought that this would have the effect of raising the prices paid by foreign buyers. Not everyone agreed with this; the Londoners argued that a home staple was far better, and that rather than set up a foreign staple, merchants should be allowed to trade wherever they liked.[10] Their arguments, however, were in vain, and it was not until 1353 that a home staple policy was once again adopted, probably as a result of pressure from the wool-growers. This policy meant that foreign buyers had to come to English ports to buy wool, and that English merchants did not have to risk trading abroad. Judging by the high levels of exports, the move was a successful one, but by 1357 a Bruges staple had re-emerged. In 1363 it was replaced by one established at Calais.

The main reason for crown interference with trade was, of course, that it provided a very convenient source of revenue. The government might, in times of emergency, seize wool with a view to exporting it and taking the profit that would in normal times have gone to the merchants. This technique was threatened by Edward I in 1294, and carried through with very limited

---

[8] Lloyd, *Wool Trade*, 30–1.   [9] Ibid. 104–14; *CCR 1313–18*, 461.
[10] *Cal. Plea and Mem. Rolls*, 53, 56–8.

success in 1297. Edward III's dealings in wool were complex; his initial plan in 1337 was to obtain a loan of 30,000 sacks of wool, which effectively amounted to a seizure. A grant made in parliament in 1338 of 20,000 sacks of wool provided another way of profiting from the main English export trade, as was a loan of a further 20,000 sacks in 1340. Seizures, however, were unpopular, and a more successful way of raising money from wool was through customs duties.

A duty was levied on exports by foreign merchants from 1266, but it was not until 1275 that a permanent customs system was introduced. In 1275 Edward I acknowledged the importance of the merchants of England in his summons to parliament, for representatives were summoned from every city, borough, and merchant town. The purpose was clear: the king wanted to obtain as full consent as possible for the new customs duties that were proposed. The idea had come from an Italian, named as Pontius de Ponto, who was probably a member of the Ricciardi company.[11] A grant was made in perpetuity, for the levy of 6s. 8d. on each sack of wool exported. Duties were also be to be paid on wool-fells and hides. The purpose of the levy was to provide a secure income from which the king could repay loans he had taken from merchants. An incidental effect of the imposition of what became known as the ancient custom was that wool exports were effectively limited to the thirteen customs ports that were set up, of which the most important were Boston, London, Hull, and Southampton. In 1294 the merchants, objecting to a planned seizure of wool, agreed to a massive increase in the levels of duty, which were raised to 40s. a sack. This *maltolt*, as it was termed, was abolished in 1297, but not forgotten. In 1303 negotiations with the foreign merchants resulted in their agreeing to pay an additional 3s. 4d. on top of the original ancient custom; these new customs also included an *ad valorem* levy on other goods both imported and exported. This duty was abolished by the Ordainers in 1311; the objection was not to the payments, but to the privileges that Edward I had granted to the foreign merchants in a charter of 1303 in exchange for the grant of customs. This charter had freed them from various regulations, notably those that limited the length of time they might stay in a given place. The revocation of the Ordinances in 1322 meant that the duties on foreign merchants could be reimposed. Edward II's reign also saw the introduction of the forced loan as a further means by which the crown could profit from the wool trade; in 1317 an additional levy of 6s. 8d. on each sack exported by English merchants, and 10s. on those exported by aliens, was imposed, as a loan, for just over year. Edward III saw the wool trade as a mainstay of his war finance. In 1336 he was granted a subsidy of 20s. a sack, and in 1338 this was raised to 40s. It was

---

[11] Ann. Dunstable, 258.

regranted and renewed on various occasions. Duties rose as high as £4 a sack for English merchants and £5 3s. 4d. for foreigners.

Edward III was also engaged in complex arrangements with consortia of merchants. The English Company, composed of thirty-three men, was set up in 1343 to receive the customs revenue and to make regular advances to the crown. In the following year two-thirds of the members of this syndicate withdrew, and in 1345 the remainder agreed to pay £50,000 a year to the king, in return for the revenues from the customs. This group was succeeded by another, headed by John Wesenham of King's Lynn, and in 1346 by Thomas Swanlond and Walter Chiriton of London, who put in a higher bid than their rivals, only to be bankrupted by 1349. These English merchants did not have sufficient financial backing to enable them to take on obligations on the scale demanded by Edward, and their syndicates did not have the solidity of the Italian merchant companies.[12]

The financial significance of the customs duties had major constitutional implications. In 1275 Edward I acknowledged the importance of the merchants of England in his summons to parliament, for representatives were summoned from every city, borough, and merchant town. The purpose was clear: the king wanted to obtain as full consent as possible for the new customs duties that were proposed. This was hardly the best way to obtain the agreement of the merchants; it made more sense to approach them in separate assemblies. The crown's attempts to make use of a separate estate of merchants were not in the end successful. In 1303 both the English and the foreign merchants were consulted about the introduction of additional customs duties, but it was only the foreigners who were agreeable to this; the crown had more to offer them in the way of privileges than it had for its own subjects. The merchants continued to be consulted separately by Edward III. In 1336 gatherings of merchants were ordered to meet at Oxford, at Northampton, and finally at Nottingham, where a subsidy of 20s. a sack, and a promise of a loan of a further 20s., were agreed. A further merchant assembly met at Nottingham in 1338, though many refused to attend, and others were held in 1340, one of which had a potential membership of 284. Not until that year was a grant of customs duties made by parliament to Edward III. In the next year, assemblies of merchants, one of as many as 110 men, were summoned to negotiate the contract by which they were to export wool in return for massive loans of £200,000 to the crown. The methods of summoning merchant assemblies paralleled those used to summon parliament. In 1347 seventy-nine merchants received individual summons, while the sheriffs were to select four or six men to accompany them. There was little unity among the merchants; those who

---

[12] Lloyd, *Wool Trade*, 193–202.

formed the consortia to advance money to the king had a different interest from the majority. Though the meetings were broadly representative, they varied considerably in composition, and were the product of the king's wishes, not of the merchants' desires. In 1351 parliament, when granting a tax, asked that any grants made out of parliament should be annulled. In 1353 a merchant assembly once again took place, but it was in a great council attended by representatives of shire and boroughs that the Ordinance of the Staple was agreed. The crown abandoned its attempts to negotiate the taxing of trade solely with the merchants, and acknowledged that this was part of the business of parliament.[13] It had seemed possible that an estate of merchants would emerge as a result of Edward III's efforts to negotiate customs duties directly with mercantile assemblies, but there was insufficient unity among the merchants, and not enough political power for them to challenge the authority of parliament. The assemblies were the creation of the king, not of any coherent community of merchants.

ITALIAN COMPANIES

Italians formed the elite of merchants operating in England in the thirteenth and early fourteenth centuries. Their resources, drawn from activities undertaken on a truly international scale, dwarfed those of English and other merchants. It was probably early in Henry III's reign that the Italians began to trade on a significant scale in England. Florentines and Sienese were active; one Florentine, Deutatus Willame, became a citizen of London. The queen, Eleanor of Provence, employed him; in 1263 he claimed to have been robbed of £600 worth of her goods that he had in store.[14] The main attraction of England for the Italians lay on the back of millions of English sheep. A merchant exporting a sack of wool which he sold for £8 might well make £2 in profit. The Italians were well placed to take advantage of the difficulties in which the Flemings found themselves from the mid-1260s. Typical deals involved advancing money to impecunious monastic houses, and buying up their wool crop for a number of years to come. The Italians took a risk on future productivity of wool and on the market price, but the profits available to them were clearly considerable. They struck hard bargains; in 1276 they insisted on a mortgage when Fountains abbey received advanced payment for four years' wool crop. In 1291 the abbey's indebtedness to the Italians stood at almost £6,500, though in 1293 and 1294 the figure was down to a more

---

[13] See G. Unwin, 'The Estate of Merchants, 1336–165', in Unwin (ed.), *Finance and Trade Under Edward III* (Manchester, 1918), 179–232; Harris, *King, Parliament and Public Finance*, 420–49.
[14] *The London Eyre of 1276*, ed. Weinbaum, 103.

manageable £3,500. Rievaulx was effectively bankrupted by the deals struck with Italian merchants, and in 1288 was taken under royal protection.[15] The abbey of Cumbermere made a deal with the Frescobaldi in 1299, under which they agreed to provide 140 sacks of wool over a twenty-year period. The house already owed the merchants 400 marks; the Italians agreed to pay 20 marks a year for the wool, a good price from their point of view.[16] In some cases, monasteries entered into a vicious circle of ever-increasing indebtedness, but in others, houses were able to use Italian loans to extend their buildings, and make effective investments in new stock and other improvements to their estates. An indication of the scale of the Italian business is provided by a planned seizure in 1295 of all the wool belonging to the Ricciardi, Frescobaldi, and Bardi in England. The total came to about 1,500 sacks, a figure that excludes those houses that had sold their entire crop to the Italians.[17] The value of this wool was about £12,000.

The companies did not confine their trading activities to wool. One small firm, the Gallerani, entered into a partnership with the vastly bigger company of the Frescobaldi to buy and sell horses. Each firm put up capital of 200 marks, and the partnership made an adequate profit of £23 8s. 2d. The Gallerani also traded English lead and Gascon wine. Wealthier and better-placed firms were engaged in trading gold and silver plate, jewels, and fine cloth.[18] Antonio Pessagno, who lent to Edward II, provided luxuries such as raisins and ginger, rich cloth and jewels, as well as medicines and horses for the royal household. He does not seem to have exported much wool, but he traded extensively in grain, providing much of what was needed for the Bannockburn campaign in 1314, and profiting from the years of famine by importing cereals from southern Europe.[19]

Successful as the Italians appeared to be, they were also highly vulnerable. They were undercapitalized and overextended, and bankruptcy was often just around the corner. The Italian companies were partnerships, which were renewed on a regular basis, but which were not static in structure. They were primarily merchants, not bankers, with their business based on trade in commodities; it has been plausibly argued that the Italian grain trade was at the

[15] E. Jamroziak, 'Rievaulx Abbey as a Wool Producer in the Late Thirteenth Century: Cistercians, Sheep, and Debts', *Northern History*, 40 (2003), 197–218; Denholm-Young, *Seigneurial Administration in England*, 55 n. 8; Knowles, *Religious Orders*, i. 68.

[16] E 368/70, m. 58.

[17] E 159/68, mm. 87–9. This seizure did not in fact take place, for the merchants made a loan of £10,000 instead: ibid., m. 84d.

[18] M. C. Prestwich, 'Italian Merchants in Late Thirteenth and Early Fourteenth Century England', in Centre for Medieval and Renaissance Studies (ed.), *The Dawn of Modern Banking* (New Haven, 1979), 99–100.

[19] Fryde, 'Antonio Pessagno of Genoa', 164–5, 170, 173.

heart of their activities. The large companies were complex. They were based on families, and exercised central control from Italy over a number of branches. As well as profiting directly from commodity trading, they took in deposits. As a result of papal prohibitions, they were not permitted to charge interest, but they could ask for payments to cover damages and costs incurred as a result of making loans, and they might also expect to receive gifts and favours. Their accounting techniques, and their financial instruments, were sophisticated. Their expertise made them ideal for tasks such as transmitting funds raised in papal taxation back to Rome. They could, if they were sufficiently skilful in reading the markets, make profits from foreign exchange. They might, for example, make a loan in one currency and ask for repayment in another, at a favourable rate. The Genoese Antonio Pessagno was accused of profiting improperly when in his accounts he claimed to have exchanged 160,000 florins lent by the pope to Edward II into precisely £25,000, a rate of 3s. 1½ d. It was argued that he had in fact obtained a rate of 3s. 4d., and that he had pocketed the difference.[20] The great firms, the Ricciardi, the Frescobaldi, the Bardi, and the Peruzzi, were very significant international merchant bankers, but there were also many much smaller Italian companies, minnows swimming alongside the big fish.

The Italians, notably the Ricciardi, Frescobaldi, Bardi, and Peruzzi, were drawn into lending to the crown on a substantial scale. This was a much less attractive business than commodity trading, given the risks involved. Repayment in full was unlikely. However, companies that were regarded with favour by the crown might gain commercial advantages as a result. Some members of the Ricciardi and Frescobaldi under Edward I were given the title of 'treasurer's valet', which gave them the status of exchequer officials and enabled the firms to use the full mechanisms of the exchequer to recover debts owing to them. Repayment of loans came in the form of grants of customs duties, paid over at the ports, and these provided the Italians with a source of cash that could be used to finance their commodity operations.

The Italians had been involved in lending to the English crown as early as the late twelfth century, and Henry III borrowed funds in Italy for the Sicilian adventure. More substantial involvement came with Edward I. The Ricciardi came to his rescue, in financial terms, during his return from crusade, advancing over £23,000. The firm were invaluable during the Welsh wars, for by using the credit that they supplied, Edward I was able to move far more quickly than he could otherwise have done. Heavy expenditure in a short period was paid for out of revenue received over a longer timescale. For the first Welsh war, the Ricciardi advanced over £22,000. It is not so easy to calculate figures

[20] Ibid. 172.

for the second war, but the company probably contributed over £50,000. When it came to the much smaller-scale operations to put down the rebellion of 1287, the Ricciardi dominated the financial arrangements, contributing £8,288 out of a total cost of some £10,600.[21] While the king was in Gascony from 1286–9, he incurred a huge debt to the company, approaching £110,000. Collapse came with the onset of war with the French in 1294, when the company could not meet all its obligations to Edward. The company of the Frescobaldi who came to take the place of the Ricciardi in Edward's financial system was never extended as far financially. Its failure in 1311 was not so much the result of financial overextension and miscalculation as of the political situation. The Frescobaldi were deeply distrusted for their links with Piers Gaveston and the substantial favours that they received from Edward II, so their expulsion from the realm was ordered by the Ordainers. Between 1297 and 1310 they lent a total of about £150,000, of which some £125,000 was repaid. More significant than the overall figures is the level at which the debt normally stood: in 1305 it was estimated that it would take eighteen months to pay what the crown owed the firm out of the revenues of the customs, which suggests a debt of about £15,000.[22]

The collapse of the Ricciardi at the start of Edward I's war with France was paralleled, to some degree, by the collapse of the two great companies that lent to Edward III, the Bardi and the Peruzzi. The Bardi had been involved, though not on a very large scale, in dealings with the crown since Edward I's reign. The Peruzzi had dealt with the Despensers, but only began to lend to Edward III in 1336. In 1338 huge sums were looked for from the companies: £20,000 in England and £100,000 in the Low Countries. In fact, they agreed to lend the king £15,000 to pay for his journey to the Low Countries, and a further £20,000 after his arrival. They would be repaid out of English wool in the Low Countries, and out of an assignment of £30,000 from the fifteenths and tenths that parliament had approved.[23] Accounts show receipts from the two firms totalling £71,500 between the king's arrival abroad on 22 July 1338 and the following Michaelmas. In less than two years the Bardi and Peruzzi had advanced about £125,000.[24] Doubt has been cast on how realistic these figures can be, for they far exceed the obvious resources available to the companies and are 'incompatible with the records and capability of the companies'.[25] One possibility is that the figures are little more than smoke and mirrors, that they

[21] Kaeuper, *Bankers to the Crown*, 76–8, 178, 190, 198.

[22] Prestwich, *Edward I*, 307, 534.

[23] E. S. Hunt, *The Medieval Super-Companies: A Study of the Peruzzi Company of Florence* (Cambridge, 1994), 198–9; Fryde, *William de la Pole*, 88.

[24] Fryde, *William de la Pole*, 89, 122.

[25] Hunt, *Medieval Super-Companies*, 201.

represent promises not payments, and that the same sum may be entered several times, so artificially magnifying the total. Gifts promised by Edward to the two companies, £30,000 to the Bardi and £20,000 to the Peruzzi, although never in practice paid, do suggest that the figures for loans by the companies were exceptionally high. Nor would the sums lent have come solely from the resources of the two companies, for they must have acted as intermediaries, raising money from other firms and merchants. The total of repayments to the Bardi and Peruzzi amounted to £104,000. By the end of this period, therefore, the companies were not left in an impossible position. Indeed, it is possible that the Peruzzi may have been as much as £8,600 in credit, when factors such as hidden payments of interest are taken into account.

After 1338 the level of Bardi and Peruzzi lending to Edward III fell back markedly. The companies were in increasingly difficulty for a range of reasons, including political problems in Florence and the decision of the papacy to shift some of the business of collecting papal taxation to the Sienese company of the Nicolucci. The companies must also have appreciated the dangers involved in making further advances to Edward at a time when his war appeared to have stalled. In 1343 the Peruzzi declared bankruptcy, and the Bardi did the same three years later. Edward III was not solely to blame for the financial collapse of the two firms, but their overextended loans to him were a significant element in it. Bankruptcy did not spell the end of the road for the Bardi in England, where members of the company continued to operate with some success, though not as a 'super-company', and not as major creditors of the crown.[26]

ENGLISH MERCHANTS

The dominance that foreign merchants exercised over English trade, which was very clear in the third quarter of the thirteenth century, was gradually eroded. Figures from the customs records of the 1270s show the domination of foreigners. The accounts for Hull for 1275/6 reveal that out of a total of 4,397 sacks, only 158 were exported by English merchants. It was the Italians who controlled more than anyone else, with 2,318 sacks. In 1291/2 the total was 4,288, with the English share now up to 546 sacks and the Italian down to 1,715 sacks.[27] By the period 1330–5 English merchants were exporting seven sacks from Hull to every one by an alien.[28] The figures for London also show the growing success of English merchants. In 1273 six out of seven wool-exporters in the city were foreigners. In the period 1304–11 the average figure for native exports was 8,836 sacks and for alien 5,367. By 1329–36 the equivalent figures

[26] Ibid. 209–10, 230–42.   [27] Lloyd, *Wool Trade*, 65.
[28] Kermode, *Medieval Merchants*, 167.

were 8,945 and 3,101.[29] Overall, it is probable that in about 1270 only about a third of the wool export trade was in English hands; half a century later the figure had risen to about two-thirds.

The reasons for this shift are not easy to explain. In part it must relate to the difficulties that the Italians faced as successive companies went bankrupt. In the case of Hull, however, it was German merchants, notably the Clipping family, who lost their share of the export trade to the English, despite the various privileges that they possessed. The economic difficulties of the famine years 1315–16 may have meant that some foreign traders lost their share of the market and were subsequently unable to recover it. It was not the policy of the English government to try to establish greater English control of trade, and it seems unlikely that the differential in export duties paid by English as against foreign merchants was sufficient to give them the commercial edge.

The most successful English wool merchants under Edward I were the Ludlows, father and son. Nicholas of Ludlow, a Shrewsbury merchant, was licensed to export up to 300 sacks of wool in 1273. His claims for compensation for losses due to Flemish piracy came to over £1,900, whereas the highest put in by a London merchant was £227. His son Laurence was used by the king to assist in the financing of the French war; he was put in charge of exporting wool forfeited by the Ricciardi, but in December 1295 his ship was wrecked and he was drowned.[30] Like most really successful merchants, Laurence began to put his profits into land and buildings; Stokesay castle in Shropshire provides evidence in stones and mortar of his accomplishments. Laurence, however, came nowhere near matching the scale of the operations of the Italians.

Under Edward II some English merchants were exporting wool on a significant scale. The Londoner William de Combemartin exported 438 sacks of wool in 1312/13, probably worth some £3,000. It was not until Edward III's reign, however, that an English merchant emerged who could rival the activities of the Italians in the wool trade. Late in 1338 William de la Pole came to the king's rescue by advancing him desperately needed funds in the Low Countries at a time when the Italians were beginning to withdraw their financial support. By October 1339 de la Pole had advanced about £111,000.[31] He was a remarkable man. He was a Hull (or possibly Ravenser) man in origin, who traded in partnership with his brother Richard until 1331. How and why William was so successful is not clear from the limited records that survive. His brother went overseas to buy corn during the famine years of 1315–16, and no doubt made a tidy profit. The two brothers were involved in

[29] Lloyd, *Wool Trade*, 123; Williams, *Medieval London*, 114.
[30] Lloyd, *Wool Trade*, 55, 79; Williams, *Medieval London*, 113.
[31] For the following section, see Fryde, *William de la Pole*, *passim*.

the wine trade, and bought wool and lead from the keepers of Lancaster's lands after the earl's execution in 1322. They showed civic solidarity in giving £306 for the construction of a town wall in Hull. Customs records show that in the 1320s William was exporting wool from Hull on a fairly substantial scale. Involvement with the crown first came when he provided £1,000 worth of French gold coins for Edward II's journey to France, selling some for more than the Bardi were demanding. In 1327 the two de la Poles began lending to the crown, advancing at least £7,200 to help pay for the Stanhope campaign. Richard, presumably in recognition of his financial services, was listed as a squire in the royal household in 1330. At the time that the partnership between Richard and William was dissolved, they were together worth over £11,200, a very impressive sum, but nowhere close to the kind of resources that the great Italian companies had behind them. As a businessman, William de la Pole was acute. His accounts show that he worked on a simple basis of unit costs, unlike his competitors. He paid his agents well, and as a result they succeeded in buying wool for him at good prices. He was well aware, as the Italians were, of the profits to be made from foreign exchange, and was accused of making a profit of over £12,000 on his loans to the king by buying florins cheaply and valuing them highly. He was ambitious, acquisitive, and entrepreneurial. As often happens to such men, he came unstuck.

William de la Pole was one of the early victims of Edward's coup against the government in England on his return from Flanders in November 1340. He was arrested, and eventually put on trial in 1341. In the following year he was released from prison, and once again began to mastermind the credit system, taking a leading part in the English Company of merchants to which the customs were farmed. Once again, things went wrong, and in 1353 de la Pole, now an old man, was put on trial, with charges brought by some of his former associates in the company. He was pardoned in the following year, but was not able to regain the great estates of Holderness which he had bought from the crown in 1338 for over £20,000, and held but briefly.

In London the main wool-traders were either foreigners or, if English, came from outside the city. London, however, had its great merchants, who profited from a wide range of trade. Gregory de Rokesley, who died in 1291, was a wine merchant, but he also traded in cloth, wool, and even fish. He was a dominant figure in the elite group that controlled London. Mayor for seven years, he served the crown in many capacities, most notably as warden of the mint, but also as a commissioner to negotiate with the Flemings, and on a wide range of judicial business. He built up a very substantial estate in London itself, and held eight manors outside the city. Henry le Waleys was another great figure, who made his fortune in the wine trade, and who was closely associated with

Edward I's government. A good marriage was part of the reason for his rise, while his investments in property no doubt stood him in good stead. Not only did he own much in London, but he also had three manors, two in Essex and one in Kent, as well as houses in Boston and Berwick. As mayor in the early 1280s he carried through, with the king's support, a radical programme intended to impose order and regulation on London.

Rare evidence of a contract made in 1304 between two merchants, William le Barber and John de Chigwell, demonstrates the range of trading activity of London merchants. Woad was bought at Amiens and, with a few other goods, sent north to Scotland for sale. With the money from this, hides, wool-fells, and wool were acquired, which were then exported to Saint-Omer.[32] Deals were tricky and might go wrong, as this one did, but there were plenty of opportunities to make good profits. Wealthy entrepreneurs continued to do well.

In Edward II's reign one of the leading London merchants was Henry Nasard, a draper who probably came from Arras. His dealings with the crown were important, and he was described as a 'king's merchant'; he provided cloth for liveries granted to members of the royal household. Marriage to a Londoner no doubt helped to make him acceptable in the city. He became a freeman, and, briefly, an alderman.[33] Men such as Nasard were major figures, not merely within London, but also on a national and even international scale. Under Edward III there were London merchants of almost legendary wealth, such as Henry Picard, a vintner, and the draper John Pulteney, who were both knighted. Thomas Swanlond and Walter Chiriton were other major figures, who headed one of the monopoly groups that farmed the customs in the late 1340s, only to suffer bankruptcy and disgrace when the scheme failed.

It is inevitable that it is the great merchants, and particularly those who had close dealings with the crown, about whom most is known. There were a great many men who traded on a lesser, but still significant, scale. Tax assessments for a fifteenth, probably that of 1275, for the port of Lynn provide some insights into the world of these smaller merchants. Philip de Bekx was a relatively wealthy man, who owned a cog, assessed at £40, a quarter share in another cog, which came to £10, and a hulk assessed at £13 6s. 8d. Chattels and merchandise he had on the ships were valued at £43. The nature of this merchandise is not specified, but he appears to have been primarily a grain merchant, for he had 104 quarters of wheat, 24 of barley, and 40 of malt in his

---

[32] Williams, *Medieval London*, 122.

[33] For summaries of these careers, see Williams, *Medieval London*, 129–30, 247, 252–3, 330, 333–5.

possession. The total value of all his goods came to £246 8s. 6½ d. Although English merchants did not form companies in the way that the Italians did, it was common practice for men to own shares in ships. Thus Henry le Irmonger had a quarter share in the *Blithe*, which was valued at 60s., and a half share in the *Gozer*, assessed at £6 13s. 4d. The merchandise he had in these two ships was worth £25. As his name suggests, he traded primarily in iron goods. This was one of the occasions when people were taxed on the money they possessed, and for this tax the assessors included not only cash, but also the value of credit in the form of tallies and written instruments. The importance of credit varied considerably between individuals, according to these assessments. Bekx had £10 in coin, and was owed only £6 6s. 8d. in credit; Thomas de Waynfleet had £8 in coin and £10 10s. in credit. It was, however, not a merchant, but a dyer, whose credit exceeded the amount he held in coin to the greatest extent. Hugh le Moigne, who had £50 worth of woad in his possession, as well as peat and firewood to heat his vats, had 13s. 4d. in coin, but £38 11s. 6d. in credit.[34]

The early fourteenth-century tax returns for Shrewsbury have been subjected to detailed analysis, enabling the main merchants in the town, such as Richard Stury, to be identified. Although, remarkably, wool barely featured in the assessments, other sources show that the wealthiest Shrewsbury men all exported wool, while some also imported wine. Two merchants traded in furs and skins, two in silk and linen, one in fish, and one in meat. Evidence of their attempts to recover debts suggest that they were much involved in providing credit, perhaps for trading partnerships, but also for wool that producers had not delivered as they had promised. Often, son followed father into trade, and it is also clear that members of the merchant oligarchy of the town tended to marry within their own circle. Profits of trade were frequently invested in property, and men of this group often undertook civic office. The evidence for smaller merchants is, inevitably, less clear; the distinction between someone manufacturing goods and someone trading in them is frequently not evident from the tax returns.[35]

Robert Gyen was a successful Bristol merchant. An immigrant to the town in the early fourteenth century, he traded in Gascon wine, and also appears to have acted as an agent for the Garter knight James Audley. He served as bailiff on four occasions, and as mayor on three. His wealth, acquired from trade, was used to purchase land and property, mostly in Somerset, where he came from, but also even as far afield as Oxford. He also invested in the afterlife, endowing

[34] G. H. Dashwood, 'Remarks on a Subsidy Roll in the Possession of the Corporation of Lynn Regis', *Norfolk Archaeology* (1847), 345, 349, 351–3.
[35] *Wealth of Shrewsbury*, ed. Cromarty and Cromarty, 53–66.

chantries on a lavish scale. Gyen died in 1354; his career was typical of the successful provincial merchant.[36] Durham was a relatively small town, which for the most part served an immediate hinterland. Yet even such a place might have its prosperous merchants. Robert de Coxside sold Durham priory malt and spices, obtained a contract in 1340 to supply the prior's household with cloth, and lent the bursar almost £80. At the same period John Cotes bought over nine sacks of wool from the priory on one occasion, and sold it almonds, sugar, wine, wax, and cloth.[37]

The role that merchants played in this period did not herald a bourgeois revolution; they were an integral part of the society of the thirteenth and fourteenth centuries, contributing to its richness and variety. Their personal lives and thoughts are largely hidden from historians, but one letter is worth quoting for the rare insight that it provides into the world of family affections. Ralf de Duram, a merchant, wrote to his mother, Agnes Grimbaud, and his sister, probably in 1282. After explaining the business difficulties he was in, he expressed his hope that there would soon be a peace or a truce, and went on to say:

Know that the thing that upsets me most is that I cannot talk to you or my wife, and there's nothing I desire more. Joan, my dear sister, I beg you that you should not be angry that I have not come to see you, since that's the thing that is closest to my heart. And please let me know how you are, when you can, and give my greetings to brother John Morel and William le Blacer. I've nothing else to tell you, except that I'm thinking of you.[38]

---

[36] S. A. C. Penn, 'A Fourteenth-Century Bristol Merchant', *Transactions of the Bristol and Gloucestershire Archaeological Society*, 104 (1986), 183–5.

[37] M. Bonney, *Lordship and the Urban Community: Durham and its Overlords, 1250–1540* (Cambridge, 1990), 158.

[38] *Receuil de lettres anglo-française 1265–1399*, ed. F. J. Tanquerey (Paris, 1916), 78. From a reference in another letter to Ralf's going twice to Wales, and staying there for more than twelve weeks while war was raging, a date of 1282–3 seems probable.

CHAPTER 20

Crime and Punishment

It might take very little for the order and restraint that controlled medieval society to collapse. In 1345 a miracle play was taking place in the marketplace at Carlisle. Two of the spectators came to blows. One was a servant of the bishop, one of a local magnate, Peter de Tillioll. The latter sent the coroner and two others to the bishop, who was in the castle, to demand justice. A body of thirty-one armed men rushed out from the castle, and with a lethal volley of arrows stopped the legal proceedings that the mayor was conducting into the affair. The mayor decided to arrest those responsible for the attack, and this led to a full-scale riot, in which the castle garrison spread terror through the town.[1] This was a society that could be close to the edge.

THE EXTENT OF CRIME

The true extent of criminal activity in the thirteenth and fourteenth centuries is hard to determine. Attempts have been made to compare medieval crime rates with those of recent times.[2] This is difficult, for it is not clear whether the proportion of crimes reported in the plea rolls was similar to that in a modern society. The figures are very different if accusations of crime are counted, or simply convictions. Since acquittal rates for those who appeared in court were extremely high, at about 80 per cent, this is a significant issue. A further difficulty is that an apparently high level of crime may represent a high level of judicial activity, not an actual increase in unlawful doings. One estimate is that in London in the first half of the fourteenth century there was a homicide rate of between 5.2 and 3.6 cases per 10,000 inhabitants. This contrasts with rates of 1.5 in mid-twentieth-century Miami, and 0.05 in later twentieth-century Britain. This calculation, however, is based on a population range of

---

[1] Summerson, *Carlisle*, i. 276–7.
[2] See e.g. J. B. Given, *Society and Homicide in Thirteenth-Century England* (Stanford, Calif., 1977), 33–40.

35,000 to 50,000 for medieval London.[3] Other estimates put London's population between 67,100 and 137,000, or even as high as between 107,900 and 176,000.[4] If the London population was 100,000, then the homicide rate was only 1.8 per 10,000. It would, however, be rash to conclude that the chance of being murdered in early fourteenth-century London was only slightly greater than that in mid-twentieth-century Miami. Another study, of homicide in fourteenth-century Oxford, suggested a very high rate, of about 11 per 10,000. While the presence of a substantial student population no doubt made matters worse than in other towns, its significance should not be exaggerated.[5] The only deduction to be drawn from the fact that there were only three larcenies in Norwich in 1313, as against 703 in Bedford, Indiana (a town of similar size), in 1975, is that the reporting of minor crime in the fourteenth century might leave a great deal to be desired.[6] Regrettably, many of the conclusions that historians have attempted to draw from the statistics are unsafe.[7]

Hard as the figures are to interpret, it is clear when they are used alongside other evidence that crime was a more serious problem at some times than others. Civil war brought crime in its wake. The conflict of the 1260s witnessed much local violence as men took advantage of the partial collapse of the institutions of government to pursue their ends by what might be euphemistically described as self-help. The marches of armies across the land, the seizure of food for supplies, the burning and looting that was an integral part of medieval warfare not only set a pattern of violence, but also instilled a desire for revenge. There were widespread attacks on the estates of prominent supporters of the crown during the rebellion, with much of the plundering done by ordinary villagers and local men. The opportunity to pay off grudges was very welcome. The Pecche brothers, Montfortian supporters and men of knightly standing, organized a regime of robbery and plunder on a widespread scale in eastern England, and there were many others like them.[8] When the tide turned in favour of the crown after Evesham, violence continued. Inquests taken after the rebellion was over reveal not only widespread seizures of land of suspected adherents of the Montfort cause, but also incidents of ordinary robberies carried out under the colour of political allegiances. William

---

[3] B. A. Hanawalt, *Crime and Conflict in English Communities 1300–1348* (Cambridge, Mass., 1979), 98.

[4] Campbell *et al.*, *A Medieval Capital and its Grain Supply*, 10.

[5] C. I. Hammer, Jr., 'Patterns of Homicide in Fourteenth-Century Oxford', *Past and Present*, 78 (1978), 11, 15–16. Hammer's high figure may be explained by the fact that he was using coroners' records, not employed by other historians to calculate homicide levels.

[6] Hanawalt, *Crime and Conflict*, 271–2.

[7] Aberth, *Criminal Churchmen in the Age of Edward III*, 66–70.

[8] Jacob, *Studies in the Period of Baronial Reform and Rebellion*, 301–2.

Barleycorn, for example, took part in the capture of Skipton castle, and was described as having robbed five people, including two parsons. One jury reported that Robert Tibetot had seized Thomas FitzWilliam's land in Plumtree (Notts.), which was worth £40, and that he had taken goods worth £20. Yet 'Sir Thomas was not a rebel but a firm supporter of the king and Sir Edward.' At Ickenham, Middlesex, John Cobus's holding of land worth 1s., with rent valued at 6s., was seized by Maurice de Berkeley 'because he went to Hampshire with Philip de Pirie to see his sister. He was never a rebel.'[9] In 1268 the king's son Edward was travelling towards Dover when he found the bodies of some murdered men in a wood near Canterbury. He had over twenty youths arrested; they were suspected because 'they banded themselves together, and because they went frequently with their fellows to the tavern, night and day, and played and drank there and quarrelled on the way home both among themselves and with those that met them, seeing that peace was insecure'. They were almost certainly not guilty of the murders, but the incident reveals the way in which the temper of the times was thought to encourage hooliganism, and with it crime.[10]

CRIME, POLITICS, AND WAR

Politics could easily turn to crime, as Edward II's reign demonstrates all too clearly. Piers Gaveston was killed in 1312 in an act that even its perpetrators must have realized lacked legality. Thomas, earl of Lancaster, conducted what amounted to a private war against Earl Warenne in 1317. Warenne's Yorkshire castles were attacked, and his lands burned. The war against the Despensers in the Welsh march in 1321–2 was accompanied by much local disturbance and crime. Lancashire was badly affected, first by the rebellion of Adam Banaster against Thomas, earl of Lancaster, in 1315, and then by the collapse of authority after Lancaster's execution in 1322, when the former Banaster supporters sought their revenge. How far such events affected the overall level of lawlessness is difficult to determine, for there were other reasons in Edward II's reign for men to turn to crime. A single example may not be typical, but does help to illustrate the connections between politics, war, and crime. Robert of Prestbury, a small Gloucestershire landowner, had expertise as a lawyer and as an estate steward. He served William de Braose in this latter capacity. Robert was involved in the death of Piers Gaveston in 1312. Two years later he occupied the tenements of his neighbour Henry de Hatherley when Henry was taken prisoner by the Scots at Bannockburn. On Henry's return, Robert, with assistance, assaulted him and held him prisoner until he

---

[9] *CIM* i, nos. 807, 850, 940, and 609–940 *passim*.   [10] *CIM* i, no. 2138.

agreed to formally hand over his lands in return for an annuity of £12 a year. He joined the Berkeleys in their attack on the earl of Pembroke's Gloucester-shire manor of Painswick in 1318, along with his brother, the rector of Minchampton. In 1321 he was with John Giffard, one of the rebellious marcher lords, and as a result forfeited his lands. He returned, however, in 1326, by which time he was an associate of Roger Mortimer. Under his patronage, Robert was able to regain the lands he had lost.[11]

Thomas of Lancaster's rebellion in 1322 provided criminals with opportun-ities they eagerly seized. Hugh Despenser the elder claimed that he lost 38,000 sheep, 1,400 oxen, 1,700 cows, 420 horses, and 300 goats in the disturbances. Evidence from Gloucestershire reveals a pattern of men pretending to have royal warrants unlawfully seizing lands and goods, and of the widespread involvement of small landowners in acts of violence at a local level.[12] The author of the life of Edward II provided an analysis of part of the problem. 'For in almost every fashion the squire strains and strives to outdo the knight, the knight the baron, the baron the earl, the earl the king. Moreover when monies fail, because their inheritance is insufficient, they turn to pillage, plunder their neighbours, fleece their tenants, and practise wicked extortions upon the servants of God.'[13] There is much evidence for the activity of criminal bands in the late 1320s and early 1330s in the north midlands, and it seems likely that this was at least in part the result of the dislocation caused by the fall of Thomas, earl of Lancaster, in 1322.

War had its impact on crime. The increase in criminal activity in Edward I's later years, for which the records of the trailbaston inquiries provide vivid evidence, can be related to war in various ways. The concentration of the government on the need to organize and finance the campaigns in Scotland meant that legal business did not receive any priority. Further, the practice, initiated in 1294, of emptying the country's gaols and recruiting their inmates into the army did little for law and order. The absence of landlords on campaign left their manors and parks vulnerable to the attention of criminal gangs. There is no doubt that one of the effects of the Scottish invasions of the north of England, particularly in the second decade of the fourteenth century, was an increase in criminal activity. The attack by a gang led by Gilbert de Middleton on the party headed by two cardinals and the bishop-elect of Durham, as they approached the city of Durham, was a striking outrage.[14] It

---

[11] S. L. Waugh, 'The Profits of Violence: The Minor Gentry in the Rebellion of 1321–2 in Gloucestershire and Herefordshire', *Speculum*, 52 (1977), 857–8.

[12] Ibid. 843–69.

[13] *Vita Edwardi*, 57.

[14] M. C. Prestwich, 'Gilbert de Middleton and the Attack on the Cardinals, 1317', in Reuter (ed.), *Warriors and Churchmen in the Middle Ages*, 179–94.

was the most notable of many crimes committed by men known as 'schaval-dours', local armed bands that made a living from pillage and extortion. There was little to choose between them and the Scottish invaders. Jack the Irishman was retained in the king's household. When in Bamburgh castle, he seized food and goods from the locality without paying for them. He was given custody of Barnard Castle, and when he had command there abducted a wealthy widow, Maud de Clifford, probably with the intention of marrying her and so acquiring her lands. As the sister of Richard de Clare, lord of Thomond in Ireland, she must have been a particularly attractive proposition for an Irishman. She was soon rescued, but despite his undoubted guilt, Jack remained a member of the royal household until his death in 1317.[15]

Foreign war had the effect of finding useful employment for criminals; under Edward III in particular some notable criminals turned their skills to their country's service overseas. The other side of the coin was seen when the return of the troops from the siege of Calais in 1347 prompted a crime wave in England. Figures from eight counties strongly suggest that the incidence of crime in the period 1340–8 was much higher than in the previous fifteen years. The link with the Hundred Years War seems clear; the general stresses the war placed on society were important in addition to the activities of returned soldiers.

Political events and foreign wars provide one explanation for levels of crime. There were also economic causes. The miserable state of the economy in the second decade of the fourteenth century undoubtedly led to much crime. The famine of 1315–16 caused dreadful hardship. When men and women did not have enough to eat, they were driven to steal. Not surprisingly, figures for reported crime in a number of counties under Edward II parallel grain prices very closely. The one explanation given by a contemporary chronicler is that many men were turned out of noble households, and, not knowing how to earn an honest living, took to crime. It is more likely, however, that ordinary peasants who simply had not enough to eat committed the great majority of offences. Such a person was Peter le Snekere who stole goods worth 2s. 6d., but who was not convicted by the jury which tried him, on the humanitarian grounds that he was suffering from poverty and hunger. The link between harvests and crime is also clearly demonstrated by the rise in crime figures following the 1321–2 drought, when grain prices doubled.[16]

[15] A. King, 'Jack the Irishman and the Abduction of Lady Clifford in November 1315: The Heiress and the Irishman', *Northern History*, 38 (2001), 187–95.

[16] Hanawalt, *Crime and Conflict*, 234–60. The eight counties that Hanawalt analysed were Northants., Essex, Norfolk, Hunts., Herefordshire, Surrey, Somerset, and Yorks.

GENTRY, CLERGY, AND WOMEN

Social change may provide an explanation for a phenomenon that has attracted much attention from historians, the involvement in crime of members of the gentry. The gangs that were led by the Folville and Coterel families in the late 1320s and early 1330s have been studied in detail. The Folvilles were a Leicestershire gentry family, but with seven sons it would have been difficult to find legitimate occupations for all. As it was, six out of the seven turned to crime. Eustace was the most notorious; he committed three or four murders, a rape, and three robberies between 1327 and 1330. Three of the Folvilles were involved in the murder of Roger Bellers, baron of the exchequer, in 1326. Another outrage was their participation, along with other gangs, in the kidnap of the justice Richard Willoughby and his ransoming for 1,300 marks. The Coterels were also involved in this incident. They were of slightly less exalted social origins than the Folvilles, but James Coterel established himself as the leader of what amounted to a confederation of gangs operating in the north midlands. They conducted a successful protection racket. One of his associates, Roger le Sauvage, extracted £20 from William Amyas, a wealthy Nottingham man, and £40 from Geoffrey Luttrell. One leader of a criminal band described himself almost poetically as 'Lionel, king of the rout of raveners', writing threatening letters from 'Our castle of the wind in the Greenwood Tower in the first year of our reign'. These groups of criminals could be hired. The Coterels were closely linked to the Lichfield cathedral chapter, and their very first commission was to attack the vicar of Bakewell on behalf of the cathedral registrar.[17] Another gentry family group active in crime was that of the Gresleys in Staffordshire. John de Swinnerton and others abducted Joanna de Gresley after the death of her first husband. She appears to have been forcibly married to Walter de Montgomery, a connection of Swinnerton's, and she and her sons were charged with the murder of her stepson. Robert de Gresley faced at least ten charges between 1320 and 1348, including four of murder. A general pardon granted in respect of his good service in Scotland enabled him to escape some charges, as did a somewhat unlikely claim to be a cleric.[18] Such gentry gangs were not a new phenomenon in the 1320s and 1330s. In 1273, for example, an inquiry was held into the losses incurred by

---

[17] E. L. G. Stones, 'The Folvilles of Ashby-Folville, Leicestershire, and their Associates in Crime', *TRHS*, 5th ser., 7 (1957), 117–36; J. G. Bellamy, 'The Coterel Gang: An Anatomy of a Band of Fourteenth-Century Criminals', *EHR* 79 (1964), 698–717; *Select Cases in the Court of King's Bench, Edward III*, v, ed. Sayles, 94.

[18] F. Madan, 'The Gresleys of Drakelowe', *Collections for a History of Staffordshire*, NS I (William Salt Archaeological Society, 1898), 43–5.

Roger Lestrange and his men in a fight with a band led by William Denyas. Lestrange's men lost seventeen horses, the most expensive worth £20. Horse armour valued at £25 was also lost along with other equipment. This was clearly an engagement on a large scale.[19] It does, however, seem that the problems caused by gangs led by members of the gentry were more acute in the years around 1330. It is probable that it was simply easier to turn to crime at that time, as a result of the political collapse at the end of Edward II's reign. It is striking that the activities that have left the strongest trace in the records are those of gangs operating in the north midland region, where Thomas of Lancaster's authority had been strong until his execution in 1322.

The clergy were less distinct from the laity when it came to crime than might be expected. This was not simply because there were a good many men of questionable character who successfully claimed, on dubious grounds, to be of clerical status. Some of the highest clerics in the land had a surprising involvement in criminal activity. Like any magnate, a bishop was expected to exercise 'good lordship', and look after his followers and associates. There might, however, be a very thin distinction between the proper exercise of patronage and support, and the unacceptable use of fraud and violence. Aymer de Valence, bishop of Winchester and one of Henry III's hated Lusignan half-brothers, was happy to use violence when he found himself in dispute with Canterbury, and sent his men to burn the archiepiscopal manor of Maidstone. Nor was this the only example of Aymer's willingness to use violence to get his own way.[20] Walter Langton, bishop of Coventry and Lichfield, and Edward I's treasurer in his final years, had a distinctly dubious reputation. Accusations that he murdered his mistress's husband with her assistance were far-fetched and unproven. However, the massive record of the cases brought against him when he no longer had Edward I to protect him shows that he was prepared to use highly unscrupulous methods in order to acquire land. Richard of St Valery owed Langton £200, but failed to pay off the debt on time. He was imprisoned, and put in irons into a deep dungeon. His house was broken into, and his property seized. He gave in, and made over one of his manors to Langton. It seems that Langton in addition made a profit of £340 on his loan to Richard.[21]

Another exalted cleric to be involved in criminal activity on a significant scale was Thomas de Lisle, bishop of Ely in Edward III's reign. An eminent Norwich citizen, Richard Spynk, accused the bishop and his men of besieging him and setting ambushes for him. They had, he claimed, stolen his sheep,

[19] CIM i, no. 951.   [20] Howell, Eleanor of Provence, 67.
[21] Prestwich, Edward I, 279.

cattle, and possessions worth £400, and terrorized him with threats of muti-
lation and imprisonment so as to prevent his bringing legal action. He also
claimed, with pardonable exaggeration, that all the important people in Cambridgeshire were either the bishop's tenants, or in receipt of fees and robes
from him. According to the bishop, Spynk was his villein, and when the case
finally reached the king's council, it found against him. Eventually an agreement was reached by arbitration. The case showed the bishop using an
unacceptable level of violence, but his actions could be justified in law.[22] Bishop
Thomas was less successful when he became involved in a feud with Joan
Wake, sister of the duke of Lancaster. This began with an arson attack on a
disputed manor, the result of a property dispute between their followers. When
the case went to court, the bishop was found guilty, even though it is unlikely
that he had been directly involved in the attack. Matters then went from bad to
worse when one of Joan's supporters was killed. The case went against him in
court, and an interview with the king proved disastrous. The bishop eventually
went into exile; he died at Avignon, where he had been attempting to win papal
support for his cause. It is clear that de Lisle's officials were responsible for
cases of abduction, false imprisonment, theft, and intimidation, and it is hard
to imagine that the bishop was unaware of what was happening. There was, it
can be argued, a fine line between the exercise of good lordship and the corrupt
maintenance of an unruly retinue, but in the bishop's case, there can be little
doubt about which side of the line he was on.[23]

   Clergy were involved in the gang activities that characterized the later years
of Edward II. In 1317 six monks from Rufford priory collected a gang together
and attacked Thomas of Holm, robbing him of his goods and demanding a
ransom of £200 for his release.[24] Master Robert Bernard was a cleric with a
superficially glittering career. He served as a chancery clerk, taught for a time
at Oxford, and was a canon of Lichfield cathedral. His participation in the
attempted migration of some scholars from Oxford to Stamford suggests that
he may have been a man of a troublesome disposition. It was at his instigation
that the Coterel gang attacked the vicar of Bakewell.[25] There were many cases
of criminal acts for which individual clerics were responsible, and some
remarkable stories were told. The rector of Manchester invited a couple and
their daughter to dine; but after dinner two of the rector's servants came
and seized the daughter, beat her so that two ribs were broken, and put her
in the rector's bed. He spent the night with her; she died a month later of her
injuries.[26] Clerics, despite their status, did not always escape punishment. In

[22] Aberth, *Criminal Churchmen in the Age of Edward III*, 95–158.
[23] Lisle's career is fully discussed in Aberth, ibid.   [24] *CPR 1317–21*, 93, 174.
[25] Bellamy, 'The Coterel Gang', 699, 712–13.   [26] *CIM* i, no. 2290.

1301–2 the bishop of Winchester had three clerks imprisoned for the whole year in his prison at Wolvesey, and a further six in the prison at Winchester, with three more there for shorter periods of time.[27]

A special problem involving clerics was presented by the universities. At Oxford in 1275 the northern students fought with the Irish, and no less than fifty were charged with homicide. More serious still were the troubles of town and gown. In 1298 there was a major riot in Oxford, in which the students ran amok in the High Street. The outcome of the legal proceedings that followed was wholly favourable to the university. After the most serious outbreak of rioting, that of St Scholastica's Day in 1355, which lasted for three days and saw much bloodshed, there was a similar outcome, with a royal charter that not only pardoned the members of the university, but gave it new and significant privileges.[28]

The role of women in crime was distinct from that of men. Only about 10 per cent of accusations were brought against women. A much higher proportion of women than men were accused of receiving, and a markedly lower proportion were charged with homicide. The figures for larceny and burglary were similar for both sexes. Not surprisingly, women were less likely to be involved in violence than men. They were less familiar with the use of arms, such as sword and bow.[29] An unusual case in 1260–1 in London was of a woman who bit a man on the finger so that his whole hand, and eventually his whole body, swelled up, and he died. She was imprisoned in Newgate prison, where she died.[30] There were a few instances where women were involved in extremely violent crimes. In 1316 Thomas Murdak, a Staffordshire knight, was hemisected, decapitated, and cut into quarters by his wife, Juliana, and a group of men led by another knight, John de Vaux. Juliana subsequently married John, but was later convicted of the murder and sentenced by the court of King's Bench to be burned. De Vaux, on the other hand, unsuccessfully claimed benefit of clergy, but was eventually acquitted nine years after the crime had been committed.[31]

THE MECHANISMS OF THE LAW

The maintenance of public order was a prime responsibility of medieval government, and there were many mechanisms through which it attempted

[27] *Pipe Roll of the Bishopric of Winchester 1301–2*, ed. Page, 359.
[28] *History of the University of Oxford*, i, ed. Catto, 143, 146–7.
[29] Hanawalt, *Crime and Conflict*, 118–19.
[30] *The London Eyre of 1276*, ed. Weinbaum, no. 113.
[31] 'Extracts from the Plea Rolls of the Reign of Edward III', ed. G. Wrottesley, *Collections for a History of Staffordshire*, 14 (William Salt Archaeological Society, 1893), 18–19; *Eyre of Northamptonshire*, ed. Sutherland, i. 217–18.

to control crime. Edward I's Statute of Winchester of 1285 laid out some of the basic principles. It explained the responsibilities of local communities for bringing accusations, and the penalties should they not do so. The statute emphasized that watch and ward in towns should be carried out in traditional manner, and ordered the widening of roads as a protection against highway robbery. In accordance with past practice, men were to possess military equipment appropriate to their rank, so as to keep the peace.[32] The statute, however, did not set out the system of courts employed by the crown. The most traditional mechanism was that of the general eyre. This was a regular visitation by royal justices, which in theory took place every seven years. It became increasingly elaborate, as the articles, or agenda, lengthened over time. The frequency of eyres varied; in Henry III's reign, after those that started in 1251, there were none until 1262. The circuits followed by the judges were not fixed, but there were usually two or three teams operating. The eyre was profitable, but not unduly so; it has been estimated that the Wiltshire eyre of 1249 may have raised approaching £800.[33] Edward I abandoned the system of holding general eyres in 1294, for, given the French war, the government had other preoccupations. It made sense, at least as a temporary measure, to abandon an unpopular procedure. As it turned out, this marked the end of the systematic use of the general eyre. The process had become cumbersome: it had taken a decade to cover the whole country in the first eyres of Edward I's reign. Sessions were becoming longer and longer. There were alternatives. Litigants willing to travel to Westminster could take civil cases to the court of Common Bench. The development of assize circuits, first set up in 1273, provided another route for civil litigation. In criminal matters, the development of justices of gaol delivery, and of special commissions of oyer and terminer, meant that the general eyre was not needed as it had been in the past.

The eyre was not wholly abandoned, however; some were still held for particular purposes. An eyre in Cambridgeshire was a good way to inquire into the liberties of the church of Ely when there was a vacancy in the bishopric, as was the case in 1299. The holding of an eyre in Cornwall in 1302 followed too neatly on the king's acquisition of the earldom on the death of Edmund of Cornwall to be a coincidence. The dispute between the king and Anthony Bek, bishop of Durham, and the confiscation of the great liberty of Durham, again provided the opportunity to institute a general eyre, though in this case the liberty was restored to the bishop before the justices had started their work. In 1311 a vacancy in Durham prompted the king to summon an eyre, but it was cancelled on payment of 1,000 marks by the local community

---

[32] Stubbs, *Select Charters*, 463–9.
[33] *Crown Pleas of the Wiltshire Eyre*, ed. Meekings, 9–11, 112.

under their new bishop. The eyre of Kent of 1313–14 took place on the death of Archbishop Winchelsey, clearly as a means of asserting the king's authority over the liberties of the see of Canterbury. The eyre of London, held in 1321, was used as a political weapon against the city, where it was bitterly resented.[34]

In 1329 the council, in a surprising move, turned back the clock and decided that the system of eyres should be revived. Chief Justice Scrope, opening the proceedings in Northamptonshire, announced that 'eyres used to be held every seven years throughout the kingdom and served to maintain and keep the peace very well and to do justice to both rich and poor'. The magnates, said Scrope, had asked for the revival of the eyre so as preserve the peace of the land.[35] There was some logic in this, for the eyre had an all-embracing remit. It would provide a thoroughgoing review of the systems for local policing, and it would look back over the whole period since a visitation had last taken place. The eyre of 1329, however, visited only four counties, Northamptonshire, Bedfordshire, Nottinghamshire, and Derbyshire, before it was abandoned. The procedures were resented in the counties, for local customs were challenged and threatened. The financial cost, though not heavy, was unaccustomed. It was felt by the local gentry that the eyre did little to deal with the fundamental problems of law and order. Its effects were temporary at best. Scrope was told this in no uncertain terms: 'Sir, many disorderly persons absented themselves from the county after the eyre was proclaimed. They will return when your court has risen, and with them will come others of their kind from Bedfordshire where an eyre is about to be held. We are very much afraid of what they may do after your court has risen.'[36] The attempt to revive the eyre as the main weapon in the crown's determination to control violence was not successful. The eyre was not, however, wholly forgotten. One began to sit in London in 1341, but was halted when the citizens agreed to pay 500 marks. Others were summoned when there were vacancies in the sees of Durham and Canterbury, but Edward III was more enthusiastic about receiving money than actually holding the proceedings.[37]

Justices of assize had a much more limited role than the eyre justices. For most of the thirteenth century their duties were to hear the petty assizes, such as *novel disseisin*, but from 1285 they had responsibility for enforcing the Statute of Winchester. Various different arrangements were made for their circuits; in 1293 a statute, *De Justiciariis Assignatis*, set out four assize circuits for England, with two justices on each. In 1310 seven circuits were created, now with three justices each. Some of these were local men, others experienced

[34] Crook, 'The Later Eyres', 250–60.
[35] *Eyre of Northamptonshire*, ed. Sutherland, vol. i, p. xxii.
[36] Ibid. 243.   [37] Crook, 'The Later Eyres', 261–8.

professionals, such as king's sergeants or justices of the central courts. A reorganization took place in 1328, and a further modification in 1330. In 1299 the process began of linking assizes to gaol delivery. Justices of gaol delivery had the task of trying criminal suspects held in prison and on bail, and so had a major role in the maintenance of order, although they did not have wider powers to inquire into offences. By the early years of Edward III's reign, assize and gaol delivery were fully merged.[38]

When there was particular alarm at the end of Edward I's reign at the state of the country, the special nationwide trailbaston commissions were set up. Edward I described their activities as being like a drink taken before medicine. The medicine would be a full-scale eyre, but that never materialized.[39] Trailbaston inquiries were instituted again on various occasions until the 1340s, but they were unpopular, and did not in the end become a permanent part of the peacekeeping machinery.

Despite these elaborate mechanisms, it was also necessary on many occasions to set up ad hoc commissions of oyer and terminer (to hear and determine) to look into specific cases. The use of these began under Edward I in 1275, with numbers rising to almost 120 a year after the second Welsh war and in the late 1290s. The explosion in the use of these commissions came under Edward II; in the second decade of the fourteenth century numbers reached about 260. There was a decline in Edward II's final years, followed by a brief burst of high activity under Isabella and Mortimer. From the early 1330s they fell steadily. There is an observable pattern under Edward I of a high level of oyer and terminer commissions at times when there was no general eyre or other nationwide inquiry. Some influence was required in order to obtain a commission of oyer and terminer. In the first few years, in the 1270s, a quarter of all the commissions were obtained by townsmen, but later it was the gentry who dominated. One minor Lincolnshire knight obtained twenty commissions in twenty-five years.[40] Frequently, it was the plaintiff who suggested appropriate men to sit on the commission. In 1315 Thomas of Lancaster wrote to the chancellor:

As, sir, we asked our lord the king if he would assign Sir John Hastang, Sir William de Dacre, Sir Hugh Louther and Sir William Trussel of Notehurst to inquire into the death of our dear and beloved sovereign vallet John de Swinnerton to hear and determine the case of those guilty of this death, we affectionately beg, sir, that no

---

[38] Musson, *Public Order and Law Enforcement*, 85–122; P. Brand, *The Making of the Common Law* (London, 1992), 138–41.

[39] Prestwich, *Edward I*, 285.

[40] R. W. Kaeuper, 'Law and Order in Fourteenth-Century England: The Evidence of Special Commissions of Oyer and Terminer', *Speculum*, 54 (1979), 734–84. See the graph on p. 741.

writ be issued for the deliverance of anyone in this matter to any other justice save those named above.[41]

Two of these men, Dacre and Trussel, were members of Lancaster's retinue, and there can be little doubt of their bias. According to a petition from William Olde, late in Edward II's reign, William de Cusance had requested a commission of oyer and terminer in the name of his lord, the earl of Chester (the future Edward III), and had then sat on it himself as a justice. Less convincing, however, was the complaint by John, Earl Warenne, who asked for suspension of a commission requested by Maud de Nerford. Maud's son was the plaintiff, and Warenne claimed that all the justices wore her robes and took fees as members of her council. What he did not explain was that Maud was his discarded mistress.[42] Few records of trials under oyer and terminer survive, but the indications are that the technique was more successful in gaining convictions than was the case with other courts. This is hardly surprising, given the influence that complainants had over the selection of justices. The decline of oyer and terminer in the course of Edward III's reign should not be seen as an indication of the failure of the crown to maintain order and listen to the pleas put forward by crime victims. Rather, it should be seen as an indication of the government's success in developing other methods of keeping the peace.

THE KEEPERS OF THE PEACE

The element of the peacekeeping machinery that has received most attention from historians is that which developed into the institution of the justices of the peace. The employment of local men to assist in the maintenance of public order goes back to the late twelfth century. In the difficult years of the 1260s keepers of the peace, often local magnates, were frequently appointed. In 1287, because the justices of assize could not go round the shires as frequently as was needed, keepers of the peace were appointed to implement the provisions of the Statute of Winchester, promulgated two years earlier. These commissions were not renewed; in these early days of the institution they were very much ad hoc arrangements. In 1300 keepers were again appointed, an initial reaction to the observed crisis in public order that shortly saw the creation of the trailbaston commissions. Under Edward II, keepers of the peace were appointed more regularly.

A powerful interpretation of the development of the keepers under Edward III set out the views of different interest groups in clear terms. The justices of the central courts wanted to have the main responsibility for the maintenance

---

[41] Davies, *Baronial Opposition*, 590.
[42] Kaeuper, 'Law and Order in Fourteenth-Century England', 768.

of order; the magnates considered that men of their stature should keep the peace in the counties; the Commons in parliament favoured the appointment of local knights to peace commissions. In the end, victory went to the Commons in parliament, for their control of the purse-strings made it impossible for the king to go against their views.[43]

In reality, the situation was much less clear-cut. The Commons wanted effective measures to control disorder, and they were not concerned to put forward class-based solutions. The different measures taken reflected the immediate concerns of the royal council; the Commons tended to accept the solutions that they were offered. The brief period from 1327 to 1330 provides a good case study. In 1327 the new government's immediate response to the very evident problems of law and order was to set up a large number of oyer and terminer commissions. Over 270 are recorded in the one year. In parliament the representatives requested the appointment of keepers of the peace, with powers to determine cases. The response was to set up keepers, but not to give them judicial authority. In addition, nobles were appointed to supervise the process. At the Northampton parliament in the following year it seems likely that the representatives complained bitterly about the disorder in the land, and the way in which men maintained by magnates were responsible for it. The solution produced was to use trailbaston commissions on a nationwide basis, and to abandon oyer and terminer commissions, for these were open to corruption and abuse. The court of King's Bench was also to be used to assist in maintaining order. By 1329 a change was made to the commissions of the peace; now they were given powers to try cases, so that the keepers of the peace became in effect justices. This was not the result of any pressure from the Commons in parliament. A very plausible argument is that it was prompted by the king's imminent departure for France, to do homage for his Continental possessions, and the need to ensure stability in his absence. When the king returned, a new, or rather old, solution was produced. The general eyre, effectively abandoned since 1294, was to be revived. The range of solutions to the problem of public order in this brief period was extraordinary. What seems to have happened is that the royal council stumbled from one expedient to another, in a desperate attempt to find an effective approach to what must have seemed an increasingly intractable problem. The evidence for political pressure from magnates and representatives to adopt particular solutions is simply not there.[44] In 1339 the Commons' view was that there was no real

[43] B. H. Putnam, 'The Transformation of the Keepers of the Peace into the Justices of the Peace, 1327–80', *TRHS*, 4th ser., 12 (1929), 19–48.
[44] A. Verduyn, 'The Politics of Law and Order During the Early Years of Edward III', *EHR* 108 (1993), 843–67.

problem, and that the existing magnate guardians had sufficient powers. Should they prove inadequate, others who were competent should be appointed with the advice of the knights of the shire present in parliament. The most serious complaint that was made was about royal grants of pardon, which gave encouragement to felons and robbers.[45]

In the succeeding years the government continued to experiment, as commissions to keep the peace were given different briefs. In 1338 no fewer than three sets of commissions were set up. The first appointments were of men mostly of gentry rank, with powers to hear and determine felonies and trespasses, and also to array men so that any possible French invasion could be resisted. A second set of appointments was of magnates to supervise the process, while a third added justices from the central courts. This, almost certainly, does not reflect arguments over who should have responsibility for peacekeeping duties, but rather a growing sense of concern and urgency. For the next ten years magnates were relatively little used on commissions, but this was a reflection of their preoccupation with the war, and not of any political issues. The view of the Commons in parliament was that the best way to keep the peace in the localities was to use local men to try criminals, but this was not the result of any hostility to the magnates. Indeed, in 1352 the Commons asked that 'the great men of the realm, earls and barons, each in his own region', should be involved in keeping the peace.[46]

There was a change in the way that gentry were used in the process of restraining criminal activity. They played an important role as justices of gaol delivery, and as justices of oyer and terminer, in the period up to about 1330; thereafter, commissions of assize and gaol delivery were increasingly the preserve of professional justices and lawyers. At the same time, members of the gentry were employed more and more to use their talents as keepers of the peace, and were becoming increasingly professional in these positions. There is no case for arguing that there was a process by which the crown was steadily devolving issues of law and order to the localities, and to amateurs. Nor was there a straightforward pattern that saw responsibilities moved from the great magnates to people of gentry status. The situation was much more complex than that.

The various different types of commission could not resolve the problems of maintaining law and order in the course of Edward III's reign. In the late 1340s there were some notorious cases. The rape and abduction of Margery de la Beche took place on Good Friday 1347, at the manor of Beams in Wiltshire.

---

[45] *Rot. Parl.* ii. 104. The interpretation put on this response by the Commons in Harriss, *King, Parliament and Public Finance*, 404, is not acceptable.

[46] Musson, *Public Order and Law Enforcement*, 65, 82 (quotation on p. 77).

The king's son Lionel, the most senior member of the royal family in England at the time, and keeper of the realm, was staying there. The crime was committed by a knight, John Dalton, and a number of associates. The charges that were brought used the language of treason and sedition. Those responsible for the crime had usurped royal power 'in manifest destruction of the regality of the crown'. This was not the only crime interpreted as amounting to treason and accroachment of royal power. John Gerberge was accused of riding in armour, with drawn sword, and of kidnapping a merchant in an act of 'manifest sedition'. In at least one other case a treason accusation was brought for what seems to have been no more than highway robbery. The policy of extending the scope of treason charges was unwelcome; the particular argument stressed in parliamentary petitions was that if such accusations were brought, then the lands, goods, and chattels of a guilty man were forfeited to the crown, rather than to his lord. The outcome was the issue of the Statute of Treason in 1352. This defined treason narrowly. No longer would it be possible to charge men with treason simply because they had ridden out, armed, with banners unfurled. There was a further background to the statute. There were recollections of the way in which treason charges had been used in the 1320s. In the specific case of John Maltravers, there was an example of a man who had been found guilty of treason for his role in the death of the earl of Kent, but who had escaped the torment of hanging, drawing, and quartering, and who had won his way back into the king's favour through good service in the French war.[47]

Most baronial and other liberties were simply brought within the national system of peacekeeping. The county palatine of Cheshire, however, was quite separate from royal government, and problems were caused by the fact that it provided a refuge to criminals from neighbouring counties, whose sheriffs could not pursue them across the county border. Attempts were made to deal with public order in Cheshire by the Black Prince, in his capacity as earl; though a general eyre was cancelled in return for 5,000 marks, a trailbaston inquiry was held. There was a need for distinct measures. In 1352 the justiciar issued a peace proclamation in the county court, and in the following year the Black Prince issued ordinances intended to reinforce order. These were proclaimed both in the county court, and in the local hundred courts. Because earlier instructions had been ignored, the prince went so far as to read them out himself.[48]

[47] J. G. Bellamy, *The Law of Treason in England in the Later Middle Ages* (Cambridge, 1970), 59–92; above, 284.

[48] R. Stewart-Brown, *The Serjeants of the Peace in Medieval England and Wales* (Manchester, 1936), 24–5; D. Green, *The Black Prince* (Stroud, 2001), 51–2.

CONVICTION AND PUNISHMENT

The effectiveness of the crown's attempts to control crime was seriously diminished by a number of problems. There were difficulties in bringing accusations. The mechanisms of the law could be used by criminals themselves to try to frighten their victims, particularly women. In a horrific case in 1319 Agnes de Haldenby was blinded by assailants, who cut out her tongue, 'and let her go inhumanly like a beast'. When she brought an accusation against her attackers, they brought an action against her and her friends in the court of King's Bench, obtaining a conviction that resulted in Agnes's imprisonment. Only after the case came before parliament was Agnes pardoned.[49]

When accusations were brought, they might not prove sustainable. A London woman was accused of poisoning her husband; she was able to prove her innocence by finding thirty-six men to swear to her innocence.[50] In Edward II's reign Edith, daughter of Robert de Grasbroke, accused five men of rape. When the case came to court, none of the defendants appeared. The sheriff of Staffordshire was ordered to attach them, and returned saying that he had served a writ on William the Clerk, bailiff of the abbot of Westminster, who had done nothing wrong. He was then ordered to attach the true culprits, but still did nothing. Eventually he was ordered to outlaw them if they did not appear, but it seems unlikely that any effective action was taken against them. Cecilia, widow of John of Narrowdale, accused another John of his murder. Because she did not specify the time or place of the deed, or the weapons used to inflict thirteen mortal wounds, the case was dismissed, and Cecilia was committed to prison for bringing it. She was then pardoned, and the crown took over the prosecution. The jury, however, found John not guilty. Margaret, widow of Robert de Esnynton, did not make the same mistake. She brought a highly circumstantial charge of murder against the men who had killed her husband. The weapons used (bows, arrows, a sword, and daggers) were described in detail, as was the way the men took turns to strike fatal blows while others held the victim down. There were problems in that some of the accused claimed to be clerics, and the case was subject to various delays. Finally, Margaret failed to appear, so all the defendants were declared quit. The crown then took over the case. Henry Spigurnel and a local knight were ordered to hear it in Stafford. The jury found all the attackers not guilty.[51] The reasons why there were no convictions, despite the apparently full details of the crimes in these and similar cases, are not always immediately clear. It is

---

[49] *CPR 1317–21*, 292, 403–4.   [50] *The London Eyre of 1276*, ed. Weinbaum, no. 209.
[51] 'Plea Rolls of the Reign of Edward I', ed. Wrottesley, *Collections for a History of Staffordshire*, 7 (1886), 10; 'Plea Rolls of the Reign of Edward II', ibid. 10 (1889), 16–19, 30, 32.

conceivable that juries knew that the accused were innocent, or that they were afraid of the personal consequences that might follow should they find them guilty. There may very well have been a reluctance to convict given the severity of the penalties that would follow. There is little evidence to suggest that juries were bribed or threatened on a significant scale.

One method of attempting to obtain convictions was to use approvers, men who turned king's evidence and brought accusations against their former comrades in crime. In these cases it was particularly difficult to convince juries. In 1328 three Northumberland men, John Turnbull, John de Pickering, and Simon of Hollingside, were charged with horse theft. Simon agreed to be an approver, and provided details of the crime. Turnbull argued that he was not guilty, and said that he was willing to prove this in battle. Accordingly, he fought Simon, and won, so providing his innocence. Simon was duly taken off and hanged. A jury was a more comfortable alternative to trial by battle, and this was Pickering's choice. He was found not guilty.[52] The use of approvers could bring in a startling number of accusations. Robert Nurry, who began his career as an approver in 1300, brought appeals against seventy-three men for forty-three crimes in no less than twenty counties.[53] The system was unreliable, for it gave encouragement to approvers to make false accusations. One Norfolk approver gave details of a dozen or so men who had assisted him in committing crimes, but it was found that he had maliciously made up their names in order to prolong his career as an approver, and his life. Evidence from this county demonstrates a vast increase in the numbers of approvers from 1315. There were three between 1299 and 1304, and fifty-four in the peak years of 1320 to 1324. Those fifty-four brought 420 appeals, which resulted in a mere seven convictions. Thirty-three of the approvers, however, were hanged.[54] Other statistics provide a similar pattern, showing large numbers of acquittals when appeals were brought by approvers. No doubt juries were reluctant to convict on the word of individuals of highly questionable honesty.

One way in which men escaped conviction was to claim that they were clerks. They might be even subjected to a reading test, but normally it was for the bishop's official to claim them as clergy.[55] If he agreed to do this, then they

[52] C. M. Fraser and K. Elmsley, 'Law and Society in Northumberland and Durham, 1290 to 1350', *Archaeologia Aeliana*, 4th ser., 47 (1969), 64.
[53] H. Summerson, 'The Criminal Underworld of Medieval England', *Journal of Legal History*, 17 (1996), 204.
[54] *Crime in East Anglia in the Fourteenth Century: Norfolk Gaol Delivery Rolls, 1307–1316*, ed. B. Hanawalt (Norfolk Record Society, 1976), no. 381; A. Musson, 'Turning King's Evidence: The Prosecution of Crime in Late Medieval England', *Oxford Journal of Legal Studies*, 19 (1999), 475, 477.
[55] 'Extracts from the Plea Rolls of the Reign of Edward III', ed. Wrottesley, *Collections for a History of Staffordshire*, 14 (1893), 59, for an example of men who the court was satisfied were clerks, because *competenter legunt ut clerici*.

would be handed over to the episcopal court, which did not have the same powers of punishment as the secular authorities possessed. Richard Wythire, charged with burglary in Durham in 1330, successfully argued that he was a cleric. The jury, as was normal, confirmed his guilt before he was handed over to the bishop's official for punishment. He was incarcerated in the bishop's prison, but succeeded in escaping and took sanctuary in Durham cathedral. Sanctuary was not a long-term solution, but it enabled criminals to abjure the realm and go into exile, rather than face trial.[56] The Church was not eager to step in to assist notorious criminals. In the early fourteenth century John of Stradsett was accused of three murders, robberies totalling £435, a burglary of goods valued at £10, and a rape. He claimed to have been ordained into the Benedictine order, but the bishop's official denied any knowledge of this.[57] When William, rector of Odell, was murdered in Bury St Edmunds in 1283, two of those responsible claimed benefit of clergy. The abbot of Bury did not claim them; instead, as they refused to plead, they were incarcerated for almost a decade.[58]

Some statistics broaden the picture of acquittals. In the 1241 Oxfordshire eyre, the majority of those accused of crimes did not appear in court. Sixty-three had fled and were not to be found. Twenty-six had taken sanctuary and had then left the country in the only course of action open to them. In thirty-three cases that did come to court, the accused were found not guilty. Only three men were hanged as a result of the proceedings. In seven cases where rape was alleged, there was only one conviction, and that was of a man who did not appear before the court. The pattern was similar in the Wiltshire eyre of 1249; of thirty-five men accused of homicide in presentments made by local juries, only twenty-four appeared in court. Of those, only one was found guilty. The conviction rate of those who did not come to court was, not surprisingly, much higher; ten out of the eleven were declared guilty. It was easier to obtain conviction for larceny; of the seventy-five who appeared in court, fifteen were found guilty. The pattern was somewhat different where individuals brought the accusations. In the homicide cases in the eyre, fifteen men were outlawed, two hanged, and seven acquitted. In nineteen cases of rape, however, there was not a single conviction.[59] Figures from the fourteenth century have been calculated in different ways, and show a varied pattern. If cases involving approvers are excluded, Norfolk gaol delivery records show that in the early 1340s the

---

[56] Fraser and Elmsley, 'Law and Society in Northumberland and Durham', 65–6.

[57] *Crime in East Anglia*, ed. Hanawalt, no. 370.

[58] Gransden, 'John de Northwold, Abbot of Bury St Edmunds', in *TCE* iii. 106–7.

[59] *The Oxfordshire Eyre 1241*, ed. J. Cooper (Oxfordshire Record Society, 56, 1989), p. xx, nos. 810, 834, 839, 840, 845, 990, 1016; *Crown Pleas of the Wiltshire Eyre*, ed. Meekings, 79–80, 95. Two of the alleged rapists were committed to prison, but in both cases the accusation had been withdrawn and the parties had come to an agreement (probably to marry).

conviction rate was as high as 60 per cent, though it was no more than 20 per cent in the years 1310–14.[60] Table 20.1 shows that the chances of escaping convictions were greater if the crime was more serious.

Where conviction was obtained, punishments might vary, although hanging was the normal penalty for felony. This was not always competently done; there are a number of cases of people who survived. In one remarkable case, the executioners had forgotten to bring either a ladder or a rope with them. In others, people were found to be alive after they had been cut down. Friars were sometimes responsible for rescuing men on their way to the gallows. In some cases, people were hanged for very minor thefts, but following a statute of 1279–80, this penalty was imposed only if stolen goods were worth more than 1s.[61] There has to be a suspicion that some articles were deliberately given a low valuation. A man found guilty of stealing a tunic worth 9d. in Lichfield was sentenced to stand in the pillory for three days. Another was guilty of stealing a pair of spurs, but as they were valued at only 3d., he only had to stand in the pillory on two market days. At the same session another man was hanged for stealing three sheep.[62] Rather than being hanged, Alice the weaver, a Cornish woman, had an ear cut off for stealing two pairs of shoes. In a Westmorland case a boy was saved from the gallows because the justices claimed that he was 12, not 14, and that he had stolen only one, not two, sheep.[63] There were special

TABLE 20.1 *Comparative crime rates (%)*

Type of crime	Wiltshire 1275–1306	Newgate 1281–91	Eight counties 1300–48
Homicide	19.8	21.0	12.4
Burglary	25.4	27.0	30.6
Robbery	26.3	31.0	31.0

Source: J. G. Bellamy, *The Criminal Trial in Later Medieval England* (Stroud, 1998), 93; Bellamy derived his figures from Hanawalt, *Crime and Conflict*, 59.

[60] These are Musson's figures, from his *Public Order and Law Enforcement*, 210. Hanawalt, by calculating on a different basis, shows much higher levels of acquittal. Where two people were indicted for one crime, she counted this as two indictments; where one person was accused of two crimes, she counted this as one indictment: see Musson, ibid. 212 n. 20; Hanawalt, *Crime and Conflict*, 13.

[61] H. Summerson, 'Attitudes to Capital Punishment in England, 1200–1350', in *TCE* viii. 123–33.

[62] 'Plea Rolls of the Reign of Edward I', ed. Wrottesley, *Collections for a History of Staffordshire*, 7 (1886), 165–6.

[63] *Crown Pleas of the Devon Eyre of 1238*, ed. H. Summerson (Devon and Cornwall Record Society, NS 28, 1985), no. 555; Summerson, 'Attitudes to Capital Punishment in England', 125–6.

local punishments. At Dover, for example, criminals were thrown from the cliffs as a form of capital punishment.[64] One of the harshest punishments, *peine forte et dure*, was reserved for men who refused to plead in court. Robert Lewer, a former member of the royal household and a notorious thug, did this after he had waged what seems to have been a one-man private war against the elder Despenser in 1323. He was given a diet of water one day, and bread the other, while at the same time he was steadily loaded with heavy weights so that eventually he was pressed to death.[65] Lewer chose his fate so as to ensure that his family would inherit his property. Had he been convicted of treason, it would have been forfeited. It is not so clear why Robert Hastang, who stabbed his relative Philip Hastang as he lay in bed one night, similarly remained silent in court, for this was not a case of treason. He, however, duly suffered the same penalty.[66]

Imprisonment was used for a range of offences, and could be used in cases where people could not pay fines. In Henry III's reign stealing deer in royal parks became an offence punishable with a year and a day in prison. From Edward I's reign onwards imprisonment was required by statute for a number of offences. Royal officials who failed in their duty were threatened with this penalty. Men found with clipped money in their possession also faced imprisonment. Lawyers who deceived the court would be imprisoned for a year; poachers faced a three-year sentence. There appears to have been a scale for imprisoning those found guilty of larceny, with a week in prison for every penny stolen.[67] Imprisonment, however, was used more often to hold suspects before they were tried than as a means of punishment. It could be appalling. Alan Blont was arrested in 1255 on suspicion of larceny, and handed over by the bailiffs of Lincoln to Alan fitzWilliam to imprison him. To ensure that he did not escape, Alan put a tight iron collar around his neck, shut the door, and left him. This was on a Friday; on the Saturday he was found dead, his neck swollen as result of the savage collar.[68] That was an exceptionally unpleasant case; but even if men were not normally tortured, they might simply starve to death, forgotten.

Not all of those found guilty suffered death or imprisonment. The use of royal pardons was seen by the Commons in the fourteenth century as a major abuse. Edward I began the practice of emptying the country's gaols in order to

[64] *The London Eyre of 1276*, ed. Weinbaum, no. 54.
[65] *Vita Edwardi*, 128–9; H. R. T. Summerson, 'The Early Development of the *Peine Forte et Dure*', in E. W. Ives and A. H. Manchester (eds.), *Law, Litigants and the Legal Profession* (London, 1983), 116–25.
[66] 'Plea Rolls of the Reign of Edward II', ed. Wrottesley, 24.
[67] R. B. Pugh, *Imprisonment in Medieval England* (Cambridge, 1968), 21–47.
[68] *CIM* i, no. 2089.

fill the ranks of his armies in 1294, and over 2,000 criminals were pardoned in this way. The Crécy campaign saw a similar number of pardons issued. In 1347 a parliamentary petition claimed, probably with some justice, that the scale of crime was increased as a result of the crown's use of charters of pardon. In 1353 the Commons pointed out that criminals pardoned on condition that they remained abroad on the king's service often swiftly returned home, to resume their misdeeds.[69] Some cases where pardons were issued certainly appear outrageous. Hugh Aston was a lay clerk of the Common Bench whose marriage was unsuccessful. In the late 1350s his wife committed adultery; Hugh persuaded his servants to seize her lover and castrate him, an offence for which he was pardoned by the king.[70]

The question of crime and how to deal with it was one of the most intractable problems that faced the English government in this period. There was, however, no complete breakdown, and there may even have been a certain pride taken in the country's traditions of lawlessness. When the captured king of France was brought on his journey to London, Edward III arranged for various people, great men and others, to encounter him in different ways. One such encounter took place close to a forest, where some 500 men were arrayed, all dressed in green. They were armed with bows and arrows, and other weapons, as if they were robbers, to the alarm of the French king.[71] The incident suggests that crime could be romanticized in a way that would later lead to the writing down of tales about Robin Hood.

---

[69] *Rot. Parl.* ii. 172, 253.   [70] Tout, *Chapters*, iii. 210.   [71] *Anon. Chron.*, 40–1.

CHAPTER 21

Population and the Black Death

In the thirteenth and fourteenth centuries the population of England underwent dramatic changes. The Black Death of 1348–9 saw a level of mortality
unprecedented in the historical record. There is surprising agreement about
the broad outlines of the demographic changes of this period. Population grew
in the thirteenth century, reached a plateau in the early fourteenth, and fell
dramatically with the great epidemic that reached England in 1348. The devil,
however, is in the detail. There are no sources that can be used to provide
global figures, no equivalent to Domesday Book of the eleventh century, or to
the poll taxes of the late fourteenth. Instead, there is a difficult jigsaw of small
pieces of evidence, and as so often happens with jigsaws where many pieces are
lost, those that remain do not all fit neatly together. This chapter will firstly
examine the period up to 1348, and secondly look at the Black Death itself.

OVERALL TOTALS

Population is controlled by birth rates, death rates, and migration. There is
very little direct evidence about the former, since there was no system for
registering births. In the early modern period there is good evidence to
demonstrate that there were very significant changes in birth rates, and it
would be foolish to suggest that, because there is no evidence, this was not
also the case in the medieval period.[1] Changes in economic circumstances may
have influenced the birth rate; if there were few opportunities for young men
and women, they might marry late, while the converse would be true in times
of prosperity. This is the most likely explanation for possible changes in birth
rates, although there are other considerations.[2] There was a lack of understanding as to how conception takes place, and this may have made it more
difficult to control. It was thought of as requiring a positive action on the part

---

[1] For changes in fertility in the early modern period, see E. A. Wrigley and R. S. Schofield,
The Population History of England 1546–1871 (London, 1981), 229.

[2] M. Bailey, 'Demographic Decline in Late Medieval England: Some Thoughts on Recent
Research', *EcHR* 49 (1996), 1–19, for a fuller discussion of the issues around fertility.

of both men and women, requiring the emission of both male and female semen. One consequence of this was the belief that if a woman conceived, she could not possibly have been raped; conception meant that she had consented. Nor was the female anatomy understood; one view was that it was similar to the male, but turned inside out. In comparison to the male, however, the female body 'hath smalle ballokkys', as a late medieval writer put it. Even odder, but well founded in classical writings, was the notion that the uterus was capable of wandering about the body, causing great problems should it lodge in an inappropriate place, such as the chest.³ There is some evidence that people tried to limit the size of their families. Herbal concoctions were no doubt used as contraceptives, probably with little effect. *Coitus interruptus* was employed, despite the weary disapproval of the Church.⁴ On the other hand, there is very little evidence of abortion. One case is recorded in London in the 1260s, in which a maidservant accused a cleric of the death of her baby by abortion. Equally, infanticide was very uncommon. Analysis of 5,000 fourteenth-century homicides yielded only three instances.⁵ The attitude of the Church may have had some effects in limiting the birth rate, for it attempted to put various hindrances in people's way. Sexual activity was prohibited on a large number of days; not only on Sundays, but also on every imaginable church festival. There is no way of knowing how effective such injunctions were. The absence of privacy possibly created greater problems for couples. One court case shows that one couple, Nicholas de Bosco and Joanna de Clapton, resolved this, as many must have done, by going out into the open, even, in their case, on a snowy night. They were, however, observed by others, and Nicholas was also seen with Matilda Goderhele, 'doing what a man does with a woman'.⁶

Death rates were affected by changes in economic circumstances. If, on a Malthusian model, food production failed to keep up with the rising population, then the resultant famine would cause a rise in death rates. One argument is that in the thirteenth century population was indeed rising faster than the means of production. Marginal land that was being brought under the plough was capable of producing adequate yields for no more than a short time, and there was no scope for further expansion. By the early fourteenth century the population had, according to such theories, reached its maximum, with decline coming with the disastrous famine of 1315–16. The epidemic disease that came

---

³ C. Rawcliffe, *Medicine and Society in Later Medieval England* (Stroud, 1995), 172–4, 197.

⁴ P. A. Biller, 'Birth Control in the West in the Thirteenth and Early Fourteenth Centuries', *Past and Present*, 94 (1982), 19–23.

⁵ *The London Eyre of 1276*, ed. Weinbaum, 51; B. A. Hanawalt, *Crime and Conflict in English Communities 1300–1348* (Cambridge, Mass., 1979), 154.

⁶ *Select Cases from the Ecclesiastical Courts of the Province of Canterbury*, ed. Adams and Donahue, 96–101.

in the wake of the famine reflected, at least in part, the result of the suscepti-
bility of a severely weakened populace. Not all changes to death rates, however,
were determined by the course of the economy. The Black Death of 1348–9
resulted from the arrival in England of a hitherto unknown infective agent, and
the disease proved to be as capable of killing the prosperous and well-fed as it
was the poor and malnourished.

Migration from overseas had no significant effect on the population in this
period, but internal movement was an important factor in determining the
population history of particular places. The growth of the urban population,
for example, is largely to be explained in terms of immigration from the
countryside. Emigration to towns and cities was a safety valve for rural
communities awash with humanity in the thirteenth century. In terms of the
overall population, however, it was birth rates, and above all death rates, that
determined its size.

The overall number of people in thirteenth- and fourteenth-century England cannot be calculated with any accuracy. The poll taxes of 1377, 1379, and
1381 provide a count of the adult population after the end of the period covered
in this book. The accuracy of that count is questionable, but by adding to the
1377 figure an estimate of the likely level of population decline that was caused
by outbreaks of Black Death from 1348 onwards, it is possible to produce a
crude calculation of the size of the population at its greatest medieval height.
Working on this basis, a figure approaching 7 million for the early fourteenth-
century population has been suggested. That was probably at least three times
the size of the late eleventh-century population, for which it is possible to make
calculations from Domesday Book. The margin of error in such estimates is
very great; the figures can do no more than give an impression of the overall
order of magnitude. Working from the same data, but with different assumptions about such factors as family size, it is equally possible to suggest a total of
no more than 3.7 million.[7]

An alternative method of suggesting a total for the population is based on a
calculation of how much food the country produced, and how many people it
could therefore support. To do this, it is necessary to make a great many
assumptions. Estimates are needed of the amount of land under the plough, of
the quantity of grain an acre would yield, of the calorific value of medieval
grain, and of the amount of grain an individual would need for subsistence.
Assumptions also have to be made about the relative productivity of peasant
and demesne land. Calculations, which assume among other things a daily

[7] M. M. Postan, 'Medieval Agrarian Society in its Prime', in *Cambridge Economic History of
Europe*, i: *The Agrarian Life of the Middle Ages*, 2nd edn., ed. M. M. Postan (Cambridge, 1966),
561–2; see also J. Hatcher, *Plague, Population and the English Economy 1348–1530* (London,
1977), 68.

intake from grain of only 1,500 calories, suggest a total population in 1300 of the order of 4 million.[8] This is worked out by piling hypothesis upon hypothesis, but provides a valuable correction to some of the higher population figures that have been suggested. Four million should probably be regarded as a minimum figure; 5 million represents a reasonable compromise between the various different methods and estimates.

Not only can a global total for the population be little more than guesswork, but it also reveals little. The more important questions are those about the way in which numbers were increasing in the thirteenth century, and the chronology and extent of the reversal of this expansionary trend. The most effective approach is to look at the population at a local level. There are many more sources and techniques that can be used, and while they may not do much to resolve the arguments over global figures for the English population, they reveal the trends upwards and downwards far more persuasively than large-scale estimates. To give one specific example, there survive two surveys for the Essex manor of Havering, one from the mid-thirteenth century, and one from the mid-fourteenth. These list the tenants, and if it is assumed that the average family size was 4.5, then the population at the time of the first was about 1,700. On the same basis, the population a century later was about 2,200. The acreage under cultivation rose from 8,500 to 9,500 between the two dates.[9]

LOCAL EVIDENCE

The rolls of manorial courts provide an important source for the reconstruction of the population of medieval rural communities. There is, however, considerable argument among historians over how they may be used, and in particular about their reliability as a source of statistics. It is possible to count the numbers of tenants from some court rolls. At Coltishall in Norfolk there were 119 tenants in 1314, 168 in 1349, and 74 in 1359. This strongly suggests that the population in this village was rising significantly until the Black Death.[10] A national survey of the numbers of holdings showed that it was rare for numbers to decline in the thirteenth or early fourteenth centuries, though one Yorkshire manor showed a startling drop of 87 per cent between 1274 and 1304, and Wiltshire evidence suggests a decline between 1280 and 1350. At the other end of the spectrum is the manor of Betley in Staffordshire,

---

[8] B. M. S. Campbell, *English Seigniorial Agriculture 1250–1450* (Cambridge, 2000), 399–406; Campbell *et al.*, *A Medieval Capital and its Grain Supply*, 37–45.

[9] M. K. McIntosh, 'Land, Tenure, and Population in the Royal Manor of Havering, Essex, 1251–1352/3', *EcHR*, 2nd ser., 33 (1980), 17–22.

[10] B. M. S. Campbell, 'Inheritance and the Land Market in a Peasant Community', in R. M. Smith (ed.), *Land, Kinship and Life-Cycle* (Cambridge, 1984), 96.

with a rise of 34 per cent between 1299 and 1308. The overall picture is one of rising numbers, though with considerable regional variation.[11] The difficulty with this type of evidence is that tenant numbers are not necessarily a good proxy for the population as a whole. If the land market was tightly controlled, tenant numbers would not go up even if the population was increasing rapidly. Nevertheless, the figures do suggest a population that, at least in some regions, was still rising when the Black Death struck.

Court rolls provide details of heriots paid by the tenants. These can be regarded as the equivalent of death duties, paid on the death of the tenants. This means that, with various qualifications, numbers of deaths can be calculated. What is instantly clear is not unexpected: the worse the harvest, the greater the number of deaths, with the obvious exception of the great epidemic of the Black Death, which was not related to grain yields. The correlation between high mortality and the famine years of 1315–16 is particularly striking, for then about twice as many tenants died as in the preceding years.[12] Any pre-industrial society is likely to be very sensitive to harvest fluctuations, but the very close correlation of deaths and prices in England in the first half of the fourteenth century suggests that there was very little spare capacity in the economy. A bad harvest pushed many into a situation in which it was hard to find enough to eat. While a count of heriots can provide indications of the death rate, it cannot provide the precise comparison between death rate and birth rate that would be needed to show whether the population was rising or falling. A further problem is that heriots might be paid not only on the death of a tenant, but also when a tenant gave up or sold his holding. In broad terms, however, this evidence suggests a high death rate for tenants. That implies an even higher rate for the population as a whole, since it excludes the poorest and most vulnerable of society, the landless poor. In turn this suggests that fertility must have been at a very high level if the population was stable or increasing.

Another technique is to count the number of individuals who appeared in the manorial courts. This was done for the manor of Halesowen, and the figures show an increase from 382 individuals in the early 1270s to a peak of 689 in 1311–15. There was then a decline, which can be attributed to the effects of the famine years, and a recovery to 675 on the eve of the Black Death. That epidemic resulted in a fall to 389.[13] A similar analysis of those named in the

---

[11] H. E. Hallam, 'Population Movements in England, 1086–1350', *Agrarian History*, ii. 508–35.
[12] M. M. Postan and J. Z. Titow, 'Heriots and Prices on Winchester Manors', in Postan, *Essays on Medieval Agriculture*, 150–85.
[13] Z. Razi, *Life, Marriage and Death in a Medieval Parish: Economy, Society and Demography in Halesowen 1270–1400* (Cambridge, 1980), 25.

TABLE 21.1 *Halesowen court appearances, 1271–1355*

Years	No. of court records	No. of individuals
1271–5	42	382
1280–2	39	463
1293–5	28	542
1301–5	44	604
1311–15	79	689
1321–5	88	582
1331–5	71	606
1345–9	66	675
1351–5	59	389

TABLE 21.2 *Broughton court appearances, 1288–1340*

Years	No. of individuals
1288–99	292
1300–9	268
1310–19	274
1320–9	249
1330–40	240

court rolls of Broughton in Huntingdonshire produced very different results.[14] There was a decline in the late thirteenth century, briefly reversed in the second decade of the fourteenth, followed by a further decline. There are obvious problems with this method of calculating population.[15] Above all, it has to be assumed that a similar proportion of peasants will appear in court over the whole period. In practice, changes in court procedures or policy might alter this proportion. Different economic circumstances might affect the number who appeared in court. The harsh years of the famine of 1315–16, and the succeeding animal murrains, undoubtedly saw a considerable rise in petty crime, with more individuals coming before the courts as a result. Some of the court rolls on the

[14] Britton, *The Community of the Vill*, 138.

[15] The difficulties are set out at length in L. R. Poos and R. M. Smith, ' "Legal Windows onto Historical Populations"? Recent Research on Demography and the Manor Court in Medieval England', in Razi and Smith (eds.), *Medieval Society and the Manor Court*, 300–8. Bennett, *Women in the Medieval Countryside: Gender and Household in Brigstock* (Oxford, 1987), 13, 224, gives similar figures for Brigstock in Northamptonshire and Iver in Buckinghamshire. She adjusts the totals to account for the different number of court rolls surviving from each period, a technique to which there are considerable methodological objections.

Ramsey abbey estates show an extraordinary, and inexplicable, increase in acts of violence in 1312, with thirty-two cases, and again in 1320, with sixty-seven. In other years the figure was under ten.[16] A further problem is that the population of a village might be affected by immigration or emigration, making it difficult to extrapolate the figures onto a wider canvas.

A more complex process of family reconstruction from the court rolls has been attempted in order to provide a fuller picture of population movements. There are various difficulties involved. One is that two or more individuals might share the same name. This was often the case with fathers and sons, while several families could carry the same occupational surname. A further problem is that a good many more men are identified in the rolls than women. Children feature rarely. The data are not full enough to make it possible to produce accurate assessments of life expectancy. Nevertheless, innovative work on the Halesowen court rolls has yielded figures for the male replacement rate; that is, the number of sons who survived their father. This stood at a very healthy level of about 1.5 until the decade 1310–19, when it dropped just below a one-for-one replacement. It then picked up in the 1320s and 1330s. Even when corrected to allow for the bias of the figures in favour of wealthier tenants, the rate was still positive in the first half of the fourteenth century, save for the years from 1310 to 1319, which strongly suggests a rising population until the Black Death. The technique and results have been criticized. Given the death rates, to have achieved the sort of growth that the calculations suggest would have required an unusual 'non-European' pattern of marriage, with villagers marrying young and having large families, with a mean size of 5.8. It is unlikely that medieval marriage patterns differed so radically from those known in later periods. It is more probable that this period was characterized by what is termed the 'European marriage pattern', in which marriage is relatively late, and far from universal. In difficult times the birth rate would fall as fewer couples married. The issue is a controversial one among historians, and remains to be finally resolved.[17]

Yet another approach to the problem is to use the data from the tithing system. All men were supposed to be in a tithing, nominally numbering ten, for the maintenance of law and order. Regular checks, known as views of frankpledge, were held. Payments were made from each tithing. In many places a fixed annual sum replaced this archaic levy, but in some manors the varying sums collected do appear to represent the actual numbers of those in the tithing system. Calculations for the manor of Taunton suggest that the adult male

---

[16] *Court Rolls of Ramsey, Hepmangrove and Bury*, ed. DeWindt, 42.
[17] Razi, *Life, Marriage and Death*, 21–6, 33–4, 63, 93. For criticism of Razi's conclusions, see Poos and Smith, ' "Legal Windows onto Historical Populations"?', 298–324.

population rose from 612 in 1209 to 1,448 in 1311. The famine of 1315–16 led to a fall in the population by over 9 per cent; it then remained static until 1330. The peak period of growth was in the years up to the mid-thirteenth century.[18] Examination of the tithing penny figures for a group of Essex manors suggests a static population from the late thirteenth century to the outbreak of the famine in 1315. Mortality from the famine varied from place to place, but averaged about 15 per cent. That was followed by years of steady population decline until the outbreak of the Black Death, which resulted in a dramatic 45 per cent fall. These various techniques for counting peasants do not produce wholly consistent results. They indicate a growing population in the thirteenth century, with the rate of increase slowing by 1300. It is not fully apparent whether, following population loss as result of the famine in the second decade, there was a continuing decline, or a recovery. It seems likely that the patterns of population movement were not the same over the whole country in the first half of the fourteenth century, but that by the 1340s levels were probably rising in many places.

Indirect evidence provides useful indicators of changes to the population. A rising population should mean an extension to the area of cultivation, and conversely, at times of falling population less land would be placed under the plough. There is ample data to show that assarting, the clearing and cultivation of areas of forest, was taking place extensively in the thirteenth century as the population grew. The acreage of arable land was increased, with expansion into marginal lands where the soil was unlikely to be able to bear good crops for many seasons. Coastal marsh and fenland was drained in the thirteenth century, under pressure from a steadily rising population, particularly in eastern England. The division of peasant holdings is one indication of the pressure that existed. The foundation of new towns provides further evidence of a buoyant, rising population.

The situation in the first half of the fourteenth century was different, particularly after the famine years of 1315–16. In Durham, to judge by grants of waste (or uncultivated) land, expansion came to a dramatic halt after the famine. Whereas forty-three such grants were made by Bishop Kellawe between 1311 and 1316, his successor made just one between 1317 and 1333.[19] Inquiries conducted in 1342 into the failure of the tax of the ninth of agricultural produce granted in the previous year are suggestive. In a number of counties the jurors, when asked why the tax had yielded so little, stated that much land had gone out of cultivation. In some cases it was because the land

[18] J. Z. Titow, 'Some Evidence of Thirteenth-Century Population Growth', *EcHR*, 2nd ser., 14 (1961), 218–23.

[19] H. M. Dunsford and S. J. Harris, 'Colonization of the Wasteland in County Durham, 1100–1400', *EcHR* 56 (2003), 48.

was too poor; in others, there were insufficient people to cultivate it, or the people were too poor. The regional distribution is curious. Bedfordshire, Buckinghamshire, and Cambridgeshire were particularly hard-hit. The Sussex coast saw much abandoned land. In Shropshire deserted land was reported in over fifty vills, and in the North Riding of Yorkshire land was uncultivated in some ninety places. Lincolnshire, on the other hand, was apparently unaffected.[20] There are some difficulties with this inquest. Those conducting it appear to have been convinced by different arguments in different parts of the country. The absence of abandoned fields in the record for Lincolnshire may reflect little more than the way the inquiry was conducted there. What the survey suggests is that much land that had been under the plough in the thirteenth century had been abandoned in the fourteenth. In Cambridgeshire alone almost 5,000 acres had gone out of production. That strongly implies a declining population. The situation was not, however, so acute that villages were being abandoned. A highly exceptional example is provided by Coldecotes in Lincolnshire, a small manor with an associated village settlement, which was ruined and depopulated as early as 1322.[21] Deserted village sites would be a familiar feature of fifteenth-century England, but not of the fourteenth. Other evidence suggests that while some soils may have become exhausted, there was no clear overall trend. In some cases, holdings were abandoned because their holders migrated, not so much driven from their lands as attracted by better opportunities elsewhere, perhaps in towns.[22]

Despite the economic difficulties evident from the returns dealing with tax of the ninth, there is some indirect evidence that suggests that the population was beginning to rise again in the 1330s and 1340s, at least in some places. The Wakefield court rolls, for example, show some enterprising peasants in the 1330s taking new land under cultivation. There is a long list of relatively small pieces of land, up to 3 acres, taken from the lord's waste in 1332. One group of tenants paid 40d. in order to enclose 18 acres of arable within a hedge.[23] Recovery, however, looks to have been slow and localized; there was no full return to the rising population trend of the thirteenth century.

Rents provide further evidence. The indications are that there was no consistent, widespread movement. There was certainly no dramatic fall that would suggest a declining population and with it substantially reduced demand

[20] A. R. H. Baker, 'Evidence in the "Nonarum Inquisitiones" of Contracting Arable in England During the Early Fourteenth Century', *EcHR*, 2nd ser., 19 (1966), 518–31. See also above, 440.

[21] Everson *et al.*, *Change and Continuity* 121.

[22] B. Harvey, 'The Population Trend in England Between 1300 and 1348', *TRHS*, 5th ser., 16 (1966), 32–7.

[23] *Court Rolls of the Manor of Wakefield*, ed. Walker, 65–6.

for land. There were, on the contrary, some cases where rents were being increased in the first half of the fourteenth century, particularly in the second quarter.[24] The indirect evidence points to a reasonably stable population in this period, in which there was some limited recovery after the difficult years of the famine of 1315–16.

THE BLACK DEATH

Such recovery in population numbers as was taking place by the 1340s was suddenly and dramatically halted in 1348 by the advent of what was probably the greatest human catastrophe that has ever affected England:

Alas, this mortality devoured such a multitude of both sexes that no one could be found to carry the bodies of the dead to burial, but men and women carried the bodies of their own little ones to church on their shoulders and threw them into mass graves, from which arose such a stink that it was barely possible for anyone to go past a churchyard.[25]

Many of the chroniclers who lived through the great pestilence of 1348–9, the Black Death, wrote about it with a brevity that suggests they found words inadequate to depict the horrors they had seen, and the grief people felt. This was the most appalling disaster, a demographic catastrophe on a scale rarely if ever seen before or since, in which up to half of the population died.

The symptoms of the disease were described by Geoffrey le Baker. Some victims had boils or abscesses. These broke out suddenly, and when lanced proved to be hard and dry. A good many survived this, either by cutting out the boils, or after a long period of illness. Others had small black pustules all over their bodies. Hardly anyone survived this form of the disease. John of Reading wrote of ulcers in the groin and armpit; these killed men in three days. An Irish account spoke of boils, abscesses, and pustules on legs and armpits, and also of a form of the disease in which men died in frenzy, or vomiting blood. Some Continental sources give more details of the symptoms. Patients might first feel cold, and suffer a tingling sensation. Then, hard solid boils would appear in the groin or armpit. A fever followed, and in some cases vomiting of blood. The most fatal form of the disease saw the patient cough up, rather than vomit, blood. The smell of the victims was particularly unpleasant.[26]

Although the symptoms appear to describe at least two different diseases, it has long been assumed that all were the result of bubonic plague, a disease well documented from the pandemic of the late nineteenth century. This plague can take varied forms. In one it is characterized by the formation of buboes, or

---

[24] Harvey, 'The Population Trend in England, 1300 to 1348', 38–40.
[25] *The Black Death*, ed. Horrox, 70, quoting William Dene's Rochester chronicle.
[26] The sources are conveniently translated by Horrox, ibid. 24–5, 40, 42, 74, 81, 84.

swellings, in the groin or armpit. In another, the pneumonic form, it affects the lungs directly, causing the patient to cough up blood. In a third, the septicaemic form, the bacillus *Yersinia pestis* infects the blood, swiftly killing the victim. The main mode of transmission of plague is the bite of an infected flea. Rodents, particularly rats, suffering from the disease harbour the fleas. The flea's gut is blocked by the bacillus, and the disease is passed on to any human it bites. Plague, however, can also be passed more directly between people by coughing, in which case it takes the pneumonic form. The disease is more likely to spread in the summer months, since the fleas are active only in warm weather. The pneumonic type, however, can be transmitted in colder weather.

There are considerable problems with the identification of the Black Death as bubonic plague.[27] The symptoms described, while similar to bubonic plague, are not identical to those described from recent outbreaks. There is surprisingly little English evidence about the precise symptoms of the victims of the Black Death, but that from miraculous cures in continental Europe, while it points to boils, buboes, and pustules, suggests that the distribution of these on the body was different from that seen in bubonic plague. Swellings were normally on the neck or throat, rather than the groin or armpit, and multiple boils were common. Small black pustules were seen as a particularly fatal symptom.[28] What is perhaps more significant is that in nineteenth- and twentieth-century outbreaks of bubonic plague the disease has not spread with the same rapidity it displayed in the fourteenth century. Nor has it had the same devastating effect on any population as the Black Death had, even though mortality among those who contract it is very high. There is no recent parallel to the 1348 outbreak.

The timing of the Black Death does not fit well with bubonic plague. While there is good evidence for high mortality in the summer months of 1349, there are also cases showing the disease raging during the winter of 1348–9. At Titchfield in Hampshire there were about 150 tenants. By the end of October 1348 eight deaths were reported, with twenty-five more by 7 November. Between then and 11 March 1349, 106 tenants died, with a further sixteen by 8 May. By the summer of 1349 the catastrophic epidemic had run its course. Similarly, at Codicote, a St Albans manor, the majority of deaths took place between November 1248 and May 1249.[29] The records of appointments to

---

[27] The most comprehensive criticism of the view that the Black Death was bubonic plague is provided by S. K. Cohn, Jr., *The Black Death Transformed: Disease and Culture in Early Renaissance Europe* (London, 2002). O. J. Benedictow, *The Black Death 1346–1353* (Woodbridge, 2004), provides a restatement of the traditional interpretation.

[28] Cohn, *The Black Death Transformed*, 78–80.

[29] D. G. Watts, 'The Black Death in Dorset and Hampshire', in T. B. James (ed.), *The Black Death in Wessex*, Hatcher Review, v. no. 46 (1998), 23–4; Levett, *Studies in Manorial History*, 249.

vacant churches in the Winchester diocese show the epidemic beginning to strike in January 1349, coming to a peak in April, when there were sixty-four such appointments, and then falling back to thirteen in August.[30] In Italy occurrences of plague were common in the hot summer months, which coincide with the low point in the lifecycle of the rat flea in a Mediterranean climate.[31] Such chronologies do not fit the classic pattern of bubonic plague.

There are also difficulties as far as rats are concerned. The rat known in medieval England was the black rat, *rattus rattus*, also known as the ship rat. It tends to live in houses, and does not range far from its nest. There is surprisingly little evidence to suggest that there was a large rat population in medieval England. On one occasion a rat-catcher killed eighteen rats at Clare castle, but such references are uncommon. Manorial accounts very rarely record depredations by rats or mice, and grain was stored in open barns with little attempt to protect it from rodents, which suggests that the animals were not very common.[32] Nor have archaeologists demonstrated that there were substantial numbers of rats throughout England. Some rat bones have been found, but not in large quantities. One unpleasant complete corpse, with fur and whiskers surviving, was found in a grave in Salisbury. Discoveries at Southampton are not surprising; a port was very likely to be infested with ship rats.[33] It is difficult to imagine that rats could have spread the disease given the speed at which it is known to have travelled. In Iceland there were no rats, yet the Black Death spread rapidly.

The answer usually given to these various difficulties is that the *Yersinia pestis* bacillus is capable of rapid mutation, and that the form it took in the mid-fourteenth century was far more virulent than that of the present day. Also, it is often suggested that the pneumonic form of plague could be transmitted in the cold weather of winter, and that it could spread very fast, unlike the type borne by rats and fleas, since it could be transmitted directly from human to human. The alternative is that this was some entirely different disease. Anthrax has been proposed, but the same objection can be made, that no modern outbreak of the disease demonstrates the same speed of spread, or very high loss of population.[34] Man, as a species, is relatively resistant to anthrax. Between 1899

---

[30] *The Register of William Edington, Bishop of Winchester 1346–1366*, ed. S. F. Hockey (Hampshire Record Office, 1986–7), vol. i, p. xiii.

[31] Cohn, *Black Death Transformed*, 176.

[32] G. Twigg, *The Black Death: A Biological Reappraisal* (London, 1984), 75–112, 131–46; Underhill, *For Her Good Estate*, 99. A rare example of the destruction of crops by rats and mice is at Bearpark, in Durham, in 1334–5, when the crop of beans and peas was lost: Durham cathedral muniments, manorial accounts.

[33] T. B. James, *The Black Death in Hampshire*, Hampshire Papers, 18 (1999), 20–1.

[34] Twigg, *Black Death*, 213–14.

and 1912, when there was widespread exposure to anthrax in industrial processes involving animal products, only 354 cases were notified. Annual case rates, not mortality rates, in four mills in the United States, where workers were regularly inhaling anthrax spores, were between 0.6 and 1.4 per cent per annum.[35] A further problem with anthrax is that, although there were many animal murrains in the fourteenth century, there is not the coincidence of animal and human deaths that would be necessary to demonstrate that the Black Death was, at least in part, an anthrax outbreak.

The most recent disease to cause a catastrophic worldwide epidemic is influenza. In the 1918 outbreak many victims turned a dark colour from lack of oxygen, and coughed up blood. Plague was at first suspected; the symptoms were far more severe than normal influenza, but did not include the plague buboes in groin and armpit. One feature of the 1918 epidemic was the extraordinary speed with which it killed its victims; this was also a feature of the Black Death. 'Few lay sick for more than two or three days, or even for half a day.'[36] It is most unlikely, however, that influenza could have caused the Black Death; neither the symptoms nor the speed with which the disease spread match sufficiently.

Another possibility that has been mooted is that the Black Death was a viral haemorrhagic disease, which vanished in the seventeenth century, and which was spread from person to person, without the involvement of any animals or insects. Calculations from late sixteenth-century evidence suggest that it had a long incubation period of some thirty-two days, followed by a five-day period up to death, when symptoms were evident. According to this scenario, people could have been infectious for as long as twenty-seven days. This would explain the way that the disease could spread as it did, for people would be infectious for as long as three weeks without being aware that they had the disease.[37] However, this can be no more than yet another hypothesis; the Black Death symptoms do not match those of today's haemorrhagic viral diseases such as Ebola. Nor does this suggestion explain the seasonality of the Black Death.

Scientific evidence could conceivably resolve the problem. It has been claimed that traces of the DNA of *Yersinia pestis* have been found in the teeth of fourteenth-century plague victims buried in a Montpellier cemetery.[38]

---

[35] World Health Organization, *Guidelines for the Surveillance and Control of Anthrax in Humans and Animals* (London, 1998).

[36] G. Kolata, *Flu: The Story of the Great Influenza Pandemic of 1918 and the Search for the Virus that Caused It* (London, 2000), 16–17, 22–3; Knighton, trans. in *Black Death*, ed. Horrox, 77.

[37] S. Scott and C. Duncan, *Return of the Black Death* (Chichester, 2004), 153–63, 218–28.

[38] D. Raoult, G. Aboudharam, E. Crubézy, G. Larrouy, B. Ludes, and M. Drancourt, 'Molecular Identification by "Suicide PCR" of *Yersinia Pestis* as the Agent of Medieval Black Death', *Proceedings of the National Academy of Sciences*, 97 (7 Nov. 2000), 12800–3.

It has not proved possible to replicate these experiments, and it is likely that they are to be explained in terms of laboratory or other contamination.[39] Whatever caused the Black Death results in no changes to bone structure, and is unlikely, given the high death rate, to have taken the form of persistent latent disease; as a result, it is unlikely that scientific or archaeological evidence will be able to determine its nature. Even if the case for the presence of *Yersinia pestis* is proven, all that the finding demonstrates is that it was present at the time of the Black Death, not that it alone caused the mass mortality.

THE COURSE OF THE EPIDEMIC

The Black Death was brought to England by sea in late June 1348, to the port of Melcombe Regis in Dorset. This is the conventional view. The sheriff of Dorset, however, did not appear at the exchequer on 16 June, as requested, and it was later stated that this was because he was so ill. All his staff died at the same time.[40] This suggests that the epidemic must have reached England a little sooner, perhaps early rather than late in June. Initially, the ravages of the disease were largely confined to the West Country and Bristol, but by November it had reached London. In the following year it spread across the whole country, with mortality particularly high in late spring and early summer. The pattern was similar in Ireland, first reached by the Black Death in the summer of 1348, and then spreading over the whole country in the following year.

Different groups of the population were not all affected by the Black Death to the same extent. The higher aristocracy were not hit as hard as the population as a whole. Only one member of the royal family succumbed, and that was the king's daughter Joan, who died at Bordeaux. No earls died. Among the parliamentary peerage, the death rate in 1348 was lower than in an average year, at 4.5 per cent. In 1349 the figure rose to 13 per cent, a level interestingly much lower than that for 1361, when with the second outbreak of the disease this group saw a mortality of 23.9 per cent.[41]

There is a good deal of evidence to show how the clergy were affected. Archbishop Stratford of Canterbury, who died in late August 1348, may have been a fatality in the great epidemic. The next two archbishops, John Offord

[39] M. I. P. Gilbert, J. Cuccui, W. White, N. Lynnerup, R. W. Titball, A. Cooper, and M. B. Prentice, 'Absence of *Yersinia Pestis*-Specific DNA in Human Teeth from Five European Excavations of Putative Plague Victims', *Microbiology*, 150 (2004), 341–54. I am grateful to Professor Cooper for sending me a copy of this paper.

[40] *Black Death*, ed. Horrox, 62–3; E. B. Fryde, 'The Tenants of the Bishops of Coventry and Lichfield and of Worcester After the Plague of 1348–9', in *Medieval Legal Records*. ed. Hunnisett and Post, 226.

[41] McFarlane, *The Nobility of Later Medieval England*, 169.

and Thomas Bradwardine, who died in 1349, certainly were. The one bishop to die was Bransford of Worcester. At the abbey of Meaux in Yorkshire, out of forty-two monks and seven lay brothers, thirty-two died.[42] Mortality of the lower clergy can be calculated from the rate of appointment of replacements for those who died. There are difficulties in working out precise figures. The bishops' registers do not always state the reason for a vacancy, and in some cases clergy may have abandoned their livings, rather than died. For York, however, mortality among the clergy was probably about 40 per cent. The figure for Hereford was similar. In the archdeaconry of Lincoln almost 45 per cent of benefices became vacant, and in the archdeaconry of Stow (also Lincolnshire) the figure was just over 57 per cent. The figure was lower for the archdeaconry of Northampton, and in Leicester, where it was just over 36 per cent. For the diocese of Ely, the mortality rate was about 47 per cent. In the diocese of Coventry and Lichfield the death rate varied from a low of 29 per cent in the Chester archdeaconry, to 57 per cent in Derby. At Worcester mortality peaked in July 1349. That month sixty-seven new appointments to church livings were made, in comparison to two in the same month of the previous year. At Norwich all the friars of the house of Our Lady died. Within the ranks of the clergy, occupational differences affected mortality. In the diocese of Coventry and Lichfield vicars (who resided in their parishes) had a 46 per cent death rate, as against rectors (who did not have to reside) with 33 per cent mortality. Monastic communities, on the other hand, may have been isolated to some extent from the secular world, but the Black Death did not respect this. At the Cistercian house of Newenham in Devon, only three monks out of twenty-six survived. In contrast, however, only four monks died at Canterbury cathedral priory.[43] One small group provides a contrast to the bulk of the evidence. Of eighty-seven theologians known to have been at Oxford in the decade prior to the Black Death, only one is known to have died from the epidemic, and only five died in 1348–9.[44] Nevertheless, the epidemic had a devastating effect on intellectual life, almost certainly causing the deaths, among others, of William of Ockham, Thomas Bradwardine, John Dumbleton, and Thomas Buckingham.

[42] *Melsa*, ii. 36–7.
[43] *Black Death*, ed. Horrox, 235; W. J. Dohar, *The Black Death and Pastoral Leadership: The Diocese of Hereford in the Fourteenth Century* (Philadelphia, 1995), 52, 86, 96–8; G. Platts, *Land and People in Medieval Lincolnshire* (Lincoln, 1985), 163–4; *A Calendar of the Register of Wolstan de Bransford, Bishop of Worcester 1339–49*, ed. R. M. Haines (London, 1966), pp. li–lii; R. A. Davis, 'The Effects of the Black Death on the Parish Priests of the Medieval Diocese of Coventry and Lichfield', *Historical Research*, 62 (1989), 85–90; J. Aberth, 'The Black Death in the Diocese of Ely: The Evidence of the Bishop's Register', *Journal of Medieval History*, 21 (1995), 275–87.
[44] W. J. Courtenay, 'The Effect of the Black Death on English Higher Education', *Speculum*, 55 (1980), 702, 708 n.

Manorial court rolls provide evidence for the rural population, for they normally listed the tenants who died. Like the other sources, they do not indicate the cause of death. These data on tenants are arguably not fully representative of the population as a whole, since the great majority of those holding land were adult males. The figures are, however, broadly in line with those showing clerical mortality. A great many examples can be provided. The levels of mortality varied from manor to manor. At Bishop's Waltham in Hertfordshire, among others, it stood at 67 per cent. The death toll from the Black Death there was twenty-six times greater than the average mortality in the previous two years. The average on twenty-two Glastonbury manors was 55 per cent. At Cuxham in Oxfordshire, of the twelve villeins alive at the start of 1349, not one survived to the end of the year. Four out of the eight cottagers died.[45] At Thornbury in Gloucestershire 163 male villeins died in 1348–9; in the previous two decades the figure had reached double figures only once.[46] At Wakefield it was coldly reported in 1350 that 'the vill of Shelf is dead'. Surveys of the estates of the bishops of Worcester show that there had been a 36 per cent fall in tenant and smallholder population between 1299 and 1349. On one manor, Hanbury by Droitwich, where there had been sixty-one tenants at the end of the thirteenth century, there were only four in 1399. In Durham 362 tenants were listed as having died in 1349, in twenty-eight townships. The total number of tenants prior to the outbreak was 718, suggesting a death rate of just over one in two. There was considerable local variation within this figure: at Jarrow the level was 78 per cent; at Monkton, close by, it was only 21 per cent.[47]

Detailed analysis of court rolls can reveal much more than a simple overall death rate. At Walsham le Willows in Suffolk the death toll was between 45 and 55 per cent. There, mortality was particularly high among those aged over 50 at almost 90 per cent, and it seems likely that the very young were also hard-hit. Those between 16 and 30 were the most likely to survive; the death rate in their generation was under 10 per cent. Few if any families in the village escaped without some deaths. Similar analysis of the tenants at Halesowen also show a death toll rising with age, though the figures are not quite so spectacular. Twenty-one per cent of those in their twenties, 35 per cent of those in their thirties, 42 per cent of those in their forties, and 62 per cent of those

---

[45] Titow, *English Rural Society*, 70; Harvey, *A Medieval Oxfordshire Village: Cuxham*, 135.

[46] P. Franklin, 'Malaria in Medieval Gloucestershire: An Essay in Epidemiology', *Transactions of the Bristol and Gloucestershire Archaeological Society*, 101 (1983), 112.

[47] *The Court Rolls of the Manor of Wakefield, 1348–1350*, ed. H. M. Jewell, Wakefield Court Rolls Series, 2 (1981), 225; Fryde, 'The Tenants of the Bishops of Coventry and Lichfield and of Worcester After the Plague of 1348–9', 229–30; R. A. Lomas, 'The Black Death in County Durham', *Journal of Medieval History*, 15 (1989), 129.

in their fifties died of the Black Death. For those above 60, the rate fell to 37 per cent. Age rates have also been calculated from the evidence for royal tenants-in-chief, and a similar pattern emerges with a relatively low mortality for young adults, with the level doubling for those in their fifties.[48]

The evidence for mortality is fuller for the countryside than it is for the towns. Normally, a major epidemic would take a greater toll of the urban population. People living close together, mostly in unsanitary, squalid conditions, were particularly liable to infection. It was later stated that one cemetery alone in London, that at West Smithfield, held 50,000 plague victims, but such a round number is not to be trusted. The chronicler Avesbury reported that 200 people were buried there each day for two months, making a total of about 12,000 in a short period of time. More reliable evidence for London is that, whereas an average of twenty-three wills a year were recorded in the decade prior to the epidemic, in 1349 there were no fewer than 352. This suggests that about half the population died. At Canterbury about two-thirds of the tax-payers disappeared from the records after the Black Death. At Winchester six parish churches were abandoned after the epidemic.[49] At Lincoln a record of wills for the period stretching from 1315 to 1376 shows an average number of just under 3.6 a year in normal years, but in 1349 there were no fewer than 105, some thirty times the average.[50] The indications, and they are no more than that, are that at the very least half the urban populace died. The overall death toll in England may well have been not far short of 50 per cent.

One major problem that faced the survivors of the great epidemic was how to deal with the huge number of corpses. That great commander Walter Mauny, with a soldier's sense of the practical, bought land in West Smithfield to serve as a cemetery, and had a chapel built on the site. Later, in 1371, he founded the London Charterhouse there. The cemetery at East Smithfield, which probably contained some 2,400 burials, was carefully laid out, with no indication of panic.[51] Care was clearly taken to try to ensure that the disease was not spread as a result of poor burial practices. At Winchester there were problems, as tempers flared over the question of burials and the claims of St Swithun's priory to monopolistic rights. In January 1349 one monk from the priory was attacked as he conducted a funeral, and in the following June the townspeople

---

[48] R. Lock, 'The Black Death in Walsham-le-Willows', *Proceedings of the Suffolk Institute of Archaeology and History*, 37 (1992), 316–29; Razi, *Life, Marriage and Death*, 109; J. C. Russell, *British Medieval Population* (Albuquerque, N. Mex., 1948), 216.

[49] R. H. Britnell, 'The Black Death in English Towns', *Urban History*, 21 (1994), 198–201; Barron, *London in the Later Middle Ages*, 239.

[50] Hill, *Medieval Lincoln*, 252.

[51] *Black Death*, ed. Horrox, 267–8; D. Hawkins, 'The Black Death and the New London Cemeteries of 1348', *Antiquity*, 64 (1990), 640–2.

attacked 'the monks of the cathedral church and men bearing bodies to the graveyard, and when these fled, followed them with noisy threats of burning the cathedral church'.[52]

THE CONSEQUENCES FOR ECONOMY AND GOVERNMENT

The chronicler Henry Knighton gave a vivid account of the consequences of the Black Death. Prices fell, wages rose. Crops rotted in the fields, unharvested. Lords were forced to pardon rent payments and to abandon labour services. Houses in towns were left vacant, and many villages abandoned. There was an acute shortage of priests.[53] The reality seems to have been less dramatic. What is most striking is the astonishing resilience of society in face of an almost unimaginable disaster.

Some of the aristocracy were able to isolate themselves from the effects of the Black Death. Elizabeth de Burgh remained for the duration of the epidemic in her castle at Usk. Her household accounts show normal levels of consumption, with feast days celebrated as usual. No efforts were made to quarantine her household from the outside world; her servants bought goods in local markets, and even continued to acquire luxuries from London. Visitors were not as many as in most years, but some, notably her close friend Marie de St Pol, continued to come to see her. Only one of her household died.[54] Yet although few great aristocrats died, and the gentry were not as hard-hit as the peasant population, the changed demographic situation had a marked and immediate effect on inheritance patterns and the land market. Noble and gentry society underwent a major change. The proportion of major landholding families that left male heirs fell strikingly as a result of the Black Death. Until 1348 roughly 70 per cent of those who died and who were recorded in inquisitions post mortem left a son to succeed them. In the decade after the outbreak the rate fell to 60 per cent. The proportion of direct female heirs rose from just over 5 per cent to over 13 per cent, though that of cases where there were co-heiresses was little changed. The number of cases where a different family took over lands on the death of the former holder doubled.[55] The case of the Lestranges of Whitchurch provides a dramatic example, for not only did John Lestrange die in 1349, but so also did his son. His son in turn died in the 1361 outbreak, and the family finally died out in the male line in 1375. Much of the family land had to be diverted to

---

[52] James, *Black Death in Hampshire*, 4–5.   [53] Knighton, 98–107.
[54] Underhill, *For Her Good Estate*, 52–3.
[55] S. J. Payling, 'Social Mobility, Demographic Change, and Landed Society in Late Medieval England', *EcHR* 45 (1992), 55.

provide for the widows of those who had died.[56] Had it not been for the Black Death, the Lestrange line would surely have lasted much longer.

At the opposite end of society the peasant land market was also transformed as a result of the Black Death. Very many holdings became vacant as the disease destroyed families. On a great many estates there is evidence that lords found surprisingly little difficulty in finding new tenants. On the St Albans manor of Abbots Langley virtually every one of the seventy-one holdings that became vacant was filled by new tenants. At Halesowen at least 82 per cent of the holdings of villagers who had died were taken up within a year. The land market was exceptionally active in the 1350s.[57] Such evidence should not be used to minimize the effects of the epidemic. England before the Black Death was overpopulated. There was a huge reservoir among the poor and the younger sons available to fill the shoes of those who died, and it is no surprise that vacant holdings were swiftly taken up. The social upheaval as new families moved in was immense; and with rising labour costs and falling food prices the economic challenges were massive.

The bishop of Winchester's hundred of Farnham provides a good case study of the immediate impact of the Black Death. The deaths of many of the tenants provided a sharp boost to the bishop's income, for entry fines in 1348-9 rose from a normal level of £8-20 to over £100. In addition, many animals were acquired as heriots when tenants died. This created a significant problem of what to do with them. Those that were sold fetched very low prices, with plough horses fetching 1s. 4d. as against a normal level of 10s., or half a mark. Much manorial activity, however, continued surprisingly unchanged, and work on repairing Farnham castle was not interrupted. In 1349-50 wages were at a very high level: whereas a tiler had been paid 2½d. to 3d., he could now expect 6d. or 8d. Harvesting costs rose to 12d. an acre, but the amount of grain brought in was little changed from earlier levels. The number of cheeses made was unchanged. In the following year wages fell somewhat. Harvesting costs at 8d. an acre were still higher than they had been before the great epidemic, when they had stood at 5d., but they were well down from the peak of the previous year.[58]

The rising cost of labour was widespread. In London, for example, a group of bakers' servants were accused of agreeing that they would no longer work unless they received two or three times their former wages. There was a similar conspiracy among the cordwainers' servants.[59] The situation led to the government's main response to the plague, the introduction of the

---

[56] *Complete Peerage*, xii/1. 343.

[57] Levett, *Studies in Manorial History*, 254; Razi, *Life, Marriage and Death*, 110.

[58] E. Robo, 'The Black Death in the Hundred of Farnham', *EHR* 44 (1929), 560-72.

[59] *Cal. Plea and Mem. Rolls*, 225, 231-2.

Ordinance of Labourers in 1349, followed by the Statute of Labourers in 1351. The purpose of this legislation was to keep wages at pre-Black Death levels. To put these measures into effect required the creation of a special set of commissions. These were recruited from the local gentry, but the whole process required organization and supervision by central government. They could succeed in this for a short time. In 1357 a number of people were prosecuted at Stratford upon Avon for accepting high wages for reaping corn; they had taken 6*d*. a day, double the level the court considered appropriate.[60] That it was possible to achieve even a modest control of wages bears witness to the energy and vitality of the regime, even at a most difficult time. It also demonstrates very clearly the fundamental desire of those in positions of power to try to maintain the structures of society that had existed before the Black Death. It would, however, prove impossible in the longer term to resist the economic forces unleashed by the transformation of the labour market that resulted from the immense loss of population.[61]

The overall patterns of settlement were not changed as a result of this first outbreak of the Black Death, serious as it was. It would be more long-term change, and a range of pressures, that caused many villages to be abandoned. A small handful of fragile villages was all that succumbed as a result of the 1348–9 epidemic. Wontley, a small settlement near Bishop's Cleeve in Gloucestershire, was one, Tilgarsley in Oxfordshire another.[62]

A full discussion of the economic effects of the Black Death would extend far beyond 1360, the terminal point for this volume. In many respects, the impact was delayed until the final quarter of the fourteenth century, as efforts to maintain the status quo gradually failed. In the short term, the consequences of high mortality were not the only problems to be faced; it is not always easy to distinguish the consequences of the Black Death from other difficulties. The early 1350s were years of severe drought, when it was claimed that there was no rain for three years. Grain yields fell to very low levels. Christ Church Canterbury priory suffered as much from this drought as it had done from the floods of 1315 and 1316. At Cuxham in Oxfordshire the grain yields of the 1350s were lower than any previous decade for which there are records. In County Durham evidence from tithes paid on the estates of the cathedral priory show that the immediate effect of the Black Death was dramatic, suggesting that the 1350 harvest yielded half the average level for the 1340s. Recovery in some places was striking, while in others, harvest levels remained

---

[60] Fryde, 'The Tenants of the Bishops of Coventry and Lichfield and of Worcester After the Plague of 1348–9', 239.

[61] Ibid. 179–80.

[62] Ibid. 237; M. W. Beresford, *The Lost Villages of England* (London, 1954; repr. 1983), 160.

low. Overall, by 1357 output had risen to over 70 per cent of that in the 1340s, though success was not sustained in the following decade.[63]

The immediate effects of the immense loss of life on the government of England appear surprisingly limited. There was very real alarm early in 1349. Parliament, due to meet in January, was postponed. The king and the treasurer left London for the country. Yet the exchequer and chancery continued to operate. So too did the courts of Common Pleas and King's Bench, although they adjourned for the Trinity term. Because so few people came to the courts, the proceeds from the fees for sealing judicial writs fell sharply. The number of top officials who died was limited. The chancellor, John Offord, died, as did three of the dozen senior clerks in the chancery. The keeper of the wardrobe died. None of the barons of the exchequer died, but the clerk of the pleas and one of the chamberlains of the receipt succumbed. By the autumn of 1349 the government was back to normal. The great series of chancery and exchequer rolls continued to be drawn up, and show no real signs of any hiatus. The resilience of the bureaucracy was astonishing. In the shires only four sheriffs died, though at a lower level mortality was higher. The sheriff of Nottingham and Derbyshire reported that all the members of his staff were either dead or dying, and his colleague of Bedfordshire and Buckinghamshire claimed that he had lost all of his. In Somerset seven tax-collectors died in rapid succession. The sheriff of Devon was unable to come to Westminster to render his accounts in 1349 because he was ill, and his under-sheriff and other staff had all died.[64] Even so, it proved possible to re-establish the bureaucratic systems of local government with remarkable speed. The evidence from taxation records is telling. The tax granted for three years in 1348 was collected with surprisingly little difficulty. Very limited relief was provided by counting the receipts raised by the justices of labourers as part of the tax, but otherwise concessions were very few. Increases in the numbers of those involved in the work of collecting the tax helped to keep the revenue rolling in. It has been calculated that, against an assessment of £38,000, the yield in the three successive years was £34,600, £31,900, and £35,300. A further tax for three years was granted in 1352.[65]

[63] M. Mate, 'Agrarian Economy After the Black Death: The Manors of Canterbury Cathedral Priory, 1348–91', *EcHR*, 2nd ser., 37 (1984), 342–3; Harvey, *A Medieval Oxfordshire Village: Cuxham*, 58; B. Dodds, 'Durham Priory Tithes and the Black Death', *Northern History*, 39 (2002), 18–21.

[64] M. W. Ormrod and P. Lindley (eds.), *The Black Death in England* (Stamford, 1996), 150, 178; M. W. Ormrod, 'The English Government and the Black Death of 1348–9', in Ormrod (ed.), *England in the Fourteenth Century* (Woodbridge, 1986), 175–80; Horrox, *Black Death*, 275; *CPR 1348–50*, 563.

[65] Ormrod, 'The English Government and the Black Death', 182, 185.

The main field of activity where the government's activity was curtailed as a result of the great epidemic was in war. The capture of Calais in 1347 was not followed up by a major English offensive before 1355. Operations continued, of course, in Gascony and Brittany, and to a lesser extent Normandy, but these amounted to little more than efforts to maintain the English position. Walter Bentley sailed with probably no more than about 300 men in 1352, and fought at Mauron that year with fewer than 1,000.[66] Even the Black Prince's expedition of 1355 was on a relatively small scale. The army that Edward III himself led out of Calais in the autumn of that year was probably only about 5,000 strong. It would have been difficult in any case to sustain the kind of effort that had gone into the campaign of 1346–7, but there can be little doubt that the epidemic had an impact on the scale of resources that could be devoted to the war with France. The level of population loss was not such that it would have been impossible to recruit large armies after the Black Death, but the degree of local disruption that the epidemic had caused must have discouraged men from coming forward to fight, and is likely to have affected the supply systems that were a vital part of the war effort.

CHURCH AND CULTURE

The impact of the Black Death on the Church is well documented. It was not easy to fill the positions made vacant by the appalling mortality, for there were insufficient unmarried men of the right age available. The chronicler Henry Knighton, whose pen was prone to an understandable degree of exaggeration, stated that soon after the outbreak of the disease 'there came into holy orders a great multitude of those whose wives had died of plague, many of them illiterate, the merest laymen, who if they were able to read at all were unable to understand what they read'.[67] Bishop Bateman of Norwich took an immediate step in 1350, when he obtained papal approval to ordain sixty young men below the normal permitted age of 25, and a further step for the future when he founded Trinity Hall in Cambridge.[68] In 1354 the abbot of Reading obtained permission to have thirty monks aged 20 ordained because so many had died of the Black Death.[69] The bishop of Hereford, John Trillek, reacted to the crisis in various ways. One was to complete Bishop Cantilupe's shrine, and proceed as rapidly as possible with the translation of the saint's bones. There were strong hopes that Cantilupe would deal with the epidemic and drive it away. Another was to ordain as many candidates as would come forward, though whether the

---

[66] Sumption, *The Hundred Years War II*, 93–4.   [67] Knighton, 102–3.

[68] C. Rawcliffe, *Medicine for the Soul* (London, 1999), 16.

[69] C. Harper-Bill, 'English Religion After the Black Death', in Ormrod and Lindley (eds.), *The Black Death in England*, 97.

gaps in the ranks of the clergy were filled with truly appropriate candidates must be open to question. Some were promoted through the ranks from acolyte to priest in less than six months. On 20 February 1350 no fewer than 262 men were ordained in a ceremony at Ledbury.[70]

As with secular administration, the resilience of the systems for running the Church and its estates is very striking. Bishop Trillek conducted a visitation of his diocese in 1353. The clerical tax demanded by the king in 1352 was duly collected, though not without some local difficulties. Clerical wages and fees were to be kept at pre-epidemic levels.[71] Estate records continued to be produced. Indeed, the Winchester pipe roll, which recorded the accounts of the vast estates of the bishopric of Winchester, was 50 per cent larger after the epidemic than in previous years, for with the deaths of so many tenants, there was much more business than normal to be noted.[72] The Church undoubtedly faced difficulties in the years following the great epidemic, but there was no danger of a collapse of the system.

Such a disaster as the epidemic of 1348–9 must have had an impact on lay piety and religion, but this is surprisingly difficult to identify. The sudden way in which the epidemic might strike people in the best of health did not persuade them to invest more to ensure success in the afterlife. There was no increase in monastic foundations, although three new Carmelite houses were founded in the decade following the advent of the Black Death. The most popular method of providing for the afterlife was to set up a chantry. The chronology of the establishment of chantries shows no acceleration as a result of the epidemic. Records show that seventy-six chantries were set up between 1327 and 1348, as against fifty-four between 1348 and 1377. The number of licences to alienate land into mortmain, grants to the Church, was 169 in the twenty years prior to the outbreak of the Black Death, and eighty-four in the thirty years following.[73] Nor did people turn to new cults to replace a religion that they might well have felt had failed them. Such extreme reactions as were seen on the Continent had little impact in England. In 1349 a large band of flagellants came to London from the Low Countries. They performed their painful ritual at St Paul's and elsewhere, flogging themselves and singing, but acquiring no new adherents from among the bemused populace.[74]

---

[70] Dohar, *The Black Death and Pastoral Leadership*, 58–60, 63, 69.

[71] Ibid. 64–7, 74.

[72] P. Arthur, '*Per Pestilenciam*: The Bishop of Winchester's Pipe Roll for 1348–9', in James (ed.), *The Black Death in Wessex*, 52.

[73] Harper-Bill, 'English Religion After the Black Death', 104, 112; J. Rosenthal, *The Purchase of Paradise* (London, 1972), 32, 162.

[74] Avesbury, 408.

People must have been traumatized by the Black Death; its psychological effects were surely immense. They are, however, difficult to detect in the surviving sources. One exceptional entry in a court record revealed an official, 'his conscience moved by the deaths and the pestilence which there then was', deciding that it had been wrong to take a horse as a payment of heriot five years previously. Various claims were made to suggest ways in which people were changed as a result of the Black Death. Fashions apparently became more extreme, with tighter and shorter clothes. Women became more lewd in their behaviour. The new generation had two fewer teeth than people had in the past. Such statements may reflect less reality than a view that things should have changed as a result of the pestilence.[75]

One tempting theory, that in the years following the great epidemic death was depicted in a far more macabre form than previously, is not warranted by the evidence. Gruesome images of death can be found in the early, as in the late, fourteenth century. The lugubrious image of the Three Living and the Three Dead was as popular before 1348 as after.[76] There were, however, changes in building style at this time. At Winchester a triple porch at the west end of the cathedral was built in Decorated style in the 1340s; above it is a very plain Perpendicular window of the 1370s. This contrast provides vivid evidence of the way in which the Black Death coincides with a stylistic shift in architecture. It is tempting to try to link the two, and see the abandonment of the naturalistic exuberance of the Decorated as the result of psychological changes. The straight lines and simplicity of the Perpendicular could reflect a sombre mood after the Black Death. This is a difficult argument to sustain. The origins of the Perpendicular can be identified in work at Gloucester and elsewhere before the Black Death, and the chronology of the transition was uneven in different parts of the country. Changes in architectural style surely proceeded from an inner momentum that would not be directly affected by the mortality of 1348–9. It is, however, likely that the high death toll accelerated change by speeding up the transition from one generation of masons and craftsmen to another. The Black Death caused the deaths of many important artists and craftsmen, and with them some traditions were extinguished, and quality lost. None of the sculptors who worked on the Lady Chapel at Ely appear to have survived the epidemic. William Ramsey, the king's master mason since 1336, who was also responsible for the chapter house and cloister at St Paul's, and who served as consultant at Lichfield cathedral, died in early June 1349, surely of the Black Death. At Lichfield cathedral stylistic change was probably the result of the deaths of one set of masons, and their replace-

---

[75] *Black Death*, ed. Horrox, 75, 127, 276.
[76] See P. Binski, *Medieval Death* (London, 1996), 123–63.

ment by men working in the new style. At Exeter the programme of sculpture was severely disrupted for a quarter of a century following the outbreak of the Black Death, and at Winchester there seems to have been a long hiatus in the building programme. It may well be that the rise in mason's wages after the Black Death, due to the comparative scarcity of skilled men, led to the popularity of building in a style which, with its simplicity and lack of exuberant carved decoration, was not labour-intensive.[77]

In many ways what seems surprising is that a demographic disaster on the almost unimaginable scale of the Black Death should not have had more immediate and obvious consequences. The survivors did their best to ensure that life continued as it had done in previous years. Society was far too resilient to collapse. This is not, however, to downplay the consequences of the epidemic. This book closes in 1360; the true impact of the Black Death lay in the long term, with the transformation of England in the fifteenth and sixteenth centuries.

[77] P. Lindley, 'The Black Death and English Art', in Ormrod and Lindley (eds.), *The Black Death in England*, 136–46; *KW* i. 207–8; James, *Black Death in Hampshire*, 17–18.

CHAPTER 22

Conclusion

England in the thirteenth and fourteenth centuries was in many ways a cosmopolitan country. Under Henry III many of the leading figures in the realm were not English in origin; not only were there the court favourites from Savoy and Poitou, but the king's main opponent, Simon de Montfort, was a Frenchman. There were many prominent foreigners in the English Church, including Boniface of Savoy, archbishop of Canterbury, Peter des Roches, bishop of Winchester, and Peter of Aigueblanche, bishop of Hereford. Westminster abbey owed its inspiration in architectural terms to France. Edward I relied greatly upon the Savoyard Otto de Grandson; Geoffrey de Geneville was another important supporter of the king. Edward's great castles in Wales owed much to the influence of the Savoyards, and above all Master James of St George. Under Edward II the king's first favourite, the unfortunate Piers Gaveston, was a Gascon; his queen, who played such a decisive role in his downfall, was French. The earl of Pembroke, Aymer de Valence, was also lord of Montignac in southwestern France. Both of his marriages were to French women. He provides one example among very many of aristocrats with strong connections across the Channel through marriage. Edward III's Order of the Garter was international in character, and among the king's captains names such as Mauny and d'Aubrichecourt have a place of honour alongside those of Audley, Bentley, or Dagworth. Italian bankers, from the Ricciardi and Frescobaldi under Edward I, to the Bardi and Peruzzi under Edward III, provided funds and expertise that were much needed by the English crown. Technical know-how was acquired from abroad: men of French and Italian origin provided the English mints with necessary skills. In Edward III's early years on the throne Flemings were encouraged to bring their proficiency in weaving to England.

NATIONAL IDENTITY

At the same time that there were these cosmopolitan elements in England, there was also a strong sense of national identity. For foreigners, there was a simple stereotype: Englishmen had tails, and were usually drunk. The English view of themselves was more complex. They might be self-critical. For Ranulf Higden, writing in the second quarter of the fourteenth century, the English were gluttonous, drunken, dishonest, and irreligious; they were also brave warriors, and highly adaptable. Southerners were more civilized than northerners.[1] The author of the *Vita* of Edward II wrote that 'I could indeed be accused of rashness if I defamed my country, my own people; but, if it is permissible or proper to speak the truth, the English race excel other nations in three qualities, in pride, in craft, and in perjury.'[2] In contrast, another chronicler placed no blame on the English, but attributed the horrors of Edward II's reign to the fact that the 'kind blood of England' had been diluted among the aristocracy by being mixed with that of other nations, France, Normandy, Spain, Hainault, Flanders, and elsewhere. This may seem a far-fetched opinion, but the view that, in ethnic terms, the English and their aristocracy were distinct was commonly held. Robert of Gloucester, writing in the early fourteenth century, was clear that the nobles were descended from Normans and the ordinary people from the Saxons.[3] In the thirteenth and fourteenth centuries, however, those nobles undoubtedly regarded themselves as English, part of the community of the land, and not as Norman interlopers.

The reality of identity was complex. There were many communities that people might identify themselves with, ranging from that of all Christendom down to those of the small local units of manor, vill, and parish. National identity or consciousness involved issues of language, law, political institutions, history, and culture; many of the topics of this book went to make up the English identity. This was not an identity new in the thirteenth century; a 'developing sense of Englishness' has, for example, been noted in the work of two of the great twelfth-century chroniclers, William of Malmesbury and Henry of Huntingdon. Nor, it has been argued, was it an Englishness born of Norman oppression, but one in which 'English men and women felt that they belonged to a Norman-French cultural community, military, secular, and courtly.'[4]

The English language was a significant element in national identity. In 1295 Edward I declared that the French intended to extirpate the English tongue from the land. Although he used this argument only on one occasion, his grandson Edward III revived this particular piece of propaganda in the 1340s.

---

[1] *Polychronicon Ranulphi Higden Monachi Cestrensis*, ed. C. Babington and J. R. Lumby (RS, 1865–86), ii. 166–72.

[2] P. Rickard, *Britain in Medieval French Literature* (Cambridge, 1956), 165–70; *Vita Edwardi*, 63.

[3] *The Brut*, ed. Brie, i. 220; *The Metrical Chronicle of Robert of Gloucester*, ed. Wright, ii. 541.

[4] J. Gillingham, *The English in the Twelfth Century: Imperialism, National Identity and Political Values* (Woodbridge, 2000), 140. For further discussion of aspects of national identity, see the articles by R. R. Davies, 'The Peoples of Britain and Ireland, 1100–1400', *TRHS*, 6th ser., 4 (1994), 1–20; 5 (1995), 1–20; 6 (1996), 1–23; 7 (1997), 1–24.

The *Cursor Mundi*, written in English about 1300, had demanded that each country should have its own language.[5] Language provided an easy means of identifying men as English: in battle in Gascony in 1297, in the twilight, it proved impossible to distinguish French from English save by the language they spoke.[6]

Ordinary people might have strong views about the use of English. In 1323 Henry Lambard was asked in court how he wished to clear himself of charges of theft. He said in English that he was a cleric, and refused to make any other answer. He was asked if he knew how to speak in Latin, or in French. He replied that he was English, and English-born, and that it was proper for him to speak in his mother tongue. He utterly refused to speak anything else but English. Henry was not convincing as a cleric; he had no tonsure, and did not wear clerical dress. He refused to give any further answer to the court, and so was committed to the Marshalsea court, to suffer *peine forte et dure*.[7] No doubt he felt doubly injured that his punishment had a French name. Lambard was anticipating a celebrated statute of 1362, which required that English be spoken in the king's courts. The statute, ironically itself written in French, had little practical effect, though it was significant as a piece of propaganda. Its issue coincided, surely deliberately, with the king's fiftieth birthday; it can also be seen as a declaration of national identity, reinforcing the concept of England as a country with its distinct and separate language.[8]

The identification of the English tongue with Englishness was, however, no simple matter. There were many different English dialects. Ranulf Higden commented on the diversity which meant that a southerner found great difficulty in understanding a northerner, especially one from Yorkshire.[9] More problematic was the fact that society was multilingual, with a French-speaking aristocracy. French was the language of gentility. Its use was socially exclusive, its speakers marked out as members of the elite. To talk or write in French was to make a statement about status, not about nationality. Even for Robert Grosseteste, whose origins were almost certainly humble, French

---

[5] S. Crane, 'Social Aspects of Bilingualism in the Thirteenth Century', in *TCE* vi. 113–14; Stubbs, *Select Charters*, 480; *Rot. Parl.* ii. 150, 158. The term *lingua*, or tongue, meant more than simply 'language'; it could also imply 'race', as when it was used in the context of the Welsh; Stubbs, *Select Charters*, 460.

[6] Guisborough, 263. In the case of the Scots in the previous year, however, it had not been possible to distinguish friend from foe by means of language; ibid. 272.

[7] *Select Cases in the Court of King's Bench Under Edward II*, iv, ed. G. O. Sayles (Selden Society, 1957), 163.

[8] M. W. Ormrod, 'The Use of English: Language, Law and Political Culture in Fourteenth-Century England', *Speculum*, 78 (2003), 751, 761, 781.

[9] *Polychronicon Ranulphi Higden Monachi Cestrensis*, ed. Babington and Lumby, ii. 160–2.

appears to have been the normal vernacular. The French spoken in England was distinct from that of France, though this may have been something that the French noticed more clearly than the English. In the thirteenth-century romance *Jehan et Blonde*, the count of Oxford's beautiful daughter had an accent, which made it plain that she was not from Pontoise, where the best French was spoken.[10] French writers made fun of the way Englishmen spoke. In *Jehan et Blonde* the count of Gloucester had no sense of proper grammar, confusing tenses and mistaking genders. A joke in a *fabliau* turned on the inability of the English to distinguish between *agnel* (lamb) and *anel* (donkey); a man sent out to buy a leg of lamb came back with a leg of donkey meat. In thirteenth- and fourteenth-century England, French was increasingly learned, rather than acquired naturally; one early treatise was written by a knight, Walter of Bibbesworth, in about 1250, with the intention of helping Denise de Muntchesney to teach her children. The French spoken in England borrowed little from English. This was not because of any desire to retain its cultural integrity; it was rather that it became an increasingly artificial language, lacking the vitality to change and develop. In contrast, from the mid-thirteenth century English saw greatly increased borrowings from French, reflecting widespread bilingualism in which English was the more widely spoken tongue.[11]

While the cultural affinities between England and northern France were close, there was a distinctive English voice emerging. A considerable number of romances survive from this period. These show that Englishness was not confined to works written in English; some were in French (or Anglo-Norman). They vary considerably in subject matter, and in style; with their English heroes, religious content, and political concerns they were markedly different from works written in France. *Gui de Warewic*, dating from about 1230, written in French with later versions in English, has a hero who fights first for love, and then for God. He successfully defends England against both the Danes and a fearsome dragon. One recurrent theme is that of the hero who struggles to recover his rightful heritage. *Havelock the Dane* probably dates from the late thirteenth century. It is a version of a story written down by Gaimar, in French, a century earlier, and tells how Havelock, son of the king of Denmark, escapes from the clutches of a wicked guardian, and is brought up as a fisherman in England. He marries Goldboru, daughter of the English king Athelwold, and the poem ends with the couple ruling England and Denmark, and producing fifteen children. The author of *Havelock* stressed that Athelwold was king of all England. Lincoln, 'the good borough' and Grimsby provide a regional setting, while the realm extended from Roxburgh to

---

[10] Rickard, *Britain in Medieval French Literature*, 170.
[11] Crane, 'Social Aspects of Bilingualism in the Thirteenth Century', 109–11.

Dover. The Englishness of *Havelock* was not forced; this was the land that the author knew and understood.[12]

The poetry of the period has no Chaucer or Langland to dominate it. Much is owed to the unknown clerk in the Ludlow region who collected together a wide range of material, from the bawdy to the spiritual, in a single manuscript, a wide-ranging anthology known unimaginatively as Harley 2253.[13] Some of the poems show a sense of place, with the Englishness emphasized by geography as well as language. They also display a love of nature. One starts:

> When the nightingale sings the woods wax green
> Leaf and grass and blossom spring in April, I wene
> And love has gone into my heart with a spear so keen.

The unrequited lover has not seen so fair a maid between Lincoln, Lindsey, Northampton, and London, and begs a sweet kiss from his love. Not all the lovers in these poems go unsatisfied; in one, a clerk successfully wheedles his way into his lady's affection, so that she concludes the poem by saying 'I am thine, and thou are mine, to do all thy will.'[14] One poem provides what is at first sight a conventional description of an ideal of womanhood, with its description of blonde hair, red lips, 'tits like apples of Paradise', and milk-white thighs, though it goes further than most such depictions in praising as being 'wondrous well-wrought' the parts he felt he could not name. The poem may, however, be an elaborate joke, for the lass had a long neck like a swan, and arms an ell, almost four feet, in length. The fact that she came from Ribblesdale almost certainly had some meaning for a medieval audience that is now lost; it certainly anchors the poem in an English locality.[15] Many of the lyrics preserved in this manuscript demonstrate the sophistication that was possible in written English, with rhyme and alliteration used in a complex manner. At the same time, others show that this was a multilingual society, even combining English, Latin, and French:

> En seynt eglise sunt multi saepe priores;
> Summe beoth wyse, multi sunt inferiores.[16]

---

[12] S. Crane, *Insular Romance: Politics, Faith and Culture in Anglo-Norman and Middle English Literature* (Berkeley and Los Angeles, 1986), 40–52, 62–5; T. Turville-Petre, *England the Nation: Language, Literature, and National Identity, 1290–1340* (Oxford, 1996), 145–9; D. B. Sands (ed.), *Middle English Romances* (Exeter, 1986), 58–129.

[13] BL, Harleian MS 2253. For analysis of this manuscript, see S. Fein (ed.), *Studies in the Harley Manuscript* (Kalamazoo, Mich., 2000).

[14] Fein (ed.), *Studies in the Harley Manuscript*, 63.

[15] *The Harley Lyrics: The Middle English Lyrics of MS. Harley 2253*, ed. G. L. Brook (Manchester, 1948), 37–9.

[16] *Political Songs*, 251.

This poetry is redolent of a sophisticated society that took pleasure in the world around it. It was no mere copy of what was being produced in France. The age may have no Chaucer, but its unknown poets, with their love of nature and of life, have a charm of their own. They also have a distinctive quality, evident above all in the lyric verse, which, though this is hard to define, can be seen as characteristically English.

ENGLISHNESS AND THE LAW

Law was an important element in English identity, for the law that operated in the secular courts was distinctive and unique. It was not codified like Roman law, though in the statutes of the thirteenth century and later a form of royal written law developed. Treatises about the law, notably that known as Bracton, were important in defining it; in 1294 Chief Justice Metingham advised a lawyer in court to 'Go to your Bracton and he will teach you.'[17] It was above all a form of law based on litigation, and the procedures and precedents of the courts. It was learned by attending the courts, particularly in London, where, at least from the 1270s, some teaching was available for those wanting to enter a profitable profession. An exception to the Englishness of law was the law of the Church. This was the Roman canon law common to all western Christendom, for which the universities provided an education.

Law was of particular importance in emphasizing a sense of identity in border regions. Where a lordship in the Welsh marches had both English and Welsh tenants, the two might be treated quite differently. The Welsh, living under Welsh law, might appear in quite different courts from their English neighbours. This had implications for a wide range of matters, such as the way in which land was inherited. In 1314 a tenant in Dyffryn Clwyd claimed that he should not be subject to the attentions of any Welsh bailiff since his land was held 'by the law of the English'. A Welshman argued in King's Bench in 1331 that his case should be heard according to Welsh, not English, law. Equally, those in the marches who were of English birth claimed that their cases should be determined according to the common law of England.[18] There were many complexities, anomalies, and difficulties, but there is no doubt that law was one key element in defining Welsh and English identities. It played, of course, as has already been shown, an important part in Edward I's disputes with Llywelyn ap Gruffudd; the English king was in no doubt about the superiority of English law.

[17] P. Brand, *The Making of the Common Law* (London, 1992), 73 (my trans.).
[18] R. R. Davies, *Lordship and Society in the March of Wales 1282–1400* (Oxford, 1978), 310 n. 35, 311.

In Ireland, too, law was important as a means of defining identity. The situation was not straightforward. The Irish who fought for the English might consider themselves entitled to use English law; the crown might grant Irishmen the right to use English law, at the same time requiring them to cut their hair in English fashion. The development of English government in Ireland brought with it a growing emphasis on the use of English law, even though English statutory legislation was not automatically valid in Ireland, where there was a separate parliament. There is no doubt, however, that English-style law was important in defining who was English and who Irish.[19]

It would be quite wrong to assume that most ordinary Englishmen and women were conscious of the differences between their legal system and those of other countries, and mistaken to think that there was a belief in the superiority of English law. The law was something to complain about, not to be proud of. One poet was clear in his opinion of the representatives of royal justice when he wrote that:

> Spigurnel and Belflour are men of cruelty;
> If they were in my charge they would not be returned.

The criticism here was directed at one specific royal measure, the introduction of the trailbaston inquiries towards the end of Edward I's reign. Other poets were cynical about the entire machinery of justice. One wrote:

> Justices, sheriffs, mayors and bailiffs, if I read aright,
> They can make out of the fair day the dark night.

Another commented that:

> And these assisers, that come to shire and to hundred,
> Damn men for silver, and that is no wonder.[20]

The law, which reached out into so many aspects of people's lives, had a profound influence. England's was a highly litigious society; the records of manorial courts demonstrate the extent to which ordinary men and women were involved in legal processes. Although there were some regional variations, it is striking that it was the same law that operated throughout the country, through both royal and private courts. The law was important in providing uniformity throughout the realm, as well as identity.

---

[19] See R. F. Frame, ' "Les Engleys nées en Irlande": The English Political Identity in Medieval Ireland', in his *Ireland and Britain 1170–1450*, 131–50.
[20] *Political Songs*, 233, 336, 344.

MYTH AND WAR

Myths, in particular those that emphasize a common descent, can be a significant element in the construction of a country's identity. In England there were different myths, which were not easy to incorporate one with another. In 1301 Edward I wrote to the pope in support of his claims to overlordship of Scotland. Initially, the historical account had begun with Edward the Elder, son of King Alfred, but an addition was made to the draft, which explained that a Trojan, Brutus, with his companions, came to a land inhabited by giants, called Albion. The unfortunate giants were defeated, and the land renamed Britain. Among the later kings of Britain was, of course, Arthur, who subjected Scotland to his will. This material was derived from the twelfth-century fantasist Geoffrey of Monmouth.[21] This story supported the belief that the whole of Britain should be incorporated into one political structure. The Brutus legend, and the subsequent history of the Britons, was included in many popular histories, notably the *Brut*. There were, however, alternative views, which stressed not Britain and King Arthur, but England and the Anglo-Saxons. For example, Bartholomew Cotton, writing at the end of the thirteenth century, appealed to the authority of Bede, Henry of Huntingdon, and William of Malmesbury, and began his history with the Anglo-Saxons and the arrival of Hengist and Horsa in England.[22] The author of the *Mirror of Justices* described the origins of England in terms of the arrival of the first Anglo-Saxon chieftains, who met together and decided to divide the land up into counties, each with its own king. They also determined that there should be one bishop.[23] The early history of England was sufficiently obscure that it could be adjusted to suit different cases, but it was the English myth that was becoming the more powerful.

A strong sense of English identity is evident in the work of Robert Mannyng of Brunne, who produced a chronicle in the later 1330s. Written in English, this was largely based on the works of Wace and Peter Langtoft, whose own rhymed chronicles had been written in French. A central thread in Mannyng's rewriting of history was that the English were oppressed by the Normans, not merely at the time of the Conquest, but through until his own day. The English were a people held in bondage. He wrote about a dismal prophetic vision that came to Edward the Confessor, and explained that William the Conqueror placed the English in servitude, cutting down the flower of freedom and

[21] E. L. G. Stones (ed.), *Anglo-Scottish Relations 1174–1328*, (1965), 97–8.
[22] Cotton, 1–2, 9.
[23] *The Mirror of Justices*, ed. W. J. Whittaker and F. W. Maitland (Selden Society, 1893).

imposing taxes that continued to be levied. Such a theme was, of course, best expressed in English rather than French or Latin, for Mannyng was very clearly addressing his book to an English-speaking audience. In addition, he wrote at the time when Edward III had just embarked on his French war, and there is no doubt that the fear of French invasion coloured his work. One of the aspects of national identity that concerned Mannying was the origin of the name England. It could be derived from Angle, the land from which the Angles came. It was more probable in his view that it was called after King Engle, who had a huge champion, Scardynk, after whom Scarborough was named, and who terrified the Angles into accepting Engle, a Briton, as their ruler. He dismissed the view that the country was named after Hengist's daughter Rowena, whose alternative name was Inge.[24]

War, as shown in earlier chapters, undoubtedly helped to give a focus to national identity. In the Welsh wars of Edward I's reign, the contrasts between the English and their foes was made very clear, above all by Archbishop Pecham, who was infuriated by the way in which the Welsh rejected his attempts to negotiate a settlement. The Anglo-Scottish war also helped to sharpen ideas of nationhood, even though the societies on either side of what was a very porous border were essentially similar, and something of a common culture was created out of the chaos of cross-border raiding. National antagonisms were built up very quickly, as concepts of the enemy were constructed. Dislike of the Scots is revealed in popular poetry from the 1290s, recorded by the chronicler Peter Langtoft:

> The foot folk
> Put Scots in the poke
> And bared their behinds
>
> .   .   .
>
> For Scots
> Tell I for sots
> And wretches unwary.[25]

'Scotland, why should I not see it sunk to the ground of hell?' wrote Robert Manning a little later.[26] Horror stories no doubt whipped up national feelings. The Luttrell Psalter of the 1340s provides, it has been suggested, a pictorial image of the Scots as the English viewed them. There are vicious scenes, with

---

[24] Turville-Petre, *England the Nation*, 75–103; Summerfield, *The Matter of Kings' Lives* (Amsterdam, 1998), 129–209.

[25] Pierre de Langtoft, 319, 323.

[26] Turville-Petre, *England the Nation*, 22.

attacks on unarmed men and women, and babies hacked to pieces; one of the assailants has half his face painted blue.[27]

The situation with the French wars in the fourteenth century was more complex. The extent to which the French war shaped and determined a sense of English identity was more limited than is often assumed, partly because attitudes were already well developed. It is also relevant that Edward III's war effort was not confined to England: Gascons made a major contribution, as of course did Welshmen. Further, as Edward claimed to be king of France, it made no sense to denigrate those he hoped would accept his rule. Frenchmen such as Robert of Artois and Godfrey of Harcourt fought on his side. The newsletters sent home from the war strike a triumphal note, but do not pour scorn on the French. Michael Northburgh, writing about the capture of Caen, described an English attack on a bridge: 'they had hard fighting; and the French defended the said bridge bravely, and bore up against them right well, before it could be taken'.[28] It is striking that the tournaments of the period, which increasingly took on the air of pageants, did not depict the Anglo–French conflict. Tatars and the papacy were seen as appropriate targets, but not the French. The kings of France, Philip VI and John II, were the adversaries, not the French people as a whole.

The French war inspired some bombastic patriotic poetry, particularly that by Laurence Minot, which is perhaps some of the worst to be produced in that undistinguished genre:

> Help me, God, my wit is thin
> Now Laurence Minot will begin[29]

Minot's poems, written in a northern dialect with ample alliteration, glorified the great events of war, from Halidon Hill to Les Espagnols sur mer. They display an obvious pride in the achievements of Englishmen, while the Scots and French were castigated for their falseness. Edward III was a hero, while Philip VI was depicted as cowardly.

> Sir Philip of France fled for doubt
> And hied him home with all his rout.
> Coward, God give him care.[30]

The sentiments in Minot are obvious enough, but interestingly show more specific hostility towards Philip VI, 'Unkind he was and uncourteous', than to Frenchmen in general.[31] There were other poems highly critical of the French, but they were in a very literary Latin, and it is difficult to know to what extent

---

[27] Camille, *Mirror in Parchment*, 284–6.   [28] Avesbury, 359, 361.
[29] *The Poems of Laurence Minot 1333–1352*, ed. T. B. James and J. Simons (Exeter, 1989), 43.
[30] Ibid. 37.   [31] Ibid. 26.

they reflect popular opinion. One takes the form of a debate, or rather a slanging match, between an Englishman and a Frenchman. The Englishman spoke an unattractive language, and ate and drank too much. The Frenchman describes himself as elegant and soft-spoken; to the Englishman he is effeminate, avaricious, and depraved. Another describes France as womanish, lynx-like, viperish, wolfish, cruel, bitter, and proud, but most of the condemnation in the poem is directed at Philip VI, rather than his subjects.[32]

Despite the complexity of the situation in which Edward III claimed to be fighting to gain the throne of France with the support of his allies, rather than simply defending England from foreign foes, there can be little doubt that many in England viewed the conflict in more straightforwardly national terms. The prayers said for the king's success, and above all the news of the triumphs in the war, must have helped to maintain a sense of patriotic pride, hard though this is to document.

ART AND ARCHITECTURE

England was part of a wider western European cultural entity, one which is normally seen, with some justification, as being dominated by France. It is also the case, however, that in the late thirteenth century a distinctively English style began to emerge, characterized by great elaboration and a keen interest in naturalistic forms. It was confident and extravagant.

The thirteenth century was an age of grand church-building in the French manner. The most important was Henry III's Westminster abbey, which had direct affinities with Reims and Amiens. Old St Paul's, where work on the choir began in the mid-thirteenth century, saw up-to-date French traceried windows constructed in the style now known as Rayonnant. At the Cistercian Tintern abbey, where the building was financed by Roger Bigod, earl of Norfolk, the magnificent tracery followed the example of St Paul's. The nave of York minster, dating from the end of the century, with its large traceried windows and unity of treatment, is a fine example of what had become an international style, though as it now stands, York gives no impression of the intensity of colour associated with Rayonnant.[33] The Angel choir at Lincoln provides another notable example of the way in which the English were adapting and using the dominant Continental style.

The royal tombs of the late thirteenth century at Westminster demonstrate the way in which a new English style began to overlay French influence, as do

[32] *Political Poems and Songs*, ed. Wright, i. 26–40, 91–3.

[33] Regensburg, where much medieval glass has survived, gives a better sense of the feel of a late 13th-century Rayonnant cathedral, as of course does the Sainte-Chapelle in Paris, on a smaller scale.

the Eleanor crosses commissioned by Edward I to commemorate the route of his first queen's funeral procession. This style has become known as Decorated; it was characterized by ornamental gables set over arches (often trilobed), elaborate carved foliage decoration, pinnacles, and complex tracery. The use of ogival arches, using an S shape, in which the curve of the arch was reversed at the top, became a particularly striking English feature. Vaults became more elaborate, with short connecting elements joining the main ribs to create increasingly complex patterns. There were clear borrowings from Islamic motifs in architecture and decoration, giving an exotic quality. With this style, it has been claimed that 'England was enjoying an unquestioned artistic supremacy over the whole of western Christendom.'[34]

A characteristic element in the English Decorated style developing in the later thirteenth century was highly naturalistic carving. There is an extraordinary exuberance and confidence displayed in the work of this period. By the early fourteenth century tombs such as that of Aymer de Valence, earl of Pembroke, in Westminster abbey show a remarkable richness of display and depth of detail. Naturalism went all the way in a remarkable crucifix carved in the 1340s at Meaux in Yorkshire, for the sculptor used a nude model. The image soon became noted for miracles, and, perhaps because of its accuracy, was a particular favourite for female devotion.[35] The Lady Chapel at Ely, built in the second quarter of the century, with its extravagant carved arcades and great vaulted roof, is testimony to the extraordinary skill of English masons. The carved foliage demonstrates a close observation of the natural world, and is combined with a sense of architectural form, employing three-dimensional ogival arches nodding forward at their apex, that almost seems to presage the baroque. The effect, when the whole was brightly painted, and lit through stained-glass windows, must have been astonishing. Ely also saw a unique and remarkable feat, with the construction in wood of the great Octagon. This surmounted the crossing, replacing the earlier tower, which collapsed in 1322. This is an astonishing piece of fourteenth-century engineering; it required a genius to see how to devise a structure that would transfer the pressures of its weight safely onto the piers of the cathedral, while at the same time disguising the way in which the great lantern was supported. This was not simply an engineering solution, for the new Octagon, which appeared to be built of stone, met every possible aesthetic requirement. William Hurley, the king's carpenter, was the man responsible for advising the monks at Ely; this alone of all his works survives.[36] (See Plates 11 and 12.)

[34] For this style, see Bony, *The English Decorated Style*, *passim* (quotation from p. 1); Coldstream, *The Decorated Style*, 1–61.
[35] *Melsa*, iii. 35–6.
[36] *KW* i. 219.

The Decorated style in architecture was just one element of the artistic achievements of the age, but because so many buildings have survived, it is the best known. Painting, on a full scale, has left little. In the far grander setting of Westminster palace, the Painted Chamber displayed the skill of thirteenth-century English artists, notably Walter of Durham; the work does not survive, but was fortunately recorded in the early nineteenth century prior to the destruction of the building in a fire fuelled by the many thousands of exchequer tallies stored below.[37] Monumental figures of Largesce and Debonerete, the latter carrying a shield with the three leopards of England, are shown standing triumphantly over Covoitise and Ira. Vigorous battle scenes depict the conflicts of Judas Maccabeus. The copies of the pictures suggest that they were somewhat stiff and stylized; Walter of Durham was no Giotto, but his paintings show that England was not a poor relation in artistic terms. Brightly painted and gilded, the Painted Chamber must have been a magnificent sight. At a very different level of society, the wall paintings at Longthorpe Tower are a fortunate survival of a type of decoration that was extremely common. They show how, in the provincial setting of a small tower built by a man who was not even of knightly standing, there might be paintings of real quality.

While few wall paintings survive, there are many examples of illustration on a small scale in magnificent manuscripts. It would be wrong to regard this work as self-consciously English, but it was distinctive. Matthew Paris provides a unique example of a chronicler who illustrated his own work. He was an artist of real ability, who employed an attractive, personal style that made interesting use of colour washes, as well as paint of full intensity. Increasingly, however, the production of fine illustrated books was a collaborative enterprise. The writing and illustration were separate operations, with the latter increasingly the work of specialized workshops. Pattern books provided illustrators with the ideas that they then developed in their own way. Various 'schools' have been identified, but the evidence that would provide proof of provenance is lacking. The so-called Queen Mary Psalter, and associated manuscripts, may well come from London. Norwich could have been the home of the workshops that produced works of the 'East Anglian school', but it has been suggested that these too may derive from London. The richness and variety of the surviving work precludes any simple generalizations. The famous page depicting the Judgement of Solomon in the late thirteenth-century Windmill Psalter contains not only beautifully drawn figures and magnificent swirling foliage patterns, but also an entirely realistic post mill and a fine picture of a peacock. Borders might contain scenes of everyday life; a page of the early fourteenth-

---

[37] See Binski, *The Painted Chamber at Westminster*. Binski argues that while some of the painting dates from Henry III's reign, the Old Testament scenes were painted in the 1290s.

century Peterborough Psalter shows huntsmen, one with dogs, the other with bow and arrow. Carefully drawn birds vie with humans for a place on the page; one man, an entertainer, makes his way on tall stilts. Some of the paintings reflect the architecture of the time, with gables, pinnacles, and ogival arches.[38] Probably the most famous manuscript from this period, partly because it has been reproduced so often, is the Luttrell Psalter, a product of the 1340s (see Plates 15 and 16). It is remarkable not so much for any advance in artistic technique as for the vivid depictions of ordinary life. At the same time, the Psalter provides a demonstration of the extraordinary imagination that medieval artists possessed, for alongside matter-of-fact pictures of village life there are fantastical beasts curling round the margins, figures with human heads and scaly tails, nightmarish in conception but bizarrely elegant in composition.[39]

Abbot Michael of St Albans, who died in the Black Death, bought a grand vestment for himself, of beautiful and expensive taffeta, powdered with gold archangels and worked with feathers, which cost 20 marks.[40] This was no doubt English work, for England was particularly renowned for the production of fine embroidered textiles using gold and silver thread, *opus anglicanum*. There is little that survives; one piece, remarkably, was signed by a nun, Joanna Beverlai, though most were almost certainly the product of London workshops with male masters. Surviving copes display considerable artistic merit, and show that the styles used by embroiderers were, not surprisingly, closely related to that which can be seen in illustrated manuscripts.[41]

INTELLECTUAL LIFE

In suggesting that there was a distinctive English identity, the case is not that the country was somehow isolated and separated from developments elsewhere in Europe, but rather that there was an identifiably English contribution to those developments. The intellectual achievements of Englishmen in this period were part of the mainstream of European culture; in Oxford and Cambridge, England possessed two of the great universities of medieval Europe.

The most remarkable English intellectual of the first half of the thirteenth century was Robert Grosseteste. There is controversy over whether he should be regarded as a product of the great intellectual centres of Paris or Bologna, or whether he was educated in the humbler surroundings of an English school,

---

[38] L. F. Sandler, *The Peterborough Psalter in Brussels and Other Fenland Manuscripts* (London, 1974), 31, 89, 133–5.
[39] The fullest discussion is by Camille, *Mirror in Parchment*.
[40] *Gesta Abbatum Monasterii Sancti Albani: A Thoma Walsingham*, ed. Riley, ii. 363.
[41] Alexander and Binski (eds.), *Age of Chivalry*, 159–60, 392.

perhaps at Hereford. The traditional view is that he was born in about 1170 and educated in the schools of Paris, and that he was elected as master of the schools at Oxford in, or soon after, 1214. The evidence for this is thin, depending largely on a recollection of 1295 that Grosseteste had said that the bishop of Lincoln was not prepared to allow him the title of chancellor, but only that of master of the schools. This is capable of different interpretations, but it seems very possible that Grosseteste was indeed chancellor of the emerging university of Oxford at some time between 1214 and 1221. The alternative interpretation sees Grosseteste as the product of English traditions, and as a late developer, the product of local schools. It is known that he was warmly recommended by Gerald of Wales for a post in the bishop of Hereford's household in the mid-1190s, but his career did not take off until 1225, when he received his first benefice from the bishop of Lincoln. For the next decade he taught at Oxford, until in 1235 he himself took over the Lincoln see. He died, full of years, in 1253.[42] This interpretation sees him as a man very much on his own, whose influence at Oxford was limited; his overall scientific and theological vision was too much at odds with the contemporary mainstream. He thought out scientific explanations from first principles. He explained the twinkling of a star in physiological terms; as the eye strains to see a distant object, so it sets up a tremor which is interpreted as twinkling. He was prepared to dismiss established authorities if they did not concur with observable reality. Aristotle's explanation that thunder was caused by fire being quenched by water in the clouds was nonsense, as a quenched fire does not make that sort of noise.[43] The argument about Grosseteste is not concluded; what is abundantly clear is that he was a remarkable man, with a vigorous and original mind. He was a unique figure whose work did not lead to the creation of a new English school of intellectual inquiry. It did help to inspire the friar Roger Bacon, who wrote a massive work on scientific matters in the 1260s, but Bacon was more a product of Paris, and of private study, than of Oxford.

The contribution of the friars to the intellectual developments of this period was immense. Duns Scotus, who studied and taught at Oxford at the end of the thirteenth century, was a major influence. The most celebrated English intellectual figure of the first half of the fourteenth century was the friar William of Ockham, who has become most famous for the logical device known as Ockham's razor, which states that the simplest explanation to a problem is the one that

---

[42] The evidence for Grosseteste's life is discussed by Southern, *Grosseteste*, 63–82. For the debate, see M. Haren, *Medieval Thought: The Western Intellectual Tradition from Antiquity to the Thirteenth Century*, 2nd edn. (London, 1992), 229–31; J. McEvoy, *Robert Grosseteste* (Oxford, 2000), 22–9; J. Goering, 'When and Where Did Grosseteste Study Theology?', in J. McEvoy (ed.), *Robert Grosseteste: New Perspectives on his Thought and Scholarship* (Turnhout, 1995), 17–51.

[43] Grosseteste's thought is skilfully analysed by Southern, *Grosseteste*, 111–232.

should be preferred. Ockham was one of the most notable products of the Oxford schools. He began his studies there around the start of Edward II's reign, and moved from Oxford to the London Greyfriars in 1320. In 1324 he was summoned to the papal court, charged with heresy by John Lutterel, a man of some notoriety, who achieved the difficult feat of being dismissed from his post of chancellor of Oxford. In 1328 Ockham left Avignon to take refuge in the court of the emperor Ludwig IV; there he produced a theory of the state that was wholly secular. He died in Munich in 1349. Much of his work, therefore, was done in Germany; his English background and his Oxford education were important for his philosophical work, but not so much for his later political writings.[44]

The central controversy for the schools of this period was that of nominalism against realism. In the nominalist position, only those things that can be observed and tested are real. Everything else is the product of the mind. The realist position was that there are absolute realities, to which actual objects can no more than approximate. Ockham was a thoroughgoing nominalist, but many scholars did not advance to his extreme position. Thomas Bradwardine was one of the great figures of fourteenth-century Oxford. He began his career there in 1321, and was a fellow of Merton College from 1323 until 1335, when he entered the service of Richard de Bury, bishop of Durham. Many of the major intellectual figures of the day, such as Duns Scotus and Ockham, were friars; Bradwardine was a secular cleric. This was important; tension between the friars and the university was a major problem in early fourteenth-century Oxford. Bradwardine's writings extended from mathematics through logic to theology; he was a thoroughgoing opponent of Ockham's ideas. Like many mathematicians, his best work was done when he was a young man. His work included a treatise, his *Tractatus de Proportionibus*, which demonstrated in a highly sophisticated way the manner in which a moving object was affected by the forces working on it, and their ratios. At Oxford he was a leading member of an astonishingly productive group of mathematicians and astronomers at Merton College, but in 1335 he moved on to service in Bury's household. He was then employed in the royal household, and gained increasingly high office in the Church. In 1349 he became archbishop of Canterbury, probably the most academically able man ever to hold that office. His tenure was, however, brief, for he died of the great pestilence shortly after returning to England from his consecration at Avignon. The work of Bradwardine and his contemporaries is not easy to comprehend; it is highly technical, and it is made the more difficult because its purpose was very different from that of the scientific method of more modern periods. Its fundamental aim was to understand the divine purpose; ultimately faith was more important than the mathematical

---

[44] *History of the University of Oxford*, i. 608–9.

rules that explained the way things worked. Bradwardine and his contemporaries were concerned with deep theological issues about God's knowledge of events, past, present, and future, and man's free actions. A fundamental question was 'Whether everything that happens, happens of necessity?' These scholars were major international figures, and the Oxford of the first half of the fourteenth century was, it can be argued, the most notable intellectual powerhouse of the time in all of Europe.[45]

The intellectual achievements of men such as Grosseteste, Bradwardine, and others were distinctive. They were not the product of some pale imitation of the great schools of Paris, but it would be wrong to think of them as self-consciously English. Just as the builders and architects of the period produced a style that was unique to England, so these great thinkers developed ideas that helped to characterize the age, and that contributed to the complex totality of English culture in this period.

CONCLUSION

At the start of this period, in 1225, England had just emerged from the traumas of civil war. There had been a very real danger that the monarchy would collapse, and the country come under French rule. Despite the achievements of William Marshal and the others responsible for guiding the country during the minority, it was potentially highly unstable. There were dangerous factional rifts among the ruling elite, and there was no clearly established mechanism for consultation with the community of the realm. Royal revenues were recovering by the mid-1220s, but the crown was not in a strong position. It was hard to increase traditional sources of income, and there was no tradition of regular and substantial taxation. In military terms, despite the success of the royalist forces at the battle of Lincoln, England was weak. Small-scale campaigns against the Welsh achieved little, and expeditions to France in 1230 and 1242 merely demonstrated the ineffective character of English armies. The Church was facing the problem of how to carry through the reform programme set out in the fourth Lateran Council. In contrast to the political situation, the economy was strong. Population was rising rapidly, and the buoyant position was demonstrated by, for example, the foundation of new towns across England. Great estates, both lay and ecclesiastical, were prospering under effective methods of management. Labour was plentiful; the group least able to take advantage of the favourable economic circumstances was the peasantry. Peasants were not in a position to demand reductions in labour services or higher wages.

[45] *History of the University of Oxford*, i. 607–13, 644–57; Martin and Highfield, *History of Merton College*, 56–8.

In 1360 the situation was reversed in almost every particular. The monarchy was politically stable. Edward III had ridden the crisis of 1340–1, and faced no challenges. Parliament provided a mechanism for consultation, not merely with the magnates, but with the nation as a whole by means of representation. Systems of direct and indirect taxation had transformed the financial basis of government; this was now a fiscal state, with substantial revenues derived above all from fifteenths and tenths, and from export duties on wool and cloth. England was a major military power. Wales had been conquered in the late thirteenth century, and although Scotland had not been subjugated, its king, freed from the captivity in which he had been placed after the battle of Neville's Cross in 1346, was in a very weak position. In France the English had achieved astonishing successes, above all at Crécy and Poitiers. Although the campaign of 1359–60 had not yielded a further triumph, the treaty of Brétigny placed immense territories in south-western France in English hands. In England the position of the Church was stable, unchallenged by heretical movements. In contrast to such successes, the economic position began to change markedly in the early fourteenth century. The foundation of new towns came to a halt. The demographic situation was turned upside down by the Black Death; the population was reduced to perhaps half its previous level, and there was no indication of recovery. Landlords were retrenching, and increasingly they were leasing out their estates, rather than running them directly. For some at least of the peasantry, however, the radically changed circumstances offered new openings, for labour was scarce and wages high.

The years from 1225 to 1360 provide both contrasts and continuity. The kings who ruled England were very different in character. Henry III was pious, autocratic, and ineffective. With the exception of the building of Westminster abbey, he could not put his grandiose ideas for the monarchy into effect. He was not without political skill in a tactical sense, but was unable to master the factions at his court, let alone find the means to deal with his opponents. His formidable son Edward I had a tough apprenticeship in the years of political upheaval and civil war. He ruled with ambition and obstinacy. He was determined to restore the authority of the crown after the traumas of the civil war in his father's reign; the *quo warranto* campaign may not have achieved all he intended, but it was a clear demonstration of the extent of royal authority over judicial matters. In 1297 Edward faced a serious crisis; it is remarkable that he insisted on carrying forward his plans for war overseas when civil conflict threatened at home. Edward II had few, if any, of the qualities his subjects looked for in a king; he was unwarlike, showed no indications of political acumen, and was all too easily influenced by favourites. Edward III was the most remarkable of the rulers of this period. He was capable of acts of rashness, both in war and politics, but he also had shrewdness and good sense. A great military leader, he also understood the art of political patronage. Edward proved to be the ideal king for an age of chivalry.

The English state suffered great upheavals. The baronial reform movement, and Simon de Montfort in particular, presented a major challenge to Henry III's government. This was fuelled both by personal grievances and by ideological differences. The crisis that Edward I faced in 1297 was not so serious; it was the result of the abnormal demands of wartime, rather than of fundamental discontent with the way in which the country was governed. Under Edward II political difficulties were acute, and led to civil war by 1321–2. The aftermath saw skeletons hanging from gallows across England, a mark of the way in which politics had reached a brutal nadir. In 1327 the monarchy went through the trauma of the deposition of Edward II. Under his son the huge demands that war placed upon the country led once more to political crisis in 1340–1.

The development of parliament did much to change the nature of politics in this period. Its importance as a court, and for presenting petitions, was undoubted, while the mechanism of representation provided an increasingly effective means by which the crown obtained consent for its policies, and above all its taxes. Through parliament, the nature of politics was transformed. It provided a forum where political argument might take place; parliamentary consent was the means by which actions could be legitimized. Consent in parliament, albeit provided solely by the baronage, was set out in the Ordinances of 1311. In January 1327 the major steps in the deposition of Edward II took place in parliament, and the assembly remained in being after the king was removed from his throne. Parliament was central to the crisis of 1340–1, and by that date it was clear that the consent of the representatives was essential.

One of the keys to political success was patronage. Under Henry III excessive favour to the Savoyard and Poitevin groups did much to discredit the government. Edward I was far less generous than his father, but grants of lands in Wales and Scotland were part of his policy of settlement. The dangers of excessive favouritism were demonstrated very forcibly under Edward II, above all with Piers Gaveston and the Despensers, but also with others. One of the central demands of Thomas of Lancaster and the king's opponents was for the resumption of royal grants. Edward III was the king who got it right. He showed that it was possible to create new earls without at the same time generating jealousies, and a policy of granting pensions and annuities meant that the crown's landed endowment was not fatally weakened.

The political vicissitudes of the 1260s, and of Edward II's reign, had surprisingly little effect on the growth of the machinery of government. England was remarkable for the way in which a sophisticated, perhaps oversophisticated, bureaucracy developed, at both central and local levels. Chancery clerks busily recorded outgoing correspondence on massive rolls;

exchequer officials kept details of payments and debts; sheriffs' offices were kept busy by the flood of writs that poured in. The process was driven by various factors. The growing complexity of the legal system, with a multiplicity of different forms of actions and of writs, was one. The pressures of war, with the consequent demands for men, money, and *matériel*, were another element. Inquiries, notably those of Edward I's reign, provided government with more information than it could possibly use, and served to create business for officials. There was throughout an almost obsessive desire to keep records of all that was done.

Finance was a key to the ability of the English state to conduct its business effectively. At the start of the period it was clear that the landed resources of the crown were inadequate to meet its needs, but no real alternative had been developed. Taxation was intermittent at best. By Edward I's reign the crown was heavily dependent upon the taxation of the wool export trade, and on regular taxes levied on an assessment of personal property. What may be called a fiscal state was emerging, and parliamentary consent to taxation was essential in that process. Taxation of the clergy was also important; this was provided in part by a compliant papacy handing over part or all of taxes it had imposed on the English Church, and in part by grants made by the English clergy. Revenues were not enough, however, to cope with the abnormal demands of war, above all in the 1290s and the late 1330s. The crown had to turn to Italian merchants in order to obtain credit; successive companies failed at least in part as a result of their involvement in English crown finance. By the 1340s and 1350s English wool merchants, rather than Italians, were assisting Edward III in providing the credit needed to pay for his French war.

The military history of the period is one of both triumphs and disasters. The lack of achievement under Henry III contrasted with Edward I's successful conquest of Wales and his successes in Scotland. These achievements were not the result of brilliant strategies or skilful tactics; they were, rather, the consequence of the ability of the English administration to mobilize resources on a massive scale. Edward II's reign saw the weaknesses of the English military machine exposed at Bannockburn, and witnessed the north of England subjected to the savagery of Scottish raids. The reversal of military fortunes under his son Edward III was startling, with victories in the battle over the Scots providing a precedent for the triumphs of the French war at Crécy and Poitiers. Rather than relying on the cautious strategies of the past, Edward, buoyed up by chivalric ideology, was prepared to risk battle in pursuit of his great enterprise. The French throne was not to be his, but the territorial position of the English in France was transformed. There are many explanations for the English triumphs. Effective tactics and well-thought-out strategy are a part of the story, as is the deployment of increasingly experienced forces.

The adept exploitation of chivalric ideas by Edward III is another element to be taken into account. Naval support and effective logistics were also important. The failings of the French are another important reason for English success, and while the contemporary explanation that God backed the English cause is no longer convincing, this does not mean that they did not also have a good share of luck in their enterprise.

The advent of the friars was a major change to the Church in the thirteenth century, but it was not a revolutionary one. The English Church proved to be remarkable stable in this period; it was wholly unaffected by heretical movements. Much work of reform was done in the thirteenth century, following the agenda set by the papacy in the fourth Lateran Council; above all, there was increased attention given to issues of pastoral care. Relations with secular authorities caused occasional difficulties, but arguments such as those between archbishops Pecham and Winchelsey, and Edward I, serious as they were, did not change the fundamental relationship of Church and State. In the second decade of the fourteenth century the bishops did much to try to calm the political storms in England. Disputes with the papacy were less important than the financial assistance given by Rome and Avignon to the crown. The attempt, however, by the papacy to make use of English resources to place a compliant ruler on the Sicilian throne in the form of Henry III's son Edmund created considerable difficulties in the 1250s.

The social structure of thirteenth- and fourteenth-century England was relatively stable. There was a constant process of change and renewal, as new families came to take the place of old ones, but although there have been arguments to suggest that there was a crisis facing the knightly class in the thirteenth century, no startling shifts took place overall. The labels of 'feudalism' and 'bastard feudalism' are not particularly helpful. In aristocratic society, however, the ties represented by the grant of fees and robes, with terms of service recorded in indentures, were increasingly important as compared with the lordship implied in the homage that men did to feudal lords for their land. In the towns the extent of conflict that can be analysed in terms of class rivalries is limited, and challenges to the established oligarchies did not lead to conflict on a widespread scale. Within the ranks of the peasantry, it is possible to discern greater differentiation taking place. Although there are examples where peasant communities challenged their lords in an effective manner, there was no widespread social upheaval, such as would occur with the Peasants' Revolt of 1381. Crime was more serious at some times, and in some regions, than in others. The years around 1330 saw particularly acute problems, especially in the north midlands, where the extent of gentry involvement in criminal activity was notable. Despite all the efforts of the government to devise effective systems, conviction rates were low. Yet the levels of disorder were not such as to threaten the fabric of society as a whole, in the manner in which the Jacquerie tore France apart in the late 1350s.

The economy saw great contrasts, but there was no threat to the power of the great landlords, who proved able to respond effectively to changing conditions. The thirteenth century was a period of economic expansion, with new towns founded, and great estates prospering under a regime of high farming. Population growth peaked by the end of the century, when it is possible that numbers reached 5 million. With the fourteenth century came economic crises. The famine of 1315–16 was a disaster, made worse by subsequent animal plagues. There was recovery in some, but not all, parts of the country, but in 1348 the Black Death arrived in England, causing what was almost certainly the greatest demographic disaster in historical times. A death toll of half the population is very probable.

The previous book in this series ended with reference to the strange beings, supernatural in character, that lived 'below the Essex fields, within the Yorkshire barrows, and beyond the Suffolk shore'.[46] The twelfth century did not have a monopoly of wonders. In 1236 ghost riders, splendidly equipped as knights, appeared by night out of the ground near Roche abbey in Yorkshire to fight tournaments, and then sank back whence they had come. In 1254 a magnificent ship, beautifully coloured, flew above St Albans in the night sky. In 1315 a boy in Bishopsgate, in London, vanished to some distant realm for twenty-four hours, and returned to tell of many marvels.[47] However, the real wonder of thirteenth- and fourteenth-century England lies not in stories such as these, but in the strength, stability, and resilience that was shown by the English people.

[46] R. Bartlett, *England Under the Norman and Angevin Kings 1075–1225* (Oxford, 2000), 692.
[47] M. C. Prestwich, 'The "Wonderful Life" of the Thirteenth Century', in *TCE* vii. 166.

Chronology

1252	Simon de Montfort recalled from Gascony and put on trial
1253	Henry III goes to Gascony
	Death of Robert Grosseteste
1254	Edward, son of Henry III, marries Eleanor of Castile
	Henry III accepts the Sicilian throne for his second son, Edmund
	Two knights summoned from each shire to attend parliament
1255	Papal tax-collector arrives in England
1256	Richard of Cornwall elected king of the Romans
1257	Rebellion in Wales
1258	Provisions of Oxford
1259	Provisions of Westminster
	Treaty of Paris
1260	Reconciliation between the king and his son Edward
1261	Treaty of Kingston
	Simon de Montfort leaves England
1262	Death of Richard, earl of Gloucester
1263	Simon de Montfort returns to England
1264	Battle of Lewes
1265	Gilbert earl of Gloucester deserts Simon de Montfort
	Edward escapes from captivity
	Battle of Evesham; death of Simon de Montfort
1266	Siege of Kenilworth
	Dictum of Kenilworth
1267	Statute of Marlborough
1268	Council at St Paul's held by the papal legate, Ottobuono
1269	Translation of the relics of the Confessor at Westminster
1270	Edward goes on crusade
1271	Death of Richard of Cornwall, Henry III's brother
1272	Death of Henry III
1273	Llywelyn ap Gruffudd building a castle at Dolforwyn; his men invade Brecon
1274	Return of Edward to England
1275	Statute of Westminster I
	Grant of customs duties of 6s. 8d. on each sack of wool exported
1276	Refusal of Llywelyn ap Gruffudd to perform homage to Edward I
1277	Edward I's first Welsh war
1278	Statute of Gloucester
1279	Statute of Mortmain
	Reform of the coinage
1280	Hard frost for seven weeks
1281	Church council at Lambeth
1282	Edward I's second Welsh war starts; death of Llywelyn ap Gruffudd

1283   Second Welsh war concluded
       Statute of Acton Burnell
1284   Statute of Rhuddlan
1285   Statute of Westminster II; Statute of Winchester; Statute of Merchants
1286   Death of Alexander III of Scots
       Edward I goes to Gascony
1287   Rebellion in Wales
1288   Major fire at Boston (Lincolnshire)
1289   Edward I returns to England from Gascony
1290   Statute of *Quia Emptores*; Statute of *Quo Warranto*
       Expulsion of the Jews
       Hearings of the Great Cause to determine succession to the Scottish throne begin
       Death of Eleanor of Castile
1291   Death of Eleanor of Provence
1292   John Balliol enthroned as king of Scots
       Death of Robert Burnell
1293   Assize circuits set up
1294   War begins with France; rebellion in Wales
       Customs duties of 40s. a sack introduced, known as the *maltolt*
1295   So-called Model Parliament held
1296   Edward I's first Scottish campaign; deposition of John Balliol in Scotland
1297   Edward I faces opposition led by the earls of Norfolk and Hereford
       Edward I goes to Flanders on campaign
       William Wallace's rising in Scotland; battle of Stirling Bridge
       Issue of *Confirmatio Cartarum*
       Maltolt abolished
1298   Campaign in Scotland, with English victory at Falkirk
1299   Further confirmation of the charters put off; Edward I complains of air pollution in London
1300   Campaign in Scotland; Caerlaverock captured
       Issue of *Articuli super Cartas*
1301   Campaign in Scotland
1302   Marriage of Edward I's daughter Elizabeth to the earl of Hereford
1303   Campaign in Scotland
1304   Surrender of Stirling castle to Edward I
1305   Settlement agreed for Scotland
1306   Robert Bruce installed as king of Scots
1307   Death of Edward I; accession of Edward II
       Piers Gaveston made earl of Cornwall
1308   Edward II's coronation; Piers Gaveston's first exile

1309	Statute of Stamford. Piers Gaveston returns to England
1310	Edward II agrees to the appointment of the Ordainers
1311	Issue of the Ordinances
	Renewed Scottish raids into the north of England
1312	Death of Piers Gaveston
1313	Settlement reached with Lancaster and the others responsible for Gaveston's death
1314	Edward II defeated at Bannockburn
1315	Famine
	Scots fail to capture Carlisle
	Scots under Edward Bruce invade Ireland
1316	Famine
	Parliament held at Lincoln
1317	Gilbert de Middleton's attack on Louis de Beaumont, bishop of Durham, and two cardinals
1318	Treaty of Leake
	Edward Bruce defeated and killed at Fochart in Ireland
1319	Edward II fails to recapture Berwick
1320	Royal seizure of Gower in south Wales
1321	War against the Despensers in the Welsh march
	Eyre of London
1322	Defeat of Thomas of Lancaster's rebellion at Boroughbridge
	Statute of York
1323	Execution of Andrew Harclay for treason
	Thirteen-year truce with the Scots agreed
1324	War of Saint-Sardos against the French begins
1325	War of Saint-Sardos concludes
1326	Isabella and Mortimer invade
1327	Edward II deposed; accession of Edward II
	Stanhope campaign against the Scots; last use of a feudal summons
1328	'Shameful peace' with the Scots
1329	Execution of the earl of Kent
	Edward III does homage to Philip VI of France
1330	Coup at Nottingham; arrest and execution of Roger Mortimer
1331	William Montague rewarded for his part in the coup of 1330, with the grant of the lordship of Denbigh
1332	Victory for the 'disinherited' at Dupplin Moor
1333	Edward II defeats the Scots at Halidon Hill
1334	What will become the standard tax assessment is made
1335	Large expedition to Scotland achieves little
1336	Edward III's rescue of the countess of Atholl

1337   War begins against France
        Creation of new earls
1338   Walton Ordinances
        Edward III in Flanders
1339   Abortive battle at Buirenfosse
1340   Battle of Sluys
        Unsuccessful siege of Tournai
        Truce of Esplechin
        Political crisis following Edward's return to England
1341   Settlement of political crisis; statute granted, and later revoked
        David II returns to Scotland
1342   Edward III's expedition to Brittany
        Battle of Morlaix
1343   Truce of Malestroit
1344   Peace negotiations at Avignon
1345   Lancaster's expedition to Gascony
1346   Battle of Crécy
        Battle of Neville's Cross against the Scots
1347   Charles of Blois defeated at La Roche-Derrien
        Capture of Calais
        Abduction of Margery de la Beche
1348   Black Death begins
        Establishment of the Order of the Garter
1349   Black Death continues
1350   Battle of Les Espagnols sur mer
1351   Statute of Provisors
1352   Statute of Treason
1353   Statute of Praemunire
        English staple ports set up, to replace the staple at Bruges
1354   Draft treaty of Guînes
1355   Black Prince's raid to Narbonne
        St Scholastica's Day riots in Oxford
1356   Battle of Poitiers
1357   David II of Scotland's ransom agreed
1358   First treaty of London
1359   Second treaty of London
        Expedition to Reims and Burgundy
1360   Treaty of Brétigny

GENEALOGICAL TABLE 1. THE ROYAL FAMILY (1)

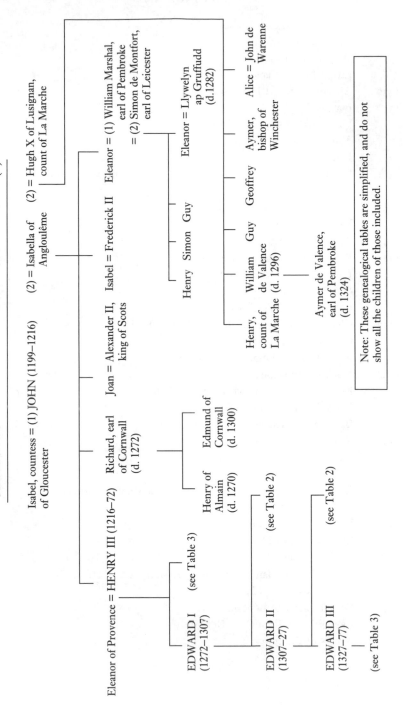

Note: These genealogical tables are simplified, and do not show all the children of those included.

GENEALOGICAL TABLE 2. THE ROYAL FAMILY (2)

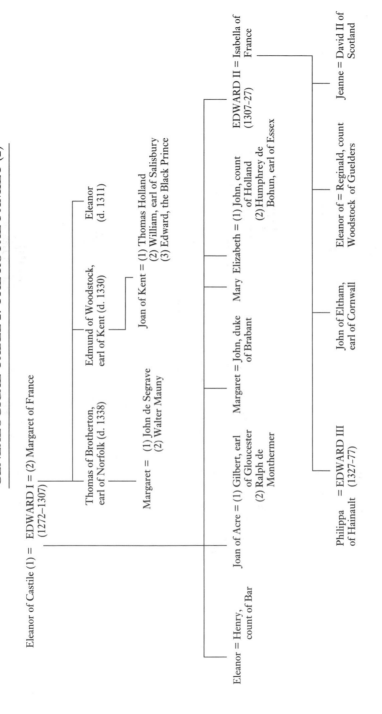

GENEALOGICAL TABLE 3. THE ROYAL FAMILY AND THE HOUSE OF LANCASTER

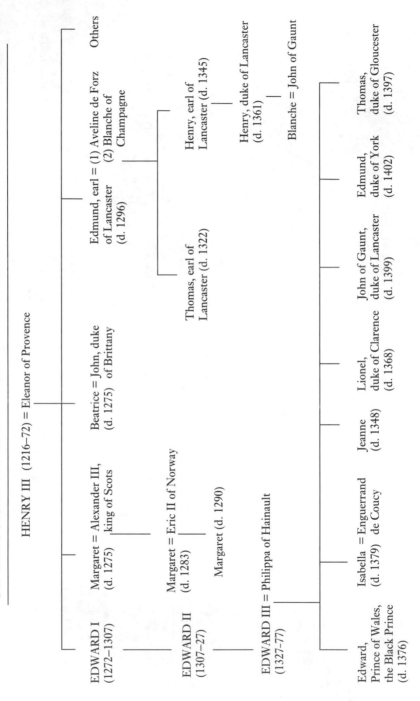

GENEALOGICAL TABLE 4. THE FRENCH MONARCHY AND THE ENGLISH CLAIM TO THE THRONE

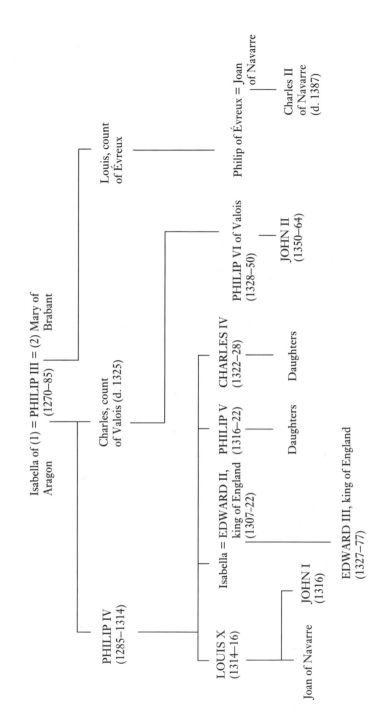

GENEALOGICAL TABLE 5. THE CLARES

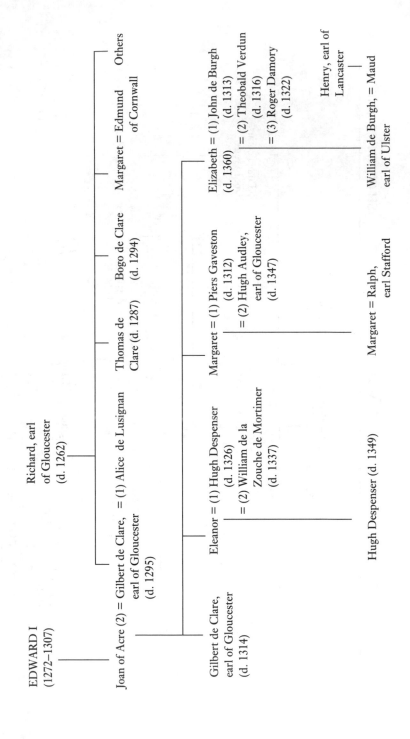

Bibliography

In this bibliography I have not followed the chapter structure of this book, but have divided up the subject matter slightly differently. I have, for example, used reigns as chronological divisions, and have included sections on the agrarian economy, women, and the Church, topics which are dealt with in several different chapters. My hope is that this will be helpful to readers. There are many works that could feature in several sections; for reasons of space, I have normally cited titles only once. Inevitably, a bibliography is highly selective, and there is much important work that does not feature in it. Nor are all works cited in the footnotes included.

In the lists that follow, the order in which titles appear reflects that of the alphabet, not their importance.

BIBLIOGRAPHIC AND OTHER AIDS

The Handbook of British Chronology, ed. E. B. Fryde, D. E. Greenaway, S. Porter, and I. Roy, 3rd edn. (London, 1986), provides essential lists of the chief government office-holders, bishops, earls, and parliaments. *The Handbook of Dates for Students of English History*, ed. C. R. Cheney (London, 1970), gives lists of regnal years, saints' days, and calendars for every year. *Texts and Calendars* lists the publications of a wide range of bodies, from the Pipe Roll Society to local historical societies. A bibliography of secondary literature is provided by *The Royal Historical Society Bibliography on CD-ROM: The History of Britain, Ireland and of the British Overseas* (Oxford, 1998). The same society provides an *Annual Bibliography of British and Irish History*, and there are annual literature surveys in the *Economic History Review*, the *English Historical Review*, and *History*. Lists of theses completed, and in progress, can be found on the Royal Historical Society's website at <http://www.ihr.sas.ac.uk>. For specifically medieval bibliographies, see C. Gross, *A Bibliography of English History to 1485*, ed. E. B. Graves (Oxford, 1975), and the annual *International Medieval Bibliography* (Leeds, 1968–) produced by the International Medieval Institute, University of Leeds.

The *Dictionary of National Biography*, ed. L. Stephen and S. Lee, 653 vols. (1885–1901), contains a wealth of material, but has been superseded by the *Oxford Dictionary of National Biography*, ed. H. C. G. Matthew and B. Harrison (Oxford, 2004). G. E. C[ockayne], *The Complete Peerage of England, Scotland, Ireland, Great Britain and the United Kingdom*, ed. V. Gibbs *et al.*, 13 vols. in 14 (London, 1910–59), provides a mine of information about the aristocracy.

PRINTED SOURCES

Collected Documents in Translation

The Black Death, ed. R. Horrox (Manchester, 1994); *Documents of the Baronial Movement of Reform and Rebellion 1258–1267*, ed. R. F. Treharne and I. J. Sanders (Oxford, 1973); *English Historical Documents*, iii: *1189–1327*, ed. H. Rothwell (London, 1975); *English Historical Documents*, iv: *1227–1485*, ed. A. R. Myres (London, 1969); *The English Manor c.1200–c.1500*, ed. M. Bailey (Manchester, 2002); *The Life and Campaigns of the Black Prince*, ed. R. Barber (Woodbridge, 1979); *The Wars of Edward III: Sources and Interpretations*, ed. C. J. Rogers (Woodbridge, 1999). See also <http://www.deremilitari.org/>.

Chronicles

Guides: A. Gransden, *Historical Writing in England c.550–c.1307* (London, 1974), and id., *Historical Writing in England*, ii: *c.1307 to the Early Sixteenth Century* (London, 1974, 1982); C. Given-Wilson, *Chronicles: The Writing of History in Medieval England* (London, 2004).

The main chronicle sources used in this volume are: *Adae Murimuth, Continuatio Chronicarum et Robertus de Avesbury De Gestis Mirabilibus Regis Edwardi Tertii*, ed. E. M. Thompson (RS, 1889); the various chronicles included in *Annales Monastici*, ed. H. R. Luard, 5 vols. (RS, 1864–9); *Bartholomaei de Cotton, Historia Anglicana*, ed. H. R. Luard (RS, 1859); *The Chronicle of Walter of Guisborough*, ed. H. Rothwell, Camden 3rd ser., 89 (1957); the works in *Chronicles of the Reigns of Edward I and Edward II*, ed. W. Stubbs (RS, 1882–3); *Chronicon Galfridi le Baker de Swynebroke*, ed. E. M. Thompson (Oxford, 1889); *Chronicon de Lanercost*, ed. J. Stevenson (Edinburgh, 1839); *Chroniques de Jean Froissart*, ed. S. Luce, G. Raynaud, L. Mirot, and A. Mirot, 15 vols. (Société de l'histoire de France, 1869–1975); *Édition critique et commentée de Pierre de Langtoft: Le Règne d'Édouard 1er*, ed. J. C. Thiolier (Créteil, 1989); *Flores Historiarum*, ed. H. R. Luard, 3 vols. (RS, 1890); *Johannis de Trokelowe et Henrici de Blaneford, monachorum S. Albani, necnon quorundam Anonymorum Chronica et Annales*, ed. H. T. Riley (RS, 1866); *Matthaei Parisiensis, Monachi Sancti Albani, Chronica Majora*, ed. H. R. Luard, 7 vols. (RS, 1872–83); *The Metrical Chronicle of Robert of Gloucester*, ed. W. A. Wright, 2 vols. (RS, 1887); *Willelmi Rishanger, Chronica et Annales*, ed. H. T. Riley (RS, 1865); *Scalacronica of Sir Thomas Gray*, ed. J. Stevenson (Maitland Club, Edinburgh, 1836); *La Vie du Prince Noir by Chandos Herald*, ed. D. B. Tyson (Tübingen, 1975); *Vita Edwardi Secundi*, ed. N. Denholm-Young (London, 1957).

Chancery records

Many rolls have been calendared in English. The most important are *Calendar of Charter Rolls*; *Calendar of Close Rolls* (those for the first part of Henry III's reign were published *in extenso* as *Close Rolls*); *Calendar of Liberate Rolls*; *Calendar of Patent Rolls*. There is much material in the *Calendar of Inquisitions Miscellaneous*, and in the

Calendar of Inquisitions Post Mortem, as well as in T. Rymer (ed.), *Foedera, Conventiones, Litterae et Acta Publica*, ed. A. Clarke and F. Holbrooke, 4 vols. (London, 1816–69).

Exchequer Records

The Pipe Roll Society has published some pipe rolls, such as *Pipe Roll 14 Henry III*, ed. C. Robinson (Pipe Roll Society, 1927), and other records for the start of this period, but, in general, few exchequer records have been published. There is, for example, only one roll, that for 1327, in the *Calendar of Memoranda Rolls, Exchequer* (London, 1968). The pipe rolls of Edward I's reign for Northumberland were published, in translation, by A. J. Lilburn, 'The Pipe Rolls of Edward I', *Archaeologia Aeliana*, 4th ser., 32–6, 38–9, 41 (1954–63).

The fullest local taxation records are *The Wealth of Shrewsbury in the Early Fourteenth Century*, ed. D. and R. Cromarty (Shropshire Archaeological and Historical Society, 1993); see also *Hertfordshire Lay Subsidy Rolls 1307 and 1334*, ed. J. Brooker and S. Flood (Hertfordshire Record Society, 1998), and G. H. Dashwood, 'Remarks on a Subsidy Roll in the Possession of the Corporation of Lynn Regis', *Norfolk Archaeology* (1847).

Household Records

Relatively few royal household accounts have been published, but *Records of the Wardrobe and Household 1285–1286*, and *Records of the Wardrobe and Household 1286–1289*, ed. B. F. and C. R. Byerley (London, 1977, 1986), *Liber Quotidianus Contrarotuloris Garderobae*, ed. J. Topham (1787), and *The Wardrobe Book of William de Norwell 12 July 1338 to 27 May 1340*, ed. M. Lyon, B. Lyon, and H. S. Lucas (Brussels, 1983), provide a good sample of final account books. *Book of Prests of the King's Wardrobe for 1294–5*, ed. E. B. Fryde (Oxford, 1962), is a subsidiary account of considerable importance.

Parliamentary Records

Parliamentary Writs and Writs of Military Summons, ed. F. Palgrave, 2 vols. in 4 (London, 1827–34), provides the writs of summons and many other documents. The rolls of parliament were published as *Rotuli Parliamentorum*, 6 vols. (London, 1783). A wholly new edition is to appear shortly, under the general editorship of C. Given-Wilson. G. O. Sayles, *The Functions of the Medieval Parliament of England* (London, 1988), contains an important selection of documents in translation. *Parliamentary Texts of the Later Middle Ages*, ed. N. Pronay and J. Taylor (Oxford, 1980), is important for the *Modus Tenendi Parliamentum*.

Legal Records

Many have been published, with translation, by the Selden Society. For the central courts, see *Select Cases in the Court of King's Bench*, ed. G. O. Sayles, 5 vols. (Selden Society, 1936, 1938, 1939, 1957, 1958). There is no equivalent for Common Bench, but many cases from this court are in *Earliest English Law Reports*, ed. P. A. Brand, 2 vols. (Selden Society, 1996). Many Year Books for Edward I's reign were published in the

Rolls Series, edited by A. J. Horwood, while for Edward II's reign, many were published by the Selden Society, edited by W. C. Bolland and others. A convenient guide to the eyre records is D. Crook, *Records of the General Eyre* (London, 1982). For printed eyre rolls, see, for example, *Crown Pleas of the Devon Eyre of 1238,* ed. H. Summerson (Devon and Cornwall Record Society, NS 28, 1985); *Crown Pleas of the Wiltshire Eyre, 1249*, ed. C. A. F. Meekings (Wiltshire Archaeological and Natural History Society, 1961); *Civil Pleas of the Wiltshire Eyre*, ed. M. T. Clanchy (Wiltshire Record Society, 1971); *The London Eyre of 1276*, ed. M. Weinbaum (London Record Society, 1976); *The Eyre of Northamptonshire, iii–iv: Edward III*, ed. D. W. Sutherland, 2 vols. (Selden Society, 97, 1981); *The Oxfordshire Eyre 1241*, ed. J. Cooper (Oxfordshire Record Society, 56, 1989); *Royal Justice and the Medieval English Countryside: The Huntingdon Eyre of 1286, the Ramsey Abbey Banlieu Court of 1287, and the Assizes of 1287–88*, ed. A. R. DeWindt and E. B. DeWindt (Toronto, 1981); *The Rolls of the 1281 Derbyshire Eyre*, ed. A. M. Hopkinson (Chesterfield, 2000). G. Wrottesley used a range of sources for his 'Plea Rolls of the Reign of Henry III', 'Plea Rolls of the Reign of Edward I', 'Plea Rolls of the Reign of Edward II', 'Plea Rolls of the Reign of Edward III', in *Collections for a History of Staffordshire* (William Salt Archaeological Society, 1883–92). For gaol delivery and assize rolls, see *Three Early Assize Rolls for the County of Northumberland*, ed. W. Page (Surtees Society, 88, 1891), and *Crime in East Anglia in the Fourteenth Century: Norfolk Gaol Delivery Rolls, 1307–1316*, ed. B. A. Hanawalt (Norfolk Record Society, 1976). More specialized inquests include *A Lincolnshire Assize Roll for 1298*, ed. W. S. Thompson (Lincoln Record Society, 1944), and *The 1341 Royal Inquest in Lincolnshire*, ed. B. W. McLane (Lincoln Record Society, 1988).

The main legal treatise from this period is *Bracton on the Laws and Customs of England*, ed. G. E. Woodbine, trans. and rev. S. E. Thorne (Cambridge, Mass., 1968).

Estate and Manorial Records

For a guide, see P. D. A. Harvey, *Manorial Records* (British Records Association, 1984). For manorial accounts referred to in this book, see *The Bolton Priory Compotus 1286–1325, Together with a Priory Account Roll for 1377–78*, ed. I. Kershaw and D. M. Smith, Yorkshire Archaeological Society Record Series, 154 (Woodbridge, 2000); *A Collection of Records and Documents relating to the Hundred and Manor of Crondall*, pt. 1, ed. F. J. Baigent (London, 1891); *The Pipe Roll of the Bishopric of Winchester 1301–2*, ed. M. Page, Hampshire Record Series, 14 (Winchester, 1996); *Wellingborough Manorial Accounts*, ed. F. M. Page (Northamptonshire Record Society, 1936).

For court rolls, see *The Court Rolls of the Manor of Wakefield* (Yorkshire Archaeological Society, various dates and editors); *The Court Rolls of Walsham le Willows 1303–1350*, ed. R. Lock (Suffolk Records Society, 41, 1998); *Select Cases in Manorial Courts 1250–1550*, ed. L. R. Poos and L. Bonfield (Selden Society, 114, 1997); *Select Pleas in Manorial and Other Seignorial Courts*, ed. F. W. Maitland (Selden Society, 2, 1888).

For treatises on estate management, see *Walter of Henley and Other Treatises on Estate Management and Accounting*, ed. D. Oschinsky (Oxford, 1971).

Ecclesiastical Records

Councils and Synods, ii: *A.D. 1205–1313*, ed. F. M. Powicke and C. R. Cheney (Oxford, 1964), includes a wide range of material. Many bishop's registers have been published, notably by the Canterbury and York Society. Those used in this book include: *A Calendar of the Register of Wolstan de Bransford, Bishop of Worcester 1339–49*, ed. R. M. Haines (London, 1966); *The Register of John de Grandisson, Bishop of Exeter*, pt. 1: *1327–30*, ed. F. C. Hingeston-Randolph (London, 1894); *The Register of William Edington Bishop of Winchester 1346–1366*, ed. S. F. Hockey (Hampshire Record Office, 1986–7); *The Register of William Greenfield, Lord Archbishop of York 1306–15*, ed. W. Brown (Surtees Society, 1931); *Registrum Epistolarum Johannis Peckham*, ed. C. T. Martin (RS, 1882–4); *Registrum Palatinum Dunelmense*, ed. T. D. Hardy, 4 vols. (RS, 1873–5).

For ecclesiastical courts, see *Select Cases from the Ecclesiastical Courts of the Province of Canterbury c.1200–1301*, ed. N. Adams and C. Donahue, Jr. (Selden Society, 1981), and *Lower Ecclesiastical Jurisdiction in Late-Medieval England*, ed. L. R. Poos (Oxford, 2001).

Private Records

Cartularies, such as *The Thurgarton Cartulary*, ed. T. Foulds (Stamford, 1994), preserve a very considerable number of charters, while a remarkable collection of documents dealing with a small estate is *The Estate Book of Henry de Bray*, ed. D. Willis, Camden 3rd ser., 27 (1916). Particularly relevant to the themes of this book are 'Private Indentures for Life Service in Peace and War', ed. M. Jones and S. Walker, *Camden Miscellany XXXII*, Camden 5th ser., 3 (1994); *Household Accounts from Medieval England*, pt. 1, ed. C. M. Woolgar (Oxford, 1992).

SECONDARY WORKS

General Works

D. A. Carpenter, *The Struggle for Mastery: Britain 1066–1284* (London, 2003); M. T. Clanchy, *England and its Rulers 1066–1272* (Glasgow, 1983); R. Frame, *The Political Development of the British Isles 1100–1400* (Oxford, 1990); A. Harding, *England in the Thirteenth Century* (Cambridge, 1993); M. H. Keen, *England in the Later Middle Ages*, 2nd edn. (London, 2004); K. B. McFarlane, *The Nobility of Later Medieval England* (Oxford, 1973); M. McKisack, *The Fourteenth Century 1307–1399* (Oxford, 1959); W. M. Ormrod, *Political Life in Medieval England, 1300–1450* (Basingstoke, 1995); F. M Powicke, *The Thirteenth Century 1216–1307*, 2nd. edn. (Oxford, 1962); S. Raban, *England Under Edward I and Edward II* (Oxford, 2000); M. C. Prestwich, *The Three Edwards: War and State 1272–1377*, 2nd edn. (London, 2003); id., *English Politics in the Thirteenth Century* (Basingstoke, 1990); W. Stubbs, *Constitutional History of England*, ii, 4th edn. (Oxford, 1906); J. A. Tuck, *Crown and Nobility, 1272–1461* (Glasgow, 1985); C. Valente, *The Theory and Practice of Revolt in Medieval England* (Aldershot, 2003).

General Works on the Economy

J. L. Bolton, *The Medieval English Economy 1150–1500* (London, 1980); R. H. Britnell, *The Commercialisation of English Society 1000–1500*, 2nd edn. (Manchester, 1996); C. Dyer, *Making a Living in the Middle Ages: The People of Britain 850–1520* (London, 2002); J. Hatcher and E. Miller, *Medieval England: Rural Society and Economic Change 1986–1348* (London, 1978); id., *Medieval England: Towns, Commerce and Crafts 1086–1348* (Harlow, 1995); M. M. Postan, *The Medieval Economy and Society* (London, 1972); S. Rigby, *English Society in the Later Middle Ages: Class, Status and Gender* (Basingstoke, 1995); P. R. Schofield, *Peasant and Community in Medieval England 1200–1500* (Basingstoke, 2003).

The Crown and the Government

Books: J. F. Baldwin, *The King's Council in England in the Middle Ages* (Oxford, 1913); A. L. Brown, *The Governance of Late Medieval England 1272–1461* (London, 1989); H. M. Cam, *Liberties and Communities in Medieval England* (Cambridge, 1944); G. P. Cuttino, *English Diplomatic Administration 1259–1339*, 2nd edn. (Oxford, 1971); J. F. Willard, W. A. Morris, and J. R. Strayer (eds.), *The English Government at Work, 1327–1336*, 3 vols. (Cambridge, Mass., 1940–7); R. Gorsky, *The Fourteenth-Century Sheriff* (Woodbridge, 2003); H. C. Maxwell-Lyte, *Historical Notes on the Use of the Great Seal of England* (London, 1926); S. K. Mitchell, *Taxation in Medieval England* (New Haven, 1951); W. A. Morris, *The Medieval English Sheriff to 1300* (Manchester, 1927); E. Peters, *The Shadow King: Rex Inutilis in Medieval Law and Literature, 751–1327* (New Haven, 1970); T. F. Tout, *Chapters in the Administrative History of Mediaeval England*, 6 vols. (Manchester, 1920–33); M. Vale, *The Princely Court: Medieval Courts and Culture in North-West Europe* (Oxford, 2001); S. L. Waugh, *The Lordship of England: Royal Wardships and Marriages in English Society and Politics 1217–1327* (Princeton, 1988); B. Wilkinson, *The Chancery Under Edward III* (Manchester, 1929); id., *Studies in the Constitutional History of the 13th and 14th Centuries* (Manchester, 1937); J. F. Willard, *Parliamentary Taxes on Personal Property, 1290 to 1334* (Cambridge, Mass., 1934).

Articles: D. A. Carpenter, 'The English Chancery in the XIIIth Century', in K. Fianu and D. J. Guth (eds.), *Écrit et pouvoir dans les chancelleries médiévales: Espace français, espace anglais* (Louvain-La-Neuve, 1997); J. L. Grassi, 'Royal Clerks from the Archdiocese of York in the Fourteenth Century', *Northern History*, 5 (1970); H. Jenkinson and M. H. Mills, 'Rolls from a Sheriff's Office of the Fourteenth Century', *EHR* 43 (1928); C. Johnson, 'The System of Account in the Wardrobe of Edward I', *TRHS*, 4th ser., 6 (1923); W. M. Ormrod, 'Accountability and Collegiality: The English Royal Secretariat in the Mid-Fourteenth Century', in K. Fianu and D. J. Guth (eds.), *Écrit et pouvoir dans les chancelleries médiévales: Espace français, espace anglais* (Louvain-La-Neuve, 1997); M. C. Prestwich, 'Exchequer and Wardrobe in the Later Years of Edward I', *BIHR* 467 (1973); id., 'English Government Records', in R. H. Britnell (ed.), *Pragmatic Literacy East and West, 1200–1330* (Woodbridge, 1997); B. Weiler, 'Symbolism and Politics in the Reign of Henry III', in *TCE* ix; J. F. Willard, 'The

Dating and Delivery of Letters Patent and Writs in the Fourteenth Century', *BIHR* 10 (1932).

Parliament

Books: J. G. Edwards, *The Second Century of the English Parliament* (Oxford, 1979); G. L. Harris, *King, Parliament and Public Finance to 1360* (Oxford, 1975); M. McKisack, *The Parliamentary Representation of the English Boroughs During the Middle Ages* (Oxford, 1932); J. E. Powell and K. Wallis, *The House of Lords in the Middle Ages* (London, 1968); H. G. Richardson and G. O. Sayles, *The English Parliament in the Middle Ages* (London, 1981); G. O. Sayles, *The King's Parliament of England* (London, 1975).

Articles: D. A. Carpenter, 'From King John to the First English Duke: 1215–1337', in R. Smith and J. S. Moore (eds.), *The House of Lords: A Thousand Years of British Tradition* (London, 1994); J. H. Denton, 'The Clergy and Parliament in the Thirteenth and Fourteenth Centuries', in R. G. Davies and J. H. Denton (eds.), *The English Parliament in the Middle Ages* (Manchester, 1981); id., 'The Making of the *Articuli Cleri* of 1316', *EHR* 101 (1987); J. G. Edwards, 'The *Plena Potestas* of English Parliamentary Representatives', in E. B. Fryde and E. Miller (eds.), *Historical Studies of the English Parliament* (Cambridge, 1970); G. L. Haskins, 'The Doncaster Petition, 1321', *EHR* 53 (1938); J. R. Maddicott, 'Parliament and the Constituencies, 1272–1377', in R. G. Davies and J. H. Denton (eds.), *The English Parliament in the Middle Ages* (Manchester, 1981); id., 'The Crusade Taxation of 1268–1270 and the Development of Parliament', in *TCE* ii; id., ' "An Infinite Multitude of Nobles": Quality, Quantity and Politics in the Pre-Reform Parliaments of Henry III', in *TCE* vii; id., 'The Earliest Known Knights of the Shire: New Light on the Parliament of April 1254', *Parliamentary History*, 18 (1999); M. C. Prestwich, 'Parliament and the Community of the Realm in Fourteenth Century England', in A. Cosgrove and J. I. McGuire (eds.), *Parliament and Community* (Belfast, 1983); K. Wood-Legh, 'Sheriffs, Lawyers and Belted Knights in the Parliaments of Edward III', *EHR* 46 (1931); id., 'The Knights' Attendance in the Parliaments of Edward III', *EHR* 47 (1932).

For the *Modus Tenendi Parliamentum*, see K. Kerby-Fulton and S. Justice, 'Reformist Intellectual Culture in the English and Irish Civil Service: The *Modus Tenendi Parliamentum* and its Literary Relations', *Traditio*, 53 (1998); M. C. Prestwich, 'The *Modus Tenendi Parliamentum*', *Parliamentary History*, 1 (1982); G. O. Sayles, '*Modus tenendi parliamentum*: Irish or English?', in J. Lydon (ed.), *England and Ireland in the Later Middle Ages: Essays in Honour of Jocelyne Otway-Ruthven* (Dublin, 1981); W. C. Weber, 'The Purpose of the English *Modus Tenendi Parliamentum*', *Parliamentary History*, 17 (1992).

Reign of Henry III

Biographical studies: D. A. Carpenter, *The Minority of Henry III* (London, 1990); N. Denholm-Young, *Richard of Cornwall* (Oxford, 1947); M. Howell, *Eleanor of Provence: Queenship in Thirteenth-Century England* (Oxford, 1998); J. R. Maddicott,

Simon de Montfort (Oxford, 1994); N. Vincent, *Peter des Roches: An Alien in English Politics 1205–1238* (Cambridge, 1996).

Other books: D. A. Carpenter, *The Reign of Henry III* (London, 1996) (a collection of articles); F. M. Powicke, *King Henry III and the Lord Edward*, 2 vols. (Oxford, 1947); R. Stacey, *Politics, Policy and Finance Under Henry III, 1216–1245* (Oxford, 1987); R. F. Treharne, *The Baronial Plan of Reform*, 2nd edn., (Manchester, 1971); *The Holy Blood: King Henry III and the Westminster Blood Relic* (Cambridge, 2001).

Articles: D. A. Carpenter, 'Simon de Montfort and the Mise of Lewes', *BIHR* 58 (1985); id., 'Westminster Abbey in Politics, 1258–1269', in *TCE* vii; C. R. Cheney, 'The "Paper Constitution" Preserved by Matthew Paris', *EHR* 65 (1950); M. T. Clanchy, 'Did Henry III Have a Policy?', *History*, 53 (1968); N. Denholm-Young, 'The "Paper Constitution" Attributed to 1244', in his *Collected Papers on Medieval Subjects* (Oxford, 1946); R. F. Frame, 'King Henry III and Ireland: The Shaping of a Peripheral Lordship', in his *Ireland and Britain 1170–1450* (London, 1998); A. Hershey, 'Success or Failure? Hugh Bigod and Judicial Reform During the Baronial Movement, June 1258–February 1259', in *TCE* v; O. de Laborderie, J. R. Maddicott, and D. A. Carpenter, 'The Last Hours of Simon de Montfort: A New Account', *EHR* 115 (2000); J. R. Maddicott, 'The Mise of Lewes, 1264', *EHR* 98 (1983); id., 'Magna Carta and the Local Community 1215–1259', *Past and Present*, 102 (1984); M. H. Mills, 'The Reforms at the Exchequer (1232–1242), *TRHS*, 4th ser., 10 (1927); H. Ridgeway, 'King Henry III and the "Aliens", 1236–1272', in *TCE* ii; id., 'King Henry III's Grievances Against the Council in 1261: A New Version and a Letter Describing Political Events', *Historical Research*, 61 (1988); id., 'William de Valence and his *Familiares*, 1247–72', *Historical Research*, 65 (1992); id., 'Mid Thirteenth-Century Reformers and the Localities: The Sheriffs of the Baronial Regime, 1258–1261', in P. Fleming, A. Gross, and J. R. Lander (eds.), *Regionalism and Revision: The Crown and its Provinces in England 1200–1650* (London, 1998); R. C. Stacey, 'The English Jews Under Henry III', in P. Skinner (ed.), *The Jews in Medieval Britain* (Woodbridge, 2003); B. Weiler, 'Matthew Paris, Richard of Cornwall's Candidacy for the German Throne, and the Sicilian Business', *Journal of Medieval History*, 26 (2000); id., 'Henry III and the Sicilian Business: A Reinterpretation', *Historical Research*, 74 (2001).

Reign of Edward I

Biographical studies: J. H. Denton, *Robert Winchelsey and the Crown 1294–1313* (Cambridge, 1980); D. Douie, *Archbishop Pecham* (Oxford, 1952); C. M. Fraser, *A History of Anthony Bek* (Oxford, 1957); J. C. Parsons, *Eleanor of Castile: Queen and Society in Thirteenth-Century England* (New York, 1995); M. C. Prestwich, *Edward I* (London, 1988).

Other books: R. Mundill, *England's Jewish Solution: Experiment and Expulsion, 1262–1290* (Cambridge, 1998); R. W. Kaeuper, *Bankers to the Crown: The Riccardi of Lucca and Edward I* (Princeton, 1973).

Articles: P. Brand, 'Edward I and the Judges: The "State Trials" of 1289–93', in *TCE* i; 'Jews and the Law in England, 1275–90', *EHR* 115 (2000); D. Crook, ' "Thieves and

Plunderers": An Anti-ministerial Protest of 1296', *Historical Research*, 67 (1994); J. H. Denton, 'The Crisis of 1297 from the Evesham Chronicle', *EHR* 93 (1978); R. Huscroft, 'Robert Burnell and the Government of England', in *TCE* vii; R. W. Kaeuper, 'The Frescobaldi of Florence and the English Crown', *Studies in Medieval and Renaissance History*, 10 (1973); J. R. Maddicott, 'Edward I and the Lessons of Baronial Reform', in *TCE* i; id., ' "1258" and "1297"': Some Comparisons and Contrasts', in *TCE* ix; M. H. Mills, 'Exchequer Agenda and Estimate of Revenue, Easter Term 1284', *EHR* 40 (1925); M. Morris, 'The "Murder" of an English Earldom? Roger IV Bigod and Edward I', in *TCE* ix; M. C. Prestwich, 'The Piety of Edward I', in W. M. Ormrod (ed.), *England in the Thirteenth Century* (Harlaxton, 1985); id., 'Royal Patronage Under Edward I', in *TCE* i; S. Raban, 'Edward I's Other Inquiries', in *TCE* ix; H. Rothwell, 'Edward I and the Struggle for the Charters', in R. W. Hunt, W. A. Pantin, and R. W. Southern (eds.), *Studies in Medieval History Presented to F. M. Powicke* (Oxford, 1948); R. Stacey, 'Parliamentary Negotiation and the Expulsion of the Jews from England', in *TCE* vi.

Reign of Edward II

Biographical studies: M. Buck, *Politics, Finance and the Church in the Reign of Edward II: Walter Stapledon, Treasurer of England* (Cambridge, 1983); P. C. Doherty, *Isabella and the Strange Death of Edward II* (London, 2003); J. S. Hamilton, *Piers Gaveston, Earl of Cornwall 1307–1312* (Detroit, 1988); R. M. Haines, *The Church and Politics in Fourteenth-Century England: The Career of Adam Orleton c.1275–1345* (Cambridge, 1978); id., *King Edward II: Edward of Caernarfon, his Life, his Reign, and its Aftermath 1284–1330* (Montreal, 2003); H. Johnstone, *Edward of Caernarvon 1284–1307* (Manchester, 1946); J. R. Maddicott, *Thomas of Lancaster 1307–1322* (Oxford, 1970); I. Mortimer, *The Greatest Traitor: The Life of Sir Roger Mortimer* (London, 2003); J. R. S. Phillips, *Aymer de Valence, Earl of Pembroke 1307–1324* (Oxford, 1972).

Other books: P. Chaplais, *Piers Gaveston, Edward II's Adoptive Brother* (Oxford, 1994); J. C. Davies, *The Baronial Opposition to Edward II* (London, 1918); N. Fryde, *The Tyranny and Fall of Edward II* (Cambridge, 1979); T. F. Tout, *The Place of the Reign of Edward II in English History* (Manchester, 1914).

Articles: W. Childs, ' "Welcome, My Brother": Edward II, John of Powderham and the Chroniclers', in I. Wood and G. Loud (eds.), *Church and Chronicle in the Middle Ages: Essays Presented to John Taylor* (London, 1991); id., 'Resistance and Treason in the *Vita Edwardi Secundi*', in *TCE* vi; G. P. Cuttino and T. W. Lyman, 'Where Is Edward II?', *Speculum*, 53 (1978); J. L. Grassi, 'William Airmyn and the Bishopric of Norwich', *EHR* 70 (1955); C. Given-Wilson, '*Vita Edwardi Secundi*: Memoir or Journal?', in *TCE* vi; J. S. Hamilton, 'Charter Witness Lists for the Reign of Edward II', in N. Saul (ed.), *Fourteenth Century England*, i (Woodbridge, 2000); G. A. Holmes, 'A Protest Against the Despensers, 1326', *Speculum*, 30 (1955); R. S. Hoyt, 'The Coronation Oath of 1308', *EHR* 71 (1956); H. Johnstone, 'The Eccentricities of Edward II', *EHR* 48 (1933); M. C. Prestwich, 'A New Version of the Ordinances of 1311', *BIHR* 57 (1984); id., 'The Ordinances of 1311 and the Politics of the Early Fourteenth Century', in J. Taylor and W. Childs (eds.), *Politics and Crisis in Fourteenth*

Century England (Gloucester, 1990); id., 'The Unreliability of Royal Household Knights in the Early Fourteenth Century', in C. Given-Wilson (ed.), *Fourteenth Century England* ii, (Woodbridge, 2002); H. G. Richardson, 'The English Coronation Oath', *Speculum*, 24 (1949); N. Saul, 'The Despensers and the Downfall of Edward II', *EHR* 99 (1984); T. F. Tout, 'The Captivity and Death of Edward of Caernarvon', in his *Collected Papers* (Manchester, 1934), vol. iii; C. Valente, 'The Deposition and Abdication of Edward II', *EHR* 113 (1998); S. L. Waugh, 'The Profits of Violence: The Minor Gentry in the Rebellion of 1321–2 in Gloucestershire and Herefordshire', *Speculum*, 52 (1977); B. Wilkinson, 'The Coronation Oath of Edward II', in J. G. Edwards, V. H. Galbraith, and E. F. Jacob (eds.), *Historical Essays in Honour of James Tait* (Manchester, 1933); 'The Sherburn Indenture and the Attack on the Despensers, 1321', *EHR* 62 (1948).

Reign of Edward III

Biographical studies: R. Barber, *Edward Prince of Wales and Aquitaine* (Woodbridge, 1978); K. Fowler, *The King's Lieutenant: Henry of Grosmont, First Duke of Lancaster, 1310–1361* (London, 1969); E. B. Fryde, *William de la Pole, Merchant and King's Banker* (London, 1988); R. M. Haines, *Archbishop John Stratford, Political Revolutionary and Champion of the Liberties of the English Church c.1275/80–1348* (Toronto, 1986).

Other books: W. M. Ormrod, *The Reign of Edward III: Crown and Political Society in England 1327–1377* (London, 1990); S. L. Waugh, *England in the Age of Edward III* (Cambridge, 1991).

Articles: J. S. Bothwell, 'Edward III and the "New Nobility": Largesse and Limitation in Fourteenth-Century England', *EHR* 112 (1997); id., 'Edward III, the English Peerage, and the 1337 Earls: Estate Distribution in Fourteenth-Century England', in J. S. Bothwell (ed.), *The Age of Edward III* (Woodbridge, 2001); E. B. Fryde, 'Parliament and the French War, 1336–40', in his *Studies in Medieval Trade and Finance* (London, 1983); A. Musson, 'Second "English Justinian" or Pragmatic Opportunist? A Re-examination of the Legal Legislation of Edward III's Reign', in J. S. Bothwell (ed.), *The Age of Edward III* (Woodbridge, 2001); W. M. Ormrod, 'Edward III and his Family', *Journal of British Studies*, 26 (1987); id., 'Edward III and the Recovery of Royal Authority in England, 1334–60', *History*, 72 (1987); id., 'The Personal Religion of Edward III', *Speculum*, 64 (1989); C. Shenton, 'Edward III and the Coup of 1330', in J. S. Bothwell (ed.), *The Age of Edward III* (Woodbridge, 2001).

Wales

Books: A. D. Carr, *Medieval Wales* (Basingstoke, 1995); R. R. Davies, *Conquest, Coexistence and Change: Wales 1063–1415* (Oxford, 1987); id., *Lordship and Society in the March of Wales 1282–1400* (Oxford, 1978); J. E. Lloyd, *A History of Wales from the Earliest Times to the Edwardian Conquest*, 2 vols. (London, 1911); J. E. Morris, *The Welsh Wars of Edward I* (Oxford, 1901); F. Suppe, *Military Institutions on the Welsh Marches: Shropshire, A.D. 1066–1300* (Woodbridge, 1994); J. B. Smith, *Llywelyn ap Gruffudd, Prince of Wales* (Cardiff, 1998); D. Stephenson, *The Governance of Gwynedd* (Cardiff, 1984); A. J. Taylor, *The Welsh Castles of Edward I* (London, 1986), reprint of his section of *The History of the King's Works*, i: *The Middle Ages* (London, 1963); D. Walker, *Medieval Wales* (Cambridge, 1990).

Articles: R. R. Davies, 'Law and National Identity in Thirteenth Century Wales', in R. R. Davies, R. A. Griffiths, I. G. Jones, and K. O. Morgan (eds.), *Welsh Society and Nationhood* (Cardiff, 1984); id., *The King of England and the Prince of Wales, 1277–84: Law, Politics and Power*, Kathleen Hughes Memorial Lectures (University of Cambridge, 2003); J. B. Smith, 'Edward II and the Allegiance of Wales', *Welsh History Review*, 8 (1976); L. B. Smith, 'The Statute of Wales, 1284', *Welsh History Review*, 10 (1980–1); id., 'The Death of Llywelyn ap Gruffydd: The Narratives Reconsidered', *Welsh History Review*, 11 (1982); D. Stephenson, 'The Laws of Court: Past Reality or Present Ideal?', in T. M. Charles-Edwards, M. E. Owen, and P. Russell (eds.), *The Welsh King and his Court* (Cardiff, 2000); R. F. Walker, 'Hubert de Burgh and Wales, 1218–1232', *EHR* 87 (1972); id., 'William de Valence and the Army of West Wales, 1282–3', *Welsh History Review*, 18 (1997).

Scotland

Books: G. W. S. Barrow, *Robert Bruce and the Community of the Realm of Scotland* (London, 1965); M. Brown, *The Wars of Scotland 1214–1371* (Edinburgh, 2004); E. L. G. Stones and G. G. Simpson (eds.), *Edward I and the Throne of Scotland, 1290–1296* (Oxford, 1978); A. Fisher, *William Wallace* (Edinburgh, 1986); C. McNamee, *The Wars of the Bruces: Scotland, England and Ireland, 1306–1328* (East Linton, 1997); R. Nicholson, *Edward III and the Scots* (Oxford, 1965); id., *Scotland: The Later Middle Ages* (Edinburgh, 1978); M. Penman, *David II 1329–71* (East Linton, 2004); F. Watson, *Under the Hammer: Edward I and Scotland, 1286–1306* (East Linton, 1998); A. Young, *Robert the Bruce's Rivals: The Comyns, 1212–1314* (East Linton, 1997).

Articles: M. Brown, 'Henry the Peaceable: Henry III, Alexander III and Royal Lordship in the British Isles, 1249–1272', in B. K. U. Weiler (ed.), *England and Europe in the Reign of Henry III* (Aldershot, 2002); J. Campbell, 'England, Scotland and the Hundred Years War', in C. J. Rogers (ed.), *The Wars of Edward III: Sources and Interpretations* (Woodbridge, 1999); A. A. M. Duncan, *The Nation of Scots and the Declaration of Arbroath*, Historical Association Pamphlet (1970); A. Grant, 'Disaster at Neville's Cross: The Scottish Point of View', in D. W. Rollason and M. C. Prestwich (eds.), *The Battle of Neville's Cross 1346* (Stamford, 1998); C. J. McNamee, 'William Wallace's Invasion of Northern England in 1297', *Northern History*, 26 (1990); C. J. Neville, 'Local Sentiment and the "National" Enemy—Northern England in the Middle Ages', *Journal of British Studies*, 35 (1996); M. C. Prestwich, 'Colonial Scotland: The English in Scotland Under Edward I', in R. Mason (ed.), *Scotland and England 1286–1815* (Edinburgh, 1987); id., 'Edward I and the Maid of Norway', *Scottish Historical Review*, 69 (1990); id., 'The English at the Battle of Neville's Cross', in D. W. Rollason and M. C. Prestwich (eds.), *The Battle of Neville's Cross 1346* (Stamford, 1998); J. Scammell, 'Robert I and the North of England', *EHR* 73 (1958); K. J. Stringer, 'Identities in Thirteenth-Century England: Frontier Society in the Far North', in C. Bjorn, A. Grant, and K. J. Stringer (eds.), *Social and Political Identities in Western History* (Copenhagen, 1994); A. Young, 'Noble Families and

Political Factions in the Reign of Alexander III', in N. Reid (ed.), *Scotland in the Reign of Alexander III* (Edinburgh, 1990).

France and England

Books: C. T. Allmand, *Society at War: The Experience of England and France During the Hundred Years War* (Edinburgh, 1973); id., *The Hundred Years War: England and France at War c.1300–c.1450* (Cambridge, 1988); A. Curry and M. Hughes (eds.), *Arms, Armies and Fortifications in the Hundred Years War* (Woodbridge, 1994); A. H. Burne, *The Crécy War* (London, 1955); A. Curry, *The Hundred Years War* (Basingstoke, 1993); E. Déprez, *Les Preliminaries de le guerre de cent ans: La Papauté, la France et l'Angleterre (1328–1342)* (Paris, 1902); D. Green, *The Battle of Poitiers 1356* (Stroud, 2002); K. Fowler (ed.), *The Hundred Years War* (London, 1971); H. S. Lucas, *The Low Countries and the Hundred Years War 1326–1347* (Ann Arbor, 1929); E. Perroy, *The Hundred Years War* (London, 1965); C. Rogers, *War Cruel and Sharp: English Strategy Under Edward III, 1327–1360* (Woodbridge, 2000); J. Sumption, *The Hundred Years War*, i: *Trial by Battle* (London, 1990); id., *Trial by Fire: The Hundred Years War*, ii (London, 1999); J. P. Trabut-Cussac, *L'Administration anglaise en Gascogne sous Henry III et Edouard I de 1254 à 1307* (Geneva, 1972); M. Vale, *The Origins of the Hundred Years War*, 2nd edn. (Oxford, 1996); N. Wright, *Knights and Peasants: The Hundred Years War in the French Countryside* (Woodbridge, 1998).

Articles: J. R. Alban and C. T. Allmand, 'Spies and Spying in the Fourteenth Century', in C. T. Allmand (ed.), *War, Literature and Politics in the Late Middle Ages* (Liverpool, 1976); A. Ayton, 'Edward III and the English Aristocracy at the Beginning of the Hundred Years War', in M. Strickland (ed.), *Armies, Chivalry and Warfare in Medieval Britain and France* (Stamford, 1998); P. Chaplais, 'Le Duché-Pairie de Guyenne', in his *Essays in Medieval Diplomacy and Administration* (London, 1981), chs. III and IV; K. DeVries, 'Contemporary Views of Edward III's Failure at the Siege of Tournai, 1340', *Nottingham Medieval Studies*, 39 (1995); K. Fowler, 'News from the Front: Letters and Despatches of the Fourteenth Century', in P. Contamine, C. Giry-Deloison, and M. H. Keen (eds.), *Guerre et société en France, en Angleterre et en Bourgogne XIVe–XVe siècle* (Villeneuve d'Ascq, 1991); C. Given-Wilson and F. Bériac, 'Edward III's Prisoners of War: The Battle of Poitiers and its Context', *EHR* 116 (2001); J. Le Patourel, 'Edward III and the Kingdom of France', in C. J. Rogers (ed.), *The Wars of Edward III: Sources and Interpretations* (Woodbridge, 1999); K. B. McFarlane, 'England and the Hundred Years War', *Past and Present*, 22 (1962); A. K. McHardy, 'Some Reflections on Edward III's Use of Propaganda', in J. S. Bothwell (ed.), *The Age of Edward III* (Woodbridge, 2001); M. W. Ormrod, 'Love and War in 1294', in *TCE* viii; M. M. Postan, 'The Costs of the Hundred Years War', *Past and Present*, 27 (1964); C. J. Rogers, 'The Anglo-French Peace Negotiations of 1354–1360 Reconsidered', in J. S. Bothwell (ed.), *The Age of Edward III* (Woodbridge, 2001); H. Rothwell, 'Edward I's Case Against Philip the Fair over Gascony in 1298', *EHR* 42 (1927); J. R. Studd, 'Reconfiguring the Angevin Empire, 1224–1259', in B. K. U. Weiler (ed.), *England and Europe in the Reign of Henry III (1216–1272)* (Aldershot, 2002); C. Taylor, 'Edward III and the Plantagenet Claim to the French Throne', in

J. S. Bothwell (ed.), *The Age of Edward III* (Woodbridge, 2001); B. J. Whiting, 'The Vows of the Heron', *Speculum*, 20 (1952).

Warfare and Military Organization

Books: A. Ayton, *Knights and Warhorses: Military Service and the English Aristocracy Under Edward III* (Woodbridge, 1994); J. R. V. Barker, *The Tournament in England, 1100–1400* (Woodbridge, 1986); J. Barnie, *War in Medieval Society* (London, 1974); D'A. J. D. Boulton, *The Knights of the Crown: The Monarchical Orders of Knighthood in Later Medieval Europe 1325–1520* (Woodbridge, 1987); K. DeVries, *Infantry Warfare in the Early Fourteenth Century* (Woodbridge, 1996); H. J. Hewitt, *The Organisation of War Under Edward III* (Manchester, 1966); M. Keen, *Chivalry* (London, 1984); N. Rogers, *The Safeguard of the Sea: A Naval History of Britain*, i: *660–1649* (London, 1997); M. R. Powicke, *Military Obligation in Medieval England* (Oxford, 1962); M. C. Prestwich, *Armies and Warfare in the Middle Ages: The English Experience* (London, 1996).

Articles: A. Ayton, 'English Armies in the Fourteenth Century', in A. Curry and M. Hughes (eds.), *Arms, Armies and Fortifications in the Hundred Years War* (Woodbridge, 1994); id., 'Sir Thomas Ughtred and the Edwardian Military Revolution', in J. S. Bothwell (ed.), *The Age of Edward III* (Woodbridge, 2001); W. H. Hudson, 'Norwich Militia in the Fourteenth Century', *Norfolk and Norwich Archaeological Society*, 14 (1901); A. King, 'A Helm with a Crest of Gold: The Order of Chivalry in Thomas Gray's *Scalacronica*', in N. Saul (ed.), *Fourteenth Century England*, i (Woodbridge, 2000); F. Lachaud, 'Armour and Military Dress in Thirteenth- and Early Fourteenth-Century England', in M. Strickland (ed.), *Armies, Chivalry and Warfare in Medieval Britain and France* (Stamford, 1998); M. C. Prestwich, 'Cavalry Service in Early Fourteenth Century England', in J. Gillingham and J. C. Holt (eds.), *War and Government in the Middle Ages* (Woodbridge, 1984); id., 'Military Logistics: The Case of 1322', in M. Strickland (ed.), *Armies, Chivalry and Warfare in Medieval Britain and France* (Stamford, 1998); A. E. Prince, 'The Strength of English Armies Under Edward III', *EHR* 46 (1931); id., 'The Indenture System Under Edward III', in J. G. Edwards, V. H. Galbraith, and E. F. Jacob (eds.), *Historical Essays Presented to James Tait* (Manchester, 1933); A. J. Taylor, 'Master Bertram, *Ingeniator Regis*', in C. Harper-Bill, C. J. Holdsworth, and J. L. Nelson (eds.), *Studies in Medieval History Presented to R. Allen Brown* (Woodbridge, 1989); T. F. Tout, 'Firearms in England in the Fourteenth Century', in his *Collected Papers* (Manchester, 1934), vol. ii; J. Vale, *Edward III and Chivalry* (Woodbridge, 1982).

Nobles and Knights

Books: M. Altschul, *A Baronial Family in Medieval England: The Clares* (Baltimore, 1965); J. M. W. Bean, *From Lord to Patron: Lordship in Late Medieval England* (Philadelphia, 1989); P. R. Coss, *Lordship, Knighthood and Locality: A Study in English Society c.1180–c.1280* (Cambridge, 1991); id., *The Knight in Medieval England 1000–1400* (London, 1993); id., *The Lady in Medieval England 1000–1500* (London, 1998); id., *The Origins of the English Gentry* (Cambridge, 2003); D. Crouch, *The Image of Aristocracy in Britain 1000–1300* (London, 1992); N. Denholm-Young, *History and Heraldry 1254 to 1310* (Oxford, 1965); id., *The Country Gentry in the Fourteenth Century* (Oxford, 1969); M. Keen, *Origins of the English Gentleman c.1300–c.1500* (Stroud, 2002); I. J. Sanders, *English Baronies: A Study of their Origin and Descent 1086–1327* (Oxford, 1960); N. Saul, *Knights and Esquires: The Gloucestershire Gentry in the Fourteenth Century* (Oxford, 1981); C. M. Woolgar, *The Great Household in Late Medieval England* (London, 1999).

Articles: P. Brand, 'Oldcotes v. Darcy', in R. F. Hunnisett and J. B. Post (eds.), *Medieval Legal Records* (London, 1978); C. Carpenter, 'Gentry and Community in Medieval England', *Journal of British Studies*, 33 (1994); D. A. Carpenter, 'Was there a Crisis of the Knightly Class in the Thirteenth Century? The Oxfordshire Evidence', in his *The Reign of Henry III* (London, 1996); P. R. Coss, 'Sir Geoffrey de Langley and the Crisis of the Knightly Class in Thirteenth Century England', *Past and Present*, 68 (1975); id., 'Knighthood and the Early Thirteenth-Century County Court', in *TCE* iii; id., 'Knights, Esquires and the Origins of Social Gradation in England', *TRHS*, 6th ser., 5 (1995); id., 'Bastard Feudalism Revised', *Past and Present*, 125 (1989); D. Crouch, D. A. Carpenter, and P. R. Coss, 'Debate: Bastard Feudalism Revised', *Past and Present*, 131 (1991); D. Crouch, 'The Local Influence of the Earls of Warwick, 1088–1242: A Study in Decline and Resourcefulness', *Midland History*, 21 (1996); N. Denholm-Young, 'Feudal Society in the Thirteenth Century: The Knights', in his *Collected Papers on Medieval Subjects* (Oxford, 1946); K. Faulkner, 'The Transformation of Knighthood in Early Thirteenth-Century England', *EHR* 111 (1996); C. J. Given-Wilson, 'Wealth and Credit, Public and Private: The Earl of Arundel 1306–1397', *EHR* 106 (1991); P. J. Jefferies, 'Profitable Fourteenth-Century Legal Practice and Landed Investment: The Case of Judge Stonor, c.1281 to 1354', *Southern History*, 15 (1993); F. Lachaud, 'An Aristocratic Wardrobe of the Late Thirteenth Century: The Confiscation of the Goods of Osbert de Spaldington in 1298', *Historical Research*, 67 (1994); J. R. Maddicott, 'Thomas of Lancaster and Sir Robert Holland: A Study in Noble Patronage', *EHR* 86 (1971); id., 'The County Community and the Making of Public Opinion in Fourteenth-Century England', *TRHS*, 5th ser., 28 (1978); id., 'Magna Carta and the Local Community 1215–1259', *Past and Present*, 102 (1984); M. Morris, 'The "Murder" of an English Earldom? Roger IV Bigod and Edward I', in *TCE* ix; J. E. Newman, 'Greater and Lesser Landowners and Parochial Patronage in Yorkshire in the Thirteenth Century', *EHR* 92 (1977); E. King, 'Large and Small Landowners in Thirteenth-Century England', *Past and Present*, 47 (1970); A. Polden, 'A Crisis of the Knightly Class? Inheritance and Office Among the Gentry of Thirteenth-Century Buckinghamshire', in P. Fleming, A. Gross, and J. R. Lander (eds.), *Regionalism and Revision: The Crown and its Provinces in England 1250–1650* (London, 1998); M. C. Prestwich, '*Miles in Armis Strenuus*: The Knight at War', *TRHS*, 6th ser., 5 (1995); J. Quick, 'The Number and Distribution of Knights in Thirteenth Century England: The Evidence of the Grand Assize Lists', in *TCE* i; N. Saul, 'A "Rising" Lord and a "Declining" Esquire: Sir Thomas de Berkeley III and Geoffrey Gascelyn of Sheldon', *Historical Research*, 61 (1988); S. L. Waugh, 'Reluctant Knights and Jurors: Respites, Exemptions, and Public Obligations in the Reign of

Henry III', *Speculum*, 58 (1983); id., 'Tenure to Contract: Lordship and Clientage in Thirteenth-Century England', *EHR* 101 (1986); K. P. Wentersdorf, 'The Clandestine Marriages of the Fair Maid of Kent', *Journal of Medieval History*, 5 (1979).

Women

Books: J. M. Bennett, *Women in the Medieval English Countryside: Gender and Household in Brigstock Before the Plague* (Oxford, 1987); P. Coss, *The Lady in Medieval England 1000–1500* (Stroud, 1998); K. M Phillips, *Medieval Maidens: Young Women and Gender in England, 1270–1540* (Manchester, 2003); F. A. Underhill, *For Her Good Estate: The Life of Elizabeth de Burgh* (London, 1999); J. C. Ward, *English Noblewomen in the Later Middle Ages* (London, 1992); P. J. P. Goldberg (ed.), *Women in Medieval English Society* (Stroud, 1997).

Articles: P. J. P. Goldberg, 'The Public and the Private: Women in the Pre-Plague Economy', in *TCE* iii; M. Howell, 'Royal Women of England and France in the Mid-Thirteenth Century: A Gendered Perspective', in B. K. U. Weiler (ed.), *England and Europe in the Reign of Henry III (1216–1272)* (Aldershot, 2002); J. C. Parsons, 'The Intercessionary Patronage of Queens Margaret and Isabella of France', in *TCE* vi; M. C. Prestwich, 'An Everyday Story of Knightly Folk', in *TCE* ix.

Demography

Books: C. Daniell, *Death and Burial in Medieval England* (London, 1997); C. Rawcliffe, *Medicine and Society in Later Medieval England* (Stroud, 1995); C. Roberts and M. Cox, *Health and Disease in Britain* (Stroud, 2003); Z. Razi, *Life, Marriage and Death in a Medieval Parish: Economy, Society and Demography in Halesowen 1270–1400* (Cambridge, 1980).

Articles: P. A. Biller, 'Birth Control in the West in the Thirteenth and Early Fourteenth Centuries', *Past and Present*, 94 (1982); J. R. Dawes and J. R. Magilton, *The Cemetery of St Helen-on-the-Walls, Aldwark* (York, 1980); P. Franklin, 'Malaria in Medieval Gloucestershire: An Essay in Epidemiology', *Transactions of the Bristol and Gloucestershire Archaeological Society*, 101 (1983); M. K. McIntosh, 'Land, Tenure, and Population in the Royal Manor of Havering, Essex, 1251–1352/3', *EcHR*, 2nd ser., 33 (1980); L. R. Poos and R. M. Smith, ' "Legal Windows onto Historical Populations"? Recent Research on Demography and the Manor Court in Medieval England', in Z. Razi and R. M. Smith (eds.), *Medieval Society and the Manor Court* (Oxford, 1996); L. R. Poos, 'The Rural Population of Essex in the Later Middle Ages', *EcHR*, 2nd ser., 38 (1985); M. M. Postan and J. Z. Titow, 'Heriots and Prices on Winchester Manors', in M. M. Postan (ed.), *Essays on Medieval Agriculture and General Problems of the Medieval Economy* (Cambridge, 1973).

The Black Death

Books: M. W. Ormrod and P. Lindley (eds.), *The Black Death in England* (Stamford, 1996); S. K. Cohn, Jr., *The Black Death Transformed: Disease and Culture in Early Renaissance Europe* (London, 2002); W. J. Dohar, *The Black Death and Pastoral Leadership: The Diocese of Hereford in the Fourteenth Century* (Philadelphia, 1995);

J. Hatcher, *Plague, Population and the English Economy 1348–1530* (London, 1977); R. Horrox, *The Black Death* (Manchester, 1994); G. Twigg, *The Black Death: A Biological Reappraisal* (London, 1984).

Articles: J. Aberth, 'The Black Death in the Diocese of Ely: The Evidence of the Bishop's Register', *Journal of Medieval History*, 21 (1995); R. H. Britnell, 'Feudal Reaction After the Black Death in Durham', *Past and Present*, 128 (1990); id., 'The Black Death in English Towns', *Urban History*, 21 (1994); W. J. Courtenay, 'The Effect of the Black Death on English Higher Education', *Speculum*, 55 (1980); B. Dodds, 'Durham Priory Tithes and the Black Death', *Northern History*, 39 (2002); M. I. P. Gilbert, J. Cuccui, W. White, N. Lynnerup, R. W. Titball, A. Cooper, and M. B. Prentice, 'Absence of *Yersinia Pestis*-Specific DNA in Human Teeth from Five European Excavations of Putative Plague Victims', *Microbiology*, 150 (2004); E. B. Fryde, 'The Tenants of the Bishops of Coventry and Lichfield and of Worcester After the Plague of 1348–9', in R. F. Hunnisett and J. B. Post (eds.), *Medieval Legal Records* (London, 1978); D. Hawkins, 'The Black Death and the New London Cemeteries of 1348', *Antiquity*, 64 (1990); T. B. James, *The Black Death in Hampshire*, Hampshire Papers, 18 (1999); R. Lock, 'The Black Death in Walsham-le-Willows', *Proceedings of the Suffolk Institute of Archaeology and History*, 37 (1992); R. A. Lomas, 'The Black Death in County Durham', *Journal of Medieval History*, 15 (1989); W. M. Ormrod, 'The English Government and the Black Death of 1348–9', in W. M. Ormrod (ed.), *England in the Fourteenth Century* (Woodbridge, 1986); D. Raoult, G. Aboudharam, E. Crubézy, G. Larrouy, B. Ludes, and M. Drancourt, 'Molecular Identification by "Suicide PCR" of *Yersinia Pestis* as the Agent of Medieval Black Death', *Proceedings of the National Academy of Sciences*, 97 (7 Nov. 2000); E. Robo, 'The Black Death in the Hundred of Farnham', *EHR* 44 (1929); D. G. Watts, 'The Black Death in Dorset and Hampshire', in T. B. James (ed.), *The Black Death in Wessex*, Hatcher Review, v. no. 46 (1998).

Agrarian Economy

Books: H. E. Hallam (ed.), *The Agrarian History of England and Wales*, ii: *The Middle Ages* (Cambridge, 1988); W. O. Ault, *Open Field Farming in Medieval England* (London, 1972); M. Bailey, *A Marginal Economy? East Anglian Breckland in the Later Middle Ages* (Cambridge, 1989); B. M. S. Campbell (ed.), *Before the Black Death: Studies in the 'Crisis' of the Early Fourteenth Century* (Manchester, 1991); K. Biddick, *The Other Economy: Pastoral Economy on a Medieval Estate* (Berkeley and Los Angeles, 1989); E. Britton, *The Community of the Vill: A Study in the History of the Family and Village Life in Fourteenth-Century England* (Toronto, 1977); B. M. S. Campbell, *English Seigniorial Agriculture 1250–1450* (Cambridge, 2000); N. Denholm-Young, *Seignorial Administration in England* (Oxford, 1937); F. R. H. du Boulay, *The Lordship of Canterbury* (London, 1966); L. Cantor, *The English Medieval Landscape* (London, 1982); C. Dyer, *Lords and Peasants in a Changing Society: The Estates of the Bishopric of Worcester, 680–1540* (Cambridge, 1980); id., *Everyday Life in the Middle Ages* (London, 1994); *Standards of Living in the Later Middle Ages: Social Change in England c.1200–1520* id., (Cambridge, 1989); P. L. Everson, C. C. Taylor, and C. J. Dunn, *Change and*

Continuity: Rural Settlement in North-West Lincolnshire (London, 1991); E. B. Fryde, *Peasants and Landlords in Later Medieval England* (Stroud, 1996); H. E. Hallam, *Rural England 1066–1348* (Glasgow, 1981); B. Hanawalt, *The Ties that Bound: Peasant Families in Medieval England* (Oxford, 1986); B. Harvey, *Westminster Abbey and its Estates in the Middle Ages* (Oxford, 1977); R. H. Hilton, *The English Peasantry in the Later Middle Ages* (Oxford, 1975); G. A. Holmes, *The Estates of the Higher Nobility in* XIV *Century England* (Cambridge, 1957); P. R. Hyams, *Kings, Lords and Peasants in Medieval England* (Oxford, 1980); W. C. Jordan, *The Great Famine: Northern Europe in the Early Fourteenth Century* (Princeton, 1996); I. Kershaw, *Bolton Priory: The Economy of a Northern Monastery 1286–1325* (Oxford, 1973); R. M. Smith (ed.), *Land, Kinship and Life-Cycle* (Cambridge, 1984); J. Langdon, *Horses, Oxen and Technological Innovation: The Use of Draught Animals in English Farming from 1066 to 1500* (Cambridge, 1986); J. R. Maddicott, *The English Peasantry and the Demands of the Crown, 1294–1341*, *Past and Present*, suppl. 1 (1975); R. M. Smith and Z. Razi (eds.), *Medieval Society and the Manor Court* (Oxford, 1996); E. Miller, *The Abbey and Bishopric of Ely* (Cambridge, 1951); M. Morgan, *The English Lands of the Abbey of Bec* (Oxford, 1946); P. D. A. Harvey (ed.), *The Peasant Land Market in Medieval England* (Oxford, 1984); M. M. Postan, *Essays on Medieval Agriculture and General Problems of the Medieval Economy* (Cambridge, 1978); J. A. Raftis, *Tenure and Mobility: Studies in the Social History of the Medieval English Village* (Toronto, 1964); id., *Peasant Economic Development Within the English Manorial System* (Stroud, 1997); Z. Razi, *Life, Marriage and Death in a Medieval Parish: Economy, Society and Demography in Halesowen 1270–1400* (Cambridge, 1980); J. Z. Titow, *English Rural Society 1200–1350* (London, 1969); id., *Winchester Yields: A Study in Medieval Agricultural Productivity* (Cambridge, 1972).

Articles: M. A. Atkin, 'Land Use and Management in the Upland Demesne of the De Lacy Estate of Blackburnshire *c*.1300', *Agricultural History Review*, 42 (1994); A. H. R. Baker, 'Evidence in the "Nonarum Inquisitiones" of Contracting Arable Lands in England During the Early Fourteenth Century', *EcHR*, 2nd ser., 19 (1966); M. Bailey, '*Per Impetuum Maris*: Natural Disaster and Economic Decline in Eastern England, 1275–1350', in B. M. S. Campbell (ed.), *Before the Black Death: Studies in the 'Crisis' of the Early Fourteenth Century* (Manchester, 1991); J. Birrell, 'Deer and Deer Farming in Medieval England', *Agricultural History Review*, 40 (1992); R. H. Britnell, 'Agricultural Technology and the Margin of Cultivation in the Fourteenth Century', *EcHR*, 2nd ser., 30 (1977); C. Dyer, 'The English Medieval Village Community and its Decline', *Journal of British Studies*, 33 (1994); H. S. A. Fox, 'Some Ecological Dimensions of Medieval Field Systems', in K. Biddick (ed.), *Archaeological Approaches to Medieval Europe* (Kalamazoo, Mich., 1984); P. D. A. Harvey, 'The Pipe Rolls and the Adoption of Demesne Farming in England', *EcHR*, 2nd ser., 26 (1973); id., 'The English Inflation of 1180–1220', *Past and Present*, 61 (1973); R. H. Hilton, 'Peasant Movements in England Before 1381', in E. M. Carus-Wilson (ed.), *Essays in Economic History*, ii (London, 1962); E. Jamroziak, 'Rievaulx Abbey as a Wool Producer in the Late Thirteenth Century: Cistercians, Sheep, and Debts', *Northern History*, 40 (2003); A. Jones, 'Caddington, Kensworth, and Dunstable in 1297', *EcHR*, 2nd ser., 32 (1979); E. D. Jones, 'The Exploitation of its Serfs by Spalding Priory Before the Black Death',

Nottingham Medieval Studies, 43 (1999); J. Kanzaka, 'Villein Rents in Thirteenth-Century England: An Analysis of the Hundred Rolls of 1279–1280', *EcHR* 55 (2002); R. A. Lomas, 'The Priory of Durham and its Demesnes in the Fourteenth and Fifteenth Centuries', *EcHR*, 2nd ser., 31 (1978); M. Mate, 'Profit and Productivity on the Estates of Isabella de Forz (1260–92), *EcHR*, 2nd ser., 33 (1980); id., 'The Farming out of Manors: A New Look at the Evidence from Canterbury Cathedral Priory', *Journal of Medieval History*, 9 (1983); id., 'Medieval Agrarian Practice: The Determining Factors?', *Agricultural History Review*, 33 (1985); E. I. N. Newman and P. D. A. Harvey, 'Did Soil Fertility Decline in Medieval English Farms? Evidence from Cuxham, Oxfordshire, 1320–1340', *Agricultural History Review*, 45 (1997); M. M. Postan, *The Famulus: The Estate Labourer in the xiith and xiiith Centuries*, *Economic History Review* suppl. 2 (1954); D. Postles, 'The Perception of Profit Before the Leasing of Demesnes', *Agricultural History Review*, 34 (1986); O. Rackham, 'The Forest: Woodland and Wood-Pasture in Medieval England', in K. Biddick (ed.), *Archaeological Approaches to Medieval Europe* (Kalamazoo, Mich., 1984); P. R. Schofield, 'Dearth, Debt and the Land Market', *Agricultural History Review*, 45 (1997); E. Searle, *Lordship and Community: Battle Abbey and its Banlieu 1066–1538* (Toronto, 1974); R. M. Smith, 'Women's Property Rights Under Customary Law: Some Developments in the Thirteenth and Fourteenth Centuries', *TRHS*, 5th ser., 36 (1986); M. J. Stephenson, 'Wool Yields in the Medieval Economy', *EcHR*, 2nd ser., 41 (1988); D. Stone, 'The Productivity of Hired and Customary Labour: Evidence from Wisbech Barton in the Fourteenth Century', *EcHR* 50 (1997); E. Stone, 'Profit-and-Loss Accountancy at Norwich Cathedral Priory', *TRHS*, 5th ser., 12 (1962); J. Z. Titow, 'Evidence of Weather in the Account Rolls of the Bishopric of Winchester 1209–1350', *EcHR*, 2nd ser., 12 (1959–60).

Towns

Books: C. M. Barron, *London in the Later Middle Ages: Government and People 1200–1500* (Oxford, 2004); M. W. Beresford, *New Towns of the Middle Ages* (London, 1967); *The Cambridge Urban History of Britain*, i: *600–1540*, ed. D. M. Palliser (Cambridge, 2000); M. Bonney, *Lordship and the Urban Community: Durham and its Overlords, 1250–1540* (Cambridge, 1990); B. M. S. Campbell, J. A. Galloway, D. Keene, and M. Murphy, *A Medieval Capital and its Grain Supply: Agrarian Production and Distribution in the London Region c.1300*, Historical Geography Research Series, 30 (Institute of British Geographers, 1993); J. W. F. Hill, *Medieval Lincoln* (Cambridge, 1948); E. Miller and J. Hatcher, *Medieval England: Towns, Commerce and Crafts 1086–1349* (London, 1995); C. Platt, *Medieval Southampton: The Port and Trading Community*, A.D. *1000–1600* (London, 1973); S. Reynolds, *An Introduction to the History of English Medieval Towns* (Oxford, 1977); J. Schofield and A. Vince, *Medieval Towns* (Leicester, 1994); H. Summerson, *Medieval Carlisle: The City and the Borders from the Late Eleventh to the Mid-Sixteenth Century* (Cumberland and Westmorland Antiquarian and Archaeological Society extra ser. 25, 1993); H. L. Turner, *Town Defences in England and Wales* (1970); G. A. Williams, *Medieval London from Commune to Capital* (London, 1963).

Articles: E. Carus-Wilson, 'The First Half-Century of the Borough of Stratford-upon-Avon', *EcHR*, 2nd ser., 18 (1965); C. Dyer, 'The Importance of Small Towns in England 1000–1540', *Historical Research*, 75 (2002); C. M. Fraser, 'Medieval Trading Restrictions in the North East', *Archaeologia Aeliana*, 4th ser., 39 (1961); E. A. Fuller, 'The Tallage of 1312 and the Bristol Riots', *Transactions of the Bristol and Gloucestershire Archaeological Society*, 19 (1894–5); R. H. Hilton, 'Small Town Society in England Before the Black Death', *Past and Present*, 105 (1984); D. Keene, 'Medieval London and its Region', *London Journal*, 14 (1989); P. Nightingale, 'The Growth of London in the Medieval English Economy', in R. H. Britnell and J. Hatcher (eds.), *Progress and Problems in Medieval England* (Cambridge, 1996); S. H. Rigby, 'Boston and Grimsby in the Middle Ages: An Administrative Contrast', *Journal of Medieval History*, 10 (1984); E. Veale, 'The "Great Twelve": Mistery and Fraternity in Thirteenth-Century London', *Historical Research*, 64 (1991).

Trade, Merchants, and Currency

Books: E. M. Carus-Wilson and O. Coleman, *England's Export Trade 1275–1547* (Oxford, 1963); W. Childs, 'The English Export Trade in Cloth', in R. H. Britnell and J. Hatcher (eds.), *Progress and Problems in Medieval England* (Cambridge, 1996); E. B. Fryde, *Studies in Medieval Trade and Finance* (London, 1983); *William de la Pole, Merchant and King's Banker* (London, 1988); E. S. Hunt, *The Medieval Super-Companies: A Study of the Peruzzi Company of Florence* (Cambridge, 1994); M. K. James, *Studies in the Wine Trade*, ed. E. M. Veale (Oxford, 1971); R. W. Kaeuper, *Bankers to the Crown: The Riccardi of Lucca and Edward I* (Princeton, 1973); J. Kermode, *Medieval Merchants: York, Beverley and Hull in the Later Middle Ages* (Cambridge, 1998); T. H. Lloyd, *The English Wool Trade in the Middle Ages* (Cambridge, 1977); id., *Alien Merchants in England in the High Middle Ages* (Brighton, 1982); J. Masschaele, *Peasants, Merchants and Markets: Inland Trade in Medieval England, 1150–1350* (New York, 1997); C. Challis (ed.), *A New History of the Royal Mint* (Cambridge, 1992).

Articles: M. Allen, 'The Volume of the English Currency, 1158–1470', *EcHR* 54 (2001); N. Fryde, 'Antonio Pessagno of Genoa, King's Merchant of Edward II of England', in *Studi in Memoria di Federigo Melis* (Florence, 1978); M. K. James, 'The Fluctuations of the Anglo-Gascon Wine Trade During the Fourteenth Century', in E. M. Carus-Wilson (ed.), *Essays in Economic History*, ii (London, 1962); R. W. Kaeuper, 'The Frescobaldi of Florence and the English Crown', *Studies in Medieval and Renaissance History*, 10 (1973); M. Mate, 'High Prices in Early Fourteenth-Century England: Causes and Consequences', *EcHR*, 2nd ser., 28 (1975); M. C. Prestwich, 'Italian Bankers in Late Thirteenth and Early Fourteenth Century England', in Centre for Medieval and Renaissance Studies (ed.), *The Dawn of Modern Banking* (New Haven, 1979); G. Unwin, 'The Estate of Merchants, 1336–1365', in G. Unwin (ed.), *Finance and Trade Under Edward III* (Manchester, 1918).

The Church and Universities

Books: A. D. M. Barrell, *The Papacy, Scotland and Northern England 1342–1378* (Cambridge, 1995); A. Brown, *Church and Society in England 1000–1500* (Basingstoke,

2003); J. Burton, *Monastic and Religious Orders in Britain 1000–1300* (Cambridge, 1994); A. Cobban, *English University Life in the Middle Ages* (London, 1999); J. H. Denton, *Robert Winchelsey and the Crown 1294–1313* (Cambridge, 1980); *The History of the University of Oxford*, i: *The Early Oxford Schools*, ed. J. I. Catto (Oxford, 1984); R. C. Finucane, *Miracles and Pilgrims: Popular Beliefs in Medieval England*, 2nd edn. (Basingstoke, 1995); K. Kamerick, *Popular Piety and Art in the Late Middle Ages: Image Worship and Idolatry in England, 1350–1500* (London, 2002); M. D. Knowles, *The Religious Orders in England*, i (Cambridge, 1948); W. E. Lunt, *Financial Relations of the Papacy with England to 1327* (Cambridge, Mass., 1939); id., *Financial Relations of the Papacy with England, 1327–1534* (Cambridge, Mass., 1962); J. McEvoy, *Robert Grosseteste* (Oxford, 2000); G. H. Martin and J. R. L. Highfield, *A History of Merton College* (Oxford, 1997); J. R. H. Moorman, *The Franciscans in England* (Oxford, 1974); D. Webb, *Pilgrimage in Medieval England* (London, 2000); W. A. Pantin, *The English Church in the Fourteenth Century* (Cambridge, 1955); J. McEvoy (ed.), *Robert Grosseteste: New Perspectives on his Thought and Scholarship* (Turnhout, 1995); R. W. Southern, *Robert Grosseteste: The Growth of an English Mind in Medieval Europe* (Oxford, 1986); J. R. Wright, *The Church and the English Crown, 1305–1334: A Study Based on the Register of Archbishop Walter Reynolds* (Toronto, 1980).

Articles: B. Golding, 'Burials and Benefactions: An Aspect of Monastic Patronage in Thirteenth-Century England', in W. M. Ormrod (ed.), *England in the Thirteenth Century* (Harlaxton, 1985); K. Edwards, 'The Social Origins and Provenance of the English Bishops During the Reign of Edward II', *TRHS*, 5th ser., 9 (1959); A. Gransden, 'John de Northwold, Abbot of Bury St Edmunds', in *TCE* iii; J. R. L. Highfield, 'The English Hierarchy in the Reign of Edward III', *TRHS*, 5th ser., 6 (1956); H. Summerson, 'The King's Clericulus: The Life and Career of Silvester de Everdon, Bishop of Carlisle, 1247–1254', *Northern History*, 28 (1992).

The Law

Books: J. Aberth, *Criminal Churchmen in the Age of Edward III: The Case of Bishop Thomas de Lisle* (University Park, Pa., 1996); J. G. Bellamy, *The Law of Treason in England in the Later Middle Ages* (Cambridge, 1970); P. Brand, *The Making of the Common Law* (London, 1992); id., *Kings, Barons and Justices: The Making and Enforcement of Legislation in Thirteenth-Century England* (Cambridge, 2003); J. B. Given, *Society and Homicide in Thirteenth-Century England* (Stanford, Calif., 1977); B. A. Hanawalt, *Crime and Conflict in English Communities 1300–1348* (Cambridge, Mass., 1979); A. Musson, *Public Order and Law Enforcement: The Local Administration of Criminal Justice, 1294–1350* (Woodbridge, 1996); id., *Medieval Law in Context: The Growth of Legal Consciousness from Magna Carta to the Peasant's Revolt* (Manchester, 2001); A. Musson and W. M. Ormrod, *The Evolution of English Justice: Law, Politics and Society in the Fourteenth Century* (London, 1999); R. C. Palmer, *English Law in the Age of the Black Death* (Chapel Hill, NC, 1993); F. Pollock and F. W. Maitland, *The History of English Law*, 2nd edn., introd. S. F. C. Milsom, 2 vols. (Cambridge, 1968); R. B. Pugh, *Imprisonment in Medieval England* (Cambridge, 1968); R. Stewart-Brown, *The Serjeants of the Peace in Medieval England and Wales* (Manchester, 1936); D. W.

Sutherland, *Quo Warranto Proceedings in the Reign of Edward I, 1278–1294* (Oxford, 1963).

Articles: B. H. Putnam, 'The Transformation of the Keepers of the Peace into the Justices of the Peace, 1327–80', *TRHS*, 4th ser., 12 (1929); D. Crook, 'The Later Eyres', *EHR* 97 (1982); J. L. Barton, 'The Mystery of Bracton', *Journal of Legal History*, 14 (1993), 1–42; J. G. Bellamy, 'The Coterel Gang: An Anatomy of a Band of Fourteenth-Century Criminals', *EHR* 79 (1964); P. A. Brand, 'Edward I and the Judges: The "State Trials" of 1289–93', in *TCE* i; id., 'The Age of Bracton', in J. Hudson (ed.), *The History of English Law: Centenary Essays on 'Pollock and Maitland'* (Oxford, 1996); C. M. Fraser and K. Elmsley, 'Law and Society in Northumberland and Durham, 1290 to 1350', *Archaeologia Aeliana*, 4th ser., 47 (1969); C. I. Hammer, Jr., 'Patterns of Homicide in Fourteenth-Century Oxford', *Past and Present*, 78 (1978); L. W. V. Harcourt, *His Grace the Steward and Trial of Peers* (London, 1907); R. W. Kaeuper, 'Law and Order in Fourteenth-Century England: The Evidence of Special Commissions of Oyer and Terminer', *Speculum*, 54 (1979); J. R. Maddicott, *Law and Lordship: Royal Justices as Retainers in Thirteenth- and Fourteenth-Century England, Past and Present*, suppl. 4 (1978); A. Musson, 'Turning King's Evidence: The Prosecution of Crime in Late Medieval England', *Oxford Journal of Legal Studies*, 19 (1999); E. L. G. Stones, 'Sir Geoffrey le Scrope *c.*1280 to 1340, Chief Justice of the King's Bench', *EHR* 69 (1954); id., 'The Folvilles of Ashby-Folville, Leicestershire, and their Associates in Crime', *TRHS*, 5th ser., 7 (1957); H. Summerson, 'Attitudes to Capital Punishment in England, 1200–1350', in *TCE* viii; 'The Criminal Underworld of Medieval England', *Journal of Legal History*, 17 (1996); A. Verduyn, 'The Politics of Law and Order During the Early Years of Edward III', *EHR* 108 (1993).

Material culture

Books: J. Alexander and P. Binski (eds.), *Age of Chivalry: Art in Plantagenet England 1200–1400* (London, 1987); P. Binski, *Westminster Abbey and the Plantagenets* (London, 1995); id., *The Painted Chamber at Westminster* (London, 1986); J. Bony, *The English Decorated Style: Gothic Architecture Transformed 1250–1350* (Ithaca, NY, 1979); R. A. Brown, H. M. Colvin, and A. J. Taylor (eds.), *The History of the King's Works*, i and ii: *The Middle Ages* (London, 1963); M. Camille, *Mirror in Parchment: The Luttrell Psalter and the Making of Medieval England* (London, 1998); M. Clanchy, *From Memory to Written Record* (London, 1979); N. Coldstream, *The Decorated Style* (London, 1994); J. Blair and N. Ramsay (eds.), *English Medieval Industries: Craftsmen, Techniques, Products* (London, 1991); C. Coulson, *Castles in Medieval Society: Fortresses in England, France, and Ireland in the Central Middle Ages* (Oxford, 2003); M. Duffy, *Royal Tombs of Medieval England* (Stroud, 2003); I. Friel, *The Good Ship* (London, 1995); E. J. Kealey, *Harvesting the Air: Windmill Pioneers in Twelfth-Century England* (Woodbridge, 1987); S. M. Newton, *Fashion in the Age of the Black Prince* (Woodbridge, 1980); L. F. Salzman, *Building in England down to 1540* (Oxford, 1952); L. F. Sandler, *The Peterborough Psalter in Brussels and Other Fenland Manuscripts* (London, 1974); N. Saul, *Death, Art and Memory in Medieval England* (Oxford, 2001); A. J. Taylor, *Studies in Castles and Castle-Building* (London, 1985).

Articles: N. Coldstream, 'Architects, Advisers and Design at Edward I's Castles in Wales', *Architectural History*, 46 (2003); P. Dixon, 'From Hall to Tower: The Change in Seigneurial Houses on the Anglo-Scottish Border After *c.*1250', in *TCE* iv; id., 'Mota, Aula et Turris: The Manor Houses of the Anglo-Scottish Border', in G. Meirion-Jones and M. Jones (eds.), *Manorial Domestic Buildings in England and Northern France* (London, 1993); B. and M. Gittos, 'Motivation and Choice: The Selection of Medieval Secular Effigies', in P. Coss and M. Keen (eds.), *Heraldry, Pageantry and Social Display* (Woodbridge, 2002); F. Lachaud, 'Liveries of Robes in England, *c.*1200–*c.*1330', *EHR* 111 (1996); J. Munby, 'Manorial Building in Timber in Central and Southern England, 1200–1550', in G. Meirion-Jones and M. Jones (eds.), *Manorial Domestic Buildings in England and Northern France* (London, 1993); M. C. Prestwich, 'English Castles in the Reign of Edward II', *Journal of Medieval History*, 8 (1982); A. J. Taylor, 'Master Bertram, *Ingeniator Regis*', in C. Harper-Bill, C. J. Holdsworth, and J. L. Nelson (eds.), *Studies in Medieval History Presented to R. Allen Brown* (Woodbridge, 1989).

National Identity

Books: S. Crane, *Insular Romance: Politics, Faith and Culture in Anglo-Norman and Middle English Literature* (Berkeley and Los Angeles, 1986); J. Gillingham, *The English in the Twelfth Century: Imperialism, National Identity and Political Values* (Woodbridge, 2000); P. Rickard, *Britain in Medieval French Literature* (Cambridge, 1956); T. Summerfield, *The Matter of Kings' Lives* (Amsterdam, 1998); T. Turville-Petre, *England the Nation: Language, Literature, and National Identity, 1290–1340* (Oxford, 1996).

Articles: S. Crane, 'Social Aspects of Bilingualism in the Thirteenth Century', in *TCE* vi; R. R. Davies, 'The Peoples of Britain and Ireland, 1100–1400', *TRHS*, 6th ser., 4 (1994); 5 (1995); 6 (1996), 7 (1997); R. F. Frame, ' "Les Engleys nées en Irlande": The English Political Identity in Medieval Ireland', in his *Ireland and Britain 1170–1450* (London, 1998); M. W. Ormrod, 'The Use of English: Language, Law and Political Culture in Fourteenth-Century England', *Speculum*, 78 (2003).

Index